MW01631044

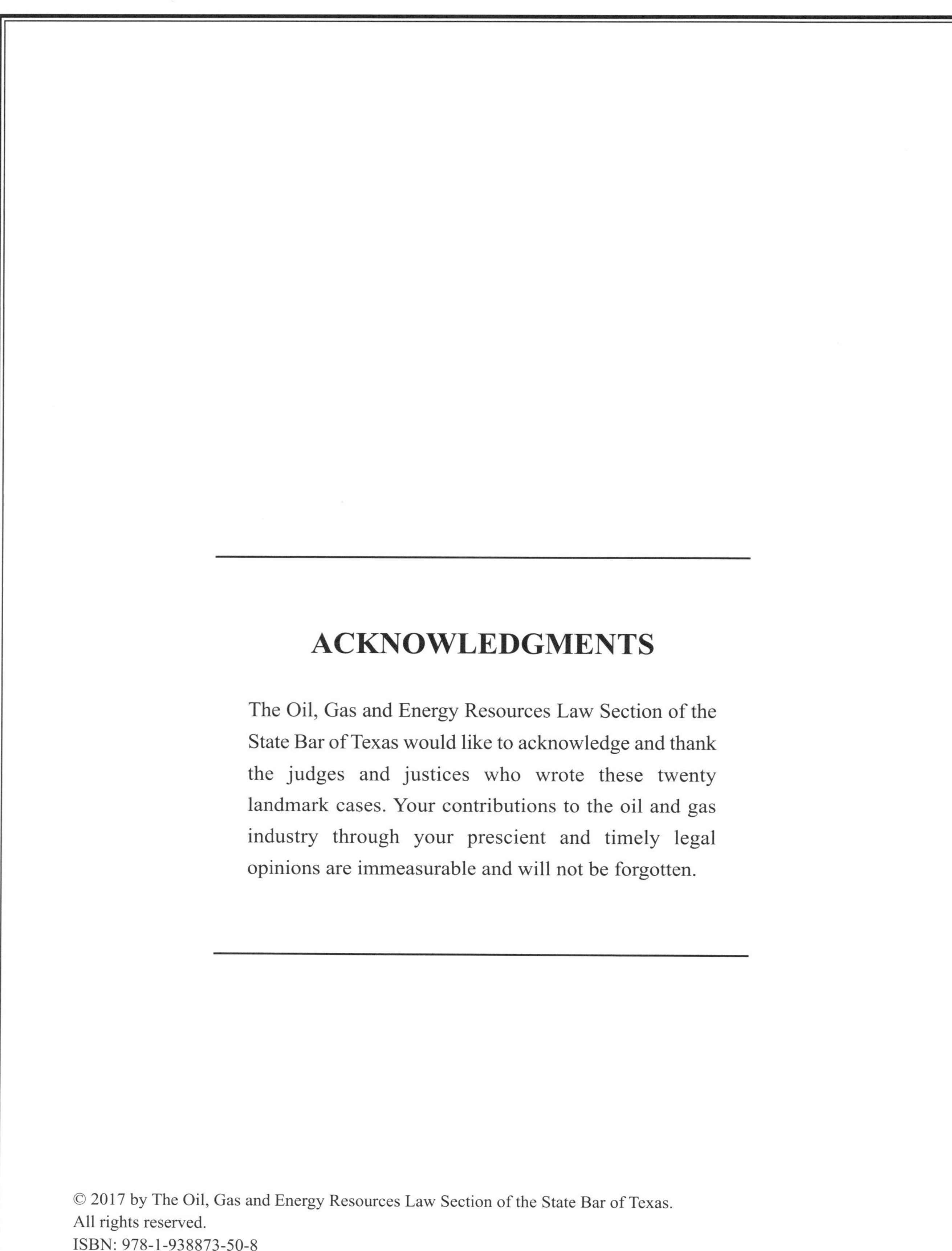

ACKNOWLEDGMENTS

The Oil, Gas and Energy Resources Law Section of the State Bar of Texas would like to acknowledge and thank the judges and justices who wrote these twenty landmark cases. Your contributions to the oil and gas industry through your prescient and timely legal opinions are immeasurable and will not be forgotten.

ISBN: 978-1-938873-50-8
LCCN: 2017942362
Printed in the United States of America.

LANDMARKS
OF A CENTURY IN
OIL AND GAS LAW

TWENTY CASES
That Shaped Texas Oil and Gas Jurisprudence

Compiled by the Oil, Gas and Energy Resources Law Section
of the State Bar of Texas

TABLE OF CONTENTS

Past Chairs of the Oil, Gas and Energy Resources Law Section of the State Bar of Texas

W.H. Francis, Dallas	1938-40
H.F. Montgomery, Houston	1940-41
A.W. Walker, Jr., Dallas	1941-42
E.E. Townes, Houston	1942-43
John E. Kilgore, Dallas	1943-44
Herman P. Pressler, Houston	1944-46
Carlos Masterson, Angleton	1946-47
J.W. Timmins, Dallas	1947-48
C.C. Small, Sr., Austin	1948-49
Herman P. Pressler, Houston	1949-50
R.E. Hardwicke, Sr., Fort Worth	1950-51
W.D. Masterson, Jr., Dallas	1951-52
Jacques P. Adoue, Montgomery	1952-53
Clayton L. Orn, Houston	1953-54
Hayden W. Head, Corpus Christi	1954-55
Paul McDermott, Fort Worth	1955-56
Gordon Brelsford, Tyler	1956-57
Joe R. Greenhill, Austin	1957-58
Cecil N. Cook, Houston	1958-59
Lee Jones, Jr., Colorado City	1959-60
Frank J. Scurlock, Dallas	1960-61
J.O. Terrell Couch, Houston	1961-62
Ira Butler, Fort Worth	1962-63
J.K. Smith, Fort Worth	1963-64
Walter C. Beardsley, Austin	1964-65
W.B. Edwards, Houston	1965-66
Lucian L. Morrison, San Antonio	1966-67
Leo J. Hoffman, Dallas	1967-68
Jack C. Hardy, Tyler	1968-69
Dean J. Cappy, Houston	1969-70
Simon M. Frank, Houston	1970-71
Hiram A. Berry, Amarillo	1971-72
Martin L. Allday, Midland	1972-73
Howard P. Coghlan, Longview	1973-74
Jesse P. Luton, Jr., Houston	1974-75
J. Burleson Smith, San Antonio	1975-76
Robert E. Rain, Jr., Dallas	1976-77
Frank Douglass, Austin	1977-78
Claude E. Upchurch, Houston	1978-79
Edward H. Hill, Amarillo	1979-80
Guy L. Nevill, Houston	1980-81
Tom Scott, Midland	1981-82
Charles B. Harris, Fort Worth	1982-83
Julius L. Lybrand, Houston	1983-84
Richard T. Brady, San Antonio	1984-85
J.R. Schneider, George West	1985-86
Ernest E. Smith, III, Austin	1986-87
Skipper Lay, Austin	1987-88
Jan E. Rehler, Corpus Christi	1988-89
H. Philip Whitworth, Austin	1989-90
Stuart C. Hollimon, Dallas	1990-91
Robert C. Grable, Fort Worth	1991-92
Tevis Herd, Midland	1992-93
Jon R. Ray, San Antonio	1993-94
Michael L. Grove, Houston	1994-95
Thomas W. Lynch, Dallas	1995-96
Richard F. Brown, Amarillo	1996-97
David G. Dunlap, Houston	1997-98
Elizabeth N. Miller, Austin	1998-99
Janice K. Hartrick, Houston	1999-00
Ernest V. Bruchez, Bryan	2000-01
Allen D. Cummings, Houston	2001-02
Kevin M. Beiter, San Antonio	2002-03
David C. Houck, Paris, France	2003-04
Laura H. Burney, San Antonio	2004-05
Brian R. Sullivan, Austin	2005-06
Arnold J. Johnson, Houston	2006-07
Dick Watt, Houston	2007-08
Michael P. Pearson, Houston	2008-09
Norma R. Iacovo, Arlington	2009-10
Fabene J. Welch, Houston	2010-11
William B. Burford, Midland	2011-12
Timothy R. Brown, Houston	2012-13
M.C. Cottingham Miles, San Antonio	2013-14
David M. Patton, Houston	2014-15
Ricardo E. Morales, Laredo	2015-16

The Oil, Gas and Energy Resources Law Section of the State Bar of Texas is dedicated to promoting excellence in the practice of oil, gas and energy resources law by (1) monitoring legal developments, (2) providing education, (3) encouraging and facilitating practice in the area, and (4) promoting ethics and professionalism; in each case coordinating as appropriate with similar professional organizations.

The Section was established in 1938 as the "Natural Resources Section" and is the oldest section of the State Bar of Texas. The Section is one of the largest and most active in the State Bar of Texas, with more than 4,000 members, and it recently celebrated its 75th anniversary.

P.O. Box 12487 | Austin, Texas 78711
www.oilgas.org

COUNCIL 2016–2017

OFFICERS

Charles W. Gordon IV, Chair
Peter E. Hosey, Chair-Elect
Kathleen E. Magruder, Vice Chair
Michael D. Jones, Secretary
Michael E. McElroy, Treasurer
Ricardo E. Morales, Immediate Past Chair

COUNCIL MEMBERS

Shonnie L. Daniel
Jeffery Adam McCarn
Jeff Weems
Jonathan D. Baughman
Lisa Vaughn Lumley
Carroll G. Martin
Rhodes Hamilton
David E. Jackson
Katy Pier Moore

Introduction

Several years ago the Oil, Gas and Energy Resources Law Section of the State Bar of Texas published for its membership a collection of the works of A. W. Walker, Jr., in which Walker analyzed many aspects of the fundamental nature of oil, gas, and mineral rights. That publication was well-received, and the Section Council began to consider whether our mission should include one or more other additions to members' libraries. The Section Council enthusiastically approved an idea first broached by then– Chairman Arnold J. Johnson to reproduce a collection of some of the most influential cases decided by Texas courts in oil and gas law, accompanied by commentary of able and experienced practitioners and scholars.

The Section Council formed a committee and tasked it first with the responsibility of identifying the cases deserving to be highlighted and then with the recruitment of commentators. The committee, composed of William B. Burford, Ernest V. Bruchez, Laura H. Burney, Cullen M. Godfrey, Stuart C. Hollimon, Norma Rosner Iacovo, Arnold J. Johnson, Elizabeth N. Miller, Joseph D. Naylor, Michael P. Pearson, Susan M. Richardson, Benjamin W. Sebree, Ernest E. Smith, and Richard D. Watt, met in person and by telephone on a number of occasions. After soliciting recommendations for the cases that should be considered and polling Section members, the committee settled on twenty cases that stood out as landmarks of Texas oil and gas jurisprudence. Those cases are presented here.

Although there could never be an indisputable tabulation of the twenty most important cases in the history of Texas oil and gas law, almost every Texas oil and gas lawyer's list would include a number of the cases presented here. Each of these cases, whether the decision broke new ground or crystallized an evident trend, has had signal influence on the development of the law. All have, in short, stood the test of time.

The cases are reproduced just as they appeared when decided, complete with all their stylistic quirks, archaic forms of citation, and even typographical errors. Any attempt at editing might have detracted from the reader's ability to grasp the courts' mode of thought and the interplay of the legal and factual circumstances of the day. They are presented mainly in chronological order, and no effort has been made, nor would any such effort be possible, to rank their importance or influence.

Our commentary authors, to whom the Section owes a debt of gratitude, are all either prominent legal scholars or practitioners who have spent their careers exploring Texas oil and gas law. Their thought-provoking observations, developed from study, discernment, and long experience, each from a unique perspective, should enable readers to consider these familiar cases with fresh insight.

Those who have contributed their efforts to the production of this work sincerely desire that readers will gain a renewed appreciation of the sources of the principles they take for granted and apply every day. These cases make us realize that there was a time when the concepts that are basic to our understanding of the law were unformed and conjectural. We hope this publication will deepen the reader's understanding of how and why the law, as we know it, came to be.

William B. Burford
Committee Chair

Preface

Over 10 years ago, in the fall of 2006, at the council meeting of the Oil, Gas and Energy Resources Law Section of the State Bar of Texas, 2006-2007 Chair Arnold J. Johnson announced that the Section would compile and provide to the Section membership a book covering the twenty (20) greatest oil and gas cases of the Twentieth Century. The result of that idea is this book – *Landmarks of a Century in Oil and Gas Law – Twenty Cases That Shaped Texas Oil and Gas Jurisprudence*. This has been a true labor of love for the Section Council.

While 2006-2007 Chair Johnson deserves credit for formulating the idea for the Landmark Book, 2011-2012 Chair William B. Burford deserves credit for the countless hours spent as Chair of the committee assigned to memorialize Chair Johnson's idea into an actual book by determining the twenty cases to be selected, and assigning the commentaries for each case to known oil and gas legal scholars. Without 2011-2012 Chair Burford's work, Arnold Johnson's wonderful idea would not be a reality and a book that we, as members of the Section, will enjoy for years to come.

As anyone who has ever assembled a compilation book before will know, while it is all well and good to have obtained the cases and commentaries for such a book, someone needs to accomplish the assimilation of the material into an actual book to be printed for mass publication. The person who has done the lion's share of that work is Tracy Nuckols, the Director for all of the State Bar of Texas Sections. While she could not have envisioned how much she would be involved in seeing this project to completion, she has nonetheless worked tirelessly to assemble all of the cases and commentaries into the book you now enjoy. The Section owes Ms. Nuckols a debt of gratitude for her efforts in seeing this project to completion.

Now that you have an insight regarding how this book grew from an idea into an actual publication, ready for you to read, I hope that as you peruse the cases and commentaries herein, that you will gain an appreciation of some of the most important foundations of Texas oil and gas law. The cases chosen for this book and the excellent commentaries of the oil and gas legal scholars involved will be an invaluable resource to each of you in your practice for years to come. I sincerely thank all of the authors for their time in drafting these commentaries, and their patience and understanding regarding the length of time they have waited to see their names and work come to fruition in this book.

The Section elected me to the Council in June 2006. The Section later elected me Chair in June 2013. It is now my great joy in 2017 (almost eleven years after I was elected to the Section Council and three years after I was Chair of the Section, to announce that the Landmark Book is completed and I look forward to all of you reading this wonderful book. I dedicate this preface and my efforts to complete the publication of the Landmark Book to the memory of my mother, Carol Cottingham Miles of San Angelo, Texas, who died on June 14, 2015. She blessed my life and the lives of so many other people. I love her and miss her.

M.C. Cottingham "Cottie" Miles

CHAPTER 1

Texas Company v. Daugherty

COMMENTARY
by Richard F. Brown

107 Tex. 226, 176 S.W. 717

1915

Texas Company
v.
Daugherty

107 Tex. 226, 176 S.W. 717

1915

Mr. Justice PHILLIPS delivered the opinion of the court.

The question presented by the case for decision is whether the interests or rights conferred upon The Texas Company in virtue of a number of so-called oil leases constituted property subject to taxation in its hands.

The instruments in question were respectively executed by owners of lands in Wichita County as grantors, duly acknowledged and recorded, the wife joining where the property constituted any part of a homestead. In each instance the grantor, by the terms of the instrument, "granted, bargained, sold and conveyed" to The Texas Company as grantee, "all the oil, gas, coal, and other minerals in and under" the particular tract of land, which was fully described, for a valuable consideration, consisting of a stated amount acknowledged to have been paid (in the particular lease shown in the record as a form and to which all of them substantially corresponded, one hundred dollars) and certain stipulated royalties, together with the exclusive right of ingress and egress at all times for the purpose of drilling, mining and operating for such minerals and the conduct of all operations, and the erection of appliances and structures in that connection, and for the laying of all pipe lines necessary for the production, mining, storing and transportation thereof, with the privilege of renewing and removing all such structures at will. Each instrument contained the following habendum clause:

> "To have and to hold, all and singular, the above described premises, rights, properties and privileges, and all such as are hereinafter specified, under the said grantee, and the heirs, successors and assigns of such, forever, upon the following terms."

Under penalty of forfeiture of "the rights and estates hereby granted," it was provided that operations for the drilling of a well for oil or gas should be begun within one year from the time of the delivery of the instrument, the forfeiture to be saved, however, notwithstanding such operations should not be commenced within that period, by the payment by the grantee of twenty-five dollars per quarter for a period not exceeding three years; with the further provision that the conveyance should be in full effect for twenty years from the discovery of oil, gas or other minerals, and as much longer as they should be produced in paying quantities, in the event the grantee, or its successors or assigns, should sink a well or shaft and make such discovery within the limits of time, or the extension thereof, stipulated. A concluding clause in each instrument was as follows:

> "This lease is not intended as a mere franchise, but is intended as a conveyance of the property and privileges above described for the purposes herein mentioned, and it is so understood by all parties hereto."

The owners of the fee of all the land described in the several so-called leases had rendered them for taxation for the current year at their fair market value, subject to the rights and privileges conferred upon the grantee under such instruments. In assessing the value of the lands against the owners of the fee, their value as oil bearing, or prospective oil bearing, lands, as evidenced by the royalty interests of such owners, under the instruments, was considered, and taxes had been paid by such owners accordingly. In that valuation, however, the value of the rights and privileges conferred by these instruments upon the grantee therein, was not included.

The question is to be resolved, in our opinion, by the determination of whether the instruments involved conferred upon the plaintiff in error an interest in the lands therein respectively described. If their effect, at most, was but the creation in its favor of a mere franchise or privilege to devote the land to a certain use, with the usufructary right, as a part of its use and enjoyment, to appropriate a portion of such oil and gas as might be discovered, such franchise or privilege was taxable against the owner of the fee as a part of the land, just as any other such valuable right or privilege belonging to land is, unless otherwise distinctly provided by statute, so taxable under article 7504, which declares that "real property, for the purpose of taxation, shall be construed to include the land itself, whether laid out in town lots or otherwise, and all the buildings, structures and improvements, or other fixtures of whatsoever kind thereon, and *all the rights and privileges belonging or in anywise appertaining thereto*, and all mines, minerals, quarries and fossils in and under the same." The rights and privileges belonging to land contribute in a very substantial way to its value. They largely cause it to yield its income, and it is the theory of our statute, therefore, that their value shall be included in the valuation of the land for taxation in the hands of the owner. They do not escape taxation by this method; on the contrary, they are subjected to its burden through the inclusion of their value in the assessment of the land; and they are taxed against the owner of the land because the Legislature has deemed it proper for him to bear the charge in view of their essential contribution to its value. This is plainly the effect of the decision in The State v. Austin & Northwestern Railroad Company, 94 Texas, 530, S.W., 62 S.W., 1050, where, before the enactment of the statute providing for the taxation of intangible assets, attempt was made to tax the franchise of a railroad company separate from its real estate. After quoting present article 7504, Chief Justice Gaines, upon this question, said:

> "It seems to us the plain purpose of the article last quoted to require that in assessing real estate for taxation, whether held by a natural person or a corporation, there shall not only be included in the valuation the value of the land itself merely as land together with the improvements thereon, but also all franchises and privileges appurtenant thereto and all the advantages for a profitable prosecution of the business to which it is appropriated. As a rule, the value of improved real estate is proportionate to the net income which it will yield. The value of a railroad is not the mere value of its right of way, road bed and superstructure, its depot grounds and structures thereon, considered by themselves, but the value of all these as an operating, 'going concern,'—this value being in general determinable by the profits which result from its operation. The statute requires all property to be assessed 'at its true and full value,' and in effect defines that value to be what it would probably sell for at a voluntary sale for cash. Persons proposing to sell or buy a railroad, in forming their opinion as to its value, would doubtless consider the condition of its physical properties, but would ultimately reach their conclusion upon the question by a careful estimate of the probable net income which its operation will produce. There are no special 'rights and privileges belonging to or in anywise appertaining' to the great mass of the real property of the State, such as farming lands and town or city lots, but the terms are applicable to the real estate of railroad companies and suggest the thought that the Legislature had such property in mind when it inserted the provision, and that it was intended that in valuing a railroad for taxation the valuation should include every right and privilege which was exercised in producing its income, and that it was not intended to disassociate the soul from the body of the living concern and value by itself the lifeless remains."

We accordingly turn to an examination of the instruments for the purpose of determining their legal effect. It will be observed that they constitute no mere demise of the premises for a given period, as in the case of an ordinary leasehold. Nor do they amount simply to a grant of the right to prospect upon the land for oil or gas and reduce those substances to possession and ownership. They deal with the oil, gas and other minerals "in and under" the land as property, in the ground, capable of ownership and subject to be conveyed, for, as such, in unmistakable terms they are "granted, sold and conveyed" to the grantee for a stated consideration acknowledged to have been paid, valuable in itself and independent of the royalties stipulated as payable to the grantor in the event of the discovery of such minerals, or any obligation imposed upon the grantee to explore for them. For the purpose of making the exploration and producing all the oil, gas and other minerals that might be within the ground, and the erection of all structures necessary thereto, as well as their storing and transportation, the possession of the land itself is likewise granted, with no limitation upon the number of wells or shafts that the grantee might sink, or the extent of its operations in that connection, and consequently no qualification of its right of possession to all such parts of the surface,—except that no well should be drilled nearer than 200 feet from the house or barn on the premises without the consent of both parties, as might be necessary to its full use by the grantee for the purposes named. The rights of the grantee are made subject to forfeiture if operations for the drilling of a well for oil or gas are not begun within one year from the delivery of the instrument, or if the payment of the amount provided in lieu of such commencement is not made; but the sinking of a well or shaft and the discovery of any of the minerals named, within the period of one year or the extension thereof provided for, in each instance renders the instrument effective for twenty years and as much longer as such minerals shall be produced in paying quantities. This constituted the entire grant as one capable of indefinite duration.

While such is the evident effect of the instruments when looked at, as they should be, from their "four corners," the parties were plainly desirous of giving further emphasis to their character as "conveyances" of property as distinguished from a mere grant of a license or privilege. With the obvious intention of placing their construction beyond the pale of any doubt, they incorporated the provision already noted, that "this lease is not intended as a mere franchise, but is intended as a *conveyance of the property* and privileges above described for the purposes herein mentioned, and it is so understood by all the parties hereto."

It will be further noted that no condition is expressed or act required of the grantee which preceded the vesting of such estates as the instruments created. Upon penalty of forfeiture of "the rights and estates *hereby* granted," the grantee was required to begin operations for the drilling of a well for oil or gas within one year or pay a stipulated amount, quarterly, during the extension period provided; but it was the manifest purpose of the parties that the estate created should constitute a present grant, and that the grantee should perform these acts after taking possession, which rendered them conditions subsequent. A fee may pass by deed upon a condition subsequent to the same extent as though the condition did not exist, subject to the contingency of being defeated according to the condition. And here, if any property was conveyed, there was a present grant but liable to be defeated by the grantee's failure to perform the requirement in respect to beginning operations for the drilling of a well for oil or gas, or, in lieu thereof, making the quarterly payment provided. The grant amounted to a defeasible title in fee to the oil and gas in the ground, if oil and gas in place are capable of ownership and conveyance.

This brings us to the consideration of the latter question, and the contention of the plaintiff in error that these substances are incapable of ownership as property until severed or extracted from the ground, and that therefore these instruments conferred upon it no more than a mere use of the surface of the ground and the right to take them from it, amounting only to a privilege belonging to the land and taxable as a part of it against the owner of the fee, but vesting it with the title to no property whatever. It may be remarked, we think, with propriety, that this position is in marked contrast with the solemn assertion of the instruments themselves, exhibited in the record by means of a common form evidently prepared by the plaintiff in error for use in its business operations, that they were not intended as "mere franchises," but as "conveyances of the property and privileges described, and were so understood by all parties thereto." However, we pass over that to the determination of the naked question.

It is no longer doubted that oil and gas within the ground are minerals. They have peculiar attributes not common to other minerals because of their fugitive nature or vagrant habit—the disposition to wander or percolate, and the possibility of their escape from beneath one part of the surface of the earth to another. Nevertheless, they are to be classed as minerals. Thornton on Oil and Gas, sec. 18; Murray v. Allred, 100 Tenn., 100, 39 L. R. A., 249, 66 Am. St., 740, 43 S.W., 355; Stoughton's Appeal, 88 Pa. St., 198; The People v. Bell, 237 Ill., 332, 19 L. R. A. (N. S.), 746, 15 Ann. Cases, 511, 86 N. E., 593. In place, they lie within the strata of the earth; and necessarily are a part of the realty. Being a part of the realty while in place, it would seem to logically follow that whenever they are conveyed while in that condition or possessing that status, a conveyance of an interest in the realty results. It is generally conceded that for the purpose of ownership and conveyance of solid minerals the earth may be divided horizontally as well as vertically, and that title to the surface may rest in one person and title to the strata beneath the surface containing such minerals in another. Because of the fugitive nature of oil and gas, some courts, emphasizing the doctrine that they are incapable of absolute ownership until captured and reduced to possession and analogizing their ownership to that of things *ferae naturae*, have made a distinction between their conveyance while in place and that of other minerals, holding that it created no interest in the realty. But it is difficult to perceive a substantial ground for the distinction. A purchaser of them within the ground assumes the hazard of their absence through the possibility of their escape from beneath that particular tract of land, and, of course, if they are not discovered the conveyance is of no effect; just as the purchaser of solid mineral within the ground incurs the risk of its absence and therefore a futile venture. But let it be supposed that they have not escaped, and are in repose within the strata beneath the particular tract and capable of possession by appropriation from it. There they clearly constitute a part of the realty. Is the possibility of their escape to render them while in place incapable of conveyance, or is their ownership while in that condition, with the exclusive right to take them from the land, anything less than ownership of an interest in the land? Conceding that they are fluent in their nature and may depart from the land before brought into absolute possession, will it be denied that so long as they have not departed they are a part of the land? Or when conveyed in their natural state and they are in fact beneath the particular tract, that their grant amounts to an interest in the land? The opposing argument is founded entirely upon their peculiar property and, therefore, the risk of their escape. But how does that possibility alter the character of the property interest which they constitute while in place beneath the land? The argument ignores the equal possibility of their presence, and that the parties have contracted upon the latter assumption; that if they are in place beneath the tract, they are essentially a part of the realty, and their grant, therefore, while in that condition, if effectual at all, is a grant of an interest in the realty. In other words, the question, it seems to us, reduces itself to this: If the oil and gas, the subject of the conveyance, are in fact not beneath or within the land and are therefore not capable of being reduced to possession, the conveyance is of no effect. But if they have not departed and are beneath it, they are there as a part of the realty; and their conveyance while in place, if the instrument be given any effect, is consequently the conveyance of an interest in the realty. There could be no warrant for denying effect to such instruments as these, and, granting them effect, they are therefore to be considered as conveyances of such an interest.

The possibility of the escape of the oil and gas from beneath the land before being finally brought within actual control may be recognized, as may also their incapability of absolute ownership, in the sense of positive possession, until so subjected. But nevertheless, while they are in the ground they constitute a property interest. If so, what is the nature of it in the hands of the original owner? It embraces necessarily the privilege or right to take them from the ground. But is that its extent, or sole character? While they lie within the ground as a part of the realty, is the ownership of the realty to be denominated, as to them, a mere license to appropriate, as distinguished from an absolute property right in the corpus of the land? With the land itself capable of absolute ownership, everything within it in the nature of a mineral is likewise capable of ownership so long as it constitutes a part of it. If these minerals are a part of the realty while in place, as undoubtedly they are, upon what principle can the ownership of the property interest which they constitute while they are beneath or within the land, be other than the ownership of an interest in the realty?

We are not dealing with conveyances of simply the right to take the oil and gas from the ground. These instruments purported to be a grant of the oil and gas themselves in the ground. If while in place they constituted an interest in the realty, that interest was subject to sale and conveyance, the purchaser assuming the risk of reducing them to possession. The instruments throughout treat these minerals in the ground as property, and bespeak the purpose to give the grantee absolute dominion over them, not merely when severed from the realty and reduced to personalty, but while in their natural state; and the interest granted was furthermore expressed as one capable of being assigned and conveyed by the grantee. There was imposed no limit upon the grantee's right to the oil and gas, save as to the royalty payable to the grantor; it could take them out to any extent, at all times, and from beneath any part of the land, with the single limitation that no well should be drilled nearer than 200 feet from the house or barn on the premises except by the grantor's consent. Such a vested interest in the minerals in the ground, forming in their natural state a part of the land, with absolute dominion over them while in that state, and with the further unlimited right to their appropriation, plainly constitute property and all that is recognized in proprietorship, and equally amount to an interest in the land itself.

As pointed out in Ohio Oil Company v. Indiana, 177 U. S., 190, 44 L. Ed., 729, 20 Sup. Ct., 576, the analogy between deposits of oil and gas and things *ferae naturae* is, at best, a limited one. The difference between them is that things *ferae naturae* are public property and all have an equal right to reduce them to possession and ownership; while the right to the oil and gas beneath his land is an exclusive and private property right in the land owner, inhering in virtue of his proprietorship of the land, and of which he may not be deprived without a taking of private property.

While there is a conflict of authority upon the question we have discussed, the views expressed are believed to be amply sustained. In Thornton on Oil and Gas, a standard work upon the subject, in section 19 it is said:

> "Oil and gas, until severed from the realty, are as much a part of it as coal or stone. So long as they remain in the ground, outside of an artificial receptacle at least, as the casing of a well or pipe line, they must be treated as a part of the realty underneath the surface of which they lie. So much so are they a part of the realty, as we shall repeatedly see hereafter, that a conveyance of them in their natural state in the earth requires all the formalities of a conveyance of any other interest in the same real estate."

Again in section 20 of the same work, this is announced:

> "The owner of the surface is the owner of the gas and oil beneath it; but if they escape into the land of another he ceases to be owner of them. They are the subject of grant or conveyance, just as much so as the grant or conveyance of coal or stone buried in the soil of the same tract of land."

In Gould on Waters, section 291, it is stated:

> "Petroleum oil, like subterranean water, is included in the comprehensive idea which the law attaches to the word land, and will be protected as a part of the soil in which it is found. Like water it is not the subject of property except while in actual occupancy, and a grant of either water or oil is not a grant of the soil or of anything for which ejectment will lie. The same is true of natural gas. A lease of land for the purposes of mining oil, coal, rock, or carbon oil passes a corporeal interest which is the proper subject of an action of ejectment, and a proportionate share of the oil to be produced by an oil well is an interest in land, a parol sale of which is void under the statute of fraud."

In Stoughton's Appeal, 88 Penn. St., 198, after adverting to the classification of oil as a mineral and its therefore being a part of the realty, the Supreme Court of Pennsylvania said:

> "In this it is like coal or any other natural product which *in situ* forms part of the land. It may become, by severance, personalty or there may be a right to use or take it originating in custom or prescription, as the right of a life tenant to work opened mines or to use timber for repairing buildings or fences on a farm, or for fire bote. Nevertheless, whenever conveyance is made of it, whether that conveyance be called a lease or deed, it is, in effect, the grant of part of the corpus of the estate and not of a mere incorporeal right."

In Blakeley et al. v. Marshall, 174 Pa. St., 425, 34 Atl., 564, the same court held:

> "An oil lease, investing the lessee with the right to remove all the oil in place, in the premises in consideration of his giving the lessors a certain per centum thereof, is in legal effect a sale of a portion of the land and the proceeds represent the respective interests of the lessors in the premises."

To the same effect is Jennings v. Bloomfield, 199 Pa. St., 638, 49 Atl., 135.

In Heller v. Dailey, 28 Ind. App., 555, 62 N. E., 490, a case which involved an oil and gas contract not materially different from the instruments in this case, and which purported to convey the oil and gas in place under a particular tract of land, the court, while fully recognizing the doctrine which forms the basis of the contention here of the plaintiff in error, that the absolute ownership of these minerals does not exist until they are reduced to actual possession, said:

> "The oil and gas in their free and natural state within the land constitute a part of it, though they be fluent and liable to depart to other land, there to be taken into possession through wells made for such purpose. The right to take such minerals from the land constitutes an interest in the land. The instrument under consideration does not create a mere personal privilege to take the minerals from the land. It is an exclusive and assignable interest in land. If with propriety it can be called a license, it must be a license coupled with an interest in land. By its terms the contract is a grant of the minerals in and under the land. If by such general terms all of a specified solid mineral, as coal, in and under the land were granted it would be a grant of real estate; but because of the fluidity and fugitiveness of petroleum and natural gas the absolute ownership of these mineral substances within the land can not be acquired without reducing them to actual control; so that a distinction must be and is made between the elusive minerals in and under the ground and the solid minerals in place in the earth. Therefore a grant of all the oil and gas in and under a tract of land is not a grant of any particular specific substance as would be the grant of the coal in and under certain land . . . . While for reasons which we have sought to state, we do not regard the contract in suit as a grant of land, or as a lease properly so called, but do regard it as a grant of a right in the nature of an incorporeal hereditament, operative from the time of its execution, and during the accomplishment of its purpose as a transfer of an exclusive right to search for, take and appropriate the minerals mentioned in the instrument, under whatever technical

> common law term it may most properly be classed, it must be held to be a conveyance of an interest in land within the meaning of our statutes."

Williamson v. Jones, 39 West Va., 231, 25 L. R. A., 222, 19 S. E., 436, affirms the same rule, it being remarked with respect to these minerals that it is only when they escape out of the possession of the owner that the right of property is gone. Wilson v. Hughes, by the same court, reported in 43 W. Va., 826, 39 L. R. A., 292, 28 S. E., 781, announces a like holding. It is contended by the plaintiff in error that Wilson v. Hughes has been in effect overruled by the Supreme Court of West Virginia in the later case of Harvey Coal & Coke Co. v. Dillon, 59 W. Va., 605, 53 S. E., 928, 6 L. R. A. (N. S.), 628, and such may be the operation of the latter decision, though it is not in terms so stated. It is to be remarked, however, that the instrument considered in the Dillon case granted merely the right to mine certain minerals without purporting to convey the minerals themselves in place, and this characteristic is more than once emphasized by the court in its opinion. Prior to the decision in the Dillon case, the same court had decided, State v. Low, 46 W. Va., 451, 33 S. E., 271, a case not adverted to in the Dillon opinion. There a conveyance of the oil and gas in place in a tract of land, of the same character as embodied in these instruments, was reviewed for the purpose of determining whether it created an interest in land which was subject to taxation against the grantees. It was held that the conveyance amounted to a defeasible title in fee to the oil and gas, taxable against the grantees as an interest in the land.

The Supreme Court of Illinois adheres to the view that these minerals in place are not capable of distinct ownership, and that a conveyance of them is not a grant of the minerals themselves in the ground, but to such part thereof as the grantee may find. Watford Oil & Gas Co. v. Shipman, 233 Ill., 9, 122 Am. St., 144, 84 N. E., 53. Yet the same court has held that such a conveyance, with the right to go upon the land and occupy it for the purpose of prospecting, if of unlimited duration, or if such right, under the terms of the lease, is capable of having unlimited duration, amounts to a grant of a freehold interest in the land. Watford Oil & Gas Co. v. Shipman; Bruner v. Hicks, 230 Ill., 536, 120 Am. St., 332, 82 N. E., 888. In *The People v. Bell, 237 Ill., 332, 19 L. R. A. (N. S.), 746, 15 Ann. Cases, 511, 86 N. E. 593*, the question was directly involved of whether the rights created by such a conveyance amounted to an interest taxable as land against the grantee, separate from the fee taxable against its owner. The conveyance there was of the oil and gas under a certain tract of land, for the consideration of the payment of a royalty to the grantors, the premises to be held for one year, and so long thereafter as oil or gas might be found thereon in paying quantities, constituting, as is the case in the instruments before us, a term capable of unlimited duration. In that state by statute such a mining right (as it is there classed) is taxable separately. The statute, however, did not undertake to define the property classification of such a right, whether it constituted personal property or an interest in land. The named question, therefore, of the character of the property right was necessary to be determined. The court held that the conveyance amounted to the grant of a freehold interest, which should be assessed and taxed as real estate against the grantees. See also Guffey v. Smith, 237 U. S., 101, 35 U. S. Ct. Rep. 527, decided April 5, 1915. According to these decisions it is immaterial whether there is any such thing as absolute ownership of oil and gas in place. They plainly announce that the conveyance of such minerals in place, with a right to the use of the land for their extraction from the earth which may prove, under the instrument, of unlimited duration, creates a freehold interest in the land itself; and the last named decision as clearly rules that such interest is taxable as realty and against the person who owns and may enjoy it.

It is assumed in the argument that because of the decision of this court in Oil & Gas Pipe Line Co. v. Teel, 95 Texas, 586, 68 S. W., 979, and its refusal of writs of error in the cases of O'Neil v. Sun Co., 123 S. W., 172, and Witherspoon v. Staley, 156 S. W., 556, it is committed to the proposition that oil and gas in place are not susceptible of grant and their conveyance creates no property interest in the land, but only a bare right or privilege to go on the land and mine for such minerals and reduce them to possession. The case of Southern Oil Co. v. Colquitt, 28 Texas Civ. App., 292, 69 S. W., 169, involved the question of whether the proper joinder of the wife was necessary in a conveyance of such minerals in place under a tract constituting a homestead, together with the right to make use of the land for the purpose of their production from the earth. The Court of Civil Appeals for the Fifth District held that it was for the reason that such a conveyance amounted to the grant of an interest in the land itself. This court refused writ of error. It could have done so only under the view that the interest created by the instrument was an interest in the realty itself, requiring for its validity the joinder of the wife because of the homestead character of the realty. In O'Neil v. Sun Company the question was the right of the Sun Company to oil from a well bored upon a tract to which it held a clear and unforfeited right under a lease. The Court of Civil Appeals for the Fourth District held that the instrument, though it purported to grant and convey the title to the oil and gas under the land, only conferred a right to exploit the ground and acquire title to the oil by its extraction from it. Under the facts of the case it was manifest that the Sun Company was entitled to the oil, whatever might be the technical classification of its right. There are essential elements of difference between the contract considered in that case and the instruments here under review. It possessed all of the characteristics of a contract for exploitation, with the right to take the oil and gas in the ground, with such right depending upon the company's performance of the contract. Here the instruments express a present grant of the minerals in place for a consideration which was valuable and independent of any obligation resting upon the grantee, emphasized by the parties as a conveyance of property and not the grant of a mere franchise by a distinct provision asserting such to be its character. The same distinction exists with respect to the instrument considered in Witherspoon v. Staley, as well as that reviewed in Oil & Pipe Line Co. v. Teel. In the former case the Court of Civil Appeals held that a forfeiture of the right created under the contract had clearly accrued. We concurred in that view and upon that ground refused the writ of error. In Oil & Pipe Line Co. v. Teel the contract was supported by only a nominal consideration other than the mere promise of the lessee to perform certain acts, but for the performance of which he was not bound. The contract was construed properly as the creation of a mere option which permitted the acquisition of an interest on performance of conditions—a mere optional right to acquire an interest in land, a character of instrument plainly distinguishable from those here presented.

It is our conclusion that these instruments had the effect to confer upon the plaintiff in error an interest in the several tracts of land described, the value of which was assessable against it for taxation. The judgments of the District Court and Court of Civil Appeals are therefore affirmed.

Affirmed.

Appellant's motion for rehearing in this case was overruled June 24, 1916.

Commentary on Texas Company v. Daugherty[1]

by Richard F. Brown

America was a very different place in 1915 when *Texas Company v. Daugherty* reached the Texas Supreme Court. In many ways, the country was indistinguishable from the country as it existed at the time of the Civil War, but changes in transportation were driving great changes in American life. The country was in the middle of the golden age of steam. The railroads were the first great revolution in ground transportation. Since the beginning of time, crossing the land was only possible by walking or by utilizing animal power. Beginning in about 1840, the railroads changed that by harnessing mechanical power to go faster and to move greater loads. Between 1840 and the early 20th century, the miles of railroad track in America increased from approximately 3,000 miles to 254,000 miles.[2] Railroads were like new rivers that suddenly brought goods, commerce, and people to remote corners of Texas, wherever the tracks were located. From approximately 1876 to 1882, Texas adopted a policy of giving away public lands to the railroads[3] as an incentive to get the railroads built and to open up the vast portions of the State that had no navigable rivers. The railroads quickly sold most of the lands to monetize the grants and capitalize the railroads. It is one of the great ironies of Texas history that if the buildout of the railroads had occurred only 20 or 30 years later, the railroads would have become the major oil companies in Texas.

By 1915, the technological change brought by the railroads was part of the fabric of American life, but the railroads were already entering the last half of the 100 years in which they would be the dominant form of transportation over land. The new competitors—the airplane and the automobile—had already arrived. The airplane was still a novelty, but the automobile was quickly finding its place in American commerce and redefining the quality of American life.

The gasoline-powered car had already defeated steam and electricity as the source of power.[4] In 1900, there were approximately 8,000 passenger cars registered in the United States[5] and 10 miles of paved road.[6] Expansion was rapid, so by 1915 there were 2,070,900 motor vehicles[7] and 226,288 miles of "improved" road.[8] By 2012, there would be 253,639,386 registered motor vehicles[9] and 2,646,000 miles of paved road.[10] This incredible transformation was in the very early stages, and its significance would not have been apparent, but the transformation of America by the automobile for at least one hundred years would be dependent upon one source of power—oil.

The first sighting of oil in Texas was recorded in July 1543 by Luis de Moscoso, a survivor of the DeSoto expedition.[11] The DeSoto expedition was forced ashore between Sabine Pass and High Island.[12] The explorers observed oil floating on the tide and collected the substance and used it to caulk their boats.[13] Seepages of crude oil would be observed and reported by Texas settlers over the next 300 years, and, during the second half of the 19th century, the discovery and production of oil would begin.[14]

On September 12, 1866, the first producing well was drilled in Texas.[15] The well was drilled about 15 miles southeast of Nacogdoches by the earliest known Texas wildcatter, Lynis T. Barrett.[16] The well was drilled 106 feet deep when oil came bubbling to the surface.[17] This discovery is not particularly well known because Barrett learned, "as so many subsequent episodes in Texas petroleum history demonstrate, it is one thing to find oil and quite another to produce it in commercially profitable quantities."[18]

In 1893, the need for water would result in the first economically significant discovery of oil in Texas.[19] In the small town of Corsicana, in Navarro County, Texas, the lack of water spurred the town into organizing a water company.[20] Drilling began in 1893, and the drillers struck oil. The Corsicana oilfield peaked in 1900, producing approximately 2,300 barrels of oil per day.[21] Although production from the Corsicana oilfield was modest compared to later discoveries, the discovery was of tremendous significance in the history of the oil and gas industry in Texas because it established the potential for commercial oil production in the State.[22] Several years later, Spindletop would produce the first oil boom in Texas.

In 1892, Patillo Higgins began promoting the possibilities of oil beneath a hill near the town of Beaumont, in southeast Texas.[23] Money ran short, and Higgins made a deal with Captain Anthony F. Lucas, who began drilling in 1899.[24] After initial testing, the two men decided to seek additional financial backing. Lucas was able to secure financing from James McClurg Guffey, a Pittsburgh oil speculator, and his partner, John H. Galey.[25] With new backing and technology, a well was spudded on October 27, 1900. On January 10, 1901, drillers reached a depth of about 1,020 feet and brought in a gusher of tremendous proportion at Spindletop.[26] Oil was flowing at 75,000 barrels per day, and the Texas oil boom was on.[27]

Texas Company v. Daugherty was decided on May 21, 1915. Just as the discovery at Corsicana and the boom at Spindletop helped shape the Texas oil and gas industry in its earliest stages, this decision helped shape the legal principles on which oil and gas law is based today. Significant events in history are frequently not perceived as historic until long after they occur. It is doubtful that any of the justices deciding *Texas Company v. Daugherty* could have appreciated that the automobile would soon transform Texas, that oil was essential to that transformation, or that, on May 21, 1915, they were deciding the case that would become the linchpin in our concept of property rights in oil and gas. The continuing relevance and efficacy of our jurisprudence is dependent upon the slow and steady evolution of the common law. But there are also seminal cases, which disproportionately affect the evolution of our jurisprudence by original and creative thought, by an abrupt change in direction, or by addressing novel issues. The new oil and gas industry would provide new challenges for the courts, and the Texas courts would respond by creating the most extensive body of oil and gas law in the world.

Fourteen years after the gusher at Spindletop, *Texas Company v. Daugherty* was the most significant oil and gas case to reach the Texas Supreme Court. Courts in Texas had decided approximately 27 cases[28] that would fit within the body of case law that A. W. Walker would first call "oil and gas" law. There was more extensive precedent available from other jurisdictions, such as Pennsylvania, that had a longer history of oil and gas commerce. Texas was beginning its own oil and gas jurisprudence with an almost blank chalkboard, but those early wildcatters from Corsicana and Spindletop had already begun the industry's rich history of heavy dependence upon the courts to resolve their differences and to define their property rights. This was not surprising because oil and gas property rights are generally defined by pieces of paper, and the law and lawyers are closely involved when important rights are determined by the intent of the parties as expressed on paper. In the new oil and gas industry, the most important and fundamental piece of paper was the oil and gas lease. Many of the early oil and gas cases were significant regardless of the issues presented simply because they were first, but *Texas Company v. Daugherty* went straight to the heart of property rights under an oil and gas lease, which guaranteed the lasting significance of the decision.

Among many of the early cases cited in footnote 28, an "unless" form oil and gas lease was generally held to be an option, and a recurring theme was the evolution of the concept of the payment of a bonus as the independent consideration to support the option to drill contained in the lease. If an oil and gas lease includes a required drilling obligation, then it is clearly supported by consideration, and a lessee can be sued for damages for failing to drill. Lessees generally do not want a required drilling obligation but instead want the right to unilaterally terminate or surrender the lease without further liability. If there is no express drilling obligation, even if the lease can be extended only by production or by paying a delay rental, there is no consideration for the option and no mutuality of obligation. The lessee could choose to neither drill nor pay, and the lessor would be without recourse. However, if the oil and gas lease is for a definite (primary) term and supported by more than nominal consideration (bonus), then there is consideration and mutuality, even if the lessee has the right to neither drill nor pay delay rental, and the lessee can simply terminate (surrender) the lease without further liability. Although these early cases developed these concepts to define the rights of the mineral owner and the mineral owner's lessee to drill and produce, they did not address the fundamental question of defining the ownership of the oil and gas in place.

The writings of A. W. Walker are the definitive source for an analysis of the significance of *Texas Company v. Daugherty*.[29] It is not possible to improve upon the depth and thoroughness of that analysis. In summary, the significance of the case is that the Supreme Court of Texas cut through the confusion and conflicts in existing Texas precedents and committed Texas to the absolute ownership theory of oil and gas in place. While conflicting views on ownership were possible prior to the decision, after *Texas Company v. Daugherty*, regardless of the correctness or advisability of this view, absolute ownership in place became a settled rule of property in Texas.

Under this theory, oil and gas in place is real property in the same sense as solid minerals or dirt. Multiple consequences flow from this fundamental concept. A conveyance of the land, without mention of the oil and gas, will pass title to the oil and gas in place.[30] Oil and gas may be severed as a separate property right.[31] The estate created may be a fee simple or some lesser estate.[32] Thus, the oil and gas "lease" in Texas generally does not create the relationship of landlord and tenant, but it is construed as a conveyance of a determinable fee in the oil and gas, severing the oil and gas from the surface estate.[33] The owner of the oil and gas in place retains such easement rights in the surface as are necessary to reasonably develop the mineral estate.[34] These are the key concepts that spring from *Texas Company v. Daugherty*. The beginning point—ownership of oil and gas in place—is essential to the analysis of many issues pertaining to oil and gas. It is essential to resolving issues of possession, adverse possession, trespass, conversion, the right to produce, correlative rights, drainage, waste, cotenancy, partition, concurrent use of the surface, due process, equal protection, eminent domain, taxation, executive rights, creditor's rights, marital property rights, rights to extraordinary relief, slander of title, damages, and the construction of deeds, wills, and trusts.

An industry, which was only beginning in Texas in 1900, but that grew to dominate the State's economy by 1950,[35] required creative thought and flexible jurisprudence to make that growth possible. *Texas Company v. Daugherty* first set the course for oil and gas property rights in Texas by adopting a theory for ownership of oil and gas in place. The theory has itself remained in place for over 100 years and has proven to be adaptable and flexible in providing a logical construct for addressing and analyzing the many issues related to the ownership of oil and gas in Texas.

---

1 107 Tex. 226, 176 S.W. 717 (1915).

2 *The Geography of Transp. Sys., Rail Track Mileage & Number of Class I Rail Carriers, United States, 1840-2007*, http://people.hofstra.edu/geotrans/eng/ch3en/conc3en/usrail18402003.html (last visited Mar. 3, 2010).

3 *See* RAILROADS, WINDMILLS, & BARBED WIRE, *IN* TEXAS ALMANAC, 1990–1991 53 (Mike Kingston), *available at* http://www.texasalmanac.com/history/highlights/railroads.

4 *See History of Hybrid Vehicles, HYBRID CARS* (June 13, 2011), http://www.hybridcars.com/ history/history-of-hybrid-vehicles.html.

5 U.S. CENSUS BUREAU, STATISTICAL ABSTRACT OF THE UNITED STATES, 1999, SECTION 31: 20TH CENTURY STATISTICS 867, 885 no.1439, *available at* http://www.census.gov/prod/99pubs/99statab/sec31.pdf.

6 *American Cultural History 1900-1909*, LONE STAR COLLEGE – KINGWOOD, http://kclibrary lonestar.edu/decade00.html (last visited Mar. 3, 2010).

7 *Latest Auto Statistics from Reports by the National Automobile Chamber of Commerce in December, 1915, in* THE WORLD ALMANAC & ENCYCLOPEDIA (1916).

8 J. Edward Schipper, *$108,191,774 for Roads in 1914*, THE AUTOMOBILE, July 22, 1915, at 139.

9 BUREAU OF TRANSP. STATISTICS, U.S. DEPT. OF TRANSP., NATIONAL TRANSPORTATION STATISTICS, tbl.1-11: Number of U.S. Aircraft, Vehicles, Vessels, and Other Conveyances, http://www.rita.dot.gov/bts/sites/rita.dot.gov.bts/files/publications/national_transportation_ statistics/html/table_01_11.html (last visited May 11, 2015).

10 BUREAU OF TRANSP. STATISTICS, U.S. DEPT. OF TRANSP., NATIONAL TRANSPORTATION STATISTICS, tbl.1-4: Public Road and Street Mileage in the United States by Type of Surface, http://www.rita.dot.gov/bts/sites/rita.dot.gov.bts/files/publications/national_transportation_ statistics/html/table_01_04.html (last visited May 11, 2015).

11 DIANA DAVIDS OLIEN & ROGER M. OLIEN, OIL IN TEXAS: THE GUSHER AGE, 1895-1945 1 (2002); Roger M. Olien, *Handbook of Texas Online, Oil and Gas Industry*, TEXAS STATE HISTORICAL ASSOCIATION, http://www.tshaonline.org/handbook/online/articles/doogz (last visited Mar. 3, 2010) [hereinafter *Handbook of Texas Online*].

12 C. A. Warner, TEXAS OIL AND GAS SINCE 1543 1 (1939); *Handbook of Texas Online, supra* note 11.

13 OLIEN & OLIEN, *supra* note 11; *Handbook of Texas Online, supra* note 11.

14 *Handbook of Texas Online*, *supra* note 11.

15 OLIEN & OLIEN, *supra* note 11. at 2-3.

16 *Id.* at 2.

17 *Id.* at 2-3.

18 *Id.* at 3.

19 JAMES PRESLEY, A SAGA OF WEALTH: AN ANECDOTAL HISTORY OF THE TEXAN OILMEN 33 (1978).

20 WARNER, *supra* note 12, at 450; *Handbook of Texas Online*, *supra* note 11.

21 DANIEL YERGIN, THE PRIZE: THE EPIC QUEST FOR OIL, MONEY & POWER 83 (1991).

22 OLIEN & OLIEN, *supra* note 11, at 7.

23 *Id.* at 26.

24 *Id.* at 28.

25 *Id.* at 29.

26 JAMES A. CLARK & MICHAEL T. HALBOUTY, SPINDLETOP 1 (1952); OLIEN & OLIEN, *supra* note 11, at 30.

27 YERGIN, *supra* note 20, at 85.

28 *See Gilmore v. O'Neil*, 107 Tex. 18, 173 S.W. 203 (1915) (lessee's title in oil and gas lease is subject to equitable title of party in possession when notice appeared of record and was visible and apparent from an inspection on the ground); *Right of Way Oil Co. v. Gladys City Oil, Gas & Mfg. Co.*, 106 Tex. 94, 99 157 S.W. 737, 738 (1913) (construes a railroad deed as conveying a right of way for railroad purposes, not a fee, and holds that a conveyance of "timber, earth, stone and mineral" within the right of way does not include oil); *Bender v. Brooks*, 103 Tex. 329, 335, 127 S.W. 168, 170 (1910) (establishes the measure of damages for production of oil by a good faith trespasser and that the mineral owner has the exclusive right to take the oil from the land, but confirms that the mineral owner has no title in the oil in place unless and until it is severed or produced, when it becomes personalty); *Swayne v. Lone Acre Oil Co.*, 98 Tex. 597, 608, 86 S.W. 740, 743 (1905) (oil before its extraction is a mineral and is a part of the land, so that the open mine doctrine is applicable to a legal life estate created by the statute of descent and distribution); *Nat'l Oil & Pipeline Co. v. Teel*, 95 Tex. 586, 68 S.W. 979 (1902) (an unless form oil and gas lease does not pass any interest in land, but is an option, and lessee, having acquired no legal title but only an equitable title, could not be a bona fide purchaser for value); *Moore v. Decker*, 176 S.W. 816 (Tex. Civ. App.—San Antonio 1915) (affirms a directed verdict on the scope of the retained acreage under a retained acreage clause in a terminated lease), *rev'd*, 220 S.W. 773 (Tex. Comm'n App. 1920, judgm't adopted) (the acreage retained by the base lessee under a terminated lease in a dispute with the top lessee presents a fact question); *McLean v. Kishi*, 173 S.W. 502 (Tex. Civ. App.—Galveston 1915, no writ) (oil and gas lease terminates when production in paying quantities, as defined in the lease, is not obtained); *Owens v. Corsicana Petroleum Co.*, 169 S.W. 192 (Tex. Civ. App.—Amarillo 1914) (an unless form oil and gas lease supported by only nominal consideration is an unenforceable option, citing *Nat'l Oil & Pipeline Co., supra), rev'd*, 110 Tex. 568, 222 S.W. 154 (1920) (an unless form oil and gas lease is an option which is necessarily unilateral, but, when granted for a definite time and supported by an independent consideration, it is enforceable, citing *Nat'l Oil & Pipeline Co., supra*); *Whited v. Johnson*, 167 S.W. 812 (Tex. Civ. App.—San Antonio 1914, writ ref'd) (a conveyance of oil "in and under" a certain tract is not invalid because it seeks to convey oil and gas in place); *McAffee v. Grubb*, 164 S.W. 925 (Tex. Civ. App.—Fort Worth 1914) (after the initial discovery, lessee is under no obligation to continue to develop during the 20-year primary term), *rev'd*, 109 Tex. 527, 212 S.W. 464 (1919) (an oil and gas lease grants an option to prospect, citing *Texas Company v. Daugherty, supra* note 1, and the implied obligation to continue to develop after the initial discovery is a covenant implied in law, not a condition, but a lease may be lost by abandonment); *Witherspoon v. Staley*, 156 S.W. 557 (Tex. Civ. App.—Austin 1913, writ ref'd) (delay rental case under an unless lease form holds that the lease was void because the lease was not a conveyance but merely grants an option without consideration or mutuality); *Burnham v. Hardy Oil Co.*, 147 S.W. 330 (Tex. Civ. App.—San Antonio 1912) (cotenant in oil and gas has the right to extract minerals from the common property without first obtaining the consent of the other cotenant, but must account to the other cotenant on the basis of the value of the minerals taken less the necessary and reasonable costs of production and marketing), *aff'd on other grounds*, 108 Tex. 555, 195 S.W. 1139 (Tex. 1917); *Hermann v. Thomas*, 143 S.W. 195 (Tex. Civ. App.—Galveston 1911, no writ) (denies the right of the winning party in possession in a title dispute to have a receiver's lease during the pendency of an appeal); *Witherspoon v. Staley*, 138 S.W. 1191 (Tex. Civ. App.—Dallas 1911, no writ) (late payment of delay rental case in which the oil and gas lease is construed as an enforceable conditional conveyance of the minerals); *Simms v. Reisner*, 134 S.W. 278 (Tex. Civ. App.—Galveston 1911, no writ) (temporary cessation of production case decided on an evidence point); *O'Neil v. Sun Co.*, 58 Tex. Civ. App. 167, 123 S.W. 172 (San Antonio 1909, writ ref'd) (lessor drilled and produced on lessee's lease, which continued under a receivership during the litigation, and lessor receives lessor's royalty cost free because lessee had no interest in the oil in the ground); *Staley & Barnsdall v. Derden*, 57 Tex. Civ. App. 142, 121 S.W.1136 (Dallas 1909, no writ) (county court without jurisdiction to grant an injunction that affects an interest and estate in land exceeds its jurisdiction by granting an injunction as to oil in place, which is realty); *J.M. Guffey Petroleum Co. v. Jeff Chaison Townsite Co.*, 48 Tex. Civ. App. 555, 107 S.W. 609 (Galveston 1907, no writ) (construes the submission of the charge in a failure-to-develop and drainage case); *Great W. Oil Co. v. Carpenter*, 43 Tex. Civ. App. 229, 95 S.W. 57 (Galveston 1906, writ ref'd) (an oil and gas lease with recital of a $1.00 nominal consideration and a firm drilling obligation is supported by consideration and therefore not an option that is void or unenforceable for want of mutuality or for lack of consideration); *San Jacinto Oil Co. v. Fort Worth Light & Power Co.*, 41 Tex. Civ. App. 293, 93 S.W. 173 (Fort Worth 1906, writ ref'd) (construes "failure of oil wells" to mean failure of the wells to produce without artificial lift when the wells made subject to the contract were originally producing under natural pressure); *J.M. Guffey Petroleum Co. v. Oliver*, 79 S.W. 884 (Tex. Civ. App.—Galveston 1904, writ ref'd) (an oil and gas lease with a surrender clause is an option for a nominal consideration, which is not supported by independent consideration and therefore unenforceable); *Hodges v. Brice*, 32 Tex. Civ. App 358, 74 S.W. 590 (Galveston

1903, no writ) (an unless form oil and gas lease reciting $4.00 as consideration and otherwise unsupported by independent consideration is an option that is void for want of consideration and does not pass an interest in land); *Roberts & Corley v. McFaddin, Weiss & Kyle*, 32 Tex. Civ. App. 47, 74 S.W. 105 (Galveston 1903, no writ) (an oil and gas lease with a surrender clause granted for no consideration is unilateral and void); *Emery v. League*, 31 Tex. Civ. App. 474, 72 S.W. 603 (Galveston 1903, writ ref'd) (an oil and gas lease is an option that conveys no title, but it was supported by consideration because lessee agreed to obtain a partition, and the lease terminates when lessee fails to timely obtain the partition); *S. Oil Co. v. Colquitt*, 28 Tex. Civ. App. 292, 69 S.W. 169 (Dallas 1902, writ ref'd) (based on precedents from other jurisdictions, an unless form oil and gas lease is not an option, but a conveyance of land, because oil in place is land); *Forney v. Ward,* 25 Tex. Civ. App. 443, 62 S.W. 108 (Galveston 1901, no writ) (commencement of a well requires actual drilling); *Fox v. Robbins*, 62 S.W. 815 (Tex. Civ. App.—San Antonio 1901, writ ref'd) (a lessee without good title, but without notice, who enters and produces oil having more value than the cost to drill and produce, cannot be a bona fide purchaser for value).

29 A. W. Walker, *Fee Simple Ownership of Oil and Gas in Texas*, 6 Tex. L. Rev. 125, 127-29 (1928); A. W. Walker, *The Nature of the Property Interests Created by an Oil and Gas Lease in Texas* (pts. 1–5), 7 Tex. L. Rev. 1, 5–7 (1928), 7 Tex. L. Rev. 539, 564–68 (1929), 8 Tex. L. Rev. 483 (1930), 10 Tex. L. Rev. 291 (1932), 11 Tex. L. Rev. 399 (1933).

30 *Taylor v. County Sch. Trs. of Eastland Cnty*, 229 S.W. 670, 672 (Tex. Civ. App.—El Paso 1921, writ ref'd).

31 *Humphreys-Mexia Co. v. Gammon*, 113 Tex. 247, 255, 254 S.W. 296, 299 (1923).

32 *Id.* at 256.

33 *See Stephens County v. Mid-Kansas Oil & Gas Co.*, 113 Tex. 160, 168, 174, 254 S.W. 290, 292, 295 (1923).

34 *Humble Oil & Refining Co. v. Wood*, 294 S.W. 197, 199 (Tex. Comm'n App. 1927).

35 *Handbook of Texas Online, supra* note 11

CHAPTER 2

Stephens County v. Mid-Kansas Oil & Gas Co.

COMMENTARY
by Cullen M. "Mike" Godfrey

113 Tex. 160, 254 S.W. 290

1923

Stephens County
v.
Mid-Kansas Oil & Gas Co.

113 Tex. 160, 254 S.W. 290

1923

Mr. Justice GREENWOOD delivered this opinion of the court.

Appellee, Mid-Kansas Oil & Gas Company sued appellants, Stephens County, and the tax collector, tax assessor, county judge, and county commissioners of Stephens County, to enjoin the assessment and collection of taxes on any separate right or interest of appellee as the assign of the Texas & Pacific Coal Company, under the following instrument:

"OIL AND GAS LEASE

"This lease made and entered into this 18th day of August, 1916, between S. R. Hill and wife, of Eliasville, County of Stephens, State of Texas, first parties, and the Texas & Pacific Coal Company, of Thurber, Erath County, Texas, second party:

> "WITNESSETH, The first parties in consideration of forty one & 25/100 dollars ($41.25) to them paid, receipt of which is hereby acknowledged, and of the covenants hereinafter contained on the part of the second party, do by these presents, let and lease to the second party the following described premises, situated in Stephens County, Texas, to-wit: Being 165 acres of land and being the east part of Sec. No. 16, Blk. No. 2, cert. No. 17/507, S. P. Ry. Co. land in said Stephens County, Texas, containing 165 acres more or less, hereby granting to second party full and exclusive authority to enter upon said premises and to dig, drill, operate for and procure natural gas and petroleum together with the right of taking upon said premises and removing therefrom at pleasure any machinery, tools, lumber, pipe, casing and other things necessary in said work, and to construct on said premises and to remove therefrom, at pleasure, pumping plants, tracks, tanks, pipe lines and other things necessary in the operation of this lease, avoiding as far as practicable damages to fences and growing crops; but in case of damage to these, second party agrees to pay such damage, the same to be fixed by appraisers, should the parties hereto fail to agree to the amount of same.

"Should second parties discover on said premises natural gas in paying quantities and the same can be marketed to advantage, second party shall pay first party a royalty of ten per cent (10%) of the market price at the wells of the amount sold.

"In the event of the sale or marketing of petroleum, second party shall deliver as royalty to first parties, in tanks near the mouth of the well or wells, without cost to the first parties, one-eighth (1/8) of such products, or pay the market price in cash thereof, at option of second parties, and the remainder of such product shall belong to the party of the second part.

"A deposit of the moneys herein provided for the credit of the first parties in The First National Bank of Breckenridge, Texas, shall be taken and accepted by them as payment.

"If gas is discovered in paying quantities on said premises, first party shall have gas free for domestic purposes for one house now on said premises.

"The second party shall have the free use of any water on said premises for drilling and operating purposes, except that no water shall be taken from any well used by the first parties without their consent.

"It is further agreed between the parties hereto, that in case natural gas or petroleum are discovered on said premises that this lease shall continue in full force and effect so long as any of these are produced in paying quantities, but in the event of second party failing to pay to first parties in advance on ten days notice in writing by first party to second party, as above provided, the ground rent due under the terms and provisions hereof, that this lease shall be null and void and the first and second parties shall be released from all liabilities mentioned.

"And whereas, second party agrees that prospect work shall begin within a term of 18 months from the date hereof, either on S. R. Hill's land, as shown by this lease, or on Geo. W. Hill's land, as shown by his lease, or on

J. W. Hill's land, as shown by his lease, or on S. H. Hill's land, as shown by his lease to said second party, and in the event said second party is not prospecting on some one of the different tracts of land named in this or Geo. W. Hill, J. W. Hill or S. H. Hill's contract within the 18 months from the date hereof, then, in that event, said second party is to pay to first party one dollar per acre instead of 25c per acre for all the time said second party shall keep or hold said lease on said land after 18 months has expired.

"The second party agrees to drill no well, except by consent of first party, within 500 hundred feet of any building now on said premises.

"It is agreed by the parties hereto, that all the terms and conditions of this lease shall extend to and be binding on their heirs, executors and assigns.

"In witness whereof the parties of the first and second parts have hereunto set their hands and seals the day and year first above mentioned."

The instrument is duly signed and acknowledged by S. R. Hill and wife.

The suit was to also enjoin the assessment and collection of taxes on any rights or interests of appellee in and to 109 additional tracts of land, as the assign of the "second parties," under instruments in substantially the same form as the writing above copied.

The trial court overruled a general demurrer to appellee's petition and rendered judgment restraining Stephens County and its officers from collecting the taxes.

Appellants perfected an appeal to the Fort Worth Court of Civil Appeals, presenting one assignment of error, complaining of the overruling of their general demurrer, on the ground that the instruments conveyed such interests in the respective tracts of land therein described as were independently taxable under articles 7503 and 7504 of the Revised Statutes.

The Honorable Court of Civil Appeals has certified to this court the single question whether appellee acquired, under the above mentioned instruments, such interests or such estates in land as were subject to separate taxation. The certificate recites that numerous suits involving the question are pending and that its authoritative determination is of the utmost importance.

Looking to the manifest intent of the parties, we do not think it difficult to arrive at a correct answer to the question. The subject matter of each contract was gas and oil in place. The principal consideration was royalties dependent on the marketing of the gas or oil. The land was leased for the purpose of prospecting for, producing, and marketing these minerals, and for no other purpose. It was solely to effectuate such purpose that the parties of the first part granted unto the parties of the second part, their heirs and assigns, full and exclusive authority to enter upon the lands and to conduct all necessary drilling and marketing operations. The gas or oil, in paying quantities, became the property of the parties of the second part, their heirs or assigns, who were obligated to pay to the parties of the first part, their heirs or assigns, the market price of one-tenth the gas sold, and to deliver to the parties of the first part, their heirs or assigns, one-eighth the oil, unless they elected to pay the market price of such oil, instead of making delivery thereof. On demand, the parties of the first part, their heirs or assigns, were also entitled to sufficient gas for domestic purposes in specified dwellings without charge. The exploratory term was eighteen months from date, subject to renewal for a reasonable time, on payment of stipulated sums per acre. The instruments were to continue in full force as long as gas or oil was produced in paying quantities.

Denial that these instruments passed separately taxable interests in lands is grounded first on the proposition that there is no such thing as ownership or conveyance of gas or oil in place, because, until the gas or oil is brought to the surface and reduced to possession, any owner of land adjacent to that containing the gas or oil may lawfully appropriate same.

The opinion in Bender v. Brooks, 103 Texas, 335, Ann. Cas., 1913A, 559 127 S. W., 168, contains an expression that the owners of the land had "no specific title" to the oil therein until its removal from the earth, but the subsequent opinion in Right of Way Oil Co. v. Gladys City Oil, Gas & Mfg. Co., 106 Texas, 103, 51 L. R. A., (N. S.) 268, 157 S. W., 737, makes clear that it was not intended to thereby deny that oil in place was capable of ownership: for both opinions were written by Judge Brown, who cites the case of Bender v. Brooks in support of the conclusion in the latter opinion that the owner of the soil owns the oil while beneath the surface, as a part of the land, though his title becomes more definite upon the oil's extraction. The court had previously held that before oil is extracted it is a part of the land like such solid minerals as iron, coal and lead. Swayne v. Lone Acre Oil Co., 98 Texas, 597, 69 L. R. A., 986, 8 Ann. Cas., 1117, 86 S. W., 740.

The opinion of the Commission of Appeals in Prairie Oil & Gas Co. v. State, 231 S. W., 1090, quotes with approval the statement in Gould on Waters that oil, like water, is not the subject of property until reduced to actual possession. This portion of the opinion is not authoritative, because the Supreme Court adopted only the judgment recommended by the Commission. As stated in McKenzie v. Withers, 109 Texas, 256, 206 S. W., 503: "Our approval of the judgment recommended by the Commission is to be understood as having no further effect than to simply adopt the view of the Commission as to the determination to be made of the cause. It is not to be considered as an approval by the Supreme Court of the opinion of the Commission in the particular case, or the reasons given in the Commission's opinion for its conclusions."

We do not regard it as an open question in this State that gas and oil in place are minerals and realty, subject to ownership, severance and sale, while embedded in the sands or rocks beneath the earth's surface, in like manner and to the same extent as is coal or any other solid mineral.

The objection lacks substantial foundation that gas or oil in a certain tract of land cannot be owned in place, because subject to appropriation, without the consent of the owner of the tract, through drainage from wells on adjacent lands. If the owners of adjacent lands have the right to appropriate, without liability, the gas and oil underlying their neighbor's land, then their neighbor has the correlative right to appropriate, through like methods of drainage, the gas and oil underlying the tracts adjacent to his own. Ry. Co. v. East, 98 Texas, 146, 66 L. R. A., 738, 107 Am. St., 620, 4 Ann. Cas., 827, 81 S. W., 279; Gillette v. Mitchell, 214 S. W., 622. Ultimate injury from the net results of drainage, where proper diligence is used, is altogether too conjectural to form the basis for the denial of a right of property in that which is not only plainly as much realty as any other part of the earth's contents, but realty of the highest value to mankind, and often worth far more than anything else on or beneath the surface within the proprietor's boundaries.

The question whether gas and oil in place were capable of separate ownership and sale was carefully considered and finally determined by this court in Texas Company v. Daugherty, 107 Texas, 234 to 240, L. R. A., 1917F, 989, 176 S. W., 717. The opinion in that case leaves no room for reasonable doubt as to the soundness of the conclusion that gas and oil in place are objects of distinct ownership and sale as a part of the land. Moreover, we regard that view as in harmony with the overwhelming weight of the authorities. The Law of Oil & Gas, Vol. 18, Michigan Law Review, p. 459.

But it is earnestly insisted that the instruments conveyed only incorporeal hereditaments appertaining to the lands, and that the terms of the instruments precluded the vesting of title to the gas and oil save as personalty after being brought to the surface.

Ownership of the gas and oil in place meant having the exclusive right to posses *(Sic)*, use and dispose of the gas and oil. The grantors were clearly divested of the right to either possess, use or dispose of the gas and oil in place in the lands described in the instruments here involved as soon as the instruments were executed. At the same instant, the right to possess, use and dispose of such gas and oil in place passed to the grantees in said instruments and to their assigns. Complete divestiture of title to the gas and oil could hardly be more clearly evinced than by the necessity for an express grant or reservation of even enough gas for domestic use in the grantors' dwellings. Dominion over a thing could not well be completer than it is in those persons who may, at their will, assign it to any other person, with or without consideration, for a time which may be forever. Sims v. Sealy, 53 Texas Civ. App., 518, 116 S. W., 630. The fact that whoever owns the gas and oil, under these instruments, is subject to certain obligations to the former owners, express and implied, with regard to exploration for, and production of, the gas and oil, and with regard to the payment of royalties, in no wise reinvests the former owners with title. Nor does the possibility of future reversions accomplish present reinvestitures of title in the former owners.

The Supreme Court of Pennsylvania decided at an early day that the grant of the right to take away coal to any extent a grantee might desire was a conveyance of no incorporal hereditament but of title to the coal. The decision rests on the following unassailable conclusion: "The grant of a thing can be no more than the grant of the full and unlimited use of it. So, too, the general power of disposal without liability to account is equivalent to ownership itself." Caldwell v. Fulton, 31 Pa. St., 483-488, 72 Am. Dec., 760.

Reaffirming the doctrine, the same court said: "Where the subject and purpose of the grant involve the mining and removing of the entire thing granted, to be held by the grantee and his heirs until it shall be so mined and removed in accord with his covenants, how can it be said that he takes for a term? What can be more uncertain than the date when the subject shall be exhausted? What greater estate in the mineral underlying the surface of a tract of land can a man have than the right in himself, his heirs and assigns, to mine and remove the whole of it? If his title is burdened with covenants and conditions insuring his payment of the purchase money, the burden does not affect the nature of the estate." Delaware, L. & W. Ry Co. v. Sanderson, 109 Pa. St., 583, 58 Am. Rep., 743, 1 Atl., 397.

In Appeal of Stoughton, 88 Pa. St., 201, approved in Blakley v. Marshall, 174 Pa. St., 429, 34 Atl., 564, and in Jennings v. Bloomfield, 199 Pa. St., 641, 49 Atl., 135, it was determined that a guardian could no more grant, without authorization of the Orphans' Court, an exclusive right to bore and dig for, and collect the oil from land of his ward, for a term of twenty-one years, than he could grant an exclusive right to mine coal from his ward's land. The opinion is to the effect that oil, like coal, is a part of the realty, which can be conveyed only on order of the Orphans' Court, and that the grant of the exclusive right to remove oil from the ward's land was "in effect the grant of part of the corpus of the estate and not of a mere incorporeal right.'"

The lease in Barnsdall v. Bradford Gas Co., 225 Pa. St., 338, 26 L. R. A. (N. S.), 614, 74 Atl. 207, was similar in many respects to the instruments before us. It demised the land for the sole purpose of operating for gas, oil and other minerals for a term of ten years and as much longer as the operations continued, in consideration of one dollar and of the delivery in the pipe lines of the equal one-eighth part of the oil produced and saved from the premises. The lessee brought an action of ejectment to recover possession against a stranger deriving no right under the lessee or lessor. The suit was defended on the ground that the lease conveyed no interest in the land but a mere license to operate for oil. In declaring that the lessee was entitled to recover, the court said: "By the agreement *the exclusive right to take and appropriate all the minerals* is conveyed, and during the term of the lease the lessor has no right to enter and operate for oil or gas. *The title to the oil, except the one-eighth thereof, is vested in the lessee, as is also the title to the gas and other minerals in the land.* Under the rule of construction established, not only in other jurisdictions, but by our own cases, therefore, the agreement creates a corporeal interest in the lessee in the demised premises, and is not merely a license to enter and operate for oil and gas." To the same effect are McIntosh v. Ropp, 233 Pa. St., 497, 82 Atl., 954, and DeWitt's Estate, 266 Pa. St., 550, 109 Atl., 699.

The case of Benavides v. Hunt, 79 Texas, 383, 15 S. W., 396, required the Supreme Court of Texas to determine the nature of the interest created by a grant of only "*the right* to mine coal or other minerals" in a certain tract of land, such right declared exclusive, with *(Sic)* habendum clause reading "to have and to hold the above described mining rights unto the parties of the second part for the full term and period of fifty years."

The grantee sued the grantors to recover possession of coal mines on the tract. The grantors based their defense in part on the statute of limitations of four years. After concluding that the grantee's suit was barred unless it was an action to recover real estate, the court, in a careful opinion by Chief Justice Stayton, decided that the grant was not of an incorporeal right but that it effected a severance of the property in the strata of minerals from the property in the remainder of the land, the mineral strata being as much *land* as the non-mineral portion of the soil. It was accordingly adjudged that the suit was not barred because the only statutes of limitations which applied were those relating to suits to recover real estate.

The portion of the opinion disposing of the question of limitations closes by citing Caldwell v. Copeland, 37 Pa. St., 430, 78 Am. Dec., 436, and Armstrong v. Caldwell, 53 Pa. St., 288. These cases involved the same grant as did Caldwell v. Fulton, supra, that is, the grant of the exclusive right to appropriate coal to any extent desired by the grantee and his assigns. It was decided in the last of the three cases, viz, *Armstrong v. Caldwell, supra*, in harmony with the decisions in the two previous cases, that the grant effected a severance of the title to the coal from the title to the remainder of the land, creating two distinct corporeal hereditaments.

We do not think that any distinction in principle lies between the title acquired under a grant of solid minerals and the title acquired under a grant in the same form of gas and oil. The reason why the grant of the exclusive right to possess, use and appropriate gas and oil should be given the same effect as a like grant with respect to solid minerals was thus stated in Hague v. Wheeler, 157 Pa. St., 341, 22 L. R. A., 141, 37 Am. St., 736, 27 Atl., 714, viz; "But it is said that the oil and gas are unlike the solid minerals, since they may move through the interstitial spaces or crevices in the sand rocks in search of an opening through which they may escape from the pressure to which they are subject. This is probably true. It is one of the contingencies to which this species of property is subject. But the owner of the surface is an owner downward to the centre, *until* the underlying strata have been severed from the surface by sale. What is found within the boundaries of his tract belongs to him according to its nature. The air and the water he may use. The coal and iron or other solid minerals he may mine and carry away. The oil and gas he may bring to the surface and sell in like manner to be carried away and consumed. His dominion is, upon general principles, as absolute over the fluid, as the solid minerals. It is exercised in the same manner, and with the same results. He cannot estimate the quantity in place of gas or oil as he might of the solid minerals. He cannot prevent its movement away from him, towards an outlet on some other person's land, which may be more or less rapid, depending on the dip of the rock, or the coarseness of the sand composing it; but so long as he can reach it and bring it to the surface, it is his absolutely, to sell, to use, to give away, or to squander, as in the case of his other property."

Much reliance is put on such expressions in the opinion in the case of Texas Company v. Daugherty, 107 Texas, 226, L. R. A., 1917F, 989, 176 S. W., 717, as that if the effect of the instruments there considered had been but the creation of a privilege to devote the land to a certain use, coupled with the right to appropriate a portion of such gas or oil as might be discovered, the privilege and right would not be separately taxable. The court's determination that the instruments before it had an altogether different legal effect makes it obvious that these expressions concerned matters not presented for decision. It was never intended that such argumentative expressions should be taken as authoritative.

There is a difference in the form of the instruments dealt with in the Daugherty case and those now under consideration. The instruments involved in the Daugherty case expressly conveyed the minerals in the lands, and granted the exclusive right to conduct operations to mine, store and transport same. They recited they were not intended to create franchises but were intended and understood to be conveyances of property and privileges. The instruments involved here lease the lands themselves and grant the exclusive right to prospect for, produce, and dispose of the minerals. The considerations for the two sets of instruments are not substantially dissimilar. Whatever was granted might be held under all the instruments as long as gas or oil was produced in paying quantities. The following statements in the opinion in the Daugherty case are equally true of the instruments now before the court, save that the distances within which wells might be located from houses were not the same, viz: "For the purpose of making the exploration and producing all the oil, gas and other minerals that might be within the ground, and the erection of all structures necessary thereto, as well as their storing and transportation, the possession of the land itself is likewise granted, with no limitation upon the number of wells or shafts that the grantee might sink, or the extent of its operations in that connection, and consequently no qualification of its right of possession to all such parts of the surface,—except that no well should be drilled nearer than 200 feet from the house or barn on the premises without the consent of both parties,—as might be necessary to its full use by the grantee for the purposes named. . . . The instruments throughout treat these minerals in the ground as property, and bespeak the purpose to give the grantee absolute dominion over them, not merely when severed from the realty and reduced to personalty, but while in their natural state; and the interest granted was furthermore expressed as one capable of being assigned and conveyed by the grantee." We find it impossible to reasonably ascribe to the two sets of instruments, disregarding mere form and looking at substance, any different legal effects as regards the transfer of title to the oil and gas in place.

Notwithstanding the distinctions attempted to be drawn in the decisions, we cannot conclude otherwise than that there is no real difference in the title conveyed, whether an instrument takes the form of a grant of the exclusive right to mine and appropriate all of a certain mineral—as in Benevides v. Hunt, supra—or takes the form of a demise of the land, for the sole purpose of mining operations, coupled with a grant of the exclusive right to produce and dispose of the mineral—as in this case—or takes the form of a grant of the mineral with the exclusive right to mine for, produce, and dispose thereof—as in Texas Company v. Daugherty, supra. The results are substantially the same to all parties at interest, whether the one or other form of instrument be used. Why hold that instruments in different forms create different estates, where there is no difference in fact with respect to that of which each divests the grantor, his heirs or assigns, nor with respect to that with which each invests the grantee, his heirs or assigns?

In Wolfe County v. Beckett, 127 Ky., 252, 105 S. W., 447, 17 L. R. A. (N. S.), 689, the Court of Appeals of Kentucky had before it leases granting "the right to drill for oil and gas for a definite term of years, and, in case oil or gas is found in paying quantities, to continue said operations so long as same is found in quantities that pay," in consideration of certain royalties in oil and gas, in holding such leases as effective as conveyances would have been to pass title to the oil and gas in place, the court said: "During the continuance of the lease, the ownership of the oil or gas is vested in the lessee; and, as the lease continues so long as oil or gas may be found in paying quantities, does not the lessor part with his title to the oil in situ for all practical purposes, for the reason that it has no value if it cannot be produced in quantities that pay? We therefore conclude that the form of contract is immaterial, and that it makes no difference whether the oil or gas privileges be conveyed by deed or lease, just so the effect of the instrument is to vest in the lessee all property rights to the oil or gas that may be found in paying quantities on the leased premises."

Mr. Hardwicke says in his work on Innocent Purchaser of Oil and Gas Lease, at page 11:

> "From a practical standpoint, the rights of the lessee in an instrument using the language 'grant, sell and convey' are the same as if holding under an instrument using the language 'lease, demise and let.' In each instance the lessee is given the right to enter and develop and to appropriate the production, and this right terminates if not exercised within a stated period, or if consideration is not paid for delay in commencing operations, and at all events the right terminates at a definite time if production is not obtained in paying quantities. Whenever production is obtained in paying quantities, the right to develop and to produce continues as long as the mineral is produced in paying quantities.

"A lessee has no more privileges under one type of instrument than he has under the other. The instruments simply provide for the development of the land and distribution of the minerals which are discovered. For this reason, the parties usually attach little or no significance to the language in the granting clause. The thing that the landowner is interested in giving, and the thing that the operator is interested in obtaining, is the right to enter on the land, to the exclusion of all others, for the purpose of discovering and producing minerals that exist, and to distribute such minerals in accordance with the lease, usually one-eighth to the landowner and seven-eighths to the operator."

While not necessary to the decision of the case, the Court of Civil Appeals announced a sound rule when it declared: "An oil lease investing the lessee with the right to remove all the oil in place, in consideration of his giving the lessor a certain per cent. thereof, is, in legal effect, a sale of a portion of the land." Southern Oil Co. v. Colquitt, 28 Texas Civ. App., 296, 69 S. W., 169.

Passing to the consideration of the precise nature of the title created by the instruments before us, it seems obvious: first, that the grants might endure forever, since the lands might never cease the profitable production of oil or gas, and, second, that it was intended by all parties that the lands should be used for no other purpose than the specified mineral exploration and production, and that the grants were to be enjoyed only while such use continued and were to immediately terminate on cessation of the use.

At common law, a grant of land for such a term and for such use and purpose—and no other—created the estate called a base, qualified, or determinable fee, defined by Kent as "an interest which may continue forever, but the estate is liable to be determined, *without the aid of a conveyance*, by some act or event, circumscribing its continuance or extent." Kent's Commentaries, Vol. IV, pp. 8, 9.

The instruments under consideration come within Tiffany's illustration of typical determinable fees, when he says: "So, when land is granted for a certain purpose, as for a schoolhouse, a church, a public building, or the like, and it is evidently the grantor's intention that it shall be used for such purpose only, and, that, on cessation of such use, the estate shall end, without any re-entry by the grantor, an estate of the kind now under consideration is created." Tiffany, Real Property, Vol. 1, p. 334.

Corpus Juris mentions as a qualification of the fee rendering it determinable that "which attaches itself to the use of the land so that the estate is held to be granted for that use and purpose only, and on the cessation of the use the estate expires." 21 C. J. 922.

In Texas & P. Ry. Co. v. Durrett, 57 Texas, 48, this court had to determine the nature of the estate created by a grant to a railway company of a right of way through and over a certain survey of land, together with the right to use the wood, timber, water, soil, gravel or stone therefrom, with a habendum clause reading "to have and to hold the same for the uses and purposes aforesaid unto said company and its successors forever." It was decided that the Railway Company took under the grant more than a perpetual easement, and that it acquired "a qualified determinable fee, liable only to be divested if the estate is used for purposes other than that contemplated by the conveyance," citing State v. Brown, 27 N. J. L. (3 Dutcher) 13.

The instruments mentioned in the certificate of the Court of Civil Appeals have passed to appellee determinable fees in the lands; leaving in the grantors, their heirs or assigns, the possibility of reacquiring the absolute fee simple titles, less whatever minerals may be meantime produced and marketed. State v. Brown, 27 N. J. L. (3 Dutcher) 20; Watford Oil and Gas Co. v. Shipman, 233 Ill., 9, 122 Am. St., 144, 84 N.E., 53; Slegel v. Lauer, 148 Pa. St., 236, 15 L. R. A. 549, 550, Atl., 996.

Our Constitution requires the taxation, in proportion to its value, of all property, save such as the Legislature is authorized to exempt. Secs. 1 & 2, Art. VIII. The owner is required to render and pay taxes on all lands and other property subject to taxation in the county where situated. Failure of owners to make the required renditions authorizes assessments at fair values by the proper officers. Sec. 11, Art. VIII. The taxes on landed property are secured by special lien thereon, and payment may be enforced by the seizure and sale of any and all property of the delinquent owner. Sec. 15, Art. VIII. In releasing the minerals to the owners of lands previously patented, the Constitution expressly declares the minerals "subject to taxation as other property." Sec. 7, Art. XIV.

Article 7509 R. S. provides that each person shall render for taxation *all* of *his* real estate, etc. Article 7504 R. S. declares: "Real property, for the purpose of taxation, shall be construed to include the land itself, whether laid out in town lots or otherwise, and all the buildings, structures and improvements, or other fixtures of whatsoever kind thereon, and all the rights and privileges belonging or in any wise appertaining thereto, and all mines, minerals, quarries and fossils in and under the same."

The cases of Texas Co. v. Daugherty, supra, and State v. Downman, 134 S. W., 787; Downman v. State, 231 U. S., 356, 357, 58 L. Ed., 264, construe these constitutional and statutory provisions to authorize the separate taxation of the value of a defeasible title in fee to gas and oil in place, when such title has been severed, by grant, from the title to the remainder of the tract containing the gas and oil. The decisions are in accord with the manifest intent of the Constitution that "the land of one person should not pay the taxes that ought properly to be paid by the land of another." Washburn v. Gregory, 125 Minn., 491, L. R. A., 1916D, 304, 147 N.W., 706. He who owns mines and minerals as land and enjoys the benefits of ownership is justly chargeable with all the burdens thereof.

Our conclusions are not in conflict with the decision in Austin Ry. Co. v. State, 94 Texas, 530, 62 S. W., 1050, that the franchise of a railroad corporation is not taxable separately from its real estate. The law forbids the severance of properties and franchises of railroad corporations on grounds having no possible relation to the ordinary severance of estates by the conveyance of minerals in place. Texas Southern Ry. Co. v. Harle, 101 Texas, 181 to 185, 105 S. W., 1107.

It is unnecessary, in disposing of this case, to decide whether taxable interests or estates in real estate are created by the usual term leases of land, for purposes of ordinary cultivation or occupancy, granting no right to appropriate any portion of the land. Such leases are essentially different in their nature and effect from conveyances of gas and oil in place. Though an oil lease be so construed as not to pass a present title to gas and oil in place, the courts recognize that it may create a separately taxable estate in land, when no such estate would be recognized under an ordinary lease providing for return of rented premises not depleted after a fixed term.

On this subject the Supreme Court of California says: "Except when held for speculative purposes, the value of land usually depends on the value of the use and occupation, and consists of a sum equivalent to a principal which, at the rate of interest usual upon safe investments, will bring a net annual income equal to that which the land will produce. The lessor or landowner annually receives a sum as rent which he deems the equivalent of this annual income, or of the value of the use of the land to him, and therefore he enjoys the entire beneficial interest in the premises, including the value of the leasehold as well as of the fee. . . .The royalty is frequently fixed before the discovery of oil, usually at a time when the existence of oil in profitable quantities is a matter of conjecture, and without regard to the adjustment between the parties of the burden of taxation upon the respective interests. The value represented by the royalty is ordinarily very small as compared to that of the right of the lessee. After the discovery of oil in such leased ground, the value of the lessor's real interest and right is much less than it would be if he had the whole estate, including all the oil thus discovered. There is no real parallel between such a case and that of a lessor under an ordinary lease for occupation and use. It is well known that such leasehold estates or interests in oil strata, after a discovery of oil, often command large prices in the market, out of all proportion to the value of the interest of the landowner receiving only the royalty and enjoying the use only for other purposes. The right of the lessee under this contract is more than that of the ordinary lessee. It is of a different character and for a different purpose. He has no right at all to the usufruct of the soil. His right extends to the extraction of a certain part of the substance of the land itself, to its permanent separation and removal and its conversion to his own use. The whole object of the contract is to effect, if not technically a sale and conveyance of a substantial and specific part of the land, at least a disposition and transfer thereof to another." Graciosa Oil Co. v. Santa Barbara County, 155 Cal., 140, 99 Pac., 483, 20 L. R. A. (N. S.), 212 to 214. See also Shaw v. Watson, 151 La., 893, 92 So., 375; Wolfe County v. Beckett, 127 Ky., 252, 105 S. W., 448, 17 L. R. A. (N. S.), 691; Transcontinental Oil Co. v. Emmerson, 298 Ill., 394, 131 N. E., 645, 16 A. L. R., 507.

Our answer to the certified question is that the appellee did acquire interests and estates in the lands which were subject to separate taxation.

Chief Justice Cureton took no part in the decision of this case.

The Taxman Cometh*:
Commentary on Stephens County v. Mid-Kansas Oil & Gas Co.

by Cullen M. "Mike" Godfrey

One of the pleasures of being an oil and gas lawyer has been the opportunity to witness active evolution and creation of a whole new body of law. Spindletop, the first major oil discovery in Texas, was completed in 1901. Since that time, Texas has created what is probably the largest and best developed body of oil and gas law of any jurisdiction in the world, and it has all been the product of an era spanning less than the past twelve decades.

I have found it to be a source of amused curiosity that the legal nature of oil and gas as a real property interest in Texas was defined in a series of cases involving ad valorem taxation. Cynics have often accused tax collectors of having an overactive imagination when it comes to their ability to identify new taxable estates,[1] and their quest to tax oil and gas in place may support that opinion. Fortunately, it led to an understanding of the oil and gas estate that has served us well over time.

The first major ad valorem tax case was the previously reviewed *Texas Co. v. Daugherty*,[2] and it might have been thought that the issue of the nature of oil and gas property rights was settled by that case. It was not, however. Oil and gas in the ground was unlike any estate with which courts had dealt previously. While hard rock minerals such as iron and coal were fixed in place, oil and gas were fugacious (i.e., they were subject to subterranean movement across property lines from where they may have once been located). Since what was here today might be gone tomorrow, many argued that oil and gas could not be owned until brought to the surface and reduced to physical possession.

The venerable A.W. Walker, Jr., in his article entitled "The Nature of the Property Interests Created by an Oil and Gas Lease in Texas: Part I,"[3] cautioned that the early analysis of the nature of the oil and gas estate must be broken into three periods. In the first period, which predated the decision in *Texas Co.*, the estate was ill-defined by the case law.[4] The second period covered the eight-year interval between the *Texas Co.* decision and the Supreme Court's decision in *Stephens County v. Mid-Kansas Oil & Gas Co.*[5] While the Court in the *Texas Company* case found that a taxable estate in oil and gas had been created by the execution of an oil and gas lease, the basis for that conclusion was found in the specific language of the lease being reviewed. As the previous article indicates, the Court first found that the landowner was also the owner of the oil and gas in place. The conclusion that a separate estate had been created in the oil and gas lessee turned on the fact that the lease's granting clause stated that the lessors "granted, bargained, sold and conveyed...all of the oil, gas, coal, and other minerals in and under" the lessors' land.[6] Moreover, the Court took special note that the lessors and lessee provided that "This lease is not intended as a mere franchise, but is intended as a conveyance of the property and privileges above described for the purposes herein mentioned...."[7]

In the intervening years prior to the *Stephens County* case, as Professor Walker points out in his article, courts were divided on the nature of the estate created and conveyed by an oil and gas lease, relying heavily on the specific language used in each instance. In addition to finding an interest in land, as in the *Texas Co.* case, courts also construed various oil and gas leases to be option contracts, licenses, and profits à prendre, among others.[8]

Out of the welter of conflicting and often contradictory opinions came the Stephens County tax collector, and one disputed tax assessment on the oil and gas in place found its way back to the Texas Supreme Court. The appellee in that case was the Mid-Kansas Oil & Gas Co., which had sued to enjoin the separate assessment and collection of ad valorem taxes on a total of 110 tracts of land as to which it had rights to explore for and recover oil and gas.

In *Stephens County*, the Texas Supreme Court reviewed the estate created by one of Mid-Kansas' oil and gas leases.[9] The single question certified to the Supreme Court was whether Mid-Kansas had acquired "such interests or such estates in land as were subject to separate taxation."[10] The opinion states that other suits were pending in addition to those involving Mid-Kansas, and their outcomes were dependent on the Supreme Court's holding.

The statute at issue in the case read:

> "Real property, for the purpose of taxation, shall be construed to include the land itself, whether laid out in town lots or otherwise, and all of the buildings, structures and

> improvements or other fixtures of whatsoever kind thereon, in any wise appertaining thereto, and all mines, minerals, quarries and fossils in and under the same."[11]

Broadly stated, the *Stephens County* case held that the estate created by lessee's oil and gas lease was a fee simple determinable that granted the lessee full and exclusive authority to enter upon the land and conduct drilling and marketing operations for gas and oil. The lessee's argument that there was no separate taxable interest rested on the proposition that there is no such thing as ownership of gas or oil in place.[12] Citing inconsistent language from prior case law, the lessee argued that gas and oil could not be owned until brought to the surface or otherwise captured.[13] The Supreme Court, however, concluded that "we do not regard it as an open question in this state that gas and oil in place are minerals and realty, subject to ownership, severance, and sale, while embedded in the sands or rocks beneath the earth's surface, in like manner and to the same extent as is coal or any other solid mineral."[14] Relying on its earlier decision in *Texas Co.*, the Court went on to say that "gas and oil in place are objects of distinct ownership and sale as a part of the land."[15]

In deciding that the interest created was a fee simple determinable, the Court found two factors to be of primary importance. First, the grant could potentially last forever, as the land could continue to produce gas or oil in paying quantities indefinitely.[16] Second, the parties' intention was that the lands conveyed in the oil and gas lease should be used exclusively for mineral exploration and production, but only for so long as such use occurred.[17] These two factors together created a fee simple determinable, defined as an estate capable of enduring forever but subject to some special limitation describing some event, which may never happen, but upon the happening of which, the fee estate is cut short and reverts, *ipso facto*, to the grantor.[18]

Finding that the estate created was a fee simple determinable, the Supreme Court reached the seminal conclusion that ordinary variations in the wording of granting clauses in conveyances of the oil and gas estate do not change the interest granted:

> "[W]e cannot conclude otherwise than that there is no real difference in the title conveyed, whether an instrument takes the form of a grant of the exclusive right to mine and appropriate all of a certain mineral, or takes the form of a demise of the land, for the sole purpose of mining operations, coupled with a grant of the exclusive right to produce and dispose of the mineral, or takes the form of a grant of the mineral with the exclusive right to mine for, produce and dispose thereof. The results are substantially the same to all parties at interest, whether the one or other form of interest is used. Why hold that instruments in different forms create different estates, where there is no difference in fact with respect to that to which each divests the grantor, his heirs or assigns, nor with respect to that which each invests the grantee, his heirs or assigns?"[19] (internal citations omitted)

Professor Walker believed it was important to distinguish between a fee simple determinable and a fee simple subject to a condition subsequent. In "The Nature of the Property Interests Created by an Oil and Gas Lease in Texas, Part I"[20], he makes clear that a fee simple determinable terminates immediately upon the occurrence of some special limitation. In the case of a producing oil and gas lease, it will automatically terminate upon the cessation of production of oil and gas in paying quantities.[21] With respect to a fee simple subject to a condition subsequent, the grantee's fee simple does not automatically terminate upon the occurrence of the condition subsequent. Rather, the beneficiary of the condition subsequent must take affirmative steps to recover possession of the property that is the subject of the condition subsequent. Professor Walker wanted to make clear that when an oil and gas lease no longer produces in paying quantities, ownership of the remaining oil and gas in place reverts to the lessor or the lessor's heirs or assigns, without any further action being required to defease the oil and gas lessee.

In order to reach its decision, the Supreme Court had to dispose of the lessee's argument that "the instruments conveyed only incorporeal hereditaments appertaining to the lands, and that the terms of the instruments precluded the vesting of title to the gas and oil save as personalty after being brought to the surface."[22] An "incorporeal hereditament" is an intangible right in land such as an easement.[23] If, as the appellee argued, its oil and gas lease was an incorporeal hereditament, the oil and gas in place should not be subject to separate ownership and separate assessment and taxation. Rejecting the argument, the Court asserted that the lessee had exclusive right to possess, use, and dispose of the gas and oil.[24] Neither the obligations owed to the lessors nor the possibility of reversion changed the nature of ownership.

How, then, did the Supreme Court deal with the possibility that oil and gas in place might migrate across a property line? The Court presumed that the primary risk of migration was through drainage from wells on adjacent lands. To that, the Court said:.

> "If the owners of adjacent lands have the right to appropriate, without liability, the gas and oil underlying their neighbor's land, then their neighbor has the *correlative right* to appropriate, through like methods of drainage, the gas and oil underlying the tracts adjacent to his own. Ultimate injury from the net results of drainage, where proper diligence is used is altogether too conjectural to form the basis for the denial of a right of property in that which is not only plainly as much realty as any other part of the earth's contents, but realty of the highest value to mankind and often worth far more than anything else on or beneath the surface within the proprietor's boundaries."[25] (emphasis added, internal citations omitted)

In the context used by the Court, Professor Walker said that the correlative right "is simply the remedy of self-help."[26] The Court's logic was so simple and so eloquent that it virtually eliminated any further debate about the issue.[27]

Four years later, the Texas Supreme Court further clarified its *Stephens County* decision in *Hager v. Stakes*.[28] That case addressed the unresolved issue of taxation of the lessor on retained interests when there was no express grant of all the minerals to the lessee. The case held that the lessor's retained right to receive royalty in kind was taxable real property.[29] The *Hager* lease is contrasted to the *Stephens County* lease, which gave the lessee the option of paying royalty in cash.[30] A similar result had been reached by the United States Supreme Court four months earlier in the case of *Waggoner Estate v. Wichita County*.[31]

More recently, the issue of ad valorem taxation of interests has arisen in context of other forms of property. It has been held that limestone is taxable separate and apart from the surface only if it is a part of an open producing excavation.[32] Conversely, underground storage facilities were held to be subject to separate taxation.[33] This, the court reasoned, was in accordance with the *Stephens County* principle that some aspects of real property can be taxed separately even though all are part of the same surface tract.

From the time of the *Stephens County* case, there has been little, if any, debate questioning whether oil and gas in place is a real property interest or whether such interest can be conveyed as a fee simple determinable. It has proven to be a sound rule of law which Professor Walker succinctly articulated in one sentence:

> "It was observed that, after a period of considerable vacillation, our courts have come to regard all ordinary types of oil and gas leases as conveyances *in praesenti* of the titles to all or part of the oil and gas in place, depending upon the wording of the royalty clauses, vesting in the lessee a corporeal estate of inheritance in these minerals, to wit, a determinable fee, and as effecting a severance of the oil and gas from the remainder of the land and the creation of two separate and distinct corporeal freehold estates, superimposed one upon the other, in a tract of land which, before the execution of the lease, had constituted the physical subject matter of but one such estate."[34]

---

* The author is grateful for the able research and assistance of Ms. Shannon Venable, a student at The University of Texas School of Law, for her contributions to this article

1 H.L. Mencken once said that "When a new source of taxation is found, it never means, in practice, that the old source is abandoned. It merely means that the politicians have two ways of milking the taxpayer where they had one before."

2 *Texas Co. v. Daugherty*, 107 Tex. 226, 176 S.W. 717 (1915).

3 A. W. Walker, Jr., *The Nature of the Property Interests Created by an Oil and Gas Lease in Texas: Part I*, 7 TEX. L. REV. 1 (1928).

4 *Id.* at 6.

5 *Stephens County v. Mid-Kansas Oil & Gas Co.*, 113 Tex. 160, 254 S.W. 290 (1923).

6 *Texas Co. v. Daugherty*, 107 Tex. at 231, 176 S.W. at 717

7 *Texas Co. v. Daugherty*, 107 Tex. at 234, 176 S.W. at 719

8 Walker, Jr., *supra* note 3, at 6-7.

9 *Stephens County*, 113 Tex. at 160, 254 S.W. at 290.

10 *Stephens County*, 113 Tex. at 166, 254 S.W. at 291.

11 *Stephens County*, 113 Tex. at 174-175, 254 S.W. at 295.

12 *Stephens County*, 113 Tex. at 166, 254 S.W. at 291.

13 *Stephens County*, 113 Tex. at 166, 254 S.W. at 291.

14 *Stephens County*, 113 Tex. at 167, 254 S.W. at 292.

15 *Stephens County*, 113 Tex. at 168, 254 S.W. at 292.

16 *Stephens County*, 113 Tex. at 173, 254 S.W. at 295.

17 *Stephens County*, 113 Tex. at 173, 254 S.W. at 295. *But see* A.W. Walker, Jr., *The Nature of the Property Interests Created by an Oil and Gas Lease in Texas; Part III*, 8 Tex. L. Rev. 483 (1930). (Walker, Jr. clarified that the Court misspoke when it said that the lands were to be used exclusively for mineral exploration and production. Rather, it was the oil and gas—not the lands—that was subject to exclusive use).

18 A.W. Walker, Jr., *The Nature of the Property Interests Created by an Oil and Gas Lease in Texas: Part II*, 7 Tex., L. Rev. 539 (1929). *But see Brazos River Conservation and Reclamation Dist. v. Adkisson*, 173 S.W. 2d 294 (Tex. Civ. App.—Eastland 1943, writ ref'd). (Justice Funderburk roundly criticized the Supreme Court's decisions in *Texas Co. v. Daugherty* and *Stephens County v. Mid-Kansas Oil & Gas Co.*, stating that the conclusion that an oil and gas lease created a corporeal interest in land was a legal fiction "smacking so loudly of judicial legislation." Justice Funderburk's view has not enjoyed wide support.)

19 *Stephens County*, 113 Tex. at 172, 254 S.W. at 294 Walker, Jr., *supra* note 3, 7-8.

20 Walker, Jr., *supra* note 3, 7-8.

21 Reversion of the oil and gas estate to the landowner upon the cessation of production in paying quantities may, of course, be subject to some contractual limitations giving the oil and gas lessee a period of time to reestablish production or to commence new drilling operations.

22 *Stephens County*, 113 Tex. at 168, 254 S.W. at 292.

23 Bryan A. Garner, A Dictionary Of Modern Legal Usage, 402 (2nd ed. 1995).

24 *Stephens County*, 113 Tex. at 168, 254 S.W. at 292.

25 *Stephens County*, 113 Tex at 167, 254 S.W. at 292.

26 A.W. Walker, Jr., *Property Rights in Oil and Gas and Their Effect Upon Police Regulation of Production*, 16 Tex. L. Rev. 370 (1938).

27 *But see* Justice Funderburk's concurrence in Note 18.

28 *Hager v. Stakes*, 116 Tex. 453, 294 S.W. 835 (1927).

29 *Hager*, 116 Tex. at 472, 294 S.W. at 842.

30 *Hager*, 116 Tex. at 471, 294 S.W. at 842.

31 *Waggoner Estate v. Wichita County*, 273 U.S. 113 (1927). *But cf., Burnet v. Harmel*, 287 U.S. 103 (1932) (which held that bonus payments for the execution of an oil and gas lease were taxable as ordinary income, not capital gains on the sale of oil and gas in place).

32 *Gifford-Hill & Co. v. Wise County Appraisal Dist.*, 827 S.W.2d 811 (Tex. 1991).

33 *Matagorda County Appraisal Dist. v. Coastal Liquids Partners, L.P.*, 165 S.W.3d 329 (Tex. 2005).

34 Walker, Jr., *supra* note 19, 539.

CHAPTER 3

Japhet v. McRae

COMMENTARY
by Terry I. Cross

276 S.W. 669

1925

Japhet
v.
McRae

276 S.W. 669

1925

POWELL, P. J.

In December, 1915, Wilbur Fisher and wife executed an oil, gas and mineral lease to the Producers' Oil Company on a certain 15-acre tract of land out of the William Bloodgood augmentation survey in a portion of what is now called Barbers' Hill oil field, in Chambers county *(Sic)*, Tex. Subsequently, Fisher, the original lessor, conveyed to Walter Keeble, one of the defendants in error here, the north 5 acres of said 15 acres. Keeble then conveyed to Charles C. McRae, the other defendant in error here, an undivided 3 acres out of his north 5 acres. Some 18 months after he sold 5 acres of the land to Keeble, Fisher, the original lessor as aforesaid, sold to the same Walter Keeble the remaining south 10 acres of the 15-acre tract. On the same day Keeble conveyed that very same 10-acre tract, for a very large profit, to Dan A. Japhet, one of the plaintiffs in error here.

The various deeds conveying these lands were in the usual form of general warranty deeds, and all referred to the lease to the Producers' Oil Company, which was itself in the usual or commercial form of oil leases. There is nothing whatever in any of the deeds providing for an apportionment of the one-eighth royalty retained by the owner of the fee among the various subdivisions of the 15-acre tract. The deeds contained no language from which it could be said that any apportionment of royalty was in the mind of the parties at the time they were executed. Keeble, undoubtedly, could have written his deed to Japhet in such a way as to provide that the latter should take the 10 acres of land by metes and bounds, but should have only ten-fifteenths of the one-eighth of any oil produced from any part of the 15 acres. But no such provision is in the deed. On the contrary, the deed expressly provided that Japhet should have all the rights which the original lessor had in the 10 acres. This is a case where it is contended that the *law itself*, in the absence of contract to the contrary, requires an apportionment of the one-eighth royalty. In this respect, it is unlike the case of *Hoffman v. Magnolia Petroleum Co., 273 S. W. 828*, very recently decided by this section of the Commission of Appeals and the Supreme Court. We will discuss this law point more fully later.

After Japhet bought the 10 acres of land, he succeeded in having the oil company, as the lessee, develop his 10 acres. Under the lease, of which all parties had notice when these various deeds were written, the lessee could develop any part of the 15 acres just as it saw fit to do. Much oil was discovered on the 10 acres. McRae and Keeble filed this suit for five-fifteenths of the one-eighth royalty from this oil, although their 5 acres had never been developed. The trial court, upon an agreed statement of facts, denied the recovery sought, and awarded all the money to Japhet. The money itself, under agreement of the parties, is being deposited in a Houston bank to await the termination of this suit.

The Court of Civil Appeals at Galveston reversed the judgment of the trial court and rendered judgment in favor of McRae and Keeble for one-third of the royalty. See *269 S. W. 829*. There is a lengthy statement of the case by the Court of Civil Appeals. We think it unnecessary to make any further statement. We have stated the facts material to a decision of the one law point which controls the judgment to be rendered in this case. We shall now discuss that one law question.

Counsel for Japhet contend that:

> "Where the lessor of land for oil and gas, subsequently to the execution of the lease, but prior to the development of the land and the production of oil or gas under the lease, sells a portion or portions of the land to others, and oil and gas are thereafter produced under the lease from some portion of the leased premises, the royalties therefrom belong to the owner of the particular tract upon which the well is located, and the owner or owners of other portions of the leased premises have no interest therein."' *(Sic)*

If this rule is correct, then the trial court's judgment should be affirmed. On the other hand, if the converse of the rule just stated is correct, as Keeble and McRae contend, the judgment of the Court of Civil Appeals should be affirmed. Which is the correct rule in this connection presents an interesting question. It is the first time the Supreme Court of Texas has ever had an opportunity to pass upon it. We have given most thorough consideration to the able briefs and arguments on file in this case and reviewed all the authorities most carefully. We have also felt unusually free, because of the importance of the question, to consult with the Supreme Court before preparing our report. We have concluded that the rule contended for by plaintiffs in error is the better one, and that the judgment of the trial court was correct. In this conclusion, we follow the great weight of authority. For instance, we are in line with the following states:

Arkansas: *Osborn et al. v. Arkansas Territorial Oil & Gas Co., 103 Ark. 175, 146 S. W. 122.*

Indiana: *Fairbanks v. Warrum, 56 Ind. App. 337, 104 N. E. 983, 1141.*

Ohio: *Northwestern Ohio Natural Gas Co. v. Ullery, 68 Ohio St. 259, 67 N. E. 494.*

Oklahoma: *Kimbley v. Luckey, 72 Okl. 217, 179 P. 928; Pierce Oil Corporation v. Schacht et al., 75 Okl. 101, 181 P. 731; Galt v. Metscher, 103 Okl. 271, 229 P. 522; Gypsy Oil Co. v. Schonwald, 107 Okl. 253, 231 P. 864.*

West Virginia: *Pittsburgh & West Virginia Gas Co. v. Ankrom, 83 W. Va. 81, 97 S. E. 593, 5 A. L. R. 1157; Musgrave v. Musgrave, 86 W. Va. 119, 103 S. E. 302, 16 A. L. R. 564.*

The only opinions contrary to our views, so far as counsel cite or we can find, are the Pennsylvania case of *Wettengel v. Gormley, 160 Pa. 559, 28 A. 934, 40 Am. St. Rep. 733,* and *184 Pa. 354, 39 A. 57*, and the Texas case of *Gillette v. Mitchell, 214 S. W. 619*. The latter case was by the Court of Civil Appeals at Galveston, and that court has again held the same way in the case at bar. It has continued to follow the Wettengel Case in Pennsylvania. The Gillette Case could go no further than the Court of Civil Appeals.

No other Texas court has passed upon this question except the Court of Civil Appeals at San Antonio in the case of *Hoffman v. Magnolia Petroleum Co., 260 S. W. 950*. That court rendered its decision upon the language of the instruments there involved. It was not necessary for the court to pass upon this apportionment of royalty rule. But the court clearly expressed its approval of the majority rule presented here by counsel for Japhet. The authorities we have cited are full and give the reasons pro and con for the conflicting views upon this issue. We shall not quote from these decisions. It would unduly lengthen our opinion. They are accessible to the attorneys in the case. We think the reasoning by the majority of the courts is sound. They answer every contention of any possible merit on the contrary side.

If the rule we approve is just in all the states where it is followed, it is also just in Texas. We are not unlike the other states in any matter of substance which affects this matter. Our Supreme Court has held that oil is a part of the realty until brought to the surface, and that it can be sold in place. Japhet unquestionably bought the realty in the 10 acres. He bought one-eighth of the oil in or under that land. The lessee had the right to take full charge of the land so far as necessary to get the oil from under it. He had the title to the oil for that purpose. But, when it was brought to the surface, Japhet had the right to his one-eighth thereof. He had an equitable title to his interest in that oil, and if the lessee had made any effort to take it away from him, Japhet would have been entitled to sue him as for conversion of his property. It seems to us that the only possible justification for permitting McRae and Keeble to participate in these royalties coming out of the Japhet wells would be on the presumption, as a matter of law, that a part of the oil from the wells on the 10 acres was being drained from their 5 acres. Should there be any such legal presumption? We think not. It is well known that oil wells and dusters are found side by side within a very few feet of each other. If the Japhet wells were draining oil from the lands of any one else, it would be impossible, in the absence of proof, to say whether such drainage was north, south, east or west of the Japhet tract. But, before the drainage could possibly affect defendants in error, it must come from the north. It is entirely possible that if McRae and Keeble should be allowed one-third of this money, they would be receiving it when there was not a drop of oil on their land. It is, in any event, unjust to take away the property apparently belonging to one party and give it to another until it is shown that the latter party has been deprived of it.

If the oil on the 15 acres in this suit should be apportioned, because the entire tract of land was under one lease, then where will we stop? Will the courts say they will apportion royalties provided the lease does not cover more than 1,000 acres, or more than 10,000, or more than some other acreage arbitrarily fixed? Or will they say that apportionment will apply, unless the contrary is expressly provided for, in all lands under the same original lease? If this rule should be enforced, we would have a situation of this kind. Upon the submission of this case, it was stated, and not questioned, that the Humble Oil & Refining Company has one lease covering 1,000,000 acres of land from the same owner. One corner of that land is 75 miles from one of its other corners. The land is in several counties. Suppose the owner of the land should sell 75 acres in one corner to a party interested in oil, and who thinks he knows oil land when he sees it. He counts confidently on the one-eighth royalty attaching to that 75-acre tract. He induces the original lessee to develop his land, and a gusher is forthcoming. Under the rule urged by defendants in error, the man discovering this 75-acre tract as the most valuable of the entire million acres for oil purposes would be entitled to only seventy-five one-millionths of the one-eighth royalty of the oil coming out of the gusher on the 75-acre tract. Can we say such a rule is just? A party owning another 75 acres, 75 miles distant, would get as much from the oil as the man whose 75 acres has the producing gusher. And yet this man without the gusher might not have a single drop of oil under his land, which is 75 miles distant from the gusher. Such a rule would, in our opinion, be entirely impracticable. Many oil leases cover thousands of acres of land. As our Supreme Court has held, oil is fugitive in its nature, and ordinarily should belong to him who captures it and brings it to the surface. The quest for it involves tremendous expense and a vast element of chance. In spite of the scientific knowledge of the geologists, the industry still partakes largely of a gamble. It seems to us that the only safe rule, and the only one free from much confusion, is one which gives the oil to the man who owns the land upon which the well is located. Clearly, it would not be right to award the oil to those who, like Keeble and McRae, offered no proof that any of it was drained from under their 5-acre tract.

Our conclusion is not unjust, as we see it, even if there were a possibility that the 5 acres were being drained by the Japhet wells. Keeble knew that the lessee had the right to drill anywhere at its pleasure. He knew that part of the 15 acres might never be developed. Still, he allowed Japhet to select 10 definite acres. He traded with his eyes wide open to the rights of the various parties. He expressly sold to Japhet the one-eighth royalty retained by the original lessor so far as the 10 acres were concerned. He must be held to have known that the 10 acres might be first developed, and, if so, that the oil thereunder would belong to Japhet and the lessee. Keeble was not required to sell any of the 15 acres. If he wanted the oil which might be found under any part of the 15 acres, he should have retained it all or expressly sold off only an undivided interest in the royalty under the entire 15 acres. That course seems fairer than to wait for others to develop a certain portion of the tract and then ask for a division of the developed tract.

While the majority rule does not seem to perpetrate any injustice on defendants in error, the contrary rule would work a grave injustice to Japhet. He paid $10,000 cash for this 10-acre tract, practically worthless except as an oil prospect. Keeble made a profit of $2,000 on the deal, and he turned it in one day. His money was not invested long. Japhet could have bought the 10 acres and accepted a deed to an undivided ten-fifteenths of the royalties in the 15 acres. But he did not do so. If he had known that Keeble wanted one-third of the oil coming from wells on the 10 acres he was buying, he doubtless would have vigorously objected to it. He bought no partnership interest in oil. It is an injustice to him to make him divide his oil after he had exercised his own best judgment and selected the 10 acres where he thought the oil was. The description of the 10 acres by metes and bounds was utterly useless under the minority rule. Under that doctrine, Japhet would get only ten-fifteenths of the oil royalty whether he bought a certain 10 acres or merely an undivided 10 acres. It is wrong to force him to do something he did not contract to do.

The various states are beginning by statute and supervision to make certain rules governing the duties of lessees. Particularly is this true with reference to the duty on the part of the lessees to drill offset wells on adjoining leases. As this great industry develops, other laws will doubtless be passed regulatory of operation by lessees. But such laws will not take away the rights of parties which have already become vested. The courts should not make contracts for people overturning those they have voluntarily and fairly made for themselves.

In the Gormley Case, the Pennsylvania court said there would be no apportionment of coal or other solid minerals. But, the court said, oil and gas were different. The court seemed to think that each of the 600 acres would probably produce an equal amount of oil. This case was written 30 years ago, and the courts did not know as much about the mysteries of oil as they do now. Actual experience shows that the Pennsylvania court is very much in error in assuming that oil is anything like equally distributed on 600 acres of land, or any other number of acres.

For the reasons stated by the great majority of all the courts which have passed upon this question, as well as those stated by ourselves, we think the judgment of the Court of Civil Appeals should be reversed and that of the district court affirmed. We so recommend.

CURETON, C. J.

The judgment recommended in the report of the Commission of Appeals is adopted, and will be entered as the judgment of the Supreme Court.

Commentary on Japhet v. McRae, and the Path Not Taken

by Terry I. Cross

The *Japhet v. McRae* opinion, handed down by the Texas Commission of Appeals in 1925,[1] decided a narrow, but fundamental, issue. If part of the land covered by an oil and gas lease is transferred, do the new owner and the transferor share royalties from all land subject to the lease, or does the new owner own royalty only in the segregated tract that it acquired and the transferor own all royalty in the retained portion? This essential question had to be answered early in the development of Texas oil and gas law, and it was definitively answered in this case. The answer is "non-apportionment." The production will not be apportioned to all of the land covered by the lease, but instead, in the absence of express language requiring a different result, the transferee's rights are limited to production from the acquired tract, and the transferor retains all royalty in the retained tract. Was the apportionment issue, like a teen-age marriage, decided too soon? Would we have gotten a different answer if the issue had been decided later?

In *Japhet*, the court actually had "two cases" before it. In the first, Humble Oil & Refining was the lessee under an oil and gas lease that covered over a million acres in West Texas, and the buyer had bought a seventy-five acre tract on one side of the ranch more than seventy-five miles from a single, producing well. The court had to decide whether the buyer of a small part of the leased acreage would share in the royalty due under that lease for a producing well seventy-five miles (and two counties) away. In the other case, Charles McRae and Walter Keeble had bought a five-acre tract in Chambers County that was subject to an oil and gas lease covering fifteen acres, and the court had to decide whether McRae and Keeble (for simplicity referred to as "McRae" below) would share in the production from two wells located on the fifteen-acre tract, at most a few hundred feet away from McRae's five-acre tract. The "case" dealing with the million-acre Humble lease was not actually before the court for adjudication,[2] but it was the "elephant in the room," and, as more fully discussed below, the court's concern for the proper adjudication of the million-acre case also decided McRae's fate with regard to his five-acre tract. In *Japhet v. McRae*, the court chose the non-apportionment rule for Texas, and McRae's royalty was limited to production, if any, from the five-acre tract.

Landmark Status

While *Japhet* is certainly a landmark because of the fundamental rule it announced, its application is very discrete. It applies only when (1) a tract is transferred subject to an oil and gas lease that covers additional land, (2) that lease does not have an "entireties clause" requiring apportionment of royalty to all portions of the leased premises, and (3) the parties to the conveyance of the segregated tract do not address the issue of whether the transferee shares in all royalty under the lease. The application of the ruling does not depend on whether production was flowing as of the transfer; but, practically, the ruling is less likely to apply if there was production because, if the transferor is receiving royalty from the lease, it is far more likely that the issue of apportionment will be expressly addressed in the transaction documents. Thus, the default rule of *Japhet* will have no place. The entireties clause has not enjoyed wide acceptance in Texas; but, obviously, a more pervasive use of that provision in oil and gas leases would diminish the application of *Japhet*.

The non-apportionment holding of *Japhet* is more important in Texas today than the non-apportionment holdings in other jurisdictions because of the unique regulatory regime in Texas. The non-apportionment result is certainly an impediment to the inattentive transferee of a tract subject to an oil and gas lease in Texas; but if *Japhet* is the "rock," then to complete the metaphor, the "hard place" is the inaccessibility of the forced-pooling statute to the transferee of the subdivided tract.[3] If the transferee of the tract could muscle into the unit for a well that is draining the acquired tract, the non-apportionment rule of *Japhet* would be of interest but would not conclusively end the transferee's right to share in production from the well. The case adopting the non-apportionment position in Oklahoma,[4] for instance, is hardly a subject for discussion today because of the statutory pooling regime in place there. By contrast, the *Japhet* case is still cited regularly and still pinches regularly in Texas. That is a landmark.

Historical Context

The non-apportionment rule had already become the majority position before the *Japhet* case was decided, but majority status was less clear when the issue was first addressed in Texas in the case of *Gillette v. Mitchell*.[5] In that case, the post-lease subdivision occurred by operation of the original lessor's will. By virtue of a retained-acreage clause that was ahead of its time, at the lessor's death the oil and gas lease had terminated except for seven-acre tracts around each of three producing wells. The lessor, through her will, bequeathed two-acre tracts to various relatives with no regard for the configuration of the seven-acre tracts around the producing wells. The *Gillette* decision relied heavily on the Pennsylvania case of *Wettengel v. Gormley*[6] and, without using the label, adopted the apportionment result, reasoning that because the lessee cannot be required to respect subsequent subdivisions by the lessor, the lessor's rights are similarly indivisible:

> When Mrs. Gaillard devised to appellant and appellees their several tracts of land burdened with the lease which gave to [the lessee] the right, by the operation of the well then producing oil from the large tract of which the two tracts constituted a part, to take all of the oil from said larger tract of which the two tracts constituted a part, to take all of the oil from said larger tract, we think the benefits as well as the burdens of this lease went proportionately to each of the tracts devised, regardless of whether the producing well was on the one or the other. Notwithstanding the adverse criticism of the decision of the Pennsylvania court in the Wettengel Case by the Supreme Courts of Ohio, West Virginia, and Indiana, we think the rule announced in the Wettengel Case is sound and should be applied in the instant case.[7]

The "benefits as well as the burdens" concept from the *Gillette* decision was pointedly relevant to McRae because the oil and gas lessee in *Japhet* had located a warehouse, office, and pipe yard on the five-acre tract to support the operations on the adjacent productive tract.[8] The Galveston Court of Appeals, which had also decided *Gillette*, stayed the course in its decision of the *Japhet* case and held that McRae would share in royalty from anywhere on the lease. The Galveston court, in *Gillette* and *Japhet* alike, saw the lessor's inability to force the lessee to recognize the subdivision by separately measuring production or operating the tracts separately, as also deciding the apportionment issue.[9] While the "single and indivisible nature of the lease"[10] concept was the basis for the decision, the use of McRae's surface is mentioned twice in different segments of the Court of Appeals decision,[11] and the burden of the entire lease falling on the non-productive tract clearly played a role in the decision.

The Commission of Appeals reversed the Galveston court in *Japhet*, adopting the non-apportionment rule and, thus, imposed the "burdens without the benefits" without any mention of the imposition that the oil and gas operations had on McRae's surface. The non-apportionment holding of *Japhet* rests on two justifications. First, the *Japhet* opinion correctly portrayed non-apportionment as the majority position, citing cases from five other states that had adopted the rule.[12] Pennsylvania, in the *Wettengel*[13] decision, was then and still is the only state that had unequivocally adopted the apportionment approach. Second, and perhaps more compelling to the court than a desire to line up with the majority, was the sense that the rule of capture required the non-apportionment result: "[T]he only safe rule, and the only one free from much confusion, is one which gives the oil to the man who owns the land upon which the well is located."[14]

<u>The Other Path</u>

Even though the *Japhet* court chose non-apportionment, the apportionment path was well charted. The *Gillette* case, though not Texas Supreme Court authority, was, for the interim between *Gillette* and the final *Japhet* opinion, the only Texas decision on the subject. The Galveston court, when the issue arose again, stuck with apportionment in its opinion in the *Japhet* case, notwithstanding the growing acceptance of non-apportionment in other jurisdictions. We have a clear vision of what the apportionment rule in Texas may have looked like, thanks to Judge Robert W. Stayton, formerly of the Commission of Appeals, who thirty years after *Japhet*, published the opinion he wrote for the Commission of Appeals that would have affirmed the Galveston court's decision in *Japhet*. Judge Stayton explains:

> Early in 1925 the writer prepared and submitted to the Supreme Court of Texas the opinion of the Commission of Appeals in a case entitled *Japhet v. McRae*. Soon afterward his term of office expired. The court, somewhat later, considered the

> opinion, declined to receive it and reassigned the case to the same section of the Commission, having conferred with Presiding Judge Powell, and instructed him to write an opinion which would reach an opposite result.[15]

Interestingly, even though the non-apportionment result was requested by the Texas Supreme Court, and Judge Powell consulted with the court while preparing the opinion,[16] the Supreme Court refrained from adopting Judge Powell's opinion and adopted the judgment only. The rejected Stayton opinion would have followed *Wettengel* and *Gillette* in affirming the Court of Appeals decision, but that proposed opinion contains thoroughly muddy analysis, and even if one were hoping for adoption of the apportionment rule, the rejected opinion would not have been a good statement of or justification for it.

If apportionment was to be the rule, the better justification would be found in the community lease cases that were to come in the 1940s in *Parker v. Parker*[17] and *French v. George*.[18] When owners of separate tracts execute a single lease covering their multiple tracts, in the absence of express contrary language, the royalty from production anywhere on the lease is apportioned to all lessors without regard to which tract yields the production. The tracts are effectively pooled by the execution of the community lease, and the allocation is based on the ratio of the acreage of each tract to the aggregate tract covered by the lease. The rule regarding community leases is the result of the courts determining the probable intent of the parties. If owners of two tracts execute the same oil and gas lease, is it likely that either of them would accept the risk that wells will be drilled only on the other tract and the respective owner would receive all of the resulting royalty payments; the lessee will not be obligated to measure production from the separate tracts or protect either tract against drainage by the other tract; the entire lease will be perpetuated indefinitely with the non-productive tract remaining burdened by the lease, perhaps even hosting operations for the benefit of the productive tract? The negative answer to those questions yielded the apportionment rule for community leases in Texas.

Certainly, there is a factual distinction between a community lease and a post-lease subdivision, as was the case of *Japhet*, but should the question regarding the parties' intent be answered differently? If the parties do not articulate their decision to adopt non-apportionment for their respective tracts, why would the court choose non-apportionment for them when no royalty owner can enforce non-apportionment on the lessee? The *Japhet* opinion supplies the default rule for parties who do not expressly address the issues without attempting to discern the probable intent of the parties or what they would have intended had they been more thoughtful about their transaction.

Of course, the problem with the query into the intent of the parties is that the intent likely varies with the size of the tracts. Professor William O. Huie wrote the definitive deconstruction of the apportionment/non-apportionment issue and is critical of *Japhet* and the non-apportionment rule.[19] Huie would make the projection of the parties' probable intent paramount and would allow different rules to apply according to the size of the tracts:

> If the intention of the parties will probably vary as the size of the tract varies, rules should be formulated reflecting this variation. Thus, even in a jurisdiction that generally adheres to the nonapportionment rule, there is no good reason to extend its application to the subdivision of a tract so small that the parties could not possibly have contemplated the drilling of more than one well to drain the entire tract.[20]

If the *Japhet* court had indulged in that type of analysis, we would not only have a different rule depending on the size of the tracts, but also a different rule for the subdivision of a productive lease versus a non-productive lease. Arguably, the failure to address the issue head-on in the transaction documents could reflect a different intent and expectation when there is flowing production, as opposed to the case where oil and gas production may be out of sight and out of mind. Clearly, the *Japhet* court wanted a single rule that would apply for large tracts and small tracts, and while either apportionment (by area) or non-apportionment would meet that requirement, the court was preoccupied with very large leases and only non-apportionment gave a satisfactory answer for the "million-acre lease." The *Japhet* decision probably decided the million-acre lease case correctly, both from an objective policy perspective and in projecting the probable intent of the parties to the hypothetical sale of a tract seventy-five miles from the only producing well. On the other hand, the court's perfunctory view of the parties' intent in the *Japhet* case presumed that the parties expected non-apportionment and would have been shocked by a different rule:

> Japhet could have bought the 10 acres and accepted a deed to an undivided ten-fifteenths of the royalties in the 15 acres. But he did not do so. If he had known that Keeble wanted one-third of the oil coming from the wells on the 10 acres he was buying, he doubtless would have vigorously objected to it.[21]

Nowhere in the opinion is there any reference to the evidence that revealed the state of Japhet's frame of mind when he bought the ten-acre tract, which preceded the drilling of any wells. Even if the court was correct in attributing geologic expertise to Japhet, the preference for non-apportionment cannot be safely projected to all parties who effectuate the post-lease subdivisions of small tracts. Rather than entertain the probable intent of parties who create small tracts post-lease, the court required a rule that could be applied without evaluation of facts, circumstances, and multiple variables. The *Japhet* opinion imposes a single immutable rule for all post-lease subdivisions. Unfortunately, the rule has not been a good fit for smaller tracts.[22]

Loose Ends: What About Drainage?

Despite the resounding adoption of the non-apportionment rule in *Japhet*, a door was left open for the owner of the non-productive tract that is being drained. The *Japhet* opinion turned on McRae's failure to prove that the five-acre tract was being drained by wells on the ten-acre tract:

> [T]he only possible justification for permitting McRae and Keeble to participate in these royalties coming out of the Japhet wells would be on the presumption, as a matter of law, that a part of the oil from the wells on the 10 acres was being drained from their 5 acres. Should there be any such legal presumption? We think not. It is well known that oil wells and dusters are found side by side within a very few feet of each other.[23]

Later in the opinion, after finding non-apportionment to be the "only safe rule" to deal with the million-acre lease, an exception was dangled for owners of a non-productive tract seeking to share royalty from elsewhere on the lease: "Clearly, it would not be right to award the oil to those who, like Keeble and McRae, offered no proof that any of [the oil produced from the ten-acre tract] was drained from under their 5-acre tract."[24]

So, what if the owners of the non-productive tract prove drainage? Does that result in apportionment on a surface acreage basis, or does it result in some other allocation depending on the severity of the drainage? In the case of *Mueller v. Sutherland*,[25] the oil and gas lease covered 224.9; and subsequent to the lease, the Muellers sold a twenty-four acre tract that had two wells located on it. The Railroad Commission had adopted field rules for the Wade City Field that required twenty-acre units in order for the lessee to receive the maximum allowable for a well. Each of the wells on the sold tract was on a unit composed of twelve acres from the twenty-four acre tract and eight acres from the retained tract. The Muellers claimed 8/20 of the royalty from each of the wells. The apportionment rule of *Wettengel* would have called for the Muellers to receive 200.9/224.9 of all royalty from the lease, but the Muellers made their claim for 8/20 of the royalty from the wells on the sold tract based on an equitable pooling theory. The equitable pooling theory would have been a logical attack under the drainage exception left open by *Japhet*. Surely, the field rules adopting twenty-acre units reflected a finding by the Railroad Commission that a well will drain twenty acres in the Wade City Field. However, the drainage exception from *Japhet* was not mentioned, and *Mueller v. Sutherland* is now the leading case for the proposition that Texas does not recognize equitable pooling. The Muellers were not entitled to any royalty from the wells bottomed on the twenty-four acre tract, notwithstanding the fact that each of the units contained the Muellers' land and the wells were draining the Muellers' land. Although the drainage exception of *Japhet* has not been expressly retracted or discredited, its vitality is subject to question, if for no other reason, by the passage of so many decades without use.

Conclusion

The non-apportionment rule in Texas stands unchanged from the 1925 *Japhet* opinion. Except for the different treatment that community leases received in the 1940s,[26] there have been no embellishments or refinements, and there is essentially no place to go from here unless the drainage exception gets traction somewhere. The logical development after adoption of the non-apportionment rule was a statutory pooling procedure that addressed the plight of the owner of the small tract being drained after the post-lease subdivision. The development of statutory forced pooling was the response generally in the other states that make up the majority position cited in *Japhet* and in the other states that adopted the non-apportionment rule after *Japhet*. The absence in Texas of those developments in the forced-pooling arena is primarily what keeps *Japhet* on the short list of important cases almost ninety years after the opinion.

---

1 *Japhet v. McRae*, 276 S.W. 669 (Tex. Comm'n App. 1925, judgm't adopted).

2 Apparently, the example of the million-acre lease was raised in the briefing: "Upon the submission of the case, it was stated, and not questioned, the Humble Oil & Refining Company has one lease covering 1,000,000 acres of land from the same owner." *Id.* at 671.

3 *R.R. Comm'n v. Coleman*, 460 S.W.2d 404 (Tex. 1970). For a discussion of the statutory amendments that followed the *Coleman* case and their failure to benefit buyers in the shoes of McRae, *see* Mark Leaverton, *Mipa...Schmipa The Foibles of Texas Forced Pooling*, State Bar of Texas, 25th Annual Oil, Gas and Energy Resources Law Course, Chapter 12 (2007).

4 *Kimbley v. Luckey*, 179 P. 928 (Okla. 1919).

5 *Gillette v. Mitchell*, 214 S.W. 619 (Tex. Civ. App.—Galveston 1918, no writ).

6 *Wittengel v. Gormley*, 160 Pa. 559, 28 A. 934 (1894).

7 *Gillette*, 214 S.W. at 622 (citations omitted).

8 *McRae v. Japhet*, 269 S.W. 829, 830 (Tex. Civ. App.—Galveston 1925), *rev'd*, 276 S.W. 669 (Tex. Comm'n App. 1925, judgm't adopted).

9 *McRae*, 269 S.W. at 837.

10 *Id.* at 832.

11 *Id.* at 830, 837.

12 "If the rule we approve is just in all the states where it is followed, it is also just in Texas." *Japhet*, 276 S.W. at 671.

13 *Wittengel*, 160 Pa. 559, 28 A. 934.

14 *Japhet*, 276 S.W. at 672.

15 Robert W. Stayton, *Apportionment and the Ghost of a Rejected View*, 32 Tex. L. Rev. 682, 682 (1954).

16 Judge Powell, like the Apostle Paul, made clear the source of his inspiration: "We have also felt unusually free, because of the importance of the question, to consult with the Supreme Court before preparing our report." *Japhet*, 276 S.W. at 670.

17 *Parker v. Parker*, 144 S.W.2d 303 (Tex. Civ. App.—Galveston 1940, writ ref'd).

18 *French v. George*, 159 S.W.2d 566 (Tex. Civ. App.—Amarillo 1942, writ ref'd).

19 William O. Huie, *Apportionment of Oil and Gas Royalties*, 78 Harv. L. Rev. 1113 (1965).

20 *Id.* at 1140.

21 *Japhet*, 276 S.W. at 672.

22 It would not have been a good answer for the two-acre tracts within the seven-acre "leases" in *Gillette v. Mitchell*, and was not good for the *Mueller v. Sutherland* facts. *See infra* note 25.

23 *Japhet*, 276 S.W. at 671.

24 *Id.* at 672.

25 *Muller v. Sutherland*, 179 S.W.2d 801 (Tex. Civ. App.—El Paso 1944, writ ref'd w.o.m.)

26 *See supra* notes 17 & 18.

4

CHAPTER 4

W. T. Waggoner Estate
v.
Sigler Oil Co.

COMMENTARY
by Jacqueline L. Weaver

118 Tex. 509, 19 S.W.2d 27

1929

W. T. Waggoner Estate
v.
Sigler Oil Co.

118 Tex. 509, 19 S.W.2d 27

1929

Mr. Justice GREENWOOD delivered the opinion of the court.

Plaintiff in error, the W. T. Waggoner Estate, brought this suit against defendant in error, Sigler Oil Company, to forfeit or cancel a conveyance of oil and gas in a certain 3000 acres of land in Wilbarger County.

On January 27th, 1919, W. T. Waggoner and others, by a writing duly executed, for a consideration of $100,000 and stated covenants and agreements, leased 85,000 acres of land in the counties of Wilbarger and Baylor, including said 3000 acres tract to W. G. Burton, "for the sole and only purpose of mining and operating for oil and gas, and of laying pipe lines and of building tanks, power stations and structures thereon to produce, save and take care of said products." The writing called a lease, stipulated for an annual rental of $100,000, payable in advance on the 27th day of each January during the life of the lease, "provided each producing well shall hold 2000 acres in a square, said well to be the center, and said 2000 acres shall be released as to further annual rental." It was expressly provided that the lease should remain in force for a term of five years from date and as long thereafter as oil or gas or either of them was produced from the land by the lessee; and, it was further provided that if no well was commenced on the land on or before the first day of June, 1919, the lease should terminate as to both parties, reasonable time being allowed for unavodiable [SIC] delays. The lessors were to receive the equal one-eighth part of all oil and gas produced and saved from the leased premises. The estate of either party under the contract was declared to be assignable in whole or in part, and the assignee of the lessee as to only a part of the leased lands was to continue payments of no more than his proportionate part of rentals. Defendant in error, Sigler Oil Company, had acquired all rights under this writing formerly held by Burton in the 3000 acres of land, and plaintiff in error, the W. T. Waggoner Estate, had likewise succeeded to the rights of the lessors in the 85,000 acres.

Plaintiff in error instituted this suit January 29, 1924, averring that the Sigler Oil Company had lost all rights and interests in and to the oil and gas in the 3000 acres: (1) by abandonment of such rights and interests, (2) by failure and refusal to use the 3000 acres for the purposes of the lease, and (3) by failure and refusal to proceed with reasonable diligence in the performance of the company's obligations to explore and develop and market the oil and gas.

Defendant in error, Sigler Oil Company, answered by pleading a general denial and specially that it had fully performed its obligations by drilling certain wells for oil and gas, including two wells which produced oil in paying quantities and from which plaintiff in error had received and was receiving royalties, and that defendant in error was entitled, in any event, to hold its rights in the oil and gas in 2000 acres, with a producing well at its center.

Answering special issues, the jury found: first, that the Sigler Oil Company and its predecessors in title prior to January 29, 1924, failed to use reasonable diligence in the development for oil of the 3000 acres of land; second, that the Sigler Oil Company, prior to January 29, 1924, breached its duty to carry out the essential purposes of the lease through reasonable development of the land; and, third, that the Sigler Oil Company did not, prior to January 29, 1924, abandon its duty of carrying out the essential purposes of the lease.

On these findings the District Court refused to cancel the lease, but decreed a kind of limited specific performance, requiring the drilling of not less than eight wells, at the rate of one each six months, and adjudged that failure to comply with the decree should result in the forfeiture of the lease.

The Court of Civil Appeals construed the stipulation for each producing well to hold 2000 acres without payment of future rentals as discharging the lessee, or his assigns, from any further obligation for mineral exploration or development of each 2000 acres containing a producing well at its center, brought in by the lessee or his assigns, at least for the fixed term of five years. The Court of Civil Appeals decided that in the absence of abandonment of its rights by the Sigler Oil Company, plaintiff in error had no remedy for any breach of duty to reasonably explore and develop the oil and gas other than an action for damages or for specific performance. Accordingly, the Court of Civil Appeals reversed the judgment of the District Court, and remanded the cause for a new trial. 276 S. W. 936.

The Commission of Appeals concluded that on the jury's findings the judgment of the District Court and of the Court of Civil Appeals should both be reversed and that judgment should be rendered for plaintiff in error, divesting the Sigler Oil Company of all interests in the 3000 acres, save as to ten acres including the two producing wells. The conclusion that the Sigler Oil Company be allowed to hold the ten acres was grounded on a concession in plaintiff in error's pleadings. The Supreme Court entered a judgment in line with the Commission's conclusions. This judgment followed the Commission's interpretation of previous opinions of the Court as holding that a lessee's failure to prosecute with reasonable diligence the essential purposes of a contract for the production of oil and gas terminated the lessee's title, aside from his intent to abandon his contract or rights. 284 S. W. 920, 926. On motion for rehearing, the case was withdrawn from the Commission and has been argued by eminent counsel.

The following propositions must be regarded as settled by repeated decisions of the Supreme Court:

> First: Such a writing as that here called a lease operated to invest the party called lessee and his assigns with title to oil and gas in place. Texas Company v. Daugherty, 107 Texas, 226; Stephens County v. Mid-Kansas Oil & Gas Company, 113 Texas, 160; Humphreys-Mexia Company v. Gammon, 113 Texas, 255.
>
> Second: The estate acquired by the so-called lessee and his assigns was a determinable fee, which was lost on cessation of the use of the land for purposes of oil and gas exploration, development, and production. Stephens County v. Mid-Kansas Oil & Gas Co., 113 Texas, 173; Texas Company v. Davis, 113 Texas, 331; Munsey v. Marnet Oil & Gas Co., 113 Texas, 220; Robinson v. Jacobs, 113 Texas, 239; Thomason v. Ham, 113 Texas, 246.
>
> Third: The estate of the lessee or of his assigns did not survive abandonment. Grubb v. McAfee, 109 Texas, 530; Munsey v. Marnet Oil & Gas Co., 113 Texas, 219; Thomason v. Ham, 113 Texas, 246.
>
> Fourth: Where a mining lease provided for oil or gas royalties and failed to define the lessee's duty as regards development after discovery of paying oil or gas, the law implied the obligation from the lessee to continue the development and production of oil or gas with reasonable diligence. Benavides v. Hunt, 79 Texas, 396; Grubb v. McAfee, 109 Texas, 530, 531; Texas Pac. Coal & Oil Company v. Barker, 117 Texas, 418, 6 S. W. (2d) 1035, 1036; Freeport Sulphur Company v. American Sulphur Royalty Company, 117 Texas, 439, 6 S. W. (2d) 1042, 1043.
>
> Fifth: Breach of the lessee's implied obligation for reasonable mineral operation will not authorize the forfeiture of the lease as for breach of condition subsequent, such obligation being a covenant. Grubb v. McAfee, 109 Texas, 530; Texas Company v. Davis, 113 Texas, 335.
>
> Sixth: The usual remedy for breach of the lessee's implied covenant for reasonable development of oil and gas is an action for damages, though under extraordinary circumstances—where there can be no other adequate relief—a court of equity will entertain an action to cancel the lease in whole or in part. Texas Pac. Coal & Oil Company v. Barker, 117 Texas, 418, 6 S. W. (2d) 1035; Freeport Sulphur Company v. American Sulphur Royalty Company, 117 Texas, 439, 6 S. W. (2d) 1045; Grubb v. McAfee, 109 Texas, 534, 535.

Analyzing and applying the principles underlying the foregoing propositions and decisions, we are satisfied that notwithstanding the stipulation that each producing well brought in under the lease on the 85,000 acres should hold 2000 acres in a square without payment of future rentals, still the Sigler Oil Company, as the assignee of the original lessee, was under an implied obligation, after the drilling of the two paying wells, to continue with reasonable diligence, during the five year term as well as thereafter, the work of exploration for, and production of, the oil and gas in the 3000 acres.

Mr. Summers shows by authorities cited that the rule is almost universally accepted which he states as follows:

> "In absence of express stipulation creating a duty to proceed with drilling after the discovery of oil and gas in paying quantities, the law, to accomplish the manifest intention of the parties, in leases where the principal consideration is royalties to be paid the lessee, implies a duty on the part of the lessee to reasonably develop the premises." Summers Oil & Gas, sec. 129, page 414, and note (48).

After the producing wells were brought in by the Sigler Oil Company no revenue whatever was to be derived from the lease of the land thereby released from rentals save through royalties.

Discussing the covenant for additional wells where the first well is a producer, Mr. Merrill says:

"It has been argued with vigor and ability that, after production is secured from the exploratory well, there should be no implied covenant for further development, other than that necessary for protection of the leased premises against drainage. The basis of this argument is that, the lessor receiving some income from the lease, the presupposition of development and payment of royalties is satisfied and further development should be left to the will of the lessee. It is submitted, with all due respect, that this is unsound. The presupposition is not satisfied by the payment of royalties from one small well if the land is clearly capable of further profitable development. The lessor assuming the presupposition for development, may justifiably claim to have his land fully developed and to realize all the royalties it is capable of producing, in the absence of an agreement to the contrary." Merrill's Covenants Implied in Oil & Gas Leases, section 117, p. 279.

Quite enough was said in the opinions in the cases of Grubb v. McAfee and Texas Compay v. Davis, supra, to demonstrate that we would do violence to what all parties plainly intended should we interpret this lease in such manner as to absolve the lessee or his assigns from the duty of reasonable development after proving that the 3000 acres contained oil in paying quantities.

Was the implied obligation for further reasonable development, while the 3000 acres was producing oil from two wells, a limitation on the estate granted? Tentative Draft No. 1 of the Restatement of the Law of Property by the American Law Institute, page 48, lines 12 to 16, uses the word "limitation" as meaning "a phrase or a number of phrases in a conveyance which delimit the duration of an interest in land."

The only clauses in the writing before us which could delimit the duration of the interests granted are as follows:

> First: The clause providing for the termination of the lease as to both parties unless a well was commenced on the land, on or before June 1, 1919;
>
> Second: The clause demising and leasing the land for the sole and only purpose of mining and operating for and producing oil and gas, and saving them for market.
>
> Third: The clause stipulating that the lease should remain in force for a term of five years from date, on payment of annual rentals, and as much longer as oil or gas was produced from the land by the lesse or his assigns.

A clause similar to the first was referred to in a dictum in Texas Company v. Davis, 113 Texas, 331, as creating a condition subsequent, that effect having been ascribed to it by distinguished counsel on both sides and by the learned judges writing the majority and minority opinions in the Court of Civil Appeals. This may have arisen from failure to recognize a distinction between the customary "drill or pay" clause and the "unless" clause. The clauses under consideration in the Davis case and here come within the class of "unless" clauses. The correct rule seems to be that while the usual "drill or pay" clause in an oil lease does introduce a condition subsequent, for the benefit of the lessor alone, yet, as said by Mr. Summers, "Where the 'unless' drilling clause is used a failure of the lesse to drill or pay a stipulated sum of money *ipso facto* terminates the lease, without the necessity of re-entry, action or their equivalents by the lessor. For this reason the interest created in the lesse by such lease cannot be one terminable by breach of condition subsequent. Some courts have designated them options or optional leases, but the interests created by them are perhaps better classified as estates upon common law limitation, wherein the interests in the grantee or lessee continue until the happening of the event upon which they terminate." Summers Oil and Gas, pages 483, 506 to 512.

However, we need not further consider this first limitation clause, because it was admittedly complied with by the commencement of an oil well on the land before June 1, 1919.

The words of the second and third clauses of limitation above mentioned not only fail to make the duration of the granted estate depend *on the degree of diligence* used in the continued exploration, development and production of oil and gas on the land, after their discovery, but such words expressly negative the termination of the lessee's interests as long as either oil or gas was actually being produced from the leased land. The express provision of the third clause is that the lease shall remain in force, i. e., shall *not* terminate, *as long as* either oil or gas is produced from the land by the lessee. We are asked to say, by judicial interpretation, that the lease shall terminate *before* the cessation of production of oil or gas from the land by the lessee, if, by reasonable diligence, more oil or gas could have been found, produced or marketed. A court should never override by implication the intention of parties expressed in a binding writing. Freeport Sulphur Company v. American Sulphur Royalty Company, 117 Texas, 439, 6 S. W. (2d) 1043 (4).

Even if the third clause did not forbid treating the measure of diligence imposed by the implied obligation for further mineral operation, as a limitation on the estate granted, we think it is more consonant with the intention of the parties not to regard the second clause as embodying in its limitation the requirement of reasonable diligence in the performance of the obligations resting on the lessee for mineral exploration, development and production.

In a case in which this Court undertook with great care to define the interests acquired by a lessee under a similar lease it was said that, "the grant was to be enjoyed only while the work of mineral exploration and production was carried on"; and that the estate granted instantly terminated when the lessee *no longer* prosecuted such work. In that case, the estate granted was adjudged terminated because "the evidence is undisputed which conclusively shows that those under whom defendants in error claim (i. e., the lessee and his assigns) *entirely and permanently* stopped and abandoned the exploration and development of the 76 1/2 acres and the production of minerals thereon." Texas Company v. Davis, 113 Texas, 331, 333, 335.

In an opinion delivered the same day the Davis case was decided, the Court again said: "It was intended by all parties that the lands should be used for no other purpose than the specified mineral exploration and production, and that the grants were to be enjoyed only while such use continued and were to immediately terminate on *cessation* of the use." Continuing, the Court quoted from both Kent and Tiffany in support of the proposition that it was *cessation* of the use for the purposes for which the grant was made, which would terminate a grant, under a clause like the second now under consideration. Stephens County v. Mid-Kansas Oil & Gas Company, 113 Texas, 173.

In Munsey v. Marnet Oil & Gas Company, 113 Texas, 219, the Court declared:

> "In our opinion, both contracts or grants passed title to corporeal property—not absolutely—but for mining purposes only, and title of such nature as to be incapable of enduring after abandonment of the contracts or abandonment of operations for mineral discovery and production."

In Robison v. Jacobs, 113 Texas, 239, it was held that the pleadings and evidence raised the issue of "termination of plaintiff in error's title and rights, through *cessation* of use for the purpose of the grant, whether or not defendant in error should prevail on the issue of abandonment."

The Court ought not to conclude that the parties intended to prescribe a test for termination of the interests granted which could only be applied with the utmost uncertainty or confusion. Yet, if reasonable diligence in performing every one of the lessee's exploring, developing, producing, and marketing operations was the test, neither lessor nor lessee could at any time have clearly or certainly known whether the estate granted was alive or ended. Such a test must inevitably diminish—if not destroy—the value of the rights of all parties derived from a mineral lease.

Considerations like the above have induced the courts to very uniformly refuse to regard obligations lacking in definiteness and certainty as introducing into grants conditions subsequent or limitations leading to forfeiture or termination of vested estates.

The Court declared, through Chief Justice Stayton, in Benavides v. Hunt, 79 Texas, 392:

> "It is further insisted that the part of the tenth paragraph which obligated appellees 'to use all economy in the conduct and management of said mining enterprise' gave another condition on noncompliance with which appellants were entitled to terminate the estate.

"'We are of opinion that this proposition can not be sustained, and if for no other reason because what would be deemed the 'use of all economy' would be too uncertain to recognize as a condition on which a forfeiture might rest.

'It would vary as much as the opinions of witnesses might vary on a matter of fact about which no fixed rule determines compliance or noncompliance. Right to forfeit estates vested can not exist by reason of the existence or nonexistence of a state of facts not clearly defined."

More recently the rule declared by Judge Stayton was reaffirmed, when the Court said:

"The authority to forfeit a vested right or estate should not rest in provisions whose meaning is uncertain and obscure. It should be found only in language which is plain and clear—whose unequivocal character may render its exercise fair and rightful." Decker v. Kirlicks, 110 Texas, 94.

In Grubb v. McAfee, 109 Texas, 532, approved in Davis v. Texas Company, 113 Texas, 335, the Court refused to hold that the implied obligation for continued development in the ordinary oil lease was a condition subsequent, quoting from the opinion of Justice Bonner in Johnson v. Gurley, 52 Texas, 227. In the latter opinion, the Court said:

"The breach of a condition does not, of itself, divest the estate of the lessee, but to do this the lessor must, by express act, take advantage of the same by re-entry, or that which in law would be equivalent thereto. (1 Wash. on Real Prop., 3d ed., marg. p. 319; Taylor's Land. and Ten., sec. 273; Fifty Associates v. Howland, 11 Met., 99; Elliott v. Stone, 1 Gray, 575.)

"A conditional limitation marks the period or event which is to determine the estate without entry of claim, and no affirmative act is necessary to vest the right in the grantor or him who has the next expectant interest. (Taylor's Land. and Ten., sec. 273, 2 Wash. on Real Prop. 3d ed., marg. p. 459.)

"In case of doubt as to the true construction of a clause in a lease, it should be held to be a covenant, and not a condition or limitation, as the law does not favor forfeitures. (1 Wash. on Real Prop., 3d ed., marg. pp. 319, 320; Taylor's Land. and Ten., sec. 273; 4 Kent's Comm., marg. p. 129; Wheeler v. Dascomb, 3 Cush., 288.)"

As a limitation, the obligation under consideration would operate more harshly than as a condition subsequent. As stated in Justice Bonner's opinion, under a limitation the estate granted is automatically terminated on the happening of stipulated events, while under a condition subsequent the lessor has the election to terminate or continue the contract after breach of the condition. It would be wholly inconsistent with this Court's previous opinions to declare that this implied obligation operated as a limitation when we had refused to regard an identical obligation as a condition subsequent because of the harshness of its operation as such in the forfeiture of vested rights.

The cases of Texas Pacific Coal & Oil Company v. Barker, 117 Texas, 418, 6 S. W. (2d) 1035, and Freeport Sulphur Company v. American Sulphur Royalty Company, 117 Texas, 439, 6 S. W. (2d) 1045, correctly recognized the right of lessors to recover damages for breaches of implied obligations for reasonable mineral production though such breaches continued for years subsequent to an initial breach. It was said in the opinion of Mr. Justice Pierson in the case last cited: "*So long as* the sulphur company breaches or violates its contractual duty to operate one plant, the royalty company may recover its compensation for the full amount of sulphur that should have been produced as contemplated in the contract." No damages could be properly awarded the lessor for any failure by the lessee to drill for or produce or protect or market minerals after they had reverted to the lessor under the operation of a limitation on the lessee's estate. Both decisions necessarily imply that the obligations breached were covenants and not limitations.

Contractual implications are justified only on the ground of necessity. 13 C. J., 558. Mr. Merrill suggests that the true basis of the whole doctrine of implied covenants in oil and gas leases may be found in the determination of courts to enforce fair dealing between lessor and lessee which could not otherwise be assured. Merrill's Covenants Implied in Oil and Gas Leases, sec. 112, page 266. While necessity and fair dealing alike require the implication of the obligation by the lessee in leases such as the one now before the Court for reasonable diligence in oil and gas exploration, development, and production, yet neither necessity nor fair dealing requires the further implication that such obligation shall operate as a limitation on the estate acquired by the lessee.

Under the doctrine that the lessee acquires no absolute but only a determinable fee, there can be no complete cessation of the use of the leased land for purposes of mineral exploration, development, and production, save at the cost of loss of the lessee's estate. It is easy to confuse this principle with that of abandonment, which implies an intention to give up the interests granted. There should be no such confusion. Regardless of the lessee's intention, his estate terminates, under its limitation, when there is complete cessation of actual use of the land for the purposes of the lease. There can be no fraudulent evasion with respect to the use which keeps the estate alive. But, it is not a partial use, nor a negligent use, nor an imperfect use—but cessation of use—which terminates the lessee's estate.

The soundness is sometimes questioned of the rule in Texas and elsewhere that interests declared to be fees in land may be lost by abandonment. Mr. Summers points out, however, that in all jurisdictions where the view prevails that an oil or gas lease creates a vested interest in the lessee, for the purposes of the lease, as soon as it is made, the courts "have not hesitated to declare such lease terminated by abandonment on that account. . . . The general rule, therefore, seems to be that an oil and gas lease, regardless of what theory the courts may take as to the nature of the interest created thereby is extinguishable by abandonment." Ample foundation for the doctrine is to be found in the very nature and object of these mineral development conveyances and contracts. Summers Oil & Gas, page 519.

Not only may the lessor recover minerals granted under the ordinary oil or gas lease, which remain unproduced, on cessation of mineral operations, or on the lessee's abandonment of his rights; but, where a solvent lessee is merely guilty of negligence, to the lessor's injury, in the conduct of the work of exploring, developing, producing or marketing the minerals, the lessor may recover his damages.

And despite our refusal to treat as a limitation or as a condition subsequent the implied covenant for reasonable development of premises leased for the mining of oil and gas, after they have been discovered, should there be a breach of such covenant for which an action for damages, for any reason, furnishes no adequate remedy, our courts, in the exercise of equitable jurisdiction, will compel the lessee to fully perform his obligation which constitutes a fundamental consideration for, and object of, the lease, or submit to cancellation of the lease. 1 Black on Rescission and Cancellation (2d ed.) sections 197, 198.

In Grubb v. McAfee, supra, we pointed out that the courts could do complete justice without adjudging a lease forfeited or terminated for breach of implied obligations, relative to development, even in cases where redress was impossible under an award of damages. On that subject, Mr. Merrill says:

> "The extreme hardship of the straight-out forfeiture and the inadequacy of damages are both avoided by a unique form of relief which has received its chief development in Kansas,—an alternative decree, requiring the lessee to do those things necessary to fulfill his obligations under the implied covenant, within a time fixed by the court, the lease to be forfeited and cancelled, in default of such performance." Merrill's Covenants Implied in Oil & Gas Leases, sec. 103, p. 246.

The verdict of the jury, construed in the light of the explanatory charges, finds no more than a breach by defendant in error of a mere covenant. This verdict furnished no proper basis for any judgment for plaintiff in error. The case was manifestly not tried in accordance with the law as it is set forth in this opinion. The Court of Civil Appeals entered the correct judgment in reversing the judgment of the District Court and in remanding the cause for a new trial. The judgment of reversal by the Court of Civil Appeals is affirmed, but the case is remanded to the District Court for a new trial in accordance with this opinion.

Commentary on *The Landmark Status of W.T. Waggoner Estate v. Sigler Oil Co.*

by Jacqueline L. Weaver

Completed November 25, 2007

No one likes a dog in the manger. The dog sleeps a lot and even though it doesn't need all the space in the soft straw, it won't let any other animal enjoy the manger's warm comforts. In 1929, the Texas Supreme Court in *W.T. Waggoner Estate v. Sigler Oil Co.*[1] announced that it didn't like such dogs hanging out in Texas oil fields; they are not the hard-working hunting dogs needed to develop oil fields properly and to effectuate the purposes of the oil and gas lease contract. Yet, over the years, this 1929 case has proven to more aptly illustrate the adage "let sleeping dogs lie." The *Waggoner* case has been all bark, no bite. Of course, merely barking a warning to complacent lessees might often be enough to get them out of the manger and working to develop a lease. Even sleeping dogs get hungry and are self-motivated to drill wells that might return a stream of black gold to them. But, should the decision to sleep or to hunt be entirely at the dog's discretion?

1. History of W.T. Waggoner Estate v. Sigler Oil Co.

The *Waggoner* case brings us back in history to the fabled ranches of yore. The Waggoner family dynasty began with a cattle kingdom sprawling across more than 500,000 acres of North Texas near Burkburnett. At age 14, W.T. "Tom" Waggoner proclaimed that "I want to run the most cattle, breed the best horses and work harder than anyone."[2] When he was 17, his father made him a full partner in the Waggoner cattle empire. By the time he was 27, Tom ran the entire enterprise. While drilling wells in search of water for his cattle, Waggoner repeatedly encountered oily water. Ever the practical businessman, he leased approximately 250,000 acres to Texaco in 1909 near the town of Beaver Switch, whose name was later changed to Electra in honor of Waggoner's daughter.

In 1918, the Red River uplift in North Texas became the next big oil play following the discovery of large fields in the Texas Gulf Coast area. Far from the coast, Fowler's Folly came in a gusher and within three weeks, 56 derricks were at work in the Burkburnett area.[3] In January 1919, W.T. Waggoner leased an 85,000-acre tract to W.G. Burton. On April 29, 1919, the Burk-Waggoner Company explored the northwest area of the Burkburnett field and found huge quantities of oil. In 1919, the Burkburnett field produced an astounding 31.6 million barrels of oil. Unproved land in the area sold for $180,000 an acre. Yet, by 1925, Waggoner had already become unhappy with the amount of drilling and development work done on parts of his ranch. The scene was set for *W.T. Waggoner Estate v. Sigler Oil Co.*

Surely, Texas practitioners (or for that matter, any legal realist, even those in ivory towers) may cynically wonder what oil company would fight this vast empire in a local court in the emperor's home base. But Sigler Oil, the assignee of 3,000 acres of the 85,000-acre lease between Waggoner and Burton, dared to fight this Goliath of a landowner. During the lengthy battle that ensued, the Texas Supreme Court pronounced the tenets of implied covenant jurisprudence in Texas oil and gas leases, especially the implied covenant to reasonably develop.

2. Its Landmark Status

Is *Waggoner* a landmark case? By the statistics, yes. Since 1929, it has been cited 189 times by the Texas courts, once by the U.S. Supreme Court, 28 times by the Fifth Circuit Court of Appeals, three times by other federal appellate-level courts, and eleven times by other states' courts.[4] Many of these citations are pro forma. This very fact may prove *Waggoner's* landmark status: its principles have been so well accepted that little more is needed but to cite it as authoritative. But, has a lessor ever won an implied covenant to develop law suit in Texas? That is a different story, as we shall see.

Moreover, the statistics mask the fact that *Waggoner* is often cited for other principles, not related to implied covenant law, which the Texas Supreme Court with evident exasperation reminded lawyers had already been decided by the Court before 1929. The Court neatly listed the blackletter rules that would define the nature of an oil and gas lease for all future time and followed each listed rule with citations to previous cases which lawyers appeared not to have read or understood, even though the Court noted that the listed propositions had been "settled by repeated decisions" of the Court. Here is the list:

1. A lease vests a lessee with title to the oil and gas in place.
2. The lease is a determinable fee.
3. The leasehold estate cannot survive abandonment.
4. When a lease provides for royalties and fails to define the lessee's duty to develop after a commercial discovery of oil or gas, the law implies a duty by the lessee to continue development and production with reasonable diligence.
5. Breach of the implied covenant to develop does not authorize a forfeiture of a lease.
6. The usual remedy for breach of an implied covenant is an action for damages, although, under "extraordinary circumstances" where no other adequate relief is possible, a court of equity may cancel the lease in whole or in part.

What were the unsettled issues, then, that faced the Court in 1929 and made the case noteworthy? The clarity in the Court's list of tenets masked the mighty struggles that the lower courts had endured over four years of wrestling with the *Waggoner* case, with quite different results in each court. The trial court, based on jury answers to special issues, rendered judgment decreeing that Sigler Oil specifically perform by drilling eight more wells in the undeveloped part of its lease or forfeit its lease, except for a small area around the two producing wells that it had drilled. (The realists and cynics say "I told you so.") Waggoner appealed because outright cancellation of the Sigler lease was not granted; Sigler appealed, arguing that it had not breached the implied covenant to develop, if such a covenant existed, and further, that a particular clause in the lease expressly negated any such implied covenant.

The Court of Civil Appeals reversed and remanded on the basis that the trial court's multi-well drilling decree was unsupported by any evidence that it was equitable or reasonable, noting in the process that the "we seriously doubt the correctness of the jury's finding that [Sigler] had not been reasonably diligent."[5] (The realists and cynics nod wisely.) Moreover, the appellate court was strongly inclined to interpret the lease provision that each producing well "shall hold 2,000 acres in a square, said well to be the center, and said 2,000 acres shall be released as to further annual rentals" as expressly negating the implied covenant to develop.[6] The Commission of Appeals, created by the legislature to assist the Supreme Court with its heavy docket, concluded that both lower courts should be reversed and that judgment should be rendered in favor of Waggoner, divesting Sigler Oil of all but ten acres around its two producing wells.[7] The Texas Supreme Court at first entered this judgment, but on motion for rehearing, withdrew the case from the commission and firmly announced the six principles listed above which should guide the trial court on remand.

At the end of the second trial, the trial court peremptorily instructed the jury to find for the lessee (who had now become Lido Oil) as to 2,000 acres and to find for Waggoner on the remaining 1,000 acres.[8] On appeal, this judgment was again reversed and remanded.[9] Who knows who won the case? Perhaps the antagonists settled, too exhausted for a third round in the trial court.

3. Its Effect in Shaping the Law

While *Waggoner* seemed to herald future victories for lessors seeking to push their lessees to work harder, sooner, the actual course of the implied covenant to develop in Texas jurisprudence is aptly summarized as follows:

> The reality of Texas law is that a lessee can allow several decades to elapse without adequate seismic testing, drilling, or development and need have little concern that its lessor will have any significant judicial recourse. Although the implied covenant of reasonable development is fully recognized by Texas courts, proof of breach is difficult and expensive, and trial court judgments are rarely upheld, even when based on jury verdicts and on jury findings of facts which, in virtually every other oil-and gas-producing state, would give rise to damages, conditional decrees, or even outright cancellation of undeveloped portions of the lease.[10]
>
> The "illusory protection" afforded by the implied covenant to develop means that lessors

> must insert express provisions in a lease to accomplish what the implied covenant fails to provide.[11] Either a "continuous development" clause or a "retained acreage" clause will cause the lessee to lose the undrilled portion of its lease, and the lessor will be free to find another lessee to work this acreage. In sum, the lessor cannot accept a lessee's model lease form and rely on implied covenant law to protect her against dog-in-the-manger lessees.

More importantly though, the overall tenor and philosophy of *Waggoner*—that implied covenants are both necessary and fair in order to give the lessor the royalty income that the land is capable of realizing—has disappeared from the language of the Texas Supreme Court in the past decade or so.[12] Indeed, the Court in its more recent decisions has turned implied covenant law on its head:landowners must become "reasonably prudent lessors" in monitoring their leases for breaches of any implied covenants, lest their causes of action be barred by statutes of limitations.[13] Further, the reasonably prudent lessor has to be a hard worker because he or she will often not be given the benefit of the discovery rule which defers accrual of a cause of action until a plaintiff knows or should know (by exercising reasonable diligence) of the facts giving rise to the cause of action.

What sorts of facts should reasonably prudent lessors discover on their own? In *HECI Exploration Co. v. Neel*,[14] the Court held that they must be vigilant in spotting the physical existence of other operators in the area and, upon seeing such, then determining whether a common reservoir underlies the land, threatening drainage of their royalty oil. Beyond drainage, lessors must exercise reasonable diligence to determine whether adjoining operators have inflicted damage on the underground reservoir by being alert to the possibility that unscrupulous rival operators in a shared reservoir might be violating commission allowable rules and destroying the maximum recovery of a field over the long term.[15]

How can lessors investigate threats to and protect their own interests? First, the Court suggests that they learn about the extent of reservoirs and competitive operations by asking for information from their own lessee. They can also search Railroad Commission records which may provide constructive notice, including filings and other publicly available material. Applying its diligent-lessor standard to the facts in the *HECI* case, the Texas Supreme Court concluded that commission information about fields in which there is competing production "indicates that injury to a common reservoir by an adjoining operator is not inherently undiscoverable."[16] Thus, the lessors' implied covenant action in *HECI* was barred by the four-year statute of limitations because the lessors did not work hard enough to monitor, not just their own lessee, but other lessees that were illicitly overproducing the reservoir and damaging it.

4. Some Musings on Its Future

What, then, can be said about the future of the implied covenant to develop or of implied covenant law in general in Texas? A few thoughts come to mind. First, because sophisticated or wealthy lessors with newer leases may have inserted express language in their leases as a substitute for reliance on an illusory covenant, future disputes over the pace of development of a tract are likely to focus on the issue of when express language in a lease negates implied covenants. Second, inside *Waggoner* lies a "sleeper" holding: that a leasehold may not survive "abandonment," regardless of the course of implied covenant law. Can this holding rescue lessors? This final section discusses these two issues and then muses about whether lessees might rue the Court's new approach to lessor/lessee relations.

(a) When Express Clauses Bar Implied Covenants

Even before deciding the *Waggoner* case in 1929, the Texas Supreme Court had addressed the issue of when an express clause would be held to bar an implied covenant. In 1928, in *Freeport Sulphur Co. v. American Sulphur Royalty Co.*,[17] the grantors had conveyed a deed to sulfur-rich land in exchange for a large cash payment of $450,000, royalties, and an express covenant that the grantee erect and operate a plant using the Frasch process within 18 months. The grantee did so and operated the plant until shutting it down for several years from 1924 to the date of trial. The Court refused to surmise whether the principal consideration for the deed was the upfront cash or the royalty; the royalty was a substantial part of the consideration which gave rise to an implied covenant to develop and operate the plant. The express clause requiring one plant negated any implied covenant to develop additional plants, but nothing barred the necessary implication of an implied covenant for continuous operation of the plant in order to realize the bargained-for royalties.

The *Waggoner* court adopted a similar approach in holding that the express clause that one well would hold 2,000 acres did not displace the implied covenant to develop; it simply acted as a "starter" provision to encourage lessees to drill early in their primary term to avoid having to pay delay rentals.[18] Any other interpretation would "do violence" to the plain intent of the parties.[19] The *Freeport Sulphur* and *Waggoner* cases were followed by two others in 1938 and 1941 which combined to establish two guiding principles: first, express clauses must very clearly bar implied covenants; and, second, express lease clauses will be interpreted against the drafter, usually the lessee.[20] Even an express clause that "development shall be at the discretion of the lessee," was interpreted by the Court to mean something quite different from the "uncontrolled will" or "inconsiderate action" of the lessee.[21] The lessee, while not required to act with the reasonable diligence demanded by implied covenant law, nonetheless was required to act in good faith according to what was "just and proper" under the circumstances and in the "honest judgment" of the lessee.

Yet, even these principles seem at risk under the Court's more recent jurisprudence. In *HECI*, the Court refused to find that the implied covenant to act as a reasonably prudent operator included a duty to protect and administer the leasehold by requiring that the lessee notify its own lessor of the need to bring suit against an adjacent operator for underground waste. No express provision barred any such implied duty, but an implied covenant to so notify the lessor was judged "not necessary to effectuate the full purpose of the lease."[22] It is difficult to square this holding with the Court's approach in the early foundational cases.

This raises the question: would the current Court have held that Sigler owed an implied duty to develop the 2,000 acres on which it had drilled?[23] Waggoner had received a bonus of $100,000 for granting the lease on 85,000 acres, and was to receive $100,000 a year as an annual rental, provided that "each producing well shall hold 2,000 acres in a square, . . . and said 2,000 acres shall be released as to further rental." Under these provisions, Waggoner had received payments totaling nearly $300,000 at the time of the lawsuit. In today's dollars, each $100,000 payment is worth roughly $1.2 million. Waggoner was a multi-millionaire from bonus and rentals alone. In 1919, the very year that Waggoner signed the 85,000-acre lease, the Relinquishment Act was passed, mandating that the state receive at least 10 cents an acre in delay rentals on the millions of acres of state-owned minerals.[24] Waggoner was receiving more than ten times this amount ($1.18 per acre) for land considered to lie in unexplored territory. Would the Court today find that an implied covenant to develop was necessary to effectuate the purpose of the Waggoner lease because Waggoner had gained such great riches from non-royalty income?

Or would the Court instead adopt Sigler Oil's interpretation of the lease as unambiguous: the lessee or its assignees had to drill 42 wells (85,000 acres divided by 2,000 acres) within a five-year period or suffer forfeiture as to each 2,000 acres not drilled on.[25] Exploration, not development, was the major purpose to be effectuated by this lease. Sigler Oil pointed to the word "and" in the lease proviso: the parties had expressly stipulated that each producing well "shall hold" 2,000 acres in the form of a square (free from any implied obligation to develop) *and* free from rentals. Thus, there was no room for an implied covenant to develop Sigler's 3,000 acres after Sigler had drilled two exploratory wells. The Court of Civil Appeals in *Waggoner* interpreted the lease this way,[26] and it may well have been a winning argument today.

(b) The Doctrine of Abandonment of Purpose

A lessor, dispirited with the state of implied covenant law in Texas, may search for another way to kick a napping dog out of the manger. If soaring oil and gas prices in the post-2001 era are not enough of a wake-up call, then perhaps a hunter with a keener scent for oil or gas can become a strategic ally and challenge the complacent incumbent, using the third of the *Wagonner* Court's six pronounced tenets: a leasehold cannot survive abandonment. A diligent lessor pursuing this quest will easily discover two recent Texas Supreme Court opinions which have cited this doctrine approvingly.

In 1994[27] and again in 2003,[28] the Texas Supreme Court reaffirmed the "abandonment of purpose" doctrine as an accepted principle of Texas oil and gas jurisprudence today. Its long lineage stems from the Court's early decision in the 1923 case of *Texas Co. v. Davis*.[29] In *Davis*, the Texas Company was the hardworking Second Lessee that drilled the first deep wells in an area which had been leased to First Lessee eighteen years earlier in 1901. This lease had a 25-year primary term which began when First Lessee discovered oil in 1901. First Lessee drilled four wells on the 76-acre tract before going bankrupt and forfeiting its corporate charter in 1905. In 1919, a month after the Texas Company drilled the first successful deep well on the acreage, the successors of First Lessee brought suit to recover their interest, arguing that the well drilled in 1901 vested them with fee simple title to the leased tract until the primary term ended in 1926.

The Texas Supreme Court in *Davis* surveyed similar cases from many other states and convinced itself that its own precedent of *Grubb v. McAfee*[30] should control the outcome in favor of the Texas Company as Second Lessee, writing:

> We are convinced: first, that [First Lessees] took only a determinable fee under the grant from [lessor], which terminated long ago, and second, that abandonment of the purpose for which [First Lessees] were invested with their title and rights in and to the minerals and land was necessarily fatal to the maintenance of the suit of [First Lessee-successors]. The evidence is undisputed . . . that [First Lessees] entirely and permanently stopped and abandoned the exploration and development of the 76 ½ acres and the production of minerals thereon. Their estate at once terminated without the need of a conveyance.[31]

Because the abandonment doctrine is brought in a suit to remove a cloud upon title which is a continuing injury, a cause of action for its removal is likewise continuing and is not barred by the statute of limitations, unlike an action for breach of covenant.[32]

In *Texas Co. v. Davis*, as in its twin case of *Munsey v. Marnet*[33] (decided the same day in 1923) and the predecessor case of *Grubb v. McAfee*, First Lessees were summarily thrown out of the manger, even though they had earned a vested conveyance in the minerals under lease by drilling initial wells. Rather than using implied covenant law to either give the First Lessee a second chance to act diligently or to cancel the lease outright based on extraordinary circumstances, the Court simply forfeited their leases. Nonetheless, despite the doctrine's proud pedigree and its prominent listing in the *Waggoner* sextet of tenets, the abandonment doctrine sank into obscurity for decades.

Astonishingly, the doctrine rose from the dead in the 1994 case of *Rogers v. Ricane Enterprises, Inc. II.*[34] In this case, the Court extensively discussed both *Davis* and what *Waggoner* said about *Davis*, explaining in no uncertain terms that its first decision in *Ricane I* "did not implicitly overrule *Davis*" and that the abandonment doctrine in *Davis* "has been repeatedly affirmed."[35] What triggered the revival of this doctrine?

If ever a dog needed to be ousted from the manger, the First Lessee in *Ricane* fit the bill. Indeed all the lower courts repeatedly held that the hardworking Second Lessee now owned the lease on a 329-acre tract. The *Ricane* cases pitted the First Lessee of a 1949 assignment of 329 acres of a 7,900-acre base lease against a Second Lessee. The 1937 base lease was held by production from wells located on land other than the 329 acres. First Lessee had drilled one well to earn the assigned acreage in 1949; the well was marginal and ceased producing in 1961. Years passed and First Lessee's property interest in the acreage was foreclosed upon by a bank when First Lessee's successor defaulted on a promissory note. In 1965, First Lessee's corporate charter was forfeited for nonpayment of franchise taxes. More years passed. In 1979, Second Lessee (Ricane Enterprises) completed a new producing well on the 320 acres having acquired the assignment of the working interest in this acreage from the bank which had foreclosed on it.

Six more years passed and in 1984, First Lessee woke up and brought a trespass to title suit against Second Lessee to recover possession of its working interest under the 1949 assignment. For ten years, from 1984 to 1994, the case made its way up and down the Texas court ladder, but always with the result in the lower courts that the *Davis* doctrine of abandonment of purpose applied to grant victory to the energetic Second Lessee.[36] Indeed the facts in *Ricane* are strikingly similar to those in *Davis*.

At the end of ten years of litigation, the Texas Supreme Court in a five-to-four decision in *Ricane II* finally ended the dispute. The Court refused to throw out the *Davis* doctrine of abandonment—but also refused to throw First Lessee off the acreage, even though the Court noted at the start of its opinion that First Lessee and its successors had not drilled any wells on the tract for 33 years. The bare majority distinguished *Davis*, writing:

> [I]n *Ricane I* we did not implicitly override *Davis*. The assignment in this case does not, by its express terms, specify a purpose for the assignment and does not contain any language limiting the duration of the assignment to "as long as" oil and gas is produced. Therefore *Davis* does not control and the jury's answer regarding abandonment of purpose is immaterial.[37]

The Court then elaborated on the meaning of *Davis* as explained in *Waggoner*, expressing concern that there not be any confusion between the theories of "abandonment of title" of fee simple estates and the doctrine of "cessation of use," which seems to be another name for the "abandonment of purpose" doctrine in the context of an oil and gas lease. The Court explained: "These are two separate doctrines. Although we do not recognize abandonment of title in Texas, the *Davis* doctrine has been repeatedly affirmed."

Having determined that *Davis* did not control the case and that the assignment created a covenant which did not automatically terminate by its own terms, the majority then proceeded to award the acreage to First Lessee on the basis that it had proved superior title in a chain derived from a common source. By a single vote, the sleeping dog won the manger.

The four dissenting justices excoriated the majority for failing to read the assignment as a whole in light of the purposes for which it was made, writing:

> If that purpose is the production of oil and gas, then a complete failure to pursue that purpose—"not a partial use, nor a negligent use, nor an imperfect use, but cessation of use" (quoting from *Waggoner*) is an abandonment of the purpose which terminates the estate. Because . . . the purpose of this contract was exploration, development and production and the jury determined that purpose was abandoned, I would apply *Davis* to conclude that the assignment automatically terminated.[38]

In the end, all nine justices affirmed the *Davis* doctrine of abandonment of purpose. Could this doctrine then become as (in)famous as the often-used *Duhig* doctrine which has created a near-endless progression of perplexing and painful interpretations of the purposes specified in deed recitals?[39] Virtually all oil and gas leases in Texas contain "so long as" language in their habendum clause and the Texas courts have repeatedly held that a lease is granted for the purpose of exploring for, developing, and producing oil and gas. The *Davis* doctrine of abandonment of purpose then would seem to clearly apply in the context of an oil and gas lease, even though it did not apply to the particular language in the *Ricane* assignment. In 2002, the Court, in its first opinion in *Anadarko Petroleum Co. v. Thompson* again cited *Davis* for its holding that "the lessee's mineral estate may continue indefinitely, as long as the lessee uses the land for its intended purpose."[40] Is there a ray of hope here for dispirited lessors that the abandonment doctrine can remove inactive lessees from their land?

Alas, lessors, the *Davis* doctrine is as illusory as implied covenant law. *Ricane II* clearly shows the Court taking great pains to avoid any finding based on abandonment: the comatose First Lessee won the prize. Similarly, the Court quickly issued an addition to its opinion on motion for rehearing in *Anadarko* to "clarify" its first opinion.[41] Gone is any language referring to the "purpose" of a lease as grounds for abandonment of purpose.[42] The facts in *Davis* (such as a lease with a 25-year term) are so unlikely to arise under a modern lease, that the Court can easily sideline *Davis*, even if the purpose of the modern lease is acknowledged to be exploration, production, and development. Indeed, all three cases of *Davis, Ricane,* and *Anadarko* are based on quirky language and peculiar facts that render them outliers to the vast body of Texas oil and gas jurisprudence.[43]

More importantly, in my opinion, the *Davis* doctrine should not be revived. It makes no sense either conceptually or practically as a device for clearing title in oil and gas leases. The essence of *Waggoner* as a landmark case is the distinction between covenants and conditions. Leases are fee simple determinables and expire if there is no production at the end of the primary term. Implied covenants are not conditions, and the remedy for their breach is not automatic termination, but damages or a conditional decree giving the lessee a second chance to be diligent. The *Davis* doctrine makes a mockery of the bright line between the happening of a condition of a fee simple determinable and breach of an implied covenant. In his early, seminal work, A.W. Walker, Jr. saw the great mischief that the *Davis* doctrine of abandonment could wreak on established property concepts and urged the Texas courts to drive a stake through its heart.[44] Indeed Professor Walker noted that an oil and gas lease cannot even be said to have an implied purpose of exploration and production because the lease expressly allows a lessee to pay delay rentals and not explore or produce.

The abandonment doctrine conflates a condition of a fee simple determinable with the lack of diligence in fulfilling the "purpose" of a lease in an implied covenant lawsuit. Using the doctrine, a lessor can bring a cause of action which might otherwise be barred by the statute of limitations and can demand lease cancellation as a remedy—two enormous advantages compared to using implied covenant law. But this third tenet in the *Waggoner* case creates a mismatched hybrid of property concepts that should not be carried into the future.

(c) A Final Thought: Ruing Recent Precedents?

The reasonably prudent operator standard embodied in implied covenant law in Texas has now been matched with a "diligent lessor" standard. Might a lessee rue this recent development as much as he might regret the rebirth of the *Davis* doctrine of abandonment? In essence, the *HECI* decision tells lessors to snoop on their lessees and on all nearby operators—to actively monitor their leases, survey their lease and lease lines, make inquiries of their lessee, troll the Railroad Commission and other records for evidence of wrongdoing,[45] and assume the worst about their lessee and all other operators in the area. Without such a cynical and negative approach, lessors may be barred by limitations from bringing an implied covenant lawsuit because what they don't know can indeed hurt them.

Similarly, might the ten-year court battle in *Ricane II* featuring the "abandonment of purpose" doctrine bring at least a gust of chill wind into the beds of near-comatose lessees? The *Davis* doctrine can so muddy the manger with mangled concepts about the purpose of a lease, its recital language, and the property interests created by it that a napping lessee may well prefer to get up and go to work than suffer nightmares from the dread of future litigation over the contours of this doctrine, especially if an energetic Second Lessee is barking so loudly that peaceful slumber is impossible.

Some lessees, now stuck with newly diligent, reasonably prudent lessors as backseat drivers who constantly question the speed and direction of the lessee at the wheel and demand thorough annual reports on the state of the oil and gas fields in the area of their tracts, might cast a rueful glance in their rearview mirror at the warmer manger they once inhabited before the Texas Supreme Court's recent precedents. Might this be at least some small comfort to the millions of Texas royalty interest owners who have neither the time nor the wherewithal to detect and then litigate breaches of implied covenants owed them by their own lessees?

---

* Editor's Note: This commentary, and the cases cited therein, was written by Professor Jacqueline Lang Weaver, A.A. White Professor of Law, University of Houston Law Center, in 2007. No further review or update of this article has occurred since that time.

1 *W.T. Waggoner Estate v. Sigler Oil Co.*, 118 Tex. 509, 19 S.W.2d 27 (1929).

2 The information in this paragraph appeared at www.waggonerranch.com/images/WaggHist.htm (last visited Sept. 9, 2007 May 16, 2013).

3 The information in this paragraph is found in Walter Rundell, Jr., Early Texas Oil: A Photographic History, 1866-1936, 93-96 (1977).

4 Based on a Lexis Nexis® "Shepardize®" search, last checked on May 16, 2013.

5 *Sigler Oil Co. v. W.T. Waggoner Estate*, 276 S.W. 936, 940 (Tex. Civ. App. —Amarillo 1925). The court cited evidence that eight dry holes had been drilled within 1.5 miles of Sigler's initial discovery well, and Sigler had expended $150,000 in exploration before being sued, resulting in only one other marginally productive well.

6 *Id.*

7 *W.T. Waggoner Estate v. Sigler Oil Co.*, 284 S.W. 921, 926 (Tex. Comm'n App. 1926), *opinion withdrawn on reh'g*, 19 S.W.2d 27 (Tex. 1929).

8 *Lido Oil Co. v. W.T. Waggoner Estate*, 31 S.W.2d 154, 157 (Tex. Civ. App. —Amarillo 1930). The Waggoner Estate sought damages of $800,000 as an additional remedy in this second round. The trial court refused to grant either damages or specific performance to Waggoner. Rather, it divided the 3,000 acres, presumably finding that Lido Oil had no further obligation to develop on the 2,000 acres held by the express provision in the lease but that Lido had lost the other 1,000 acres. Both parties appealed. The appellate court remanded because the trial court had failed to ask the jury whether there had been reasonable development of the entire 3,000 acres, and if not, what would constitute such development. The evidence showed that damages were entirely too speculative to be ascertained.

9 *Id.*

10 Ernest E. Smith & Jacqueline Lang Weaver, The Texas Law Of Oil And Gas, §5.2[B][2], p. 5-22 to 5-23 (2007). The lessor bears the burden of proof in implied covenant cases. In *Atlantic Richfield Co. v. Gruy*, 720 S.W.2d 121 (Tex. App.—San Antonio 1986, writ ref'd n.r.e.), the court reversed a jury finding that the lessee had breached the implied covenant to develop because the lessor had not met this burden, at the same time stating: "We acknowledge that the argument that ARCO's failure to drill in over 26 years is grounds to cancel the lease is persuasive."

11 *Id.* at § 5.2[B][3].

12 The Texas Supreme Court in *Waggoner* quoted extensively from Maurice Merrill's treatise on Covenants Implied In Oil And Gas Leases, a treatise which generally supports a pro-lessor position.

13 *HECI Exploration Co. v. Neel*, 982 S.W.2d 881 (Tex. 1998). Indeed, sleepy lessors may well find that their own lessees have adversely possessed the very leasehold mineral estate which had earlier reverted to the lessor when the lessee ceased production. *See Natural Gas Pipeline Co. v. Pool*, 124 S.W.3d 188 (Tex. 2003).

14 *HECI*, 982 S.W.2d 881.

15 Sometimes, competitive drainage may be relatively easy to spot. E.g., in *Amoco Prod. Co. v. Alexander*, 622 S.W.2d 563 (Tex. 1981), the lessors appeared to have noticed a drastic reduction in their royalties as production on their tract plummeted from 600 barrels of oil per day in 1972 to a mere 35 barrels per day in 1976. In 1973, crude oil prices skyrocketed because of the OPEC oil embargo, and any lessor might have wondered why their royalty payments weren't soaring as well. In *Amoco*, the lessors proved breach of the implied covenant to protect against drainage; indeed their own lessee was the very cause of much of the drainage, as it deliberately embarked on a plugback program to quickly push oil away from its competitor, Exxon, to Amoco's own leases updip from Exxon and the plaintiff-lessors. (These facts appear in the appellate opinion of *Amoco Prod. Co. v. Alexander*, 594 S.W.2d 467, 471 (Tex. App.—Houston [1st Dist.] 1979), *judgment modified*, 622 S.W.2d 563 (Tex. 1981)).

The lessors in *HECI* faced a quite different situation: a rival operator on an adjacent tract violated Railroad Commission rules and overproduced the reservoir. The lessor's own lessee, HECI, noticed the overproduction and sued the rival operator. *HECI* received $1.7 million in actual damages and $2 million in punitive damages after a jury trial, representing lost revenues equal to 100% of the diminution in value of the reserves in place, but never told its lessors about the lawsuit. The lessors' future royalties would clearly be lower because of this reservoir damage. The lessors learned about the lawsuit between HECI and the rival operator shortly after the statute of limitations for a cause of action against the rival had passed. The lessors then sued their own lessee under implied covenant law for failure to notify them either that (a) it was suing the operator, or (b) that the lessors should bring their own suit. The Court in HECI ruled that the second cause of action was barred by limitations, and that the first cause of action did not exist because the implied covenant to so notify was "not necessary to effectuate the full purpose of the lease." The Court further noted that "notwithstanding any excess recovery by HECI," the lessors could not claim unjust enrichment because they should have sued the rival operator themselves in a timely manner. *HECI*, 982 S.W.2d at 886. Now, suppose the drainage in *Amoco* had not been so drastic and had been masked by the offsetting increase in crude oil prices, so that royalty payments increased, but not as much as they would have absent the drainage. Should a diligent lessor have noticed the offset drilling being done by Exxon next door to counter Amoco's moves and made further inquiries about drainage? The Texas Supreme Court's answer, after *HECI*, is clearly "yes."

16 *HECI*, 982 S.W.2d at 887.

17 *Freeport Sulphur Co. v. Am. Sulphur Royalty Co. of Tex.*, 117 Tex. 439, 6 S.W.2d 1038 (1928).

18 *W.T. Waggoner Estate v. Sigler Oil Co.*, 118 Tex. 509, 518, 19 S.W.2d 29, 29 (1929). The Court noted that the implied covenant would not be barred either during or after the primary term.

19 *Id.*

20 The *Freeport Sulphur Co.* case and the other early foundational cases are fully discussed in Jacqueline Lang Weaver, *When Express Clauses Bar Implied Covenants, Especially in Natural Gas Marketing Scenarios*, 37 Nat. Resources J. 490, 497-502 (1997).

21 *See id.* at 501 (discussing Cowden v. Broderick & Calvert, Inc., 114 S.W.2d 1166 (Tex. 1938)); *also*, A.W. Walker, Jr., *The Nature of the Property Interest Created by an Oil and Gas Lease in Texas*, 11 Tex. L. Rev. 399, at 407-08 (1933).

22 *HECI Exploration Co. v. Neel*, 982 S.W.2d 881, 883 (Tex. 1998); *see supra* notes 13-15 and accompanying text.

23 The two wells which Sigler had drilled were so close to each other that a square of 2,000 acres around each well enclosed only about 2,000 acres of the 3,000-acre lease assignment.

24 Relinquishment Act, 36th Leg., 1st and 2d Called Sess., ch. 81, 1919 Tex. Gen. Laws 249.

25 Brief for Appellant (Sigler Oil) at 19-20, *Sigler Oil Co. v. W.T. Waggoner Estate*, 276 S.W. 936 (Tex. Civ. App.—Amarillo 1925) No. 2532 (copy from the Texas State Archives in author's files). The appellant's brief is the only one of record in the archives.

26 *Sigler Oil Co. v. W.T. Waggoner Estate*, 276 S.W. 936, 940 (Tex. Civ. App.—Amarillo 1925).

27 *Rodgers v. Ricane Enters., Inc. II*, 884 S.W.2d 763 (Tex. 1994).

28 *Anadarko Petroleum Corp. v. Thompson*, 94 S.W.3d 550 (Tex. 2003).

29 *Tex. Co. v. Davis*, 113 Tex. 321, 254 S.W. 304 (1923).

30 *Grubb v. McAfee*, 109 Tex. 527, 212 S.W. 464 (1919).

31 *Tex. Co. v. Davis*, 113 Tex. 321 at 335, 254 S.W. 304, 309 (1923).

32 *Id.* 113 Tex. at 336, 254 S.W. at 309.

33 *Munsey v. Marnet*, 113 Tex. 212, 254 S.W. 311 (1923).

34 *Rodgers v. Ricane Enters., Inc. II*, 884 S.W.2d 763 (Tex. 1994).

35 *Id.* at 767.

36 The trial court granted summary judgment in Ricane's favor finding that the lease automatically terminated because of cessation of use, abandonment, laches, and statute of limitations. The Court of Appeals affirmed on the cessation of use theory. The Texas Supreme Court in *Ricane I* reversed the summary judgment and remanded for a trial on the merits, holding that the assignment language created a covenant, not a condition, and breach of covenant could not result in automatic termination. On retrial, the trial court rendered a take-nothing judgment on First Lessee's claim for trespass to try title and conversion. The appellate court affirmed after concluding that the lease had terminated based on the jury's finding of abandonment of purpose. First Lessee then argued that the appellate court had erred in applying the Supreme Court's holding in *Ricane I* that the assignment had not terminated automatically, a holding which implicitly rejected the *Davis* doctrine of abandonment. The Texas Supreme Court in *Ricane II* felt compelled to explain its first holding and its relationship to *Davis*.

37 *Ricane II*, 884 S.W.2d at 767-68.

38 *Ricane II*, 884 S.W.2d at 770-71 (Hightower, J., dissenting).

39 Ernest E. Smith & Jacqueline Lang Weaver, The Texas Law Of Oil And Gas §3.7(C)(2007).

40 *Anadarko Petroleum Corp. v. Thompson*, 94 S.W.3d 550, 554 (Tex. 2002), *clarified on motion for reh'g*, 94 S.W.3d 558 (Tex. 2003) (per curiam). The Court denied the motion for rehearing, but went on to clarify its opinion.

41 *Id.*

42 In *Anadarko II*, the Court analyzed *Davis* as follows: "In *Davis*, the lessee abandoned all operations on the lease after the wells it had drilled ceased to produce and there was no production for about fourteen years. There was also evidence that the lessee had expressly released the lease. This Court held the lease had terminated." *Id.* at 560.

43 The lease in *Anadarko* was for a term of one year and "as long thereafter as gas is or can be produced."

44 A. W. Walker, Jr., *The Nature of the Property Interests Created by an Oil and Gas Lease: Part II*, 7 Tex. L. Rev. 539, 589-96 (1929); and *Part III*, 8 Tex. L. Rev. 483, 484-511 (1930).

5

CHAPTER 5

Sheffield v. Hogg

COMMENTARY
by Scott Lansdown

124 Tex. 290, 77 S.W.2d 1021

1934

Sheffield v. Hogg

124 Tex. 290, 77 S.W.2d 1021

1934

Mr. Justice GREENWOOD delivered the opinion of the court.

The above styled two cases will be determined under one opinion. In their consequences, the cases affect directly the subject matter of mineral royalties in Texas, which furnish an important basis for the State's oil industry. Involving the correct solution of taxation of royalties on minerals—liquid, solid, and gaseous—they require the determination of the rights acquired by lessors and lessees under conveyances and contracts under which much of our minerals of untold value are owned and held. The questions presented by the two cases are logically too closely related for much that is said in one case not to apply to what is said in the other.

For convenience, in this opinion cause No. 6001 will be called the "Hogg case," and cause No. 6130 will be called the "Federal Royalty Company Case."

The questions for decision in the "Hogg Case," save some relating to the manner and validity of the assessment of the properties, may be sufficiently discussed under the concise statement of the nature and result of the suit and the statement of the undisputed facts, contained in that part of the opinion of the Court of Civil Appeals, which is copied as follows:

"This suit was brought by appellants against the tax collector of Brazoria county, the county of Brazoria, two independent school districts, and a navigation district in said county, the commissioners' court, and all the officials of said county and districts having to do with the assessment of property for taxation and the collection of taxes in said county, to enjoin the collection of taxes levied and assessed upon one-eighth of the oil and other minerals in lands owned by appellants in said county for the year 1927.

"Five private oil corporations engaged in the production of oil on the lands of appellants in the county were also made defendants.

"Before the trial in the court below the state of Texas intervened in the suit and sought recovery against appellants for alleged delinquent taxes due for the year 1927, with interest, penalties, and costs.

* * * * * *

"Plaintiffs are, and were on January 1, 1927, the owners of the lands in Brazoria county described in their petition, in and under which the oil and other minerals assessed for taxes by the tax assessor of the county for that year as plaintiffs' and defendant oil companies' property was situated. On June 6, 1913, plaintiffs being then the owners of these lands, executed to John Hamman the contract of sale and lease referred to in plaintiffs' petition. This instrument, which is denominated a 'Mineral Lease Contract,' in its first contractual paragraph declares: 'That, for and in consideration of the sum of One Dollars ($1.00) cash in hand to first parties paid by second party, the receipt whereof is acknowledged, and of the covenants and agreements herein embraced and hereby undertaken by second party, first parties do transfer and set over, sell and convey (under the terms and conditions hereof, and for the period and purpose herein set forth) all the gas, oil, sulphur and other minerals and mineral substances whatsoever on, in and under the hereinafter described land, and the exclusive right and privilege to go on and upon said land, and to take possession thereof, for the purposes of drilling for and prospecting therefor, and, after the finding thereof, the development and production of same, and to that end, shall have the right to do and perform all proper and desired acts and things in the premises, especially the right to use all necessary water thereon or therein, and to erect any and all works and buildings, construct derricks, place machinery, and construct and place all manner of tanks and pipe lines desired."

The Court of Civil Appeals here refers to paragraph fifth of the contract of sale and lease, which reads as follows:

> "Fifth: (a) In consideration of this lease second party agrees that first parties shall have the following royalty of the gross production of all oil or gas wells on said lands, to-wit: one-eighth of all oil and one-eighth of all gas; and first parties' one-eighth royalty interest in all oil and gas marketed from said land to be paid over to them by second party at the end of each month, or whenever second party shall receive pay therefor, such royalty to be delivered by second party to the credit of first parties in any pipe-line or pipe-lines which said first parties may designate, and which connect with the wells or connect with the settling tanks of second party, free of any charge to first parties, or into said first parties' own private

> storage upon said land, or upon their other land adjoining, at the expense of said first parties; and first parties shall have one-eighth interest in all money realized from gas marketed from said land, as a royalty to be paid over to them, or their order, at the end of each month, or whenever second party shall receive pay therefor.

"(b) If sulphur or other minerals are produced on said land, second party shall pay first party $1.00 per ton of 2240 pounds for each ton thereof produced and saved from said land; quarterly settlements to be made by second party with first parties by either the payment to them in person of proper amount or by its deposit to their credit in their bank, or its successor in business."

After referring to paragraph fifth, the Court proceeds with its statement of undisputed facts, as follows:

> "Plaintiffs, none of whom are residents of Brazoria County, rendered for taxes for the year 1927 all of their property in the county of Brazoria, both real and personal. This rendition of their property did not list or include any part of the unproduced oil or other minerals underlying the lands described in their petition, but contained the following notation by them: 'Note: It is not the intention to render any of the oil, gas, sulphur or other minerals in the above lands, as said minerals were transferred, set over, sold and conveyed by Will C. Hogg, Miss Ima Hogg, Mike Hogg, and Tom Hogg to John Hamman per instrument dated June 6, 1913, recorded in Book 125, pages 53 et seq., of the Deed Records of Brazoria County, which instrument covers all of said land.'

"This rendition was accepted and approved by the tax assessor and commissioners' court of the county, and all taxes levied on the property therein rendered were paid by plaintiffs in December, 1927. The tax assessor, however, placed upon the unrendered roll and assessed for taxes for that year against plaintiffs and the defendant oil companies, jointly, one-eighth of the oil and minerals underlying these lands. None of the taxes accruing upon this rendition and assessment were paid by plaintiffs or the defendant oil companies. These are the taxes the collection of which from them plaintiffs ask to be enjoined, and for which, with interest, penalties, and costs, the intervener, the state of Texas, sought and recovered judgment against plaintiffs in the court below.

"The defendant oil companies, each of whom held under transfer and conveyance from John Hamman separate portions of the oil and other minerals conveyed to him by plaintiffs by the instrument before set out, rendered for taxes and paid the taxes for the year 1927 on seven-eighths of the oil and minerals in and under the several tracts of land described in the respective conveyances to them from Hamman."

The main question to be decided in the "Hogg Case" is the correctness of the proposition in the Argument for defendants in error W. C. Hogg and others, viz.:

> "The rule of construction applicable to the Hogg-Hamman instrument should be this: Because of the fact that the parties thereto did use apt words of conveyance of all the minerals in place, and because there is no ambiguity in such language in the instrument, and because there is no language in the instrument that can fairly be construed, either as an exception of any of the minerals expressly conveyed, or as a reservation of title by defendants in error of any such minerals, therefore no other fair construction of such instrument can be made than that the parties thereto meant what they clearly stated in the granting clause of the instrument, wherein Miss Ima Hogg et al. 'do transfer and set over, sell and convey * * * *all* of the gas, oil, sulphur and other minerals and mineral substances whatsoever on, in and under the hereinafter described land, and the exclusive right and privilege to go on and upon said land, and to take possession thereof for the purpose of drilling for and prospecting therefor, and, after the finding thereof, the development and production of same.'"

In the "Federal Royalty Company Case," the brief and argument for Plaintiff in Error in the Supreme Court states the controlling facts as follows:

> "There are three leases involved in the instant case. One covering Section 60, Block 1, I. & G. N. Railway Co., a patented railroad survey; another covering Section 101, Block 194, G. C. & S. F. Railway Co., a patented railroad survey; and the third covering Section 32, Block 194, G. C. & S. F. Railway Co., an unpatented State school survey.

"The leases, in so far as general form and provisions are concerned, are identical. Each lease contains the same granting clause, to-wit: 'Have granted, demised, leased and let and by these presents does grant, lease and let unto the said lessee for the sole and only purpose of mining and operating for oil and gas, and of laying pipe lines and of building tanks, power stations and structures thereon to produce, save and care for said production, all that certain tract of land,' etc.

"The royalty provision is as follows: 'In consideration of the premises the said lessee covenants and agrees: To deliver to the credit of the lessor free of cost, in the pipe line to which he may connect his wells the equal one-eighth part of all oil produced and saved from the leased premises.'

"The lease covering Section 32 differs from the other two leases in that it is executed by the lessor individually and as agent for the State of Texas and recites that it is made by virtue of authority granted by Articles 1 and 2, Chapter 81 of the Acts of the 36th Legislature, second called session, and Article 1, Chapter 38 of the Acts of the 37th Legislature, first called session.

"The lease covering Section 60 contains the additional provision: 'It is expressly agreed that and understood that grantors by a prior conveyance conveyed to Lee Hager of Harris County, Texas, a one-sixteenth royalty interest in all oil and gas in and under said land, but reserving the rights for grantors to lease said lands, and all future rentals to be paid to grantors under the terms of said royalty deed. But it is understood that one-half of the one-eighth royalty provided for shall be paid to the said Lee Hager, his heirs or assigns.

"In other words, the one-eighth royalty herein provided shall be divided equally between the said Lee Hager and the said Ira G. Yates and words "lessors" as used herein, relative to the one-eighth royalty, shall refer to both said Yates and said Hager.'"

The brief and argument states, at page 14:

"The real question in this case is whether a royalty interest under an ordinary oil and gas lease, is a taxable interest in real estate. And by the expression 'ordinary oil and gas lease' is meant any one of the several forms of contract which gives to the lessee the exclusive dominion and control over the *oil and gas in place in the ground* and provides for the delivery of a fractional part of the oil, after it is produced, to the lessor."

(1) At the outset, it must be regarded as finally settled in this state, as stated in Waggoner's Estate v. Sigler, 118 Texas, 517, 19 S. W. (2d) 27, that the ordinary oil lease operates to invest the lessee with a determinable fee in oil and gas in place. The question before us, accepting that postulate, is what was the interest of the lessors under the instruments through which they claim in each of the cases now before us? Despite differences in their phraseology and forms, we have concluded, after careful consultation and deliberation, that the lessor's interest, sought to be taxed in each instance in these cases, or that of his assign, was an interest in land, subject to taxation as such in the counties in which the respective tracts of land are situated.

Let us consider the contracts in the order we have referred to them. The fifth clause of the Hogg-Hamman contract states that as consideration therefor the lessors "*shall have*" a certain royalty, being 1/8 of the oil produced and 1/8 of the gas produced on the lands, the oil to be delivered in any pipe-lines the lessors may designate, connected with the wells or into the lessor's private storage upon the leased land or any adjoining land; while for the gas the lessors "*shall have" one-eighth interest* in all money realized from gas marketed from said land, and for the sulphur or other minerals $1.00 for each ton produced and saved from the land, under quarterly cash settlements.

(2, 3) Endeavoring to reach the true purpose and intent of parties we can draw no substantial difference, so far as taxation is concerned, between an agreement *excepting* from a grant or a lease a certain fractional portion of minerals, or an agreement *reserving* the same portion, or an agreement that the lessor "*shall have*" or *rather shall continue to have* the same portion, or an agreement that the lessees *shall yield or shall deliver to the lessor* exactly the same portion. In either instance, the title to the specified mineral portion is intended to remain or vest, and does actually remain or vest in the lessor. It logically can make no difference, as may have been intimated in this justice's and in other far greater jurists' reasoning, whether the oil is retained by the lessor as oil and gas, readily convertible into cash on the market, or whether the lessee is given a power to sell all of the oil and gas, always accounting for a fixed royalty portion to the lessor. Sound principle, supported by the highest authority, goes further and compels us to accede to the proposition that dealing with oil and gas or dealing with solids in place, like sulphur, lignite, salt, coal, or lime, the lessor owning the entire fee simple title to the land, and his assigns, who have been careful to secure to themselves, their heirs or assigns, (by exception or reservation or by contract for "having" or yielding or paying, or for delivery, or by what-not similar contractual clause), the right to a portion of the proceeds or profits derived from the lessee's or his assigns' authorized sale of the minerals, throughout the duration of a determinable fee, which may be perpetual, have and own a fee simple interest in land, or at least have a right belonging or appertaining to the horizontal strata of the land in which the minerals are embedded. Humphreys-Mexia Co. v. Gammon, 113 Texas, 247, 254 S. W., 296; Freeport Sulphur Co. v. American Sulphur Royalty Co., 117 Texas, 458,

6 S. W. (2d) 1039. We therefore hold that all the property interests of ascertainable value, secured to the lessors or their assigns under the Hogg-Hamman lease, are subject to taxation as real estate in the county wherein the land lies, as adjudged by the District Court.

The oil industry in Texas is largely dependent for development, growth, or prosperity, on the doctrine that the interests we are considering—such as the lessee's and the lessor's estates under contracts which are in customary use in Texas—are interests in land; and hence not subject to parol sale, but have the protection of the statute of frauds, the statutes regulating conveyances and mortgages of real estate, and the statutes requiring the record of instruments affecting title to or liens on land, so that purchasers can rely on deed and lien records and can execute and receive transfers and conveyances in reliance on true abstracts of title and lawyers' correct opinions thereon. Were the stability furnished by these rules withdrawn and the fundamental contracts, on which the oil business so largely rests, be adjudged by the Supreme Court to create mere rights in personalty at some uncertain date in the future, the structure of the business would be seriously, if not fatally, jeopardized.

At least in so far as we are dealing with leases under which the lessors are entitled "to have," or to require "the delivery of," a fraction of the oil itself, (as does each lease involved in these two cases), our conclusion is the same as was reached in Hager v. Stakes, Tax Collector, 116 Texas, 453 to 472, 294 S. W., 835. One paragraph of that opinion reads:

> "Assuming, as does the certificate of the Honorable Court of Civil Appeals, that the lessor in each of these leases owned each tract of land leased, or an undivided interest therein, at the time each lease was executed, and bearing in mind that the minerals or any portion thereof could be severed and separately owned, and that the minerals or a fraction of same could be conveyed, in place, only as part of the realty, there is no escape from the conclusion that the portion of the oil and other minerals not conveyed but required to be delivered to the lessor *continued* to belong to the lessor, and *continued to be realty*."

Another paragraph of the opinion, considering questions arising where the lease was made "*subject to* the royalties hereinafter *reserved*," reads:

> "We think a dominant purpose of the parties was to make impossible any other disposition of 1/8th of 17/18th of this petroleum than its delivery to the lessor, or his assigns, as the property of the lessor or his assigns. Hence, no matter how poorly expressed, there being words disclosing such purpose, there is excepted from the grant the one-eighth part of the seventeen-eighteenths of the petroleum. It is obvious that the instrument negatives the view that the obligation to deliver a portion of the oil was intended to be a mere personal covenant of the lessee or its assigns. Likewise, the obligation was not meant to enure to the personal benefit of the lessor. *It was meant to benefit the owner of an estate in the land and to permanently run with the land*." (Italics ours).

At page 470 of the opinion in Hager v. Stakes, Tax Collector, supra, we expressly approved a former opinion of the Court which is decisive as to the nature of the title to a fraction of oil which the lessor under such a lease as that under consideration may require the lessee to deliver. For we said:

> "The court in an opinion of Chief Justice Phillips stated the legal effect of a lease to be to invest the grantee with 'the right to seven-eighths of the oil if found.' That lease contained language less clear than that now before us to *except* from the grant or to *reserve* to the lessor one-eighth of the minerals. For that lease 'recited that the grantors, in consideration of $28.20 paid by the grantee, the receipt being acknowledged, had granted, sold, etc., unto the grantee *all* the oil, gas, coal, and other minerals in and under the land described, with the exclusive right to drill, mine and operate thereon for producing oil, gas, coal, and other mineral to be held by the grantee for the term of ten years from the date of the instrument and as much longer as oil, gas or other minerals were produced in paying quantities; *yielding* to the grantors the 1/8th part of all oil produced and saved from the premises.' Corsicana Petroleum Company. v. Owens, 110 Texas, 570, 571, 222 S. W., 154, 155."

Nevertheless we are cognizant that language was used in Hager v. Stakes, supra, and in Ehlinger v. Clark, 117 Texas, 557, 558, 8 S. W. (2d) 666, which is or may seem repugnant to some holdings we now make. Some of this language was doubtless unnecessary to reach the adjudications made. Our attention has also been called by counsel to frequent other declarations by Texas appellate judges, which cannot be reconciled with our present holdings. We cannot discuss them in detail, and no very good result would follow therefrom. Most such declarations appear to have been occasioned by earnest attempts to follow something appearing in a Supreme Court or Commission opinion, which at times was dicta. It is enough to say that declarations contrary to what is necessarily decided in this opinion are disapproved.

Japhet v. McRae, 276 S. W., 669, 670, held that the lessor, after making a lease of oil, reserving a royalty of one-eighth, conveyed such royalty by his deed *to the land*. No such pronouncement could have been made had the royalty been regarded as personalty or a chose in action. It passed by deed to the land only because it was land or some interest belonging or appertaining thereto. The opinion of Presiding Judge Powell in that case was not only expressly approved, but he states in its context that the opinion followed full and free consultation with the justices of the Supreme Court. The opinion further states that it is supported by the "great weight of authority" after its author had "reviewed all the authorities most carefully." After such review, the opinion, expressly sanctioned by the Court, says:

> "Japhet unquestionably bought the *realty* in the 10 acres. He bought one-eighth of the oil in and under the land. * * * If the lessee had made any effort to take it away from him, Japhet would have been entitled to sue him as for conversion of his property." 276 S. W., 671.

Commenting on the rule laid down in Japhet v. McRae, supra, Mr. A. W. Walker, Jr., of the faculty of the University of Texas, says:

> "The only way to justify the passage of unaccrued royalties by the sale of the surface estate when they are unmentioned in the conveyance is because they are interests in land, and this is true whether they are regarded as passing because incidental to the surface estate or, as the writer contends, because included within the description in the deed (admitting the description to be sufficient for this purpose). But if they are interests in land the assignment thereof comes within the provision of the statutes requiring conveyances of interests in land to be recorded in order to be valid as to subsequent bona fide purchases and creditors. All of the foregoing problems and complications and the resulting confusion of land titles can be avoided by a holding that all royalties and delay rentals, regardless of the method of payment, are interests in land within the meaning of the registration statutes Volume VII, No. 1, Texas Law Review, Dec., 1928, p. 49.

The Japhet case is followed in Bibb v. Nolan, 6 S. W. (2d) 157, W. of E. ref.; Humble Oil & Ref. Co. v. Davis (Tex. Com. App.), 296 S. W., 287.

Reynolds v. McMan Oil & Gas Company, 11 S. W. (2d) 780, was decided under an opinion of the Commission by Judge Speer, approved by the Supreme Court at page 787, wherein it is said that the cases of Waggoner v. Wichita County, 273 U. S., 113, 47 S. Ct., 271, 71 L. Ed., 566, and Hager v. Stakes, supra, do affirmatively decide that the extent of the estate granted in such instruments as were before the courts in those cases is the oil and gas, less the exception contained in the royalty clause, *which exception is real estate and remains* the property of the lessor.

In the late case of Jackson v. United Producers' Pipe Line Company, 33 S. W. (2d) 541, the Court, per Mr. Justice Dunklin, said:

> "On April 16, 1917, J. W. Langford and wife, Letha Langford, executed to J. W. Lynch an oil and gas lease on 125 acres of land in Eastland County. In that lease a royalty interest of one-eighth of the oil to be produced was reserved by the grantors. The interest so reserved by the lessors was an interest in realty, and the same is true of the leasehold interest conveyed to Lynch, as is well settled by the decisions of the Supreme Court of this state, as shown in Hager v. Stakes, Tax Collector, 116 Texas, 453, 294 S. W., 835, and numerous decisions there cited. The legal effect of that conveyance was to vest in Lynch and his assignees seven-eighths of the oil to be produced from the land and to reserve to the lessor one-eighth of the oil."

To like effect, see Taylor v. Higgins Oil & Fuel Co., 2 S. W. (2d) 288.

Our decision is in accord with opinions, carefully prepared, of the U. S. Supreme Court, and of the Circuit Court of Appeals for the district including Texas, and with late opinions of the U. S. Judges in Texas Districts, such as the valuable opinion of Judge Atwell, 298 Fed., 821.

Waggoner's Estate v. Wichita County, 273 U. S., 113, is the last case from the Supreme Court of the United States in point, to which we have been directed. Attorneys on each side argue it supports their respective contentions. The leases before the Court obligated the lessees "*to deliver to the lessor*, free of charge, in the pipe line to which said lease may be connected, *the equal one-eighth part of all the oil and gas produced on said premises*, settlement to be made not later than the tenth day of each month for the preceding month." The leases also contained an express covenant for the lessee to pay seven-eighths of all increase in taxes assessed against the land. Construing such leases, the Court gave its own independent conclusion, speaking through Mr. Justice Stone, as if there were no controlling authority in the Texas decisions, that "we find in the terms of the leases themselves no basis for the contention that the lessor granted or conveyed away his entire interest in the oil." The opinion closes with the significant words: "See, also, United States v. Noble, 237 U. S., 74, 80; Barnsdall v. Bradford Gas Co., 225 Pa. St., 338, 343."

Following the reference in Justice Stone's opinion to Barnsdall v. Bradford Gas Co., supra, we find the opinion of the Supreme Court of Pennsylvania states the contract before the court and determines its legal effect in these words:

> "The lease was to remain in force for a term of ten years, and as much longer as the premises were operated for oil or gas or as the rent for failure to commence operations was paid. The consideration was the delivery in pipe lines to the credit of the first party the equal one-eighth part of all the oil produced and saved from the premises. * * * By the agreement the *exclusive* right to take and appropriate *all* the minerals is conveyed, and during the term of the lease the lessor has no right to enter and operate for oil or gas. The *title* to the oil *except the one-eighth thereof* is vested in the lessee, as is also the title to the gas and other minerals, in the land. Under the rule of construction established, not only in other jurisdictions, but by our own cases, therefore, the agreement creates a *corporeal* interest in the lessee in the demised premises, and is not merely a license to enter and operate for oil and gas." (Italics ours).

Following the first reference at the close of Justice Stone's opinion to the case of U. S. v. Noble, 237 U. S., 74, 59 L. Ed., pp. 846-849, we find an opinion by Mr. Justice Hughes, which removes all doubt of the correctness of our every holding in the cases now under consideration.

We quote only such portion of the statement of the controlling facts by Mr. Justice Hughes as will make plain the Court's precise, unanimous conclusion, when wholly unhampered by state authorities. Such portion follows:

> "The act of 1895 contained the following restriction: 'Provided that said allotments shall be inalienable for a period of twenty-five years from and after the date of said patents.'

"Lease dated January 11, 1902 (from an Indian allottee to A. W. Abrams, for ten years from date, in consideration of the sum of $10, and a royalty of five per cent. of the market value of all minerals mined or removed (except gas, for which there was to be paid $40 per annum for each paying well), with the proviso that there should be a minimum rental of $20 a year in case the royalties did not exceed that amount. On August 13, 1903, the lease was assigned by Abrams to the Iowa & Oklahoma Mining Company.

* * * * * *

"Grant or assignment, dated August 16, 1902, to the appellee, Charles F. Noble, of all the allottee's 'right, title and interest in and to the royalty, rent and proceeds' of the mining lease dated January 11, 1902, made to Abrams, described in paragraph (1). It was further agreed, by said instrument, that if the Abrams lease 'should be surrendered and become void the within lease should hold good for the period of ten years.' On the same date, Noble assigned 'a one-half interest in the above-described instrument' to John M. Cooper."

The parts of the opinion determining the nature of the interest retained under the above lease, in the language of the Supreme Court of the United States follows:

> "In the act of ratification of 1895 Congress imposed the restriction upon alienation which has been quoted. The guardianship of the United States continues, notwithstanding the citizenship conferred upon the allottees; * * * and where Congress has imposed restrictions upon the alienation of an allotment, the United States has capacity to sue for the purpose of setting aside conveyances or contracts by which these restrictions have been transgressed. (Authorities omitted).

"We may first consider *the assignments of rents and royalties*. Under his patent, the allottee took an estate in fee, subject to the limitation that the land should be 'inalienable for the period of twenty-five years' from date. This restriction bound the land for the time stated, whether in the hands of the allottee or his heirs. Bowling v. United States, supra. It put it beyond the power of him, or of them, to *alienate the land, or any interest therein*, in any manner except as permitted by the acts of 1896 and 1897. See Taylor v. Parker, 235 U. S., 42, 35 Sup. Ct. Rep., 22. The comprehensiveness of the restriction was modified only by the power to lease; and while the allottee could make leases, as provided in these acts, they gave him no power to dispose of *his interest in the land subject to the lease, or of any part of it. The rents and royalties were profit issuing out of the land.* When they accrued, they became personal property; *but rents and royalties to accrue were a part of the estate remaining in the lessor. As such, they would pass to his heirs, and not to his personal representatives*. 1 Washb. Real Prop., 337; Wright v. Williams, 5 Cow., 501. * * *

"It necessarily follows that the allottee in the present case, having no power to convey *his estate in the land*, could not pass *title to that part of it which consisted of the rents and royalties*. It is said that the leases contemplated *the payment of sums of money, equal to the agreed percentage of the market value of the minerals, and thus that the assignment was of these moneys; but the fact that rent is to be paid in money does not make it any the less a profit issuing out of the land.* The further argument is made that the power to lease should be construed as implying the power to dispose of the rents to accrue. This is wholly untenable. The one is in no way involved in the other; the complete exercise of the authority which the statute confers would still leave *the rents and royalties to accrue as part of the estate remaining in the lessor*. It was the intent of Congress that the allottees, during the period of restriction, should be secure in their actual enjoyment *of their interest in the land*," citing Heckman v. United States, 224 U. S., 413.

The principle underlying the determination in United States v. Noble, supra, that the mineral royalties there under discussion constituted *interests in land* had been announced in that tribunal as far back as 1823, when, in an opinion by Mr. Justice Story, the Court said:

> "*A right to land essentially implies a right to the profits accruing from it, since, without the latter the former can be of no value. Thus a devise of the profits of land, or even a grant of them, will pass a right to the land itself.* Shep., Touch., 93 Co. Litt., 4, b. '*For what*,' says Lord Coke, *in this page, 'is the land, but the profits thereof?*'"

In Kendall v. Ewert, 259 U. S., 149, U. S. v. Noble, supra, was cited with approval.

The Circuit Court of Appeals in Judge Walker's opinion in the case of W. T. Waggoner Estate v. Wichita County, 3 Fed. Rep. (2d) 962, affirmed by the United States Supreme Court in 273 U. S., 113, declared:

"From the facts that, prior to the making of the leases now in question, the lessor was the owner of the oil in or under the land described, and that nothing contained in those instruments evidences the lessor's consent that the leases *have or retain* as owner the part of the oil produced which the lessee was required to *deliver to the lessor*, it follows that the lessor was the owner of that part of the oil both before and after it was brought to the surface. His property right to mineral oil in or under land owned by him was taxable as real property. Vernon's Sayles' Texas Civil Statutes, 1914, Annotated, art. 7504."

Circuit Judge Hutcheson, in the case of Evans v. Mills et ux., 67 Fed. (2d) 840, was squarely confronted with the necessity to determine whether "A standard oil and gas 'unless' lease * * * for a primary term of ten years, and as long thereafter as oil or gas is produced by the lessee, providing for a money rental during the primary term of $47 annually, in default of drilling, *and reserving a one-eighth royalty*," left in the lessors using the leased premises for the purposes of a residence homestead any mineral estate in land, which could be conveyed only as is land constituting the family homestead. In adjudging that the lessors continued to have title to an interest in land, Judge Hutcheson rejected as "mistaken" the argument that the effect of the lease reserving the one-eighth oil royalty was to convey away entirely all their present estate in the minerals, upon consideration of the royalty to be paid *as personalty* for part of the oil the lessee severed and brought up, and *by way of money* for the gas, leaving in plaintiffs no right, title, or interest in the minerals in place, except the possibility of reverter, and working an abandonment of the homestead as to these contingent interests. The opinion then declares that the lessors' interest, including the 1/8 mineral royalty, "does not pass to the lessee; *it remains owned as realty* by the lessor," citing the Waggoner Estate case (273 U. S., 113); Hager v. Stakes, Tax Collector, supra, and others, including Reynolds v. McMan Oil & Gas Co., supra.

On the subject of rents and profits from lands Mr. Thompson says: "Rent is said to be a certain yearly profit arising out of land and tenements as compensation for the use thereof. * * * Unaccrued rents are not personal property. They are incorporeal hereditaments. They are an incident to the reversion. They pass with a sale or devise of the land. If transferred apart from the land the provision of the statute of frauds relating to sales of land applies. In fact, though separable from the reversion, they are, *until such separation, part of the land*. And it is held that they are real estate under provisions of a tax law providing for the taxation of real estate." Vol. 1, Thompson on Real Property, sec. 240, p. 313, sec. 240, p. 314.

"Thus, if the grantor conveys a fee simple title in the land, reserving rent, he himself has a fee simple in the rent. * * * A rent *reserved* upon a conveyance of land with words of inheritance" (and such is a conveyance of a determinable fee in minerals in place in Texas), "*is real property* and passes to the heirs or devisees of the grantor. * * * *If a rent is reserved, no particular words of reservation need be used*, though such words as *'reserving,' 'rendering,' 'returning,' 'yielding,'* or *'paying'* are used; but *other words* showing the intent will be sufficient." Vol. 1, Thompson on Real Property, sec. 246, p. 320; sec. 247, p. 321; sec. 248, p. 322.

Mr. Tiffany is in full accord with Mr. Thompson. According to Mr. Tiffany: "A rent reserved upon the grant of a fee simple estate in land is *real property* passing to the heir or devisee. * * * Both the benefit and the burden of a covenant to pay rent upon a demise leaving a reversion in the lessor, run with the land. * * * An assignment of rent already due is an assignment of the rent, that is, of the right to the installments as they come due in the future, is properly *not* an assignment of a chose in action, but is a transfer of an *interest in land*." Vol. 1, Tiffany on Real Property (2d ed.), sec. 407, p. 1474; sec. 407, p. 1471; and sec. 407, p. 1470.

On the subject of taxation of interests under oil and gas leases, Mr. Summers significantly notes that: "Where, under the ordinary lease, the lessor retains a certain share of the oil or gas as a royalty, the value of such interest may be added to the agricultural value *of the land* for the purpose of making the assessment." Summers, Oil & Gas, sec. 212.

The possibility of reverter is said in Tentative Restatement of the Law of Property (Draft No. 1, sec. 25, p. 56), to be itself a *nonpossessory interest in land*.

We are cited to opposite views found in Thornton's Law of Oil & Gas to sustain the proposition that the properties under consideration should be taxed as personalty. To our minds, no stronger argument against Mr. Thornton's view can well be made than is embodied in his own deductions therefrom. Mr. Thornton says: "Royalty is a certain percentage of the oil after it is found, or so much per gas well developed. * * * Royalty is personal property. * * * The legal effect of a provision in a deed excepting and reserving out of and from a grant at all times thereafter and forever, unto the grantor, his heirs and assigns one-tenth of all the mineral oil that may be obtained by the grantee, his heirs and assigns, from the land granted, to be delivered on the land to the grantor, his heirs and assigns, his or their agent, free of expense, except the furnishing of barrels or other means of transportation, *is to except and reserve in the grantor, his heirs and assigns*, to be delivered as stimpulated, a royalty of one-tenth of all the oil produced, *possessing the same quality of estate as royalty received in an ordinary lease for oil and gas purposes*. * * * A royalty may be assigned or conveyed by the lessor without necessarily assigning the lease or conveying the lease by deed. The assignment does not create an interest in the land; for royalty is personal property. * * * A contract for the sale of royalty arising out of an oil lease does not come within the statute of frauds. *It may be an oral contract*." 1 Thornton's Law of Oil & Gas (4th ed.), sec. 253, pp. 668, 669; sec. 256, p. 676; sec. 287a, pp. 721, 722. (Italics ours).

What we have said determines that all the royalties in both cases must be taxed as interests in land. So much is substantially conceded when plaintiffs in error frankly and rightly assert in their brief and argument, on page 14, that "the real question in this case is whether a royalty interest under an ordinary oil and gas lease, is a taxable interest in real estate."

We will add a few words as to the royalty interest involved under the lease of the unpatented school land survey, which is, as said in plaintiffs in error's argument, "executed by the lessor individually and as agent for the State of Texas."

After upholding the *validity* of the "Relinquishment Act" in Greene v. Robison, the Supreme Court, in an adopted opinion by Judge Sharp, for the first time definitely determined the nature of the interests of the agent-lessor and of his assigns in words concise, clear and unambiguous, viz.:

> "In the case of Greene v. Robison, 117 Texas, 533, 8 S. W. (2) 655, it was held that by the terms of the Relinquishment Act it is meant that *the oil and gas in place* shall not vest in the owner of the soil as his property, but that *it means that fifteen-sixteenths of the minerals and one-half of any and all amounts received above 10 cents per acre per annum as rental shall be allowed the owner of the land for his service as agent of the State in making the mineral leases*. In our opinion, the Act when fairly and reasonably construed, also means that all minerals not disposed of go with the title of the land, subject to the provisions of the Act. That when a valid and binding lease or conveyance of the minerals is made by the owner of the land, as the agent of the State, then in that event *he receives the foregoing*

> *amounts as compensation for his services. His share of the rentals, royalties and bonuses derived from the leases executed by him become property rights during the period of time for which the lease runs*. Prior to the making of the mineral lease the owner of the land has no right to assign or convey any mineral rights in the property. It is the intention of the law that the owner of the land shall be the agent of the State to execute mineral leases. Whenever a mineral lease executed by a prior owner terminates, the then owner of the land becomes the agent of the State with authority to sell or lease the oil and gas mineral rights, as provided for in the Relinquishment Act.

"The rule is well established that it is not the policy of the law of this State to favor restraints upon alienation of property. *The Courts of this State have established the rule that rents or royalties payable under oil and gas mineral leases are severable and separable from the ownership of the surface estate and are property rights, and having established this with respect to such property, we think, under the policy of the law of this State, that they are assignable by the owner thereof.*" Lemar v. Garner, 121 Texas, 502, 512, 513, 50 S. W. (2d) 769.

The Court could not, without overruling Lemar v. Garner, supra, and the settled law re-affirmed therein, and recapitulated in Waggoner's Estate v. Sigler, supra, prescribe a different rule for the rights for the agent-lessor or his assigns, under lease of the unpatented school land surveys from the rule governing such rights under leases of patented lands.

There is another reason which forbids our holding that the interests of the lessors or their assigns are not taxable in Texas as real estate. No one in either case questions that such interests are property. Section 1 of Article VIII of the Constitution plainly provides for the taxation of *all* property. The entire debate is about whether these interests are taxable as personal property or real property. Our statutes declare:

> "Art. 7147. 'Personal property.' Personal property, for the purposes of taxation, shall be construed to include all goods, chattels and effects, and all moneys, credits, bonds, and other evidences of debt owned by citizens of this State, whether the same be in or out of the State; all ships, boats and vessels belonging to inhabitants of this State, if registered in this State, whether at home or abroad, and all capital invested therein; all moneys at interest, either within or without the State, due the person, to be taxed over and above what he pays interest for, and all other debts due such person over and above his indebtedness; all public stock and securities; all stock in turn-pikes, railroads, canals and other corporations (except national banks) out of the State, owned by inhabitants of this State; all personal estate of moneyed corporations, whether the owners thereof reside in or out of this State, and the income of any annuity, unless the capital of such annuity be taxed within this State; all shares in any bank organized or that may be organized under the laws of the United States; all improvements made by persons upon lands held by them, the title to which is still vested in the State of Texas, or in any railroad company, or which have been exempted from taxation for the benefit of any railroad company, or any other corporation whose property is not subject to the same mode and rule of taxation as other property." Article 7147, R. S., 1925.

These interests cannot come within the definitions of money or credits as defined in article 7149, R. S., 1925.

"Real property," says the statute, "for the purpose of taxation, shall be construed to include *the land itself*, whether laid out in town lots or otherwise, and all buildings, structures and improvements, or other fixtures of whatsoever kind thereon, and a*ll the rights and privileges belonging or in any wise appertaining thereto, and all mines, minerals, quarries and fossils in and under the same*." Article 7146, R. S., 1925.

Reading the Constitution and Statutes together there is no escape from the conclusion that interests here involved are meant to be taxed as real estate. Classify them as you may, they are at least rights or privileges belonging or in some wise appertaining to real property, and the Legislature has provided that they be taxed as such. Bracken v. Zan Yandt County, 74 S. W. (2d) 540.

Under practically the same taxation statutes, the Supreme Court of Minnesota, considering minerals in place as "part of the land," and defining royalties on the portion of ore which might be removed annually therefrom, not as purchase money, but as "rents," said:

> "Our conclusion is that *unaccrued rents* are real estate, that they are taxed under our tax laws by taxation of the real estate, and that they are not taxed as personal property, and are

> not to be listed or taxed as 'credits.'" State v. Royal Mineral Association, 132 Minn., 232, 156 N. W., 128, 1918 Anno. Cas., 145, 148. (Italics ours).

(4) In the "Hogg Case," the principal complaint in the voluminous attack on the valuations and assessments of the lessors' interests in the land leased is based on the fact that the interest of the lessors was not figured at precisely the same amount as the same fraction of minerals which was conveyed to the lessees and their assigns. Under the very terms of the contract, the lessees having to pay all expenses of exploration and production, each one-eighth out of their seven-eighth mineral interest was necessarily worth less than the one-eighth interest of the lessor. The Court takes judicial knowledge of such differences in values in numberless sales from the beginning of the State's oil industry. On the whole, as we read the undisputed facts, the commissioners' court fairly and without discrimination valued and assessed the interest of or under the lessors, in each instance before us. In the "Federal Royalty Company Case," we are satisfied with the disposition made by the Court of Civil Appeals of the Eighth District of the complaints relative to the means adopted to arrive at correct values by the Commissioners' Court of Pecos County, as well as with that Court's disposition of all other matters not herein specifically discussed.

For the reasons above stated, it follows that in Cause No. 6001, to which reference is made throughout this opinion as the "Hogg Case," the judgment of the Court of Civil Appeals should be reversed and the judgment of the District Court should be affirmed; and, it further follows, that in Cause No. 6130, to which reference is made throughout this opinion as the "Federal Royalty Company Case," the judgment of the District Court and that of the Court of Civil Appeals should be affirmed. It is so ordered.

ON MOTION FOR REHEARING

PER CURIAM.—The motions for rehearing and the several arguments filed in connection therewith have been carefully examined and considered and are overruled.

(5) It has been suggested in a motion filed in connection with the motions for rehearing that the opinion be clarified by pointing out more particularly the nature of the royalty interest in Section 32 involved in the "Federal Royalty Company Case" and which section is, for convenience, referred to in in the opinion as an unpatented school land survey.

That section, after being classified as mineral, was sold by the State with reservation to the State of all of the minerals. It remained unpatented. The owner of the land under such sale leased the land for oil and gas, acting as agent of the State by the authority conferred in Section 2 of Chapter 81, Acts 2nd Called Session of 36th Legislature, commonly known as the "Relinquishment Act." Under the terms of that Act, one-half of the royalty reserved in the lease belongs to the State and one-half to the owner of the soil, the agent-lessor. A part of the agent-lessor's royalty reserved in such lease of Section 32 was conveyed to Federal Royalty Company, and that royalty so acquired and owned by said company is held by the opinion to be taxable like all the other royalties in both cases as an interest in land. The opinion does not undertake and was not intended to draw a distinction in connection with the taxation of royalties between patented and unpatented sold school land. The State's ownership of the minerals in public school land sold with reservation of the minerals, the land owner's right to lease such land for oil and gas under the Relinquishment Act, and the nature of the royalties reserved in such leases are the same whether the land is patented or unpatented.

Commentary on Sheffield v. Hogg

by Scott Lansdown[1]

Sheffield v. Hogg[2] dealt with the nature of the royalty interest created under an oil and gas lease; it is one of a series of cases in Texas that addressed the nature of interests in oil and gas and the nature of the interests created by oil and gas leases. In order to understand the context of *Sheffield*, a brief mention of the cases that preceded it in Texas is appropriate. As Professor A. W. Walker observed in his seminal series of articles on the subject, prior to the decision in *Texas Co. v. Daugherty*[3] there were two lines of authority, one which held that an oil and gas lessee did not obtain an interest in land but only an option contract and one which held that the lessee acquired an interest in land but did not make any attempt to define the nature of the interest.[4] In *Daugherty* the court adopted the ownership in place theory and held that the lease involved in that case conveyed a defeasible title to the oil and gas in the ground.[5] As Professor Walker noted, *Daugherty* did not definitively conclude that all oil and gas leases were intended to convey such an interest in oil and gas, but rather held that the nature of the interest conveyed was dependent upon the intent of the parties, which led to "the endeavor on the part of the courts to determine the nature of the lessee's property interest by an examination of the wording of the granting clause in each particular lease."[6]

Then, in *Stephens County v. Mid-Kansas Oil & Gas Co.*[7] the Texas Supreme Court rejected the concept that the nature of the interest granted under an oil and gas lease was dependent upon the specific wording of the lease's granting clause, and held instead that the parties' intent was always that an oil and gas lease operate as a present conveyance of the oil and gas in place.[8] These cases did not, however, address the nature of the royalty interest retained under an oil and gas lease.

As Professor Walker observed (in a discussion that predated *Sheffield*), efforts to classify the royalty interest were complicated by the fact that royalty was payable in different ways. Royalty on oil could be paid by delivering a portion of the oil to the lessor, or the lessee could pay the lessor the market price of the oil. Discussing *Hager v. Stakes*,[9] in which the Texas Supreme Court held that the effect of a royalty clause that provided for the payment of royalty in kind was that the royalty owner remained the owner in fee simple of the royalty portion of the oil, Professor Walker noted that the inference of that case was that if an oil royalty clause provided for the payment of money, title to all of the oil in place passed to the lessee, and the lessor's interest was personalty.[10] In addition, Professor Walker concluded that since royalty on gas was always payable in money, under the logic of *Hager v. Stakes*, such royalty was also personalty.[11] Professor Walker discussed some of the problems raised by this classification scheme, including the question of whether the interest in question was taxable as personalty or real property, whether the statute of frauds would be applicable to a transfer of such interest, and the applicability of the recordation statutes, concluding that it would be "highly desirable that all royalty interests should be regarded as interests in land...."[12]

As Professor Walker noted in the fourth article in his series,[13] doubt with regard to the nature of the royalty interest was created by the Texas Supreme Court case of *Ehlinger v. Clark*,[14] in which the court indicated that title to all minerals passed to the lessee regardless of whether the royalty was payable in kind or in money.[15] Professor Walker then characterized the decision by the court of civil appeals in *Hogg v. Sheffield* as an effort to reconcile *Hager v. Stakes* and *Ehlinger v. Clark*. In the court of civil appeals decision in *Sheffield*, the court, discussing *Hager*, focused on the language in that decision finding that an oil and gas lease providing for in-kind royalty payment "negatives the view that the obligation to deliver a portion of the oil was intended to a mere [sic] personal covenant of the lessee or its assigns. Likewise, the obligation was not meant to inure to the personal benefit of the lessor. It was meant to benefit the owner of the estate in the land and to permanently run with the land."[16] The court of civil appeals then noted that there was no language in the lease before it similar to the language that was relied upon by the *Hager* court and stated that *Ehlinger v. Clark* supported "the conclusion that appellants in this case conveyed to [the lessee] all of the oil in and under the land, and only became the owners of a one-eighth royalty interest in the oil after it was produced."[17]

All of the foregoing culminated in the Texas Supreme Court case of *Sheffield v. Hogg*. In that case, addressing the payment in kind versus payment in money issue the court held the distinction immaterial:

> It logically can make no difference, as may have been intimated in this justice's and in other far greater jurists' reasoning, whether the oil is retained by the lessor as oil and gas, readily convertible into cash on the market, or whether the lessee is given a power to sell *all* the oil

> and gas, always accounting for a fixed royalty portion to the lessor. Sound principle, supported by the highest authority, goes further and compels us to accede to the proposition that dealing with oil and gas or dealing with solids in place, like sulphur, lignite, salt, coal or lime, the lessor owning the entire fee-simple title to the land, and his assigns, who have been careful to secure to themselves, their heirs or assigns (by exception or reservation or by contract for "having" or yielding or paying, or for delivery, or by what-not similar contractual clause), the right to a portion of the proceeds or profits derived from the lessee's or his assigns' authorized sale of the minerals, throughout the duration of a determinable fee, which may be perpetual, have and own a fee-simple interest in land, or at least have a right belonging or appertaining to the horizontal strata of the land in which the minerals are embedded.[18]

The court thus held that all of the interests retained by the lessors were subject to taxation as real estate in the county in which the land in question was located.[19] Although the court did not engage in an extensive discussion of the arguments for and against the proposition before it, it did note that the health of the oil industry in Texas was dependent upon treating interests such as those of the lessee and lessor as interests in land and "hence not subject to parol sale, but [having] the protection of the statute of frauds, the statutes regulating conveyances and mortgages of real estate, and the statutes requiring the record of instruments affecting title to or liens on land, so that purchasers can rely on deed and lien records and can execute and receive transfers and conveyances in reliance on true abstracts of title and lawyers' correct opinions thereon."[20]

The issue in *Sheffield* was whether a royalty interest was real property or personalty for the purpose of determining the applicability of property taxes; in fact, the application of property taxes was the issue in most of the early cases addressing the nature of interests in oil and gas. Interestingly, as Williams & Meyers notes, "Such problems of classification are usually not of major consequence inasmuch as early action by a state legislature may be expected to make taxable any interest in minerals which it is believed has improperly escaped taxation by reason of its classification."[21] Along similar lines, Williams & Meyers also notes, "With the increased importance of the oil and gas industry in many states there has been considerable legislation dealing specifically with oil and gas interests as regards such matters as taxation, mechanics liens, partition, and the like. Such statutes materially reduce the significance of the realty-personalty classifications."[22]

However, Smith & Weaver, after noting the significance of the realty-personalty cases in the context of taxation, expands on their importance:

> The adoption of the ownership-in-place doctrine has had other significant legal implications. Because oil and gas are realty until extracted, a landowner whose interests in oil and gas are adversely affected by the actions of another party is entitled to bring the same civil actions for title, injury to real estate, or other actions as the owner of any other type of real property.[23]

It is also important to note that although a royalty interest is an interest in land, it is a non-possessory (or incorporeal) interest;[24] thus the owner of a royalty generally may not bring a suit for partition[25] or seek possessory remedies such as trespass to try title.[26]

A review of the cases and commentary subsequent to *Sheffield* suggests that not all issues related to the nature of the royalty interest have been resolved, particularly in the area of remedies for damage to the mineral interest. Addressing the general question of whether the nature of the landowner's interest in oil and gas is significant in the context of an action for negligent or wasteful loss of hydrocarbons, Williams & Meyers concludes that the question is probably not significant in determining whether a landowner is liable to other landowners overlying a common reservoir for the loss of otherwise recoverable hydrocarbons or for negligent injury to the producing formation, but that the question is significant in determining how the damages in each situation may be measured.[27]

The latter point was illustrated by the case of *Elliff v. Texon Drilling Co.*[28] That case was an action by the royalty owners in a tract of land based on a blowout on adjoining land caused by the negligent actions of the operator on that land. The Texas Supreme Court, in what is generally regarded as the key holding in *Elliff*, rejected the court of civil appeals' conclusion that the rule of capture precluded the royalty owners from recovery. With regard to the question of damages, the court of civil appeals had noted that the royalty owners' position was that "their action is essentially one of an action for damages to real property and not an action for oil and gas wrongfully taken and converted."[29] Indeed, the court of civil appeals acknowledged that the royalty owners' "paramount property right was the ownership of a certain undivided portion of the oil and gas in place within a specific tract of land."[30] Interestingly, the court apparently assumed that the royalty interest was an interest in the minerals in place, not even bothering to cite *Sheffield*:

> Since a surface estate in land is real property and a mineral estate in land is likewise real property, there seems to be no logical or compelling reason why the monetary loss occasioned by the injury or destruction of said estates should be determined by different standards. In our opinion the rule that where land is permanently injured, the usual measure of damages is the depreciation in value occasioned by the wrongful act, is applicable to mineral estates.[31]

The Texas Supreme Court, however, held that there had been no assignment of error on the measure of damages, so that the court of civil appeals was without authority to review that question; the supreme court also refused to pass on that issue.[32] Upon remand of the case to the court of civil appeals, that court somewhat confusingly held that "[t]he Supreme Court's opinion supports the theory that appellees may recover for gas and distillate wrongfully lost or destroyed."[33]

In an article shortly after the *Elliff* decision, Professor Walker noted that it appeared that "no issue was made during the trial of the fact that the plaintiffs were mere royalty owners and that, as a consequence, if the existing lease was in the usual form providing for the payment of a monetary royalty on gas, title to all of the gas that escaped was in the lessee of the plaintiffs and not in the plaintiffs."[34] Professor Walker specifically noted that *Sheffield v. Hogg* "merely held, and properly so, that even though a royalty is payable in money, it is nevertheless an incorporeal interest in land in the nature of a common law rent, and, therefore, taxable as real estate."[35] Thus, Professor Walker criticized the holding in *Elliff* with regard to the measure of damages, noting that the plaintiff royalty owners in that case "did not have 'title' to, or any possessory interest in, the property alleged to have been converted."[36]

Secondary authority on the proper measure of damages in cases such as *Elliff* is somewhat confusing. For example, Williams & Meyers notes that in states that have not adopted the ownership in place theory, damages should not be measured by the value of the hydrocarbon that migrated as the result of the wrongful conduct of the landowner, but rather by the "the difference between the market value of the plaintiff's interest in his land or minerals before and after the defendant's wrongful conduct."[37] Williams & Meyers goes on to note, however, that "the normal measure of damages for a permanent injury to real property is the difference between the fair market value before and after the negligent act."[38] This certainly appears to be the same measure of damages as the measure that Williams & Meyers asserts should be used in the states where the ownership in-and place theory has not been adopted.

In *Amoco Production Co. v. Alexander*,[39] the case in which the Texas Supreme Court upheld an action for "field-wide drainage," the lessee had argued that the royalty owners could not recover exemplary damages, contending, among other things, that such damages were not recoverable under a cause of action for waste. Rejecting that argument the court, citing *Elliff*, stated, "The common law theory of waste must not be confused with an action for negligent waste or destruction of minerals which may be maintained by a mineral or royalty owner."[40] The court then noted that the royalty owners held a fee simple interest in land, citing *Sheffield*, and concluded that it was not faced with a waste case.

Apache Corp. v. Moore,[41] like *Elliff*, involved an action by royalty owners against the operator of a well on an adjoining tract for lost royalties due to a blowout of the operator's well. The operator argued that the royalty owners' interest was an interest in real property and that the injury to the royalty owners was a permanent injury to realty for which the only proper measure of damages was the difference in the value of the royalty interest before and after the blowout. The court held that the second court of civil appeals opinion in *Elliff* had rejected the concept that damages for a loss of royalty due to the negligence of an adjacent land owner could only be measured by the depreciation in value of the mineral estate.[42] The court also noted that the reduction in market value measure was inappropriate because the injury in the case before it was temporary and "[t]he proper measure of damages for temporary injuries to realty is the amount of damages which accrued during the continuance of the injury."[43] In light of the jury finding that the damages in the case were the result of the defendant's gross negligence, the court also upheld an award of exemplary damages.[44]

Williams & Meyers refers to the conceptual problem noted by Professor Walker with regard to *Elliff*, indicating that "[i]f the lessor has leased all of his or her interest (8/8ths), then the lessee should bring the suit against the negligent operator and the lessor should recover from the lessee."[45] However, as the treatise goes on to note, "this leads to the further problem that under the *Bruni* line of cases, a lessee generally owes royalty only on *production* and damage to the reservoir may not count as production and loss of production by the actions of the adjacent operator may not count as production by or on behalf of the lessee."[46]

As Williams & Meyers observes, the questions raised by *Elliff* are posed in the case of *HECI Exploration Co. v. Neel*.[47] Prior to *Neel*, a lessee had brought an action against an adjacent producer based on overproduction that had damaged the reservoir and had recovered damages, as well as injunctive relief; the lessors subsequently brought a claim for royalty on the amount the lessee recovered. The Austin court of appeals rejected the contention that the lessors had an action for royalty on the recovery but held that they might have a claim for the lessee's failure to notify the lessors of the lessor's potential claim.[48] As Williams & Meyers notes, the court of appeals opinion in *Neel* appears to suggest (without directly saying) that the lessors continued to own a share of the oil and gas in place because the lessors would have their own claim against the adjacent producer.[49] As Williams & Meyers also notes, the court of appeals almost seemed to say that both the lessee and the lessor owned the lost reserves/production in some independent fashion, which, the treatise observes, "strikes us as conceptually incoherent."[50] Although the Texas Supreme Court disposed of the case largely based on its rejection of the application of the discovery rule to toll the statute of limitations, it did engage in some discussion of the nature of the royalty interest; unfortunately that discussion does not appear to have been consistent: addressing the question of whether HECI and the royalty owners were in privity, the court stated that "A royalty interest is an interest in real property that is a distinct part of the mineral estate (citation omitted). Although royalty is payable only as minerals are produced, a royalty owner is entitled to compensation for damage to a reservoir underlying an oil and gas lease (citing *Elliff*)."[51] Later, however, the court stated that "[t]he [court of appeals] analysis of what [the lessee] owned fails to recognize that *although [the lessee] did own all the reserves in place*, that interest was burdened with royalty obligations to the [royalty owners]." (Emphasis added.)[52] As Williams & Meyers notes, this appears to conflict with both *Elliff* and the holding in *Sheffield v. Hogg* that royalty owners own a real property interest subject to property taxes.[53] In fact the statement also appears to conflict with the supreme court's own earlier observation that the royalty interest is an interest in real property that is a distinct part of the mineral estate.

The issue of the nature of the interest of a royalty owner was also raised in *Coastal Oil & Gas Corp. v. Garza*,[54] in which royalty owners asserted a claim of trespass based on an operator's hydraulic fractures extending across the lease boundaries. The operator asserted that the royalty owner did not have standing to assert an action for trespass, in part because the royalty owner had "only 'a royalty interest and the possibility of a reverter.'"[55] The court rejected this argument, however, indicating that the law allowed recovery for damages to non-possessory interests, such as reversions; in a footnote, the court cited the language from *HECI v. Neel* quoted above to the effect that even though royalty is payable only as production occurs, a royalty interest is an interest in real property that is a part of the mineral estate.[56] The court in *Garza* did eventually reject the royalty owners' claim on the grounds that it was precluded by the rule of capture.[57]

As the foregoing discussion illustrates, eighty years after the decision in *Sheffield v. Hogg* there continues to be a lack of clarity concerning the specific nature of the royalty interest reserved in an oil and gas lease. One reason for this may be that courts have been more interested in reaching what they felt was a "fair and just" result and that they basically adopted whatever view of the question assisted in reaching that result. There also appear to have been relatively few cases that have raised the issue; compared, for example, to the extremely large number of cases that have turned on the questions around the proper method for calculating royalty on natural gas, there are only a handful of cases in which the nature of the royalty interest was a significant factor. It is possible, although by no means certain, that the recent resurgence of the oil and gas industry in Texas will provide future opportunities for the courts to address this question.

---

1 Counsel, XTO Energy Inc., Fort Worth Texas. The views expressed herein are those of the author and do not necessarily reflect the views of XTO or any of its affiliates.

2 77 S.W.2d 1021 (Tex. 1934).

3 176 S.W. 717 (Tex. 1915).

4 A. W. Walker, Jr., *The Nature of the Property Interests Created by an Oil and Gas Lease in Texas,* 7 TEX. L. REV. 1, 6 (1928) [hereinafter Walker I].

5 176 S.W. at 720-22.

6 Walker I at 6.

7 254 S.W. 290 (Tex.1923).

8 *Id.* at 294-95.

9 294 S.W. 835 (Tex. 1927).

10 Walker I at 33.

11 *Id.* at 34-35.

12 *Id.* At 35-37.

13 A. W. Walker, Jr., *The Nature of the Property Interests Created by an Oil and Gas Lease in Texas*, 10 TEX. L. REV. 291, 305 (1932).

14 8 S.W. 2d 666 (Tex. 1928).

15 *Id.* at 670. The court in *Ehlinger* acknowledged that the fact that the one-eighth royalty on oil was to be delivered in kind provided some "theoretical ground" for the argument that the lease did not cover the full mineral estate, but it dismissed this argument on the grounds that the right to one-eighth of the oil was worthless without the right to explore for and produce the oil, which right had been granted away by the lease.

16 *Hager v. Stakes* 294 S.W. 835, 841 (Tex. 1927).

17 *Hogg v. Sheffield*, 38 S.W.2d 353, 359 (Tex. Civ. App. –Galveston 1931), *rev'd, Sheffield v. Hogg*, 77 S.W.2d 1021 (Tex. 1934).

18 77 S.W.2d 1021, 1024 (Tex 1934).

19 *Id.* at 1030.

20 *Id.* at 1024.

21 2 Patrick H. Martin & Bruce M. Kramer, *Williams & Meyers Oil & Gas Law* § 213.3, at 142 (2013) [hereinafter Williams & Meyers]. The treatise also observes, "Federal taxation of interests in oil and gas does not depend on the realty-personalty classification or other technical distinctions of common law estates." *Id.*

22 *Id.* § 213, at 134-35.

23 Ernest E. Smith & Jacqueline Lang Weaver, *Texas Law of Oil and Gas* § 1.2(B) at 1-17 (2d ed. 2013) [hereinafter Smith & Weaver]. Smith & Weaver also notes, "All or part of [the landowner's] interest in oil and gas in the ground may be granted or reserved, and the deed in which he makes the grant or reservation must comply with the same rules that are applicable to conveyances of real estate generally." *Id.*

24 Williams & Meyers §209, at 96-97; Smith & Weaver §2.4(E).

25 *Chaffin v. Hall*, 210 S.W.2d 191 (Tex. Civ. App–Eastland 1948, writ ref'd n.r.e.).

26 *T-Vestco Litt-Vada v. Lu-Cal One Oil Co.*, 651 S.W.2d 284 (Tex. App.–Austin 1983, writ ref'd n.r.e.)

27 Williams and Meyers § 204.7.

28 210 S.W.2d 558 (Tex. 1948).

29 *Texon Drilling Co. v. Elliff*, 210 S.W. 2d 553, 556 (Texas App.–San Antonio 1947) *rev'd, Elliff v. Texon Drilling Co.*, 210 S.W.2d 558 (Tex. 1948).

30 210 S.W.2d. at 556-57.

31 *Id.* at 557.

32 210 S.W.2d at 560.

33 *Texon Drilling Co. v. Elliff*, 216 S.W.2d 824, 829 (Tex. Civ. App.–San Antonio 1948, writ ref'd n.r.e.).

34 A.W. Walker, Jr., *Important Oil and Gas Decisions*, 11 TEX. B. J. 479, 499 (1948).

35 *Id.*

36 *Id.* at 502.

37 Williams & Meyers § 204.7, at 72.2.

38 *Id.* at 72.3.

39 622 S.W.2d 563 (Tex. 1981).

40 *Amoco Prod. Co. v. Alexander*, 622 S.W.2d 563, 572 (Tex. 1981).

41 891 S.W.2d 671 (Tex. App.–Amarillo 1994, writ denied), *cert. granted*, 517 U.S. 1217 (1996), *judgmn't vacated and remanded for reconsideration in light of BMW of North Am. v. Gore*, 517 U.S. 559 (1996).

42 *Id.* at 679.

43 *Id.* at 680.

44 The original award of $562,500 to each of three plaintiffs was vacated by the United States Supreme Court, and the case was remanded in light of that court's decision in *BMW of North America v. Gore*, 517 U.S. 559 (1996). On remand, the Texas court of appeals reduced the exemplary damages to a total of $43,340. *Apache Corp. v. Moore*, 960 S.W.2d 746, 750 (Tex. App.—Amarillo 1997, writ denied).

45 Williams & Meyers §204.7, at 72.10.

46 *Id.* The *Bruni* line of cases was a group of cases that held that a royalty owner was not entitled to recover royalty on payments made to settle amounts owed under "take-or-pay" contracts, on the grounds that royalty was only payable on gas that was severed from the ground. *Killam Oil Co. v. Bruni*, 806 S.W.2d 264 (Tex. App.—San Antonio 1991, writ denied). *See also Mandell v. Hamman Oil & Refining Co.*, 822 S.W.2d 153 (Tex. App.—Houston [1st Dist.] 1991, writ denied); *Hurd Enterprises, Ltd. v. Bruni*, 828 S.W.2d 101 (Tex App.–San Antonio 1992, writ denied).

47 982 S.W.2d 881 (Tex. 1998).

48 *Neel v. HECI Exploration Co.*, 942 S.W.2d 212, 218 (Tex. App.—Austin 1997) *rev'd, HECI Exploration Co. v. Neel*, 982 S.W. 2d 881 (Tex. 1998).

49 Williams & Meyers §204.7, at 72.11.

50 *Id.*

51 982 S.W.2d at 890.

52 982 S.W.2d at 891.

53 *Id.* at 204.7, at 72.12 & n. 20.6.

54 268 S.W.3d 1 (Tex. 2008)

55 *Id.* at 9.

56 *Id.* at 10 & n. 25.

57 *Id.* at 12-13.

6

CHAPTER 6

Duhig et al.
v.
Peavy-Moore Lumber Co., Inc.

COMMENTARY

by Ernest E. Smith, III

135 Tex. 503, 144 S.W.2d 878

1940

Duhig et al.
v.
Peavy-Moore Lumber Co., Inc.

135 Tex. 503, 144 S.W.2d 878

1940

Mr. Judge SMEDLEY of the Commission of Appeals delivered the opinion to the court.

Through conveyance from the executor of the estate of Alexander Gilmer, deceased, W. J. Duhig became the owner of the Josiah Jordan survey in Orange County, subject, however, to reservation by the grantor of an undivided one-half interest in the minerals. Thereafter Duhig conveyed the survey to Miller-Link Lumber Company, and in the deed it was agreed and stipulated that the grantor retained an undivided one-half interest in all of the mineral rights or minerals in and on the land. Peavy-Moore Lumber Company became the owner of whatever title and estate Miller-Link Lumber Company acquired by the deed from Duhig in 574 3/8 acres of the said survey.

The suit is by defendant in error, Peavy-Moore Lumber Company, against plaintiffs in error, Mrs. W. J. Duhig and others, who claim under W. J. Duhig, for the title and possession of the 574 3/8 acres in the Jordan survey. The trial court's judgment was that the plaintiff, Peavy-Moore Lumber Company, recover the title and possession of the land, except all minerals and mineral rights therein, and that as to the minerals and mineral rights, it take nothing against the defendants. On appeal by Peavy-Moore Lumber Company, the Court of Civil Appeals reversed the judgment of the trial court and rendered judgment in favor of that company. 119 S.W.(2d) 688.

The ownership by Gilmer's estate, and its assignees, of an undivided one-half interest in the minerals in the land through the reservation in the first deed, which was duly recorded, is admitted by the parties. Plaintiffs in error, Mrs. Duhig and others, make no claim of title to the surface estate, but their contention, sustained by the trial court and denied by the Court of Civil Appeals, is that W. J. Duhig, their predecessor, reserved for himself in his conveyance of the land to Miller-Link Lumber Company the remaining undivided one-half interest in the minerals. Defendant in error, Peavy-Moore Lumber Company, takes the position that the deed last referred to did not reserve to or for the grantor such remaining one-half interest in the minerals, but that it in effect excepted only the one-half interest that had theretofore been reserved by Gilmer's estate and invested the grantee with title to the surface estate and an undivided one-half interest in the minerals.

The deed from W. J. Duhig to Miller-Link Lumber Company is a general warranty deed, describing the property conveyed as that certain tract or parcel of land in Orange County, Texas, known as the Josiah Jordan Survey, further identifying the land by survey and certificate number and giving a description by metes and bounds. After the metes and bounds the following matter of description is added: "* * * and being the same tract of land formerly owned by the Talbot-Duhig Lumber Company, and after the dissolution of said company, conveyed to W. J. Duhig by B. M. Talbot". After the habendum and the clause of general warranty and constituting the last paragraph in the deed, appears the following: "But it is expressly agreed and stipulated that the grantor herein retains an undivided one-half interest in and to all mineral rights or minerals of whatever description in the land."

(1-4) We cannot agree with plaintiffs in error's contention that the granting paragraph of the deed purports to convey only the surface estate and an undivided one-half interest in the minerals. It is our opinion that the statement in the deed, that the land described is the same tract as that formerly owned by Talbot-Duhig Lumber Company and conveyed to Duhig by Talbot, is not intended to define or qualify the estate or interest conveyed but that it is inserted to further identify the tract or area described by metes and bounds. The deed, of course, does not actually convey what the grantor does not own. Richardson v. Levi. 67 Texas 359, 365, 3 S.W. 444. But the granting clause in this deed describes what is conveyed as the tract or parcel of land known as the Jordan survey. This description includes the minerals, as well as the surface, and thus the granting clause purports to convey both the surface estate and all of the mineral estate. Holloway's Unknown Heirs v. Whatley, 133 Texas 608, 131 S.W.(2d) 89; Schlittler v. Smith, 128 Texas 628, 101 S.W.(2d) 543; Bibb v. Nolan, 6 S.W.(2d) 156 (application for writ of error refused.) Likewise the clause of general warranty has reference to "the said premises", meaning the land described in the granting clause, and, but for the last paragraph of the deed retaining an undivided interest in the minerals, would warrant the title to the land including the surface estate and all of the minerals.

(5) The writer believes that the judgment of the Court of Civil Appeals should be affirmed for substantially the same reasons as those set out in the opinion of that court, that is, that the language of the deed as a whole does not

clearly and plainly disclose the intention of the parties that there be reserved to the grantor Duhig an undivided one-half interest in the minerals in addition to that previously reserved to Gilmer's estate, and that when resort is had to established rules of construction and facts taken into consideration which may properly be considered, it becomes apparent that the intention of the parties to the deed was to invest the grantee with title to the surface and a one-half interest in the minerals, excepting or withholding from the operation of the conveyance only the one-half interest theretofore reserved in the deed from Gilmer's estate to Duhig. It is the court's opinion, however, that the judgment of the Court of Civil Appeals should be affirmed by the application of a well settled principle of estoppel.

The granting clause of the deed, as has been said, purports to convey to the grantee the land described, that is, the surface estate and all of the mineral estate. The covenant warrants the title to "the said premises". The last paragraph of the deed retains an undivided one-half interest in the minerals. Thus the deed is so written that the general warranty extends to the full fee simple title to the land except an undivided one-half interest in the minerals.

(6, 7) The language used in the last paragraph of the deed is that "grantor retains an undivided one-half interest in * * * the minerals". The word "retain" ordinarily means to hold or keep what one already owns. 54 C.J. p. 738; Words & Phrases, Second Series, Vol. 4, p. 371, Fourth Series, Vol. 3, p. 400; Websters New International Dictionary. If controlling effect is given to the use of the word "retains", it follows that the deed reserved to Duhig an undivided one-half interest in the minerals and that the grantee, Miller-Link Lumber Company, acquired by and through the deed only the surface estate. We assume that the deed should be given this meaning. When the deed is so interpreted the warranty is breached at the very time of the execution and delivery of the deed, for the deed warrants the title to the surface estate and also to an undivided one-half interest in the minerals. The result is that the grantor has breached his warranty, but that he has and holds in virtue of the deed containing the warranty the very interest, one-half of the minerals, required to remedy the breach. Such state of facts at once suggests the rule as to after-acquired title, which is thus stated in American Jurisprudence:

"It is a general rule, supported by many authorities, that a deed purporting to convey a fee simple or a lesser definite estate in land and containing covenants of general warranty of title or of ownership will operate to estop the grantor from asserting an after-acquired title or interest in the land, or the estate which the deed purports to convey, as against the grantee and those claiming under him." Vol. 19, p. 614, Sec. 16. See also Robinson v. Douthit, 64 Texas 101; Baldwin v. Root, 90 Texas 546, 40 S.W. 3; Jacobs v. Robinson, 113 Texas 231, 254 S.W. 309; Caswell v. Llano Oil Company, 120 Texas 139, 36 S.W.(2d) 208; Moore v. Crawford, 130 U.S. 122, 32 L.Ed. 878.

The case last cited quotes from a decision of the Michigan court the following clear statement of the rule and the reasons supporting it:

"When one assumes, by his deed, to convey a title, and by any form of assurance obligates himself to protect the grantee in the enjoyment of that which the deed purports to give him, he will not be suffered afterwards to acquire or assert a title and turn his grantee over to a suit upon his covenants for redress; the short and effectual method of redress is to deny him the liberty of setting up his after-acquired title as against his previous conveyance; that is merely refusing him the countenance and assistance of the courts in breaking the assurance which his covenants had given."

In the instant case Duhig did not acquire title to the one-half interest in the minerals after he executed the deed containing the general warranty, but he retained or reserved it in that deed. Plaintiffs in error, who claim under him, insist that they should be permitted to set up and maintain that title against the suit of defendant in error and to require it to seek redress in a suit for breach of the warranty. What the rule above quoted prohibits is the *assertion* of title in contradiction or breach of the warranty. If such enforcement of the warranty is a fair and effectual remedy in case of after-acquired title, it is, we believe, equally fair and effectual and also appropriate here.

(8) We recognize the rule that the covenant of general warranty does not enlarge the title conveyed and does not determine the character of the title. Richardson v. Levi, 67 Texas 359, 365-366, 3 S.W. 444; White v. Frank, 91 Texas 66, 70, 40 S.W. 962. The decision here made assumes, as has been stated, that Duhig by the deed reserved for himself a one-half interest in the minerals. The covenant is not construed as affecting or impairing the title so reserved. It operates as an estoppel denying to the grantor and those claiming under him the right to set up such title against the grantee and those who claim under it.

For the foregoing reasons, the judgment of the Court of Civil Appeals is affirmed.

Opinion adopted by the Supreme Court, October 16, 1940.
Rehearing overruled December 18, 1940.

Commentary on Duhig et al. v. Peavy-Moore Lumber Co., Inc.

by Ernest E. Smith, III[1]

Few, if any, title doctrines have been as widely followed in other jurisdictions while simultaneously generating as many exceptions and as much misunderstanding as the doctrine enunciated in *Duhig v. Peavy-Moore Lumber Co.* The *Duhig* case presents a classic example of what is often referred to as "overconveyancing," i.e., a grantor executes a deed that governs a larger interest in the land than the grantor actually owns. This situation is not uncommon in areas where there have been widespread conveyances of fractional mineral interests, and the facts of the case illustrate the simplest example of this situation. The initial owner of the land had previously conveyed the land in question to Duhig, reserving an undivided one-half interest in the mineral estate. Duhig subsequently reconveyed the land by a deed containing a reservation of an undivided half interest in the minerals in himself but making no reference to the initial owner's outstanding interest. Facially, the deed appeared to govern 100% of the land, with Duhig reserving half the mineral estate and the grantee receiving the other half of the mineral estate plus the entire surface estate. This result is, of course, impossible because of the existing outstanding interest in the initial grantor, which was properly recorded. The court resolves the constructional issue by concluding that the grantee received all interest in the land other than the interest retained by the original grantor.[2]

Duhig is not limited to the limited fact situation presented by the facts of the original case. In the closely analogous situations where the party in the position of the original *Duhig*[3] owns a significant fractional share of the minerals, but not enough to completely satisfy both the grant and the reservation and the situation where that party's fractional interest is too small to satisfy the entire grant, the grantee's interest is satisfied first, and the grantor retains whatever fractional interest, if any, remains.[4] *Duhig* has also been applied where the Duhig grantor executes a deed in which he purports to reserve an interest but fails to except an outstanding royalty from the deed's coverage. Regardless of whether the *Duhig* party's reserved interest is a royalty or a fractional interest in the mineral fee, it bears the entire burden of the outstanding royalty.[5]

Although the *Duhig* decision is based primarily upon a breach-of-warranty theory and an analogy to the doctrine of after-acquired title, at least one Texas court has applied the doctrine to a no-warranty deed. In *Blanton v. Bruce*, the *Duhig* grantor reserved a one-half mineral interest in a deed that purported to "grant, sell and convey" the property but failed to except an outstanding one-fourth interest in the mineral estate.[6] The court held that the grantor's successors were estopped from asserting title to the reservation to the extent that the reservation was inconsistent with making the grantee whole. It reasoned that a general covenant of warranty is not essential to the estoppel doctrine, which should apply to any deed that purports to convey a definite interest in the property. The North Dakota Supreme Court reached the same result where a special warranty deed was used.[7]

Much of the criticism of the *Duhig* doctrine stems from this use of estoppel in support of the result. The standard estoppel-in-pais doctrine presupposes that the party benefiting from estoppel had neither actual nor constructive notice of the salient facts; whereas the *Duhig* doctrine applies even when the grantee is clearly on constructive notice of the outstanding interest, as is the case when the outstanding interest has been properly recorded[8] or is contained or referenced in an instrument forming a necessary link in the grantee's chain of title.[9] As a result, although the *Duhig* doctrine has been widely followed in other states, some courts have used the analysis preferred by the decision's author, rather than the majority's breach-of-warranty/estoppel theory,[10] and at least one state has rejected *Duhig* outright.[11]

The dissent in *Peterson v. Simpson*, where a majority of the Arkansas Supreme Court opted to follow *Duhig* as it applied to subsequent purchasers from the original *Duhig* grantee, provides a good example of the criticism of the doctrine. As the dissenting judge stated,

> If the fifty percent mineral reservation, outstanding at the time of the deed questioned here, was made in a recorded deed, subsequent grantees had constructive notice of it. If it was not recorded, subsequent grantees may be bona fide purchasers in good faith without notice. The *Duhig* rule has nothing to do with either situation. . . . [A]pplication of the *Duhig* rule . . . relieve[s] the ultimate grantee of having to pursue his remedy on the warranty by construing the deed to achieve a result *contrary* to the intent of the grantor.[12]

Unfortunately, attorneys who are otherwise knowledgeable but are unfamiliar with the specialized doctrines applicable to mineral titles occasionally make the same analysis as suggested by the dissent in *Peterson* in construing *Duhig*-like conveyances. In many instances the original parties to the conveyance are dead, and an attorney drafting a re-conveyance for the heirs or other successors of the *Duhig* grantee construes the conveyance as written. The attorney concludes that the grantee, who was on constructive notice of the prior recorded interest in the third-party, received no interest in the mineral estate. As a result, subsequent grants by the successors of the *Duhig* grantee may result in "underconveyancing:" the deed is either limited to the surface estate, in which event the grantor of that deed unwittingly retains an interest in the mineral estate; or, the conveyance is not limited to the surface, but specifically excepts both the outstanding interest in the original grantor (the party in the position of the executor of Gilmer's estate from the *Duhig* case) and the interest in the *Duhig* grantor, who, of course, owns no interest. Such a conveyance is entirely reasonable from the standpoint of an attorney who is unfamiliar with the *Duhig* rule. It is drafted to protect his client from a potential suit for breach of warranty, but the deed results in an additional complexity in an already complex chain of title.

As of the time of this writing, there was no clear judicial resolution of how the re-conveyances just described should be construed. It seems reasonably likely, however, that the ultimate judicial conclusion will be that the grantee of the reconveyance from the *Duhig* grantee's successors receives the *Duhig* interest. Such a result is consistent with the doctrines that there can be no reservations in strangers[13] and that a deed is construed in favor of the grantee.[14] Of course, title attorneys can not safely rely on possible but uncertain outcomes, and may well continue to draft subsequent re-reconveyances on the assumption that a prior party in the chain of title may own the *Duhig* interest. Their clients are protected against breach-of-warranty claims, but the title's complexity is now compounded, and clear ownership of the *Duhig* interest will remain uncertain until a title action is brought.

Several of the limitations on the application of the *Duhig* rule recognize that a grantee who is on actual or inquiry notice of a prior recorded interest in a third party should not be able to take advantage of the doctrine. However, these limitations are restricted to situations where the deed makes some express reference to the outstanding interest. The most obvious situation is where the *Duhig* grantor specifically excepts the outstanding interest in the third party from the conveyance. Exceptions to *Duhig* have also been made where the conveyance was made subject to a prior deed "shown of record" at a specified volume and page number in the county deed records, but understated the size of the outstanding fractional interest,[15] and where the *Duhig* grantor merely referred to the prior deed containing the outstanding interest "for all purposes."[16]

The same result has been reached, at least from a practical standpoint, where the *Duhig* deed not only purported to reserve a fractional interest at a time when there was an existing interest in a third party, but also spelled out the incidents of the reserved fraction. In *Benge v. Scharbauer*, the grantors, who owned land subject to an undivided one-fourth mineral interest in a third party, executed a conveyance in which they reserved an undivided three-eighths mineral interest.[17] The deed also contained a stipulation that future leases "shall provide for the payment of three-eights (3/8ths) of all the bonuses, rentals and royalties to the grantors." In subsequent litigation, the Texas Supreme Court held that although the *Duhig* doctrine applied to give the grantee an undivided five/eighths of the mineral estate, the grantors, who were left with only a one-eighth interest, were nonetheless entitled to three-eighths of all lease benefits. The court justified this result on the ground that parties to a deed may agree to participate in lease benefits in different proportions from their actual fractional ownership in the mineral estate and that the express stipulation in the deed was a contractual agreement that the parties would do so. Because a reservation of a three-eighths mineral interest carries with it a right to three-eighths of lease benefits unless the parties stipulate to the contrary, it is not clear why merely spelling out that the retained interest is entitled to three-eighths of such benefits constitutes an enforceable contract that the grantor is entitled to such benefits; whereas silence on the matter transfers all but one-eighth of lease benefits to the grantee.

There are, of course, other limitations on the application of the *Duhig* doctrine. Because the doctrine is one of estoppel rather than substitution, it clearly does not apply where a grantee seeks to substitute a mineral interest reserved by the grantor in one portion of land for a mineral interest purportedly but ineffectively granted in another portion of the land.[18] There is authority in other states that *Duhig* does not apply if a quitclaim deed is used,[19] and the reasoning in *Blanton v. Bruce* supports the same conclusion in Texas.[20] This result is entirely consistent with *Duhig*, for if a true quitclaim is used, neither basis of the *Duhig* rationale is present. A quitclaim contains no warranty and does not purport to grant a specific fractional interest in the mineral estate, but merely "whatever right title and interest" the grantor owns after his reserved interest is excluded.

A much more significant exception has resulted from the refusal to apply the doctrine to oil and gas leases.[21] This result has been justified on the ground that leases are typically prepared by the lessee, rather than the lessor and are often executed under extreme time pressures before the parties have an opportunity to do a thorough title examination. Hence, they often purport to cover the entire mineral estate, although both parties are aware that the lessor probably owns less than 100% of that estate. Leases executed in this situation typically provide adequate protection for the lessee under the proportionate-reduction clause that reduces the lessee's royalty obligation to the proportionate interest actually owned by the lessee. Somewhat confusingly, an exception to this exception exists. If the lease is executed at a time when the outstanding interest is an NPRI rather than a fractional mineral interest, the lessee's royalty obligation is limited to the royalty set out in the lease, which bears the entire burden of the NPRI.[22]

Whereas the basic exception for leases can be justified on grounds of equity, several other exceptions are less explicable. A good example is the "co-tenant" exception. *Duhig* has been held to be inapplicable to partition deeds, even though the division into severalty of the co-owned land is done by warranty deeds. The rationale advanced by one court[23]—that a partition is not a conveyance of title—is difficult to reconcile with the fact that each party conveys all of his or her interest in a specific portion of the land to another party. Indeed, *Duhig* unquestionably governs transactions where a co-tenant conveys her interest to a third party.

In addition to "underconveyancing," which has been previously mentioned, there are other fact patterns that raise potential *Duhig* issues, but have not yet been addressed by Texas courts. Suppose, for example, that the *Duhig* grantee owns the outstanding interest that the deed fails to reference. Can he nonetheless assert estoppel against a grantor who reserves an interest in the deed? In *Gilstrap v. Jane Eisele Warren Trust*, the Wyoming Supreme Court held that the interest owned by the grantee should be subtracted from the estate warranted by the grantor, which in that case reduced the warranty's coverage to an undivided half interest in the minerals.[24] Whether Texas and other courts will agree with the Wyoming conclusion remains uncertain.

---

1 Ernest E. Smith, Rex G. Baker Centennial Chair in Natural Resource Law, The University of Texas School of Law.

2 *See Duhig v. Peavy-Moore Lumber Co.*, 144 S.W.2d 878 (Tex. 1940).

3 In subsequent examples, the person in this position will usually be referred to as the "*Duhig* grantor" and his grantee called the "*Duhig* grantee." The interest that the *Duhig* grantor attempts to reserve is referred to as the *Duhig* interest.

4 *See e.g., Scarmardo v. Potter*, 613 S.W.2d 756 (Tex. Civ. App.—Houston [14th Dist.] 1981, writ ref'd n.r.e.). Professor Willis Ellis has called application of *Duhig* to these latter situations as the "allocation of shortage rule." Willis H. Ellis, *Rethinking the Duhig Doctrine*, 28 Rocky Mtn. Min. L. Inst. 947 (1982).

5 *Haddad v. Boon*, 557 S.W.2d 805 (Tex. Civ. App.—Amarillo 1977), *appeal after remand*, 609 S.W.2d 609 (Tex. Civ. App.—Amarillo 1980, writ ref'd n.r.e.); *Selman v. Bristow*, 402 S.W.2d 520 (Tex. Civ. App.—Tyler 1966), *writ ref'd n.r.e.*, 406 S.W.2d 896 (Tex. 1966).

6 *Blanton v. Bruce*, 688 S.W.2d 908 (Tex. App.—Eastland 1985, writ ref'd n.r.e.).

7 *See Miller v. Kloeckner*, 600 N.W.2d 881 (N.D. 1999).

8 *See Cherry v. Farmers Royalty Holding Co.*, 160 S.W.2d 908 (Tex. Comm'n App. 1942).

9 *See Westland Oil Dev. Corp. v. Gulf Oil Corp.*, 637 S.W.2d 903 (Tex. 1982).

10 *See e.g., O'Brien v. Village Land Co.*, 794 P.2d 246 (Colo. 1990) (en banc).

11 *See Hartman v. Potter*, 596 P.2d 653 (Utah 1979). North Dakota initially adopted the doctrine; later repudiated it, and then re-adopted it a few years later. *See Sibert v. Kubas*, 357 N.W.2d 495 (N.D. 1984).

12 *Peterson v. Simpson*, 690 S.W.2d 720, 724-25 (Ark. 1985) (Holt, C.J., dissenting) (emphasis in original).

13 *See e.g., Little v. Linder*, 651 S.W.2d 895 (Tex. App.—Tyler 1983, writ ref'd n.r.e.); Ernest E. Smith & Jacqueline Lang Weaver, The Texas Law of Oil and Gas, § 3.9 (2d ed. 1998 & 2008).

14 *See* Tex. Pac. Coal & Oil Co v. Masterson, 334 S.W.2d 436 (Tex. 1960).

15 *See Helms v. Guthrie*, 573 S.W.2d 855 (Tex. Civ. App.—Fort Worth 1978, writ ref'd n.r.e.).

16 *See Harris v. Windsor*, 294 S.W.2d 798 (Tex. 1956).

17 *Benge v. Scharbauer*, 259 S.W.2d 166 (Tex. 1953).

18 *See Forrest v. Hanson*, 424 S.W.2d 899 (Tex. 1968).

19 *See e.g., Opaline King Hill v. Gilliam*, 682 S.W.2d 737 (Ark. 1985); *Rosenbaum v. McCaskey*, 386 So.2d 387 (Miss. 1980); *Young v. Vermillion*, 992 P.2d 917 (Okla. Civ. App. 1999).

20 *Blanton v. Bruce*, 688 S.W.2d 908 (Tex. App.—Eastland 1985, writ ref'd n.r.e.).

21 *See e.g., McMahon v. Christmann*, 303 S.W.2d 341 (Tex. 1957).

22 *See e.g., Klein v. Humble Oil & Ref. Co.*, 86 S.W.2d 1077 (Tex. 1935) (refusing to apply the lease's proportionate reduction clause in this situation). For the effect of applying the proportionate reduction clause, rather than *Duhig, see E.H. Lester Leasing Co. v. Griffith*, 779 S.W 2d 226 (Ky. Ct. App. 1989); *also* Owen L. Anderson, Discussion Notes, 107 O&GR 254 (1991) (criticizing the holding).

23 *Zapatero v. Canales*, 730 S.W.2d 111 (Tex. App.—San Antonio 1987, writ ref'd n.r.e.).

24 *Gilstrap v. Jane Eisele Warren Trust*, 106 P.3d 858 (Wyo 2005).

CHAPTER 7

Elliff et al.
v.
Texon Drilling Co. et al.

COMMENTARY

by Bruce M. Kramer

146 Tex. 575, 210 S.W.2d 558

1948

7

Elliff et al.
v.
Texon Drilling Co. et al.

146 Tex. 575, 210 S.W.2d 558

1948

MR. JUSTICE FOLLEY delivered the opinion of the court.

This is a suit by the petitioners, Mrs. Mabel Elliff, Frank Elliff, and Charles C. Elliff, against the respondents, Texon Drilling Company, a Texas corporation, Texon Royalty Company, a Texas corporation, Texon Royalty Company, a Delaware corporation, and John L. Sullivan, for damages resulting from a "blowout" gas well drilled by respondents in the Agua Dulce Field in Nueces County.

The petitioners owned the surface and certain royalty interests in 3054.9 acres of land in Nueces County, upon which there was a producing well known as Elliff No. 1. They owned all the mineral estate underlying the west 1500 acres of the tract, and an undivided one-half interest in the mineral estate underlying the east 1554.9 acres. Both tracts were subject to oil and gas leases, and therefore their royalty interest in the west 1500 acres was one-eighth of the oil or gas, and in the east 1554.9 acres was one-sixteenth of the oil and gas.

It was alleged that these lands overlaid approximately fifty per cent of a hugh reservoir of gas and distillate and that the remainder of the reservoir was under the lands owned by Mrs. Clara Driscoll, adjoining the lands of petitioners on the east. Prior to November 1936, respondents were engaged in the drilling of Driscoll-Sevier No. 2 as an offset well at a location 466 feet east of petitioners' east line. On the date stated, when respondents had reached a depth of approximately 6838 feet, the well blew out, caught fire and cratered. Attempts to control it were unsuccessful, and huge quantities of gas, distillate and some oil were blown into the air, dissipating large quantities from the reservoir into which the offset well was drilled. When the Driscoll-Sevier No. 2 well blew out, the fissure or opening in the ground around the well gradually increased until it enveloped and destroyed Elliff No. 1. The latter well also blew out, cratered, caught fire and burned for several years. Two water wells on petitioners' land became involved in the cratering and each of them blew out. Certain damages also resulted to the surface of petitioners' lands and to their cattle thereon. The cratering process and the eruption continued until large quantities of gas and distillate were drained from under petitioners' land and escaped into the air, all of which was alleged to be the direct and proximate result of the negligence of respondents begin here in permitting their well to blow out. The extent of the emissions from the Driscoll-Sevier No. 2 and Elliff No. 1, and the two water wells on petitioners' lands, was shown at various times during the several years between the blowout in November 1936, and the time of the trial in June 1946. There was also expert testimony from petroleum engineers showing the extent of the losses from the underground reservior, which computations extended from the date of the blowout only up to June 1938. It was indicated that it was not feasible to calculate the losses subsequent thereto, although lesser emissions of gas continued even up to the time of the trial. All the evidence with reference to the damages included all losses from the reservoir beneath petitioners' land without regard to whether they were wasted and dissipated from above the Driscoll land or from petitioners' land.

The jury found that respondents were negligent in failing to use drilling mud of sufficient weight in drilling their well, and that such negligence was the proximate cause of the well blowing out. It also found that petitioners had suffered $4,620.00 damage to sixty acres of the surface, and $1,350.00 for the loss of 27 head of cattle. The damages for the gas and distillate wasted "from and under" the lands of petitioners, due to respondents' negligence, was fixed by the jury at $78,580.46 for the gas, and $69,967.73 for the distillate. These figures were based upon the respective fractional royalty interests of petitioners in the whole amount wasted under their two tracts of land, and at a value, fixed by the court without objection by the parties, of two cents per 1,000 cubic feet for the gas and $1.25 per barrel for the distillate.

The findings as to the amount of drainage of gas and distillate from beneath petitioners' lands were based primarily upon the testimony of petitioners' expert witness, C. J. Jennings, a petroleum engineer. He obtained his information from drilling records and electric logs from the high pressure Agua Dulce Field. He was thereby enabled to fairly estimate the amount of gas and distillate. He had definite information as to porosity and bottom-hole pressure both before and after the blowout. He was able to estimate the amount of gas wasted under the Elliff tract by calculating the volume of the strata of sands and the voids which were occupied by gas. Under his method of calculation the determining factor was the decrease in bottom-hole pressures of the sands caused by the blowout. He estimated that 13,096,717,000 cubic feet of gas had been drained from the west 1500 acres of the Elliff land, and that 57,625,728,000 cubic feet had been drained from the east 1554.9 acres as a result of the blowout. The distillate loss was calculated by taking the gas and distillate ratio from the records of the Railroad Commission. Jennings estimated that 195,713 barrels had been drained from the west 1500 acres and 802,690 barrels from the east 1554.9 acres, as a result of the blowout.

On the findings of the jury the trial court rendered judgment for petitioners for $154,518.19, which included $148,548.19 for the gas and distillate, and $5,970.00 for damages to the land and cattle. The Court of Civil Appeals reversed the judgment and remanded the cause.

The reversal by the Court of Civil Appeals rests upon two grounds. The first was that since substantially all of the gas and distillate which was drained from under petitioners' lands was lost through respondents' blowout well, petitioners could not recover because under the law of capture they had lost all property rights in the gas or distillate which had migrated from their lands. The second theory was that the recovery cannot stand because the trial court had submitted the wrong measure of damages in that petitioners' claim "is for trespass in and to a freehold estate in land and the proper measure of damage is the reasonable cash market value before and after the occurrence complained of."

(1) In our opinion the Court of Civil Appeals was without authority to pass upon the propriety of the measure of damages adopted by the trial court for the simple reason that no such assignment was presented to that court. Although such an objection was raised in the trial court, we do not find an intimation of it brought forward to the Court of Civil Appeals. The question is therefore not before us, and our subsequent conclusions as to the rights of the parties are without reference to the correctness of the measure of damages, and we express no opinion on that question.

Consequently, our attention will be confined to the sole question as to whether the law of capture absolves respondents of any liability for the negligent waste or destruction of petitioners' gas and distillate, though substantially all of such waste or destruction occurred after the minerals had been drained from beneath petitioners' lands.

(2) We do not regard as authoritative the three decisions by the Supreme Court of Louisiana to the effect that an adjoining owner is without right of action for gas wasted from the common pool by his neighbor, because in that state only qualified ownership of oil and gas is recognized, no absolute ownership of minerals in place exists, and the unqualified rule is that under the law of capture the minerals belong exclusively to the one that produces them. Louisiana Gas & Fuel Co. v. White Bros., 157 La. 728, 103 So. 23; McCoy v. Arkansas Natural Gas Co. 175 La. 487, 143 So. 383, 85 A.L.R. 1147, cert. den. 287 U.S. 661, 53 Sup. Ct. 220, 77 L.Ed. 570; McCoy v. Arkansas Natural Gas Co. 184 La. 101, 165 So. 632. Moreover, from an examination of those cases it will be seen that the decisions rested in part on the theory that "the loss complained of was, manifestly, more a matter of uncertainty and speculation than of fact or estimate." In the more recent trend of the decisions of our state, with the growth and development of scientific knowledge of oil and gas, it is now recognized "that when an oil field has been fairly tested and developed, experts can determine approximately the amount of oil and gas in place in a common pool, and can also equitably determine the amount of oil and gas recoverable by the owner of each tract of land under certain operating conditions." Brown v. Humble Oil & Refining Co., 126 Texas 296, 83 S.W.(2d) 935, 940, 87 S.W.(2d) 1069, 99 A.L.R. 1107, 101 A.L.R. 1393.

(3) In Texas, and in other jurisdictions, a different rules [SIC] exists as to ownership. In our state the landowner is regarded as having absolute title in severalty to the oil and gas in place beneath his land. Lemar v. Garner, 121 Texas 502, 50 S.W.(2d) 769; Humphreys-Mexia Co. v. Gammon, 113 Texas 247, 254 S.W. 296, 29 A.L.R. 607; Waggoner Estate v. Sigler Oil Co., 118 Texas 509, 19 S.W.(2d) 27; Texas Co. v. Daugherty, 107 Texas 226, 176 S.W. 717, L.R.A. 1917F, 989. The only qualification of that rule of ownership is that it must be considered in connection with the law of capture and is subject to police regulations. Brown v. Humble Oil & Refining Co., supra. The oil and gas beneath the soil are considered a part of the realty. Each owner of land owns separately, distinctly and exclusively all the oil and gas under his land and is accorded the usual remedies against trespassers who appropriate the minerals or destroy their market value. Peterson v. Grayce Oil Co., 37 S.W.(2d) 367, affirmed 128 Texas 550, 98 S.W.(2d) 781; Comanche Duke Oil Co. v. Texas Pac. Coal & Oil Co., (Tex.Com.App.) 298 S.W. 554; Calor Oil and Gas Co. v. Franzell, 128 Ky. 715, 109 S.W. 328; Louisville Gas Co. v. Kentucky Heating Co., 117 Ky. 71, 77 S.W. 368, 70 L.R.A. 558, 111 Am.St.Rep. 225; Id. 132 Ky. 435, 111 S.W. 374; Ross v. Damm, 278 Mich. 388, 270 N.W. 722; 31A Tex.Jur. 911, Sec. 530; Id. 924, Sec. 537; 24 Am.Jur. 641, Sec. 159.

(4, 5) The conflict in the decisions of the various states with reference to the character of ownership is traceable to some extent to the divergent views entertained by the courts, particularly in the earlier cases, as to the nature and migratory character of oil and gas in the soil. 31A Tex.Jur. 24, Sec. 5. In the absence of common law precedent, and owing to the lack of scientific information as to the movement of these minerals, some of the courts have sought by analogy to compare oil and gas to other types of property such as wild animals, birds, subterranean waters, and other migratory things, with reference to which the common law had established rules denying any character of ownership prior to capture. However, as was said by Professor A. W. Walker, Jr., of the School of Law of the University of Texas: "There is no oil or gas productive state today which follows the wild-animal analogy to its logical conclusion that the landowner has no property interest in the oil and gas in place." 16 T.L.R. 370, 371. In the light of modern scientific knowledge these early analogies have been disproven, and courts generally have come to recognize that oil and gas, as commonly found in underground reservoirs, are securely entrapped in a static condition in the original pool, and, ordinarily, so remain until disturbed by penetrations from the surface. It is further established, nevertheless, that these minerals will migrate across property lines towards any low pressure area created by production from the common pool. This migratory character of oil and gas has given rise to the so-called rule or law of capture. That rule simply is that the owner of a tract of land acquires title to the oil or gas which he produces from wells on his land, though part of the oil or gas may have migrated from adjoining lands. He may thus appropriate the oil and gas that have flowed from adjacent lands without the consent of the owner of those lands, and without incurring liability to him for drainage. The non-liability is based upon the theory that after the drainage the title or property interest of the former owner is gone. This rule, (at first blush, would seem to conflict with the view of absolute ownership of the minerals in place, but it was otherwise decided in the early case of Stephens County v. Mid-Kansas Oil & Gas Co., 113 Texas 160, 254 S.W. 290, 29 A.L.R. 566 (1923). Mr. Justice Greenwood there stated; (113 Tex. 167).

"The objection lacks substantial foundation that gas or oil in a certain tract of land cannot be owned in place, because subject to appropriation, without the consent of the owner of the tract, through drainage from wells on adjacent lands. If the owners of adjacent lands have the right to appropriate, without liability, the gas and oil underlying their neighbor's land, then their neighbor has the correlative right to appropriate, through like methods of drainage, the gas and oil underlying the tracts adjacent to his own."

(6) Thus it is seen that, notwithstanding the fact that oil and gas beneath the surface are subject both to capture and administrative regulation, the fundamental rule of absolute ownership of the minerals in place is not affected in our state. In recognition of such ownership, our courts, in decisions involving well-spacing regulations of our Railroad Commission, have frequently announced the sound view that each landowner should be afforded the opportunity to produce his fair share of the recoverable oil and gas beneath his land, which is but another way of recognizing the existence of correlative rights between the various landowners over a common reservoir of oil or gas.

It must be conceded that under the law of capture there is no liability for reasonable and legitimate drainage from the common pool. The landowner is privileged to sink as many wells as he desires upon his tract of land and extract therefrom and appropriate all the oil and gas that he may produce, so long as he operates within the spirit and purpose of conservation statutes and orders of the Railroad Commission. These laws and regulations are designed to afford each owner a reasonable opportunity to produce his proportionate part of the oil and gas from the entire pool and to prevent operating practices injurious to the common reservoir. In this manner, if all operators exercise the same degree of skill and diligence, each owner will recover in most instances his fair share of the oil and gas. This reasonable opportunity to produce his fair share of the oil and gas is the landowner's common law right under our theory of absolute ownership of the minerals in place. But from the very nature of this theory the right of each land holder is qualified, and is limited to legitimate operations. Each owner whose land overlies the basin has a like interest, and each must of necessity exercise his right with some regard to the rights of others. No owner should be permitted to carry on his operations in reckless or lawless irresponsibility, but must submit to such limitations as are necessary to enable each to get his own. Hague v. Wheeler, 157 Pa. 324, 27 A.H., 717, 22 L.R.A. 141, 37 Am.St.Rep. 736.

While we are cognizant of the fact that there is a certain amount of reasonable and necessary waste incident to the production of oil and gas to which the non-liability rule must also apply, we do not think this immunity should be extended so as to include the negligent waste or destruction of the oil and gas.

(7) In Summers, Oil and Gas, Permanent Edition, Volume 1, page 142 correlative rights of owners of land in a common source of supply of oil and gas are discussed and described in the following language:

"These existing property relations, called the correlative rights of the owners of land in the common source of supply, were not created by the statute, but held to exist because of the peculiar physical facts of oil and gas. The term 'correlative rights' is merely a convenient method of indicating that each owner of land in a common source of supply of oil and gas has legal privileges as against other owners of land therein to take oil or gas therefrom by lawful operations conducted on his own land; that each such owner has duties to the other owners not to exercise his privileges of taking so as to injure the common source of supply."

In 85 A.L.R. 1156, in discussing the case of Hague v. Wheeler, supra, the annotator states:

"* * * The fact that the owner of the land has a right to take and to use gas and oil, even to the diminution or exhaustion of the supply under his neighbor's land, does not give him the right to waste the gas. His property in the gas underlying his land consists of the right to appropriate the same, and permitting the gas to escape into the air is not an appropriation thereof in the proper sense of the term."

In like manner, the negligent waste and destruction of petitioners' gas and distillate was neither a legitimate drainage of the minerals from beneath their lands nor a lawful or reasonable appropriation of them. Consequently, the petitioners did not lose their right, title and interest in them under the law of capture. At the time of their removal they belonged to petitioner and their wrongful dissipation deprived these owners of the right and opportunity to produce them. That right is forever lost, the same cannot be restored, and petitioner are without an adequate legal remedy unless we allow a recovery under the same common law which governs other actions for damages and under which the property rights in oil and gas are vested. This remedy should not be denied.

(8) In common with others who are familiar with the nature of oil and gas and the risks involved in their production, the respondents had knowledge that a failure to use due care in drilling their well might result in a blowout with the consequent waste and dissipation of the oil, gas and distillate from the common reservoir. In the conduct of one's business or in the use and exploitation of one's property, the law imposes upon all persons the duty to exercise ordinary care to avoid injury or damage to the property of others. Thus under the common law, and independent of the conservation statutes, the respondents were legally bound to use due care to avoid the negligent waste or destruction of the minerals imbedded in petitioners' oil and gas-bearing strata. This common-law duty the respondents failed to discharge. For that omission they should be required to respond in such damages as will reasonably compensate the injured parties for the loss sustained as the proximate result of the negligent conduct. The fact that the major portion of the gas and distillate escaped from the well on respondents' premises is immaterial. Irrespective of the opening from which the minerals escaped, they belonged to the petitioners and the loss was the same. They would not have been dissipated at any opening except for the wrongful conduct of the respondents. Being responsible for the loss they are in no position to deny liability because the gas and distillate did not escape through the surface of petitioners' lands.

We are therefore of the opinion the Court of Civil Appeals erred in holding that under the law of capture the petitioners cannot recover for the damages resulting from the wrongful drainage of the gas and distillate from beneath their lands. However, we cannot affirm the judgment of the trial court because there is an assignment of error in the Court of Civil Appeals challenging the sufficiency of the evidence to support the findings of the jury on the amount of the damages, and another charging that the verdict was excessive. We have no jurisdiction of those assignments, and, since they have not been passed upon, the judgment of the Court of civil [SIC] Appeals is reversed and the cause remanded to that court for consideration of all assignments except those herein decided. McKenzie Construction Co. v. City of San Antonio, 131 Texas 474, 115 S.W.(2d) 617; Ritchie v. American Surety Co. of New York, 145 Texas 422, 198 S.W.(2d) 85, and authorities cited.

Opinion delivered March 3, 1948.
Rehearing overruled May 12, 1948.

Commentary on a Restatement of the Rule of Capture and a Missed Opportunity to Create a New Cause of Action
Elliff et al. v. Texon Drilling Co. et al.

by Bruce M. Kramer

Elliff v. Texon Drilling Co. is a watershed case for many reasons. The court makes clear its commitment to the rule of capture notwithstanding the rule's inconsistency with the absolute ownership doctrine that had been adopted some 30 years earlier.[1] It also sets forth the parameters of the rule of capture's non-liability regime. Finally, the court recognizes the correlative rights doctrine as impacting the rule of capture ownership jurisprudence. But what the court does not do is either provide a clear recognition of the type of cause of action that may arise when a common source of supply is injured through the acts of a lessee or develop an appropriate damage model for this type of injury.

The case is deceptively simple in its facts, but in both the initial court of civil appeals opinion and the supreme court decision the courts omit the fact that the defendant was the lessee of the Elliff tracts, as well as the tract where the negligently drilled well that blew out was located.[2] That explains why no suit was ever brought by the Elliffs' lessee who was losing 7/8ths of the natural gas and condensate, while the Elliffs were only losing 1/8th. The court reiterates its adherence to the absolute ownership or ownership-in-place doctrine whereby the mineral owner has "absolute title in severalty to the oil and gas in place beneath his land." Of course, that absolute ownership is subject to two qualifications, the rule of capture and police power regulation. It is unfortunate that the court does not expressly add a third qualification to the absolute ownership doctrine, namely correlative rights, although it does discuss the impact of correlative rights on the mineral owner's bundle of sticks in a later portion of its opinion. Relying on *Stephens County*, the court does not resolve the inconsistency between the rule of capture and the absolute ownership doctrine. Its tautological explanation ignores the reality that the essence of property ownership, or the most important stick in the bundle of sticks making up that ownership, is the right to exclude others from possessing or using that property interest. The application of the rule of capture to an absolute ownership theory, however, results in the non-sequitur that what is Alpha's absolute property interest today may be Beta's property interest tomorrow and that Alpha's right to exclude Beta and the rest of the world from possessing its oil and gas is solely the function of Alpha's being able to go out and drill as many wells as possible to prevent the drainage of hydrocarbons. It is hard to come up with another type of property interest where one can lose "title" to that interest through the actions of a third party. While there are many benefits that flow from classifying oil and gas interests as corporeal real property interests, ideological or doctrinal consistency is not one of those benefits.

Besides the restrictions placed on the absolute ownership of oil and gas by the rule of capture and police power regulation, the court finds a third restriction, namely that drainage may not be caused by illegitimate, reckless, negligent, or lawless actions. Clearly, the operator of a directional well bottomed on the land of another is not given the protection of the rule of capture nor is the producer of hydrocarbons in violation of a Railroad Commission order. This is a socially beneficial result because it discourages, through the possibility of litigation, negligent, reckless, or criminal behavior by oil and gas operators.[3] Since the jury concluded that Texon was negligent in drilling its off-lease offset well, the drainage of natural gas and condensate through the blown-out wellbore on the neighboring tract did not fall within the protections afforded by the rule of capture. Without coming out definitively in recognizing that absolute owners of oil and gas over a common source of supply owe a duty to other absolute owners over that same common source of supply, the court clearly implies that the correlative rights doctrine is a fourth restriction on the absolute owner of the oil and gas. The court had the opportunity to reinforce the earlier decision in *Peterson v. Grayce Oil Co.*,[4] which dealt with both illegal production in violation of a Commission order and the use of production techniques that injured the common source of supply. It chose not to clarify the dual bases of the *Peterson* decision so that either of the two factors would, independent of each other, not be protected by the rule of capture.

The court relies on a case that is clearly inapposite to the point that it is making, however, *Hague v. Wheeler*.[5] In *Hague,* two adjacent oil and gas operators sought to enjoin a third operator from allowing natural gas to be flared or to dissipate into the air because the third operator lacked a market. The Pennsylvania Supreme Court refused to issue the injunction and relied on the rule of capture to conclude that once brought to the surface the natural gas is owned by the operator who is free to do with it what it desires. Hague does not represent a correlative rights holding but a "pure" rule of capture holding that says once captured the personal property of the capturer may be disposed of, including by flaring, as the capturer sees fit. Notwithstanding the mis-citation, the principle that the absolute ownership doctrine is qualified by considerations of waste and injury to the common source of supply is an important part of Texas oil and gas jurisprudence largely because of the *Elliff* opinion. Prior to this time, the jurisprudence of the state was unclear in its adherence to the correlative rights doctrine that clearly recognizes that each absolute owner's rights or privileges are constrained by the rights or privileges of other absolute owners over the common source of supply.

The *Elliff* opinion is also a critical linchpin in the holdings of two later Texas Supreme Court decisions that more clearly defined the rights of royalty owners to bring suits to protect their interests. A. W. Walker, Jr., in commenting on *Elliff,* criticized the reference to the fact that the royalty owners had "title" to the natural gas and condensate that was being lost through the blown-out well.[6] This reference to "title" was the basis of a motion for rehearing by Texon, which claimed that earlier Texas Supreme Court decisions clearly held that with a payment-type royalty clause, title to 8/8ths of the natural gas passed to the lessee at the time the lease was executed.[7] The court also said that the usual remedies against "trespassers" who appropriate the minerals or destroy their market value would be available to royalty owners. Prior to this case, it is clear that while a royalty interest in the ground is an incorporeal interest, and that after being produced it becomes a personal property interest, the *Elliff* opinion appears to change the status of the owner to an owner of an interest in real property. In fact, the court of civil appeals decision emphasizes that the Elliffs' claim is grounded in damage to real property, a claim belied by their status as royalty owners, as well as by the measure of damages awarded by the trial court. By recognizing that royalty owners have a cause of action for injury to the common source of supply, the *Elliff* opinion set the stage for a similar finding in *Neel v. HECI Exploration Co.*[8] By using the term "trespass", the court also presaged the supreme court's opinion in *Coastal Oil & Gas Corp. v. Garza Energy Trust*,[9] whereby the court differentiated between trespass *quare clasum freget,* which is applicable to possessory interests, and trespass on the case, which is applicable to non-possessory interests. It would have been better had the supreme court recognized that a royalty owner also owns a possibility of reverter in the mineral estate which is subject to a claim for damages based on a trespass on the case claim. In fact, one could reasonably argue that there has been an injury caused to both the royalty interest and the possibility of reverter. That would justify the conclusion that the owner of a freestanding royalty interest or an overriding royalty interest would have standing to sue, where an operator negligently or recklessly injured the common source of supply. While there would be some overlap in the damage models used for the injury to the royalty interest and the possibility of reverter, recognizing that both are property interests that are protected against negligent, wasteful, or reckless behavior would better allow the court to come up with an appropriate damage theory in these kinds of cases.

The most troubling aspect of the *Elliff* decision is the way it handled the damages issue. The trial court essentially awarded "conversion" damages based on an expert's testimony that a specified volume of natural gas and condensate had been lost through the blown-out well. The court of civil appeals reversed the damage recovery based on its application of the rule of capture, with dicta that the damages recoverable should be the same for mineral estates as they are for surface estates when it comes to trespass, namely, the difference in value of the estate prior to and after the trespass. The supreme court said that the court of civil appeals lacked jurisdiction to question the propriety of the trial court's damage award because apparently there was no assignment of error presented to that court. Thus, the supreme court, without expressing an opinion on the matter, said that the damage award must stand. Notwithstanding this admonition by the supreme court, the court of civil appeals on remand treated the supreme court's decision as concluding that liability for the "taking or destruction of gas and distillate" was a settled fact and affirmed the original damage award.[10]

The question of damages might have been resolved had the court decided that essentially the cause of action held by either a royalty owner or a possibility of reverter owner is negligent injury to the common source of supply that arises from the correlative rights doctrine. Had it done so, the issue of whether trespassory or conversion damages should be awarded would have been clear. Under the facts in *Elliff*, a claim for conversion is clearly inappropriate because Texon is not in possession of personal property owned by the Elliffs. A different circumstance would apply if there were a directional well wrongly bottomed case, giving on the Elliff mineral estate that produced gas sold by Texon. In that Elliffs the value of the converted personal property would be entirely appropriate. But since Texon was never in "possession" of the natural gas, it having escaped into the atmosphere, the conversion measure of damages was seemingly inappropriate unless it could be used as a surrogate measure for the damage or injury to the common source of supply.

Giving the royalty owners the full value of the lost hydrocarbons overcompensated the owners because there was no evidence that those volumes could have been produced in the time frame involved. There should have been a discount rate used to give them the current value of a future income stream from the royalties to be paid as the natural gas and condensate was being produced. In addition, at the time this case was decided the Railroad Commission had allowable or proration regulation that might have restricted the ability of Texon to produce from the existing Elliff wells and thus stretched out the period of time over which the Elliffs would have received their royalty income. None of those matters appears to have been taken into account by the trial court.

Had this been a drainage case, it is also clear that the Elliffs would not have been entitled to recover for the gross amount of hydrocarbons that were lost into the atmosphere through the blown-out well. As more recently decided by the Texas Supreme Court, a party asserting drainage is not entitled to recover the total amount of hydrocarbons drained because that would over-compensate the royalty owner.[11] The royalty owner in an *Elliff*-type situation would have to show that its lessee could have produced all of the hydrocarbons that escaped through the blown-out well. Depending on the applicable Railroad Commission well spacing regulation and the nature of the reservoir, it might be difficult for a royalty owner to prove that it could have recovered all of the lost hydrocarbons.

A.W. Walker proposed two possible measures of damages in an *Elliff*-type case.[12] The first would be the traditional measure of damages for injury to real property interests, namely the difference in value before and after the injury. That was the approach taken by the court of civil appeals in *Elliff*. A lease covering a portion of a common source of supply that has been drained of hydrocarbons is certainly worth less than a lease covering a portion of a common source of supply with more hydrocarbons still in place. But there may be additional damages recoverable because the blown-out well not only reduced the amount of recoverable hydrocarbons but also may have made it more expensive to produce the remaining hydrocarbons. While the royalty interest owner is obviously indifferent about the cost of production, a lessee is not and therefore may produce less hydrocarbons because the well may not produce sufficient revenue to meet the increased costs of having to institute secondary or enhanced recovery techniques in order to produce the remaining hydrocarbons. Another issue that might lead to a determination that the royalty owner has suffered additional damages is whether or not an enhanced recovery project may be implemented without having to pool or unitize the royalty owner's interest with adjacent lands. If the leasehold interest becomes encumbered with additional transaction costs, it becomes less valuable and the value of the possibility of reverter becomes further diminished.

The second measure of damage would give the royalty owner the value of the destroyed property. For example, if a person negligently causes a fire that destroys a neighbor's stand of growing timber, the measure of damages would be the value of the lost timber. That value, however, would not be the value of cut and finished wood but the value of the timber as it stood prior to the fire. As applied to a royalty owner, however, that measure of damages would not fully compensate the royalty owner since the royalty owner has a cost-free interest. It would compensate unleased mineral owners in the position of the Elliffs, who would otherwise not be able to develop their now-lost hydrocarbons unless they expended the funds necessary to drill a well or leased the land to another and received a fractional royalty interest.

Elliff is a watershed case because it is one of the first cases dealing with a factual scenario involving a negligent injury to the common source of supply. By recognizing that the royalty owner has a cause of action for such an injury, the court takes a giant step forward in advancing the notion that the correlative rights doctrine must be considered when applying the rule of capture. The unique qualities of oil and gas, including both their fugacious nature and their location in common sources of supply that are typically owned by multiple parties, led the *Elliff* court to create a common law claim when one owner over that common source of supply negligently or wantonly injures the common source of supply.

---

1 *See, e.g., Stephens County v. Mid-Kansas Oil & Gas Co.*, 113 Tex. 160, 254 S.W. 290 (1923); *Humphreys-Mexia Co. v. Gammon*, 113 Tex. 247, 254 S.W. 296 (1923); *Texas Co. v. Daugherty*, 107 Tex. 226, 176 S.W. 717 (1915).

2 This point is raised in the remand decision of the court of civil appeals in San Antonio in its discussion of some allegedly prejudicial statements made by counsel for Texon, who was claiming that Texon came to the Elliffs' rescue by leasing the premises in order to avoid a tax foreclosure sale. 216 S.W.2d 824, 827, 829 (Tex. Civ. App.—San Antonio 1948, writ ref'd n.r.e.).

3 The author of a casenote on Elliff disagreed with the above statement and concluded, "[The court] adds a contingent costly burden, depending upon a jury finding of ordinary negligence to the oil-producing industry." John E. Thomason, *Liability in Texas for Wrongful Drainage of Oil and Gas*, 27 Tex. L. Rev. 349, 360 (1948).

4 37 S.W.2d 367 (Tex. Civ. App.— Fort Worth 1931), *aff'd*, 128 Tex. 550, 98 S.W.2d 781 (1936).

5 27 A. 714 (Pa. 1893). Hague is discussed at Bruce M. Kramer & Owen L. Anderson, *The Rule of Capture –An Oil and Gas Perspective*, 35 Env'tl L. 899, 907-09 (2005).

6 A.W. Walker, Jr., *Important Oil and Gas Decisions*, 11 Tex. B.J. 479, 499 (1948). Dean Eugene Kuntz read *Elliff* to hold in fact that the royalty owner "does not lose title to the drained substances and can recover their value." Eugene Kuntz, *Correlative Rights in Oil and Gas*, 30 Miss. L.J. 1, 3 (1958).

7 Robert E. Hardwicke, *Problems Arising Out of Royalty Clauses in Oil and Gas Leases in Texas*, 29 Tex. L. Rev. 790, 793 (1951). Those cases are *Hager v. Stakes*, 116 Tex. 453, 294 S.W. 835 (1927), and *Sheffield v. Hogg*, 124 Tex 290, 77 S.W.2d 1021 (1934).

8 942 S.W.2d 212 (Tex. 1997).

9 268 S.W.3d 1, 12 (Tex. 2008).

10 216 S.W.2d at 826.

11 Coastal Oil, 268 S.W.3d at 18-19.

12 Walker, *supra* note 4, at 501.

CHAPTER 8

Lillie M. Clifton et al., Petitioners
v.
R. W. Koontz et al., Respondents

COMMENTARY

by Stuart C. Hollimon

160 Tex. 82, 325 S.W.2d 684

1959

Lillie M. Clifton et al., Petitioners,
v.
R. W. Koontz et al., Respondents

160 Tex. 82, 325 S.W.2d 684

1959

MR. JUSTICE SMITH delivered the opinion of the court.

This suit brought by petitioners, Lillie M. Clifton, individually and as executrix of the estate of her husband, J. H. Clifton, deceased, et al., seeks the cancellation of an oil, gas, and mineral lease on the theory that after the expiration of its ten-year primary term, the lease terminated due to cessation of production.

In the alternative, and only in the event the Court should find that production had not ceased, petitioners sought cancellation of the lease (other than for 40 acres around the existing well) on the theory that the owners of the lease (the working interest) breached an implied covenant to reasonably develop the property and to "reasonably explore the same for the production of minerals therefrom * * *." It was their contention that the owners of the working interest, in the event the alternative plea should be sustained, would forfeit all rights under the lease (except as to 40 acres around the producing well) upon failure within a reasonable time, to commence and continue the drilling of wells to a depth sufficient to test all known horizons in the general area. Petitioner also sought damages because of breaches of express and implied covenants of the lease.

The lease was executed in 1940. It covers two tracts of land encompassing 350 acres owned by the Cliftons, in Wise County, Texas. In 1949, during the primary term, a well was drilled which produced both oil and gas but very little oil. The Railroad Commission classified the well as an "associated" (with oil) gas well. Other than its acidization in 1950, no other drilling or reworking operations were carried on during the intervening years until September 12, 1956, when it was successfully reworked by "sandfracting". This date was subsequent to the filing of the present case.

The judgment of the trial court, entered after a trial before the court, without the aid of a jury, contains the court's findings of fact upon the basic questions. The court found that the existing gas well had at all material times continuously produced gas in paying quantities. Accordingly, the oil and gas lease was held to be in full force and effect, thus denying petitioners' prayer for judgment that the lease had terminated. The judgment recites a finding to the effect that petitioners were damaged by the failure of respondents to rework the existing well and to drill, but that such damages were speculative and could not be ascertained with any degree of certainty. Judgment for damages was therefore denied.

The judgment decreed "that unless on or before the expiration of 60 days after the date this Judgment shall become final, the owners of the working interest shall commence and thereafter drill with reasonable diligence and in a good and workmanlike manner a test well looking to the production of oil and/or gas on said land, the drill site to be selected by said working-interest owners and said well to be drilled to a total depth of 5600 feet below the surface of said land unless production of oil and/or gas in paying quantities be by them found at a lesser depth, this lease shall terminate and re-invest in Plaintiff and her assigns except as to the conglomerate formation found in the stratigraphic interval from 5300 to 5600 feet, from which the present well is now producing, such section being generally known as the Atoka (Morris Field) conglomerate; and as to all of such section, strata, or formation, the lease shall continue in full force and effect, as to appearing parties herein, so long as it continues producing oil, gas or other minerals conformably with the terms of the lease instrument."

Both petitioners and respondents appealed. The Court of Civil Appeals affirmed the trial court's judgment denying termination of the oil and gas lease and petitioners claim for damages, but held that respondents were not required to drill a second well. Therefore, the judgment of the trial court requiring such drilling was reversed and rendered. 305 S.W.2d 782.

We have concluded that the judgment of the Court of Civil Appeals must be sustained. We first consider the primary question, which is: Was there any evidence to sustain the finding of the trial court that production in paying quantities had not ceased?

(1) One of the rules in determining this question is the well settled rule that if there is any evidence reasonably tending to prove, either directly or by permissive inference, the essential facts, the judgment rendered thereon must

be sustained. Woodward v. Ortiz, 150 Texas 75, 237 S.W.2d 286; Benoit v. Wilson, 150 Texas 273, 239 S.W.2d 792.

We have examined the entire record and in doing so have viewed the evidence in the light most favorable to the respondents; discarding all adverse evidence, and giving credit to all evidence favorable to the findings and judgment of the court, the trier of the facts, and have reached the conclusion that there is evidence of probative force supporting the judgment of the trial court that the gas well had continuously produced in paying quantities.

Petitioners base their contention that the well had ceased to produce in paying quantities upon the showing that for the period of time from June 1955 through September 1956, the income from the lease was $3,250.00 and that the total expense of operations during the same period was $3,466.16-thus, a loss of $216.16 for the sixteen months' period selected by petitioners. During the period of time indicated, some months showed a gain and some a loss. For the months of July, August, and September 1956, the total net loss amounted to $372.37. These were the months immediately following June 1956, the date respondent, Koontz, acquired his 52 per cent interest in the lease. Beginning July 1, 1956 he began making financial arrangements, securing the services of third parties, and commenced saving all oil produced from the lease to be used in reworking the well. The holding from the market of this oil accounts materially for the losses in the operations during the months of July, August, and September 1956. The record shows that for years, in view of the low allowable on gas, the oil production had made the difference between operating at a profit and at a loss. The respondent, Koontz, testified that from two to three months were required to accumulate a tank of oil and that after such accumulation a sale would be made. Respondents' evidence reflects that through 1955 and 1956 there was but little variation in gas production. For the same period of time there was a great variation in oil production, resulting in a showing of a profit in months when oil sales were made.

(2) It is undisputed that reworking operations were commenced on September 12, 1956, and that such operations resulted in an 1800 per cent increase of production. Reworking operations having thus been commenced on September 12, 1956, the evidence that there was a small operating loss for the period of time from July 1956 through September 1956 is not controlling in determining whether or not there had been a cessation of production in paying quantities through July 12, 1956, a date 60 days prior to the beginning of reworking operations. The question, therefore, is: Was there production in paying quantities from the existing well through July 12, 1956? Evidence, as contended for by the petitioners, as to profit or loss subsequent to July 12, 1956, is immaterial in determining whether or not there was production in paying quantities through that date. If there was production in paying quantities at all times through July 12, 1956, then the clause contained in the lease, which permits reworking within 60 days following cessation of production, if it ever came into operation, was complied with when reworking operations were begun on September 12, 1956, and later successfully completed. Thus, by considering only the evidence relative to production prior to July 12, 1956, we find that the lessee operated at a profit in the sum of $111.25, for the period of time beginning in June 1955 and continuing through July 12, 1956. The record shows a loss during the months of April and May 1956. The record further shows that for the year 1954, a profit was earned each month, and that the aggregate profit was the sum of $1575; that in 1955 the operations were profitable during nine months of the year, with a net profit of $894.00 for the year; and that for the first six months' period of 1956, the lease was operated at a profit of $145.00. These factual situations, when considered in the light most favorable to the findings of the trial court, support its finding and judgment that there was not a cessation of production in paying quantities through July 12, 1956.

Petitioners argue that it is settled under the Texas law that, after the primary term, the ordinary oil and gas lease absolutely terminates when its income no longer exceeds the cost of its operation, and that since the operations showed a loss for the months of April and May 1956, the lease terminated. Citing Garcia v. King, 139 Texas, 578, 164 S.W.2d 509, and Holchak v. Clark, Texas Civ.App., 284 S.W.2d 399, er.ref. Also Freeman v. Magnolia Petroleum Company, 141 Texas 274, 171 S.W.2d 339; Cox v. Miller, Texas Civ.App., 184 S.W.2d 323, er.ref. The further argument is made that such established rule applies as well to a lease with a 60-day termination clause, except a period of 60 additional days is allowed in which to begin additional drilling or reworking operations. The lease under consideration does contain such a clause which is directly related to the petitioners' argument relating to the determination of cessation of production:

> "* * * or if after discovery of oil, gas or other mineral the production thereof should cease from any cause, this lease shall not terminate if lessee commences additional drilling or re-working operations within sixty (60) days thereafter. * * *"

We agree with petitioners that if production in paying quansities ceased, the 60-day clause applies. However, the facts in the instant case compel a different result than that contended for by petitioners.

(3) It is only in the event of a finding of cessation of production in paying quantities that the trial court would be called upon to determine whether, if within 60 days from the date of such cessation, reworking operations

were begun and resulted in profitable production thereafter. After cessation of production in paying quantities, the lessee has 60 days of "grace" in which to save his leasehold, however, if production never ceased, as is the case here, the 60-day clause is not definitive of the period over which the trier of the facts must determine whether a lease is producing in paying quantities. There can be no arbitrary period for determining the question of whether or not a lease has terminated for the additional reason that there are various causes for slowing up of production, or a temporary cessation of production, which he courts have held to be justifiable. See Texas Pacific Coal & Oil Co. v. Bratton, Texas Civ.App., 239 S.W. 688 (1921), no writ history; also Midwest Oil Corp. v. Winsauer, 159 Texas, 560, 328 S.W.2d 944. We again emphasize that there can be no limit as to time, whether it be days, weeks, or months, to be taken into consideration in determining the question of whether paying production from the lease has ceased. To apply the 60-day clause as contended by petitioners would mean that the respondents would have been required to immediately commence drilling operations, upon sustaining a slight loss for one month, without regard to whether they believed the next month's production might be profitable for the reason that if they were in error and suffered another slight loss, the lease would terminate. The petitioners cite the case of Stanolind Oil & Gas Company v. Newman Brothers Drilling Company, 157 Texas 489, 305 S.W.2d 169, as supporting their position. That case has no application to this question since it was concerned primarily with whether the 60-day clause and the 30-day clause contained in an oil, gas, or mineral lease are cumulative in application or separate and distinct provisions. No attempt was made in that case to settle the question of over what period of time paying quantities should be determined. However, the opinion does state that "the sixty-day provision would be brought into play by a cessation of such production."

(4) The lease instrument involved in this suit provides by its terms that it shall continue in effect after commencement of production, "as long thereafter as oil, gas, or other mineral is produced from said land." While the lease does not expressly use the term "paying quantities", it is well settled that the terms "produced" and "produced in paying quantities" mean substantially the same thing. Garcia v. King, 139 Texas 578, 164 S.W.2d 509.

The generally accepted definition of "production in paying quantities" is stated in the Garcia case, supra, to be as follows:

> "If a well pays a profit, even small over operating expenses, it produces in paying quantities, though it may never repay its costs, and the enterprise as a whole may prove unprofitable."

In the case of a marginal well, such as we have here, the standard by which paying quantities is determined is whether or not under all the relevant circumstances a reasonably prudent operator would, for the purpose of making a profit and not merely for speculation, continue to operate a well in the manner in which the well in question was operated.

In determining paying quantities, in accordance with the above standard, the trial court necessarily must take into consideration all matters which would influence a reasonable and prudent operator. Some of the factors are: The depletion of the reservoir and the price for which the lessee is able to sell his product, the relative profitableness of other wells in the area, the operating and marketing costs of the lease, his net profit, the lease provisions, a reasonable period of time under the circumstances, and whether or not the lessee is holding the lease merely for speculative purposes.

(5) The term paying quantities involves not only the amount of production, but also the ability to market the product (gas) at a profit. See Benedum-Trees Oil Co. v. Davis, 107 F.2d 981 and Hanks v. Magnolia Petroleum Co., (Tex.Com.App.) 24 S.W.2d 5. Whether there is a reasonable basis for the expectation of profitable returns from the well is the test. If the quantity be sufficient to warrant the use of the gas in the market, and the income therefrom is in excess of the actual marketing cost, and operating costs, the production satisfies the term "in paying quantities". In the Hanks case, supra, the trial court found that the well completed by Hanks did not produce in paying quantities within the contemplation of the terms of the lease, and this Court upheld such finding, holding that there was no evidence showing that there were any facilities for marketing the gas or any near-by localities or industries which might have furnished a profitable market therefor. The Court went further and pointed out the complete failure of the evidence to show what the gas could have been sold for at any probable market, and that there was no evidence "tending to show that the well was situated in such proximity to any prospective market which would justify the construction of a pipe line for marketing same."

In the present case we have a finding of the trial court that there was production in paying quantities, and that the lease had not terminated. The evidence supports the finding. Evidence of marketing facilities and that the gas was sold at a profit is present in the instant case, whereas the Hanks case, supra, was wholly devoid of such evidence.

(6) Proration rules adopted by the Texas Railroad Commission are a factor in determining the productive capacity of a particular lease. The Railroad Commission may by its order, for example, permit the taking of a greater

percentage of the daily volume from nonassociated gas wells to the end that adequate quantities of gas may be delivered during the winter months when the demand therefor is the greatest, and by its order reduce the percentage to be taken during the summer months when a much less quantity of gas is needed. Relative to individual lease or gas units, the Commission has taken the position that it may by its order allow an overproduction for a period of time to meet the market demand for that period, and, in order to balance such overproduction, it takes the position that it may order that the well be cut down to a minimum volume of production.

(7) Petitioners contend that the trial court's finding that production in paying quantities had not ceased is erroneous because the profit and loss figures heretofore considered do not include charges for depreciation as an operating expense. We are of the opinion that the trial court correctly excluded depreciation as an operating expense in determining whether and when production in paying quantities ceases. The petitioners contend that depreciation of the original investment cost should be taken into consideration as a part of the expense in operating the well. With this contention we do not agree. We do not have before us the question of whether or not depreciation on producing equipment should be charged as an operating expense, and, therefore, do not decide the question.

As the Garcia case, supra, indicates, the term "paying quantities", when used in the extension clause of an oil lease habendum clause, means production in quantities sufficient to yield a return in excess of operating costs, and marketing cost, even though drilling and equipment costs may never be repaid and the undertaking considered as a whole may ultimately result in a loss. The underlying reason for this definition appears to be that when a lessee is making a profit over the actual cash he must expend to produce the lease, he is entitled to continue operating in order to recover the expense of drilling and equipping, although he may never make a profit on the over-all operation. Depreciation is nothing more than an accounting charge of money spent in purchasing tangible property, and if the investment itself is not to be considered, as is held by this Court, then neither is depreciation.

In Transport Oil Co. v. Exeter Oil Co. Ltd., 84 Cal.App.2d 616, 191 P.2d 129, it was held that operation of an oil and gas leasehold at an annual profit of about $4,300.00, without deduction of reserves for depletion and depreciation and after exclusion under terms of the lease and operating agreement of overriding royalties as an operating expense, was in "paying quantities" within the habendum clause of the lease. By not including depreciation as an operating expense, we more nearly accomplish a just result for lessors and lessees alike, for, if the rule were otherwise, many leases would be terminated and the lessees' incentive to drill decreased, regardless of the magnitude of the investment.

Petitioners present two cases to support their argument that depreciation should be treated as an expense item, but they are both distinguishable. In Persky v. First State Bank, Texas Civ.App., 117 S.W.2d 861, no writ history, the Court of Civil Appeals merely held:

> "We *might* take judicial knowledge that all property of this kind has some depreciation from year to year, but we could not, in the absence of testimony to support it, take judicial knowledge of the percentage or amount of such depreciation." (Emphasis supplied.)

It is not held that depreciation is to be considered as operation expense, and, as such, is to be deducted from income. Also, we do not have pumping machinery involved in the case at bar, as was true in the Persky case.

The other case relied upon is United Central Oil Corporation v. Helm, 11 F.2d 760 (5 Cir.), certiorari denied, 271 U.S. 686, 70 L.Ed. 1151, 46 S.Ct. 638. The Court in that case held that depreciation and overhead expenses are to be considered in determining paying quantities at the time of abandonment of a lease, in an action for damages against the lessee by the lessor. However, the lease was for a period of four years rather than "so long thereafter as oil and/or gas are produced." The holding in the Helm case does not conflict with our holding in the present case. The case merely demonstrates the variable meaning applied to the phrase "paying quantities."

(8) Petitioners contend that the 8 per cent overriding royalties outstanding, as shown by the record, should be excluded from the total income attributable to the working interest in determining whether or not production is being obtained in paying quantities. We do not agree. The entire income attributable to the contractual working interest created by the original lease is to be considered. Petitioners cite no Texas case, and we have found none, which supports their argument. While apparently there is no Texas decision in point on the particular question, we believe the case of Transport Oil Co. v. Exeter Oil Co. Ltd., supra, is authority supporting our view. In that case the basic oil and gas lease on a tract of land executed in 1921 required certain drilling operations and the payment of 16-2/3rds per cent royalty to the lessor based upon the gross income. After several assignments of the lease in which overriding royalties had been reserved, the plaintiff in the action became the owner of the lease subject to the overriding royalty. Thereafter, the plaintiff, Transport Oil Company, assigned this lease to the defendant, Exeter Oil Company, in which assignment the defendant obligated itself to pay out of the gross income from the lease, the basic landowner's royalty, the overriding royalty reserved in previous assignments, and the override to the plaintiff totaling almost

50 per cent of the income per well. In 1942 the defendant plugged the well and abandoned the property, due to declining production. The abandonment terminated the plaintiff's interest as an overriding royalty owner, and it brought suit to recover damages. The court held that overriding royalty could not be excluded from the total income in determining whether there was production in paying quantities. See also, Vance v. Hurley, 215 La. 805, 41 So.2d 724 (1949).

We come now to consider the question of whether the petitioners are entitled to a cancellation of the lease (other than for 40 acres around the existing well) on the theory advanced by the petitioners that the owners of the lease (the working interest) breached an implied covenant to reasonably develop the property and to "reasonably explore the same for the production of minerals therefrom * * *." The petitioners take the position that the implied covenant to further develop the property required and obligated the working-interest owners to rework the existing well.

The findings of fact incorporated in the trial court's judgment, bearing directly upon this question, are as follows:

> "1. That the working interest owners likewise impliedly covenanted and were obligated to develop the lease and to further explore said land for other such reservoirs and formations which might be so productive, in both instances in the manner and with the diligence of a reasonably prudent operator under all the surrounding facts and circumstances;
> "2. That the implied covenant first above stated [to reasonably develop] required and obligated the working interest owners to rework the existing well two years before they actually did so in September, 1956;
> "3. That the implied covenant second above stated [to further explore] required and obligated said working interest owners to drill a second or additional well on said land as a test well looking to the production [of] oil, gas or other minerals therefrom prior to this date;
> "4. That said working interest owners have violated both said implied covenants by failing so to rework the existing well and drill the second well within the times respectively specified therefor;"

The courts generally have recognized the implied covenant to reasonably develop the premises after production is obtained. Such implied covenant requires a lessee, after production is discovered on the premises, to conduct further development with reasonable diligence, to the end that such operations would result in a benefit or profit for both the lessor and the lessee. The petitioners first sought damages for the breach of the implied covenant to reasonably develop by failing to rework the existing well. Their pleadings were sufficient to admit proof that the owners of the working interest had violated such implied covenant to further develop the leased premises. The pleadings were that the owners of the working interest had full knowledge that the existing gas well had ceased to produce in paying quantities, and that the lease had terminated because of such cessation of production; that Koontz "belatedly began the reworking of well Number 1, and as a result of its reworking, production of oil and * * * gas was increased manifold, which reworking should have been done at least three years prior to the filing of this suit on August 11, 1956, and, had it been done, the parties at interest would have received royalties, in addition to what they did receive, in excess of the amount herein elsewhere alleged."

Admitting that respondents failed to rework the existing well for two years before it was actually reworked on September 12, 1956, and that the petitioners sustained damages because of such failure, we cannot agree with petitioners' contention that the evidence showing an increase in production and income after the reworking of the well would support a judgment for damages. The trial court held that such damages were too "speculative to be ascertained with any degree of certainty." The evidence supports such a finding. Respondents contend that the judgment as contained in the transcript omits the phrase "and that such damages have not been proved with any degree of certainty." Petitioners contend that had the well been reworked, two years before reworking was actually begun, they would have received monthly royalty in the sum of $270.00, and that such payments would have been continuous for the 2-year period. They contend that the failure to earlier rework the existing well amounted to a breach of the covenant to reasonably develop the premises. With this contention we cannot agree. There is no evidence in this record that the petitioners will not recover all of their undivided interest in the gas reservoir under the land involved; neither is there any evidence that earlier reworking of the existing well would have resulted in the production of any greater quantity of gas. It is entirely speculative and uncertain as to the life of the field. The record does not disclose any factual or evidentiary basis upon which damages can be assessed with certainty.

Petitioners next contend that the respondents breached the implied covenant to reasonably develop by failing to drill additional wells for the purpose of developing all formations for the production of oil and/or gas, and that the evidence supports such contention. With this we cannot agree. Charles Kadane, one of the petitioners, testified that he was willing to take a chance and drill a well on the Clifton lease. His decision to enter into a contract to drill on the Clifton lease was reached after he had drilled the "Sipes" well. This well was located about 1200 feet north of the north line of the Clifton 350-acre tract involved in this suit. Mr. Kadane testified that the showing of oil in the Sipes well was in the Strawn formation, that the test was successful, but that at the time of the trial he was not producing anything from the Strawn formation. However, he testified that he anticipated "producing at some later date should the lower production run out." He testified further that there were three different conglomerates below the Strawn formation, and that he tested the conglomerate in two places, making a total of three tests. The tests in the two conglomerates were made to a depth of approximately 5600 feet. Mr. Kadane testified that the Marble Falls and Ellenburger formations are both below 5600 feet, but that he did not test either of those formations. He stated that no wells had been drilled close to either of those formations, but that he thought there was a 'likelihood' of production being obtained from those formations in the area of the Sipes and Clifton leases. The nearest well producing from such formations or sands was some 2 1/2 miles east of the tract involved in this suit. The evidence fails to show that any tests were made on the 350-acre Clifton tract, and that production of oil or gas could be produced in paying quantities from either the Strawn formation, which is a stratum above the present production, or the Marble Falls and Ellenburger formations, which are strata below present production. There is no evidence in the record of any geological formation or horizon in the area of the 350-acre Clifton lease, other than the conglomerate, from which production is being obtained in paying quantities. Mr. Kadane's contract with Mrs. Clifton to drill a well, if cancellation of the present lease was obtained, was premised upon obtaining a release of acreage, and not upon a release of horizons under acreage.

(9) The gas well now in production is located in the Morris Field. There is no evidence that reasonable development required that an additional well be drilled to this stratum to obtain production of either oil or gas. The field rules prescribed by the Railroad Commission were introduced in evidence. They were adopted by the Railroad Commission on February 28, 1955, and provide for 320-acre units with 10 percent tolerance so that a maximum of 352 acres may be assigned. Consequently, on this particular 350-acre tract only one well could be permitted to be drilled to the Morris sand. Rule 3, as promulgated by the Railroad Commission for this field, provides that gas shall be allocated to each well in the ratio that the product of bottomhole pressure times acreage bears to the summation of this product for all wells in the reservoir. Thus, it is seen that if a second well had been drilled on the 350-acre lease to the Morris sand, then the total allowable for the two wells would have been no greater than the allowable for one.

We conclude from all of the above circumstances that the respondents did not violate the implied covenant to reasonably develop the lease by the drilling of additional wells. The petitioners did not discharge the burden which rested upon them to prove, as required, that the lessees failed to measure up to the standard of the prudent operator. While it is true that each separate stratum or horizon would be entitled to separate development, yet it is equally true that the burden rests upon the lessor to prove that the producing stratum required additional wells, or that strata different from that from which production is being obtained, in reasonable probability, exist, and that by the drilling of additional wells there would be a reasonable expectation of profit to the lessee. Under such circumstances, the lessee's obligation as to development is measured by the rule of reasonable diligence or what an ordinarily prudent and diligent operator would do, and he is not required to continue in the performance of these duties or to engage in the performance of such implied duties unless there is a reasonable expectation of profit, not only to the lessor, but also to the lessee. Texas Pacific Coal & Oil Co. v. Barker, 117 Texas 418, 6 S.W.2d 1031, 60 A.L.R. 936; Brewster v. Lanyon Zinc Co., 140 Fed. 801 (8th Cir.); Rhoads Drilling Co. v. Allred, 123 Texas 229, 70 S.W.2d 576.

This Court in the case of Texas Pacific Coal & Oil Co. v. Barker, supra, quoted with approval the holding in the case of Brewster v. Lanyon Zinc Co., supra, wherein the Court said:

> "The large expense incident to the work of exploration and development, and the fact that the lessee must bear the loss if the operations are not successful, require that he proceed with due regard to his own interests, as well as those of the lessor. No obligation rests on him to carry the operations beyond the point where they will be profitable to him, even if some benefit to the lessor will result from them. It is only to the end that the oil and gas shall be extracted with benefit or profit to both that reasonable diligence is required."

However, it should be noted that we do not have a factual situation where the lease covers several thousand acres and an effort is being made to hold such vast acreage by showing production from a comparatively small area. Neither are we confronted with a situation where an unreasonably long length of time has elapsed since the last development of the leased premises. Therefore, we do not pass upon these questions.

(10) We turn now to the holding of the trial court that the working-interest owners impliedly covenanted to further explore the land for other reservoirs and formations, and that such implied covenant was violated, and that

such violations obligated the respondents to drill a second or additional well. Petitioners contend that there is an implied covenant to explore as distinguished from the implied covenant to conduct additional development after production is once obtained. Petitioners argue that there is a distinction between development and exploration. They urge this Court to approve of the holding in the case of Willingham v. Bryson, Texas Civ.App., 294 S.W.2d 421, no writ history, wherein an implied covenant of exploration as opposed to the implied covenant of development was adopted. We do not believe this case to be authoritative or in harmony with the rule announced in the Texas cases. Our examination of the Texas cases reveals that the corpus of the oil and gas law, as it has developed, treats the covenant of development as covering all additional drilling requirements after production is once obtained on the lease, except those for protection from offset wells which are draining the premises.

The issue in Willingham v. Bryson, supra, was whether there is an implied covenant to "explore" as distinguished from the covenant to "develop", and if there be such a covenant, what is the lessor's burden to show that he is entitled to further exploration or to a cancellation. The court held that there is an "implied covenant reasonably to explore a lease after production has been obtained" as distinguished from the covenant reasonably to develop. The court continues by stating that it is not necessary for the lessor to prove that additional drilling would probably result in profit, but that the prudent operator rule was satisfied by a showing that no well had been drilled to a deeper sand, "coupled with the testimony of one witness that he would be willing to drill another well."

The Court of Civil Appeals in the Willingham case, supra, cites the case of Sauder v. Mid-Continent Petroleum Corporation, 292 U.S. 272, 54 S.Ct. 671, 78 L.Ed. 1255, 93 A.L.R. 454, in support of its theory of the existence of a covenant to explore. However, the court in the Willingham case makes no reference to the clearly stated issue in the Sauder case, at page 278 of the opinion.

"The question for decision is whether the respondent failed to comply with an implied covenant to develop the tract with reasonable diligence."

The court did not treat exploration as a separate covenant, but instead followed the basic theory in the case of Brewster v. Lanyon, supra. The latter case dealt solely with the development covenant. In addition, the court in the Sauder case, justifies its holding upon the peculiar circumstances surrounding the drilling on the disputed lease where drilling had been so long delayed.

(11) We hold that there is no implied covenant to explore as distinguished from the implied covenant to conduct additional development after production in paying quantities has been obtained. Petitioners argue that the lease involved *expressly* provides for exploration. We agree that, under the terms of the lease, the lessee has the right to explore, but it does not necessarily follow that the lessee is under a duty to explore. To follow petitioners' argument would be to adopt the theory advanced in their "Outline of Argument", filed in this Court, that "In an oil and gas lease, the implied covenant reasonably to explore obligates the lessee to drill when a ready, able and willing operator would drill regardless of the certainty of profit." In support of this theory the petitioners cite the case of Willingham v. Bryson, supra, and Meyers, "The Implied Covenant of Further Exploration", 34 Texas Law Rev. 553. This theory is untenable and is diametrically opposed to our established "prudent operator" rule where expectation of profit is an essential element. See Texas Pacific Coal & Oil Co. v. Barker, supra. We decline to follow the theory advanced that there is an implied covenant to explore as distinguished from the implied covenant to develop. There being no implied covenant to explore, the respondents were under no duty to drill a second or additional well, as found by the trial court.

The judgment of the Court of Civil Appeals is affirmed.

Commentary on Lillie M. Clifton et al. v. R. W. Koontz et al.

by Stuart C. Hollimon

Clifton v. Koontz, 325 S.W.2d 684 (Tex. 1959), is a landmark case on two issues — the meaning of production in paying quantities in the context of the habendum clause of an oil and gas lease, and whether or not Texas recognizes a separate implied covenant for further exploration.

Clifton v. Koontz concerned a 1940 oil and gas lease with a primary term of 10 years, covering 350 acres of land in Wise County. In 1949, the lessee drilled a well that produced gas and a small amount of oil, but the well was never very profitable after the first two or three years. Over a period of years, ownership of the lease had become broken up into fractional interests. Koontz, who had been employed by the lessees, saw potential in the well. In the summer and fall of 1956, he acquired and consolidated ownership of the lease for the purpose of attempting to increase production by reworking the well and seeking to change the classification of the well in order to qualify for a higher allowable from the Railroad Commission. He obtained the reclassification of the well and performed the reworking operations in late September and early October of 1956. His efforts were extremely successful, resulting in an 1800 percent increase in production.

Shortly before Koontz reworked the well, Charles Kadane, who operated adjoining land, completed a successful well to the same producing formation. Encouraged by his success, Kadane entered into a contract with Mrs. Clifton to drill a well on her land if the existing lease were cancelled. In August of 1956, Mrs. Clifton, joined by Kadane, filed suit against Koontz for that purpose. The lawsuit claimed:

> (1) that the lease had terminated for cessation of production in paying quantities; (2) that the lessee had breached its implied covenant to reasonably develop the lease; and (3) that the lessee had breached a separate implied covenant to further explore the lease by failing to drill test wells penetrating formations deeper than the one in which the existing well was completed. The suit sought damages and cancellation of the lease.

Finding that damages had not been proved with adequate certainty, the trial court denied recovery of damages, but found that Koontz had breached the implied covenants to reasonably develop and reasonably explore the lease. On that basis, the court conditionally granted forfeiture of the lease, except as to the producing formation, unless Koontz drilled a well to a depth below that formation within sixty days from the date of the judgment.

Disposition of the development claim on appeal was unremarkable — simply stated, there was no evidence that a prudent operator would drill an additional well into the producing formation with an expectation of profit, and the damages attributable to the lessee's failure to rework the existing well sooner were too speculative to be ascertained. But the other two claims — alleging cessation of production in paying quantities and breach of an implied covenant to further explore the lease — both resulted in landmark rulings by the Supreme Court.

Production in Paying Quantities

The habendum clause of the lease in *Clifton v. Koontz* provided that the lease could be extended beyond its 10-year primary term by production. The lease also contained a 60-day clause under which the lease would remain in force despite a cessation of production if, within sixty days after the cessation, the lessee commenced additional drilling or reworking operations. The habendum clause did not expressly provide that production must be "in paying quantities" in order to hold the lease beyond the expiration of the primary term. But the Supreme Court had already considered a similarly worded habendum clause in *Garcia v. King*, 164 S.W.2d 509 (Tex. 1942) and had held that, in the habendum clause, the term "produced" means "produced in paying quantities." *Id.* at 510-11. *Garcia* also recognized that "if a well pays a profit, even small, over operating expenses, it produces in paying quantities, though it may never repay its costs, and the enterprise as a whole may prove unprofitable." *Id.* at 511.

While *Garcia* established that "production" means "production in paying quantities," and that this requires at least a small profit over operating expenses, it left many questions unanswered. For example, *Garcia* did not address what time period is used to measure production in paying quantities, or the relationship between the requirement for production in paying quantities and other savings clauses, such as the 60-day clause. *Clifton v. Koontz* earned landmark status on the issue of production in paying quantities by answering many of the questions left open by *Garcia*.

Factual differences between the two cases help explain why the Supreme Court in *Clifton v. Koontz* found it necessary to go beyond the issues decided in *Garcia*. For a continuous period of eight months — beginning approximately three months before the end of the primary term, and continuing for five months after the primary term — the lease in *Garcia* did not produce in paying quantities because the lessee's entire seven-eighths share of the production was taken by a contract operator as compensation. Despite receiving none of the income, the lessee continued to pay taxes and incur other expenses during that eight-month period, so rather than paying a profit, however small, to the lessee during that period, the lease was operating at a loss from the lessee's perspective. Under those circumstances, it was relatively easy to conclude that the lease was not producing in paying quantities.

The issue was far less clear-cut in *Clifton v. Koontz*. Prior to reclassification of the well and Koontz's completion of the reworking operations, the lease had either been barely profitable or was operated at a slight loss, depending upon the period examined. Clifton's contention that the well had ceased to produce in paying quantities was based upon the sixteen-month period from June 1955 through September 1956, during which the income from the lease was $3,250 and the total expense of operations was $3,466.16, resulting in a loss of $216.16 for the period. Despite this slight loss over that sixteen-month period taken as a whole, the well's performance was not consistently unprofitable at all times during that period. Instead, a month or two of profitable operations would be followed by a month or two of losses.

Several factors contributed to that pattern. For one thing, the gas allowable was so low that the oil production, which fluctuated from month to month, made the difference between operating at a profit or at a loss. Also, it took two or three months to accumulate sufficient oil for sale, so there were profits in months when the oil was sold, and losses while the oil was being produced and stored. Finally, in the months preceding the reworking operations, Koontz saved oil for use in those operations, so there were losses in those months.

The Supreme Court began its analysis of the "paying production" issue by holding that, due to the effect of the 60-day clause, the last two months of the sixteen-month period that Clifton identified as being unprofitable should not be included in determining profitability. The Court explained that after a cessation of production in paying quantities, the lessee had a 60-day "grace" period in which to save his leasehold by commencing drilling or reworking operations. 325 S.W.2d at 690. Koontz began his reworking operations on September 12, 1956, so the Court concluded that the controlling issue was whether there had been a cessation of production in paying quantities through July 12, 1956, which was the date sixty days prior to commencement of the reworking operations. The existence of a small operating loss between July 12 and September 12 was not controlling in determining whether there had been a cessation of production in paying quantities through July 12. *Id*. at 689.

Considering only the evidence relevant to production prior to July 12, 1956, the Court found that the lease operated at a small profit for the period from June 1955 through July 12, 1956. *Id*. at 689. That finding was not the end of the story, however, because, due to the factors already noted, there were periods of operating losses between June 1955 and July 12, 1956, even though there was an aggregate profit for the period. Due to this see-saw pattern of profitable and unprofitable periods, the Court took a closer look at the rules for determining whether a marginal property is producing in paying quantities, including the relevant period for measuring whether a lease has ceased to produce in paying quantities, and the types of factors to be taken into account when making that determination.

While *Garcia* established that a well is producing in paying quantities if it pays even a small profit over operating expenses, *Clifton v. Koontz* established that failure to produce a profit for a period of time does not necessarily mean that there has been a cessation of production such that the lease should be terminated. Instead, under these circumstances, a court should determine whether a reasonably prudent operator would continue to operate the well for the purpose of making a profit. The Court explained this as follows:

> In the case of a marginal well, such as we have here, the standard by which paying quantities is determined is whether or not under all the relevant circumstances a reasonably prudent operator would, for the purpose of making a profit and not merely for speculation, continue to operate a well in the manner in which the well in question was operated.
>
> In determining paying quantities, in accordance with the above standard, the trial court necessarily must take into consideration all matters which would influence a reasonable and prudent operator. Some of the factors are: The depletion of the reservoir and the price for which the lessee is able to sell his produce, the relative profitableness of other wells in the area, the operating and marketing costs of the lease, his net profit, the lease provisions, a reasonable period of time under the circumstances, and whether or not the lessee is holding the lease merely for speculative purposes.

325 S.W.2d at 691. Other relevant factors that the Court identified were the ability to market the production at a profit and applicable proration rules. The Court held, however, that depreciation of the original capital investment

should not be treated as an operating cost in determining whether production from the lease is sufficient to yield a return in excess of operating and marketing costs. The Court reasoned that "depreciation is nothing more than an accounting charge of money spent in purchasing tangible property, and if the investment itself is not to be considered, as is held by this Court, then neither is depreciation." *Id.* at 692. The Court expressly reserved judgment on whether depreciation on producing equipment should be treated as an operating cost because the case did not present that issue. The Court resolved that issue three years later in *Skelly Oil Co. v. Archer*, 356 S.W.2d 774, 781 (Tex. 1962), holding that depreciation on salvable producing equipment, which was not a part of the original drilling and completion expense, should be treated as an operating cost in determining whether there is production in paying quantities.

On the income side of the test balancing income against expenses, the Court held that the entire income attributable to the working interest created by the lease, including amounts paid under overriding royalties carved out of that interest, is to be considered in determining whether production is being obtained in paying quantities. 325 S.W.2d at 692-93.

Rather than identify a time period within which this determination must be made, the Court concluded that there can be no arbitrary period for determining the question of whether or not a lease has terminated due to a cessation of production in paying quantities. *Id.* at 690. Thus, how long a prudent operator would continue to hold the lease under the circumstances for the purpose of making a profit is one of the factors that must be considered.

Taken together, *Garcia* and *Clifton v. Koontz* establish a two-part test for determining whether there has been a cessation of production in paying quantities. If the income from production exceeds operating and marketing costs, even slightly, then the first part of the test is satisfied and the lease survives. If, however, the lessee is not realizing any profit, then the second part of the test becomes applicable, and the court must determine whether a reasonable prudent operator would continue to operate the lease under the circumstances. The party seeking to terminate the lease has the burden on both parts of the test. That is, the party seeking termination must prove that the lessee is not making a profit, and if that burden is met, then that party must make a further showing that a reasonable prudent operator would not continue to operate the lease under the circumstances. *Skelly Oil Co. v. Archer*, 356 S.W.2d 774, 783 (Tex. 1962) (op. on rehg.).

Subsequent cases have clarified that this two-part test does not apply if there has been a total cessation of physical production for the period specified in the cessation-of-production clause of the lease. Under those circumstances, the lease automatically terminates, without regard to whether a reasonable prudent operator would continue to hold it, unless drilling, reworking, or other types of operations contemplated by the lease are commenced before the expiration of specified period. *Brown v. Reeter*, 170 S.W.3d 151, 155 (Tex. App.—Eastland 2005, no pet.); *Ridenour v. Herrington*, 47 S.W.3d 117, 122 (Tex. App.—Waco 2001, pet. denied); *Bachler v. Rosenthal*, 798 S.W.2d 646, 650 (Tex. App.—Austin 1990, writ denied).

Implied Covenant to Further Explore the Lease

The other issue on which *Clifton v. Koontz* holds landmark status is whether or not Texas recognizes a separate implied covenant for further exploration. Texas law on the issue was unsettled prior to *Clifton v. Koontz*. The earlier cases that had considered the issue can best be described as a hodge-podge of inconsistent cases reaching every conceivable conclusion on the issue. The Williams and Meyers treatise suggests that the Texas cases on the issue prior to *Clifton v. Koontz* fell into five general categories: (1) a case that seems to repudiate an obligation to explore; (2) cases in which the facts seem to raise the issue of further exploration, but which deny relief due to lack of proof of probable paying production without expressly discussing the issue of further exploration; (3) further exploration cases that refuse to award the remedy of absolute lease cancellation, but which stop short of either expressly recognizing or expressly repudiating the exploration covenant; (4) cases that arguably recognize an implied covenant to explore, without requiring proof of probable paying production; and (5) *Willingham v. Bryson*, 294 S.W.2d 421 (Tex. Civ. App.—Fort Worth 1956, no writ), which expressly held that there is an implied covenant of further reasonable exploration, and that proof that additional drilling would probably result in a profit is not required to establish a breach of the covenant. These five categories of cases, with citations, are discussed more fully at 5 Williams & Meyers Oil and Gas Law § 845.6.

Of the exploration covenant cases decided prior to *Clifton v. Koontz, Willingham*, which pre-dated *Clifton v. Koontz* by only a couple of years, is the one that addressed the issue in the most unequivocal terms. The Supreme Court discussed *Willingham* at some length in *Clifton v. Koontz* and summarized the key holdings in *Willingham* as follows:

The issue in *Willingham v. Bryson, supra*, was whether there is an implied covenant to "explore" as distinguished from the covenant to "develop," and if there be such a covenant, what is the lessor's burden to show that he is entitled to further exploration or to cancellation. The court held that there is an "[implied] covenant reasonably to explore a lease after production has been obtained" as distinguished from the covenant reasonably to develop. The court continues by stating that it is not necessary for the lessor to prove that additional drilling would probably result in profit, but that the prudent operator rule was satisfied by a showing that no well had been drilled to a deeper sand, "coupled with the testimony of one witness that he would be willing to drill another well."

325 S.W.2d at 696. The Court then squarely rejected each of the principal *Willingham* holdings. On the existence of a separate implied covenant to explore, the Supreme Court said: "We hold that there is no implied covenant to explore as distinguished from the implied covenant to conduct additional development after production in paying quantities has been obtained." *Id*. The Court concluded that, once production is obtained, the development covenant covers all additional drilling requirements, with the exception of the lessee's obligation to protect the lease against drainage. *Id*.

On the other key holding in *Willingham*, the Court in *Clifton v. Koontz* rejected the proposition that under the implied covenant to explore, the lessee must drill when a ready, able, and willing operator would drill, regardless of the certainty of profit. The Court concluded that this proposition "is untenable and is diametrically opposed to our established 'prudent operator' rule where expectation of profit is an essential element." 325 S.W.2d at 696. The Court explained the burden of proof on that element as follows:

> While it is true that each separate stratum or horizon would be entitled to separate development, yet it is equally true that the burden rests upon the lessor to prove that the producing stratum required additional wells, or that strata different from that from which production is being obtained, in reasonable probability exist, and that by the drilling of additional wells there would be a reasonable expectation of profit to the lessee. Under such circumstances, the lessee's obligation as to development is measured by the rule of reasonable diligence or what an ordinarily prudent and diligent operator would do, and he is not required to continue in the performance of these duties or to engage in the performance of such implied duties unless there is a reasonable expectation of profit, not only to the lessor, but also to the lessee.

Id. at 695. Despite these clear holdings on the absence of a separate exploration covenant and on the requirement for proof of an expectation of profit, one brief passage in *Clifton v. Koontz* seemed to leave the door open to proof of a breach of the development covenant based on a failure to explore, without requiring proof of a reasonable expectation of profit, if a large lease was being held by production from a small area. In that passage, the Court said:

> However, it should be noted that we do not have a factual situation where the lease covers several thousand acres and an effort is being made to hold such vast acreage by showing production from a comparatively small area. Neither are we confronted with a situation where an unreasonably long length of time has elapsed since the last development of the leased premises. Therefore, we do not pass upon these questions.

Id. at 696. In *Sinclair Oil & Gas Co. v. Masterson*, 271 F.2d 310 (5th Cir. 1959), the Fifth Circuit relied upon this language in affirming a trial court judgment that ordered conditional cancellation of unexplored portions of a 90,000-acre lease unless a specified number of additional wells were drilled annually, even though there was no proof that the drilling could be done with a reasonable expectation of profit.

In the nearly fifty years since *Clifton v. Koontz* and *Masterson* were decided, however, Texas state courts have not followed *Masterson* in recognizing any such large lease "exception" under *Clifton v. Koontz*; and, with the passage of time, it seems increasingly doubtful whether any such exception actually exists. In *Felmont Oil Corp. v. Pan American Petroleum Corp.*, 334 S.W.2d 449 (Tex. Civ. App.—El Paso 1960, writ ref'd n.r.e.), which was decided less than a year after both *Clifton v. Koontz* and *Masterson*, the court refused to grant relief to a lessor who showed that only a small portion of a 31,000-acre lease had been developed, but who failed to show that other portions of the lease could be explored with a reasonable expectation of profit. In reaching that result, the court concluded that *Masterson* failed to either follow *Clifton v. Koontz* or adequately distinguish it.

Thirty-one years after the decision in *Clifton v. Koontz*, the Supreme Court in *Sun Exploration & Prod. Co v. Jackson*, 783 S.W.2d 202 (Tex. 1989), had an opportunity to clarify whether *Clifton v. Koontz* required development of unexplored portions of a large lease without requiring proof of a reasonable expectation of profit, but the Court's opinion is silent on that issue. The decision in Jackson concerned a 10,000-acre lease on which only the Oyster

Bayou Field, which was confined to a 1,100-acre portion of the lease, had been developed. The *Jacksons* contended that Sun had neglected to explore and develop the larger remaining part of the lease. Based upon jury findings that Sun had not failed to reasonably develop the lease, but had failed to reasonably explore the portions of the lease that were outside the Oyster Bayou Field, the trial court rendered a judgment for the Jacksons that: (1) unconditionally cancelled the portion of the lease on which Sun had not drilled; and (2) conditionally cancelled the lease below the depth to which Sun had drilled in the smaller developed area. The court of appeals affirmed the unconditional cancellation and reversed and remanded as to the conditional cancellation. *Sun Exploration & Production Co v. Jackson*, 715 S.W.2d 199 (Tex. App.—Houston [1st Dist.] 1986).

In reversing the judgment of the court of appeals, the Supreme Court reaffirmed the holdings in *Clifton v. Koontz* that no implied covenant of further exploration exists independent of the implied covenant of reasonable development, that the covenant of reasonable development encompasses the drilling of all additional wells after production on the lease is achieved, and that the critical question is whether the lessor can prove a reasonable expectation of profit to the lessor and the lessee. 783 S.W.2d at 204. Based upon those principles, the Court held that the jury finding that Sun had not failed to reasonably develop the lease was dispositive of the case. Even though, factually, *Sun v. Jackson* involved a large lease that was being held by production from a comparatively small area, the Court's opinion does not suggest that any different burden of proof should be applied under such circumstances. *Sun v. Jackson* therefore reinforces the principal holdings in *Clifton v. Koontz*, and in doing so it casts further doubt on whether vast acreage held by production from a comparatively small area should be treated any differently.

Conclusion

Clifton v. Koontz would be deserving of recognition as a landmark case if the only issue that it resolved had been the meaning of production in paying quantities in the context of the habendum clause of an oil and gas lease. It would be equally deserving of such recognition if the only issue that it resolved had been that Texas does not recognize an implied covenant of further exploration independent of the implied covenant of reasonable development and that proof of a breach of such covenant requires proof of a reasonable expectation of profit. But *Clifton v. Koontz* resolved both of those issues, and it did so in such decisive terms that very little clarification or refinement has been required on either point. It therefore continues to stand as the definitive authority on each of those issues

CHAPTER 9

Atlantic Refining Company et al., Appellants, v. Railroad Commission of Texas et al., Appellees.

9

COMMENTARY

by H. Philip "Flip" Whitworth

162 Tex. 274, 346 S.W.2d 801

1961

Atlantic Refining Company et al., Appellants,
v.
Railroad Commission of Texas et al., Appellees.

162 Tex. 274, 346 S.W.2d 801

1961

MR. JUSTICE HAMILTON delivered the opinion to the court.

This suit was brought in the 98th District Court of Travis County by The Atlantic Refining Company, Tidewater Oil Company, Mrs. James R. Dougherty, a widow, Dudley T. Dougherty, Rachael D. Vaughan and husband, Ben F. Vaughan, Jr., and May D. Carr, a widow, hereinafter collectively referred to as appellants, to annul an order of the Railroad Commission of Texas, hereinafter called the Commission, prorating gas and condensate production from the Slick, Luling and First Massive pay zones among wells in the Normanna Gas Field, Bee County. On December 16, 1957, field rules were enacted for the Slick, Luling and Second Massive pay zones in the Normanna Field. At a second hearing on February 26, 1958, field rules were adopted for the First Massive pay zone in said field. Atlantic at both of these hearings protested the adoption of the 1/3-2/3 rule, and introduced the same evidence at both hearings, except at the first hearing the First Massive was not shown to be productive. Said field rules included a proration formula for production in said field on the basis of 1/3 per well and 2/3 according to the amount of acreage. Specific complaint was made of such order in so far as it allows the production of gas, including the liquid content thereof, or the condensate, from a well drilled by Bright & Schiff, a partnership, hereinafter called appellee, on a lot in the Normanna Town site 79 feet wide and 130 feet long. Although this tract contains something less than 3/10 of an acre, it will be referred to hereinafter as the .3-acre tract, or the "Town Lot." W. G. Darsey, Jr., Joe T. Darsey and Walter R. Koch intervened in this suit and assumed the status of defendants.

Trial was to the court without a jury. Subsequent to judgment being entered for appellees, the following finding of fact was filed:

> "Production of gas and condensate from the well drilled by defendant Bright & Schiff upon its lease containing approximately .3 acre under the rules of defendant Railroad Commission of Texas prorating the production of gas from the reservoirs in the Normanna Field, Bee County, Texas, will result in the drainage of a tremendous quantity of gas and condensate from other leases and tracts in the field, including leases and tracts in which plaintiffs own an interest, to said .3 acre lease, the precise amount of said drainage being incapable of ascertainment; and said drainage will not be compensated by drainage of gas and condensate from said lease containing approximately .3 acre to said other leases and tracts in the field, including leases and tracts in which plaintiffs own an interest."

Among the conclusions of law filed by the court is the following:

> "2. Under the rule of unlimited right of capture laid down in *Ryan Consolidated Petroleum Corp. v. Pickens* 285 S.W.2d 201, the orders of defendant Railroad Commission of Texas complained of by plaintiffs are not invalid, even though production of gas and condensate under said orders will result in the uncompensated drainage of a tremendous quantity of gas and condensate from other leases and tracts in the Normanna Field, including leases and tracts in which plaintiffs own an interest, to the .3 acre lease upon which defendant Bright & Schiff has drilled its well."

A direct appeal from the adverse judgment holding the Commission's order valid and denying the plaintiffs the injunctive relief prayed for was brought to this court under Article 1738a, V.A.C.S., and Rule 499a, T.R.C.P. We hold that the order complained of is invalid.

In establishing the spacing pattern for the Normanna Field, it was determined that one gas well could reasonably drain 320 acres, and the Railroad Commission established a 320-acre spacing pattern in accordance with that determination. This spacing pattern is not at issue in this action.

Appellee Bright & Schiff applied for a permit to drill a well on its .3-acre tract under exception to Rule 37 on the ground that it was necessary to prevent confiscation of the oil and gas in and under its tract of land. On that ground the Railroad Commission granted the permit. There was expert testimony presented by appellant to the effect that a reasonable estimate of the value of gas in place under said tract was $7,000, and that if appellee Bright & Schiff is allowed to produce a well under this order some two and one-half million dollars' worth of gas will be produced in twenty years, the estimated life of the field. Such evidence further showed that this order will allow said well to produce at a rate of over 200 times as much gas per acre as a well on the 320-acre unit would produce.

The 1/3-2/3 formula means that 1/3 of the total field allowable must be divided equally among all the wells in the field and that 2/3 of the total field allowable will be divided among all the wells on a per acreage basis. Under this formula a well on a .3-acre tract would be allowed to produce many times more gas per acre than would a well on a 320-acre tract be allowed to produce. The Railroad Commission introduced no evidence at the trial. Appellee Bright & Schiff used two expert witnesses. The substance of their testimony was that there were not enough known facts available on which to base an estimate of the total field reserves in the Slick, Luling and First Massive sands, the three pay zones in the Normanna Field which are here involved, and the reserves under the Bright & Schiff tract. Both of appellants' expert witnesses and both of Bright & Schiff's expert witnesses testified that the extent of the field to the south had not been determined, and based partly upon this fact appellee's witnesses said that the total field reserves could not be determined. Appellants' witnesses from the known facts estimated what in their opinion would be the extent of the field, and based on their estimate of the size of the field determined the total field reserves, using the volumetric method. This is a complicated formula which takes into consideration various factors such as porosity, connate water, pressure, condensate within the given volume of gas samples, abandonment pressure, productive acre feet, etc. Appellee's witnesses testified that there were not enough wells drilled and the wells had not produced long enough to furnish the information for this system to be accurate. They contend that too many assumptions had to be made to fill in for the unknown factors. For instance, appellants' witnesses estimated reserves under the Bright & Schiff town lot by assuming that a well on that tract would be an average well. There was no testimony at the trial as to what kind of well Bright & Schiff made on their tract. The well had not been drilled at the time of the Railroad Commission hearings, but it had been drilled at the time of the trial, and appellee did not choose to introduce any evidence as to whether said well was as good as an average well in the field. Appellee's witnesses do not say that the calculations made by appellants' witneses of a $7,000 value of gas in place under the Bright & Schiff town lot are incorrect, but say that from the evidence introduced at the trial an estimate of such reserves could not be made. They do not say that the estimate of $2,500,000 value of the gas which will be produced by Bright & Schiff under the 1/3-2/3 formula in twenty years is incorrect, but that it is not sufficient data upon which to base such estimate. Appellee's witnesses made no estimate whatsoever of the field reserves and made no estimate of reserves in place under the town lot well. There was no evidence introduced which would show that the town lot had any more gas per acre under it than was on the average under the other tracts in the reservoir. It appears from the record that whether the estimate of the field reserves made by appellants' witnesses was over estimated or under estimated, that there is not the slightest doubt but what there would be enormous drainage from the other tracts in the field, including those of appellants, to the Bright & Schiff tract under the 1/3-2/3 proration formula.

The statute which gives the Railroad Commission authority to regulate gas fields is Article 6008, V.A.C.S. The following is the substance of the sections of said act which are here pertinent:

> Section 1 of said article states that the purpose of the act is to protect public and private interests against certain evils by prohibiting waste and compelling ratable production.
>
> Section 10 enjoins the Commission to so regulate production as to prevent waste and adjust correlative rights.
>
> Section 11 provides that the Commission shall exercise its authority to prevent waste when the presence of waste or imminence of waste is found, and shall exercise its authority to adjust correlative rights when the market demand for gas is exceeded by the capacity of the wells to produce gas from any reservoir.
>
> Section 12 provides that when the Commission has determined that conditions in a gas reservoir exist which give it authority to regulate, then it shall proceed to regulate and prorate the gas production in such reservoir on a reasonable basis, and that the allowable allocated to each well shall be such as to give each well its fair share of the gas to be produced from such reservoir.

> Section 13 provides that the Commission shall, in determining the allowable production for each well, take into consideration the size of the tract on which the well is located and the daily producing capacity of the well and "all other factors which are pertinent."
>
> ection 15 provides that nothing contained in the article shall require the Commission to fix the allowable for any well below 50,000 feet per day, provided said well has a producing capacity of 200,000 feet or more, and not less then 25% of its open natural flow when it is less than 200,000 feet per day.
>
> Section 22 provides that the Commission shall have broad powers to effectuate the provisions and purposes of the act.

Appellants maintain that the proration rule adopted by the Railroad Commission, viewed in the light of the substantial evidence rule, is unreasonable, arbitrary and confiscatory, and does not allow appellants to produce their fair share of the gas from the reservoir, and for this reason the order should be declared invalid and that its enforcement should be enjoined. Appellee contends in effect that the Railroad Commission can take into account what a .3-acre tract could have produced under the rule of capture before conservation laws restricted drilling and production in fixing a proration formula, and even though such formula results in an enormous drainage from the larger tracts to the small tract, the order is valid.

Appellants, in support of their contention that the Commission, in adjusting correlative rights in a gas field which it has undertaken to regulate, is required to so prorate as to prevent substantial drainage from one tract to another, cite the case of Corzelius v. Harrell, 179 S.W.2d 419, in which the Supreme Court granted writ of error, but dismissed it as moot, 143 Tex. 509, 186 S.W.2d 961. In that case Harrell owned about 94.8 per cent of the gas reserves in the Bammell Field, and Corzelius owned about 4.1 per cent thereof. Harrell was cycling gas, that is, was producing about 35 million cubic feet of gas per day from his leases, was extracting the liquid content therefrom, and was injecting the remaining dry gas, about 33 million cubic feet, into the reservoir from which it had been produced. As the result of this cycling operation Harrell was drying up the wet gas reserves beneath the lease owned by Corzelius. Corzelius, on the other hand, was producing between four and five million cubic feet of gas per day from his lease, and was transporting this gas to an industrial fuel market in the City of Houston. Harrell had requested the Commission to prorate production of gas as required by Article 6008, V.A.C.S. The court held that the Commission was under the duty of fairly prorating gas production as between Harrell and Corzelius, not only the gas in the reservoir, but the liquid content thereof. In discussing this situation the court said:

> "The record shows that Corzelius is producing by volume in excess of his fair share of the total net volume allowable from the field, and to that extent is creating a local net drainage, by volume, from Harrell's holdings. Harrell, on the other hand, though withdrawing by net volume only 2 MMCF daily, is processing 35 MMCF, extracting therefrom the valuable liquids, and is already reducing (draining) the liquid content of the gas from Corzelius' holdings. Corzelius is entitled to produce his fair share of the recoverable liquids, as well as his fair share of the volume of recoverable gas. Thus each is draining from the other's holdings, though of different elements of the total gas content." [179 S.W.2d 425]

The court goes on to hold that it was the duty of the Railroad Commission to prorate production from the reservoir in question so that Corzelius' operations would not drain from Harrell's holdings, and that Harrell's operations would not drain from Corzelius' holdings. In support of its holding in the Corzelius case the court cited and quoted extensively from Henderson v. Terrell, D.C., 24 Fed. Supp. 147. That case involved an order of the Railroad Commission of Texas prorating the production of sour gas for carbon black in the West Panhandle Field and involved the construction of Article 6008a, V.A.C.S., which directed the Commission to so allocate production between wells as to prevent cognizable and preventable drainage of gas from tracts of land in sour gas producing areas. However, the court in the Harrell case construed that opinion as being applicable to the situation here, where the Commission is required by said Article 6008 to allocate production between the wells so as to allocate to each well its fair share of gas from the reservoir. The court quoted with approval the following from the opinion in Henderson v. Terrell:

> "We think the statute is simply and clearly phrased to give effect to a public policy, and to exercise the police power in respect to matters which the courts of Texas and of the United

> States uniformly hold it is the right of the state by statute, to control. This right extends to preventing one person from unduly draining from under the lands of another, oil and gas lying in a common pool equally when the undue drainage is for wasteful uses, and when the rule of capture no longer applying, because of lawful statutory limitation, one of the owners, by drawing more than his due proportion of the limited share, is draining the lands of his co-owners.
>
> "We find nothing unreasonable in the statute, nothing unreasonable in the orders. For all that the statute does, all that the orders do, is to make limitation and prorartion effective by putting an end to an existing unreasonable drainage condition, and preventing its continuance in the future. Neither the statute nor the order operates retrospectively, either punitively or reparatively; both operate prospectively. So operating, they merely say to plaintiffs 'you may produce from your wells of the total amount limited in a due proportion with every other well in the field. You may not produce more.'"

After this quotation the Court of Civil Appeals said in the Corzelius case: "The decision in that case (Henderson v. Terrell) rests, in our opinion, upon sound and well-established legal doctrine which controls the issues in the instant case." [179 S.W.2d 425]

While the Supreme Court granted a writ of error in the Corzelius case and dismissed it as moot in [143 Texas 50a] 186 S.W.2d 961, the opinion of the Supreme Court did not in any way disturb the holding of the Court of Civil Appeals. It appears that at the time the Supreme Court passed on the matter a new and different order had been entered by the Railroad Commission and the order passed on by the Court of Civil Appeals was not then in effect. However, the Supreme Court, in Corzelius v. Harrell, 143 Texas 509, 186 S.W.2d 961, at p. 968, did have this to say:

> "To adjust correlative rights' [SIC] the Commission is authorized by this law to consider many items that relate to the production of gas, and it further provides that the Commission shall consider 'all other factors which are pertinent.' The courts have frequently sustained the exception to Rule 37 'to prevent confiscation of property', (originally 'to protect vested rights'). The criterion fixed by the Legislature relating to the adjustment of correlative rights is as definite as that fixed by law to authorize the Commission 'to prevent confiscation of property' under Rule 37. Trapp v. Atlantic Refining Co., Tex.Civ.App., 169 S.W.2d 797; Nash v. Shell Petroleum Corporation, Tex.Civ.App., 120 S.W.2d 522; Atlantic Oil Production Co. v. Railroad Commission, Tex.Civ.App., 85 S.W.2d 655; Gulf Land Co. v. Atlantic Refining Co., 134 Tex. 59, 131 S.W.2d 73."

Appellants also cite the case of Marrs v. Railroad Commission, 142 Texas 293, 177 S.W.2d 941, by this court. This was an oil proration case, but it involved the question of drainage such as we now have before us. The case was concerned with a proration order affecting the McElroy and Church Fields in Crane and Upton Counties, in Texas. The Church Field, which was initially considered to be separate from the McElroy Field, was densely drilled on a 10-acre pattern and was substantially depleted at the time proration became effective, only 15% of its original recoverable reserves remaining. The Inside McElroy, which was later discovered and was being drilled and developed on a spacing pattern of 17.8 acres, was revealed as connecting up the McElroy and Church Fields. At the time proration went into effect 80% of the recoverable reserves of the Inside McElroy Field remained in the ground. Prior to the effective date of proration, and to protect the Inside McElroy from drainage to wells in the Church Field area, the Gulf Oil Company drilled a tier of wells along its southern boundary which it permitted to flow at full capacity. However, under the restricted allowables established by the Commission this was no longer possible, and Gulf and Marrs asked the Commission to annul the proration order, which allowed the Church Field to produce almost as much as the McElroy, on the ground that the oil in place under their leases was being confiscated through uncompensated drainage to the Church Field. In setting aside the order, the court said:

> "Under the settled law of this State oil and gas form a part and parcel of the land wherein they tarry and belong to the owner of such land or his assigns (31 Tex.Jur. 518; Texas Co. v. Daugherty, 107 Tex. 226, 176 S.W. 717, L.R.A.1917F, 989; Stephens County v. Mid-Kansas Oil & Gas Co., 113 Tex. 160, 254 S.W. 290, 29 A.L.R. 566; Lemar v. Garner, 121 Tex. 502, 50 S.W.2d 769; Hager v. Stakes, 116 Tex. 453, 294 S.W. 835); and such owner has the right

> to mine such minerals subject to the conservation laws of this State. Every owner or lessee is entitled to a fair chance to recover the oil or gas in or under his land, or their equivalent in kind, and any denial of such fair chance amounts to confiscation. Gulf Land Co. v. Atlantic Ref. Co., 134 Tex. 59, 131 S.W.2d 73; Railroad Commission of Texas et al. v. Gulf Production Co., 134 Tex. 122, 125, 132 S.W.2d 254.
>
> "Under the findings of the trial court the allowables as fixed by the Railroad Commission for the two areas are entirely out of proportion to the potentials thereof. They are not in proportion to the oil under the different areas. It is very evident that petitioners are not being permitted to mine their just proportion of the oil. There is several times as much oil underlying petitioners' land as there is under the land in the Church-Fields area, yet those in the Church-Fields area are being permitted to mine nearly as much oil as are petitioners. As the oil is taken from the depleted Church-Fields area it is replaced by oil drained from petitioners' property. If petitioners were free to fend for themselves they could mine the oil under their land and thus prevent its escape to the adjoining area. But the orders of the Railroad Commission here complained of prevent petitioners from so doing. As a result, petitioners are being forever deprived of their property. It is the taking of one man's property and the giving it to another."

Appellants also cite Brown v. Humble Oil & Refining Company, 126 Tex. 296, 83 S.W.2d 935, 99 A.L.R. 1107, which is a case involving the construction of Rule 37 and the exceptions thereto. In an exhaustive opinion holding invalid the Commission's order in granting a permit under exception to Rule 37 the court said:

> "Conditions may arise where it would be proper, right and just to grant exceptions to the rule so as to permit wells to be drilled on smaller tracts than prescribed therein. Also, conditions may arise where it would be proper, right and just to permit tracts to be subdivided and such subdivisions drilled after the adoption of the rule; but in all such instances it is the duty of the commission to adjust the allowable, based upon the potential production, so as to give to the owner of such smaller tract only his just proportion of the oil and gas. By this method each person will be entitled to recover a quantity of oil and gas substantially equivalent in amount to the recoverable oil and gas under his land. * * *
>
> "The commission, in order to prevent waste, has the power to limit the rate of flow in the same way that it has the power to regulate spacing. See Champlin Refining Co. v. Corporation Commission, 286 U.S. 210, 52 S.Ct. 559, 76 L.Ed. 1062, 86 A.L.R. 403; Danciger Oil & Refining Co. v. Railroad Commission (Tex.Civ.App.) 49 S.W.(2d) 837. This right to control the rate of flow in order to prevent waste also enables the commission to offset the advantage obtained by one who is given an exception to the spacing rule by limiting his allowable production to the extent necessary to overcome this advantage. In this way the commission, by controlling the oil stored in the common reservoir, is enabled to carry out the dominant purpose of preventing waste, and, at the same time, permit each owner to enjoy the opportunity fully to realize upon his estate by developing and recovering his oil and gas. * *"

In the case of Railroad Commission of Texas et al. v. Gulf Production Company, 134 Tex. 122, 132 S.W.2d 254, the question involved was the validity of a Railroad Commission order granting a permit under exception to Rule 37 which had been granted "to prevent the confiscation of property." The application was for a third well on a 4.77-acre tract. In holding that the order was invalid, this court said:

> "In the Gulf Land Company case, supra, [Gulf Land Company v. Atlantic Refining Company, 134 Tex. 59, 131 S.W.2d 73] we held that the term 'confiscation,' as used in Rule 37, refers principally to drainage. We also held that every owner or lessee is entitled to a fair chance to recover the oil or gas in or under his land, or their equivalents in kind, and that any denial of such fair chance would be confiscation. We still adhere to such holdings. We think it would follow from the above rule that when an owner or a lessee has been given a fair chance to recover his oil and gas, as above defined, he has received his legal rights in regard thereto. We think the opinion of the Court of Civil Appeals demonstrates that the facts of this record

> show, as a matter of law, that the two wells Tippett already has on this tract of land will protect him against confiscation, -that is, will insure him a fair chance to recover the oil and gas in and under his land, or their equivalents in kind. We think the opinion of the Court of Civil Appeals further demonstrates that the facts of this record show, as a matter of law, that a third well on this tract would enable Tippett to recover more than his fair share of the oil and gas in or under his land, or their equivalents in kind. Under such a record, the granting of this permit to prevent confiscation was an abuse of power on the part of the commission, and therefore unlawful."

In Magnolia Petroleum Co. v. Railroad Commission, 93 S.W.2d 587, writ refused, the court in considering Magnolia's right to drill an eleventh well on its tract said:

> "The right of each individual leaseholder extends no further than the opportunity to extract his fair share of the oil, measured by a reasonable approximation of the amount of oil in place under his leasehold."

In Atlantic Oil Production Co. v. Railroad Commission, 85 S.W.2d 655, writ dismissed, the court in considering the right of the operator to drill a third well on his tract said:

> "Appellee is entitled, and entitled only, to be accorded an equal opportunity with surrounding lessees to recover his fair share of the recoverable oil; or, stated differently, to recover the approximate amount of oil lying in place under his lease."

In addition to the case of Ryan Consolidated Petroleum Corporation v. Pickens, 155 Tex. 221, 285 S.W.2d 201, cited by the trial court in support of its judgment, the appellees rely principally upon the Hawkins Field case, Railroad Commission v. Humble Oil & Refining Co., 193 S.W.2d 824, writ refused, n. r. e., and the Yates Field case, Standard Oil Co. v. Railroad Commission, 215 S.W.2d 633, writ refused, n. r. e. The Ryan case was not a proration case. It was a contest between Ryan on the one hand and Pickens and Coffield on the other over the production from four lots in the Hawkins Townsite. These lots originally constituted a tract under single ownership, and were subdivided after Rule 37 became effective. Pickens acquired a lease on Lots 10 and 11 and Ryan on Lots 12 and 13. Both applied to the Commission for permits to drill on the four lots. The application of Pickens was granted and that of Ryan was denied. After considerable litigation over the validity of the permits Pickens' permit was upheld in court, and he drilled his well upon Lots 10 and 11. Ryan filed suit for equitable relief, alleging confiscation of the oil and gas under Lots 12 and 13 by Pickens and Coffield. The only issue presented in the court was that of "who was entitled to the production from the Pickens well". The court said:

> "Petitioner's contention that this case is one for equitable relief should not be sustained for the further reason that its position is inconsistent with the law of capture, which is a well-settled rule of property in this jurisdiction. The rule of capture is simply this-that the owner of a tract of land acquires title to the oil and gas which he produces from wells drilled thereon, though part of such oil or gas may have migrated from adjoining land. The Railroad Commission is without power from the Legislature or by decisions of this Court to do anything more than declare illegal the drilling of wells which are prohibited by Rule 37. The Railroad Commission cannot change the law of Texas. The Legislature of this State has heretofore conferred broad, extensive and exclusive regulatory powers upon the Railroad Commission of Texas in the regulation of the oil industry of this State, but the Commission has not been given the power to determine property rights as between litigants. The courts, whether sitting as court of law or equity, determine such matters in accordance with existing laws in Texas." [155 Tex. 221, 285 S.W.2d 207]

As can be determined from this language, the court defined "the rule of capture" in clear and unmistakable terms, and as defined "the rule of capture" is simply this: the owner of a tract of land acquires title to the oil which he produces from wells thereon, although part of such oil or gas may have migrated from the adjoining land. The permit to drill was granted for the four lots. Whichever one got the permit and drilled the well was entitled to all the oil produced. The court refused to recognize the voluntary subdivision of the lots after Rule 37. The court in its definition clearly followed the law as declared by the Commission of Appeals in Japhet v. McRae, 276 S.W. 669, in which the court said:

> "It seems to us that the only safe rule, and the only one free from much confusion, is one which gives the oil to the man who owns the land upon which the well is located."

The effect of the holding in this case was that Pickens and Coffield, having been granted the well permit for the four lots, could legally produce the oil under the four lots, and under "the rule of capture" as defined above they owned all of the oil produced from the well. Except for the voluntary segregation of Lots 10 and 11 from Lots 12 and 13 after Rule 37, Pickens and Coffield would not have had the exclusive right to produce the oil from under all four lots. Prior to Rule 37 Ryan could have drilled a well and produced oil from under Lots 12 and 13. It was the application of Rule 37 which gave Pickens and Coffield the right to produce such oil and not the rule of capture. It was, however, the rule of capture which prevented Ryan from collecting damages from Pickens and Coffield for the oil drained from beneath Ryan's lots.

In the case presently before the court The Atlantic Refining Company et al. are not seeking to collect damages from Bright & Schiff for gas drained from beneath their lease, but are seeking to have an order of the Railroad Commission declared invalid, the enforcement of which they allege will necessarily result in the drainage of gas from their leases to the Bright & Schiff lease. If we should hold valid the Railroad Commission order, of which The Atlantic Refining Company et al. herein complain, The Atlantic Refining Company et al. would have no recourse for damages against Bright & Schiff regardless of the alleged drainage. The rule of capture as defined in Ryan Consolidated Petroleum Co. v. Pickens and Coffield et al. would prevent such relief. The gas produced by Bright & Schiff would belong to them regardless of the fact that 199/200 of the gas produced may have come from the leases of appellants. We therefore say that the Ryan case is not authority for the trial court's conclusion of law set forth, supra, nor the holding of the court that the Railroad Commission order is valid.

As we construe the opinion in the Humble case, 193 S.W.2d 824, the court held in that case that the Commission could, in fixing well allowables, take into consideration certain factors such as the cost of production to the owner of a small tract and the savings realized by owners of large tracts who would not be required to drill wells to offset drainage in administering conservation laws. Further, that court said that the allowable to an owner of a small tract could not be reduced to the point where his well could not be drilled and operated at a reasonable profit. The opinion elsewhere, however, after citing Brown v. Humble Oil & Refining Company, 126 Tex. 296, 83 S.W.2d 935, 87 S.W.2d 1069, and Corzelius v. Harrell, 186 S.W.2d 961, recognizes the restrictions which the conservation laws have placed upon the common law right of an owner to drill as many wells on his land as he pleases and to produce as much as he pleases. At page 832 of 193 S.W.2d the court commented:

> "Any restriction upon the number of wells drilled or the amount of production therefrom is essentially an infringement upon the right of private property, and can only be upheld as a conservation measure. In the exercise of this right of curtailment it is generally recognized that the rules and regulations adopted must, as far as practical, and within reasonable limitations, afford the several property owners a fair opportunity to produce the recoverable oil underlying their lands or its equivalent."

The record in the Humble case shows that the Railroad Commission's rules had been in effect in that field for a considerable period of time without the validity of such rules having been challenged in the courts.

The Standard Oil Company case (Standard Oil Co. v. Railroad Commission, 215 S.W.2d 633, error refused, n. r. e.), involved oil proration in the Yates Field. The Yates Field was discovered long prior to the conservation laws and the Standard Oil Company had concurred with the rules established and agreed to by the operators in that field. After proration became effective the Railroad Commission merely adopted the rules which had already been set up with the recommendation and consent of the operators. In upholding the order of the Railroad Commission the court pointed to the fact that there were sharp conflicts in the testimony of witnesses as to the effect of the Commission's order, and that the parties had complied for a long period without protest or objection.

(1) We are in agreement with the reasoning of the courts in the Humble and Standard Oil Company cases in holding that where producers have acquiesced in and have failed to complain of the Commission's proration orders for a long period, during which time other operators have expended vast sums in exploration and drilling operations, such producers should not be heard to complain.

In the case of Railroad Commission v. Mackhank Petroleum Co., 186 S.W.2d 351, cited by appellee, the court held that under the field spacing pattern the complaining party could drill additional wells and protect himself from drainage. The opinion of the Supreme Court in 144 Tex. 393, 190 S.W.2d 802 did not deal with the allocation issue.

In the Rowan and Nichols cases Railroad Commission v. Rowan & Nichols Oil Company, 310 U.S. 573, 60 Sup.Ct. 1021, 84 L.Ed. 1368, and Railroad Commission v. Rowan Oil Company, 311 U.S. 570, 61 Sup.Ct. 343, 85 L.Ed. 358, both of which involved oil proration orders in East Texas, and which are cited and relied on by appellee, the Supreme Court reversed the judgment of the lower courts setting the Commission orders aside. In so doing the court pointed out serious conflicts in the testimony, saying that in the face of such conflicts Federal Courts should not substitute their judgments for those of the Commission. In effect, it concluded that the validity of such orders should be left to the final decision of the courts of Texas.

(2) After reviewing and considering the principles expressed in the cases above referred to in connection with the plain provisions of Article 6008, V.A.C.S., we feel compelled to hold, under the facts of this case, that the 1/3-2/3 proration formula promulgated by the Railroad Commission for the Normanna Field is invalid. The order allows a well on a .3-acre tract to produce gas at a rate many times greater per acre than a well on a 320-acre tract is allowed to produce, and we find no substantial evidence in the record justifying such a wide discrepancy in the rate of production. Viewing all the facts in the light of the substantial evidence rule, we think the 1/3-2/3 proration formula is an unreasonable basis upon which to prorate the gas production from this reservoir. It does not come close to compelling ratable production; neither does it afford each producer in the field an opportunity to produce his fair share of the gas from the reservoir. Appellee says that prior to the conservation laws one could drill as many wells as he pleased and produce as much gas as he pleased, and under that situation may have been able to drain as much or more gas from his neighbors as this proration order will allow it to do, and that for that reason this proration order is valid. They contend that whatever advantage a small tract would have had prior to conservation laws, it is entitled to a similar advantage under the proration laws. We do not think the principles stated in the cited cases by this court support that view.

As pertaining to the question generally before this court see: Vol. 31, Texas Law Review, pp. 113 to 122; article entitled "Oil-Well Spacing Regulations and Protection of Property Rights", by Robert E. Hardwicke; Vol. 12, Baylor Law Review, article entitled "A Century of Correlative Rights", by R. O. Kellam; Vol. 16, Texas Law Review, article entitled "Property Rights in Oil and Gas and Their Effect Upon Police Regulations", by A. W. Walker.

(3) It has been suggested in some of the briefs that this court might set some rule or standard by which the Commission should be guided in regulating the production of gas. This the court will not undertake to do. We recognize that the Railroad Commission alone is authorized to make the rules regulating the production of oil and gas. While such rules are subject to review by the courts, a court cannot substitute its judgment for that of the Commission. A court can only pass on the validity of a rule or order when properly presented to it for review. The responsibility rests with the Commission to devise some rule of proration which will conserve the gas in the field in question and at the same time be fair and just to all parties without depriving any of them of his property. As is provided in said Article 6008, Section 22, the Commission is given broad discretion in accomplishing the purpose of giving each party an opportunity to produce its fair share of the gas in the reservoir.

The judgment of the trial court is reversed and this cause is remanded with instructions to enter judgment declaring the proration order of the Commission invalid and granting the injunction preventing the enforcement thereof.

ASSOCIATE WALKER and STEAKLEY, not sitting.

MR. JUSTICE SMITH, joined by JUSTICE GRIFFIN, dissenting, ON MOTION FOR REHEARING

Assuming that the Supreme Court of Texas has jurisdiction of this case, it is our duty to decide the controlling questions presented. These questions necessarily must be decided in the light of the entire record. The Appellees, Bright & Schiff et al., have, in my opinion, filed a very able brief in support of their motion for rehearing. I might add that thorough and exhaustive briefs have been filed by Appellants, as well as amicus curiae briefs in support of and against the motion. The Attorney General of Texas, in behalf of the Railroad Commission of Texas, has continued to defend the order of the Commission. The Attorney General not only joins Bright & Schiff in its motion for rehearing, but has filed a compelling and forceful supplemental brief in support of the motion.

A review of the record has led me to believe that the motion for rehearing should be granted for the reasons now to be stated.

The plaintiffs, Atlantic Refining Company et al. shall hereafter be referred to as plaintiffs. The defendants, Bright & Schiff et al. shall hereafter be designated as defendants, and the defendant, The Railroad Commission of Texas, shall hereafter be referred to as the Railroad Commission or the Commission.

This suit was brought by the plaintiffs in the Ninety-Eighth District Court of Travis County, Texas, against the defendants to annul certain orders of the Commission. In a trial to the court, without the intervention of a jury, the Commission's orders were held to be valid and all injunctive relief as prayed for by the plaintiffs was denied.

The plaintiffs have perfected a direct appeal to this court under Article 1738a, Vernon's Annotated Civil Statutes, and Rule 499a, Texas Rules of Civil Procedure. They complain, as they did in the trial court, of orders of the Rairoad Commission entered on December 16, 1957, and May 13, 1958, the first of which orders adopting field rules for the Normanna (Slick Sand) Field, the Normanna (Luling Sand) Field, and the field rules for the Normanna (Second Massive Wilcox) Field, and the second of which orders adopting field rules for the Normanna (First Massive Wilcox) Field. Plaintiffs do not attack the orders in their entirety. Plaintiffs object only to that portion of said orders that allocate the allowable production among all wells in each reservoir on the basis of "two-thirds, one-third"; that is to say, two-thirds of the total allowed gas production for the entire reservoir is allocated to the wells therein in that proportion that the acreage assigned to a well bears to the sum of the acreage in the reservoir, and one-third of such total allowed gas production is allocated equally among the wells in the reservoir. This portion of the order is contained in "Rule 3". It was this portion of the field rules that was labeled by the plaintiffs as being "illegal, unjust, arbitrary, unreasonable, and discriminatory". Plaintiffs sought in the trial court and seek here the following relief: "(1) That the court adjudicate that the provisions of the special field rules adopted by the Commission for the Normanna Field, Bee County, Texas, that allocates production among the wells therein are null and void; and that the same are set aside and cancelled *and the Commission enjoined from granting production to said wells on the basis thereof;* (2) that plaintiffs have their cost and any other and further relief to which they may show themselves entitled." (Emphasis added.)

The question occurs: What is the exact form of the relief that plaintiffs request? Is the injunctive relief sought that the Railroad Commission be enjoined merely from granting production under these particular allocation orders only, or do the plaintiffs request that the Railroad Commission be enjoined from granting production to any operators in the field under any circumstances until an order is adopted by the Commission that will give to each operator only his gas in place? It cannot be that plaintiffs desire the first. Incidentally, the Railroad Commission does not "grant" production to wells under the orders. It neither grants nor denies production to wells in any given field. Therefore, the mere allocation of the allowable on the basis of a "two-thirds, one-third" rule will not cause any immediate and irreparable injury to the plaintiffs. Production, and only production, will cause such injury.

This court has held that portion of the orders that allocates the allowable production invalid and has instructed the trial court to grant an injunction "preventing the enforcement thereof". Neither this court nor the trial court can write a new order. This court's opinion, of course, does not make the slightest suggestion as a guide to the Railroad Commission. Naturally, any suggestion would have been meaningless. This court knows that the plaintiffs were not asking for relief that would merely require inaction on the part of the Railroad Commission. What would be the result if the Commission took no action at all? Until field rules are set by the Commission, production in the Normanna Fields will be automatically governed by statewide Rule 25, which allows each well to produce 25 percent of its open flow. The witness, Bellanfonte, testified that the Bright & Schiff (defendants) well will be entitled to produce *three times* as much under the statewide rule. Plaintiffs admit that all wells in the field are average wells. Therefore, the statewide rule would place all wells in the field, including the Bright & Schiff well, on an equal basis, in so far as the production is concerned.

What the plaintiffs are actually requesting here is that the production from the Normanna Fields be stopped. It must be admitted that they cannot just stop the production from the Bright & Schiff well and allow production to continue under the other wells in the field. The field rules are applicable to all wells alike. Plaintiffs are not asking for an injunction directly against the operators prohibiting all production. They are seeking an injunction against the Railroad Commission to restrain it from "*granting*" production on any basis to the wells in the fields.

In any event, this is not a situation such as existed in the cases of Railroad Commission v. Shell Oil Co., 146 Tex. 286, 206 S.W.2d 235 (1947), and Railroad Commission v. Sterling Oil & Refining Co., 147 Tex. 547, 218 S.W.2d 415 (1919). In those cases the plaintiffs sought an injunction to restrain the Commission from enforcing orders against them. Here the plaintiffs are asking, in effect, that this court issue an injunction ordering the Railroad Commission to shut in the production from the Normanna Fields.

Basically, the questions for determination are: Can the owner of any separate tract, no matter how small, which is not an illegal subdivision, be compelled by the Commission to unitize his tract with adjoining lands; and (2) if he is entitled to drill at least one well on his separate tract, and cannot be compelled to unitize, then what amount of gas can he produce from his well?

It is well established that there can be no compulsory unitization in Texas. To grant the injunction in the present case would practically effect unitization.

The argument presented by the plaintiffs has been consistently and uniformly rejected by the courts. It has been consistently held that the owner of a small tract (.3 of an acre), not an illegal subdivision, *as a matter of law* is entitled to a well upon his tract, no matter how small the tract may be. Dailey v. Railroad Commission, Tex.Civ.App., 133 S.W.2d 219, wr. ref.; Stanolind Oil & Gas Company v. Railroad Commission, Tex.Civ.App., 96 S.W.2d 664, no writ hist.; Nash v. Shell Petroleum Corporation, Tex.Civ.App., 120 S.W.2d 522, wr. dism.; Railroad Commission v.

Delhi-Taylor Oil Corporation, Tex.Civ.App., 302 S.W.2d 273, wr. ref. n. r. e.; Holbouty v. Darsey, Tex.Civ.App., 326 S.W.2d 528, wr. ref. n. r. e.; Foster v. Railroad Commission, Tex.Civ.App., 326 S.W.2d 533, wr. ref., n. r. e.

All of the above cases, just as our case, relate to the right of the owner of a small tract to drill his first well on his tract. They are not cases which involved the right to drill *additional* wells. The court cites several of these additional wells cases. They are not in point. The court quotes from such cases as Magnolia Petroleum Company v. Railroad Commission, Tex.Civ.App., 93 S.W.2d 587, wr. ref.; Atlantic Oil Production Company v. Railroad Commission, Tex.Civ.App., 85 S.W.2d 655, wr. dism., and Railroad Commission v. Gulf Production Company, 134 Tex. 122, 132 S.W.2d 254. These cases involved the right to drill an eleventh well in the first case, and the last two cases involved the right to drill a third well. No question of the right to drill additional wells on the Bright & Schiff tract is involved here.

The lack of authority of the Railroad Commission to compel pooling or unitization, and the uniform holding that the Commission has no authority to compel pooling or unitization is made clear by the provisions of paragraph (g) of Article 6014, which reads as follows:

> "(g) Waste or loss incident to, or resulting from, the unnecessary, inefficient, excessive or improper use of the reservoir energy, including the gas energy or water drive, in any well or pool; however, *it is not the intent of this Act to require repressuring of an oil pool or that the separately owned properties in any pool be unitized under one management control or ownership.*"

This statute should be construed in connection with Article 6008(b), Vernon's Annotated Civil Statutes, which authorizes the establishment of pooled units for certain purposes. Section 1 of Article 6008(b), supra, however, contains an express provision that no person shall be compelled or required to enter into any such pooling agreement:

> "Such agreements shall not bind any land owner, royalty owner, lessor, lessee, overriding royalty owner or any other person who does not execute them, but shall bind only the persons who execute them, their heirs, successors, assigns and legal pepresentatives; *but no person shall be compelled or required to enter into such an agreement.*" (Emphasis added.)

See Pickens v. Ryan Consolidated Petroleum Corporation, Tex.Civ.App., 219 S.W.2d 150, wr. ref. n. r. e.; Ryan Consolidated Petroleum Corporation v. Pickens, 266 S.W.2d 526, affirmed in Ryan Consolidated Petroleum Corporation v. Pickens, 155 Tex. 221, 285 S.W.2d 201; Nale v. Carroll, Tex.Civ.App., 266 S.W.2d 519, affirmed in Nale v. Carroll, 155 Tex. 555, 289 S.W.2d 743. In this latter case, the Court of Civil Appeals held:

> "It is well established that there can be no compulsory unitization in Texas, and to yield to the claims of appellants in this case would practically effect unitization."

In the Ryan case, this court said:

> "The petitioner knew that the Railroad Commission did not have the power to cause a merger or unitization of the separately owned leasehold rights of respondents in Lots 10 and 11 with those of petitioner." (155 Tex. 221, 285 S.W.2d 207.)

In the recent case of Halbouty v. Darsey, supra, the Court of Civil Appeals held that the granting of a permit by the Railroad Commission on a .48 acre tract under spacing Rule 37 was not improper because oil and gas from surrounding tracts would drain to the tract, since such drainage would be part of the law of capture. This court refused the application for writ of error. It is true the refusal was with the notation n. r. e. However, undoubtedly this court approved the holding, otherwise it would have granted the writ.

The plaintiffs would have us believe that this is a cause between small tract owners and large tract owners. The opposite is true. At the time of the Railroad Commission hearing the plaintiffs were just as much "small tract owners" as was Bright & Schiff's predecessors in title. The plaintiffs, Atlantic, Tidewater, and Dougherty owned an undivided interest in all of the town lots in the townsite area and owned small lots throughout the field. The plaintiffs could have exercised their own right of capture, but they elected to unitize their small tracts and emerged as "large tract" owners. The question arises: Is the Railroad Commission under such circumstances required to nullify the rights of the owner of a small tract by so limiting his production that he will have no incentive to take the risk of going ahead and drilling his own well? It is inconsistent to say that the Railroad Commission is required to take away with one hand what the law says it has to give with the other hand.

The right of the owner of a well depends fundamentally upon the law of property. The Texas law of property in oil and gas has been defined by this court as embracing *two* parts of *equal force and dignity*: the *law* of ownership in place, and the *law* of capture.

The majority opinion quotes from Brown v. Humble Oil & Refining Company, 126 Tex. 296, 83 S.W.2d 935, but, in my opinion, it misses the basic statement of the law in that case which is applicable here:

> "The rule in Texas recognizes the ownership of oil and gas in place, and gives to the lessee a determinable fee therein. Lemar v. Garner, 121 Tex. 502, 50 S.W.2d 769; Humphreys-Mexia Co. v. Gammon, 113 Tex. 247, 254 S.W. 296, 29 A.L.R. 607; Waggoner Estate v. Sigler Oil Co. 118 Tex. 509, 19 S.W.2d 27; Texas Co. v. Dougherty, 107 Tex. 226, 176 S.W. 717, L.R.A.1917 F, 989."
>
> "Owing to the peculiar characteristics of oil and gas, the foregoing rule of ownership of oil and gas in place should be considered in connection with the law of *capture*. This rule gives the right to produce all the oil and gas that will flow out of the well on one's land; and *this is a property right*. And it is limited only by the physical possibility of the adjoining landowner diminishing the oil and gas under one's land by the exercise of the same right of capture. * * * *Both rules are subject to regulation under the police power of a state.*" (Emphasis added.)

The expression of the court, supra, when it said "by the exercise of the same right of capture" simply means that the answer to the rule of capture *is* the rule of capture. "The correlative right to the law of capture was the law of capture." Ralph B. Shank, "Present Status of Law of Capture", Proceedings of the 6th Annual Institute on Oil & Gas Law and Taxation, 257 at 272. This court in the Brown v. Humble case summed up the answer to the plaintiffs here, when it said: "And it [the law of capture] is limited only by the phsyical [SIC] possibility of the adjoining landowner diminishing the oil and gas under one's land by the exercise of *the same right of capture.*"

The plaintiffs in this case have, through closely related litigation, fought Bright & Schiff at every turn. They contested the granting of the permit. As early as December 1958, and after Bright & Schiff was granted the right to drill on its small tract, plaintiffs sought to intimidate drilling contractors and to construct buildings and structures on land adjacent to the Bright & Schiff drill site and to drill a water well thereon. Bright & Schiff had obtained a surface lease on two lots and part of a third lot to accommodate the necessary pits, pumps, tanks, and equipment to be used incident to the drilling of a well on the lot under which they owned the minerals. Bright & Schiff sought injunctive relief against the plaintiffs asking that they be restrained from interfering with their drilling activities. The Bee County District Court found that the activities of the plaintiffs were conducted for the sole and only purpose of willfully and unlawfully obstructing, hampering and preventing the Bright & Schiff drilling operations. The injunction followed, and the trial court's judgment was affirmed by the Court of Civil Appeals. See The Atlantic Refining Company et al. v. Bright & Schiff, Tex.Civ.App. 321 S.W.2d 167, wr. ref. n. r. e.

The plaintiffs made the contention in that case that the use of the surface to the three lots would enable Bright & Schiff to complete a gas well on *its small lot* which will drain minerals from beneath the lots under which the plaintiffs owned the minerals. One of the plaintiffs, The Atlantic, emphasized that the gas reserves beneath the Bright & Schiff lot was worth only $15,000, whereas a completed well would be worth a million dollars because gas would flow from beneath the Atlantic's leases. The Court of Civil Appeals disposed of this contention with the terse statement that "The trial court found that Atlantic would suffer no drainage at all. [The court was referring to the same well we are concerned with here]. Drainage presents no new problem. The rule of capture is settled law. Ryan Consolidated Petroleum Corp. v. W. L. Pickens, 155 Tex. 221, 285 S.W.2d 201; Eliff v. Texon Drilling Co., 146 Tex. 575, 210 S.W.2d 558. *Under that rule*, an injunction may not be used as an instrument to protect a lessee from the risk of drainage. Prairie Oil & Gas Company v. State, Tex.Com.App., 231 S.W. 1088."

This court refused a writ of error, n. r. e., in spite of the contention of Atlantic et al. in its application for writ of error that "Drainage of petitioner's minerals was established as a matter of law." By our action in refusing the writ, we sustained the contention that drainage is not illegal in and of itself. Thus, in my opinion, we followed our holding in Ryan v. Pickens, supra, that 'Petitioner's contention that this case is one for equitable relief should not be sustained for the reason that its position is inconsistent with the law of capture, which is a well-settled rule of property in this jurisdiction. The rule of capture is simply this-that the owner of a tract of land acquires title to the oil and gas which he produces from wells drilled thereon, *though part of such oil or gas may have migrated from adjoining land.*' 285 S.W.2d at p. 207. The rule of capture has become a property right." This rule was not first announced in Ryan v. Pickens, supra. It has been the rule at least since Brown v. Humble, supra, was decided by this court in June 1935. Plaintiffs' attempt here to destroy the effect of what the courts have said in Brown v. Humble, and Ryan v. Pickens, supra, by claiming that the law of capture is nothing more than a rule of convenience or a rule of nonliability for damages for drainage. The plaintiffs, however, seem to level their attack only against Ryan v. Pickens, supra, as it indicated by the conclusion of law number 2, filed undoubtedly by the trial court at the instance of the plaintiffs. They have chosen to ignore the many other cases by this court and the courts of civil appeals.

Plaintiffs apparently are proceeding without regard to the significant holding of the court in Brown v. Humble, supra, on motion for rehearing in 87 S.W.2d at page 1069. In its original opinion the court used language to the effect that the Commission has the duty "to adjust the allowable" so as to give the owner of a small tract "his just proportion of the oil and gas" and that by this method "each person will be entitled to recover a quantity of oil and gas substantially equivalent to the recoverable oil and gas under his land." (83 S.W.2d at page 944).

On motion for rehearing, the court in explanation of this statement said in 87 S.W.2d at page 1069:

> "It appears that the first quotation above and a part of the second have been construed by some to mean that this court has undertaken to prescribe them as rules and standards by which to determine property rights and as standards to control the Railroad Commission in promulgating conservation rules and orders relating to oil and gas. Others have construed the language, or part of the language, above quoted from the opinion to amount to a ruling that acreage must be used as the sole or controlling factor in determining how many oil and gas wells may be drilled on, or how much oil or gas may be taken from, a tract of land, or to hold in effect that whenever a well or wells are permitted to be drilled upon a small tract under the exception in rule 37, the allowable from such wells must always be adjusted so that the tract will be permitted to produce only a quantity of oil measured by the proportion which its acreage bears to the acreage of tracts developed under the general provisions of the rule.
>
> "These are erroneous constructions of the opinion. The language quoted was used, not for the purpose of prescribing rules or standards, but merely in a discussion of the validity and purpose of the rule and its exception, as showing that the rule and the exception with respect to vested rights are reasonable; and that, while it is "impossible to measure the quantity of oil and gas beneath each tract of land", or to "give exact justice to all land owners," the rule and the exception can be so administered as to prevent the invasion of property rights by fairly and reasonably, but of course not exactly, protecting each owner in the ownership of, and in the opportunity to save and produce, the oil and gas which according to the decisions in this state he has a right to take."

It is plausible to conclude that Brown v. Humble stands for the proposition that the owner of a small tract is not limited simply to the oil or gas, or their equivalent, beneath his tract. The court said that the conservation laws should be administered so as to prevent the invasion of property rights by giving each owner "the opportunity to save and produce the oil and gas which according to the decisions in this state *he has a right to take*." The court without doubt was referring to the law of capture, a property right. The opinion on motion for rehearing makes it clear that there is no basis for a claim that proration must be in proportion to either acreage or reserves in place.

I feel that it is necessary to discuss all of these cases as they have a direct bearing upon the action of the Railroad Commission in determining the issue before it. The issue before the Railroad Commission at the first hearing was the question of adoption of field rules for all four vertically separated reservoirs, the Slick Sand Field, the Luling Sand Field, the First Massive and the Second Massive Wilcox Field. This hearing was requested by Midstates, a proponent of a 100 percent acreage formula. At the hearing, Midstates offered a "waste" argument to justify the adoption of field rules and especially an allocation formula based 100 percent upon acreage times bottom hole pressure. Midstates contended that some 80 townsite lots would be drilled if field rules were not enacted and substantial "waste" would occur since (1) danger of "blow-outs" would be increased and (2) the concentrated withdrawals would cause a reduction of pressure in the townsite area and there would be a "dewing out" and loss of liquids.

Atlantic apparently contended for a different formula, and presented some figures as to the amount of money that a well drilled on a town lot would produce under different allocation formulas from the Slick, Luling, and First Massive formations. However, no evidence was presented at the first hearing showing that the First Massive was productive. This accounts for the fact that in the order of December 16, 1957, field rules were enacted for only the Slick Sand Field, the Luling Sand Field, and the Second Massive Wilcox Field. This order recited that the Commission "finds that waste as the term is defined in the applicable statutes, will take place in said field unless rules are adopted by the Commission for the prevention thereof, and the following field rules are necessary to prevent such waste and to provide for a more orderly develoment and operation of said field." In this connection, a great volume of testimony was introduced by both plaintiffs and defendants, Bright & Schiff. It would be impractical to attempt to set out all the testimony. It is sufficient to say that in my opinion the orders complained of are reasonable [SIC] supported by substantial evidence and are not illegal, unjust, arbitrary, unreasonably, or discriminatory. I may add that the finding of fact by the trial court that "Production of gas and condensate from the well drilled by defendant Bright & Schiff * * * under the rules of the * * * Railroad Commission * * * prorating [2/3-1/3 formula] the production of gas from the reservoirs in the Normanna Field, Bee County, Texas, will result in the drainage of a tremendous quantity of gas and condensate from other leases and tracts in the field, including leases and tracts in which plaintiffs own an interest *to* said .3 acre [Bright & Schiff] lease, * * *" cannot be material because the plaintiffs wholly failed to prove their theory. The plaintiffs failed to make out their case for calculating the reserves and the production to the Bright & Schiff well, in that the finding of the trial court shows that they failed to prove the amount, whatever that amount may be, of drainage. The court said in its finding "the precise amount of said drainage being incapable of ascertainment." The plaintiffs should not be permitted to destroy the orders of the Railroad Commission merely because of an irrelevant finding made by the trial court to the effect that a tremendous quantity of gas and condensate from other leases in the field will be drainage to the .3 acre Bright & Schiff tract. No showing was made as to the quantity of deainage [SIC], if any, which would flow from plaintiffs' leases. There is no way of knowing from the evidence what quantity of gas or condensate would flow to the plaintiffs' leases as a result of their drilling operations. On the other hand, Bright & Schiff witnesses testified to facts showing conclusively that no drainage could be computed and no field reserves could be computed "at this time." If a question of fact was presented as to whether or not reserves can be computed, then such question of fact must be determined in the first instance by the Commission. The case of Corzelius v. Harrell, 143 Tex. 509, 186 S.W.2d 961, supports the contention of the defendants that the power to make rules rests exclusively with the Commission and the courts may only adjudge that a rule of the Commission is valid or invalid. The courts cannot make new rules, and by the same token cannot determine fact issues in the first instance. The alternative argument made by the plaintiffs to the effect that there is tremendous drainage or "enormous drainage" cannot prevail. In the first place there are no pleadings raising such question-next, the finding of "tremendous drainage" or "enormous drainage" is indefinite, ambiguous and cannot be the basis for a workable order by the Railroad Commission, the agency responsible for the administration of the oil and gas laws in the State of Texas. What I have said applies with equal force to the second order. This order followed Atlantic's request to the Commission on January 26, 1958 for the adoption of special field rules for the First Massive Sand. The only additional evidence to that presented at the first hearing was that the First Massive was then in production. This was a "waste order" like the first order. Neither of the orders were "correlative rights" orders. No evidence was introduced at either hearing concerning the market demand or any prospective market demand. Likewise, no finding was made by the Commission as required by Article 6008, Section 11, Vernon's Annotated Civil Statutes, that "the aggregate lawful volume of the open flow or daily potential capacity to produce of all gas wells located in" each common reservoir was "in excess of the daily reasonable market demand from gas wells that may be produced" from such reservoir. This matter is given emphasis in order that the court will know that the orders of the Commission now under consideration are strictly "waste orders" and that the rules were entered solely for the purpose of preventing "waste". The Commission was presented with no evidence to support a "correlative rights" order under Article 6008, supra. The first time the plaintiffs attempted to present a case based upon the "correlative rights" was when they presented evidence before the District Court that the sum total of the potentials for all of the wells excluded any reasonably expected market demand for gas. The Commission and the District Court have rejected plaintiffs' argument that the reference in Article 6008, supra, to the adjustment of "correlative rights" means that "the Commission should allow each producer to produce ultimately an amount of oil or gas substantially equivalent to that in place beneath his tract." The contention was rejected because the plaintiffs failed to discharge their burden on the only issue and that was to establish that their "waste" formula was supported by substantial evidence. Attention is again directed to the fact that regardless of what was meant by the term "adjust correlative rights" as contained in Section 11, Article 6008, and even if plaintiffs' version is correct (which I do not admit), the Commission has never invoked its jurisdiction under Section 10 (b) of said Article. Section 10 of Article 6008 requires the Commission to prorate and regulate production (a) in the prevention of "waste", and (b) "in the adjustment of correlative rights and opportunities of each owner of gas in a common reservoir to produce and use or sell such gas as permitted in this Article". If you will read the second paragraph of Section 11, Article 6008, supra, you will readily ascertain that the Commission only exercises its authority to accomplish the purpose designated under item (b) [adjustment of correlative rights] "*When evidence introduced at a hearing [for that purpose] will support a finding made by the Commission that the aggregate, lawful volume of the open flow or daily potential capacity to produce of all gas wells located in a common reservoir, as in excess of the daily reasonable market demand for gas from gas wells that may be produced from such common reservoir, to be utilized as permitted in this Article.*" The opinion of the majority constitutes a departure from the well-established rules of procedure as laid down by the statutes governing the Commission in adopting field rules. I trust that other members of the Court will join me in admitting our grievous error in basing our original opinion upon the theory of adjustment of correlative rights, when plaintiffs failed to introduce any evidence supporting such theory.

In the case of Brown v. Humble, supra, this Court, in discussing the rules of ownership of oil and gas in place and the rule of capture, a property right, said that "Both rules are subject to regulation under the police power of the state." However, the Commission has no authority in the exercise of the police power to inject issues into the hearing which are not raised by the pleadings and the evidence. Since the "correlative rights" issue has never been presented to the Commission, this Court is without jurisdiction to consider much less reverse the case on such grounds. We have here the sole question of whether the orders of the Commission are supported by substantial evidence. The plaintiffs have elected to request the Commission to act only under the "waste" prevention powers granted to it under item (a) of Section 10 or under Section 7 of Article 6049c, relating to waste.

I realize that a great fight is being waged against the substantial evidence rule. The majority opinion in this case lends itself to the theory which has never before been recognized that the courts through judicial review have the authority not only to substitute their judgment or discretion for that of the Commission, but to go a step further and test the validity of the Commission's order on the matter which was not raised before the Commission. It has long been held that the courts will set aside a Commission order only where it deprives the complaining party of property rights. See Railroad Commission v. Rowan & Nichols Oil Company, 310 U.S. 573, 60 S.Ct. 1021, 84 L.Ed. 1308; Railroad Commission v. Rowan & Nichols Oil Company, 311 U.S. 570, 61 S.Ct. 343, 83 L.Ed. 358. While it is true that in these cases the primary attack on the orders was on the basis that the proration orders deprived the owners of larger tracts of their property without due process of law in violation of the Fourteenth Amendment to the United States Constitution, nevertheless, these cases definitely decided that even a straight proration order, in view of the Texas Law of property, including the law of capture, did not constitute a taking of the property of the large tract owners. These cases involved proration orders for the East Texas field. They definitely settled the validity of the Commission's proration order in the East Texas field, where proration was and still is substantially on a per well basis. In those cases, as in this case, the contention was made that the proration order was invalid because it enabled the owners of wells on small tracts to drain away oil beneath the larger tracts. The Court in both cases carefully considered the Texas cases, including Brown v. Humble, supra, and stated the Texas law as it had been announced in this latter case. The Court said in the first Rowan case:

> "In Texas, according to conventional doctrine, the holder of an oil lease 'owns' the oil in place beneath the surface. * * * But equally recognized is the 'rule of capture' which subjects the lessee's interest to his neighbors' power to drain his oil away. Therefore, to speak of ownership in its relation to oil, is to imply a contingency of control not applicable to ordinary interests in realty."

The Commission in determining the issue of waste must necessarily be guided by the case law on the subject. It, no doubt, in considering the type of order to be entered here, took into consideration the reasoning of the Court in the first Rowan case wherein it said "* * * To deny the holders of these [small] tracts permission to drill might subject them to the risk of losing their oil in place or of being put at the mercy of adjoining holders. [compulsory pooling]. In many instances, therefore, the Commission has granted exceptions to its general spacing rule on the basis of which investments have been made and wells drilled. If these wells, most of them small, were restricted to production on the basis of an hourly potential formula, it might be unprofitable to operate them at all. *Not only are the individual interests of these small operators involved*, but their effect on the State's economy is an appropriate factor to be taken into account when plans are devised to keep the well open."

The only case in which the Supreme Court of Texas has nullified a proration order of the Railroad Commission is Marrs v. Railroad Commission, 142 Tex. 293, 177 S.W.2d 941. The proration formula in that case was on the basis of 50 percent per well and 50 percent average potential productivity as applied to unitized acreage and other factors. The basic premises of the Marrs opinion that the trial court had a right to make an independent review of the evidence, was expressly overruled by this Court in Trapp v. Shell Oil Company, 145 Tex. 323, 198 S.W.2d 424, 434. The Marrs case was a departure from the substantial evidence rule. Not only that, it completely ignored the law of capture as a part of the law of property in oil and gas. It should be noted, also, that the complaining parties in that case were not "free to fend for themselves". It was in the light of this situation that the Court emphasized that each owner is entitled "to a fair chance" to recover such oil and gas and that the denial of "such fair chance" amounted to confiscation. In our case, we do not have a situation where the plaintiffs cannot fend for themselves. The plaintiffs, instead of developing their tracts separately as they had a right to do, have voluntarily elected to pool their tracts. I think it is not unreasonable to say that they elected not to drill eighty wells in order to save themselves drilling and operating expenses. The drilling of ten or eleven wells, of course, is much less expensive than the drilling of eighty, thereby making it more profitable for the plaintiffs. If the plaintiffs can compel the defendant, Bright & Schiff, under the guise of "correlative rights" to suffer a drastic reduction in the allowable assigned to its well, then they will make even a still larger profit.

Although the Court in the present case recognized the applicability of the substantial evidence rule, yet, it failed to apply it. Such failure, together with an unintentional misinterpretation of the authorities, has again led us into the repudiated Marrs, supra, and we have forgotten the generally recognized fact that where the order of the agency under attack involved the exercise of the sound judgment and discretion of the agency in a matter committed to it by the legislature, the Court will sustain the order if the action of the agency in reaching such conclusions is reasonably supported by substantial evidence. See Alamo Express v Union City Transfer, Tex. 309 S.W.2d 815, 822, 823.

It is well for the courts to review and keep constantly in mind that the issue is not whether or not the Commission came to the proper fact conclusion on the basis of conflicting evidence, but whether or not it acted arbitrarily and without regard to the facts. It is well to remember that the Court does not act as an administrative body to determine whether or not it would have reached the same fact conclusions that the Commission reached, but will consider only whether the action of the Commission in its determination of the facts is reasonably supported by substantial evidence. The question is one of law. To permit the Court to substitute its fact finding on the controverted issues of fact (issue of waste) we have here destroys all uniformity of Commission administration. See 31A Tex.Jur. (Oil and Gas) Sec. 431, p. 758.

It is also necessary to remember that the validity of the orders involved is to be tested by the conditions as they existed at the time the orders were made, and is not to be tested by the conditions on appeal. The orders are the subjects of review. The Commission lost jurisdiction when the orders were appealed. It might be well to recall our recent opinion in Southern Canal Company v. State Board of Water Engineers, Tex. 318 S.W.2d 619, wherein it was declared that the legal test of reasonableness of an order of an administrative agency is whether it is reasonably supported by substantial evidence and not whether it is supported by a preponderance of the evidence, and, an administrative order is reasonable, as a matter of law, if it is supported by substantial evidence. This declaration of the proper legal test followed the Trapp case, supra, rather than the Marrs case, supra.

It is only where the evidence as a whole is such that reasonable minds could not have reached the conclusion that the agency must have reached in order to justify its actions, that the order must be set aside.

The preceding sentence has been lifted from this Court's opinion in the Trem Carr case, Railroad Commission v. Shell Oil Co., 139 Tex. 66, 161 S.W.2d 1022, 1029. In addition, the following from the Trem Carr case was quoted with approval in the Trapp case, supra, at page 441:

> "* * * In such a case the issue is not whether or not the agency came to the proper fact conclusion on the basis of conflicting evidence, but whether or not it acted arbitrarily and without regard to the facts. Hence it is generally recognized that where the order of the agency under attack involves the exercise of the sound judgment and discretion of the agency in a matter committed to it by the Legislature, the Court will sustain the order if the action of the agency in reaching such conclusion is reasonably supported by substantial evidence. *This does not mean that a mere scintilla of evidence will suffice, nor does it mean that the Court is bound to select the testimony of one side, with absolute blindness to that introduced by the other.* * * *
>
> "The authority to regulate the natural resources of oil and gas is in virtue of Section 59 (a) of Article XVI of the Constitution. The problem of conservation of these resources has been recognized by this Court to be 'complex', 'intricate', and 'exacting'. Corzelius v. Harrell, 143 Tex. 509, 186 S.W.2d 961, and authorities there cited. It is not the function of this Court to pass upon the wisdom of delegating authority to administrative agencies. That is a legislative

> function. It has been previously stated by this Court that "the Railroad Commission must be fair and render justice to the parties." When the Commission fails in its duty, we should have no hesitancy in declaring its order or rule invalid but, under the decisions of this Court and on the evidence which we summarized according to the views of the respective parties in this case, it clearly appears that the action of the Railroad Commission in granting the permit in review is reasonably supported by substantial evidence. In such a case the trial court should not substitute its judgment for that of the Commission." (Emphasis added.)

In the present case and in the light of the evidence presented by both parties, and in view of the decisions of this Court, I cannot see that the Commission *failed in its duty in* making the orders under review.

There is substantial evidence to uphold the orders of the Commission. It is to be noted from the evidence that because of the exceptional faulting in the field otherwise recoverable gas in the field would be lost to the detriment of the lessees, the landowners, and the State, if Rule 37 were not applied, as required.

It seems to me that the 1/3 per well factor is sound. The drilling of wells, as stated by the Honorable James A. Ludlum in his brief, provides the only real "known" and it is the per well factor that gives the inducement to take the costly chance and drill the well. "It affords a reasonable pay-out and is effective in determining underground reservoir conditions and the limits of the field. It furnishes the assurance that in a field of this type oil or gas will be sought, discovered and utilized, for the benefit of all." I agree with Mr. Ludlum's statement that "In this case the 1/3 per well allowable does not mean that a well on a small tract will get, under that factor, as much gas as is allowed a full unit under the 1/3 per well factor. The smaller the amount of acreage assignable to a well, the less credit the well gets on the 2/3 acreage factor, and certainly a well on a fraction of an acre would receive an insignificant allowable return from that portion of the formula." Thus, there is no justification for the conclusions we reached in our original opinion relative to the particular economics of the well on the Bright & Schiff lease. The field must be viewed as a whole and not just from the standpoint of one small tract in the field.

Section 22 of Article 6008, supra, gives the Commission broad discretion in administering the law. Under that Section the Commission is vested with "a broad discretion in administering this law, and to that end shall be authorized to adopt any and all rules, regulations or orders which it finds are necessary to effectuate the provisions and purposes of said law." The paramount and controlling importance of this Section over the other sections of Article 6008, does not seem to have been fully appreciated when we wrote our original opinion.

I agree with the defendants and the able briefs in support of their motion for rehearing that the result sought by the plaintiffs can only be obtained through the Legislature. The way was expressly pointed out by this Court more than five years ago in Ryan v. Pickens, supra. If what was said there came as a shock to some of the oil fraternity, surely they have had ample time to obtain their remedy. The plaintiffs boldly advocate here compulsory pooling, yet, the Legislature has met in 1957, 1959, and 1961, without enacting statutes such as were adopted in Mississippi, and discussed in Ryan v. Pickens, supra.

This Court has, through the years, with the exception of the Marrs case, consistently refused to destroy existing property rights, and has throughout all the litigation involving oil and gas upheld the orders of the Commission when supported by substantial evidence.

The Normanna Case:
Commentary on Atlantic Refining Co. v. Railroad Commission

by H. Philip "Flip" Whitworth

Background:

From the inception of significant oil and gas discoveries that made this state the nation's leading oil producer, Texas was the political home of the wildcatter and small-tract driller. At least in part as a result of this political influence, and prior to the Texas Supreme Court decision of *Atlantic Refining Co. v. Railroad Commission* (the *Normanna* Case),[1] the Railroad Commission (RRC) routinely adopted special field rules for gas reservoirs that assigned gas allowables on the basis of the "1/3 – 2/3 formula."[2] Under this formula, 1/3 of the entire field's monthly allowable was divided equally among each well in the field, while 2/3 of the field allowable was allocated among the wells on an acreage basis. Such an allocation formula provided a significant advantage to wells drilled on town lots or tracts smaller than the field density rule required and allowed those short acreage wells to drain many times the reserves underlying their tracts.[3] These allocation formulae, which were heavily weighted for simply having a well in the field regardless of the acreage owned by the drilling operator and available for assignment to the well, not only authorized but encouraged small-tract drilling.

Since the mid-1930s, noted commentators like Robert Hardwicke[4] and A.W. Walker[5] pointed out the abuses resulting from small-tract drilling and the need for a compulsory-pooling law in Texas.[6] Despite the introduction of compulsory-pooling bills in each session of the Texas Legislature for decades, the political muscle of Texas independents and wildcatters prevented each of these legislative attempts from becoming law—until the *Normanna* case was decided on March 8, 1961.

Facts of Case:

In the *Normanna* case, Atlantic appealed an adverse Travis County district court judgment directly to the Texas Supreme Court. Atlantic sought to invalidate Railroad Commission orders adopting the 1/3 – 2/3 formula for several different reservoirs in the Normanna Gas Field in Bee County. Atlantic showed that a well Bright & Schiff had permitted as an exception to Rule 37 on a 0.3-acre tract would produce over 200 times the gas per acre that a well on a standard 320-acre tract would recover.[7] The Atlantic experts estimated that the value of the gas in place under the Bright & Schiff tract was approximately $7,000 but that a well drilled on this tract, if allowed to produce under the RRC's order, would recover some $2.5 million worth of hydrocarbons over the field's 20-year expected life.[8]

Court Holding:

On March 8, 1961, a date of historic importance to oil and gas regulatory law in Texas, the Supreme Court held that, under these facts, the 1/3 – 2/3 formula was invalid by allowing a well on a 0.3-acre (substandard) tract to produce at a rate many times greater than a well on a 320-acre (standard) tract was allowed to produce.[9] The court further noted that the formula did "not come close to compelling ratable production" nor did it "afford each producer in the field an opportunity to produce his fair share of the gas from the reservoir."[10]

Historical Significance:

The *Normanna* decision was the first time the Texas Supreme Court invalidated a "standard" allocation formula routinely adopted by the RRC that provided a tremendous advantage to the small-tract operators/lessees. This case was followed by the Supreme Court's opinion in *Railroad Commission v. Shell Oil Co.* (the *Quitman* Case)[11] that struck down the RRC's 50/50 allocation formula in the Quitman Field in Wood County. This 50/50 formula had provided the same kind of advantage to small-tract producers in oil fields as the 1/3 – 2/3 formula did in gas fields.

The *Normanna* decision also removed much of the incentive for small-tract operators to oppose force-pooling legislation and paved the way for the passage of the Mineral Interest Pooling Act (MIPA) in 1965.[12] From the time of the Texas Supreme Court's decision in the *Normanna* case forward, small-tract owners became supporters instead of opponents to compulsory pooling to protect their small-tract leases, which could no longer be profitably drilled under acreage allocation formulas, from being drained by wells on larger tracts.[13] Indeed, in passing the MIPA, the

Texas Legislature specifically prevented this statute from being used or applied to any reservoir "discovered or produced prior to March 8, 1961."[14] As noted above, this cutoff date is the same date the Texas Supreme Court rendered the *Normanna* decision.

Thus, the *Normanna* case struck down the method for assigning allowables that the RRC had been following for decades which allowed small-tract operators to produce vastly more of a reservoir's reserves than their fair share. In rendering this landmark decision, the Supreme Court established basic principles of oil and gas regulatory law that are still followed today and removed the political opposition that had prevented the adoption of a forced-pooling statute in Texas.

---

1 *Atl. Ref. Co. v. R.R. Comm'n*, 346 S.W.2d 801, 811 (Tex. 1961).

2 The RRC similarly adopted special field rules for oil reservoirs that allocated oil allowables on the basis of the "50/50 formula." Under this rule, a well received 50% of its yardstick allowable for having a valid drilling permit with the remaining 50% of the yardstick allowable being determined on the basis of acreage, thus enabling operators with wells or small tracts or lots to produce vastly more oil and casinghead gas than the volume of hydrocarbons under their leases.

3 *See Halbouty v. Darsey*, 326 S.W.2d 528, 530 (Tex. Civ. App.—Austin 1959, writ ref'd n.r.e.) (where the gas and condensate reserves underlying the drillsite were valued at $20,000 and the cost to drill the well was $250,000); *Foster v. R.R. Comm'n*, 326 S.W.2d 533, 534 (Tex. Civ. App.—Austin 1959, writ ref'd n.r.e.) (where the value of the reserves under the drillsite tract was only $250 and the cost of drilling the well was at least $75,000); *Atl. Ref. Co. v. R.R. Comm'n*, 330 S.W.2d 494, 494-95 (Tex. Civ. App.—Austin 1959, writ ref'd n.r.e.) (where the value of the reserves under the drill site tract was $5,000 and the cost to drill the well was at least $160,000); *Stanolind Oil & Gas Co. v. R.R. Comm'n*, 96 S.W.2d 664, 664-65 (Tex. Civ. App.—Austin 1936, no writ) (where the value of the oil underlying the tract in question was $2500 and the cost to drill the proposed well was $10,000).

4 Robert E. Hardwicke, *The Rule of Capture and Its Implications As Applied to Oil and Gas*, 13 Tex. L. Rev. 391, 393 (1935).

5 A.W. Walker, *The Problem of the Small Tract Under Spacing Regulations*, 17 Tex. B.A. Proc. 157, 167-69 (1938).

6 Ernest E. Smith, *The Texas Compulsory Pooling Act*, 43 Tex. L. Rev. 1003, 1009 (1965).

7 *Normanna*, 346 S.W.2d at 803. The RRC had determined that wells in these reservoirs would reasonably drain 320 acres and therefore adopted a 320-acre gas unit density rule.

8 *Id.*

9 *Id.* at 811.

10 *Id.*

11 *R.R. Comm'n v. Shell Oil Co.*, 380 S.W.2d 556, 560-61 (Tex. 1964).

12 *See* Tex. Nat. Res. Code Ann. §§ 102.001-102.112 (West 2011).

13 E. Smith & Jacqueline Lang Weaver, The Texas Law of Oil and Gas, § 12.4 (2d ed. 2002).

14 Tex. Nat. Res. Code Ann. § 102.003 (West 2011).

CHAPTER 10

Elizabeth L. Cox and Jake L. Hamon, Petitioners, v. Leland Davison et al., Respondents.

Jake L. Hamon et al. v. Leland Davison et al.

10

COMMENTARY

by Allen D. "Al" Cummings

397 S.W.2d 200

1965

Elizabeth L. Cox And Jake L. Hamon, Petitioners,
v.
Leland Davison et al., Respondents.

Jake L. Hamon et al.
v.
Leland Davison et al.

397 S.W.2d 200

1965

NORVELL, Justice

The Texas rule is that a cotenant who produces minerals from common property without having secured the consent of his cotenants is accountable to them on the basis of the value of the minerals taken less the necessary and reasonable cost of producing and marketing the same. Burnham v. Hardy Oil Co., 147 S.W. 330 (Tex.Civ.App., 1912), affirmed, 108 Tex. 555, 195 S.W. 1139 (1917); Stroud v. Guffey, 3 S.W.2d 592 (Tex.Civ.App., 1927), affirmed, 16 S.W.2d 527, 64 A.L.R. 730 (Tex.Sup., 1929); White v. Smyth, 214 S.W.2d 953 (Tex.Civ.App., 1947), affirmed, 147 Tex. 272, 214 S.W.2d 967, 5 A.L.R.2d 1348 (1948); Davis v. Atlantic Oil Producing Co., 87 F.2d 75 (5th Cir. 1936). The controlling question in this case is whether under the facts here presented interest charges are a part of the necessary and reasonable cost of producing and marketing.

Leland Davison and others, respondents here, are the producing cotenants. The petitioners, Elizabeth L. Cox and Jake L. Hamon are the nonconsenting cotenants. Judgments in two cases (Nos. 6269 and 6270 on the District Court's docket) were rendered by the trial court in favor of Leland Davison and his associates. These judgments were affirmed by the Court of Civil Appeals in one opinion as the legal questions in both cases were identical. 385 S.W.2d 864.

It was stipulated that respondents, Leland Davison and those allied with him owned 28/32 of 13/16 leasehold working interest in and to the four quarter sections involved in the two suits under lease from others than petitioners; that petitioners Elizabeth L. Cox and Jake L. Hamon owned 3/32 of all oil, gas and other minerals in and under the [SIC] that may be produced from said four tracts; that the Cox-Hamon interest was not under lease; that respondents desired to develop the tracts by drilling thereon, but petitioners refused to join in the proposed program, whereupon respondents at their own expense drilled wells upon the premises and completed the same as producers. By this stipulation the dispute was reduced to one involving interest charges. As stated by the Court of Civil Appeals, the only question presented for decision is whether respondents in an accounting with petitioners, the nonconsenting cotenants were entitled to a credit claim of six per cent interest on petitioners' proportionate part of the money advanced by respondents to pay for producing and selling the minerals from the lands held by the parties as tenants in common.

We are unable to agree with the holdings of the trial court and the Court of Civil Appeals. Interest is an incident of debt and is not payable in the absence of an obligation binding one person to pay money to another. Barker v. Torrey, 69 Tex. 7, 4 S.W. 646 (1887); Maryland Casualty Co. v. Lee, 165 S.W.2d 135, (Tex.Civ.App., 1942, wr. ref.). The obligation may be expressly set forth in a contract or it may be implied in law. Where one cotenant decides to develop a common property, the law raises no obligation binding a nonjoining cotenant to pay a part of the costs of development. However, when mineral property is developed by one cotenant and as a result thereof he acquires minerals which at one time underlay the common property, the problem of accounting to the nonconsenting cotenant arises. Cases dealing with debts or obligations implied by law are not directly applicable. In Shaw & Estes v. Texas Consolidated Oils, 299 S.W.2d 307 (Tex.Civ.App.1957, ref. n. r. e.) the distinction between circumstances wherein a cotenant may be bound by the doctrine of implied obligation and situations in which he may not was discussed. Following Stephenson v. Luttrell, 107 Tex. 320, 179 S.W. 260 (1915), the Court of Civil Appeals in an opinion by Mr. Justice Gannon said:

> (W)ith reference to money necessarily and beneficially spent, the (Supreme Court in Stephenson v. Luttrell) continues: '* * * the principle of contribution has no element of speculation in it. In cases of this kind it is implied that the person seeking contribution had

> authority from his cotenant to expend the money that was actually spent. It is the same as if he had been actually instructed by his cotenant to expend that much money for him in improving the lot. This much is implied by law.' Because the principle is so well known, it is unnecessary to cite authority for the proposition that a cotenant incurring speculative expense in connection with exploration and development of oil, gas, and mineral properties is not entitled to a personal judgment against his cotenant for reimbursement, but only to be reimbursed out of production if and when production results.'

Both the trial court and the Court of Civil Appeals recognized that Cox and Hamon owed no debt or personal obligation to respondents. As there is no debt or enforceable personal obligation, it follows that a claim for interest as such cannot be supported. Under our view of the case it would be immaterial whether respondents actually borrowed money and paid interest thereon in order to prosecute their drilling operations. We perceive no good reason when accountability is the problem at hand, why a distinction should be made between an operator who borrows money to hire a drilling rig and one who pays such rental charges out of his own funds.

We realize that in equitable accounting between cotenants, it is not essential that legal concepts be technically or strictly construed. Ordinarily, money will make money and it is probable that had the producing cotenants put their money to work in some other business undertaking, they probably would have realized some returns therefrom. Arguments may be and have been marshalled to support the equitable claim of the producer. It is he who takes the risk and, if successful, he usually produces financial gain for both himself and his cotenants. However, there is something to be said for the nonjoining cotenant. Actual production of minerals is not the only way by which benefits may be obtained from the ownership of mineral interests in land. Drilling may and often does condemn property for mineral purposes. A tenant in common as the owner of property is legally entitled to make such use of it as he sees fit, subject to those qualifications necessarily imposed by society for the promotion of the public good and those dictated by the qualities of the property and the characteristics of its ownership. The right of one cotenant to appropriate the property of another is sanctioned only because the mineral estate is such that necessarily the rights of one contenant must be interfered with if another cotenant is to be permitted to exercise those rights properly belonging to him. As between the producing cotenant and the non-joining cotenant a balance of equities has been struck. The rule of accountability is the proportionate market value of the product less the proportionate necessary and reasonable costs of producing and marketing. This measure in its present form does not include interest and we decline to rewrite the formula.

In both cases, the judgments of the trial court and the Court of Civil Appeals are reversed and judgments here rendered that respondents take nothing.

On Motion for Rehearing

NORVELL, Justice.

The respondents in their motion for rehearing say that our original opinion tends to leave the impression that the rule announced therein is one of long standing, whereas this case is actually one of first impression. Particular emphasis is laid upon the statement that the 'measure (of accountability) in its present form does not include interest and we decline to rewrite the formula'. It is urged that this Court has never held that interest is not a recoverable cost of production and consequently it would not be a rewriting of the formula to now say that interest is a recoverable cost of production.

To allow interest as a part of the production costs would constitute a variance from the established formula to the extent of going contrary to the general rule that interest will not be allowed in the absence of an obligation to pay money owed by the person sought to be held upon an interest charge. This is the rule supported by the Texas cases. Of course the essential obligation to pay may be either expressed or implied by law. The argument urged here and accepted by the Court of Civil Appeals, as evidenced by the cases cited in its opinion, is that under the factual situation presented by the record, the law has in effect implied an obligation binding the non-consenting cotenants to pay interest charges to the operating cotenant. But, here the obligation runs the other way. The operating cotenant has taken and sold petroleum products belonging to the non-consenting cotenant. However, because of the peculiar legal relationship existing between the parties,-they being cotenants of oil producing property, the usual rule of conversion is not applied. The problem is one of accounting and we have held that in accounting the operating cotenant is entitled to a credit for his necessary and reasonable cost of producing and marketing the same. This, of course, does not mean that the non-consenting cotenant owed an obligation of any kind to the operating cotenant. This case is not analogous to one involving the payment of taxes or the discharge of any other legal obligation owed by the non-consenting cotenant. No implied obligation can arise upon the theory that the operating cotenant has with the consent or upon the implied request of petitioners, expended money for the mutual benefit of the estate held in common by the parties. The petitioners here are non-consenting cotenants. For these reasons we say that interest is not a part of the accounting formula. Invariably, the reports of the Texas decisions which allow a claim of reimbursement asserted by one cotenant against another, will disclose that some obligation of the nonpaying cotenant was lessened or discharged, or that the non-paying cotenant expressly or impliedly consented to an expenditure for the mutual benefit of the estate from which an obligation to repay could be implied. Such is not the situation here.

Respondents' motion for rehearing is overruled.

POPE, Justice (dissenting).

The former dissenting opinion is withdrawn and this one is substituted for it.

The majority refuses to allow the producing cotenants to recover legal interest upon the capital they advanced to drill sixteen producing wells in which the nonproducing cotenants proportionately participate. The basis for this result appears to be either that (1) the nonproducing cotenants did not agree to pay the cost for which reason there is no debt, or (2) costs are recoverable only in nonspeculative beneficial advances, and the drilling of oil wells is speculative, or (3) policy reasons, with respect to interest only, forbid reimbursement of costs to the active cotenant who took all the risk. We shall examine these reasons.

Petitioners Cox and Hamon own 3/32 of the oil, gas and other minerals in the tracts on which Davison drilled sixteen producing wells. The parties have agreed that Davison advanced $114,069.54 for the sole benefit of the passive cotenants as their share of the costs, and that the active cotenants vainly sought the joinder of the nonoperators in the drilling venture. Despite some disturbing language in the course of the majority opinion, it is the settled law of Texas that an active cotenant may recover out of the production his necessary and reasonable cost of producing and marketing the product. We arrive, therefore, at a statement of the narrow issue. Is interest on the capital advanced by the active cotenants recoverable as an item of cost or expense? It is my judgment that the majority at once falls into error by posing a variant and misleading question. It asks: Are costs expended by the active cotenants for the benefit of the passive cotenants in the nature of debts? Concluding that they are not debts the majority holds that interest is not collectible. In my opinion, the issue is shifted from, 'Is the interest on capital advanced a cost?' to 'Is the capital advanced a debt?' The latter is not the real problem at all. The basis for the settled law that the passive cotenant must account to the active one upon successful completion of a well, is that it restores to the active cotenant the funds he expended in the venture, the costs he incurred for the benefit of all cotenants. The extent to which this rule applies and the range in which the passive cotenant's share is held accountable is illustrated in Burnham v. Hardy Oil Co., 147 S.W. 330, 334 (Tex.Civ.App.1912), affirmed 108 Tex. 555, 195 S.W. 1139 (1917):

> 'As to the appellee the Rio Bravo Oil Company, which asks for an affirmance of the judgment in its favor, we think it would be improper to do so. Concerning its liability to plaintiffs with reference to oil taken from the land, we think the Texas Land & Cattle Company, having an unquestioned undivided interest in the league, had, by virtue of its undivided ownership in the land, the right to extract oil from the tract. In case oil was not found, it would have to bear the loss of its experiment and could not call on a nonparticipating cotenant for contribution. But where it found oil and marketed the same, the cotenant requiring it to account to him for his interest in the product, measured by his interest in the land, would be required to allow his proportion of the necessary cost of producing and marketing the product. Wolfe v. Childs, 42 Colo. 121, 94 P. 292, 126 Am.St.Rep. 152. This reasonable expense would include the cost of the machinery and appliances and other means necessary and proper to the production. In other words, all reasonable expenses incurred in the production and marketing would have to be deducted from the gross value, before a division of the proceeds between the cotenants. The result of the above is that the Texas Land & Cattle Company, or its lessees of the land, had the right to pay and to charge to the fund derived from the product the reasonable cost of what was necessary to be done in producing and marketing the oil. This being so, it, or its lessee, had the right to contract with the Rio Bravo Oil Company for a pumping plant and a pipe line for utilizing the oil and to pay for the same, either in money or in oil; and in a suit by other cotenants against the producing cotenant for its share of the value of the oil, the cost of the plant and pipe

> line to the extent that it is fair and reasonable should be allowed. And the Rio Bravo Oil Company would not be liable to plaintiffs for the oil it received for such necessary improvements, if it was a fair equivalent therefor. * * *.'

Many cases hold that the passive cotenant must pay his share of the costs but they do not do so because the items are debts. The recovery by the active cotenant is not as a creditor. He recovers costs as a charge against the proceeds of the oil or other commodity. He recovers his costs, not his debt. Stroud v. Guffey, 3 S.W.2d 592 (Tex.Civ.App.1927), affirmed 16 S.W.2d 527, 64 A.L.R. 730 (Tex.Com.App.1929); Durham v. Scrivener, 259 S.W. 606, 614 (Tex.Civ.App.1923), affirmed 270 S.W. 161 (Tex.Com.App.1925); Rosse v. Northern Pump Co., 353 S.W.2d 287 (Tex.Civ.App.1962, writ ref., n. r. e.); Estes v. Texas Consolidated Oils, 266 S.W.2d 272, 275 (Tex.Civ.App.1954, no writ).

The majority cites cases which hold that interest is an incident of debt, which is true; and then concludes no debt, no interest. That is not true. Interest is a statutory creature in Texas. Article 5069 says that "Interest' is the compensation allowed by law or fixed by the parties to a contract for the use or forbearance or detention of money * * *.' What the majority overlooks is that interest can arise by law as well as by contract. Bell v. C. J. Gerlach & Bro., 205 S.W. 470, 471 (Tex.Civ.App.1917, no writ). We shall mention a few instances. In Donaldson v. Meyer, 261 S.W. 369 (Tex.Com.App.1924), Donaldson furnished funds to Meyer under a contractual arrangement that failed by reason of Meyer's mental incompetence. Donaldson's prayer for contractual eight per cent interest on the sum of his advancements was denied but he was allowed six per cent legal interest, the Court saying:

> '* * * The right of Donaldson to recover the $3,000 used by Meyer and wife as necessaries is not based on the contract that Meyer entered into, it having been ascertained that he was incapable of entering into a binding contract, but the relief given Donaldson is on the equitable ground that he is entitled to recover the money he had paid to Meyer, and which had been used by Meyer and his wife for necessaries, and, the right to recover not being based upon any contract of Meyer, then Donaldson could not recover the rate of interest mentioned in the contract, but could recover only the legal rate of 6 per cent.'

Norris v. Vaughn, 278 S.W.2d 582 (Tex.Civ.App.1955, no writ) allowed interest on a cotenant's advancements for oil development and in so holding relied upon Schluter v. Sell, 194 S.W.2d 125, 133 (Tex.Civ.App.1946, no writ). Schluter sums up the reason for these holdings:

> 'It is the general rule that one who lends money to or makes advancements for another is entitled to interest, although nothing is said about interest. Parsons v. Parsons, Tex.Com.App., 284 S.W. 933; and in 40 Tex.Jur. 210, it is said that where 'one co-tenant pays taxes on property jointly owned (he) is entitled to contribution, and the state's lien for such taxes passes to him so that he has a lien on his co-tenant's interest.' Where pleaded interest is usually allowed on taxes paid by one having an interest in land from the date of payment. McDermott v. Steck Company, Tex.Civ.App., 138 S.W.2d 1106.'

In Hensel v. Kegans, 8 Tex.Civ.App. 583, 28 S.W. 705 (1894, no writ) the Court cited Freeman on Cotenancy for the principle that one cotenant who pays title expenses and advances taxes on behalf of another cotenant, upon principles of equity may recover his advancements, and enforce an implied lien. The Court's order for remand was 'with direction to the district court to ascertain and fix the amounts expended with lawful interest. * * *' Accord: Wooley v. West, 391 S.W.2d 157, 161 (Tex.Civ.App.1965, writ ref. n. r. e.); Robinson v. Moore, 1 Tex.Civ.App. 93, 20 S.W. 994 (1892, no writ), cited with approval in Dakan v. Dakan, 125 Tex. 305, 83 S.W.2d 620, 627 (1937); Winn v. Winn, 131 Neb. 650, 269 N.W. 376, 379 (1936).

Hill v. Moore, 85 Tex. 335, 19 S.W. 162, 167 (1892) also concerned obligations imposed by law. A contenant who advanced funds to perfect title and pay taxes was entitled to reimbursement and the Court decreed the manner:

> '* * * Looking to the relation of the parties to the land, and to the certificate by virtue of which it was acquired, we are of [SIC] opinion that appellee will be entitled to the reasonable cost of procuring title to so much of the land as appellants may recover, with interest thereon from time title was obtained; and, in addition to this, will be entitled to recover the sum paid as taxes on the lands appellants recover, with interest on same from time several payments may have been made. * * *.' (Emphasis added.)

The second reason suggested by the majority opinion for denial of interest upon the capital advanced for the benefit of the passive cotenants is that the drilling of oil wells is speculative. Unless this is so, I can see no reason for the quotation from Stephenson v. Luttrell, 107 Tex. 320, 179 S.W. 260 and Shaw & Estes v. Texas Consolidated Oils, 299 S.W.2d 307 (Tex.Civ.App.1957). To the present time, the test has been one of viewing the situation after the drilling was completed. If the venture is unsuccessful it is speculative and the one taking all the risk suffers all the cost. If the well is completed as a producer, it is regarded as nonspeculative and the passive cotenant's share is accountable proportionately. The elements of speculation are squeezed out by the time the venture is finished. This is the holding and the settled law as announced both in Luttrell and Texas Consolidated Oils. If it is the opinion of the majority that the drilling of sixteen producing oil wells, viewed after the fact, is speculative, it should clearly so state.

The third reason for the majority's rejection of interest as a valid cost is based on policy. 'Something (is) to be said for the nonjoining cotenant,' says the opinion, 'Actual production of minerals is not the only way by which benefits may be obtained from the ownership of mineral interests in land. Drilling may and often does condemn property for mineral purposes.' Interest has not been allowed in the past and the Court declines 'to rewrite the formula.' In a case of original impression about interest as a cost item, we hardly are rewriting anything. But the real fallacy of such an approach is the inherent inconsistency in applying the rule. The majority concedes that costs are recoverable and then, after assuming that interest is a cost, gives its reasons for rejecting this isolated cost item. Are we reduced to a case by case determination of policy on which items of costs will be allowed or disallowed? Whether interest is a cost at all is the question. The majority holds, however, that even if it be a cost, on policy grounds, it will not be allowed. For each claimed item of cost, the Court in the future will now determine anew the policy and equity of the many cost items.

We return to the only issue in the case. In a case in which it is admitted that the active cotenants advanced $114,069.54 for the passive cotenants who, without any risk of capital, became 3/32 owners of sixteen producing oil wells and were therefore benefited in a venture which in law was nonspeculative, are the active cotenants entitled to legal interest as costs for the 'use or forbearance or detention of money'? We have cited a number of Texas authorities which have in fact allowed interest as costs.

On principles of cost accounting, interest on the funds advanced, if uncollected, is a loss. An active cotenant who already has employees and a drilling rig, nonetheless can charge off as costs the wages he pays and a fair rental for the use of his rig.

'Just as rent is the return for the use of land, and wages the return for the workman's labor, so interest is considered as the return for the use of capital. Included in the proponents of this argument are economists, engineers, plant managers and owners who adhere to the economic interpretation of profits. 'Net profit' to them usually means pure profit, which is the profit that is attributed to the compensation for the risk taken in carrying on a business enterprise. Girded with this argument, the interest-inclusionist maintains that the interest upon the capital investment is just as logically a production cost item as is wages. To exclude it as an item of cost causes the production cost to be understated. By treating interest as a production cost (overhead expense), the resultant net profit is a pure profit or return for the business risk only. There is really a good argument for including interest as a cost, for to do so segregates the profit allocated to the use of capital goods from the profit attributed to the risk involved in the business venture. Certainly, if the production costs of two different enterprises in a given industry are to be comparable, where one business rents its plant and the other owns it, then interest on plant investment should be treated as a cost by the later concern. This is true because the rent paid by a tenant invariably includes an interest investment charge. Also, the interest on plant investment must be considered by the management in the long run, when selling prices are established, if an adequate return on the owner's capital investment is to be earned.' Van Sickle, Cost Accounting-Fundamentals and Procedures, p. 270 (1938); See note, 3 Houston Law Review, 109, 112-113.

Whether interest is a proper item of cost is new to us. This is our first case. It is not new in other areas of the law. A patent owner can recover the revenues earned by an infringer, but he must allow the infringer his production costs. In those cases interest as a cost item has often been closely examined. Even though the infringer is a wrongdoer, he may claim interest upon his capital outlay as a necessary cost item. He may do so whether he actually borrows money or merely furnishes his own capital to produce the sales. International Industries v. Warren Petroleum Corp., 248 F.2d 696, 702 (3rd Cir. 1957); W. H. Miner, Inc. v. Peerless Equipment Co., 115 F.2d 650 (7th Cir. 1940); Barber Asphalt Paving Co., v. Standard Asphalt & Rubber Co., 30 F.2d 281 (7th Cir. 1928); Permutit Co. v. Refinite Co., 27 F.2d 695 (7th Cir. 1927); Producers' & Refiners' Corporation v. Lehmann, 18 F.2d 492, 502 (8th Cir., 1927). International Industries, supra, cites many authorities for the rule and also states the reasons for it:

> '* * * The interest on the capital which the appropriator invests in his endeavor is allowed in an effort to arrive at a realistic determination of the actual costs in the standard of

> comparison analysis. This is a practical business problem to be solved by a method as accurate as possible, and the disallowance of interest would merely distort the actualities of the money expended.'

I would affirm.
HAMILTON, J., joins in this dissent.

Accounting Among Cotenants:
Commentary on Cox v. Davison

by Allen D. "Al" Cummings

In the 1965 decision *Cox v. Davison*[1], the Texas Supreme Court addressed accounting among cotenants in the oil and gas estate. The narrow issue before the court was whether interest charges are part of the reasonable and necessary costs of marketing and production, which the operating cotenant may deduct in accounting to a non-consenting cotenant for the value of the minerals taken. This is not the first Texas decision on this issue. Accounting among cotenants had been earlier addressed in several cases listed by the Court in its opinion, the most familiar of which are *Burnham v. Hardy Oil Co.*[2] and *White v. Smyth.*[3] And yet *Cox v. Davison* is the case most often cited on accounting among cotenants in the oil and gas estate. What then is the significance of the opinion in *Cox v. Davison* – what new ground did the Texas Supreme Court cover that had not been earlier addressed? And further, how well developed is accounting among cotenants in the oil and gas estate, and why is it an important aspect of Texas oil and gas law?

In *Burnham*, the appellate court, for the first time in Texas oil and gas jurisprudence, declared the right of and the rationale for a single cotenant to explore for and develop oil and gas in a jointly owned estate:

> It seems to us that the peculiar circumstances of a cotenancy in land upon which oil is discovered warrant one cotenant to proceed and utilize the oil, without the necessity of the other cotenants concurring. Oil is a fugitive substance and may be drained from the land by well on adjoining property. It must be promptly taken from the land for it to be secured to the owners. If a cotenant owning a small interest in the land had to give his consent before the others could move towards securing the oil, he could arbitrarily destroy the valuable quality of the land.[4]

This holding put Texas among the majority of oil and gas producing states that do not treat operations by a single cotenant as waste. The Court went on to state the accompanying accounting obligation of the operating cotenant:

> In case oil is not found, it would have to bear the loss of its experiment and could not call on a nonparticipating cotenant for contribution. But where it found oil and marketed the same, the cotenant requiring it to account to him for his interest in the product, measured by his interest in the land, would be required to allow his proportion of the necessary cost of producing and marketing the product . . . . In other words, all reasonable expenses incurred in the production and marketing would have to be deducted from the gross value, before a division of the proceeds between the cotenants.[5]

However, the court of appeals holding in *Burnham* was affirmed by the Texas Supreme Court on other grounds – it addresses only adverse possession issues and does not discuss accounting among cotenants.

In *White*, the Texas Supreme Court addressed the duty of a co-owner to account to his cotenant for solid minerals taken from jointly-owned property. The court cited *Burnham* as authority for the duty to account for crude oil taken from jointly-owned property, but it did not rely on *Burnham* in reaching its decision. *White* was, in fact, a partition case. The *White* opinion contains extensive discussion concerning the properties and mining of rock asphalt and how this affects a finding that the common property could not be partitioned in kind, but must be partitioned by sale. The Texas Supreme Court affirmed the lower court decisions requiring the operating cotenant to account to his nonparticipating cotenants according to the "net profits" realized from the common property. The result is similar to, but not the same as, the cotenant accounting rule stated in *Burnham*. The difference results in large part from the difference between oil, which the *Burnham* court called a "fugitive substance," and rock asphalt.When *Cox v. Davison* reached the Texas Supreme Court in 1965, Texas oil and gas law recognized the right of a single cotenant to develop commonly-owned property without committing waste and the obligation of the operating cotenant to account to his co-owners. However, the Texas Supreme Court had never expressly addressed these issues and there had not been many cases applying these concepts to fact. Therefore, *Cox v. Davison* is the first case in which the Texas Supreme Court directly addressed the nature and scope of the accounting obligation among cotenants in the oil and gas estate. While the narrow issue before the court was whether interest is a reasonable and necessary cost incurred by the operating cotenant, in examining this issue the court provided oil and gas practitioners a broader understanding of the rights and obligations of an operating cotenant.

Elizabeth L. Cox and Jake L. Hamon, the petitioners, together owned an undivided and unleased 3/32 of the oil and gas in four tracts. The respondents Leland Davison and his co-owners of an undivided 28/32 of 13/16 oil and gas leasehold working interest desired to develop these tracts by drilling wells. Cox and Hamon refused to lease or to join in the drilling. Davison and his co-owners drilled 16 oil and gas wells and completed them as producers. In the appellate court, there was not any dispute about whether Davison and his co-owners had the right to withhold from Cox and Hamon's share of production the expenses they incurred for drilling and producing the wells. However, Davison, et al. attempted to recover six percent (6%) interest on the money they advanced for drilling and producing the wells. The trial and appellate courts held that the operating cotenants could recover interest based on a theory that interest was analogous to payment of taxes by a cotenant, which benefitted the common property and gave rise to a right of contribution from the other cotenants for the amount of taxes paid, together with interest thereon. The appellate opinion did not cite either *Burnham* or *White*[6]. Cox and Hamon appealed the holding that interest is a reasonable and necessary cost of drilling and producing the wells that is recoverable by an operating cotenant.

The Texas Supreme Court reversed the judgments of the trial and appellate courts, holding that interest is not a reasonable and necessary cost of an operating cotenant in drilling and producing wells. But it is not this simple holding that makes this case significant – it is the analysis set forth in the majority and dissenting opinions and in the opinion on rehearing that flesh out the rather simplistic statement of an operating cotenant's rights and obligations with respect to its cotenants declared in *Burnham*. The court begins its opinion by restating the rule:

> The Texas rule is that a cotenant who produces minerals from common property without having secured the consent of his cotenants is accountable to them on the basis of the value of the minerals taken less the necessary and reasonable cost of producing and marketing the same.[7]

This formulation is found in the cases relying on *Cox v. Davison*. But following this simple rule, the court makes a series of declarations, some from other cases, that set out boundaries for the rights and obligations of an operating cotenant:

> . . . the law raises no obligation binding a nonjoining cotenant to pay a part of the costs of development.[8]
>
> . . . it is implied that the person seeking contribution had authority from his cotenant to expend the money that was actually spent.[9]
>
> . . . a cotenant incurring speculative expense in connection with exploration and development of oil, gas and mineral properties is not entitled to a personal judgment against a cotenant for reimbursement, but only to be reimbursed out of production if and when production results.[10]
>
> Drilling may and often does condemn property for mineral purposes.[11]
>
> The right of one cotenant to appropriate the property of another is sanctioned only because the mineral estate is such that necessarily the rights of one cotenant must be interfered with if another cotenant is to be permitted to exercise those rights properly belonging to him.[12]
>
> The operating cotenant has taken and sold petroleum products belonging to the non-consenting cotenant. However, because of the peculiar legal relationship existing between the parties — they being cotenants of oil producing property, the usual rule of conversion is not applied.[13]
>
> . . . Texas decisions which allow a claim of reimbursement asserted by one cotenant against another, will disclose that some obligation of the non-paying cotenant was lessened or discharged, or that the non-paying cotenant expressly or impliedly consented to an expenditure for the mutual benefit of the estate from which an obligation to repay could be implied[14]

Taken together, these statements clearly establish that the operating cotenant is not liable to the nonconsenting cotenant and, likewise, the nonconsenting cotenant is neither expressly nor impliedly liable to the operating cotenant for any of the costs incurred by the operating cotenant in exploration and development of the common property for oil and gas. The operating cotenant assumes the risk that its costs will not be recovered from production. The nonconsenting cotenant's share of production is chargeable with the reasonable and necessary costs incurred by the operating cotenant, so there is a risk that the nonconsenting cotenant may never receive any share of the production from the common property if the operation does not pay out.

Notwithstanding the reasoning in Justice Pope's dissent, the court expressly rejects any claim that interest on the monies advanced by the operating cotenant are analogous to payment of taxes or discharge of a lien by a co-tenant. Because payment of taxes or discharge of a lien benefits the common property, they give rise to an implied obligation of contribution or reimbursement by the nonpaying cotenant. This obligation of contribution or reimbursement bears interest. The dissenting opinion asserts that the funds expended and costs incurred by the operating cotenant are for the benefit of all cotenants. Therefore, although not in the nature of a debt or contribution obligation, interest can and should be recovered by the operating cotenant, not as a matter of contract, but by operation of law. The dissenting opinion also attacks the majority opinion's characterization of drilling wells as speculative. Justice Pope reasoned that once a well is completed as a producer the speculative element has been wrung out of the equation. Justice Pope asserted that the completion of a producing well confers a benefit to the nonconsenting cotenant, without any risk of capital. Therefore, interest should be recoverable on capital put at risk by the operating cotenant as a component of the reasonable and necessary cost of producing and marketing production from the common property. It should be noted, however, that no benefit would, in fact, be conferred on the passive cotenant by the completion of a producing well, unless and until the proceeds of production from such a well actually pays the reasonable and necessary costs incurred by the operating cotenant.

After *Cox v. Davison*, there is little controversy about the right of an operating cotenant's ability to explore for and develop oil and gas in a common property without the consent of all cotenants. In fact, in later cases, the aggrieved party will attempt to characterize the relationship between the litigants as something other than cotenancy. For example, in *Byrom v. Pendley*[15], Pendley sought to characterize Byrom, who had drilled a producing well on common property, as a bad-faith trespasser because at the same time Byrom was contesting the validity of Pendley's title. The Texas Supreme Court reversed the appellate court holding that Byrom was a bad-faith trespasser. Relying on the characterization of the relationship between the operating and nonjoining cotenant declared in *Cox v. Davison*, the Waco Court of Appeals, in *Bomar Oil & Gas, Inc. v. Loyd*[16], declined to hold that Loyd, the nonconsenting cotenant, was a consumer under the Texas DTPA.

What is less clear after *Cox v. Davison*, and what continues to be a source of controversy, is whether costs sought to be recovered by an operating cotenant are reasonable and necessary – that is, are the costs reasonable and necessary for producing and marketing production from the common property and are they reasonable and necessary in amount? This is illustrated by at least two recent cases. In *Wagner & Brown v. Sheppard*[17], after termination of the pooled Sheppard oil and gas lease, Sheppard disputed whether landman fees, lease bonus, recording fees, title-opinion expenses and overhead expenses, to the extent they related to other unit tracts rather than solely to Sheppard's tract, could be recovered by Wagner & Brown from Sheppard's share of production. The court's holding that such costs could be recovered turned on whether Sheppard's oil and gas estate remained subject to the pooled unit, rather than on cotenancy. The court remanded the case to the trial court for further proceedings on what costs incurred by the operating cotenant after the Sheppard lease termination were reasonable and necessary and whether those costs were reasonable and necessary in amount.

It has never been clear whether costs of the operating cotenant may be aggregated and recovered from the aggregate production from the common property, or whether costs must be considered on a well-by-well basis. *Cox v. Davison* did not directly address this issue. However, sixteen producing wells had been drilled and were producing from the common property. There is not any indication that the court looked at the reasonable and necessary cost issue on a well-by-well basis, but rather, the court; at least implicitly, considered the four tracts as representing a common property. However, because the court decided the narrow issue of whether interest could be recovered as a reasonable and necessary cost, it could be that the "well-by-well vs. common property" issue never really came up. Sheppard argued in the trial court, and the trial court ruled, that costs could only be recovered from production on a well-by-well basis. The trial court's holding was not appealed, therefore, it remains unclear how the courts would rule if presented with this exact issue.

In another recent case, *Bomar*, the non-consenting cotenant, Loyd, claimed that overhead supervision (such as rent, telephone, employees, and other costs of running a business) and engineering fees (such as evaluating the well bore, checking pressures, designing fracture treatments, and other engineering-type work) were unrelated to producing and marketing and were not, therefore, recoverable as reasonable and necessary costs. The court upheld jury findings, based on the lack of evidence that overhead supervision and engineering fees were directly related to production, that such costs could not be charged to the unleased mineral owner. The court also upheld jury findings that the unleased mineral owner's interest in production may not be charged with (i) purchase of wells and their equipment, (ii) unsuccessful testing operations, and (iii) an unnecessary and unreasonable hydraulic fracture treatment which did not increase the flow rate of the well. These jury findings may be a result of how the case was presented – each of these issues was the subject of conflicting expert testimony about whether they were reasonable and necessary. Nonetheless, this case demonstrates that what costs fall within the ambit of "reasonable and necessary for producing and marketing" is not settled.

Cox v. Davison is also significant in Texas because Texas does not have a robust compulsory-pooling statute, like most other oil and gas producing states. The court's holding that the operating cotenant is not liable to the nonconsenting cotenant and, likewise, the nonconsenting cotenant is neither expressly nor impliedly liable to the operating cotenant for any of the costs incurred by the operating cotenant in exploration and development of the common property for oil and gas, is a solid basis for (i) an operator to assume the risk of unleased mineral interests in their operations and (ii) for unleased mineral owners to acquiesce in such operations.

The operating cotenant's exemption from liability for exploring and developing common property without the consent of all cotenants and the nonconsenting cotenant's exemption from any personal obligation to pay for such operations is the most significant and settled aspect of *Cox v. Davison*. However, what constitutes reasonable and necessary costs of producing oil and gas and whether those costs are necessary and reasonable in amount is and will continue to be a subject of disagreement.

---

1 *Cox v. Davison*, 397 S.W.2d 200 (Tex. 1965).
2 *Burnham v. Hardy Oil Co.*, 147 S.W. 330 (Tex. Civ. App.—San Antonio 1912), *aff'd*, 195 S.W. 1139 (Tex.1917).
3 *White v. Smyth*, 214 S.W.2d 953 (Tex. Civ. App.—San Antonio 1947), *aff'd*, 214 S.W.2d 967 (Tex. 1948).
4 *Burnham*, 147 S.W. 330 at 335.
5 *Id.* at 334
6 *Cox v. Davison*, 385 S.W.2d 864 (Tex. Civ. App.—Eastland 1964, no writ).
7 *Davison*, 397 S.W.2d at 201.
8 *Id.*
9 *Id.* at 202.
10 *Id.*
11 *Id.*
12 *Id.* at 203.
13 *Id.*
14 *Id.*
15 *Byrom v. Pendley*, 717 S.W.2d 602 (Tex. 1986).
16 *Bomar Oil & Gas, Inc. v. Loyd*, No. 10-08-00016-CV, 2009 WL 2136404 (Tex. App.—Waco July 15, 2009, no pet.).
17 *Wagner & Brown Ltd. v. Sheppard*, 282 S.W.3d 419 (Tex. 2008).

CHAPTER 11

Mildred Mitchell Jones et vir, Petitioners, v. S. H. Killingsworth et al., Respondents.

COMMENTARY

by Dick Watt

11

403 S.W.2d 325

1965

Mildred Mitchell Jones et vir, Petitioners,
v.
S. H. Killingsworth et al., Respondents.

403 S.W.2d 325

1965

John A. Pace, Edward Kliewer, Jr., Dallas, for petitioners.
Ralph Shank, Prentice Wilson, Dallas, Murph Wilson, F. Wilbert Lasater, Ramey, Brelsford, Hull & Flock, Frank L. McClendon, with above firm, Tyler, for respondents.

SMITH, Justice.

ON MOTION FOR REHEARING

Our opinion delivered on June 23, 1965, is withdrawn and the following opinion is substituted therefor.

The question presented for our determination is whether or not the lands owned by the petitioner, Mildred Mitchell Jones, and described in an oil, gas and mineral lease executed by Mildred Mitchell Jones and her husband, Harry C. Jones, as lessors, to S. S. Long, as lessee (later assigned to S. H. Killingsworth), on August 16, 1951, were effectively pooled into what is known as the Hunt Oil Company et al.—West Poynor Unit. The trial court, without a jury, held that Killingsworth effectively pooled the acreage covered by the lease in accordance with authority granted in the lease, and for that reason the lease did not terminate on August 16, 1961, the date of the expiration of the primary term. A take-nothing judgment rendered against the petitioners has been affirmed by the Court of Civil Appeals. 379 S.W.2d 362.

The judgments of both the trial court and the Court of Civil Appeals are reversed and judgment is rendered for the petitioners.

Mildred Mitchell Jones and her husband filed this suit against S. H. Killingsworth and owners of leases in the immediate vicinity of the Mitchell-Long lease. These owners will be referred to as 'Hunt Petroleum Corporation.' On July 12, 1961, at a time when the Mitchell-Long lease was in effect and was owned by and the title thereto was vested in S. H. Killingsworth, subject to certain overriding royalty interests, Killingsworth, joined by the above-mentioned owners of other leases, entered into a pooling agreement establishing a unit hereinafter referred to as the 'West Poynor Unit.' The two tracts of land described in the Mitchell-Long lease were included within this unit designation. These tracts contained, in the aggregate, 20.55 acres. It was stipulated that the created unit contained 170.86 acres. However, the parties deal with this unit as though it contains only 160 acres.

It was stipulated that the unit owners commenced drilling operations on the West Poynor Unit and completed a producing oil well on or about August 16, 1961, which 'unit well' has continued to produce oil in paying quantities. It was agreed that 'no well in search of oil, gas or other minerals has been drilled by S. H. Killingsworth and the other defendants on the lands actually described by metes and bounds in the Long lease, and that no oil, gas or other minerals in paying quantities has been produced from any well actually located on the lands actually described in the Long lease.'

Although lessors contend that they are not bound by the terms of the Unit Declaration and the Amended Unit Declaration, it is agreed that Killingsworth and the other unit owners in the unit acted in good faith in forming the unit, in securing a permit to drill and in drilling the well on the unit.

The habendum clause of the Mitchell-Long lease provides that:

> 'Subject to the other provisions herein contained, this lease shall be for a term of ten (10) years from this date * * * And as long thereafter as oil * * * is produced from * * * land with which said land is pooled hereunder.'

The pertinent pooling provisions of the lease are to be found in the first two sentences of paragraph 4 of the Mitchell-Long lease. These sentences read as follows:

> 'Lessee, at its option, is hereby given the right and power to pool or combine the acreage covered by this lease, or any portion thereof as to oil and gas, or either of them, with other land, lease or leases in the immediate vicinity thereof to the extent, hereinafter stipulated, when in Lessee's judgment it is necessary or advisable to do so in order properly to develop and operate said leased premises in compliance with the spacing rules of the Railroad Commission of Texas, or other lawful authority, or when to do so would, in the judgment of Lessee, promote the conservation of oil and gas from said premises. Units pooled for oil hereunder shall not substantially exceed 40 acres each in area, and units pooled for gas hereunder shall not substantially exceed in area 640 acres each plus a tolerance of 10% Thereof, provided that should governmental authority having jurisdiction prescribe or permit the creation of units larger than those specified, units thereafter created may conform substantially in size with those prescribed by governmental regulations.'

The issue in this case is not whether the pooling clause granted authority to pool the Jones' land into an oil unit consisting of more than 40 acres. The issue, properly defined, is whether the pooling clause granted authority [SIC] pool the Jones' land into an oil unit containing 170.86 acres. The lessors take the position that authority to pool their land into an oil unit consisting of 170.86 acres was not granted by the lease, and that the attempt to pool did not effectively extend the term of the lease beyond the terminal date provided therein. We agree with the lessee that the pooling provision confers authority on the lessee to pool the lessors' land, but, we do not agree that the Extent to which the power to pool may be exercised is entrusted solely to the lessee's judgment. The lessors' land may be pooled only to the extent stipulated in the lease. The second sentence of the pooling provision provides that 'units pooled for oil * * * shall not substantially exceed 40 acres each in area, and units pooled for gas * * * shall not substantially exceed in area 640 acres each plus a tolerance of 10% Thereof. * * *' However, this provision must be construed in the light of the further provisions which is to the effect that in the event a governmental authority having jurisdiction should 'prescribe or Permit the creation of units larger than those specified units thereafter created may conform substantially in size with those Prescribed by governmental regulations.' (Emphasis added.) Absent this proviso, perhaps it could well be said that the lessee was given authority to pool the lessor's land for oil only in units not substantially exceeding 40 acres in area for either the purpose of complying with spacing rules or to promote the conservation of oil, the two situations mentioned in the first sentence wherein the power to pool is left exclusively to lessee's judgment. In order to ascertain the true intention of the parties to this lease, the Court should take into consideration all of the pooling provisions contained therin, as well as the rules and regulations governing the Fairway (James Lime) Field in which lessors' land is located. (The rules adopted by the Railroad Commission governing that field have the express purpose of 'permitting only one well to each eighty (80) acre proration unit.' The field rules only encourage larger units by Permitting an operator 'to assign tolerance of not more than eighty (80) acres of additional unassigned lease acreage to a well on an eighty (80) acre unit and shall in such event receive allowable credit for not more than one hundred sixty (160) acres.') It is argued that these Railroad Commission rules provide for proration units of not less than 80 acres [SIC] more than 160 acres, and that by reading the rules into the lease contract, paragraph 4 of the lease would read: 'the size of the units thereafter created may not be substantially less than 80 acres nor substantially more than 160 acres.' We disagree with this construction of the lease contract. The lessors did not consent to enlarge an oil proration unit to any size Permitted by governmental regulations. They gave their consent to enlarge a unit of substantially 40 acres, but only to the extent of the size of units Prescribed by the regulatory authority. The fact that the Railroad Commission may Permit a much larger unit cannot be read into the lease contract when, as here, the authority to create larger oil units is expressly limited to units of the size Prescribed by the Railroad Commission. The Commission Prescribed a unit of 80 acres. (The field rules clearly say that there Must be a proration unit of at least 80 acres, and there May be larger units of not more than 60 acres.) It is true that the pooling provision contains the word 'permit' as well as the word 'prescribe.' It is not unreasonable to assume that the parties to the lease contract intended, by the use of both words, to give each a distinctly different meaning. The parties obviously knew when the lease contract was executed that a Permitted oil proration unit could conceivably be much larger in area than one Prescribed by governmental authority. To say that a lessee can pool lessors' land with units of any size Permitted by the Railroad Commission would defeat the intention of the parties to restrict the size of the units to the size Prescribed by governmental authority. Absent express authority, a lessee has no power to pool interests in the estate retained by the lessor with those of other lessors. See Brown v. Smith, 141 Tex. 425, 174 S.W.2d 43 (1943); Gulf Oil Corporation v. Marathon Oil Co., 137 Tex. 59, 152 S.W.2d 711 (1941); Knight v. Chicago Corporation, 144 Tex. 98, 188 S.W.2d 564 (1945). Since the lands were pooled without authority, the habendum clause in the Mitchell-Long lease cannot be used to extend the term of the lease beyond August 16, 1961, the terminal date of the primary term of the lease.

Killingsworth and the Hunt Petroleum Corporation contend that the pooling clause in the Mitchell-Long lease created a relationship of principal and agent, or at least created a relationship similar to the of principal and agent, and that performance by the lessee is to be measured by the standard of good faith. It is true that the lessee acted in good faith. It is true that the lessee was given authority to pool. It is equally true that the permit granted by the Railroad Commission is unquestionably valid. Even so, the acts of the Railroad Commission cannot be said to operate effectively to extend the restrictive terms of the lease. The orders of the Railroad Commission cannot compel pooling agreements that the parties themselves do not agree upon. The Railroad Commission has no power to determine property rights. See Ryan Consolidated Petroleum Corp. v. Pickens, 155 Tex. 221, 285 S.W.2d 201 (1955); Magnolia Petroleum Co. v. Railroad Commission, 141 Tex. 96, 170 S.W.2d 189 (1943); Nale v. Carroll, 155 Tex. 555, 289 S.W.2d 743 (1956).

(The judgments of the trial court and the Court of Civil Appeals are both reversed and judgment is rendered declaring the Mitchell Long lease terminated as of August 16, 1961, and the title and possession of the lands described in said lease is awarded to Mildred Mitchell Jones. Respondents' motion for rehearing is overruled. A second motion for rehearing may be filed within fifteen days.)

GRIFFIN, HAMILTON and POPE, JJ., dissenting.

HAMILTON, Justice (dissenting).

I withdraw the dissenting opinion heretofore filed in this cause on June 23, 1965, and file the following opinion, respectfully dissenting:

I disagree with the Court's construction of the pooling agreement in the oil and gas lease under consideration and with the application of the pooling agreement to the rules and regulations adopted by the Railroad Commission. Construing the pooling agreement in its entirety simply means that the lessee was given authority to pool the lessor's land with other land in units, the size of which are controlled by the rules and regulations of the Railroad Commission.

The applicable rules and regulations for the development of the Fairway (James Lime) Field, in which the pooling unit in question is located, are set out in Railroad Commission Order No. 6—45, 322. Rules 1 and 2 of that order are as follows:

'RULE 1: No well for oil or gas shall hereafter be drilled nearer than eighteen hundred fifty (1850) feet to any well completed in or drilling to the same reservoir on the same lease, unitized tract or farm, and no well shall be drilled nearer than six hundred sixty (660) feet to any property line, lease line or subdivision line; provided, however, that the Commission will, in order to prevent waste or to prevent the confiscation of property grant exceptions to permit drilling within shorter distances than herein prescribed whenever the Commission shall have determined that such exceptions are necessary either to prevent waste or to prevent the confiscation of property. When exception to this rule is desired, application therefor shall be filed and will be acted upon in accordance with the provisions of Commission Statewide Rules 37 and 38, which applicable provisions of said rules are incorporated herein by reference.

'The aforementioned distances in the above rule are minimum distances to allow an operator flexibility in locating a well, and the above spacing rule and the other rules to follow are for the purpose of permitting only one well to each eighty (80) are [SIC] proration unit.

'In applying this rule, the general order of the Commission with relation to the subdivision of property shall be observed.

'RULE 2: The acreage assigned to the individual oil well for the purpose of allocating allowable oil production thereto shall be known as a proration unit. No proration unit shall consist of more than eighty (80) acres except as hereinafter provided, and the two farthermost points in any proration unit shall not be in excess of forty two hundred (4200) feet removed from each other; provided, however, that in the case of long and narrow leases or in cases where because of the shape of the lease such is necessary to permit the utilization of tolerance acreage the Commission may after proper showing grant exceptions to the limitations as to the shape of proration units as herein contained. All proration units, however, shall consist of continuous and contiguous acreage which can reasonably be considered to be productive of oil.

'Provided, however, that operators may elect to assign tolerance of not more than eighty (80) acres of additional unassigned lease acreage to a well on an eighty (80) acre unit and shall in such event receive allowable credit for not more than one hundred sixty (160) acres.

'Operators shall file with the Commission certified plats of their properties in said field, which plats shall set out distinctly all of those things pertinent to the determination of the acreage credit claimed for each well; provided that if the acreage assigned to any proration unit has been pooled, the operator shall furnish the Commission with such proof as it may require as evidence that interests in and under such proration unit have been so pooled.'

The petitioner does not contend, nor does the opinion say, that the proration unit in question does not comply with the regulations of the Railroad Commission. The opinion simply assumes, without giving a reason why, that the regulations of the Railroad Commission under which the unit in question was created were not Prescribed by governmental regulations.

The court, in discussing the provisions of the regulations, does not fully cover all the size units provided in said regulations. Since the authority given by lessor to pool is governed largely by these regulations, it is thought that it well [SIC] be helpful to more fully analyze them.

At the time the unit in question was formed, Railroad Commission Order No. 6—45, 322 was in effect and governed the Fairway (James Lime) Field. One of the Commission's preliminary findings set out in the order, preceding the adoption of field rules, was an express finding to the effect that certain observations and calculations made with reference to the discovery well in the field had indicated that the well was producing oil in an area outside the radius of a 160-acre circle around the well. From this and other findings the Commission proceeded to adopt proration rules which established a maximum proration unit of 160 acres for which full acreage allowable credit would be given. Thus, it was implicit that the Commission had determined that the basic drainage pattern for the field was 160 acres or, in other words, that a 160-acre unit would be reasonably drained by a single well.

The Commission order did something more. It expressly recognized that smaller units would also be given full acreage allowable credit, if they met certain requirements. One of the provisions of the rules established, in effect, that if an operator had as much as 80 acres in a single lease, 80 acres would then be considered as the minimum proration unit, the inclusion of additional acreage, up to the total maximum of 160 acres, being optional with the operator. But another provision, relating to distance spacing, also established that, still without the necessity of any hearing or exception, any square tract of 40 acres or more would also serve as an acceptable proration unit, if that were all the acreage the operator possessed in the particular property, and if there had been no illegal subdivision. The 40-acre minimum standard was implicit in the rule that no well be drilled nearer than 660 feet from any property line. Thus, the Commission Order in effect recognized that, without special hearing and exception, the maximum standard proration unit, i.e., the area which could reasonably be drained by a single well, was 160 acres, while the minimum standard unit, i.e., the smallest to be allowed, was 40 acres. Pickens v. Railroad Commission, 387 S.W.2d 35, 38, 39 (Tex.Sup.Ct.1965).

The court's opinion says 'The Commission prescribed a unit of 80 acres', inferring that all other size units provided for in said regulations were permitted by the Railroad Commission or permitted by the regulations, I am not sure which. To be sure, an 80-acre unit is prescribed by the regulations. But I do not agree that it is the only unit prescribed. As shown above, the regulations provide for units from 40 acres to 160 acres in size.

The pooling unit in question comes squarely within the limits as to size with the provisions of the governmental regulations just as much so as does the 80-acre unit referred to above.

This brings us to a discussion of the interpretation to be given the proviso of the pooling unit, which we here quote:

> '* * * provided that should governmental authority having jurisdiction prescribe or permit the creation of units larger than those specified, units thereafter created may conform substantially in size with those prescribed by governmental regulations.'

The first clause of the proviso governs the condition under which the lessee may create units larger than those specified, (40 acres), that is, when government authority has prescribed rules and regulations for the creation of larger units or when governmental authority has permitted the creation of larger units. Under the facts of this case the governmental authority has prescribed rules and regulations providing for the creation of larger units, but it has not permitted the creation of larger units. No permit was requested nor was one needed. As a general rule the Railroad Commission permits the creation of units only as exceptions to established rules and regulations. The last clause of the proviso governs the size of units created under either prescribed regulations or governmental authority permission. As said above, it is not questioned but that this unit was created in compliance with the established regulations and not by permission of the Railroad Commission as an exception to the regulation.

It has been argued before this court that since the first clause in said proviso uses the term 'permit' and the second clause does not use the term, that 'prescribed' must necessarily have a special meaning of 'required' in order to leave room for permissive units to be formed, and since the last clause did not establish a size for permissive units, no authority was given to form any permissive units. This reasoning seems to be the basis of the court's holding. Under this line of reasoning we wonder why the parties used the term 'permit' at all in the first clause of the proviso. It is fundamental that in contracts all the terms used should be given meaning if possible. Should a governmental authority lay down rules and regulations for the creation of larger units, it is reasonable to say the governmental authority has Prescribed. If the governmental authority allows the creation of a larger unit as an exception to the prescribed rules and regulations it can be said that governmental authority has Permitted the creation of larger units. In fact, the term 'permit' is the universal term applied to authority granted as an exception to regular rules and regulations governing the development of oil and gas fields. The fact that the word 'permit' is not used in the second clause of the proviso does not destroy the import of the word 'permit' in the first clause.

This construction of the proviso allows us to give the usual and ordinary meaning to the word 'prescribe' as defined by Webster:

'prescribe (L. praescribere, praescriptum, fr.prae before—scribere to write, see scribere.) * * *

'2. To lay down authoritatively as a guide direction or rule of action; to impose as a peremptory order; to dictate; direct; ordain; as, to prescribe regular hours of study. 3. To keep within limits or bounds; to restrain; to confine * * *.

'Syn.—Limit, control, order, guide.'

I think that the authority granted by the lessor for pooling necessarily had to be stated in broad and general terms because it could not be foreseen what the circumstances in the future might be, what the regulations of the Railroad Commission might be nor in what terms they might be stated. For that reason a liberal interpretation should be given to the pooling provision to accomplish the purpose for which it was intended, that is, to promote conservation beneficial both to the lessor and the lessee. It can be reasonably concluded that from said pooling provision the parties intended for the authority to pool to extend to any unit size substantially conforming to any unit standard officially established by the Railroad Commission in the exercise of its spacing proration function.

This court, in construing an oil and gas lease in the recent case of Grady L. Fox et al. v. Julia Thoreson, 9 Tex.Sup.Ct.J. 26 (1965), used the following language:

> '* * * Another sound rule of interpretation is that language used by the parties to an oil and gas lease will not be held to impose a special limitation on the grant unless it is clear and precise and so unequivocal in nature that it can reasonably be given no other meaning.'

The court's opinion in the instant case has given a narrow and restricted meaning to the pooling provision in question when there is no language in said pooling provision which compels such construction to be placed thereon. So long as the lessor's pooling unit is confined to the size of the pooling units authorized by the rules and regulations of the Railroad Commission, it can reasonably be said that the unit complies in size with the prescribed regulations. This would be a reasonable construction of the pooling provision rather than a strained one.

In Texaco, Inc. v. Letterman, 343 S.W.2d 726, 732 (Tex.Civ.App.1961), the court in construing a pooling provision in an oil and gas lease said:

> 'That pooling or unitizing of oil and gas leases is a standard practice in the industry can not be questioned. It is equally recognized that unitization is often a more feasible method of operation from an engineering and scientific point of view. Unitization can be said to be advantageous to both lessors and lessees. We think these facts lead to the conclusion that in the absence of clear language to the contrary, pooling clauses should not be construed in a narrow or limited sense.'

And in Tiller v. Fields, 301 S.W.2d 185, 187 (Tex.Civ.App.1957), the court said:

> 'Anticipatory provisions in leases for the committment by the lessee of such leases to unitization, of necessity must be in general terms. Neither the lessor nor the lessee has any way of knowing at the time the lease is taken the facts with respect to which it will be necessary for the lessee to apply his power. It is not practicable for the lessee to await the ascertainment of such facts. He knows from experience that because of the possibility of many changes in ownership of the lessor's interest as time goes on, it may be difficult to effect an agreement if the right to unitize is not included in the lease itself. Phillips Petroleum Co. v. Peterson, 10 Cir., 218 F.2d 926. The Texas courts, as well as other courts, have recognized these basic facts, and have consistently sustained the basic validity of lease pooling provisions and units formed under their authority.'

In Phillips v. Petroleum Co. v. Peterson, 218 F.2d 926, 933, (10th Cir. 1954), the court reasoned as follows:

'Thus, it will be seen that unitization is a conservation measure which benefits both lessor and lessee and tends to prevent waste of a natural resource. * * *

'The practice of unitization by a power granted the lessee in advance, if faithfully carried out, will be fair and profitable both to the lessor and lessee, and is vital to the oil and gas industry in the interests of the conservation of both natural and material resources. It should be upheld, although the grant of power is in general terms, because it is subject to implied terms that will prevent arbitrary and unfair dealing, will require compliance with the implied covenants in the lease for the benefit of the lessor and will impose a rigid standard of good faith on the part of the lessee.'

In construing this pooling provision of the oil and gas lease we should recognize that this does not only affect the litigants involved here, but affects the oil industry as a whole for the simple reason that the form of the pooling unit used is in wide use in Texas and has been for many years.

The pooling clause which we have before us for construction has been in use in Texas for many years. Tolerance type proration units have been prescribed for various oil and gas fields in Texas for many years. The result has been the creation of many pooled units in numerous fields which are now shadowed. The confusion, uncertainty, and possible title failure is not limited to the lessee who may have formed the unit. It extends to royalty owners in the unit, overriding royalty owners, and to some extent to the purchasers of production and the financial institutions which furnish capital for the development and enjoyment of the mineral resources. Furthermore, there is affected by the court's opinion the new Texas Compulsory Pooling Act by the Legislature, Art. 6008c, Rev.Civ.Stat.Ann. (1965). See discussion by Ernest E. Smith, Tex.Law Rev. Vol. 43 pp. 1003—1021.

I think a reasonable construction of the pooling clause does not require that we strike it down, and I would affirm the judgments of the trial court and Court of Civil Appeals.

GRIFFIN, J., joins in this dissent.

POPE, Justice (dissenting).

The fault that I find with our holding in this case is that we are trying to fit the meaning of terms used by private parties to a lease into a supposed technical terminology used by the Railroad Commission in making its rules and orders. This is the sequence of events. First the parties made the oil and gas lease and in it they provided:

> 'Units pooled for oil hereunder shall not substantially exceed 40 acres each in area, and units pooled for gas hereunder shall not substantially exceed in area 640 acres plus a tolerance of 10% Thereof, provided that should governmental authority having jurisdiction Prescribe or permit the creation of units larger than those specified, units thereafter created may conform substantially in size with those Prescribed by governmental regulations.'

Several years later the Commission order was passed which stated:

> '* * * No proration unit shall consist of more than eighty (80) acres except as hereinafter provided, * * * 'Provided, however, that operators may elect to assign tolerance of not more than eighty (80) acres of additional unassigned lease acreage to a well on an eighty (80) acre unit and shall in such event receive allowable credit for not more than one hundred sixty (160) acres.'

The thrust of our opinion is that the Commission 'prescribes' certain things, and it also 'permits' certain things. The majority then tries to determine which the Commission did in this instance and holds that the Commission 'prescribed' eighty acres but did not 'prescribe' 160 acres. The fact is that the Commission passed its rules without regard to whether it was 'prescribing' or 'permitting,' as those terms are used by the private contracting parties. The term 'permitted' actually does two things: It permits but it also prohibits all that is beyond that which is permitted. Every permit carries an inherent prescription, proscription, and prohibition of things beyond the permit. What the Commission did in passing its Rule 2 was to authorize certain units. Those units could be formed without any further recourse to the Commission. To the extent that Rule 2 was complied with, a unit was authorized. To the extent that it was beyond what Rule 2 authorized, it was prohibited. To the extent that it was prohibited, it was 'prescribed,' if we want to squeeze the Commission order into the contractual mold. In my opinion the word 'prescribed' is more applicable to the 160-acre unit than the 80-acre unit because the only prohibition or direction is against creating a unit of more than 160 acres.

I respectfully dissent.

Commentary on Jones v. Killingsworth

by Dick Watt

The Texas Supreme Court's 1965 decision in *Jones v. Killingsworth*, 403 S.W.2d 325 (1965) earns its status as a "landmark" decision because of its effect on the development of the pooling clause in oil and gas leases, and because it establishes clear and well-reasoned "bright-line" principles applicable to the requirements of voluntary pooling in virtually all oil and gas leases. Of equal importance, it makes clear the consequences of failing to follow those requirements.

The importance of this decision is magnified because it was decided in 1965, a time when voluntary pooling clauses were still a relatively new concept in oil and gas leases, having come into common use in Texas only after the end of the Second World War in 1945. As a result, although voluntary pooling was certainly a common practice by 1965, case law on this topic was scarce.[1]

The Background: Echoes of the East Texas Field

In a sense, understanding the circumstances surrounding the discovery and development of the East Texas Field is necessary for a complete understanding of *Jones v. Killingsworth*. Until 1930, East Texas generally was a sleepy and largely impoverished rural area, having neither the vast cattle ranches of South and West Texas, nor the large plantations and other agricultural enterprises of the Deep South. Instead, with the exception of large tracts owned by lumber companies, most land was owned locally in small tracts and farms of little economic value, thus many formalities customarily used to perfect title were often overlooked or ignored.[2]

All of this changed overnight in September of 1930, when in the western part of Rusk County, the Daisy Bradford No. 3 well announced to the world the discovery of the giant East Texas Field, the world's largest oil discovery at that time, stretching for over 30 miles from north to south to cover parts of five East Texas counties. The discovery of such enormous wealth, in an area where the ownership of land was often poorly documented, encouraged a generation of oilmen, lawyers and land men to quickly learn to scrutinize every facet of the recorded deeds, leases and other title documents that determined who owned the prolific Woodbine oil formation, lying less than a mile below the hardscrabble East Texas countryside. Many of those who grew rich learned quickly that if the common law was properly utilized, then its emphasis on the sanctity of contract and real property rights—stronger probably nowhere than in Texas at this time—could produce wealth as surely as the drill bit.

At the same time, they also learned dramatic lessons about the danger and difficulties of drilling wells on each small tract that competed to produce the oil, as seen in familiar pictures from that time of downtown Kilgore, with row after row of tightly packed oil derricks—a practice that eventually led to the imposition of martial law in the East Texas Field.[3] Moreover, in large part, these lessons from the 1930s soon led the oil industry to include provisions in leases that allowed pooling, so that the leases could be combined into units with one well that could produce and perpetuate multiple leases and acreage. They also led to the Railroad Commission promulgating various rules aimed at regulating production and preventing waste—the sort made the *casus belli* in *Jones v. Killingsworth*.

The Fairway (James Lime) Field

Keeping this background in mind, *Jones v. Killingsworth* has its origins in nearby Henderson and Anderson Counties, where the Fairway Field was discovered in 1960, just one county to the west of the East Texas Field. The Fairway Field was a prolific oil discovery in the James Lime formation and was discovered by independent operators out of Tyler, all well acquainted with the pitfalls and opportunity found when leasing mineral rights in this area.[4] This was certainly true with a discovery of the magnitude of the Fairway Field, one of the major discoveries in East Texas in the last half of the 20th century, and has to date produced well over 100,000,000 barrels of oil. As will be seen, in such an area where the memories of the countless lawsuits involving title in the East Texas Field were still fresh, many veterans of those battles regularly scrutinized every oil and gas lease when it was recorded in the Courthouse.

But the story of *Jones v. Killingsworth* begins in 1951, nine years before the Fairway Field was discovered, when on August 16, 1951, a lady named Margaret Mitchell leased her 20-acre tract to S.S. Long. This oil and gas lease, called the Long Lease, was located in the far eastern part of Henderson County, near the Neches River between Athens and Tyler, south of Chandler and slightly to the east of the little community of Poyner.[5] The Long Lease was for a 10-year primary term, and common to the time, contained provisions that generally allowed it to be pooled with other leases to form voluntary units for an oil well up to a maximum of 40 acres in size.[6]

By the time of the Fairway Field's discovery in 1960, the Long Lease was still within its 10-year primary term, and by then had been assigned by Long to a man named Killingsworth.[7]

By 1961, the oil boom was on in the Fairway Field, and wells were rapidly being drilled to develop it. As it happened, Hunt Oil Company out of Dallas had quickly become a significant player in the field and wanted to drill a well on a lease it owned, which was directly adjacent to the Long Lease. To accomplish this, Hunt agreed with Killingsworth to pool Hunt's lease with the Long Lease to form a unit called the Hunt Oil Company—West Poyner Unit, composed of a total of 160 acres.[8] With this done, Hunt drilled a producing oil well on its lease within the Unit—but not located on the Long Lease.

Oil Proration and the Long Lease

Although perhaps difficult to imagine at the time of this writing (2008), in that long ago time when Hunt drilled its well, the production of oil was regulated, or "prorated," by the Texas Railroad Commission to give each well an "allowable" amount of oil that it could produce each month. This was done so that the total amount of production in Texas each month would approximate the estimated market demand for oil. Under this system of proration, generally each oilfield was apportioned its share of the expected market demand for oil each month, and then in turn, each well in the field was allowed to produce its share of the amount of oil allocated to the field.

This allocation was based on the Railroad Commission's field rules for each field, which determined this amount of production allocated to each well based on allotments of acreage called "proration units." Thus, the amount of oil each well was allowed to produce each month was based on whether its "proration unit" contained enough acreage to meet the requirements established by the Railroad Commission's field rules. As will be noted, a proration unit is based on leased acreage owned by an oil company and allocated to a well. But it does not concern or affect the ownership of the leases, and in that sense, is a "unit" in name only.

Of particular importance to *Jones v. Killingsworth*, the Railroad Commission's field rules for the Fairway Field prescribed 80-acre proration units—that is, 80 acres was required to be allocated to a well if that well was to produce its maximum amount of oil each month.[9] Additionally, these rules encouraged larger proration units—and more production—by permitting—but not requiring—an operator to assign as much as an additional 80 acres to form a 160-acre proration unit, and thus gain an even greater "allowable" for oil produced from that well each month.[10]

Thus, the motivation was clear for Killingsworth to agree with Hunt Oil to form the 160-acre West Poyner Unit: they wanted to hold with one well an amount of allocated acreage necessary to obtain the highest allowable production of oil from that well.[11] However, because more than one leased tract was necessary to meet this 160-acre allocation requirement, it was necessary to pool both of the leases, so that they could both be perpetuated by production from the single well located on Hunt Oil Company's lease.

Shortly after the 160-acre West Poyner Unit was formed and production commenced, the primary term of the Long Lease expired. Thus, because there was no well on the Long Lease, that lease was perpetuated solely by *production from the well on the adjacent acreage with which it had been pooled.*[12]

Of course, the creation of the Unit benefited Hunt and Killingsworth, as well as Mrs. Mitchell, the lessor of the Long Lease, whose name by then was Margaret Mitchell Jones, and did so by allowing the well on the Unit to produce the maximum amount of oil each month allowed by the Railroad Commission rules. However, at the same time, the Unit was detrimental to Mrs. Jones' interest in that it significantly reduced her royalty, diluting it from a full 1/8th down to approximately 20/160 of 1/8th, that is, from 12-1/2% to about 1-1/2%. At this juncture, one may be curious, because normally a lessor without a well on her land wants to *get in* a unit, not *get out*. As will be shown later, at this time many operators were eager to pay large bonuses for unleased tracts, on which they could drill new, non-unitized wells.

Mrs. Jones obviously preferred a bonus money payment and a larger amount of royalty from a new well, instead of the greater amount of production and diluted royalty from the Hunt well. Accordingly, she filed suit in the District Court of Henderson County seeking a declaration that the Long Lease had terminated for lack of production when its primary term expired, because there was no well located on it.[13]

Her argument focused on the pooling clause of the Long Lease, and what it authorized, which lies at the heart of *Jones v. Killingsworth*. This provision, common at the time and even now found in older leases, provides that:

> Lessee, at its option, is hereby given the right and power to pool or combine the acreage covered by this lease . . . with other land . . . to the extent hereafter stipulated . . . in order to *properly develop and operate* . . . in compliance with the *spacing* rules of the Texas Railroad Commission . . . when to do so would, in the judgment of Lessee, *promote the conservation of oil and gas from said premises* . . . (*emphasis added*).[14]

Then comes the crux of the case, where the pooling clause then continues to limit the size of such a Unit, and then also provides an exception to this size limitation:

> Units pooled for oil *shall not substantially exceed 40-acres* . . . provided that if (the Railroad Commission) should *prescribe* or *permit* larger units, . . . (then) units *may conform* substantially in size to those *prescribed by governmental regulations* (emphasis added).[15]

The Trial Court Decision

Mrs. Jones' argument in the trial court was basically this: it did not matter that the Long Lease had been included in a unit with a producing well, because the unit in which it had been pooled exceeded the 40-acre maximum unit size authorized by the pooling clause in the Long Lease. Of course, while the pooling clause prohibited units larger than 40 acres for oil wells, it also allowed larger units. The Long Lease made this exception by providing that if such units were "prescribed or permitted" by Railroad Commission rules, then units could be formed larger than 40 acres—if they were "prescribed" by those Railroad Commission rules. Taking this into account, Mrs. Jones urged that while the Railroad Commission rules "prescribed" or "permitted" units larger than 40 acres, the Long Lease only allowed such larger units under one condition: the Railroad Commission must actually "prescribe" such larger units.[16] Accordingly, she argued that the 160-acre unit that was actually formed was not "prescribed," and thus not required, because the Railroad Commission's field rules merely "permitted" a 160-acre unit in order to obtain the extra allowable.[17]

Thus, her claim was that because a unit of 160 acres exceeded—and thus violated—the pooling authority granted by the lease, the unit should be cancelled because it had never been validly formed in the first place and was void from the beginning. Mrs. Jones reasoned that if this were done, the Long Lease, with no well located on it, would have expired by its own terms at the end of its primary term on August 16, 1961.

Hunt Oil, Killingsworth, and the other working interest owners disagreed with her argument. Instead, they urged that the Long Lease had been properly pooled under its express provisions because the pooling clause must be read in conjunction with the Railroad Commission Rules, which they argued allowed for units larger than 40 acres if these conditions were met: (1) units larger than 40 acres were "prescribed or permitted" by the RRC, and (2) such units were "prescribed" in order to gain the maximum allowable.[18]

Based on this, the working interest owners argued that this was precisely the case with the Long Lease, and moved for summary judgment that the Long Lease had not terminated, i.e., it had been properly unitized.

This motion squarely presented the crucial question: where the Railroad Commission clearly "prescribed" and "permitted" units larger than 40 acres—it required 80-acre units, but permitted optional 160-acre units—how did those rules mesh with the pooling provisions of the Long Lease? The District Judge, the Honorable Jack Y. Hardee of Athens, agreed with the working interest owners and without elaboration granted that motion for summary judgment, ruling in effect that the Long Lease had been properly pooled, and thus was held by production from the unit well located on Hunt's lease.[19]

On to Tyler: The Court of Appeals Decision

Mrs. Jones disagreed. She continued to maintain that larger units were allowed only when actually "prescribed" by the Railroad Commission rules, and not when merely "permitted," like the optional 160-acre unit in question. On this basis, she appealed to the Tyler Court of Civil Appeals, which affirmed the trial court.[20] The Tyler Court's decision was based on a construction of the lease language that reflected its perception of the parties' overall intent, as expressed by the language in the pooling clause—to allow units larger than 40 acres if the Railroad Commission rules either "prescribed" or "permitted" larger units, and holding that the Railroad Commission had in reality actually "prescribed" the optional 160 acre units.[21]

More specifically, the Tyler Court focused on the stated purposes found in the pooling clause, which allowed the formation of units in order to "comply with spacing rules" of the Railroad Commission or when in Lessee's judgment larger units would "promote the conservation" of oil and gas.[22] In doing this, the Court reasoned that further language in the Long Lease clearly recognized that the regulations of the Railroad Commission might "prescribe" or "permit" larger units. If this were so, as it was here, then the authority to pool found in the lease would be extended to allow the formation of a unit larger than 40 acres, if that unit conformed in size to what such regulations either "prescribed" or "permitted."[23]

Moreover, based on this and the other parts of the pooling clause quoted above, the Court further deduced that this would apply to both "spacing" units and "proration units" if such were "prescribed" or "permitted" by the Railroad Commission.[24] This result was based primarily on the Tyler Court's definition of "prescribe," which it held meant to "lay down authoritatively as a guide, direction or rule of action."[25] Using this definition, the Court concluded that even if the Railroad Commission regulations only "permitted" a 160-acre unit to obtain an additional allowable, this regulation was laid down "authoritatively as a guide, direction or rule," and therefore the size of the unit was "prescribed."[26]

In short, the Tyler Court held that in these circumstances, "permitted" actually meant the same as "prescribed," and thus because a 160-acre unit was "permitted," it also was "prescribed" by the Railroad Commission rules. Consequently, the 160-acre unit did not exceed the authority to pool granted in the lease.[27]

The Tyler Court's ruling seems to be firmly rooted in its recognition that the language of pooling clauses in oil and gas leases "should not be construed in a narrow or limited sense" and that the language in such clauses, together with prior court decisions, indicate that the "power to pool lease (sic) by the Lessee should be given broad powers . . . ."[28] Relying on this assumption, the Tyler Court obviously determined the meaning of this provision by utilizing a liberal contract construction approach reflecting both what it viewed as the parties' general intent, as well as proper public policy regarding pooling.

The Supreme Court Opinion

Mrs. Jones then appealed this decision to the Texas Supreme Court, which disagreed and reversed both of the lower courts.[29]

The Supreme Court's opinion and its rationale are important not only because of its effect on all voluntary pooling, but because both the majority and dissenting opinions contain reasoned and precise analyses that explain the interaction between real property principles, regulatory rules, and common law rules of contract construction.

The majority opinion first focused on the language of the pooling clause—the clear-cut prohibition that units for oil well must not exceed 40 acres in size.[30] Determining that much was very clear, the Court then addressed the exception to this prohibition, the language that would allow larger units, and greater dilution of the Lessor's royalty: that if the Railroad Commission rules "prescribe or permit *larger* units," then units "may conform substantially in size" with those larger units that were actually "prescribed" by those rules.[31]

The majority then decided the case based on the following rationale: although the Railroad Commission rules clearly allowed units larger than 40 acres because those rules "prescribed" 80-acre proration units, those same rules only "permitted" a 160-acre unit—it was optional—thus under the pooling clause, units larger than 40 acres were allowed only when "prescribed" by the rules. Stated another way, the Supreme Court appeared to reason that to authorize a lessee to pool the lessor's land with units of any size that were merely "permitted" by the Railroad Commission rules would defeat the obvious intention of the parties to restrict the size of the units to 40 acres unless larger units were actually "prescribed." In short, the Court essentially held that units larger than 40 acres were authorized by the lease only when mandated or required by law, as opposed to being simply permitted, arguably at a lessee's whim.

The majority explains this result and its reasoning with the following:

> "The lessors *did not consent* to enlarge an oil proration unit to any size *Permitted* by governmental regulations. *They gave their consent* to enlarge a unit of substantially 40 acres, but only to the extent of the size of units *Prescribed* by the regulatory authority. The fact that the Railroad Commission may *Permit* a much larger unit *cannot be read into the lease contract* when, as here, the authority to create larger oil units is expressly limited to units of the size *Prescribed* by the Railroad Commission. . . . It is true that the pooling provision contains the word 'permit' as well as the word 'prescribe.' It is *not unreasonable to assume that the parties to the lease contract intended, by the use of both words, to give each a distinctly different meaning."* (*Emphasis added*—note capital "Ps" for "prescribe" and "permit" in opinion).[32]

-- -- --

Although the Supreme Court opinion clearly reflects the same goal of contract construction sought by the Tyler Court of Civil Appeals—to discern the parties' intent from the language they used—the Supreme Court obviously adhered to a much more narrow view of contract construction. This narrow view undoubtedly reflected a strong adherence to real property principles of ownership and sanctity of contract. As to ownership and principles of real property, the Court concluded that:

> *Absent express authority*, a lessee has *no power to pool interests in the estate* retained by the lessor with those of other lessors. (*emphasis added*)[33]

By this, the majority opinion clearly was concerned with the loss of a vested interest in real property—the lessor's royalty would be diluted by the larger unit. Such a dramatic event obviously could not be allowed to happen unless the Lessor—the lawful owner of the royalty—expressly authorized it.

Moreover, the sanctity of contract is preserved only if contracts are enforced as written by the parties. In this respect, while the Opinion never expressly reverses the Tyler Court's expanded definition of "permit," the majority clearly did not intend to allow a liberal contract construction to allow an interest in real property to be diluted by a lease's somewhat uncertain reference to regulatory action. Additionally, the majority was obviously concerned that such vague language in a lease might tacitly imply that uncertain bureaucratic regulations would actually impact more clear-cut agreements concerning real property. Accordingly, the majority strongly expressed this sentiment, stating that it would not allow "orders of the Railroad Commission" to "*compel pooling agreements* that the *parties themselves do not agree upon*" (*emphasis added*).[34]

In summation, the Supreme Court's rationale obviously reflects two bedrock principles deeply embedded in the common law:

1. *Private property rights are paramount*. Just as a man's home is his castle, interests in real property such as royalty cannot be casually or impliedly taken away or diminished. Instead, the lessor who owns the property must clearly and unequivocally authorize such a dilution and an uncertain reference in a lease to Railroad Commission "rules" and what they "permitted" does not constitute such a clear authorization.[35]

2. *The sanctity of contract must be preserved*. Agreements are enforced as written, and if the words used don't mean what their scriveners may have intended them to mean, then any judicial construction

of the meaning of those words should not expand their definition.[36] In short, "permitted" does not mean "prescribed."

With this decided, the Court then proceeds to an equally important topic: what happens when a lessee exceeds the lease's authority to pool? On this point, the Court logically deduces, with little discussion, that when pooling is done improperly, i.e., in a manner that exceeds the authority granted in the lease, the following results:

> Since the lands were pooled *without authority*, the habendum clause in the Mitchell-Long Lease *cannot be used to extend the term* of the lease beyond August 16, 1961, the terminal date of the primary term of the lease (*emphasis added*).[37]

In short, here the Court looks at the habendum clause in the lease, and notes that it requires production from the lease at the end of the primary term to be extended. This being so, the Court then holds that because there was no well located on the Long Lease at the end of its primary term, then there was no production to extend it beyond its primary term.[38] The Court concludes this with very little discussion, and those justices writing the majority opinion in 1965 probably felt that no extended discussion of such an obvious point was necessary. But what about the unit well on the Hunt tract? On this point, they conclude essentially that there was no unit: that if a lessee forms a unit that exceeds the pooling authority granted in the lease, then its action is a nullity—no pooling has ever occurred and this means the unit is void *ab initio*—that is, it never existed.

Implicit in this reasoning, though not stated expressly, is an assumption that the Railroad Commission's concept of proration of production and allowing wells to produce more depending on how much acreage was "allocated" to a proration unit, or requiring certain distances for a spacing unit, had absolutely nothing to do with the parties' agreement as to real property interests.[39]

Bad-Faith Pooling

In this respect, it should be noted that *Jones v. Killingsworth* contains no contention of bad-faith pooling, as it was stipulated by all parties that the West Poyner Unit had been formed in good faith.[40]

Despite this, and never decided or mentioned in the opinion, this same result—the cancellation of the unit *ab initio*—occurs when bad-faith pooling is proved. Again, this is because a unit formed improperly is considered not to be formed at all, and *Jones v. Killingsworth* is often cited for this proposition in bad-faith pooling cases.[41] In those cases, of course, unlike Mrs. Jones, the plaintiff is always a lessor under the drillsite tract where the well is located, who seeks an undiluted royalty share of that well's production, rather than a release of the lease itself, as occurred in *Jones v. Killingsworth*.

The Dissenting Opinions

The Supreme Court's decision in *Jones v. Killingsworth* also earns its distinction as a "landmark" case because it contains two cogent and well-reasoned dissents, which squarely confront and rationally address the rationale of the majority opinion. Both of these dissents basically advocate a more liberal contract interpretation process to find a broader intent, in contrast to the stricter real property and sanctity of contract emphasis of the majority.

For example, Justice Hamilton in the first dissent argued that because the first clause of the last sentence in the pooling clause used both "prescribe and permit," the use of only the word "prescribe" in the second clause does not destroy the use of "permit" in the first.[42] In the second dissent, Justice Griffin joined by Justice Pope argued along the same lines that to "permit" something is essentially the same as to "prescribe" it, in that "permit" is a verb that "prohibits all that is not permitted," i.e., as used, "permit" is really no different from "prescribe."[43]

Subsequent Legal History and Effect on Pooling Provisions

Despite the two well-reasoned dissenting opinions, the majority opinion in *Jones v. Killingsworth* has stood unchallenged since 1965 for its two basic principles: (1) for a unit to be valid, the authority to pool in a lease must be followed exactly, and (2) if not followed exactly, then no unit has been formed. These rules, though sometimes harsh in their result, are fair and logical, and furnish landowners, oil companies, and the legal profession clear guidelines as to pooling. As a result, though *Jones v. Killingsworth* has been cited in nearly forty reported cases and several treatises and law review articles, to this author's knowledge, neither the decision nor its reasoning has ever been seriously criticized. As to pooling clauses in leases, while many such clauses found in so-called standard form leases have been modified to overcome the lessee's difficulties in *Jones v. Killingsworth*, identical clauses are still often found in older leases held by production, and the lessons of *Jones v. Killingsworth* may still prove relevant to an entire new generation of operators, landmen, and lawyers who now deal with those leases.

However, a case with exactly the same facts is unlikely to arise again for at least two reasons:

(a) First, in direct response to the *Killingsworth* decision, the Railroad Commission adjusted the use of its terminology for optional proration units and, in many gas units, no longer uses an acreage factor in establishing an allowable;[44] and

(b) Second, lease forms after *Jones v. Killingsworth* that still used the "prescribed or permitted" language, have been modified to remove any distinction between "prescribed" and "permitted."

The Aftermath: Oil, Law, and Ingenuity

Any notion that *Jones v. Killingsworth* is dry legalese quickly evaporates when the reality of its immediate result is considered: that, conceivably, hundreds of leases overlying the prolific and now proven James Lime oil reservoir would be open and available, and one naturally wonders what effect such a decision must have had in the Fairway Field, which by the time of the Supreme Court's decision in 1965 contained numerous producing wells and stretched over thousands of acres, composed of numerous small farms and parcels. Because most of those leases contained pooling clauses substantially identical to the Long Lease, and had been unitized in 160-acre units, it was clear that *such tracts without wells located on the leased tract* itself might no longer be held under the lease.

If so, these tracts could then be leased and drilled with a 100% chance of making an excellent James Lime oil well.[45]

As might be expected, the decision initially resulted in a flurry of activity involving opportunistic operators, landmen, and lawyers. Upon reading the decision, they reasoned—quite logically—that if they could find leases in the rich Fairway Field that contained pooling clauses like the Long Lease, and most did, and those leases had been pooled, like the Long Lease, into a unit that exceeded the size stated in the pooling clause, and many did, then unless there was a well actually located on the lease, such leases would have expired for lack of production.

Fortunately, or unfortunately, depending on one's viewpoint, a substantial obstacle quickly presented itself in the form of the field-wide unitization of the Fairway Field, which had occurred by the time that *Jones v. Killingsworth* was decided.[46] As a result, most lessors and royalty owners had signed a ratification of the Fieldwide Unit Agreement and a Fieldwide Unit Operating Agreement covering the Fairway Field.[47] Those agreements contained references to the existing leases and units, and as a result, the landowners' signatures to such agreements effectively ratified any units or leases that otherwise might have run afoul of *Jones v. Killingsworth*.

Thus, many thought this cured any problem for the working interest owners. However, such an assumption ignored the human ingenuity that is almost universally exhibited when great riches are at stake, and perhaps like nowhere else will such ingenuity come forward as in the midst of a large oil and gas discovery.

In this instance, in Athens, Texas, a very smart and well-respected lawyer named Willis D. Moore pondered this problem at length. Eventually, the solution hit him: Moore reasoned that even if a royalty owner had signed both agreements—the Fieldwide Unit Agreement and Fieldwide Unit Operating Agreement—*but that royalty owner did so at a time after he had sold all of his royalty*, then that royalty owner could maintain that he had not ratified the otherwise offending unit. Instead, such an owner could assert that (1) he had not ratified the agreements as a royalty owner, because he owned no royalty; and (2) instead, he signed them as a working interest owner who owned not a mere lease, but owned the unleased fee minerals, and because his lease had expired before signing the agreements, it could not be later ratified or revived.

Armed with this idea, Moore enlisted the services of a pleasantly eccentric and extremely knowledgeable Athens fixture named Billy Wofford, who possessed astonishing knowledge of the land in Henderson County and the people who owned it. Moore asked Wofford to comb the Henderson County Deed Records for just such facts as required to fit Moore's theory: a lease with no well on it, in a unit with a size that exceeded the lease's pooling authority, with a lessor who had sold all of his royalty before signing the two fieldwide agreements. After examining the deed records at length, Wofford ultimately identified a small number of lessors and leases which fit Moore's required scenario.

With this information, Moore then acted, and on behalf of a well-heeled client who was not averse to risk, Moore bought top leases from the lessors who fit the situation that Wofford had spotted. Next, Moore secured the aid of a gifted oil and gas lawyer from Dallas named Edward Kliewer, Jr., and they filed suit against Hunt Oil Company and various other lessees to establish their title, basing their claim on *Jones v. Killingsworth* and the unique facts of Moore's theory.[48]

While the resulting legal war is far beyond the scope of this paper, ultimately Moore and his client were very successful in some instances.[49]

In closing, it is hoped that beyond this case's obvious legal significance, the reader has gained some flavor of the rich and continuing panorama of the oil and gas business. As a result of this case, certainly every lawyer who deals with oil and gas leases never again casually uses the words "prescribe" and "permit," and always keeps the lessons of *Jones v. Killingsworth* in the back of his or her mind.

---

1 There are only eleven Texas Court of Appeals cases and five Texas Supreme Court cases that are related to the voluntary pooling practice before 1965. *See, e.g., Ward v. Gohlke*, 279 S.W.2d 422 (Tex. Civ. App.—San Antonio 1955, writ ref'd).

2 *See* James A. Clark & Michel T. Halbouty, *The Last Boom, the Exciting Saga of the Discovery of the Greatest Oil Field in America* (1st ed. 1972).

3 *Id.*

4 The factual and legal history concerning its discovery, who did what to whom, and the subsequent litigation, in itself is worthy of a book, or perhaps a television series.

5 *Jones v. Killingsworth*, 379 S.W.2d 362, 364 (Tex. Civ. App.—Tyler 1964, writ granted).

6 *Id.*

7 *Id.*

8 The unit was described at various times as containing various amounts of acreage; for purposes of its opinion, the Supreme Court assumed it to be 160 acres, *see Jones v. Killingsworth*, 403 S.W.2d 325, 326 (1965).

9 *See Hunt Oil Co. v. Moore*, 656 S.W.2d 634, 638 (Tex. Civ. App.—Tyler. 1983writ ref'd n.r.e.).

10 *Jones*, 403 S.W.2d at 327.

11 For an example of this in practice, *see People's Petroleum Producers v. Smith*, 1 F.Supp. 361, 361 (1932) (the court held that the acreage of the oil field affects the highest allowable production of oil from that well).

12 *See Jones*, 379 S.W.2d at 362.

13 *Id.* at 364.

14 *Id.* at 365.

15 *Id.* This language was common at the time. At least one commentator believes it was originated in the early 1950s in Humble Oil & Refining Company leases, which were widely copied. J. Robert Goldsmith, Jr. *Selected Title Exam Issues*, Advanced Oil, Gas and Mineral Course (1994). However, this author has seen identical language in at least some of the Pound Printing & Stationery, Houston, Texas forms dating from at least the late 1940s.

16 *Jones*, 379 S.W.2d at 366.

17 *Id.*

18 *See Id.*

19 *Jones*, 403 S.W.2d at 326.

20 *Jones*, 379 S.W.2d at 362.

21 *Id.* at 368.

22 *Id.* at 369.

23 *Id.*

24 *Id.*

25 *Id.*

26 *Id.*

27 *Id.*

28 *Id.*

29 *Jones*, 403 S.W.2d at 325.

30 *Id.* at 327.

31 *Id.*

32 *Id.* at 328.

33 *Id.*

34 *Id.*

35 *See id.*

36 *See id.*

37 *Id.*

38 *See id.*

39 *See id.*

40 For example, in *Jones*, the court held that:"it is true that the lessee acted in good faith." *Id.* at 328.

41 *See generally Union Gas Corp. v. Gisler*, 129 S.W.3d 145 (Tex. App.—Corpus Christi—Edinburg 2003, no pet.) (the plaintiff claimed that defendant involved in bad-faith oil drilling); *Jones v. Hunt Oil Co.*, 456 S.W.2d 506 (Tex. App.—Dallas 1970, writ ref'd n.r.e.); *Tittizer v. Union Gas Corp.*, 171 S.W.3d 857 (Tex. 2005); *Southeastern Pipe Line Co., Inc. v. Tichacek*, 997 S.W.2d 166 (Tex. 1999).

42 *Jones*, 403 S.W.2d at 331.
43 *Id.* at 333.
44 The larger unit is now "prescribed" and the smaller "permitted."
45 *See Westbrook v. Atlantic Richfield Co.*, 502 S.W.2d 551, 553 (1973).
46 *Id.*
47 *See Hunt Oil Co.*, 656 S.W.2d at 637.
48 *See Id.* at 635.
49 *See Westbrook*, 502 S.W.2d at 551. *But see Hunt Oil Co.*, 656 S.W.2d at 634. For an additional sampling of the flavor of this legal donnybrook, *see generally Jones,* 456 S.W.2d at 506; *Atlantic Richfield Co. v. Westbrook*, 491 S.W.2d 207 (Tex. Civ. App.—Tyler 1972, writ granted), *rev'd*, 502 S.W.2d 551 (1973); *Hunt Oil Co. v. Jones*, 436 S.W.2d 186 (Tex. Civ. App.—Eastland 1968, writ dism'd w.o.j); *Atlantic Richfield Co. v. Hilton*, 437 S.W.2d 347 (Tex. Civ. App.—Tyler 1969, writ ref., n.r.e.), *cert den'd*, 396 U.S. 90 (1969); *Hilton v. Atlantic Refining Company*, 327 F.2d 217 (1964).

CHAPTER 12

W. R. Montgomery, Petitioner, v. Charles Edgar Rittersbacher et al., Respondents.

COMMENTARY

by Bruce M. Kramer

424 S.W.2d 210

1968

W. R. Montgomery, Petitioner,
v.
Charles Edgar Rittersbacher et al., Respondents.

424 S.W.2d 210

1968

Kelley, Looney, McLean & Littleton, L. C. McLean, Edinburg, for petitioner.

Aldrich, McDonald & Stewart, B. R. Stewart, Edinburg, for respondents.

SMITH, Justice.

Petitioner, W. R. Montgomery, brought this suit to establish his right to accumulated and prospective royalty under an oil, gas and mineral lease. The material facts are undisputed. The trial court in a nonjury trial rendered judgment that Montgomery take nothing. The Court of Civil Appeals affirmed. 410 S.W.2d 925. We reverse the judgments of the courts below and remand the cause to the trial court with instructions.

In 1945 Montgomery conveyed approximately eighty (80) acres of land, designated in the record as 'First Tract,' to Respondents' predecessors in title but reserved for himself a non-participating royalty interest. The title to the property, including the royalty interest not reserved by Montgomery, became vested in Respondents, who also owned land hereinafter designated as 'Second Tract' which is contiguous to 'First Tract.' Montgomery owned no interest in this 'Second Tract.' Respondents were the owners of the executive rights under 'First Tract' and 'Second Tract' as well as some of the royalty rights under 'Second Tract' and the royalty rights not owned by Petitioner under 'First Tract.'

In 1953 Respondents filed for record an oil, gas, and mineral lease dated September 4, 1951, covering both 'First Tract' and 'Second Tract.' Since Respondents held the executive rights of 'First Tract,' it was not necessary for Montgomery to join, nor did he, in the lease executed by Respondents. The lease contained a pooling clause whereby lessee was permitted to combine the leasehold estate with any other mineral estate in order to create appropriate operating units. The lease further provided that production on any tract of land within any unitized area formed under the pooling provision should constitute full compliance with the development, drilling, and producing obligations expressed in the lease. Additionally, the lease contained the following entirety clause:

'If the leased premises are now or shall hereafter be owned in severalty or in separate tracts, the premises, nevertheless, shall be developed and operated as one lease, and all royalties accruing hereunder shall be treated as an entirety and shall be divided among and paid to such separate owners in the proportion that the acreage owned by each such separate owner bears to the entire leased acreage.'

The lessee, Sun Oil Company, formed several units out of the original leased acreage by combining some of the land under the lease with land Sun held under other leases. A portion of 'Second Tract' was unitized with a tract known as the Crutchfield tract, land not owned by Respondents and not covered by the lease. A producing well was completed on the Crutchfield tract in October, 1956, from which commercial production was begun in May, 1958. 'First Tract' was placed in a unit on which a dry hole was drilled in July, 1961.

Montgomery brought this suit in May, 1964, against Sun Oil Company, the lessee, and Respondents, the holders of the executive rights, claiming by virtue of the entirety clause a share of the royalties which were accruing under the lease. Since 'Second Tract' is in the Crutchfield pool, it receives a proportionate share of the royalties that are produced from the Crutchfield well. This royalty, according to the terms of the entirety clause in the lease, is 'divided among and paid to such separate owners in the proportion that the acreage owned by each such separate owner bears to the entire leased acreage.' Consequently, Montgomery seeks the proportion of the royalties accruing under the lease that his non-participating interest bears to the leased acreage. He contends that the entirety clause in the lease by its express terms applies to and includes his non-participating royalty interest; and since he has ratified the lease, Respondents cannot now deny the effect of the contract entered into between Respondents and Sun.

Respondents contend and the Court of Civil Appeals has held that Respondents did not have the power to bind Montgomery's non-participating royalty interest with an entirety clause; Montgomery did not properly ratify the lease; and, Montgomery did not qualify to recover as a third party beneficiary of the lease. We agree that the Respondents, the holders of the executive rights, did not have the power to bind Montgomery's non-participating royalty interest by virtue of the entirety clause alone, but do not agree with their contention that the Petitioner has not 'properly' ratified the lease. We are of the opinion that the enlargement or diminishment of the rights of a prior non-participating royalty owner can be accomplished by the holder of the executive rights executing an oil, gas, and mineral lease which includes either a pooling clause or an entirety clause, provided the non-participating owner ratifies such action.

This Court has held that pooling effects a cross-conveyance among the owners of minerals under the various tracts of royalty or minerals in a pool so that they all own undivided interests under the unitized tract in the proportion their contribution bears to the unitized tract. Veal v. Thomason, 138 Tex. 341, 159 S.W.2d 472 (1942). The mere reservation of a non-participating royalty interest under a tract does not show that the royalty owner intended to give to the holder of the executive rights the power to diminish the royalty owner's interest under that tract. Consequently, pooling on the part of the holder of the executive rights cannot be binding upon the non-participating royalty owner in the absence of his consent. Minchen v. Fields, 162 Tex. 73, 345 S.W.2d 282 (1961); Brown v. Smith, 141 Tex. 425, 174 S.W.2d 43 (1943); and Nugent v. Freeman, 306 S.W.2d 167 (Tex.Civ.App.—Eastland 1957, writ ref'd n.r.e.), cited with approval in Minchen v. Fields, supra. We can see no distinction between the pooling clause, insofar as it has the effect of changing the aggregate ownership of the non-participating royalty owner, and the entirety clause, which, in effect, would allow the holder of the executive rights to either diminish or enlarge the ownership of that of the royalty owner. In either case, the consent of the owner must be obtained.

Respondents argue that although the lease in question covered Montgomery's non-participating interest, the entirety clause in the lease did not. They contend that since they did not have the power to diminish Montgomery's interest in 'First Tract' and thereby to obtain a proportional share of any royalties accruing to that tract, they did not intend for Montgomery to use the entirety clause to share proportionally in royalties accruing to their tracts. Furthermore, Respondents claim that one of the reasons that they inserted a proportional reduction clause in the lease was to make the entirety clause operative only on those interests which they had authority to cover by the entirety clause.

We are unable to agree with Respondents' contention. The lease executed by Respondents and the original lessee explicitly described the entire tract in which Montgomery had a non-participating interest as being covered by the lease. The unambiguous entirety clause clearly indicates that it was to apply to all the interests covered by the lease. The clause points out that even if the premises are owned in severalty At the time of the execution of the lease, as the premises were in this case, 'the (leased) premises, nevertheless shall be developed and operated As one lease, and All royalties accruing hereunder shall be treated as an entirety and shall be divided among and Paid to such separate owners in the proportion that the acreage owned by each bears to the entire leased acreage.' (Emphasis added.) This Court has held that an 'are now' entirety clause as was contained in the present lease applies to minerals held in severalty at the time of the execution of the lease. Thomas Gilcrease Foundation v. Stanolind Oil & Gas Co., 153 Tex. 197, 266 S.W.2d 850, 853 (1954).

Respondents, in exercising the executive rights, had a duty to protect the nonparticipating royalty owner. See Jones, Nonparticipating Royalty, 26 Texas L.Rev. 569, 580—85 (1948) and Elliott, The Executive Right, 42 Texas L.Rev. 865 (1965). Had Respondents not intended to include Montgomery's non-participating interest within the provisions of the entirety clause, they could have easily taken affirmative steps to exclude the interest from the operations of the clause. The insertion of a proportionate reduction clause in the lease does not indicate an intention to exclude 'First Tract' from the express terms of the entirety clause. The lessee, in this case, operated as if 'First Tract' was covered by all of the terms contained in the lease. 'First Tract' was placed in a unit and a well was drilled on that unit, even though the lessor could not pool the non-participatingroyalty interest. Therefore, we view it as conclusively established that in executing the lease in question, Respondents purported to bind Montgomery's interest by the entirety clause—whether or not they had the authority to do so.

RATIFICATION

This suit was filed on May 12, 1964. Prior to the filing of suit, Petitioner claimed and made demand upon Sun Oil Company for his pro-rata share of royalties payable under the terms of the lease. The parties stipulated that, 'W. R. Montgomery by his attorney informed a representative of Sun Oil Company during the last week of January, 1959, that the said W. R. Montgomery was offering to sign a ratification of the Charles E. Rittersbacher, et al., lease to P. V. Hitt, dated September 4, 1951 (the lease in controversy) * * *.' The parties agreed that the affidavit of Montgomery would be acceptable in lieu of requiring him to appear in person as a witness. In the affidavit, Montgomery stated: 'I am and have been willing to ratify the said lease and have offered and agreed with Bettis & Shepherd, Sun Oil Company's predecessor in title, as well as Sun Oil Company, to execute any division order or ratification necessary or proper with regard to any royalty interest, if such be needed.' Respondents contend that this evidence does not establish actual ratification, but only amounts to an offer to make the ratification—the contention being that an offer, absent acceptance, does not meet the requirement that there must be actual ratification. Respondents further take the position that Montgomery's offer to ratify was conditional and was never fully binding upon Montgomery. This evidence demonstrates Montgomery's intention to ratify the lease, and by filing suit to enforce the lease as written, Mongomery, as a matter of law, has exercised his option to ratify the lease. We think that the manner in which he has exercised his option is analogous to the manner by which a principal can ratify the unauthorized actions of an agent—bringing a suit to enforce the unauthorized act. In such a situation it has been held that the bringing of the suit constitutes an implied ratification of the unauthorized act. Lyons v. Texorado Oil & Gas Co., 91 S.W.2d 375, 377 (Tex.Civ.App.—Amarillo 1935, writ ref'd); Ziegler v. Southwest Film Laboratory, Inc., 351 S.W.2d 636, 641 (Tex.Civ.App.—Texarkana 1961, writ ref'd n.r.e.); Commercial Standard Ins. Co. v. Nelson Mortg. Co., 138 S.W.2d 169, 173 (Tex.Civ.App.—Eastland 1940, writ dism'd jdgmt cor.); James v. Klar & Winterman et al., 118 S.W.2d 625, 627 (Tex.Civ.App.—Dallas 1938, no writ); Steele v. Butler, 227 S.W. 506, 510 (Tex.Civ.App.—Amarillo 1921, no writ); Lechenger v. Merchants' Nat. Bank, 96 S.W. 638, 643 (Tex.Civ.App.—Houston 1906, writ ref'd); 2 C.J.S. Agency s 61, 2 Tex.Jur.2d Agency s 95.

This Court has never been called upon to decide the question of whether a holder of non-participating royalty has an option to make an entirety clause operative on his interest. We think that the nonparticipating royalty owner, so far as the existence of an option is concerned, occupies a comparable position to that of a cotenant under a lease made by his cotenant or a non-participating royalty owner under a pooling agreement made by the holder of the executive rights. As to the cotenant, it has been held that he has the right to ratify or repudiate a lease made by his cotenant which covers his interest. Ryan Consolidated Petroleum Corp. v. Pickens, 155 Tex. 221, 285 S.W.2d 201 (1955); Loeffler v. King, 149 Tex. 626, 236 S.W.2d 772 (1951); Gill v. Bennett, 59 S.W.2d 473 (Tex.Civ.App.—El Paso 1933, writ ref'd); Van Deventer v. Gulf Production Co., 41 S.W.2d 1029 (Tex.Civ.App.—Beaumont 1931, writ ref'd); Texas & Pacific Coal & Oil Co. v. Kirtley, 288 S.W. 619 (Tex.Civ.App.—Eastland 1928, writ ref'd); Duval v. W. T. Carter & Bro., 207 S.W.2d 962 (Tex.Civ.App.—Beaumont 1948, writ ref'd n.r.e.). Likewise, in the pooling area, if a non-participating royalty owner ratifies a pooling agreement, either by joining in the execution of the agreement or by accepting royalties from the pool, his interest is bound by the pooling agreement. Minchen v. Fields, supra, 162 Tex. at 77, 345 S.W.2d at 285; Guaranty Nat. Bank & Trust Co. v. May, 395 S.W.2d 80, 82 (Tex.Civ.App.—Waco 1965, writ ref'd n.r.e.); Nugent v. Freeman, supra, 306 S.W.2d at 170—171. Therefore, we hold that the non-participating royalty owner has the option to ratify or repudiate a lease containing provisions which as to his interest the holder of the executive rights had no authority to insert in the lease.

Montgomery, in bringing this suit, seeks two things under the lease—royalties that have already accrued and royalties that are to accrue in the future. We have held that Montgomery has ratified the lease in question by filing suit; consequently, he is only entitled to receive royalties accruing from and after May 12, 1964, the date this suit was filed. In this connection, we point out that Montgomery, having thus ratified the lease, is as much bound thereby as if he had joined in the original execution thereof. As long as the lease is in force, he is not free to claim his full 1/2 non-participating interest under 'First Tract.'

We come now to the judgment to be entered. The cause must be reversed and remanded to the trial court with instructions. There is an agreed order in the record which is to be used by the trial court in determining the percentage of royalty to be awarded Montgomery and the amount of accrued royalty in dollars and cents due him from May 12, 1964. The order, Plaintiff's Exhibit No. 7, reflects that the Plaintiff and Defendants agreed and the court found that if successful in this suit, Montgomery would own 19.59% Of [SIC] the total royalty payable on the production allocated to the 80 acres of 'Second Tract' placed in the Crutchfield Gas Unit; that the interest amounts to .006122 royalty interest of the production from said unit; and that the accrued royalty allocable to the Montgomery interest amounted to $1706.05 on runs from date of first production through October 31, 1964. Under our holding, Montgomery will not be entitled to royalty accruing prior to May 12, 1964, the date of filing of suit. The amount of money due Montgomery accruing under the lease subsequent to May 12, 1964, is to be determined in accordance with the above mentioned order, other pertinent stipulations in the record, and this opinion.

Reversed and remanded to the trial court with instructions. All costs are adjudged against the Respondents. Dissenting opinions by CALVERT, C.J., and GRIFFIN and WALKER, JJ.

CALVERT, Chief Justice (dissenting).

I join in the dissenting opinion filed by Justice Walker. I append the following comment.

The holding of the court is that the filing of suit of Montgomery on May 12, 1964, constituted a ratification of the lease. The parties stipulated that a well was completed as a producer on the Crutchfield Unit on October 9, 1956, and that shut-in royalty was paid from that date until May, 1958, when actual production was begun. The record reflects that Montgomery knew as early as July, 1957, that the well had been completed. The record thus reflects that Montgomery waited nearly seven years before he ratified the lease.

By agreeing that ratification has been effected by the judgment herein, I do not wish to be understood as agreeing that a non-participating royalty owner, with full knowledge of his rights, cannot lose his right to ratify through laches. See Nugent v. Freeman, 306 S.W.2d 167 (Tex.Civ.App.—Eastland 1957, n.r.e.). There was no plea of laches in this case.

GRIFFIN, Justice (dissenting).

I respectfully dissent. The entirety clause in a lease was never intended to convey and does not convey any interest owned by any land owner or mineral owner in any tract of land in any lease. It merely provides for each person to receive such part of the common production as was the ownership of the one who receives in his original tract of land or minerals.

WALKER, Justice (dissenting).

In my opinion petitioner has heretofore done nothing that would irrevocably bind him to the terms of the lease, and he will not be bound thereby until his tender of ratification is made effective by the judgment rendered in this case. I would hold that he is entitled to his proportionate share of royalties accruing from and after the date of judgment.

CALVERT, C.J., joins in this dissent.

A Needed Response to the Rule of Brown v. Smith: Commentary on Montgomery v. Rittersbacher

by Bruce M. Kramer

In *Montgomery v. Rittersbacher*, the Texas Supreme Court took a needed step to ameliorate the anti-pooling bias that had arisen out of its earlier decision in *Brown v. Smith*.[1] The continued importance of this case has been diminished somewhat by the enactment of the Mineral Interest Pooling Act in 1965[2], but its pro-pooling policies are nonetheless still relevant so long as there are non-executive mineral interests outstanding. *Montgomery* can only be understood in the context in which it arose, namely Texas's embrace of the non-apportionment rule and the rule in *Brown v. Smith* whereby non-executive interests could not be pooled without the further consent of the non-executive owner.

The adoption of the non-apportionment rule for royalties serves as a predicate for both the rule in *Brown v. Smith* and *Montgomery*. The non-apportionment rule deals with the post-lease subdivision of the mineral estate. Where such a subdivision occurs, the only royalty owners who are entitled to royalty are those who own the mineral estate upon which the drillsite tract or tracts are located. Texas adopted the non-apportionment rule in *Japhet v. McRae*,[3] based on the court's conclusion that it was "the only safe rule, and the only one free from much confusion. . . ."[4] The non-apportionment rule deals with post-lease transfers of the possibility of reverter and royalty interest that cover a smaller geographic area than that conveyed by the lease. For example, in *Japhet* the lessor conveyed a 5-acre tract to one party and a 10-acre tract to a second party. Two wells are drilled on the 10-acre tract and no wells are drilled on the 5-acre tract. Applying the non-apportionment rule, the court concludes that the royalty owner of the 10-acre tract is entitled to 100% of the royalties while the royalty owner on the 5-acre tract receives nothing. The non-apportionment rule is the majority rule in the United States with only Pennsylvania clearly adopting the apportionment rule. While the original leasing parties are free to contract around the non-apportionment rule through the inclusion of an entirety clause, if the lease is executed without such a clause, or if the clause is inapplicable, then the non-apportionment rule applies.[5] The non-apportionment rule provides support for the more generalized concept that tracts of land and interests may be segregated for purposes of sharing or not sharing in production from a particular well.

This general notion of areal or geographic segregation of interests was at the heart of the decision in *Brown v. Smith* that did not deal with the problem of post-lease conveyances but the problem created by the existence of non-executive interests that may have antedated the execution of the lease. In *Brown*, Lee reserved a 1/32nd royalty interest in a 20-acre tract of land she otherwise conveyed to the Smiths. The Smiths negotiated a community lease with Brown that purported to include Lee's royalty interest. Upon learning of the Lee interest, Brown refused to execute the lease. The Texas Supreme Court clearly holds that the owner of the executive power does not have the power to execute a lease on behalf of non-executive owners without their consent. The Smiths could certainly lease their 20-acre tract, but they could not through the execution of a community lease pool the Lee interest. This basic principle that would deny the executive the power to pool directly the non-executive interest would also apply to the more common situation in which the executive enters into a lease with a pooling clause.[6] Brown was able to withdraw his leasing offer because of the existence of this non-pooled or non-communitzed interest. In effect, Brown had he executed the lease would have had two leases, one covering all of the interests except for the Lee non-executive interest that would be communitized and a second lease covering the tract of land upon which the Lee interest would be a non-pooled burden.

The Texas Supreme Court in *Brown v. Smith* did not consider the problems it created for the pooling of outstanding non-executive interests.[7] The holding makes it more difficult to pool, discourages the efficient development of oil and gas, and encourages non-executive owners to hold out for higher payments or not lease their interests. It can also lead to the situation where even though one lease has been executed if there are non-executive interests outstanding that cover only a portion of the leasehold acreage, the court will treat the one lease as several leases since the non-executive owners will not be bound by the terms of the pooling clauses. This was the situation in *Minchen v. Fields*, a Texas Supreme Court decision issued in 1961.[8]

One way to ameliorate the potentially harsh results of the rule in *Brown v. Smith* is to allow the non-executive owner to ratify a lease with its pooling and/or entirety clause and therefore receive the benefits that flow from such clauses. In *Nugent v. Freeman*,[9] a court of civil appeals suggested that a non-executive owner might voluntarily and unilaterally choose to pool its interest without meeting the formal requirements of a pooling agreement. In *Nugent* the court rejected the non-executive's claim that by filing a lawsuit seeking apportioned royalties where the drillsite tract was off of the tract burdened by the non-executive interest but nonetheless stated that under a different set of facts such a unilateral ratification of a community lease or a pooling clause in a lease would be valid. There is some language in the opinion that does not want to allow the non-executive owner to wait around and see whether the well will be drilled on its tract as an initial matter and then to wait around and see if the well is productive.[10] While apparently concerned about the "windfall" of a non-executive owner's delay in ratification, the *Nugent* court is apparently not concerned about the non-executive owner's "wipe-out" should the well not be located on that owner's tract.

While the *Nugent* court clearly suggested that the non-executive owner could ratify a lease and therefore have its interest pooled pursuant to the leasehold pooling clause, another court of civil appeals placed a substantial impediment to exercising the ratification power. In *Guaranty National Bank & Trust v. May*,[11] there were several non-executive owners within the five tracts covered by the lease. While several of the non-executive owners attempted to ratify the lease before production was achieved, other non-executive owners did not. While it was clear that under the rule in *Brown v. Smith* that the non-ratifying owners would not have their interests pooled, the court added that, where there is more than one non-executive owner, only the unanimous ratification by all of those owners would be effective.[12] The court said, "[T]he royalty interests could not be unitized or communitized without the joinder or ratification of *all* of the royalty owners. Ratification by less than *all* of the owners does not effectuate the pooling, and there is no communitization as a matter of law."[13]

Montgomery v. Rittersbacher liberalized the rules relating to ratification of leases and made it clear that the lease ratification could entail more than just the pooling clause but the entirety clause as well. It also disapproved of the laches or undue delay argument that had led the *Nugent* court to find that there was not a ratification of the lease. It also expanded the scope of the ratification to clearly include entirety clauses as well as land that is outside the lease that covers the non-executive owner's interest. The lease covered two tracts of land and contained both an entirety and a pooling clause. It was executed in 1951. The non-executive's interest was on the smaller 80-acre First Tract. The lessee, acting under the pooling clause, pooled a portion of the 124.19-acre Second Tract with land owned by third parties. A producing well was drilled off the Second Tract but within the pooled unit. Eighty acres from the Second Tract were included in the pooled unit. In July 1961, the lessee placed the entire First Tract in a pooled unit and drilled a dry hole. From 1951 through May 1964, the non-executive owner did nothing but then filed this action claiming that by virtue of the entirety clause he was entitled to a pro rata share of the royalties from the producing well that included acreage from the Second Tract.

The court immediately expands the *Brown v. Smith* rule by stating that there is no distinction between the non-executive owner's interest being diminished by the leasehold pooling clause and being diminished by the leasehold entirety clause.[14] The impact of an entirety clause is to overcome the application of the non-apportionment rule by requiring that royalties be paid on an apportioned or pro rata basis. That would clearly diminish the non-executive owner's royalty interest in a portion of a larger tract that is leased with an entirety clause. If the well is drilled on the tract covered by the non-executive interest under an entirety clause, the interest would be apportioned. While *Brown v. Smith* did not deal expressly with an entirety clause, the *Montgomery* court extends the rule to cover entirety clauses since the impact on the non-executive's interest would be the same. At no time did the *Montgomery* court give any support to the overruling of *Brown v. Smith* and the adoption of the Louisiana approach which gives the executive the power to make non-executive interests subject to a community lease, a pooling clause, or an entirety clause.[15]

Where, as in this case, the well is not drilled on the tract burdened by the non-executive interest, *Montgomery* clearly holds that the non-executive owner may ratify the lease and receive the benefits of the entirety and/or pooling clauses. In giving the non-executive owner the power to ratify the lease with its attendant beneficial clauses, the *Montgomery* court also sweeps away some of the court-imposed restrictions on the ratification power. It accomplishes that task by analogizing the situation with non-executive owners to the situation where you have a leasing cotenant and unleased cotenants. Since any one cotenant may lease its own interest without the consent of the other cotenants, the non-leasing cotenants have the option to remain as unleased cotenants and receive their pro rata share of the revenue less their pro rata share of the costs or may ratify the lease and become lessors, subject to all of the leasehold terms.[16] The power to ratify would no longer be strictly construed.

In this case the act that ratified the lease was the filing of the lawsuit seeking to share in the royalties from the pooled unit wells' production. The suit would be justified only if the non-executive owner received the benefit of both the leasehold pooling and entirety clauses. By seeking to be covered by the entirety clause in its requested relief, the non-executive owner is impliedly ratifying the lease so as to fall under the coverage of the entirety clause. The court relies on principal-agent ratification analysis to support the proposition that the filing of a lawsuit is an implied ratification of what had been an unauthorized act. Thus a formal, written request to ratify is not required.

Earlier cases had suggested that a long wait by the non-executive would prevent an effective ratification through a laches-type argument. The facts in *Montgomery* show a 13-year delay between the time the lease was executed and the filing of this litigation. The non-executive waited six years from the time of first production on the pooled unit well and even waited three years after the dry hole was drilled on his tract. Chief Justice Calvert in a dissenting opinion noted the lengthy delay in the ratification in *Montgomery* but said that because the defendants had not raised the laches affirmative defense, it could not be used to defeat the ratification although he was in favor of allowing such a defense where a proper plea and proof were made.[17]

Montgomery also stands for the proposition, albeit somewhat implicitly, that when a non-executive owner attempts to exercise its power to ratify the lease it must do so unconditionally. The non-executive may not choose to ratify a portion of the lease or make its ratification conditioned on certain events occurring. The defendants had argued that the ratification attempt was conditional and not binding on the plaintiff. But the court rejects that claim, without stating it in an affirmative manner but merely by referring to the principal-agent and cotenant ratification cases where it is made clear that only an unconditional ratification will suffice. This concept of unconditional ratification applies not just for non-executive interests but for those who seek to ratify a pooling or joint operating agreement.[18]

Ratification by the non-executive is not a unilateral offer that may be rejected by the lessee. As long as the ratification is unconditional, the lessee does not possess the power to reject it. The act of bringing the lawsuit seeking pooled or apportioned royalties from lands not subject to the non-executive interest is, as a matter of law, sufficient to ratify the earlier unauthorized act of pooling the non-executive interest.

Montgomery clarified how a non-executive interest owner may ratify a lease. It erased some of the earlier limiting and sometimes conflicting views of the courts of civil appeals regarding this unilateral ratification power. It extended the scope of the ratification power to include entirety clauses. It also reinforced the *Brown v. Smith* rule regarding the lack of power by executive rights owners over outstanding non-executive interests. The cases that have followed *Montgomery* have been true to its holding, with limited exceptions, making this area of the law much more certain in its application. This surely has reduced the frequency of litigation regarding the rights of non-executive owners to ratify leases.[19]

---

1 141 Tex. 425, 174 S.W.2d 43 (1943).

2 1965 Tex. Gen. Laws ch. 11, at 24 (codified at Tex. Nat. Res. Code Ann. §§ 102.001-102.112 (West 2011)).

3 276 S.W. 669 (Tex. Comm'n App. 1925, judgm't adopted).

4 *Id.* at 672.

5 For a discussion of entirety clauses see 1 Bruce M. Kramer & Patrick H. Martin, The Law of Pooling & Unitization § 7.04 (3d ed. 2009). The non-apportionment doctrine has been criticized by some and approved of by others. *Compare* Robert W. Stayton, *Apportionment and the Ghost of a Rejected View*, 32 Tex. L. Rev. 682 (1954), *and* William O. Huie, *Apportionment of Oil and Gas Royalties*, 78 Harv. L. Rev. 1113 (1965)(critical), *with* Owen L. Anderson, et al., *Hemingway Oil and Gas Law and Taxation* 462-63 (4th ed. 2004).

6 The extension of the *Brown v. Smith* holding to the pooling clause situation was identified by A.W. Walker, Jr., *Developments in the Law of Oil and Gas in Texas During the War Years—A Resume*, 25 Tex. L. Rev. 1, 16-18 (1946). *See generally* Kramer & Martin, *supra* note 5, at § 7.05.

7 For a critical review of the *Brown v. Smith* decision see Howard R. Williams, *Stare Decisis and the Pooling of Nonexecutive Interests in Oil and Gas*, 46 Tex. L. Rev. 1013 (1968). Raymond Myers offered a rebuttal to Professor Williams's analysis in Raymond M. Myers, *Stare Decisis and the Pooling of Nonexecutive Oil and Gas Interests: A Reply*, 47 Tex. L. Rev. 1379 (1969).

8 *Minchen v. Fields*, 162 Tex. 73, 345 S.W.2d 282 (1961).

9 306 S.W.2d 167 (Tex. Civ. App.—Eastland 1957, writ ref'd n.r.e.).

10 *Id.* at 170.

11 395 S.W.2d 80 (Tex. Civ. App.—Waco 1965, writ ref'd n.r.e.).

12 395 S.W.2d at 82.

13 *Id.*

14 424 S.W.2d at 215. The court of civil appeals rejected the non-executive owner's claim based on *Brown v. Smith* and the lengthy delay in the ratification attempt. 410 S.W.2d 925 (Tex. Civ. App.—Corpus Christi 1966).

15 *LeBlanc v. Haynesville Mercantile Co.*, 230 La. 299, 88 So.2d 377 (1956).

16 *See* Kramer & Martin, *supra* note 5, at § 7.05[2][a].

17 424 S.W.2d at 215 (Calvert, C.J., dissenting).

18 *See, e.g.*, *Stable Energy, L.P. v. Newberry*, 999 S.W.2d 538, 547 (Tex. App.—Austin 1999, pet. denied); *Sun Expl. & Prod. Co. v. Pitzer*, 822 S.W.2d 294 (Tex. App.—Eastland 1991, writ denied).

19 *See, e.g.*, *Amoco Production Co. v. Wood*, 113 S.W.3d 462 (Tex. App.—Texarkana 2003, no pet.); *London v. Merriman*, 756 S.W.2d 736 (Tex. App.—Corpus Christi 1988, writ denied); *Verble v. Coffman*, 680 S.W.2d 69 (Tex.App.—Austin 1984 no writ); *Ruiz v. Martin*, 559 S.W.2d 839 (Tex. Civ. App.—San Antonio 1977, writ ref'd n.r.e.); *but cf. De Benavides v. Warren*, 674 S.W.3d 353 (Tex. App.—San Antonio 1984, writ ref'd n.r.e.).

CHAPTER 13

Texas Oil & Gas Corporation et al., Petitioner v. Juan M. Vela et al., Respondent.

COMMENTARY

by Michael P. Pearson

(See Chapter 14 for a combined commentary)

429 S.W.2d 866

1968

Texas Oil & Gas Corporation et al., Petitioners-Respondents,
v.
Juan M. Vela et al., Respondents-Petitioners.

429 S.W.2d 866

1968

Geary, Brice & Lewis, W. S. Barron, Jr., Dallas, G. C. Mann, Laredo, Robert R. Barton, Kerrville, for Texas Oil and Gas Corp. and others.
Meer, Chandler & Carlton, Dean Carlton, Dallas, for Delhi-Taylor Oil corp.
Turner, Hitchins, McInerney, Webb & Hartnett, James J. Hartnett, Dallas, for Texas Oil and Gas and Delhi-Taylor.
Fansler & Fansler, C. N. Fansler, Jr., Laredo, for Hannah D. Gaines et vir.
Mann, Cronfel & Mann, John E. Mann, Laredo, Bobbitt, Brite, Bobbitt & Allen, Robert Lee Bobbitt, Jr., San Antonio, for Juan M. Vela and others.
W. Pat Camp, San Antonio, for L. A. Nordan.

Opinion
WALKER, Justice.

This case involves an oil and gas lease executed in 1933 and covering 1,500 acres of land in Zapata County. Under its terms the lessee is obligated to 'pay to lessor, as royalty for gas from each well where gas only is found, while the same is being sold or used off of the premises, one-eighth of the market price at the wells of the amount so sold or used.' Gas has been produced and sold from the leased premises since 1935. In that year the owners of the working interest entered into contracts 'for the life of the lease' by the terms of which the gas was sold at a price of 2.3¢ per mcf. Royalties have been paid on that basis, but more recent contracts for the sale of gas from the same field provide for substantially higher prices.

Subject to certain non-participating royalty interests, the title of the original lessors is owned by Juan M. Vela et al, [SIC] hereinafter referred to as the Velas. They instituted suit to recover alleged deficiencies in royalty payments on gas sold from the leased premises during the period from February 1, 1960, to January 31, 1964, and for additional relief on the theory that the premises were being drained and had not been properly developed. The principal defendants, who will be referred to individually by name and collectively as respondents, are Delhi-Taylor Oil Corporation, the American-Texas Group, and Texas Oil & Gas Corporation. These respondents were owners of the working interest at different times during the four-year period. One member of the American-Texas Group is Mrs. Hannah D. Gaines, who owns a three-sixteenths non-participating royalty interest in the land. The named defendants also include L. A. Nordan, who owns a one-fourth non-participating royalty interest. Nordan and Mrs. Gaines, who will be referred to by name or as petitioners, answered and sought a recovery of any additional royalties to which they might be entitled. They and the Velas compromised and settled their claims against several defendants referred to as the Venture Group. Under and in accordance with the terms of the settlement agreement, judgment was rendered against the Venture Group for deficiencies in royalty payments with the understanding that no execution would issue thereon.

After a non-jury trial the district court rendered judgment: (1) awarding the Velas, Nordan and Mrs. Gaines a total of $55,750.13 for unpaid royalties and interest; (2) denying a recovery of damages for past drainage; (3) declaring that the working interest operators are obligated to pay as royalty one-eighth of the market price at the wells, at the time produced, of all gas sold or used off the premises after February 1, 1964; and (4) directing Texas Oil & Gas Corporation, the present owner of the working interest, to drill certain additional wells or suffer cancellation of the lease. The Court of Civil Appeals: (a) affirmed the money award in favor of the Velas but modified the judgment of the trial court to provide that the recovery against the members of the American-Texas Group should be several and not joint; (b) upheld the denial of damages for past drainage; (c) reversed and rendered judgment that Nordan and Mrs. Gaines take nothing by their suit for additional royalties; (d) modified the declaratory portion of the judgment to provide that the operators would be obligated to pay royalties on the basis of market price from and after the date of judgment; and (e) held that the royalty owners could be adequately compensated by an award of damages for drainage and failure to develop after the operator was notified of its failure to comply with the implied covenants of the lease. The judgment of the trial court, in so far as it directed Texas Oil & Gas Corporation to drill additional wells or suffer cancellation of the lease, was accordingly reversed, and that part of the case was severed and remanded to the district court for a determination of the amount of damages. 405 S.W.2d 68.

Applications for writs of error were filed by the Velas, Nordan, Mrs. Gaines, Delhi-Taylor, the American-Texas Group, and Texas Oil & Gas Corporation. All applications were granted, and the case was argued orally and submitted to the Court for decision. Some time after argument a joint motion was filed by the Velas, Texas Oil & Gas Corporation. [SIC] Delhi-Taylor and the American-Texas Group stating that all claims and controversies between them have been settled and praying that the cause be dismissed as moot but without prejudice to the claims of Nordan and Mrs. Gaines against Texas Oil & Gas Corporation, the American-Texas Group and Delhi-Taylor. This motion is granted as here-inafter set out, but there are a number of questions to be decided in disposing of the claims of Nordan and Mrs. Gaines.

As indicated above, Nordan and Mrs. Gaines each own a fractional non-participating royalty interest. Their pleadings indicate that they would have been content if the claims of the Velas had been denied, but in the alternative they adopted the Velas' first amended original petition and prayed that they be given their portion of any relief granted by the court. In a later pleading they alleged their royalty ownership more specifically and prayed that they recover damages from Texas Oil and Gas Corporation and certain other defendants in proportion to any amount awarded the Velas on the basis of their second amended original petition. As we construe the pleadings and in so far as they affect the questions to be decided here, Nordan and Mrs. Gaines were seeking in the trial court substantially the same relief as the Velas. They brought forward a number of points of error to the Court of Civil Appeals and also adopted the brief filed there by the Velas.

Although the Court of Civil Appeals upheld the award of additional royalty to the Velas, it concluded that Nordan and Mrs. Gaines are equitably estopped from asserting their right to a similar recovery. This question will be discussed later. Respondents make two other basic contentions with respect to the action for the recovery of additional royalty: (1) that the contract price of 2.3¢ per mcf at which they sold the gas is the market price within the meaning of the lease; and (2) that even if this is not so, there is no evidence to support the trial court's finding that the market price of the gas during the four-year period was 13.047¢ per mcf. These contentions will be considered in the order in which they have been stated.

The leased premises are located in the Lopeno Field, which was discovered in 1934. The first gas well on the land was brought in shortly after that time, and six wells have now been completed thereon. These wells produce from the Upper Queen City sand. Another and lower Queen City sand located at a depth of about 2,700 feet was recognized in 1963 as a separate reservoir from the upper Queen City. There was no pipeline in the Lopeno Field and no market for the gas when it was first discovered. Nordan & Morris, a partnership composed of L. A. Nordan and John G. Morris, acquired various leases in the field. They entered into a gas sales contract with United Gas Public Service Company on November 20, 1934. Under its terms Nordan & Morris agreed to establish the commercial possibilities of the field by completing at least three gas wells capable of delivering a combined total of five million cubic feet of gas daily. United agreed to construct a pipeline to the field and was granted the exclusive right to purchase on a ratable basis all gas produced from land in the field in which Nordan & Morris owned or acquired an interest. This right was to exist for the terms of the leaseholds and any renewals or extensions thereof. The stipulated price was 3 1/2¢ per mcf, computed at a base pressure of two pounds per square inch above an assumed atmospheric pressure of 14.4 pounds per square inch.

Nordan & Morris then entered into gas purchase contracts with various operators in the field. All owners of the working interest in the lease now in question executed such contracts, agreeing to sell the gas produced from the leased premises in accordance with their terms. There are three of these contracts, two of which were executed in 1935 and the third in 1937. They provide for an effective rate of 2.3¢ per mcf at standard measurement, and for a term during the life of the leases covered thereby. All of the contracts were consummated, and all gas sold from the leased premises as well as from the surrounding land has been marketed pursuant to their terms.

The only producing formations in the Lopeno Field from the time of its discovery until 1960 were the Queen City sands. In 1950 Wilcox production was discovered in the area, the Wilcox formation being a deep sand found at depths below

6,500 feet. Additional pipelines were then built into the area, and there are now three companies purchasing gas from the Lopeno Field. They are Delhi Gas Pipeline Corporation, the successor to United, Tennessee Gas Transmission Company, and Alamo Gas Supply Company. The net prices paid by the last two companies range from 13¢ to 17.24¢ per mcf.

When the Nordan & Morris contracts were made, however, United was the only commercial purchaser of gas in the field. The operators could market their gas only on a 'life of the lease' basis, and the price stipulated is the only price that could be obtained at that time. Respondents also point out that gas is not sold on a day-to-day basis, and that any substantial volume can be marketed only under a long-term contract that fixes the price to be paid throughout its term. The trial court found that the contracts in this case were made in good faith, and the finding has not been attacked. Petitioners argue that in these circumstances, the market price of gas within the meaning of the lease is the price contracted for in good faith by the lessee in pursuance of its duty to market gas from the premises. We do not agree.

Mrs. Gaines may well have been obligated to sell gas in accordance with the terms of the contracts while she owned part of the working interest, but none of the royalty owners has ever agreed to accept royalties on the basis of the price stipulated in the contracts. The royalties to which they are entitled must be determined from the provisions of the oil and gas lease, which was executed prior to and is wholly independent of the gas sales contracts. In addition to the gas royalty clause quoted above, the lease binds the lessee:

'1st. To deliver to the credit of lessor, free of cost, in the pipe line to which lessee may connect its or his wells, the equal one-eighth part of all oil produced and saved from the leased premises.

'3rd. To pay to lessor as royalty for gas produced from any oil well and used by lessee for the manufacture of gasoline, one-eighth of the market value of such gas. If such gas is sold by lessee, then lessee agrees to pay lessor, as royalty, one-eighth of the net proceeds derived from the sale of said casinghead gas at the wells.'

It is clear then that the parties knew how to and did provide for royalties payable in kind, based upon market price or market value, and based upon the proceeds derived by the lessee from the sale of gas. They might have agreed that the royalty on gas produced from a gas well would be a fractional part of the amount realized by the lessee from its sale. Instead of doing so, however, they stipulated in plain terms that the lessee would pay one-eighth of the market price at the well of all gas sold or used off the premises. This clearly means the prevailing market price at the time of the sale or use. The gas which was marketed under the long-term contracts in this case was not 'being sold' at the time the contracts were made but at the time of the delivery to the purchaser. See Martin v. Amis, Tex.Com.App., 288 S.W. 431, 433. We agree with the Court of Civil Appeals, therefore, that the contract price for which the gas was sold by the lessee is not necessarily the market price within the meaning of the lease. See Foster v. Atlantic Refining Co., 5th Cir., 329 F.2d 485; Wall v. United Gas Public Service Co., 178 La. 908, 152 So. 561.

The lease obligation may prove financially burdensome to a lessee who has made a long-term contract without protecting itself against increases in market price. This was considered in Foster, where the court said:

'The inability of Atlantic to make a gas sales contract with escalation provisions is beside the point. The obligation of Atlantic to pay royalties is fixed and unambiguous. It made the gas sales contract with full knowledge of this obligation and did nothing to protect itself against increases in price. The fact that its purchaser would not agree to pay the market price prevailing at the time of the delivery does not destroy the lease obligation.

'When it made the gas sales contract, Atlantic took the calculated risk of that contract producing royalties satisfactory to the lease terms. The fact that increases in market prices have made the lease obligations financially burdensome is no defense.

'Atlantic argues that it is only required to use reasonable diligence in selling the Foster royalty gas and that the 1950 contract was not improvident. These arguments beg the question. The royalty provision is clear. Granting that the 1950 contract was provident when made, that fact does not change the royalty provisions.

'Stripped of all the trimmings Atlantic's position is simply: We cannot comply. This is no answer. The lease calls for royalty based on the market price prevailing for the field where produced when run. The fact that the acertainment

[SIC] of future market price may be troublesome or that the royalty provisions are improvident and result in a financial loss to Atlantic 'is not a web of the Court's weaving.' Atlantic cannot expect the court to rewrite the lease to Atlantic's satisfaction.'

We are in general agreement with these conclusions and turn now to respondents' second basic contention. As indicated above, the trial court found that the market price of the gas during the four-year period was 13.047¢ per mcf. This finding, if it has any support in the evidence, must rest upon the testimony of Mr. Jack K. Baumel. Our statement concerning the witness and his testimony is taken largely from the opinion of the Court of Civil Appeals. Baumel is a consultant petroleum and natural gas engineer who had been employed by the Railroad Commission of Texas and by other governmental agencies. He had been familiar with the Lopeno Field for for [SIC] many years, and before testifying in this case he made a study of production and sales of gas from the field. The records of sales in the office of the Comptroller of Public Accounts were the principal source of his information, but he also considered the gas sales contracts made by the various producers in the field.

Mr. Baumel ascertained the amounts of gas sold from each well in the field during the four-year period and the amount received for the same. This included production from the Upper Queen City sand, the 2,700-foot Queen City sand, and the Wilcox sand. By mathematical calculation he determined that the average price received for all gas sold during the period, except that marketed under the Nordan & Morris contracts, was 16.047¢ per mcf. He stated that the amounts received pursuant to the Nordan & Morris contracts were disregarded because such contracts were too far out of line. Since the gas from the Upper Queen City sand was of low pressure, he deducted a compression charge of 3¢ per mcf from the average price, and testified that 13.047¢ per mcf was the market price of the Vela gas.

The parties agree that the market price of gas is to be determined by sales of gas comparable in time, quality and availability to marketing outlets. See Phillips Petroleum Co. v. Bynum, 5th Cir., 155 F.2d 196. Respondents contend, however, that Baumel's conclusion as to market price is nothing more than the mathematical average of the amounts received from noncomparable sales involving vastly different factors and circumstances. They also say that there is no demand whatever for the Vela gas at the price found by the trial court.

We have already pointed out that all wells on the leased premises produce only from the upper Queen City sand. The prices used by Baumel in making his calculations are those paid by Tennessee and Alamo under their contracts with various producers. These contracts were made in 1960 and 1961 before the lines of the particular company were laid into the field. They cover some Queen City gas, but most of the wells produce from the Wilcox formation. The estimated reserves committed thereunder to each company amount to approximately 300 billion cubic feet of gas, and the Alamo contract covers 14 different fields located in five counties. The latter contract was made to enable Alamo to fulfill another contract in which it agreed to supply the public consumer gas requirements of the City of San Antonio for a period of twenty years. Tennessee has five contracts which were presented as a package to the Federal Power Commission, apparently in connection with an application for authorization to extend its pipeline to the Lopeno Field.

The Queen City sands in the Lopeno Field are about two-thirds depleted and have remaining reserves of from 50 to 60 billion cubic feet of gas. The original flowing pressure of wells producing therefrom was approximately 1,000 pounds per square inch, but the same has now fallen to an estimated range of from 150 to 200 pounds. Wilcox gas is of sufficient pressure to enter a 1,000 pound line without compression. It also appears that Queen City gas is extremely dry and that Wilcox gas has some distillate in it.

As pointed out by the Court of Civil Appeals, these differences were fully developed by petitioners in their cross-examination of Baumel. He recognized that the market price of gas might be affected by the type and quality of the gas, pressure, reserves and deliverability. The witness stated, however, that reserves are not a significant factor when pipelines have already been laid into the field, and that the remaining Queen City reserves are sufficient to justify a market. He further testified that there is no substantial difference between the Queen City gas and that produced from the Wilcox formation, and that the deliverability of the Vela wells is better than average for the field. Queen City gas and Wilcox gas are intermixed by the purchasers in their pipelines, and the 'end use' of gas produced from each source is the same. The witness also stated that after an allowance of 3¢ per mcf was made for compression charges, the pressure differential is not material. There is no contention that the amount allowed as a compression charge is not reasonable.

Baumel had not tested the BTU content of the Wilcox gas. He reasoned that Wilcox gas and Queen City gas are of similar type and quality because they were mixed by purchasers in the same pipeline and devoted to the same ultimate use. We do not attempt to determine whether his conclusion in that respect is entirely valid, because it appears that since 1960 at least 10 additional wells have been drilled to the Queen City sands. These were dedicated by the producers under amendments to the existing contracts at net prices ranging from 13.047¢ to 14.24¢ per mcf. In the light of such facts and the other circumstances mentioned above, the trial court was not required as a matter of law to reject Baumel's opinion that there is no substantial difference in the quality or market value of Queen City and Wilcox gas.

We agree with the Court of Civil Appeals that the mathematical average of all prices paid in the field is not a final answer to the difficult problem of determining market price at any particular time. But see Wall v. United Gas Public Service Co., supra, and Arkansas Natural Gas Co. v. Sartor, 5th Cir., 78 F.2d 924. In this instance, however, both the witness and the trial court were required to fix a figure that would be used in determining the amount that should have been paid to the royalty owners over a period of four years. If the rate of production were constant, that figure would be the average market price for the period. Baumel's conclusion as to the market price of the gas in question is corroborated, moreover, by the sales of Queen City gas under amendments to the existing contracts. As for respondents' contention that there is no demand for Queen City gas at the price found by the trial court, it does not appear that any well in the field is shut in for lack of a market. In these circumstances and where purchasers have amended their contracts to cover additional Queen City wells at equal or greater prices, it may fairly be inferred that there was a demand for the Vela gas at 13.047¢ per mcf.

Respondents rely upon Phillips Petroleum Co. v. Bynum, supra; Arkansas Natural Gas Co. v. Sartor, supra; Shamrock Oil & Gas Corp. v. Coffee, 5th Cir., 140 F.2d 409; and Sartor v. United Gas Public Service Co., 186 La. 555, 173 So. 103. These cases are to be distinguished on the facts. The gas involved in Bynum was used for the extraction of gasoline and other products. There was no market for the same from companies which dealt in gas for heating and fuel, and it was held that the amounts paid by such companies was not competent evidence of market price. Certain contracts were held inadmissible in Arkansas Natural Gas, because the undisputed testimony showed that the guaranty to deliver large quantities of gas from another field constituted part of the consideration for the price paid and there was no evidence that would enable the jury to determine what this amounted to. The court went on to say, however, that:

> 'It is also apparent that the stipulation as to average prices paid under contracts substantially similar to the lease in suit was improperly excluded. The same is true in respect to the testimony of Hargrove wherein his opinion as to the established market price at the well and the prices paid in other sales, under substantially similar conditions, was sought to be elicited.'

In Coffee it was held that market price is to be determined by comparable sales and not by the opinions of witnesses as to what the purchasers could or should have paid. The contracts introduced in United Gas Public Service imposed obligations upon the producers so different from those assumed by the plaintiffs that the court concluded the same did not constitute evidence as to the market price of the plaintiffs' gas. Here the record shows the prices paid by other purchasers in comparable sales, and in our opinion the evidence supports the finding of the trial court as to market price.

Although neither Tennessee nor Alamo began taking gas until the latter part of 1960, the Tennessee contracts were executed on or about February 5, 1960. It also is clear that the prices mentioned by Baumel were net to the producer. There is no merit then in respondents' argument that the trial court erred in granting a recovery for the period prior to December 1, 1960, and in failing to deduct gathering costs in addition to the compression charge.

After awarding a money recovery for deficiencies in royalty payments for the period from February 1, 1960, to January 31, 1964, the judgment of the trial court declares that from and after February 1, 1964, those holding under the lessee are obligated to pay as royalty one-eighth of the market value of all gas sold or used off the premises. The Court of Civil Appeals held that since there is no evidence of market price between the date of filing suit and the date of judgment, the declaratory judgment should be modified to provide that the operator is required to pay royalty on the basis of market price from and after the date of judgment. Petitioners say that this was erroneous, because it will deprive them of any right to recover a deficiency in royalty payments between the date of filing suit and the date of judgment.

The Velas contended in the Court of Civil Appeals that the trial court properly gave prospective as well as retrospective operation to the finding that the market price of the gas was 13.047¢ per mcf. This contention is unsound for the reasons pointed out by the intermediate court, but implicit in the argument so advanced is an erroneous construction of the trial court's judgment. It was the latter that probably led to a modification of the declaratory portion of the judgment. As we construe the judgment of the trial court, it does not purport to give prospective operation to the finding of a market price. Such finding is not determinative of the rights of the parties with respect to gas produced after January 31, 1964. On the basis of that construction, we think the declaratory part of the trial court's judgment should be affirmed. Petitioners are not precluded by the judgment in this case from recovering deficiencies in royalty payments on gas produced after January 31, 1964, upon proof of the prevailing market price at the time such gas was sold or used off the premises. Ben C. Jones & Co. v. Gammel-Statesman Pub. Co., 100 Tex. 320, 99 S.W. 701, 8 L.R.A.,N.S., 1197.

The Court of Civil Appeals also held that the royalty owners were properly denied a recovery of damages for drainage which occurred prior to the time they gave written notice to the lessee as required by the terms of the lease. The lease contains the following provisions:

> 'In the event lessor considers that lessee has not complied with all its obligations hereunder, both express and implied, before production has been secured or after production has been secured, lessor shall notify lessee in writing, setting out specifically in what respects lessee has breached this contract. Lessee shall then have sixty (60) days after receipt of said notice within which to meet or commence to meet all or any part of the breaches alleged by lessor. The service of said notice shall be precedent to the bringing of any action by lessor on said lease for any cause and no such action shall be brought until the lapse of sixty (60) days after service of such notice on lessee. Neither the service of said notice nor the doing of any acts by lessee aimed to meet all or any of the alleged breaches shall be deemed an admission or presumption that lessee has failed to perform all its obligations hereunder.'

Provisions of this nature are included in the lease primarily to protect the lessee against a forfeiture for breach of some express or implied obligation. The parties could not have intended that the lessor would be forever barred from recovering damages sustained prior to the giving of notice, and we hold that the first two sentences quoted above apply only to actions to cancel the lease and not to suits for damages. See Shell Oil Co. v. Stansbury, Tex.Civ.App., 401 S.W.2d 623 (wr. ref. n.r.e., Tex.Sup., 410 S.W.2d 187); General Crude Oil Co. v. Harris, Tex.Civ.App., 101 S.W.2d 1098 (wr. dis.). The purpose of the requirement that the lessee be given notice as a condition precedent to the bringing of suit is to enable the lessee to prepare his defense. Failure to comply therewith may be grounds for abating the suit, but it does not bar the right or constitute a basis for entering a take nothing judgment. See Philadelphia Underwriters' Agency of Fire Insurance Association of Philadelphia v. Driggers, 111 Tex. 392, 238 S.W. 633. The notice provisions quoted above do not constitute a defense to the suit for damages, and the courts below erred in denying a recovery on that ground. The opinions in Kinnear v. Scurlock Oil Co., Tex.Civ.App., 334 S.W.2d 521 (wr. ref. n.r.e.), and Burnett v. R. Lacy, Inc., Tex.Civ.App., 293 S.W.2d 674 (wr. ref. n.r.e.) are disapproved to the extent that they are inconsistent with the views here expressed. This part of the case must be remanded, however, because the trial court made no finding as to the amount of damages for past drainage.

Although the trial court awarded Nordan and Mrs. Gaines a recovery of additional royalty, the Court of Civil Appeals held that they are equitably estopped from claiming that they are entitled to be paid on the basis of market price for the period involved in this suit. The royalty interests owned by such parties were purchased by Nordan and John G. Morris from the Velas in 1934 after the discovery of gas in the field but before a well was drilled on the leased premises. Shortly after acquiring such royalty interests, Nordan & Morris entered into the gas purchase and sale contracts mentioned above. Morris, who was the husband of Mrs. Gaines, died in 1937 and left her all of his estate. Nordan and Mrs. Gaines retained their rights under the contracts with the lease operators until 1950, when they sold the same to Joe C. Palmer.

The working interest in certain portions of the leased premises was formerly owned by the American Texas Oil Company, which entered into one of the contracts with Nordan & Morris. The company was dissolved in 1941, and its assets were conveyed to the stockholders in proportion to their interests. These conveyances were executed by L. A. Nordan, as surviving President and Director of the company, and by Mrs. Gaines, as surviving Director and Liquidating Trustee thereof. One of the conveyances was to the daughter of L. A. Nordan, and another was to

Mrs. Gaines. The latter thereby received a one-fourth interest in the American-Texas Group, and thus became an owner of part of the working interest in addition to her non-participating royalty interest. All of such conveyances expressly ratify and confirm the gas purchase contract.

There is no basis in the record for an ordinary estoppel in pais against either Nordan or Mrs. Gaines. The trial court did not find, and the evidence does not establish as a matter of law, a prejudicial change of position on the part of the working interest owners in reliance on any misrepresentation or silence when there was a duty to speak. It is argued, however, and the Court of Civil Appeals held, that Nordan and Mrs. Gaines are equitably estopped by their acceptance of the benefits of the gas purchase contracts. The court concluded that these parties, after accepting the benefits of contracts which obligated the lease operators to sell all gas produced from the leased premises at a price of 2.3¢ per mcf, could not claim that they are entitled to be paid royalty on the basis of 13.047¢ per mcf. We do not agree.

According to the doctrine relied upon by the Court of Civil Appeals, sometimes called quasi estoppel, a party who has accepted the benefits of a transaction is precluded from later repudiating the accompanying or resulting obligation. See Theriot v. Smith, Tex.Civ.App., 263 S.W.2d 181 (wr. dis.); United Fidelity Life Ins. Co. v. Fowler, Tex.Civ.App., 38 S.W.2d 128 (wr. dis.); 28 Am.Jur.2d Estoppel and Waiver s 59; 31 C.J.S. Estoppel s 107. Nordan and Mrs. Gaines are not attempting to repudiate or escape any obligation of the gas purchase contracts. In the light of subsequent events the terms of these agreements make the royalty provisions of the lease financially burdensome to the operators, but this affords no basis for denying to Nordan and Mrs. Gaines the right to recover their share of the royalty as provided in the lease. The operators acquired their interests in the leased premises with actual or constructive knowledge of the provisions of the contracts and the lease. It also is clear that the gas purchase contracts were made in good faith, and as previously indicated the royalty owners have never agreed that royalty should be paid on the basis of the price stipulated therein. In our opinion they are not precluded from insisting upon their rights under the lease by the fact that they or their predecessors in title were parties to and accepted the benefits of the contracts.

The position of Mrs. Gaines is different from that of Nordan in one respect. While the latter has had no interest in the leased premises since 1950 other than his nonparticipating royalty, Mrs. Gaines also owned part of the working interest until after the present suit was filed. That circumstance does not, however, deprive her of the right to be paid royalty in accordance with the terms of the lease. She is a party to the suit in two different capacities, one as a royalty owner and the other as owner of part of the working interest in some of the land. The trial court awarded her a recovery of her full share of the deficiency in royalty payments against the American-Texas Group, which includes herself. Since she owned 25% Of [SIC] the working interest, this part of the judgment should have been in her favor against the other members of the Group for 75% Of [SIC] the deficiency in royalty paid on gas produced by such Group.

It is also argued that the judgment in favor of Nordan and Mrs. Gaines cannot stand because they did not prove the amount of royalty they received during the period involved in this suit. The record shows that the Velas were paid on the basis of the price of 2.3¢ stipulated in the gas purchase contracts. There being no evidence to the contrary, the trier of fact could reasonably conclude that all royalty owners were paid on the same basis.

Delhi-Taylor insists that the trial court erred in denying a jury trial on the demand therefor filed by the attorneys representing the Jamison Estate interest. As pointed out by the Court of Civil Appeals, the case was regularly called for trial on February 23, 1965. A jury was available but no demand therefor had been made at that time. The owners of the Jamison Estate interest moved for a continuance, and it was agreed that the case would be postponed until a special non-jury setting on April 12th. The demand for the jury was filed and the jury fee was paid on April 2nd. It was overruled by an order entered on April 9th in which the trial court found that the request was not made a reasonable time in advance of the date set for trial. The court further found that granting the request would require that the case be continued until September, would interfere with the handling of the court's business, and would prejudice the other parties who had made arrangements for the attendance of their witnesses.

Rule 216, Texas Rules of Civil Procedure, requires that the demand for a jury be made and the necessary fee paid 'on or before appearance day or, if thereafter, a reasonable time before the date set for trial of the cause on the non-jury docket, but not less than ten days in advance.' We agree with the Court of Civil Appeals that a demand made ten days in advance is not necessarily timely as a matter of law, and that in view of the circumstances mentioned the trial court did not err in denying a jury trial in this case.

Nordan and Mrs. Gaines recognize that they are not entitled to recover any deficiency in royalty payments accruing prior to October 1, 1960, and accordingly filed a remittitur in the Court of Civil Appeals. No complaint has been made concerning the action of the Court of Civil Appeals with respect to the conditional decree provisions of the trial court's judgment, nor is there any attack on its holding that the liability of the members of the American-Texas Group for unpaid royalties is several and not joint. The cause will be severed into three parts so as to preserve these rulings, grant the motion to dismiss, and give Nordan and Mrs. Gaines the relief to which they are entitled here.

The judgment of the Court of Civil Appeals is accordingly set aside, and it is ordered:

(1) That all claims and controversies between Juan M. Vela, Carlos Vela, Ernestina Vela, Emma Vela de Garcia and husband, Jesus M. Garcia, on the one hand, and Texas Oil & Gas Corporation, Claudia L. Eaves and husband, Jack R. Eaves, Anita Nordan Lindsay and husband, Sidney A. Lindsay, Marian Nordan Hudson and husband, Harold W. Hudson, individually and as members of the partnership of Nordan & Company, Hannah D. Gaines and husband, Arthur Gaines (but only in her capacity as a defendant-operator and not in her capacity as a plaintiff-royalty owner), Mrs. Leo G. Moss and husband, Leo G. Moss, Raymond Gibbs, administrator of the estate of C. T. Jamison, deceased, Jessie Faye Gibbs Jamison, a widow, individually and as guardian of the persons and estates of Michael E. Jamison and Patrick Jamison, minors, C. A. Reiter, and Delhi-Taylor Oil Corporation, on the other, be severed, and as to all such claims and controversies the judgment of the trial court is set aside and the cause is dismissed as moot without opinion or adjudication on the merits;

(2) That the judgment of the trial court in so far as it denies L. A. Nordan and Mrs. Hannah D. Gaines any recovery for past or future drainage or the failure to reasonably develop the leased premises, directs Texas Oil and Gas Corporation to drill additional wells and provides that the lease shall be cancelled and terminate in the event additional wells are not drilled in the manner and within the time therein provided, is reversed. These parts of the case are also severed, and as to them the cause is remanded to the district court;

(3) That as to the remainder of the cause:

(a) The judgment of the trial court in favor of L. A. Nordan for royalties due and unpaid is reformed to provide that he recover from Delhi-Taylor Oil Corporation the sum of $1,411.76, from the Venture Group the sum of $4,077.39, from Texas Oil & Gas Corporation the sum of $1,726.95, from Mrs. Hannah D. Gaines the sum of $1,363.12, from Nordan & Company the sum of $1,363.12, from Mrs. Leo G. Moss the sum of $1,226.81, from the C. T. Jamison Estate the sum of $1,226.81, and from C. A. Reiter the sum of $272.62, with interest on each of said amounts from April 12, 1965, at the rate of six per cent per annum;

(b) The judgment of the trial court in favor of Mrs. Hannah D. Gaines for royalties due and unpaid is reformed to provide that she recover from Delhi-Taylor Oil Corporation the sum of $1,058.83, from the Venture Group the sum of $3,057.86, from Nordan & Company the sum of $1,022.34, from Mrs. Leo G. Moss the sum of $920.11, from the C. T. Jamison Estate the sum of $920.11, from C. A. Reiter the sum of $204.47, and from Texas Oil & Gas Corporation the sum of $1,295.21, with interest on each of said amounts from April 12, 1965, at the rate of six per cent per annum; and

(c) The judgment of the trial court as so reformed is affirmed.

The costs of appeal are taxed one-sixth against the Velas, one-sixth against Nordan and Mrs. Gaines, jointly, and two-thirds against Texas Oil and Gas Corporation, Delhi-Taylor Oil Corporation, and the American-Texas Group, jointly.

Dissenting opinion by HAMILTON, J., in which GRIFFIN, SMITH and GREENHILL, JJ., join.

Dissenting opinion by GRIFFIN, J.

DISSENTING OPINION

HAMILTON, Justice.

I respectfully dissent.

I cannot agree with the Court's holding that the 'market price' mentioned in the royalty clause must be determined as of the date of delivery of the gas. While I agree with the Court's holding that the price in the gas sales contracts is not Necessarily [SIC] controlling, it could very well be, depending on the circumstances under which the contract price was determined. The burden is on those suing for royalty deficiencies to show that such contract price is not equivalent to the 'market price' called for in the lease royalty provision. That burden cannot be discharged by showing the average price for which gas is sold in other long-term gas contracts of sale, unless they are comparable in time (and otherwise) with the contracts under attack. Phillips Petroleum Company v. Bynum, 155 F.2d 196, 201 (5th Cir.1946).

In the oil and gas lease in question the lessees obligated themselves:

'To deliver to the credit of lessor, free of cost, in the pipe line to which lessee may connect its or his wells, the equal one-eighth part of all oil produced and saved from the leased premises.

'To pay to lessor, as royalty for gas from each well where gas only is found, while the same is being sold or used off of the premises one-eighth of the market price at the wells of the amount so sold or used, * * *

'To pay to lessor as royalty for gas produced from any oil well and used by lessee for the manufacture of gasoline, one-eighth of the market value of such gas. If such gas is sold by lessee, then lessee agrees to pay lessor, as royalty, one-eighth of the net proceeds derived from the sale of said casinghead gas at the wells.'

It is the second royalty provision we are primarily concerned with here. It will be noted by that provision royalty is to be paid for gas 'while same is being sold or used off the premises,' as distinguished from gas used by the lessee on the premises for operational purposes, and gas used by the lessor for domestic purposes. For these uses the lease elsewhere provides no royalty is to be paid. The provision says, further, that such royalty shall be one-eighth the 'market price' at the wells. No one contends that this means a 'market price' established by daily sales at the wells. I quote from the Court of Civil Appeals, Texas Oil & Gas Corporation et al., v. Vela et al., Tex.Civ.App., 405 S.W.2d 68 (1966).

> 'The royalty to be paid for gas presents a most difficult problem because of the nature of the gas sales, and has been the subject of much litigation. The Courts have recognized, and the undisputed evidence in this case confirms, that the practicalities of the gas industry require that gas be sold under long-term contracts because the pipelines must have a committed source of supply sufficient to justify financing, construction and operation. Therefore, the rules of daily sales and daily quotations have no application. Foster v. Atlantic Refining Co., 5 Cir., 329 F.2d 485, Phillips Pet. Co. v. Bynum, 5 Cir., 155 F.2d 196; Gex v. Texas Co., Tex.Civ.App., 377 S.W.2d 820, n. wr. hist.'

The phrase 'market price at the well' means market price received by lessee less the necessary expense, if any, of processing and transporting the gas from the well to pipeline of purchaser. Le Cuno Oil Co. v. Smith, Tex.Civ.App., 306 S.W.2d 190, n.r.e.; Hemler v. Union Producing Co., D.C.La. 1941, 40 F.Supp. 824, affirmed in part and reversed on other grounds in part, 134 F.2d 436 (5th Cir.); Clear Creek Oil & Gas Co. v. Bushmaier, 165 Ark. 303, 264 S.W. 830.

Since it appears that the royalty provision fails to state as of what time the 'market price' is to be determined, I think, we must look to common practices in the industry at the time the lease contract was made in 1933 to ascertain what was the intention of the parties with reference to this matter. All parties agree and this Court so holds that at such time the only sales for gas from wells producing gas only were made on long-term contracts or for the life of the lease. The parties, when they entered into the lease contract, knew how such gas had to be marketed; it had to be marketed under a contract similar to the one before us. Consequently, when the parties entered into the lease contract they all knew that the term 'market price' necessarily meant the price prevailing for gas on long-term contract as of the time the sale contract should be made. They knew it could only be sold at a price to be fixed in the contract for gas to be delivered in the future. If the gas contracts in question have provided for a price which at the time was below the prevailing 'market price' for gas sold on lease life-time contracts then the lessors would have cause to complain. In the absence of such showing they have no cause for complaint.

This Court in holding that when gas is marketed under a long-term contract the sale is deemed to have been made at the time of delivery to the purchaser, refers to Martin v. Amis, Tex.Com.App. 288 S.W. 431, 433. In this case the lessee executed a written contract to sell raw gas to a gasoline plant in consideration of twenty-five percent of the proceeds of the gasoline manufactured therefrom, and one-half of the proceeds of the residue gas. Lessor contended that he was entitled to one-eighth of all the gasoline manufactured, and one-eighth of all the residue gas as royalty, because the lessor was still the owner of the gasoline and residue gas when sold—no sale ever having been made to the gasoline plant. The gasoline plant, he contended, was a mere servant of the lessor. The Court held that when the gas was delivered to the plant under the terms of the executory contract of sale, an executed sale was thereby effected. Thus, it appears the sale was complete when the gas was delivered, but it took both the contract of sale and its delivery to constitute the sale.

Likewise, in the instant case the mere delivery of gas does not constitute the sale; it takes both the contract of sale plus the delivery to constitute the sale.

The Court, also, relies on the case of Foster v. Atlantic Refining Company, (5th Cir.) 329 F.2d 485, in support of its holding. In that case the court said:

'Atlantic urges that the market price is the price at which the gas was sold in 1950. Developing this point it first says that the phrase 'when run' applies to oil but not to gas on the theory that a 'run' is a transfer of crude oil from stock tanks to a pipeline. We see no reason why the phrase may not apply to gas and mean the time of delivery of gas from the well to the pipeline. Indeed, a witness for Atlantic so testified.' (emphasis supplied)

It is noted that the court does not hold that the 'market price' is to be determined as of the time of sale, which under long-term contract is deemed to be at the time of delivery, as held by this Court in the instant case. The Foster lease only had one royalty provision which covered both oil and gas, and the Court based it's [SIC] opinion solely on the provision in the royalty contract, which specifically said that the gas must be sold at the 'market price' prevailing when the gas was run. The royalty provision is in part as follows:

> 'The conventional royalties to be paid by Lessee are: (a) on Oil [SIC] and gas, including all hydro-carbons, one-eighth (1/8th) of that produced and saved from said land, the same to be delivered to the credit of the Lessor into the pipe line and to be sold At [SIC] the market price therefor prevailing for the field where produced when run; * * *.'

It will be noted under the royalty provision the lessee did not even have authority to sell lessor's one-eighth (1/8th) interest in the gas until it had been delivered to the credit of the lessor in the pipeline. The parties in effect contracted against long-term gas sales contracts. We have no such limitation in the lease before us. Under the terms of the lease the lessee owns all the gas, and it was contemplated by the parties that it would be sold in the usual and customary manner, that is, under long-term contracts.

It is obvious, therefore, that the Foster case should have no persuasive force in determining the question before us in the instant case. There is no intimation that the 5th Circuit would have reached the same result if the contract made by Atlantic had not contained the words 'market price when run,' thus, clearly and unambiguously obligating it to pay royalties based on market price existing on the date the gas was run or delivered. In fact, it is submitted that there is a clear intimation expressed in the Court's opinion that the 'market price' specified in the sales contract (made in good faith, and at the best prices and terms available when the lessee-producer was compelled to 'market' the gas) did establish the 'market price' for royalty payment purposes if it were not for the peculiar royalty provision requiring a different conclusion.

Although, the lessee in the instant case put himself in no such bind as Atlantic did in its lease, this Court reasons that the lessee is in the same bind that Atlantic was, and has unnecessarily put itself into a strait jacket which it feels compels it to hold as the 5th Circuit felt it was compelled to hold in the Foster case. The problem before us is by no means the problem that the 5th Circuit had in the Foster case. In that case the lessee bound itself to pay the prevailing 'market price' in the field when the gas was delivered. In the case before us the lessee bound itself to pay 'market price' for gas sold (necessarily sold under long-term contracts). The lessee did not agree to pay the 'market price' prevailing in the field at the time of delivery, but agreed to pay the 'market price' of gas sold; that is, sold under long-term contract at a price determined as of the time the contract was made. If the parties understand that the price for which gas was to be sold under long-term contracts had to be determined as of time of making the contract, is it not reasonable to say that they understood that market-price [SIC] was to be determined as of the same time?

Most of all of the legal commentators who have written on the subject before us favor the view presented here by this dissent. Siefkin, Rights of Lessor and Lessee With Respect to Sale of Gas and as to Gas Royalty Provisions, Fourth Annual Institute on Oil and Gas Law and Taxation, pp. 181, 188—91; Bounds, Division Orders, Fifth Annual Institute on Oil and Gas Law and Taxation, pp. 91, 116—17; Brown, The Law of Oil and Gas Leases, Section 6.09, p. 118 (1958); Gregg, Analysis of Usual Oil and Gas Lease Provisions, 5 South Texas Law Journal 1, 14; 43 Tex.Jur.2d 48, Sec. 389.

I would hold that the lessors recover nothing by virtue of their suit for additional royalties. I concur in the Court's holding on their suit for damages for nondevelopment and its remand of the cause to the trial court.

GRIFFIN, SMITH and GREENHILL JJ., join in this dissent.

DISSENTING OPINION

GRIFFIN, Justice.

I agree with the Court of Civil Appeals in the disposition it made of the recovery sought by Nordan and Mrs. Gaines. Mrs. Gaines' predecessor in title and Nordan purchased gas under the original contract, and at the price therein set out, and paid the owners of the various royalties and mineral interests under this contract. When the corporation was dissolved in 1941 and its assets distributed to Mrs. Gaines and Nordan, they expressly ratified and confirmed the original contract of sale of the gas. In my opinion, Mrs. Gaines and Nordan cannot recover.

ON MOTION FOR REHEARING

WALKER, Justice.

In their motions for rehearing, respondents correctly point out:

(1) That since L. A. Nordan did not give notice of appeal or except to the trial court's judgment, he is not in position to complain of the action of that court in denying him a recovery for past drainage, West Texas Utilities Co. v. Irvin, 161 Tex. 5, 336 S.W.2d 609;

(2) That neither Nordan nor Mrs. Gaines complained in their motions for rehearing in the Court of Civil Appeals of the modification by that court of the declaratory portion of the trial court's judgment; and

(3) That the judgment of the trial court includes interest on the several money recoveries to November 1, 1965, rather than to April 12, 1965, as we thought when our original opinion was handed down.

The motions for rehearing are accordingly granted, in part, our former judgment is set aside, and judgment is now rendered as follows:

The judgment of the Court of Civil Appeals is set aside, and it is ordered:

(1) That all claims and controversies between Juan M. Vela, Carlos Vela, Ernestina Vela, Emma Vela de Garcia and husband, Jesus M. Garcia, on the one hand, and Texas Oil & Gas Corporation, Claudia L. Eaves and husband, Jack R. Eaves, Anita Nordan Lindsay and husband, Sidney A. Lindsay, Marian Nordan Hudson and husband, Harold W. Hudson, individually and as members of the partnership of Nordan & Company, Hannah D. Gaines and husband, Arthur Gaines (but only in her capacity as a defendant-operator and not in her capacity as a plaintiff-royalty owner), Mrs. Leo G. Moss and husband, Leo G. Moss, Raymond Gibbs, administrator of the estate of C. T. Jamison, deceased, Jessie Faye Gibbs Jamison, a widow, individually and as guardian of the persons and estates of Michael E. Jamison and Patrick Jamison, minors, C. A. Reiter, and Delhi-Taylor Oil Corporation, on the other, be severed, and as to all such claims and controversies the judgment of the trial court is set aside and the cause is dismissed as moot without opinion or adjudication on the merits;

(2) That the action of L. A. Nordan to recover damages for drainage that may have occurred prior to April 12, 1965,

the date of trial, is severed, and as to this part of the case the judgment of the trial court is affirmed;

(3) That the judgment of the trial court in so far as it denies L. A. Nordan and Mrs. Hannah D. Gaines any recovery for future drainage or the failure to reasonably develop the leased premises, denies Mrs. Hannah D. Gaines any recovery for past drainage, directs Texas Oil & Gas Corporation to drill additional wells and provides that the lease shall be cancelled and terminated in the event additional wells are not drilled in the manner and within the time therein provided, is reversed. These parts of the case are also severed, and as to them the cause is remanded to the district court;

(4) That as to the remainder of the cause:

(a) The declaratory portion of the trial court's judgment is reformed as provided in the judgment of the Court of Civil Appeals;

(b) The judgment of the trial court in favor of L. A. Nordan for royalties due and unpaid is reformed to provide that he recover from Delhi-Taylor Oil Corporation the sum of $1,411.76, from the Venture Group the sum of $4,077.39, from Texas Oil & Gas Corporation the sum of $1,726.95, from Mrs. Hannah D. Gaines the sum of $1,363.12, from Nordan & Company the sum of $1,363.12, from Mrs. Leo G. Moss the sum of $1,226.81, from the C. T. Jamison Estate the sum of $1,226.81, and from C. A. Reiter the sum of $272.62, with interest on each of said amounts from November 1, 1965, at the rate of six per cent per annum;

(c) The judgment of the trial court in favor of Mrs. Hannah D. Gaines for royalties due and unpaid is reformed to provide that she recover from Delhi-Taylor Oil Corporation the sum of $1,058.83, from the Venture Group the sum of $3,057.86, from Nordan & Company the sum of $1,022.34, from Mrs. Leo G. Moss the sum of $920.11, from the C. T. Jamison Estate the sum of $920.11, from C. A. Reiter the sum of $204.47, and from Texas Oil & Gas Corporation the sum of $1,295.21, with interest on each of said amounts from November 1, 1965, at the rate of six per cent per annum; and (d) The judgment of the trial court as so reformed is affirmed.

In all other respects the motions for rehearing are overruled. The parties will have 15 days from this date within which to file motions for rehearing.

Commentary on Texas Oil & Gas Corporation et al., Petitioners-Respondents

v.

Juan M. Vela et al., Respondents-Petitioners (1968)

Over the years the cases of *Texas Oil & Gas Corporation et al., Petitioners-Respondents v. Juan M. Vela et al., Respondents-Petitioners* (1968) and *Exxon Corporation et al., Petitioners, v. Triphene Middleton et al., Respondents* (1981) have become so intricately intertwined, that it would be an injustice to comment separately on these two decisions. Please see the commentary following the *Middleton* case in Chapter 14 (beginning on page 197), by Michael P. Pearson, for a commentary on both *Vela* and *Middleton*.

14

CHAPTER 14

Exxon Corporation et al., Petitioners, v. Triphene Middleton et al., Respondents.

COMMENTARY

by Michael P. Pearson

613 S.W.2d 240

1981

Exxon Corporation et al., Petitioners,
v.
Triphene Middleton et al., Respondents.

613 S.W.2d 240

1981

Baker & Botts, Frank G. Harmon, Walter B. Morgan and Louis Bagwell, Houston, Orgain, Bell & Tucker, John G. Tucker, Beaumont, Herf M. Weinert and Julius L. Lybrand, Dallas, for petitioners.

Bracewell & Patterson, William Key Wilde and Charles G. King, Houston, for respondents.

ON MOTION FOR REHEARING

CAMPBELL, Justice.

Our opinion and judgment dated October 1, 1980, are withdrawn and set aside.

Exxon Corporation, formerly Humble Oil and Refining Company, (Exxon) secured three oil and gas leases from A. D. Middleton in 1933 and 1934 and one lease from members of the White family in 1935. Sun Oil Company of Delaware (Sun) obtained two oil and gas leases from A. D. Middleton and others in 1940 and 1941, one lease from R. M. White in 1933, one lease from Lily Mae Hamilton and O. B. Hamilton in 1933, and two leases from Felix Jackson and others in 1933 and 1938.

Three lawsuits involving these leases were filed in 1974. The first was by the successors in interest to A. D. Middleton (Middletons) against Exxon. The second was by the successors in interest to R. M. White (Whites) against Exxon and Sun. The third was brought by the successors in interest to Felix Jackson (Jacksons) against Sun. These separate suits alleged a deficiency in the amount of royalties paid by Exxon and Sun, as lessees, for the years 1973, 1974 and 1975. The three original lawsuits were consolidated into a single suit, which was tried to the court in January of 1977, and judgment was rendered for the plaintiffs. The Court of Civil Appeals reversed the trial court judgment and remanded the cause in part and rendered judgment in part. 571 S.W.2d 349, Tex.Civ.App.

The problem begins with the gas royalty clause. That clause in the Exxon lease with the Middletons and Whites provides that royalties

> ... on gas, including casinghead gas or other gaseous substances, produced from said land and sold or used off the premises or in the manufacture of gasoline or other product therefrom, shall be the market value at the well of one-eighth of the gas so sold or used, provided that on gas so sold at the wells the royalties shall be one-eighth of the amount realized from such sale.

The gas royalty clause in the Sun-Middleton, White and Jackson leases provides that Sun would pay

> ... on gas, including casinghead gas or other gaseous substances, produced from said land and sold or used off the premises, or used in the manufacture of gasoline or other products therefrom, by lessee, the market value at the well of one-eighth of the gas so sold or used, provided that on gas sold at the wells, the royalty shall be one-eighth of the amount realized from such sale.

The first question is "What is a sale at the wells?" or "What is a sale off the premises?" The Exxon leases are located in the Anahuac Field, Chambers County. Some of the natural gas produced from the Middleton and White leases was processed at Exxon's Anahuac Gas Plant. This plant is not located on any of the Middleton or White leases but is in the Anahuac Field. The processed gas was delivered by Exxon at the tailgate of its Anahuac Gas Plant to the City of Anahuac, the Houston Pipeline Company and the Exxon Gas System. Twenty percent of the processed gas was sold to the City of Anahuac and the Houston Pipeline Company. The remainder was delivered to the Exxon Gas System and was sold to Exxon's "eastend customers," and is marketed to fifteen industrial customers. The Exxon Gas System delivered gas to each eastend customer at the customer's "plant gate."

The distinction between "sold or used off the premises" or "sold at the wells" now becomes important because the oil and gas royalty clause provides two standards for computing royalties, market value and amount realized. The royalty clause provides

> (1) ... on gas ... sold or used off the premises ... the market value at the well of one-eighth of the gas so sold or used.

The clause further provides

> (2) ... that on gas sold at the wells the royalties shall be one-eighth of the amount realized from such sale ....

The parties agree that on gas "sold at the wells" royalties are based on the amount realized.

Exxon argues that its sale to the City of Anahuac and Houston Pipeline Company at the tailgate of the Anahuac Plant, not located on the Middleton or White leases, but within the Anahuac Field is a sale at the wells. Therefore, the royalties should be based on the amount realized from such sales. The Middletons and Whites argue that the Anahuac Plant is not on the leased premises and the royalties should be based on market value because a sale off the leased premises is not a "sale at the wells."

Stated another way, the issue with regard to Exxon's sales to Houston Pipeline Company and the City of Anahuac is whether a sale in the field, but not on the premises of the lease, is a sale "off the premises" or a sale "at the wells." If the former, the royalty is calculable on the basis of market value; if the latter, the royalty is payable on the basis of the proceeds received by Exxon for the sale of that gas.

The trial court found Exxon's sales to Houston Pipeline Company and the City of Anahuac at the tailgate of the Anahuac Gas Plant were "sales at the wells." The Court of Civil Appeals reversed that finding and held that gas sold at the tailgate of the Anahuac Gas Plant were sales "off the premises."

The court stated:

> The court's finding that the gas was sold at the tailgate of the Anahuac Gas Plant is inconsistent with, and better supported by the evidence than the finding that the gas was "sold at the wells."

It is undisputed that "off the premises" means off the leased premises. However, the question is whether the boundary lines of the leased premises determines which royalty clause is applicable, market value or amount realized.

The market value provision of the royalty clause stated:

> ... on gas ... sold or used off the premises ... the market value at the well of one-eighth of the gas so sold or used.

The Whites and Middletons argue this clause provides royalties based on market value for all gas sold off the leased premises and based on the amount realized for all gas sold within the leased premises (sold at the wells). They argue that in the phrase "sold or used off the premises" off the premises modifies both "sold" and "used." Because the market value standard includes all sales off the leased premises, they contend that, by implication, the phrase "sold at the wells" includes all sales which occur "on the premises."

Exxon contends that "off the premises" modifies the word "used" only. It contends the phrase "sold at the wells" is neither defined nor limited by any language in the lease, and that the parties intended a sale at the well to include any sale which occurred in the field of production.

Exxon's contention that the words "off the premises" modifies the word "used" and not the word "sold" is weakened by looking at the entire clause.

> ... on gas ... sold or used off the premises ... the market value at the well of one-eighth of the gas so sold or used.

The words "so sold" imply the gas has been sold in a certain manner. In Webster's Third International Dictionary, "so" is defined as "in a manner or way that is indicated or suggested." If, as Exxon insists, "off the premises" modifies the word "used" only, parallel construction would rewrite the phrase to provide a royalty calculated on "the market value at the well of one-eighth of the gas sold or so used."

Exxon's construction creates royalty standards which overlap. According to Exxon, the market value standard applies to all sales wherever they occur, whereas, the amount realized standard applies only to sales at the wells even though sales at the wells are covered by the market value standard. Exxon's construction would cause the royalty clause to read as follows:

> On gas ... produced from said land and sold ... the market value at the well of one-eighth of the gas so sold provided that on gas sold at the wells the royalty shall be one-eighth of the amount realized.

We conclude "off the premises" modifies both "sold" and "used." The "premises" is the land described in the lease agreement. Therefore, sold "off the premises" means gas which is sold outside the leased premises. Thus, "sold at the wells" means sold at the wells within the lease, and not sold at the wells within the fields.

Our construction in no way conflicts with Texas Oil and Gas Corporation v. Vela, 429 S.W.2d 866 (Tex.1968). In Vela, the royalty clause obligated Texas Oil and Gas:

> To pay to lessor, as royalty for gas from each well where gas only is found, while the same is being sold or used off the premises, one-eighth of the market price at the wells of the amount so sold or used, ... (emphasis added).

Gas produced from the Vela leases was sold on the leased premises. The sole standard for calculating royalties was market value, regardless of where the sale took place. Under those circumstances the phrase "off the premises" did not modify sold, and the words "so sold" as used in that context referred to all sales.

Exxon relies heavily on Butler v. Exxon Corporation, 559 S.W.2d 410 (Tex.Civ.App. El Paso 1977, writ ref'd n. r. e.). In Butler, supra, the royalty clause is almost identical to the one in issue. Gas produced from the Butler leases was sold off the leased premises, but within the field of production. The trial court interpreted the phrase "sold at the wells" to include sales which occurred anywhere in the vicinity of the field and found the gas sold from the Butler leases was "sold at the wells." The Court of Civil Appeals expressly approved this finding. It noted the parties did not use mutually exclusive terms such as "on the premises" and "off the premises" or "at the well" and "away from the well," and that the clause based on "amount realized" from a sale "at the well" had no limiting language requiring the sale to be "on the premises." The court relied primarily on expert testimony about what constituted a "sale at the well" as understood in the oil and gas industry. To the extent the Court of Civil Appeals' interpretation of the royalty clause in Butler, supra, conflicts with our interpretation of this clause, it is disapproved.

In Skaggs v. Heard, 172 F.Supp. 813 (D.C.Tex.1959), it was held, under a gas royalty clause, that a sale at a separator on the leased premises, but 320 feet from a wellhead, was a sale "at the well" as opposed to being a sale not at the well and off the leased premises. Also, in Kingery v. Continental Oil Company, 434 F.Supp. 349 (D.C.1977), the Court, in construing a gas royalty provision similar to the one in question, held that a sale off the premises was not a sale at the wells. In that case the point of delivery was located off the premises approximately 31/2 miles from the nearest line of the leased premises.

Having determined that Exxon must pay royalties based on the market value of all the gas sold off the White and Middleton leases, we turn to the question of when and how market value is determined.

MARKET VALUE

All parties agree market value is determined when the gas is sold. The problem is "when is it sold." Before 1972, most natural gas was marketed under long-term contracts at fixed prices. Exxon contends the date its gas contracts became effective is the time the gas is sold and therefore the time market value is determined. Relying on our decision in Texas Oil & Gas Corporation v. Vela, 429 S.W.2d 866 (Tex.1968), the Court of Civil Appeals rejected this contention and held that Exxon must pay royalties of one-eighth of the market value of the gas when delivered, and not the market value when Exxon's gas contracts became effective.

Exxon argues Vela, supra, is distinguishable because the language of the Vela royalty clause supports the position that the parties intended market value to be determined when the gas was delivered to the purchaser. That clause provided that a royalty equal to one-eighth of the market value at the wells would be paid on gas produced on the lessor's land "while the same is being sold or used off the premises." Exxon insists no such intention can be ascertained from the language of the White and Middleton royalty clause. We disagree.

Under the express terms of the clause, for royalty to become payable, gas must be "produced from said land and sold or used off the premises...." Production means actual physical extraction of the mineral from the land. Monsanto Co. v. Tyrrell, 537 S.W.2d 135 (Tex.Civ.App. Houston 1976, writ ref'd n. r. e.). Under the royalty clause, production of gas is a prerequisite to its sale or use. The gas purchase contracts became effective before the gas was produced and sold. The clause also employs the words "sold" and "used" in the same tense. Gas is "used" when delivered or consumed. The time gas is "sold" is the same time gas is "used" when it is delivered. Because Exxon must pay royalties based on market value for gas "used off the premises," that same royalty clause cannot permit Exxon to pay royalties on "gas sold off the premises" on any basis other than its market value when delivered. The wording of the royalty clause, therefore, negates the idea of a sale of gas on the effective date of a gas contract for royalty purposes. Just as gas was "being sold" when delivered to the gas purchasers in Vela, so was gas "sold" when delivered by Exxon to its customers.

Exxon insists the practicalities of the natural gas industry require us to construe "sold" to mean the time the gas becomes committed to a bona fide long-term gas contract. We are not unmindful of the realities of the gas industry; however, our resolution of this problem is based upon the recognition of two separate and distinct transactions, the lease agreement and the gas contract. Although as between Exxon and its customers, the gas may have been sold when the contracts became effective, there is no basis in the royalty clause for applying such a definition to the lease agreements. Exxon's royalty obligations are determined from lease agreements which were executed prior to and wholly independent of the gas contracts. Vela, supra. When Exxon negotiated the gas contracts, it took the risk that the revenue therefrom would be sufficient to satisfy its royalty obligations. That subsequent increases in market value have made these obligations financially burdensome is no reason to compel this Court to disregard the plain and unambiguous terms of the royalty clause and rewrite it to conform to the meaning that Exxon, as drafter of the language, says was intended. See Foster v. Atlantic Refining Company, 329 F.2d 485 (5th Cir. 1964). Exxon's royalty obligations are fixed and unaffected by its gas contracts. If the parties intended royalties to be calculated on the amount realized standard, they could and should have used only a "proceeds-type" clause.

(The lessees) might have agreed that the royalty on gas produced from a gas well would be a fractional part of the amount realized by the lessee from its sale. Instead of doing so, however, they stipulated in plain terms that the lessee would pay one-eighth of the market value at the well of all gas sold or used off the premises. This clearly means the prevailing market price at the time of the sale or use. Vela, supra, at 871. (emphasis added)

The parties did not use "market value" and "amount realized" interchangeably and we reject Exxon's assertion that the parties intended "market value" to have essentially the same meaning as "amount realized."

> It is clear then that the parties knew how to and did provide for royalties ... based upon ... market value, and based upon the proceeds derived by the lessee from the sale of gas. Vela, supra.

We now turn to the question of how the market value is determined.

In Texas, a gas pipeline purchaser is required each month to file a Purchaser's Monthly Gas Tax Report with the State Comptroller of Public Accounts. These reports, commonly called "Form 60-150's" contain the name of the purchaser and seller; the month and year of each purchase; the lease and county from which the gas was produced; the quality of the gas or whether it is produced from an oil well or gas well; the volume purchased; and the price. The Middleton's expert, Mr. William S. Hudson, reviewed over 30,000 of these reports to arrive at an opinion of market value. He considered the relevant market area for the gas sold from the White and Middleton leases to be Texas Railroad Commission Districts (TRC) 2, 3, and 4. He arrived at his opinion by taking the arithmetical average of the three highest prices paid from quarter to quarter for any quantity of gas anywhere in the relevant market area.

Exxon's expert, Mr. Frederick M Perkins, testified that Exxon's "field price" was the market value of the gas. Exxon's "field price" for the Anahuac Field is computed from sales in TRC #3 plus the seven adjoining counties of Lavaca, Jackson, Milam, Robertson, Angelina, San Augustine, and Sabine. The field price is calculated by taking the total price paid for one month in each quarter for the gas currently delivered to all major purchasers and dividing it by the total volume of gas delivered.

The trial court determined market value based on Mr. Hudson's expert opinion testimony. The Court of Civil Appeals disagreed. It held the method used by Hudson failed to satisfy the requirements for determining market value as set forth in Vela, supra:

> Hudson did not define the relevant market area as the Anahuac Field. He refused to give weight to any contracts for sale of gas from this field. The sales that he considered were not shown to be comparable in time, quality and availability to marketing outlets. He selected only the highest prices paid in TRC Districts 2, 3 and 4 that satisfied his criteria. He made no mathematical average of all prices paid in the field, nor did he seek to corroborate such an average with comparable sales as defined by the supreme court. His consideration of price data compiled on a quarterly, rather than monthly, basis is inconsistent with the time period at issue in the case.

The Court of Civil Appeals also rejected Exxon's contention that its "field price" conclusively established the market value of the gas because the "field price" is computed in part on the basis of sales of gas in interstate commerce. The parties stipulated that during the years 1973-1975 all of the gas from these leases was sold in intrastate markets in Texas.

Market value is defined as the price property would bring when it is offered for sale by one who desires, but is not obligated to sell, and is bought by one who is under no necessity of buying it. Polk County v. Tenneco, Inc., 554 S.W.2d 918 (Tex.1977). To determine the market value of gas, the gas should be valued as though it is free and available for sale.

Market value may be calculated by using comparable sales. Comparable sales of gas are those comparable in time, quality, quantity, and availability of marketing outlets. Vela, supra.

Sales comparable in time occur under contracts executed contemporaneously with the sale of the gas in question. Sales comparable in quality are those of similar physical properties such as sweet, sour, or casinghead gas. Quality also involves the legal characteristics of the gas; that is, whether it is sold in a regulated or unregulated market, or in one particular category of a regulated market. Sales comparable in quantity are those of similar volumes to the gas in question. To be comparable, the sales must be made from an area with marketing outlets similar to the gas in question. Gas from fields with outlets to interstate markets only, for instance, would not be comparable to gas from a field with outlets only to the intrastate market.

Comparable sales should be drawn from a relevant market. The Court of Civil Appeals interpreted our decision in Vela to mean that the relevant market must be the field from which the gas is produced. In Vela, the plaintiff's expert determined market value by analyzing comparable sales from the field of production. Although the field was used as the relevant market, this Court did not hold that the relevant market is confined to the field. Rather we held it was proper, not necessary, for the trial court to consider the expert's testimony on market value and that the evidence of the expert supported the finding of the trial court.

The size of a relevant market depends on the facts in each case. Mr. Hudson testified that Texas Railroad Commission Districts (TRC) 2, 3, and 4 was the relevant market. He testified that within this area sales comparable in time, quality, quantity, and availability of marketing outlets occurred. He also testified that gas production, facilities for gathering and transporting gas, and consumption of gas were present in this area.

Mr. Hudson's testimony was substantially corroborated by the testimony of Sun's expert, Mr. H. J. Gruy. Moreover, there was testimony that price redetermination clauses of many gas purchase contracts use TRC #2, 3, and 4 as the relevant market for gas produced along the Gulf Coast. We hold there was some competent testimony to support the trial court's finding of TRC #2, 3 and 4 as the relevant market. Applying the test of comparability to the market value formula urged by the parties, we hold that Mr. Hudson's testimony is competent testimony which supports the trial court's determination of market value.

The sales used by Mr. Hudson are comparable in quality. He testified that most of the gas produced within the relevant market is sweet gas. Mr. Gruy and Mr. Perkins also testified that the quality of gas in TRC #2, 3 and 4 was comparable. The Gas Purchaser Reports show that most of the sales used by Mr. Hudson were sales of sweet gas. Moreover, Mr. Hudson adjusted the sales he used according to the btu content of the gas to make them comparable. Also, the sales used were intrastate sales, and therefore comparable in legal quality.

Although he used sales of varying volumes, Mr. Hudson testified that during 1973, 1974, and 1975 in TRC #2, 3, and 4, the price of gas was comparable regardless of the volumes sold. Mr. Perkins testified that during the period in question quantity did not make any difference. Mr. Hudson testified if one knew the btu value of the gas and made the necessary adjustments, that sales could be made comparable regardless of quantity.

The sales used by Mr. Hudson are comparable in their availability to marketing outlets. He testified the gas fields in TRC #2, 3, and 4 are interconnected through a great network of pipelines, both intrastate and interstate.

The sales used by Mr. Hudson are comparable in time. The parties stipulated that the market value of the gas was to be determined quarterly. Mr. Hudson selected the three highest prices for the first month of each quarter, made btu adjustments, averaged them arithmetically, and determined the market value for that quarter. The three highest prices were used because gas prices were increasing and if you wanted the most current price you would look at the highest prices because they represented the most recent transactions. Mr. Hudson also stated that most gas purchasers set their initial price or redetermined price by taking the highest prices in the area.

Exxon argues that Mr. Hudson's method is flawed because it, in effect, values the gas as if it were free and available for sale each quarter. Exxon insists the gas was committed to the performance of its gas contracts and, therefore, the sales used by Mr. Hudson were not comparable. The terms of a gas contract between Exxon and a third party will not lessen Exxon's duty to pay royalties based on market value. We hold the trial court did not err in valuing the gas as if it were free and available for sale.

Exxon's "field price" fails to establish conclusively the market value. The sales used in its computation were not comparable in quality. All gas produced from the White and Middleton leases was sold within the State. Exxon's field price, however, includes interstate sales. Intrastate and interstate gas prices are not comparable in quality. They are conceptually and legally different. The price of interstate gas during the period in question was regulated by the Federal Power Commission ("FPC"). While this evidence may be admissible, such evidence does not bind the fact finder as a matter of law in its determination of market value.

Moreover, Exxon's "new vintage gas" concept supports our holding that its "field price" was not binding on the trial court in its determination of the market value of gas produced from the White and Middleton leases. Exxon treats gas discovered and produced after January 1, 1972, as new vintage gas and computes the royalty on this gas in a manner completely different from its field price. In fact, the formula used by Exxon for calculating royalties on new vintage gas is remarkably similar to Mr. Hudson's market value formula. Market value for Exxon's new vintage gas is determined, by Exxon, by taking the arithmetic average of the three highest prices paid by a pipeline for sales over one million cubic feet per day, with adjustments for btu content. In 1962, Sun, through arbitration, agreed the representative prices to be submitted to arbitrators were the three highest prices paid in Railroad Commission District 3. When Sun's agreement with Amoco ended it sold gas to United Texas Transmission Co. pursuant to a negotiated agreement that contained a price redetermination provision pursuant to which Sun sells its gas for the arithmetic average of the three highest prices paid for gas in Railroad Commission Districts 2, 3 and 4. This was almost the same method used by the trial court.

Sun's expert, Buford Koehler, testified

> "I wouldn't have too much quarrel about his method here to determine the three highest prices paid for it for the purposes of redetermining under the contract."

Exxon's methods of calculating royalties reflect one market value for gas produced from wells discovered before January 1, 1972 and another market value for gas discovered and produced after that date. This distinction is inconsistent with our holdings that under the White and Middleton royalty clause gas is sold when delivered and market value is determined from sales comparable in time, quantity, quality, and availability of markets. The determination of market value is not dependent on when the gas is discovered.

The Court of Civil Appeals criticized Hudson's method because he made no mathematical average of all prices paid in the field nor did he seek to corroborate such an average with comparable sales. We do not share the Court of Civil Appeals' views on this point. We specifically stated in Vela, supra, that a mathematical average of all prices paid in the field is "not a final answer to the difficult problem of determining market value at any particular time."

The complexity of the oil and gas industry makes it difficult to establish a formula to determine the market value of gas in each field in Texas. The market value of gas may be established by expert testimony. Once experts qualify, their testimony is to be considered by the fact finder. Objections to the basis of their testimony goes to its weight, not to its admissibility. Weymouth v. Colorado Interstate Gas Company, 367 F.2d 84 (5th Cir. 1966). In Weymouth, supra, the lessors asserted that the lessees' experts based their opinion of market value on sales which were not comparable. The Fifth Circuit rejected the lessors' attempts to confine the experts' testimony to sales of exact comparability:

> This view is too restrictive for the situation of an expert witness explaining his opinion. Lessors' heavy reliance on the Sartor cases would bind upon us and all experts the rules applicable to introduction of direct evidence of comparable sales. This is simply unrealistic where we deal with an expert who, once he establishes his qualifications and he gives his broad, general opinion, needs to be able to reveal the basis for his opinion in his own language without too many communication-crippling legal barriers thrown in his way. 367 F.2d at 91.

The lessees' experts testified that the prices they utilized were fairly comparable. The court held that objections against uncomparable sales went only to the weight which the fact finder should attach to the experts' opinion. We hold there was some evidence to support the trial court's determination of market value.

SUN OIL COMPANY'S DIVISION ORDERS

The leases between the Middletons, Whites and Jacksons (royalty owners) and Sun were executed during the years 1933 through 1941.

Except for gas produced from the R. M. White lease,[7] the gas produced from the Sun leases was processed off the lease premises at Union Texas Petroleum's Winnie Plant. During the years 1973, 1974, and 1975, gas was delivered by Sun to Pan American Gas Company, a predecessor of Amoco Gas Company, at the tailgate of the Winnie Plant pursuant to a gas contract dated July 5, 1951, and amended July 22, 1965. The price paid by Pan American under the contract was 17.58¢. Sun calculated and paid royalties to the royalty owners on the contract price. The royalty owners contend the royalties were payable on the market value at the well of the gas.

The gas royalty clause of these leases is identical and obligates Sun to pay:

> ... on gas, including casinghead gas or other gaseous substances, produced from said land and sold or used off the premises or in the manufacture of gasoline or other product

> therefrom, the market value at the well of one-eighth of the gas so sold or used, provided that on gas sold at the wells the royalties shall be one-eighth of the amount realized from such sale .... (emphasis added).

Because the gas is sold off the leased premises, Sun was obligated to pay one-eighth of the market value of the gas. Instead, Sun calculated and paid royalty to the lessors on the amount realized. The payment of royalties calculated on the amount realized was at all times during the period in question in conformity with certain documents, denominated "division orders," executed by the royalty owners or their predecessors in 1952. These documents were directed to Sun as operator of the leases, and in effect, changed the basis of the royalty standards of the leases. The documents also provided for the monthly payment of royalties, and required Sun to make available charts and records at all reasonable times. Finally, the documents stated they were binding on all parties, their heirs, successors, and assigns, and would remain in force during the life of the respective leases. The documents did not refer to any specific gas contracts executed by Sun.

The trial court found the "division orders" did not amend the leases to provide for royalties payable on proceeds. The trial court considered the division orders revocable, and found they were, in fact, revoked by the royalty owners on March 30, 1974, the date their petitions were served on Sun. The trial court concluded that the payments made by Sun and accepted by the royalty owners prior to March 30, 1974, were made pursuant to agreements supported by consideration and therefore, binding. However, the trial court also found that payments made and accepted after March 30, 1974, were not supported by consideration and therefore were not binding.

Thus, the trial court held the royalty owners were entitled to judgment for the difference between the royalty paid and one-eighth of the market value of the gas produced from the leases only from and after March 30, 1974.

The Court of Civil Appeals held the "division orders" were valid written agreements modifying the gas royalty clause, were supported by consideration before and after March 30, 1974, and were irrevocable.

Sun argues the trial court correctly held, under well-settled law that these instruments were binding for the time the parties acted under them. We agree.

After this Court's decision in Chicago Corporation v. Wall, 156 Tex. 217, 293 S.W.2d 844 (1956), the Texas law has been that payments made and accepted under an agreement such as these were effective until the agreement was revoked. See R. HEMINGWAY, THE LAW OF OIL & GAS s 7.5 (1971).

Federal courts, have on a number of occasions, been required to apply Texas law in division order cases. Phillips Petroleum Company v. Williams, 158 F.2d 723 (5th Cir. 1946), is particularly applicable, wherein the Court held:

> As to contention one, the division and transfer orders, with their definite declaration that the market value of the gas at the mouth of the well is to be the measure of lessors' rights and lessee's obligations, and their clear and full provisions for precisely arriving at the value, we agree with defendant, that, until withdrawn or modified, they constitute the precise and definite basis for payments, and payments made in accordance with them are final and binding. The very existence of this and the other numerous other litigations which have arisen over the meaning and effect of market price or rate provisions and over what was the market price or value of the gas, and the fact that these agreements fix, as due, sums which may from time to time be more or less than the prevailing market price, give full support to and make binding payments and settlements thereunder. Binding as they are, however, in respect of payments made and accepted under them, these division or transfer orders did not rewrite or supplant the lease contract. They are binding only for the time and to the extent that they have been, or are being acted on and made the basis of settlements and payments and from the time that notice is given that settlements will not be made on the basis provided in them, they cease to be binding.

In Pan American Petroleum Corporation v. Long, 340 F.2d 211 (5th Cir. 1964), the Court held that a division order, whether called a contract or not, until revoked, is binding on the parties. In J. M. Huber Corporation v. Denman,

367 F.2d 104 (5th Cir. 1966), the Court, referring to division orders similar to these, held "they do, of course, constitute a precise and definite basis for payments so that payments made in accordance with them are final and binding,"and cited this Court's opinion in Chicago Corp. v. Wall, supra, as one of its authorities for this holding.

MIDDLETONS' AND WHITES' DIVISION ORDERS

Our holding on Sun's division orders applies to Exxon's division orders executed by Middletons and Whites. We hold as a matter of law the division orders were revoked on March 29, 1974, when these royalty owners served Exxon with copies of their pleadings.

"GAS SOLD ON THE UNIT"

Portions of the Middleton leases belong to the Anahuac Main Frio Gas Unit No. 1. Gas produced from this unit is sold at the Anahuac Gas Plant which is located within the boundaries of Unit No. 1.

Amici Curiae argue that we should hold, as a matter of law, that gas sold anywhere within Unit No. 1 is a sale at the well because the creation of a unit obliterates all lease lines and that the unit becomes, in effect, one "amalgamated" lease. The unit lines rather than the lease lines limit or define the scope of each royalty standard. This argument ignores the express wording of the Unit No. 1 Agreement.

Article 3.4 which deals with the effect of the Agreement provides:

> Operations, including drilling operations, conducted with respect to the Unitized Formation on any part of the Unit Area, or production from any part of the Unitized Formation, except for the purpose of determining payments to Royalty Owners, shall be considered as operations upon or production from each Tract, and such operations or production shall continue in effect each lease or term royalty or term mineral interest as to all of the lands covered thereby just as if such operations had been conducted and a well had been drilled on and was producing from each Tract.

Article 8 provides:

> For the purpose of determining the royalties to which Royalty Owners are entitled on the gas produced from the Unitized Formation, the following method shall be used, to-wit:
>
> The volume of gas from said Tracts remaining and not used for injection operations, lost or used in handling or consumed or lost in plant operations in connection with extraction of liquids or liquid hydrocarbons therefrom or flared, shall be deemed to be dissolved gas to the extent of the total volume of dissolved gas produced from said Unitized Formation from all Tracts after deducting from such total dissolved gas produced a volume equal to the calculated volume of dissolved gas which was used or consumed in plant operations; and the remainder of said volume of gas so remaining, if any, shall be deemed to be free gas. The total dissolved gas so remaining shall be prorated among and deemed attributable to each Tract in the Unit Area in the ratio or production that the dissolved gas produced from such Tract bears to the total dissolved gas produced from all such Tracts. In like manner, the total free gas, if any, so remaining shall be apportioned among and allocated to the several Tracts within the Unit Area in accordance with the respective Tract Participations effective hereunder. From the gas so attributable to each Tract, there shall be deducted the volume of gas returned to the Tract for operations thereon or supplied to the Lessor under the terms of the lease covering such Tract ; and after all such computations and deductions have been accomplished, settlement shall be made for royalties on the remaining volume of gas, or so much thereof as if sold or used off the premises, in accordance with the terms and provisions of each lease or other instrument creating Royalty Owners' interests. (emphasis added)

We construe these provisions to mean that in determining each lessee's royalty obligation the terms of the leases are considered. Under the Middleton leases, the scope of each royalty standard is determined by the lease lines. The Unit Agreement does not substitute the Unit lines for the lease lines. Article 8, in fact, expressly provides that the gas attributable to each unitized tract shall for royalty purposes be considered as sold or used off the premises.

PREJUDGMENT INTEREST

Exxon contends the trial court erred in awarding prejudgment interest on the difference between the amount of royalties paid the Whites and Middletons and the amount which should have been paid. Exxon argues that a gas royalty dispute is not a proper case for an award of prejudgment interest because the market value standard does not provide a measure of ascertaining a sum payable at a date certain.

This Court held in Black Lake Pipeline Co. v. Union Construction Co., 538 S.W.2d 80 (Tex.1976), that prejudgment interest is recoverable when damages are established at a definite time and the amount of damages is definitely determinable.

Here, the damages are established at a definite time. However, the problem is that the amount of damages was not definitely determinable. In view of the uncertainty that has existed in the oil and gas industry with respect to the method of determining market value of oil and gas, we hold that prejudgment interest is not recoverable in this case.

FACTUAL INSUFFICIENCY

Both Exxon and Sun urge points in the Court of Civil Appeals which complain that the evidence is factually insufficient to support the trial court's determination of market value. The Court of Civil Appeals did not rule on these points. Because these factual insufficiency points are within the exclusive jurisdiction of the Court of Civil Appeals, we remand the cause to that court for determination of the points. Custom Leasing, Inc. v. Texas Bank & Trust Company of Dallas, 491 S.W.2d 869 (Tex.1973).

JUDGMENT

A. EXXON CORPORATION.

That part of the judgment of the Court of Civil Appeals holding that Exxon is liable to the Middletons and Whites for the difference in the royalties paid based on amount realized and the royalties due based on market value prior to March 29, 1974 is reversed.

That part of the judgment of the Court of Civil Appeals holding that plaintiffs failed to prove the market value of the gas sold from the White, Middleton, and Jackson leases is reversed and the cause is remanded to the Court of Civil Appeals to determine the insufficient evidence points presented to the Court of Civil Appeals. The insufficient evidence points of error shall be considered only to evidence of market value of gas after March 29, 1974.

That part of the judgment of the Court of Civil Appeals holding that the division orders executed by the Whites and Middletons do not vary Exxon's royalty obligation under the gas royalty clause of the lease agreements prior to March 29, 1974, is reversed.

B. SUN.

That part of the judgment of the Court of Civil Appeals holding that the Whites, Middletons, and Jacksons take nothing in their actions against Sun is reversed and the cause is remanded to the Court of Civil Appeals to consider the insufficient evidence points.

The cause is remanded to the Court of Civil Appeals to enter judgment in accordance with this opinion.

The motions for rehearing on behalf of Exxon and Sun Oil Company are granted. The motion for rehearing on behalf of Triphene Middleton et al. is overruled.

Commentary on *Vela* and *Middleton*: Tracing the Arc of the Concept of Market Value Royalty in Texas

by Michael P. Pearson[1]

When I was asked to write about *Texas Oil & Gas Corporation v. Vela*[2] ("*Vela*") and *Exxon Corporation v. Middleton*[3] ("*Middleton*") for this publication, it brought back, oddly enough, some childhood memories. By way of background, I am an oil company brat. For forty-four years (interrupted by World War II), my father was a distinguished oil and gas lawyer with, first, Humble Oil & Refining Company and, after its merger into Standard Oil of New Jersey, Exxon Corporation. Like many men of his era, Dad enjoyed "talking shop" at the dinner table. Many nights, rather than considering the recent exploits of Mickey Mantle, Hank Aaron, or the Texas Longhorns (my topics of choice), Dad would launch into detailed explanations of the latest royalty, or unitization, or pipeline right-of-way, or other oil and gas issue to come across his desk. Although she was not an oil and gas lawyer, my mother had been an accomplished businesswoman before she and Dad married, and she enjoyed the business-oriented conversations as well. Grudgingly, I had no choice except to absorb some of what was discussed.

I still recall the consternation with which Dad, who was a true "company man," greeted the Texas Supreme Court's 1968 decision in *Vela*. Dad appeared genuinely concerned that the "Veela" decision (his pronunciation) would ultimately bankrupt many oil and gas producers. On the other hand, I have always thought that there were probably children sitting at the dinner tables of royalty owners or royalty owner lawyers during this time who heard conversations in which *Vela* was viewed as opening a new era of economic opportunity for royalty owners and leveling the royalty calculation playing field between gas producers and royalty owners.

What was it about *Vela* that engendered this much emotion? To understand the answer to this question, we must review the manner in which gas was marketed at that time.

I. Historical Gas Marketing Practices

In the early days of the oil and gas industry, natural gas was generally regarded as an unwelcome by-product of oil production, rather than a valuable resource in its own right. Until the 1920s, most gas was flared at or near the wellhead.[4] The discovery of the great Panhandle Field in Texas in 1918 ushered in an era in which the apparently vast reserves of natural gas available in the Panhandle Field became viewed as a clean and efficient source of heating and electric power generation fuel for cities and municipalities in other parts of the country. The evolution of this demand for gas sparked the construction of the large and complex "interstate" pipeline system, which by the end of World War II was transporting gas to residential heating, industrial, manufacturing, and power generation markets in the eastern and midwestern portions of the country.[5] The development during and after World War II of a market for liquid hydrocarbons extracted from gas by processing further fueled the increasing demand for gas.[6]

Because the pipelines provided the only path to move gas to its markets, the modern natural gas industry became premised upon the merchant role of the pipeline companies — that is, pipelines as purchasers of natural gas from the gas producers and as resellers of such gas to public utilities, industrial users, local distribution companies ("LDCs"), and other end users. By the late 1930s, the United States government had become concerned about the development of the gas pipeline industry as a "natural monopoly,"[7] in response to which Congress passed the Natural Gas Act of 1938 ("NGA").[8] The NGA subjected to the jurisdiction of the Federal Power Commission ("FPC") so-called "natural gas companies" – primarily pipelines engaged in the transportation of gas in interstate commerce and/or the sale in interstate commerce of gas for resale for ultimate public consumption.[9] The NGA did not establish federal jurisdiction over the production or gathering of gas, gas transportation solely within a single state ("intrastate" transportation), direct gas sales to end users, or the activities of LDCs.[10]

Wellhead sales of gas did not become subject to the FPC's jurisdiction under the NGA until the United States Supreme Court so ruled in *Phillips Petroleum Co. v. Wisconsin* in 1954.[11] As the result of *Phillips*, producers desiring to sell gas in the interstate market were required to obtain from the FPC certificates of public convenience and necessity pursuant to which their leases and leased acreage were dedicated to serve the interstate market,[12] and the FPC was required to establish "just and reasonable" rates for such sales.[13]

As a result of this economic and regulatory structure, interstate pipelines sought to assure themselves of an acceptable return on the significant investment involved in pipeline construction and adequate supplies of gas for their customers by entering into long-term gas purchase contracts with producers (for the life of the underlying reserves, or, at a minimum, for terms of as much as 15-20 years) pursuant to which the producers committed to sell to the pipelines all of the gas produced from wells dedicated to the contracts. Producers desiring to sell gas in the interstate market embraced this approach because it gave them an assured market for their production which, in turn, facilitated their ability to obtain financing and otherwise to conduct their business planning from a position of economic stability.[14] The pipelines performed essentially all of the off-lease gas management services required to assure the delivery of the producer's gas to the pipeline's customers, including transportation, pooling, balancing, storage, exchanges, and similar functions.[15]

Ultimately, the FPC's NGA-based regulation of wellhead gas sales proved incapable of responding in a timely manner to changing market conditions. Increasing prices for crude oil and oil products in the late 1960s and the early 1970s increased demand for natural gas. The artificially low gas prices applicable to gas sold in the interstate market, however, discouraged the development of new gas reserves and their dedication to interstate service. At the same time, the higher deregulated prices available for gas sold to intrastate pipelines incentivized producers to develop reserves for sale in that market. Consequently, by the late 1960s, there had evolved two separate and very distinct gas markets in most producing states – a lower-priced, highly regulated interstate gas market and a higher-priced, unregulated (or more lightly regulated) intrastate gas market.[16]

In *Middleton*, the court of civil appeals thus described the "custom and usage" regarding royalty calculation and payment that developed between producers and royalty owners against this commercial and regulatory backdrop:

> Throughout the history of the industry a "custom and usage" had developed under which royalty owners were compensated by payment of a designated percentage of the "proceeds" of the sale of gas. From these proceeds were deducted severance taxes and, where applicable, the cost of compression or other processing of the gas needed to bring it up to pipeline specifications and to obtain the liquid content by-product. This so-called "custom and usage" largely ignored the exact language of the oil and gas leases and their gas royalty provisions . . . . The complacency of the lease operators was shattered, however, by the holding of the Supreme Court of Texas in the case of *Texas Oil & Gas Corporation v. Vela*, 429 S.W.2d 866 (Tex. 1968).[17]

II. The *Vela* Decision

The facts at issue in *Vela* describe a fairly typical scenario encountered by gas producers selling gas under long-term sales contracts in the 1960s and early 1970s. In *Vela*, the lessees under several mid-1930s oil and gas leases covering lands in the Lopeno Field in Zapata County contracted in 1934 to sell the gas to a utility for the life of the leases at a fixed price of $0.035 per Mcf without future escalation. The lessee/sellers then entered into gas purchase contracts with various operators in the field, pursuant to which they purchased the operators' gas for resale to the utility for the lives of the leases at a fixed price of $0.023 per Mcf without escalation. By the early 1960s, the net prices being paid for gas under newly negotiated contracts in the Lopeno Field — both interstate pipelines and intrastate pipelines — ranged from $0.13 to $0.1724 per Mcf.[18]

The leases in *Vela* obligated the lessee to "pay to lessor, as royalty for gas from each well where gas only is found, while the same is being sold or used off the premises, one-eighth of the market price at the wells of the amount so sold or used."[19] The lessee in *Vela* argued that, because gas produced from the Lopeno Field in the 1930s could not be sold on a day-to-day basis, but could only be marketed under long-term, fixed-price sales contracts, the market price of gas within the meaning of the quoted royalty clause could only be the price contracted for in good faith by the lessees under their long-term contracts.[20]

The Texas Supreme Court rejected the lessee's position and, in so doing, turned the world of market-value royalty analysis on its ear. Among the fundamental principles established by *Vela* were the following:

- The lessee's royalty obligation must be determined from the terms of the underlying oil and gas leases, which were executed prior to, and were transactions wholly independent of, the lessee's gas sale contracts.[21]

- With respect to gas "sold or used off the premises," royalty is calculated under the quoted provision based on the prevailing market price of the gas at the time of the sale of the gas to the purchaser thereof.[22]

- The sale of the gas took place at the time of delivery of the gas to the gas purchaser. Thus, the applicable market price was the prevailing market price at the time of the delivery of the gas to the purchaser, and not at the time of the execution of the sales contract. As stated by the court, "The contract price for which the gas was sold by the lessee is not necessarily the market price within the meaning of the lease."[23]

- Market price should be established by reference to sales of gas comparable in time, quality, and availability of marketing outlets.[24] The mathematical average of all prices prevailing in a field does not necessarily yield the market price at any particular point in time, however.[25] Based on the evidence presented, the court upheld the trial court's determination that the market price of the gas during the period in question was $0.13047 per Mcf.[26]

In support of its decision, the Texas Supreme Court relied heavily on *Foster v. Atlantic Refining Co.*,[27] a 1964 Fifth Circuit decision applying Texas law. In *Foster*, the Fifth Circuit, in considering how market value should be determined under a gas royalty clause providing for a 1/8 royalty on gas "produced and saved from said land, the same to be . . . sold at the market price therefor prevailing for the field where produced *when run*"[28] (emphasis added), affirmed the district court's judgment and held that the lessee must account to the lessor for royalty on gas production based on the value of the gas when produced and delivered, rather than on the price received by the lessee under its twenty-year term gas sales contract entered into several years before.[29] In so holding, the court rejected the lessee's defense that it was impossible for the lessee to have included in the gas sales contract, at the time of its execution, price escalation provisions to match prevailing market prices for gas during the life of the contract, stating that "the fact that the ascertainment of future market price may be troublesome or that the royalty provisions are improvident and result in a financial loss to Atlantic 'is not a web of the Court's weaving.'"[30]

It should be noted that *Vela* was a 5-to-4 decision, and the criticism of the majority's opinion, including, in particular, its reliance on *Foster*, is eloquently expressed in Justice Hamilton's dissenting opinion (joined by three other judges). After noting that the lessors and lessees in 1933 knew that gas production could only be marketed under long term or life-of-lease sales contracts similar to the contracts in controversy, Justice Hamilton stated:

> The problem before us is by no means the problem that the 5th Circuit had in the *Foster* case. In that case the lessee bound itself to pay the prevailing 'market price' in the field when the gas was delivered. In the case before us the lessee bound itself to pay "market price" for gas sold (necessarily sold under long-term contracts). The lessee did not agree to pay the "market price" prevailing in the field at the time of delivery, but agreed to pay the "market price" of gas sold; that is, sold under long-term contract at a price determined as of the time the contract was made. If the parties understand that the price for which gas was to be sold under long-term contracts had to be determined as of time of making the contract, is it not reasonable to say that they understood that market price was to be determined as of the same time?[31]

When one analyzes the economic impact on the lessee in *Vela* of being required to pay royalty based on a price of $0.13047 per Mcf when the lessee was actually receiving $0.035 per Mcf for the sale of its gas, it is easy to see why my father feared that this result might very well trigger a "doomsday" economic scenario for the oil and gas industry and why many royalty owners may have viewed *Vela* as providing the roadmap to El Dorado.[32]

III. From *Vela* to *Middleton*

Thirteen years elapsed between *Vela* and the Texas Supreme Court's 1981 decision in *Middleton*. In the interim, *Vela* generated extensive legal commentary, much of it negative;[33] the revolution in the regulatory and commercial structures of U.S. gas marketing began; the Texas courts addressed some of the many secondary issues raised by *Vela*, including, in particular, the effect of Federal wellhead price regulation on the determination of market value; and courts in other states began to address and resolve on their own the market value issues addressed in *Vela*.

A. Movement Toward Price Deregulation

The first shots fired in the revolution in the U.S. gas market related to the decontrol of wellhead gas prices. In response to increasingly significant shortages of available natural gas supplies in the interstate gas market resulting from the bifurcated interstate/intrastate gas markets existing in the early 1970s, Congress and the Federal Energy Regulatory Commission ("FERC"), which had succeeded to the regulatory responsibilities of the former FPC,[34] undertook numerous legislative and regulatory initiatives intended to provide price and other incentives for increased production and sales of natural gas in the interstate market, including Congress's enactment of the Natural Gas Policy Act of 1978 ("NGPA").[35]

The NGPA established a series of "maximum lawful prices," subject to statutorily prescribed annual escalations, applicable to several categories of newly drilled wells, regardless of whether gas from these wells was sold in the interstate or the intrastate markets, that would expire in 1985.[36] The NGPA also incorporated as separate categories of maximum lawful prices certain existing FPC/FERC approved rates applicable to existing gas production being sold into the interstate market,[37] as well as the prices being paid under existing intrastate gas sales contracts.[38]

In large part, the NGPA worked. The separate and distinct interstate and intrastate gas markets, and their associated price disparities, were eliminated over a period of years, resulting in additional gas-focused exploration and development activity and the discovery of significant new gas reserves.[39]

B. Regulated Prices and Market Value

A key issue in the analysis of market value royalty during this period was the effect of federal regulation of wellhead gas prices under the NGA and, later, the NGPA on the determination of market value for gas royalty purposes. If the market value of gas sold in the interstate market were determined by reference to applicable FPC rates or NGPA maximum lawful prices, rather than by reference to the value of the gas in a hypothetical market free of regulation, the royalty exposure under the *Vela* analysis of lessees selling gas in the interstate market would be reduced or at least capped.

Although the market value evidence presented in *Vela* included testimony about the prices being paid under gas sale contracts in both the interstate and intrastate markets, the Texas Supreme Court was, somewhat surprisingly, otherwise silent on this issue.[40] The federal courts, however, had been considering the impact on the determination of "market value" or "market price" of the FPC's NGA jurisdiction over wellhead sales of gas in the interstate market for several years.

Initially, the question whether a producer, whose gas sales were price-regulated by the FPC under the NGA, could be required to pay royalty under a market value royalty clause on a price basis greater than the regulated rate received by the producer from an interstate pipeline was analyzed based on whether the producer's royalty obligation constituted a sale of gas in interstate commerce by the royalty owner subject to the primary jurisdiction of the FPC under the NGA.[41] In *J. M. Huber Corporation v. Denman*[42] and *Weymouth v. Colorado Interstate Gas Company*,[43] both decided on the same day in 1966, the Fifth Circuit deferred the determination of the actual "market prices" until the parties obtained a ruling from the FPC concerning whether, *inter alia*, (i) the FPC had jurisdiction over the payment of royalties for gas sold for resale in interstate commerce and (ii) a royalty owner's transaction with its lessee was a sale of gas subject to FPC jurisdiction under the NGA when incident to a sale for resale in interstate commerce.[44] This line of inquiry ended, mercifully, when, in *Mobil Oil Corp. v. Federal Power Commission*,[45] the D. C. Circuit held that the FPC did not have jurisdiction under the NGA over the payment of gas royalties under a typical oil and gas lease.

In short order, there followed a series of federal court cases, most of which applied Texas law, in which the courts concluded that sales of gas in the intrastate market were not "comparable sales" for purposes of determining the market value of gas sold in the interstate market and that, indeed, the market value of interstate gas must be determined by reference to gas of the same regulatory classification and vintage under applicable FPC regulations and orders.[46] Consistent with these results, after the enactment of the NGPA, the federal courts consistently held that the market value of gas subject to NGPA maximum lawful prices may not exceed the applicable maximum lawful price under the NGPA.[47] The leading Texas case on this point is the Texas Supreme Court's decision in *First National Bank of Weatherford v. Exxon Corporation*[48] ("*Weatherford*"), decided in 1981 shortly after *Middleton*. *Weatherford* will be discussed in more detail as part of the *Middleton* analysis below.

C. Market Value in Other States

In an excellent 1974 paper appearing in the proceedings of the Southwestern Legal Foundation's Institute on Oil and Gas Law and Taxation, the distinguished jurist Judge Joseph W. Morris argued that *Vela* stood "alone in its construction of this [market price] language" in the royalty clause in controversy in *Vela* and "should not be followed by the courts in other jurisdictions."[49] Beginning in the late 1970s, however, state supreme courts in Kansas,[50] Montana,[51] West Virginia,[52] and North Dakota,[53] as well as the Fifth Circuit applying Mississippi law,[54] adopted the reasoning in *Vela* and held that, under typical market value royalty clauses, "market value" or "market price" refers to current market value or market price at the time gas is produced.

The Oklahoma Supreme Court, on the other hand, in *Tara Petroleum Corp. v. Hughey*,[55] expressly rejected the *Vela* reasoning and held that the phrase "market price at the well" in the oil and gas lease in controversy did not refer to current market value, but rather to the price received by the lessee under its long-term gas sale contract. The court's reasoning was similar to the argument made by Justice Hamilton in his dissent in *Vela*.[56] Similar positions were taken by the courts in Louisiana[57] and Arkansas.[58]

IV. The *Middleton* Decision

By 1981, the Texas Supreme Court appears to have determined it was time to reaffirm, as well as to elaborate upon and clarify, its holding in *Vela*, and it chose the appeal of the Houston Court of Civil Appeals (14th District) decision in *Exxon Corp. v. Middleton*[59] as the vehicle for doing so.

Like *Vela*, the lessees in *Middleton* entered into several oil and gas leases during the 1930s, this time in the Anahuac Field in Chambers County, Texas. During 1973 through 1975, the period complained of by the royalty owner/plaintiffs, some of the gas produced by defendant Exxon was processed at Exxon's Anahuac Gas Plant in Chambers County, Texas, which was not located on the leased premises. Exxon delivered the processed gas at the tailgate of its Anahuac Plant under three intrastate sales contracts to, respectively, the City of Anahuac, Houston Pipeline Company, and Exxon Gas System (an intrastate pipeline serving industrial end-users).[60] Under its contract with Houston Pipeline, Exxon received a negotiated price. Under its contracts with the City of Anahuac and Exxon Gas System, however, Exxon received its "field price," a projected, or "forward," volume-weighted average price determined according to the prices received by twenty-six major pipeline purchasers in Texas Railroad Commission District 3 and seven adjoining counties. In all cases, Exxon paid royalty based on the proceeds it received under its gas sales contracts.[61]

The leases in *Middleton* each obligated the lessee to pay as royalty:

> On gas, including casinghead gas or other gaseous substances, produced from said land and sold or used off the premises, or used in the manufacture of gasoline or other products therefrom, by lessee, the market value at the well of one-eighth of the gas so sold or used, provided that on gas sold at the wells, the royalty shall be one-eighth of the amount realized from such sale.[62]

Exxon argued, *inter alia*, that the gas sold at the tailgate of its Anahuac Plant was sold "at the well," so that the "amount realized" royalty standard under the leases in controversy was applicable.[63] Alternatively, Exxon argued that the royalty clause in *Vela*, which required royalty to be paid on gas "while the same is being sold or used off the premises," was distinguishable from the quoted royalty provision in the *Middleton* leases, and that under the *Middleton* leases gas was "sold," for royalty purposes, on the dates of execution of Exxon's long-term gas sales contracts.[64]

The Texas Supreme Court's decision in *Middleton* rejected Exxon's positions on these points and stated the following principles:

- The obligation to pay royalty on gas does not accrue until there has been both (a) production of gas and (b) the sale or use of the gas produced. In this regard, production of gas does not occur until the physical severance of the gas from the ground,[65] and the sale of gas that triggers the obligation to pay royalty does not occur until the physical delivery of the gas to the purchaser thereof.[66]

- In the phrase "sold or used off the premises," the words "off the premises" refer to both the sale and the use of gas.[67] The word "premises" refers to the "leased premises," or the lands covered by the relevant oil and gas lease.[68] Therefore, if gas is delivered for sale within the leased premises, it will be deemed to be sold "at the well" for royalty calculation purposes, but if gas is delivered for sale at a point outside the leased premises, it will be deemed to be sold "off the premises," even if the sales delivery point is a central point in the field (such as Exxon's Anahuac Gas Plant).[69]

- If gas is "sold or used off the premises," royalty is calculated based on the market value at the well of the gas so sold or used, determined at the time of delivery of the gas to the purchaser thereof.[70]

- Market value at the well is a hypothetical concept — the price property would bring when it is offered for sale by one who desires, but is not obligated, to sell and is bought by one who is under no necessity of buying it. To determine the market value of gas, the gas should be valued as though it is free and available for sale.[71]

- The preferred method of establishing market value is by evidence of comparable sales — i.e., sales comparable in time, quality (including regulatory character), quantity, and availability of markets.[72]

The court also made several significant pronouncements about the nature and effect of division orders, which will be discussed later in this chapter.

In terms of issues considered and resolved, *Middleton* is an extremely "rich" opinion to which another one hundred pages of analysis could easily be devoted. Since I have not been given that much space, however, let us focus on the following two points.

A. "Off the Premises" v. "At the Wells" (Herein of *Butler v. Exxon Corp.*)

First, *Middleton* clarified the meanings of the phrases "off the premises" and "at the wells" as used in the *Middleton* lease royalty provision. *Vela* did not address this issue. The first meaningful appellate treatment of this issue in Texas appears to have been the 1977 court of civil appeals decision in *Butler v. Exxon Corporation ("Butler")*.[73] In *Butler*, the gas in controversy was delivered to the gas purchaser at the tailgate of Exxon's central separation, dehydration, and treatment facility in the Atkinson Gas Field in Karnes and Live Oak Counties, Texas, which was located approximately one hundred feet west of the boundary of the land from which the gas was produced.[74] In interpreting a royalty provision virtually identical to the *Middleton* lease royalty provision[75] (which provided for an "amount realized" royalty payment standard for gas sold "at the wells"), the El Paso Court of Civil Appeals expressly approved the trial court's findings of fact[76] to the effect that "the term 'at the wells' means gas delivery which occurs in the vicinity of the field of production where the wells are located. . . . [Delivery] need not occur at the 'Christmas tree' on top of the well casing, nor is there any requirement that delivery occur on the particular lease or unit from which the gas is produced."[77]

This result was very favorable to producers, because the larger the circle within which sales "at the well" occur, the more likely it is that the amount realized, and not the market value, royalty payment standard will apply. In *Middleton*, however, the Texas Supreme Court, in holding that gas produced from a particular lease that is sold anywhere on the leased premises is deemed to be sold "at the well," but that gas sold at any point outside the leased premises is sold "off the premises,"[78] expressly rejected the holding in *Butler* on this point, stating, "To the extent the Court of Civil Appeals' interpretation of the royalty clause in *Butler, supra*, conflicts with our interpretation of this clause, it is disapproved."[79] The supreme court continued by holding that, even when oil and gas leases have been included in a pooled unit, the "leased premises," for royalty calculation purposes, are determined not by reference to the entire unit, but to the lands covered by each individual lease in the unit.[80]

B. Comparable Sales and the Regulatory Character of Gas

Middleton also elaborated upon the concept of "comparable sales" established in *Vela* as the basis for determining market value. According the Texas Supreme Court in *Middleton*:

> Sales comparable in time occur under contracts executed contemporaneously with the sale of the gas in question. Sales comparable in quality are those of similar physical properties such as sweet, sour, or casinghead gas. Quality also involves the legal characteristics of the gas; that is, whether it is sold in a regulated or unregulated market, or in one particular category of a regulated market. Sales comparable in quantity are those of similar volumes to the gas in question. To be comparable, the sales must be made from an area with marketing outlets similar to the gas in question. . . . Comparable sales should be drawn from a relevant market. . . .[81]

The court's statement regarding gas quality involving not only the physical, but the legal, characteristics of the gas was the first recognition by the Texas courts of the impact of federal regulation of wellhead gas prices on the determination of market value, a subject that had already received extensive attention by the federal courts.[82] Unlike the prior federal court cases, however, the issue of federal wellhead price regulation was not the central issue in *Middleton*. In *Middleton*, Exxon appears not to have argued in favor of a specific contract price as the measure of market value, but rather that its method of calculating market value, which produced a lower price basis for royalty calculation purposes, was more accurate than the plaintiffs'.[83] The plaintiffs' expert reviewed over 30,000 monthly gas tax reports filed with the Comptroller of Public Accounts covering gas sales in a market area consisting of Railroad Commission Districts 2, 3, and 4, and then arrived at his opinion regarding market value by calculating the arithmetic average of the three highest prices paid in such market area during each calendar quarter under review. Exxon's expert testified that Exxon's "field price" for the Anahuac Field (calculated as the total price paid for one month out of each calendar quarter for gas delivered to major purchasers in Railroad Commission District 3 and the seven surrounding counties, divided by the total volume of such gas delivered for sale) constituted the market value.

The trial court accepted the plaintiffs' expert opinion on market value, concluding that Exxon's "field price" did not satisfy the "comparability test" because it included both interstate and intrastate sales while all of the gas in controversy was sold in the intrastate market.[84] Although the court of civil appeals found fault with both expert opinions,[85] the Texas Supreme Court ultimately upheld the trial court's finding.[86] In so holding, the court stated: "Exxon's field price . . . includes interstate sales. Intrastate and interstate gas prices are not comparable in quality. They are conceptually and legally different . . . . While this evidence may be admissible, such evidence does not bind the fact finder as a matter of law in its determination of market value."[87]

The last sentence of the quoted language suggests that, in a case involving the determination of the market value of gas sold in the intrastate market, the requirement of comparability of legal or regulatory characteristics goes not so much to the admissibility of evidence of regulated interstate gas prices, but to the weight that the fact finder may choose to give to that evidence. The Texas Supreme Court took a more definitive stance on this issue in *Weatherford*[88] decided five months after *Middleton*. In *Weatherford*, the court addressed directly the question whether gas sales in the intrastate market constitute comparable sales for purposes of determining the value of gas dedicated to the interstate market.[89] After citing *Middleton* as the controlling authority, the court quoted the second and third sentences, but not the last sentence, of the language quoted above and stated, "We hold that intrastate sales of gas are not comparable to interstate sales regulated by the Federal Power Commission."[90]

V. The Rest of the Story (Almost)

Middleton brought to a close an extremely active, thirteen-year period of royalty litigation attempting to define the parameters of the *Vela* decision. As we will see, the continuing dramatic changes in the U.S. gas market occurring after *Middleton* eliminated, for the most part, the market conditions that gave rise to *Vela* and *Middleton* in the first place. But royalty calculation is almost always complicated, and frequently there are significant amounts of money involved. Not surprisingly, therefore, *Vela* and *Middleton* did not represent the end of the story, but rather the "jumping off point" for a number of other royalty disputes involving the concept of market value. Once again, I have not been given enough space to review all of these subsequent disputes, but this chapter would be incomplete if we did not complete our brief description of the revolution in the U.S. gas market begun in the late 1970s and review the two most significant market value royalty decisions rendered by the Texas Supreme Court after *Middleton* and their aftermath.

A. Continued Evolution of the U.S. Natural Gas Market

As discussed above, the enactment of the NGPA ultimately eliminated the separate and distinct interstate and intrastate gas markets in the United States, together with their associated price disparities, and ushered in an era of increased gas-focused exploration and development that resulted in the discovery of significant new gas reserves. These increased gas reserves were a two-edged sword, however. By 1982, the increase in gas reserves, together with a world-wide recession, mild winters, and legislative and regulatory initiatives favoring the switching by industrial users to fuels other than gas, created a situation of weakened demand for, and excess supply of, gas.[91] These changed economic circumstances had adverse impacts on both the pipelines and their customers.

The principal source of the pipelines' difficulties was the presence of so-called "take-or-pay" provisions in virtually all of their gas purchase contracts with producers. Take-or-pay provisions obligated a pipeline purchaser to take certain minimum quantities of gas on an annual basis (the "minimum contract quantity"), or, if the pipeline was unable to take all of the minimum contract quantity, to pay the producer for the difference between the minimum contract quantity and the volume of gas actually taken by the pipeline. Most contracts also gave the pipeline the right, over a period of succeeding years, to credit gas taken in excess of the minimum contract quantity for a particular year against previous take-or-pay payments.[92] As the demand for gas from the pipelines' end user customers decreased, the pipelines' economic exposure to producers under take-or-pay provisions increased dramatically. Pipelines adopted a range of responses to this circumstance, including unilateral reductions of the volumes of gas taken from producers and unilateral reductions in the price paid for gas taken. As a result of these actions, numerous lawsuits were filed by producers against pipelines pursuant to which producers sought damages for the pipelines' failure to comply with the take-or-pay and other provisions of the relevant gas purchase contracts and, when appropriate, the repudiation by the pipelines of such contracts.[93] With very few exceptions, producers prevailed in these lawsuits.[94]

In response to these changed conditions in the natural gas industry, the FERC and Congress implemented several legislative and regulatory initiatives intended further to reshape the natural gas industry. In a series of orders beginning in 1984, including Order No. 436 in 1985[95] and its landmark Order No. 636 in 1992,[96] the FERC undertook, first, to transform the role of the interstate pipelines from the role of gas merchant to the more limited role of gas transporter,[97] and later, to require the unbundling of the interstate pipelines' sales and transportation services, which permitted pipeline shippers and customers to contract only for the specific service or services – such as dehydration, compression, treating, storage, and the like – required to transport that party's gas, thus lowering the transportation costs of the shipper or customer.[98]

During the same period, Congress passed the Natural Gas Wellhead Decontrol Act of 1989,[99] pursuant to which all remaining NGA-regulated rates and NGPA maximum lawful prices applicable to wellhead gas sales were eliminated by January 1, 1993.

A complete discussion of these FERC orders is beyond the scope of this chapter.[100] Suffice it to say that the foregoing market, legislative, and regulatory developments utterly changed the face of the domestic natural gas industry.[101] As wellhead prices became deregulated and the pipeline industry was restructured, a national free market for gas rapidly evolved. As a result, it is now possible readily to identify at any time the current market sale price, or "spot" price, for gas reported by both interstate and intrastate pipelines at any one of numerous locations on the national pipeline grid. Technological advances have permitted the development of instantaneous electronic trading of both gas and pipeline capacity as truly fungible commodities.[102] Interstate pipelines now perform relatively few gas management functions, with most of these functions having been assumed either by gas producers or gas aggregators — marketing companies (that may be producer affiliates) that own no transportation facilities, but that purchase gas at the wellhead or in the field, arrange for transportation, engage in gas trading activities, and contract for the ultimate sale of the gas to an LDC or other end user. Under these circumstances, sales of gas in which producers are the sellers now generally fall into one of three general categories:

- wellhead sales to a gas processor, gas gatherer, or intrastate pipeline, involving a commitment by the seller of reserves to the contract, a "firm"[103] commitment by the purchaser to take the gas (usually up to a maximum daily quantity), and pricing based on a designated index price (plus or minus the applicable basis differential), with delivery to be made at the wellhead, one or more central delivery points in the field, or the tailgate of a gas processing plat;

- short term sales, usually to gas aggregators, at daily index prices (plus or minus the applicable basis differential) at delivery points on the transporting pipeline, in most cases without a contractual commitment of reserves ("non-source specific"); and

- short, intermediate, or long term, non-source specific, direct, firm sales to end users, also known as "warranty contracts", made at delivery points on the transporting pipeline or at the inlet of the purchaser's facilities, at a fixed price, or at prices determined by reference to designated price indices (plus or minus the applicable basis differential) or a "forward" price curve based on gas futures prices on the New York Mercantile Exchange ("NYMEX"), or a combination thereof.[104]

B. Does the Elevator Also Go Down?

Vela and *Middleton* teach us that, in a period of rising gas prices, market value royalty provisions may work to the advantage of royalty owners and the disadvantage of producers, requiring producers to account to royalty owners for royalties on a price basis that may be higher than that received by the producer under the applicable gas sale contract. Does the same analysis apply when the lessee sells gas for *more* than the market value of such gas? In one of the two most significant market value royalty decisions since *Middleton*, the Texas Supreme Court answered "yes."

In *Yzaguirre v. KCS Resources, Inc.*,[105] the leases in controversy, executed in 1973, contained *Middleton* lease royalty provisions. In 1979, the lessees entered into a 20-year gas purchase contract with Tennessee Gas Pipeline Co., under which Tennessee agreed to purchase gas produced from the leases at a fixed price subject to automatic price escalations (the "*Tennessee Contract*"). Gas produced from the leases was processed several miles from the leased premises and sold to Tennessee at the tailgate of the plant. As such, the gas was "sold or used off the leased premises," and royalty was, therefore, payable based on the market value standard. By the 1990s, when substantial production from the leases was obtained as the result of the development of the Bob West field, the automatic price escalations in the Tennessee Contract had caused the price paid for gas sold thereunder to far exceed the current market value of the gas.[106]

The lessees filed suit seeking a declaratory judgment that royalty on production from the leases was payable based on the market value of the gas, rather than the higher price paid under the Tennessee Contract. The trial court rendered judgment in favor of the lessees, and the court of appeals and the Texas Supreme Court affirmed. According to the Texas Supreme Court, citing *Vela* as controlling precedent:

> The parties to these leases, in unambiguous terms, based the royalty on the amount realized for gas sales at the well and on market value for sales that occurred off the premises. This clearly means the prevailing market price at the time of the sale or use. Because the *Vela* lease's plain terms specified a market price royalty, we rejected the lessee's argument that the "market price of gas within the meaning of the lease is the price contracted for in good faith by the lessee in pursuance of its duty to market gas from the premises." Instead, we held that the plain terms of the lease required the lessee to pay a market value royalty even though the lessee received less than market value under its long term sales contract. The same plain terms that fixed the lessee's duty to pay royalty also defined the benefit the lessor is entitled to receive. Thus under the leases, Yzaguirre and the other royalty owners are entitled to a market value royalty, not an amount realized royalty. [107]

Two years later, the Texas Supreme Court leaned heavily on its decision in *Yzaguirre* in *Union Pacific Resources Group, Inc. v. Hankins*,[108] a class action suit brought by royalty owners alleging that the lessee, which sold gas produced from the leases in controversy to affiliates at specified index prices, had improperly paid royalties based on the index prices used in the inter-affiliate sale, rather than the higher prices received by the lessee's affiliates on the resale of the gas. In concluding that the plaintiffs' class failed to satisfy the "commonality" requirement for class certification under Texas Rule of Civil Procedure 42,[109] the supreme court rejected the plaintiffs' argument that, regardless of whether a "market value" or "amount realized" royalty standard was applicable under a particular lease, royalty was payable based on the resale proceeds received by the lessee's affiliates.[110] According to the court:

> Could the trial court . . . infer that the third party sale price represented both market value and the best price reasonably attainable? No, because the marketing affiliates may have been able to receive a price higher than market value, either through a long-term contract as in *Yzaguirre* or simply through extraordinary negotiation and sales efforts that exceeded the results reasonably obtainable by an ordinary lessee. Under this scenario, the proceeds

> owner would be entitled to share in the lessee's good fortune, while the market-value owners would not be. [*Citations omitted*] Conversely, the third-party sale price might conceivably be lower than market value, in which case the proceeds owners would receive less than the market-value owners . . . Further analysis would be needed to determine whether market-value owners were indeed paid market value.[111]

As one might suspect, the Texas Supreme Court's decisions in *Yzaguirre* and *Hankins* were roundly criticized by royalty owners and their lawyers.[112] As a general proposition, however, the results in *Yzaguirre* and *Hankins* seem to represent the logical extension of the market value analysis of *Vela* and *Middleton*. If the market value standard calls for the payment of royalty based upon current comparable sales of gas utilizing the model of the willing buyer/willing seller, without reference to the proceeds actually received by the producer under the applicable gas sale contract, then in a period of declining gas prices, the producer who contracts for the sale of its gas at a price in excess of market value should be entitled to retain the full amount of that premium.[113] Stated differently, under the *Vela-Middleton* market value formulation, the producer bears the commodity price risk of the gas for royalty purposes during periods of increasing prices, and the royalty owner bears this commodity price risk during periods of declining prices.[114]

Yzaguirre also addressed the applicability of the implied covenant to market[115] when royalty is calculated based on the market value standard, an issue not considered in either *Vela* or *Middleton*. In *Cabot Corp. v. Brown*,[116] the Texas Supreme Court had characterized the implied covenant to market as being two-pronged: the lessee must (a) market the production with due diligence and (b) obtain the best price reasonably possible.[117] In *Cabot*, decided six years after *Middleton*, the Texas Supreme Court had stated, in dictum, that under a gas royalty clause providing for royalties based on market value, the lessee has an obligation to obtain the best current price reasonably available."[118]

In *Yzaguirre*, however, after concluding that the plaintiff/royalty owners were entitled, under the terms of the applicable lease royalty clause, to be paid royalty based upon the lower current market value of the gas rather than the higher sale price received by the lessee under the Tennessee Contract,[119] the Texas Supreme Court rejected the royalty owners' argument that the lessee's failure to pay royalty based on the Tennessee Contract proceeds constituted a breach of the implied covenant to market the gas.[120] After noting that implied covenants do not come into existence when the lease expressly covers the subject matter of the implied covenant, the court stated:

> In this case, the parties entered into a lease requiring a market value royalty. Because the lease provides an objective basis for calculating royalties that is independent of the price the lessee actually obtains, the lessor does not need the protection of an implied covenant. Depending on future market behavior, this may be financially beneficial to the lessor, as it was in *Vela*, or it may be less advantageous, as here. In either event, the parties received the benefit of their bargain. . . . [U]nder these circumstances, we do not believe the *Cabot* dicta should override our decisions in *Vela, Pyote*, and *Middleton*.[121]

Yzaguirre's treatment of the *Cabot* dictum has been criticized by some because, to the extent that the court in *Cabot* remanded the case to the trial court to give the plaintiffs the opportunity to recover on their implied covenant claim for the period after the division orders had been revoked, the plaintiffs' implied covenant claims had been preserved, and because the court did not expressly overrule the quoted dictum from *Cabot*.[122] While there may be merit to these criticisms, it seems that *Yzaguirre's* statement that "we do not believe the *Cabot* dicta should override our decisions in *Vela, Pyote,* and *Middleton*" clearly indicates that the quoted dictum from *Cabot* is no longer the law in Texas and that the implied covenant to market does not obligate the lessee to obtain the best current price reasonably available if a market value royalty standard is in effect.[124]

This holding has been followed in a number of subsequent cases and played a particularly significant role in several of the class action lawsuits filed by royalty owners in Texas during the late 1990s and early 2000s. One of the requirements for certifying a class in a class action brought in Texas is that there be "commonality" among the members of the proposed class – that is, there must be questions of law or fact common to the class.[125] Because most of these cases involved royalty owner claims arising under both market value and amount realized royalty provisions, the applicability, as the result of *Yzaguirre*, of the implied covenant to market only to royalty owners claiming under amount realized royalty provisions has been held to be sufficient to defeat class certification due to lack of "commonality" among the members of the proposed class.[126]

C. Proving Market Value (Herein of *Heritage Resources*)

Regardless of whether one agrees or disagrees with the Texas Supreme Court's decisions in *Vela, Middleton, Yzaguirre,* and *Hankins*, they appear to establish a reasonably well defined analytical framework for the determination of market value royalty that possesses a certain internal logic.[127] That framework was clearly, although perhaps unintentionally, called into question by the Texas Supreme Court's 1996 decision in *Heritage Resources, Inc. v. NationsBank*,[128] the second of the two most significant market value decisions since *Middleton*.

1. Comparable Sales. It seems fair to characterize the core concepts underlying *Vela, Middleton,* and *Yzaguirre* as follows: (i) "market value" is defined not by oil and gas industry custom and practice but by the applicable oil and gas lease language; and (ii) the "typical" market value royalty provision calls for the determination of market value based on evidence of comparable sales – sales comparable in time, quality (including regulatory character), quantity, and availability of markets – by expert testimony utilizing the model of the willing seller/willing buyer, which amount may be wholly unrelated to the actual proceeds received by the producer under its gas sale contract.[129] Once experts are qualified, their testimony is to be considered by the trier of fact, who can determine the weight to be given to the evidence.[130]

An interesting issue in this regard is, notwithstanding *Vela's* admonition that "the contract price for which the gas was sold is not necessarily the market price within the meaning of the lease,"[131] whether evidence of the price actually paid for the gas in controversy is admissible as one of the "comparable sales" evaluated by the market value expert. In *Vela*[132] the defendant's market value expert was permitted to include in his analysis the old, fixed-price contracts under which the defendant's gas was being sold, although he ultimately excluded the prices paid under such contracts from his market value calculation because they were "too far out of line."[133] In *Middleton*, it is unclear whether the plaintiff's market value expert reviewed the gas sales contracts under which Exxon sold the gas in controversy, although nothing in the Texas Supreme Court's opinion expressly indicates that they were excluded from evidence.

In *Yzaguirre*, on the other hand, the Texas Supreme Court affirmed the trial court's decision to exclude evidence of the price received by the defendant for gas sold under the Tennessee Contract.[134] In so holding the court stated:

> According to the [Tennessee Contract], Tennessee was obligated to purchase [the defendant's] gas at an ever-escalating price, regardless of its value on the open market. The gas was not free and available for sale, and its price was negotiated in 1979, not contemporaneously with the deliveries. Under these circumstances, the [Tennessee Contract] price was not evidence of market value, and the trial judge properly excluded it.[135]

As before, this holding has been roundly criticized by royalty owners and their counsel, and with some justification. At a minimum, it seems that evidence of the actual sales price paid for the gas in controversy is at least relevant in a market value case and should be admissible. The lesson of these cases may be that the older the vintage of the gas sales contract, the less relevant the price paid under such contract will be in determining current market value. That issue relates to the weight to be given to the evidence, however, and not its admissibility. The court in Vela appears to have had the better approach when it admitted evidence of the actual sales prices paid for the gas in controversy but upheld the expert's decision to exclude such sales prices from his calculation of market value.[136]

2. Net-Back Method. Establishing market value based on evidence of comparable sales can make for expensive litigation. In addition, it may be difficult, in some circumstances, to develop sufficient evidence of comparable sales to support a determination of market value at the well. Is there, then, a permissible alternative method of determining market value? In *Heritage Resources*,[137] the Texas Supreme Court answered "yes" to this question and endorsed the "work-back" or "net-back" valuation method.[138]

In *Heritage Resources*, although the royalty provisions in the leases in controversy each differed in certain respects, all of the royalty provisions required royalty to be paid based upon the market value at the well of gas produced or produced and sold from the leased premises, subject, however, in each case to the following proviso:

> Provided, however, that there shall be no deductions from the value of the Lessor's royalty by reason of any required processing, costs of dehydration, compression, transportation, or other matter to market such gas.[139]

Based upon the inclusion in each lease of the foregoing proviso, the royalty owner objected to the lessee's deduction of certain transportation expenses from royalty payments made on production from such leases.[140] The lessee argued that the proper calculation of market value in royalty provisions of this type requires that transportation costs between the wellhead and the point of delivery must be taken into account, and that the enforcement of a provision disallowing the deduction of transportation costs when such a market value royalty payment standard is applicable would result in the payment of royalty on a basis other than that contracted for in the lease.[141] Thus, the lessee argued that the foregoing proviso was intended only to prevent the lessee from deducting more than the "reasonable" costs of transporting the gas to market.[142]

The El Paso Court of Appeals rejected this argument, concluding that the lessee's argument rendered the quoted proviso meaningless. Attempting to harmonize and give meaning to all provisions of the affected leases, the court held the proviso to be enforceable, concluding that the parties had contemplated gas sales and, consequently, the calculation of royalty, away from the wellhead, and that the royalty owners would not absorb any post-production costs.[143]

The Texas Supreme Court reversed the holding of the court of appeals and held that the provisions of the affected leases required the lessee to pay royalties based on the market value of the production at the well, taking into account appropriate deductions for transportation costs.[144] According to the majority opinion of the court, written by Justice Baker and joined in by Chief Justice Phillips and Justices Cornyn, Enoch, and Spector, the most desirable method of determining market value is the use of comparable sales, but when information about comparable sales is not readily available, courts use a second method, which "involves subtracting reasonable post-production marketing costs from the market value at the point of sale."[145] The court then stated that the well accepted trade meanings of the terms "royalty" and "market value at the well," both of which contemplate the deduction of transportation and other post-production costs in calculating royalty, rendered the quoted "no post-production cost" proviso mere "surplusage as a matter of law."[146] The court stated further that the court of appeals' interpretation improperly converted the royalty clauses in issue from provisions requiring payment of royalty based on the "market value at the well" to provisions requiring the payment of royalty based on the "market value at the point of sale with no deductions for post-production costs."[147] To avoid this result, the court characterized the quoted proviso as "merely stating existing law" to the effect that the lessee cannot pay "the lessor less than his fractional share of the value of the comparable sales price (market value)."[148]

Like *Middleton, Heritage Resources* is also a very "rich" opinion that addresses several issues (in controversial fashion) beyond recognizing the net-back method of determining market value. Indeed, we would be remiss if we did not devote at least some attention to Justice Owen's concurring opinion, joined by Justice Hecht, which elaborated extensively on the issue of post-production costs.[149] After undertaking an exhaustive review of the authorities in Texas and other states concerning the deductibility of post-production costs in calculating royalty,[150] Justice Owen found persuasive the Fifth Circuit's analysis in *Piney Woods* that the phrase "at the well" is intended to distinguish between gas sold in the form in which it emerges from the wellhead and gas that thereafter has value added by transportation or processing.[151] Justice Owen further expressly rejected the so-called "marketable condition" rule adopted by the Oklahoma, Kansas, and Colorado courts to the effect that the implied covenant to market imposes upon the lessee the obligation to pay the costs associated with post-production activities, such as compression, dehydration, gathering, and, in some cases, transportation.[152]

Having concluded that post-production costs are to be shared by the royalty owners under a "market value at the well" royalty provision, Justice Owen next addressed the effect of the proviso purporting to prohibit the deduction of such costs as follows:

> The concept of deductions of marketing costs from the value of gas is meaningless when gas is valued at the well. Value at the well is already net of reasonable marketing costs. The value of gas "at the well" represents its value in the market place at any given point of sale, less the reasonable costs to get the gas to that point of sale, including compression, transportation, and processing costs. . . . As long as "market value at the well" is the benchmark for valuing the gas, a phrase prohibiting the deduction of post-production costs from that value does not change the meaning of the royalty clause. . . . It could not be said that under that circumstance that the clause is ambiguous. It could only be said that the proviso is surplusage.[153]

In a vigorous dissent, Justice Gonzalez, joined by Justice Abbott, strongly objected to the majority's decision "to ignore the unequivocal intent of sophisticated parties who negotiated contractual terms at arm's length," and concluded that both the trial court and the court of appeals had correctly held that the quoted proviso prevented the lessee from deducting transportation costs in the calculation of the market value of the gas for royalty purposes.[154] Justice Gonzalez continued his criticism of the majority and concurring opinions in a second dissent filed in conjunction with the supreme court's order overruling the lessor's motion for rehearing in March 1997.[155] In his second dissent, Justice Gonzalez was joined by Justices Cornyn and Spector, who had originally joined in the majority opinion, as well as Justice Abbott. Justice Gonzalez argued that, *inter alia*, because the court was without a majority in the case, the judgment should control only the case at bar and otherwise have limited precedential value.[156]

3. So, Where Are We Now? Where *Middleton* addressed and answered numerous legal issues with genuine clarity, Heritage Resources raises and leaves unanswered almost as many questions as it answers. For example:

a. What Is the Precedential Value of *Heritage Resources*? The question of the precedential value of *Heritage Resources* beyond the dispute in that case is legitimate. As pointed out by Justice Gonzalez, when Justices Cornyn, Spector, and Abbott joined in his second dissent filed in conjunction with the Texas Supreme Court's March 1997 order overruling the lessor's motion for rehearing, the court's original "majority" opinion was no longer supported by a majority of the Justices.[157] It is noteworthy, in this regard, that *Yzaguirre*, decided by the Texas Supreme Court five years after *Heritage Resources*, does not contain a single citation or other reference to *Heritage Resources*.

Recently, the United States Court of Appeals for the Fifth Circuit directly addressed such a challenge to the precedential value of *Heritage Resources* in *Potts v. Chesapeake Exploration, L.L.C.*[158] In rejecting the lessor's challenge, Judge Owen, who authored the concurring opinion in Heritage Resources before her appointment to the Fifth Circuit, stated, "Because rehearing was denied, the court's opinion in Heritage was not withdrawn. The Texas court's decision in Heritage remains binding law . . ."[159] Indeed, *Heritage Resources* has been cited as controlling precedent for one proposition or another in a number of subsequent appellate decisions applying Texas law in addition to *Potts*.[160]

b. Why Did the Court Resort to the Net-Back Method to Determine Market Value? In *Heritage Resources*, neither party complained about the price the lessee received for the sale of its gas, and no comparable sale or other market value evidence was introduced at trial. The case is therefore not a traditional "market value v. actual sale price" controversy like *Vela* or *Middleton*. Rather, the plaintiff's claim for underpayment of royalties was limited to its claim that transportation charges had been improperly deducted. The court was thus left with no conceptual framework for its market value analysis. The net-back method appears to have provided that framework in a manner that fit the needs of the case.[161]

c. Is a Showing That Comparable Sales Evidence Is Not Readily Available Required Before The Net-Back Method May Be Used? In market value royalty cases, the burden to prove market value at the well is on the plaintiff.[162] In *Heritage Resources*, the court noted that the lessor had offered no evidence of comparable sales and had conceded that the transportation costs deducted were reasonable, while the lessee had conceded that the price received from the sale of the gas was the market price at the point of sale. In the absence of evidence of comparable sales, the court stated that the net-back method would be used to determine the market value of the gas, but did not indicate whether a showing on this point was required.[163] Although market value at the well cases decided based on comparable sales evidence have not totally disappeared from the landscape,[164] most of the subsequent decisions involving determinations of market value at the well that have invoked the principles of *Heritage Resources* have contained similar statements regarding the unavailability or lack of comparable sales evidence.

For example, in *Ramming v. Natural Gas Pipeline Company of America*,[165] a case involving lessor allegations of underpayment of royalties based on the lessee's alleged improper deduction of certain post-production costs, the Fifth Circuit stated that comparable sales provides the preferable method of determining market value at the well, and that the net-back method was to be used only when comparable sales are not available.[166] In rejecting the lessor's claims and approving the lessee's determination of market value at the well (including the lessee's deduction of gathering and transportation charges), the court noted that "the plaintiff offer[ed] no evidence of comparable sales or evidence that the gathering charge deducted was not reasonable."[167] Similarly, in *Potts v. Chesapeake*

Exploration, L.L.C.,[168] the Fifth Circuit affirmed a district court holding approving Chesapeake's calculation of market value at the well using net-back methodology after neither Chesapeake nor the plaintiff lessor were able to make any evidentiary showing of comparable sales at the wellhead.[169] On the other hand, in *French v. Occidental Permian Ltd.*,[170] a case involving the determination of market value at the well of gas production from a carbon dioxide waterflood unit based on a *Middleton* royalty clause, the Texas Supreme Court adopted the net-back methodology without any reference whatsoever to any evidentiary showing, or lack thereof, with respect to comparable sales.[171]

Based on the cases reviewed, the courts do not appear consistently to be requiring an evidentiary showing of no comparable sales as a condition precedent to applying the net-back method to determine market value at the well. Nonetheless, it seems like good practice for litigants desiring to use the net-back method, rather than comparable sales, to determine market value at the well to attempt to demonstrate why comparable sales information is unavailable.[172] Conversely, it seems incumbent on litigants attempting to avoid the application of the net-back method to make a convincing showing of market value at the well based on comparable sales at the well.

d. <u>Did the Court Really Intend To Establish "Market Value at the Point Of Sale" as the Starting Point for the Net-Back Method</u>? As discussed above, the majority opinion in *Heritage Resources* stated that the net-back method of determining market value at the well "involves subtracting reasonable post-production marketing costs from the *market value at the point of sale*" (emphasis added).[173] Several commentators have suggested that the Texas Supreme Court erred in not using the "actual price" received at the point of sale as the starting point for the net-back calculation,[174] as courts in some other jurisdictions have done,[175] arguing that the reference to "market value" produces "an illogical and circular result."[176]

While several aspects of *Heritage Resources* have an "Alice Through the Looking Glass"[177] character to them, I am not sure that this issue is one of them. Conceptually, it is certainly possible to calculate market value at any of a number of points – at the wellhead, at the tailgate of a processing plant, or at other points of sale or resale. As such, the use of a market value "at the point of sale" as the starting point for a net-back calculation of market value "at the well" does not, in and of itself, appear to produce a circular result.

The "market value at the point of sale" formulation is consistent with the description of the net-back method in *Piney Woods*[178] and has been incorporated faithfully into several post-*Heritage Resources* decisions in Texas.[179] In particular, *Potts* serves as a roadmap for how such an analysis would work. In *Potts*, COI, the lessee's operating company affiliate, as agent for the lessee, sold the gas produced from the relevant lease to CEMI, the lessee's marketing affiliate, at the wellhead. CEMI then caused the gas to be gathered, transported, and delivered for resale to unaffiliated gas purchasers at one or more pipeline hubs located substantial distances from the leased premises. The applicable lease royalty clause required the payment of royalty on gas production based on "the market value at the point of sale of the gas sold or used . . ."[180] The lease also provided that the royalty would be calculated "free of all costs and expenses related to the exploration, production and marketing" of such gas production, including compression, dehydration, treatment, and transportation costs.[181]

Rather than simply paying royalty based on the sales proceeds received by COI from CEMI at the wellhead, the lessee paid royalty based on a net-back calculation of market value at the well equal to the volume weighted average sales price received by CEMI from its downstream resales of gas to unaffiliated gas producers <u>less</u> the post-production costs incurred between the wellhead and the points of delivery to the gas purchasers.[182] In the absence of comparable sales evidence to the contrary, the Fifth Circuit upheld the lessee's determination of market value at the well.[183]

Indeed, the "market value at the point of sale" formulation is consistent with the Texas courts' recognition that there is a difference between the market value and the amount realized royalty payment standards.[184] The use of the "actual sales price" as the starting point for a net-back market value determination would erode the distinction between the two royalty payment standards. The court's "market value at the point of sale" formulation ostensibly prevents that result from occurring.

e. <u>Does the Net-Back Method Produce a Different Market Value than Comparable Sales Evidence</u>? In many circumstances, almost certainly. It should be kept in mind that in virtually all of the cases reviewed, the net-back method is the "second choice" for determining market value at the well in the absence of suitable comparable sales evidence and is characterized as an "indirect means" of determining market value at the well.[185] Inherent in that characterization is the acknowledgment – perhaps even the expectation – that the net-back method is likely only to approximate the market value at the well determined based on comparable sales evidence.

f. Does the Use of the Net-Back Method Affect the Implied Marketing Covenant Analysis with Respect to Market Value? Some commentators have suggested that the use of the net-back method may reopen the issue of the applicability of the implied covenant to market when royalty is based on the market value at the well. The argument assumes that the "true" starting point for the net-back calculation is the actual price from the sale. As such, the higher the actual sale price, the higher the market value at the well following the net-back. Therefore, so the argument goes, the implied covenant to market should operate, as it does in the case of an amount realized royalty clause, to require the lessee to obtain the best price reasonably possible for the gas.[186]

While this argument obviously provides some "red meat" for royalty owners and their lawyers with respect to the implied marketing covenant issue, it should be noted that, based on the cases we have reviewed, the Texas courts have never endorsed the actual sale price received at the point of sale as the starting point for a net-back calculation of market value at the well. On the contrary, the Texas courts have consistently used the "market value at the point of sale" as the starting point for the net-back analysis.[187] Consequently, it seems unlikely that the use of the net-back method will have any impact on the issue of the applicability of the implied covenant to market to the determination of market value at the well.

g. Must Not the Parties in *Heritage Resources* Have Intended *Something* by the Inclusion of the "No Post-Production Costs" Provisions in their Leases? The conclusion of the El Paso Court of Appeals in *Heritage Resources* that "no post-production costs" provision in the lease in controversy moved the point of royalty calculation away from the wellhead downstream to the point of sale[188] seems to be a reasonable reconciliation of that provision with the market value at the well royalty clause. Even if one does not accept that reconciliation, however, the inclusion in a conventional market value royalty clause of a provision expressly prohibiting the deduction of post-production costs appears to create a patent ambiguity that should have permitted the application of the customary rules of contract interpretation relating to ambiguous agreements, including the introduction, if appropriate, of extrinsic evidence of the intent of the parties. Neither the El Paso Court of Appeals nor the Texas Supreme Court, however, found the relevant royalty clauses ambiguous in any way, even though the courts reached completely different conclusions concerning their meanings.[189] It is these courts' refusal to identify such an ambiguity that is the most "Alice Through the Looking Glass" aspect of *Heritage Resources* for this author.

At the end of the day, however, *Heritage Resources* and the subsequent cases applying its principles appear clearly to have established as the law in Texas that:

- the phrase "at the well", when used in the calculation of gas royalty – whether pursuant to a "market value",[190] "amount realized",[191] "net proceeds",[192] or other royalty clause – refers to gas in its natural state as produced and that has not been increased in value by gathering, processing, or transportation;

- when the net-back method is used to determine the amount owed as royalty on gas production "at the well", costs of gathering, processing, transportation, and other "reasonable post-production costs" must be applied against the market value of, or the amount realized or gross proceeds from the sale of, the gas at its point of sale in order to determine the market value of, or the amount realized or net proceeds from the sale of, such gas "at the well"; and

- attempts to prevent contractually post-production costs from being subtracted in the net-back calculation of royalty valued "at the well" almost certainly will be treated as "surplusage as a matter of law" and not enforced by the courts.

The key, then, for lessors attempting to insulate themselves from post-production costs appears to be to stop providing for the calculation of royalty "at the well." As Justice Owen stated in her concurring opinion in *Heritage Resources*:

> If [the parties] had intended that the royalty owners would receive royalty based on market value at the point of *delivery* or *sale*, they could have said so. If they had intended that *in*

> *addition* to the payment of market value at the well, the lessee would pay all post-production costs, they could have said so. They did not.[193]

To date, royalty owner attempts to insulate themselves from post-production costs by using royalty clauses different from the *Middleton* lease model have met with limited success, mostly because of their inability to eliminate completely the "at the well" concept from their leases. For example, recall that in *Potts*,[194] the applicable lease required the payment of royalty on gas production based on "the market value at the point of sale of the gas sold or used . . .", subject to a no-post-production costs provision.[195] Because the gas was sold at the wellhead, however, the Fifth Circuit determined that the market value royalty must be determined "at the well".[196] Then, applying the net-back method as described in *Heritage Resources*, the court upheld the lessee's calculation of market value at the well as the volume weighted average sales price received by the lessee's marketing affiliate upon its resale of the gas to unaffiliated gas purchasers less the post-production costs incurred between the wellhead and the points of delivery to the gas purchasers, notwithstanding the presence of the no-post-production costs provision.[197]

Similarly, in *Warren v. Chesapeake Exploration, L.L.C.*,[198] the lease in controversy required the payment of royalty on gas production based on "the amount realized by Lessee, computed at the mouth of the well . . .," subject to a no-post-production costs provision similar to that in *Potts*.[199] Because royalty was required to be determined "at the mouth of the well", the Fifth Circuit, once again applying *Heritage Resources*, held that royalty should be calculated, pursuant to the net-back method, based on the amount realized by the lessee upon the sale of the gas production less the post-production costs incurred between the wellhead and the points of sale, again notwithstanding the presence of the no-post-production costs provision.[200]

The most interesting current case dealing with these issues is *Chesapeake Energy, L.L.C. v. Hyder*.[201] In *Hyder*, the applicable lease contained a non-standard royalty clause that provided, in pertinent part:

> (b) for natural gas, including casinghead gas and other gaseous substances produced from the Leased Premises and sold or used on or off the Leased Premises, twenty-five percent (25%) of the price actually received by [Lessee] for such gas . . . . *The royalty reserved herein by [Lessors] shall be free and clear of all production and post-production costs and expenses, including but not limited to, production, gathering, separating, storing, dehydrating, compressing, transporting, processing, treating, marketing, delivering, or any other costs and expenses incurred between the well-head and [Lessee's] point of delivery or sale of such share to a third party.* [emphasis added][202]

The lease also provided that the holding in *Heritage Resources* "shall have no application to the terms and provisions of this Lease."[203]

Gas was sold by the lessee, using the same marketing path as described in *Potts*.[204] The lessors alleged that the lessee underpaid royalties because it interpreted the quoted royalty clause to permit the deduction of post-production costs incurred between the "points of delivery" of the gas by the lessee's marketing affiliate into various interstate transporting pipelines and the "points of sale" of the gas to unaffiliated gas purchasers.[205]

After discussing the holding in *Heritage Resources* (including an acknowledgement that the Texas Supreme Court did not directly address "the apparent conflict" between the definition of "market value at the well" and the no-post-production costs provision in the *Heritage Resources* lease),[206] the San Antonio Court of Appeals rejected the lessee's interpretation of the *Hyder* lease, holding that an interpretation of such lease that permitted the deduction of post-production costs between the "points of delivery" and the "points of sale" was "contrary to the plain reading of the royalty clause."[207] In so holding, the court upheld the no-post-production costs language in the *Hyder* lease, concluding that the holding in *Heritage Resources* did not apply based on the terms of the *Hyder* lease.[208]

The Texas Supreme Court has granted the lessee's petition for review in *Hyder*, and oral arguments were heard in March 2015.[209] As this publication goes to press, the supreme court has not issued its opinion in this case. It appears that the court of appeal's holding in *Hyder* has a good chance of surviving the Texas Supreme Court's review because the *Hyder* lease contains no language that drives the determination of royalty back to the wellhead.

VI. The Issue of Division Orders (The "Real" Rest of the Story)

Our discussion tracing the arc of the market value royalty analysis in Texas ends with consideration of the Texas Supreme Court's holdings with respect to division orders in *Middleton* and two significant subsequent judicial treatments of the issue, as well as, finally, the Texas division order statute.

A. Why *Middleton* Was Important to Division Order Analysis?

Before diving into *Middleton's* treatment of division orders, some background is appropriate. Prior to *Middleton*, the Texas courts, and the Federal courts applying Texas law, had consistently treated division orders – regardless of whether the division order purported to act as a contract of sale, passing title to the covered substance from the interest owner to the hydrocarbon purchaser, or simply as a written direction for the party obligated to make revenue distributions concerning to whom, and in what percentages, such distributions should be made – as creating a contractual relationship among the parties that (a) does not modify the terms of the underlying lease, (b) may be unilaterally revoked by the party entitled to receive payment thereunder, and (c) like the payments made and accepted thereunder, are effective, final, and binding between the parties until revoked.[210]

The leading Texas case was the 1956 Texas Supreme Court decision in *Chicago Corp. v. Wall* ("*Wall*").[211] The principle underlying these rules is detrimental reliance. If the purchaser or lessee who prepares the division order underpays one interest owner and overpays another interest owner in reliance upon the interest owners' agreement to the terms of the division order, and the underpaid interest owner is not estopped by its execution of the division order from asserting a claim for underpayment against the purchaser or lessee, the lessee could have double liability for the amount of the overpayment, an unfair result.[212]

None of these cases considered, however, the question whether a division order would be effective and binding if the division order established a royalty payment standard different from that in effect under the relevant lease. In *Butler v. Exxon Corporation*,[213] the court of civil appeals addressed this question and answered "no." In *Butler*, although the leases provided for a market value royalty standard for gas sold "off the premises" and an amount realized royalty standard for gas sold "at the wells," the plaintiff/royalty owners and Exxon, following first production, executed division orders that provided that settlements for "gas sold at wells or at a central point in or near the field where produced shall be based on the net proceeds at the wells."[214] The original division orders were later revoked and replaced by new division orders providing for settlements in accordance with the royalty provisions of the applicable leases.[215]

The trial court concluded that the original division orders and the royalty distributions made pursuant thereto were binding until the division orders were revoked, but the court of civil appeals reversed the trial court's judgment on this point, holding that the plaintiff/royalty owners' acceptance of royalties pursuant to the original division orders did not estop them from claiming royalties based on the higher market value of gas during the period before the original division orders were revoked.[216] In so holding, the court relied on *Craig v. Champlin Petroleum Co.*,[217] a 1969 federal district court case out of Oklahoma; refused to follow the contrary results reached in *J.M. Huber Corp. v. Denman*[218] and *Phillips Petroleum Co. v. Williams*[219] (both of which applied Texas law); and distinguished *Wall* based on the notion that, unlike *Wall*, there was no detrimental reliance by Exxon, as the lessee/payor under the original division orders, because the original division orders were executed without consideration.[220]

In *Middleton*, Sun Oil Company of Delaware, in addition to Exxon, was also a defendant. Gas produced from Sun's leases was processed off the leased premises at Union Texas Petroleum's Winnie, Texas Plant.[221] During the period in controversy (1973-1975), Sun sold its gas production under a fixed price gas sale contract executed in 1951 and amended in 1965 that established the sales/delivery point as the tailgate of the Winnie Plant. Sun's leases contained royalty clauses substantially identical to the royalty clauses in the Exxon leases.[222] Sun calculated and paid royalty based on the amount received from the sale of the gas in conformity with the terms of several division orders executed by the plaintiff/royalty owners in 1952,[223] which provided that royalty on processed gas would be calculated as the sum of the applicable royalty fraction of the liquids recovered by processing plus "the proceeds derived from the sale of residue gas."[224] The terms of the division orders thus effectively changed the otherwise applicable "market value" royalty standard to an "amount realized" royalty standard.

The trial court concluded that: (a) the division orders in controversy did not permanently amend the applicable royalty provisions to provide, in all cases, for the payment of royalty based on the amount realized standard; (b) until withdrawn or revoked, however, the division orders were supported by consideration and, therefore, binding on the plaintiff/royalty owners; (c) the division orders were revoked by the plaintiff/royalty owners when they filed suit against Exxon and Sun on March 30, 1974; (d) all royalty payments made by Sun prior to March 30, 1974, were final and binding on the plaintiff/royalty owners; and (e) royalty payments made thereafter were not final and binding, and the plaintiff/royalty owners were entitled to recover the excess of the market value of the gas over the amount of such post-March 30, 1974 royalty payments.[225]

Butler was clearly on the mind of the Houston Court of Civil Appeals (14th District) in *Middleton* when it considered the issues relating to Sun's division orders. After agreeing with *Wall* that Sun's division orders created a contractual relationship between Sun and the plaintiff/royalty owners,[226] the court went to considerable lengths to conclude that, unlike the division orders in *Butler*, Sun's division orders were supported by consideration in the form of several reporting and record keeping obligations on the part of Sun provided for therein. The court of civil appeals concluded, however, that because Sun's division orders were supported by consideration, the division orders effectively modified the terms of the underlying leases and, therefore, could not be unilaterally revoked by the plaintiff/royalty owners.[227]

The Texas Supreme Court reversed the court of civil appeals judgment and held that: (a) the division orders were effective to establish the basis on which royalty payments were made; (b) the division orders were unilaterally revocable by the plaintiff/royalty owners; and (c) payments made pursuant to the division orders were final and binding on the parties until the division orders were revoked.[228] In so holding, the court reaffirmed the holding in *Wall*[229] and then, quoting from the Fifth Circuit's opinion in *Phillips Petroleum Co. v. Williams*,[230] stated:

> [U]ntil withdrawn or modified, [the division orders] constitute the precise and definite basis for payments, and payments made in accordance with them are final and binding. . . . . Binding as they are, however, in respect of payments made and accepted under them, these division or transfer orders did not rewrite or supplant the lease contract. They are binding only for the time and to the extent that they have been, or are being acted on and made the basis of settlements and payments and from the time that notice is given that settlements will not be made on the basis provided in them, they cease to be binding.[231]

As such, the plaintiff/royalty owners' rights under the leases in controversy to receive royalty based on a market value standard were modified by the division orders to authorize royalty payments based on the amount realized by Sun under its long-term contract until the division orders were revoked by the filing of suit by the plaintiff/royalty owners.

Almost seven years later, the Texas Supreme Court, in *Cabot Corp. v. Brown*,[232] once again held that division orders and the payments made and accepted thereunder were effective against the royalty owner until revoked, even though the division orders provided for royalty settlement based on FPC-approved rates that were lower than the current market value that otherwise would have been the basis for royalty settlement under the terms of the applicable leases, citing *Middleton* as controlling precedent. As the result of *Wall, Middleton*, and *Cabot*, then, producers routinely employed gas division orders to authorize royalty settlements based on the price received by the producer under the applicable gas sale contract, notwithstanding an otherwise applicable market value royalty payment standard in the relevant lease, and to specify the post-production costs that would be borne by the royalty owner.

B. Subsequent Limitations on *Middleton* and *Cabot*

The Texas courts have, from time to time, placed limits on the scope of the holdings in *Middleton* and *Cabot*, however. In *Gavenda v. Strata Energy, Inc.*,[233] for example, the Texas Supreme Court held that, when the lessee had erroneously prepared division orders crediting certain royalty owners with only a portion of the interest to which they were entitled and then retained the underpaid royalties for its own account, the effective division orders did not bar the royalty owners' recovery from the lessee of the amount of the underpaid royalty retained by the lessee because it profited from its error. To permit the lessee to retain the benefits of its error would result in unjust enrichment.[234] In so holding, the supreme court distinguished its earlier holding in *Middleton* based on two factors. First, even though the division orders in Middleton provided for a royalty payment standard different from that provided for in the applicable leases, Exxon could not have detrimentally relied on the division orders' representations in entering into its long-term gas contracts, since these contracts were executed long before the royalty owners had executed the division orders. More importantly, however, Exxon did not benefit from the difference in the royalty standards expressed in the division orders and the applicable leases because they paid to the royalty owners the proper royalty fraction of the proceeds received from the gas purchaser.[235]

More recently, in *Heritage Resources*,[236] the applicable lease expressly provided that there would be no deductions from the value of the lessor's royalty payable thereunder for transportation and several other types of post-production costs, while the division orders executed with respect to this lease authorized the deduction of these costs.[237] There does not appear to have been any issue concerning the revocation of the division orders. Nevertheless, the El Paso Court of Appeals held that the royalty owners were not bound by the division orders and that the lessee was obligated to reimburse the royalty owners for improperly withheld transportation costs.[238] The court's conclusion was based upon (a) the presence in the division orders of language disclaiming an intent to alter or amend the provisions of the applicable lease, and (b) a finding that the lessee profited from the "erroneous" inclusion of language in the division orders authorizing the deduction of transportation costs because the president and sole shareholder of the lessee also was the majority shareholder of the pipeline purchaser of the gas, citing *Gavenda* in support of this conclusion.[239]

On appeal, the Texas Supreme Court, after citing *Gavenda* for the proposition that division orders are not binding when prepared in a manner that allocates payments among the interest owners in a manner different from the lease provisions and the operator retains the benefits,[240] modified the opinion of the court of appeals on the division order issue concerning the extent of the liability for underpayments of royalties by the defendant lessee.[241] Since there were other working interest owners who benefited from the improper deduction of transportation charges from the royalties paid to the lessor who were not defendants in this case, the supreme court concluded that the defendant/lessee could be held liable only for the portion of the unpaid royalties that it had retained.[242]

It is difficult to know what to make of *Heritage Resources*' holdings on division orders. At first blush, *Heritage Resources* appears to represent a retreat from the principles stated in *Middleton* regarding the effect of division orders to modify the express provisions of an oil and gas lease until the division orders are revoked. The use (indeed, I would suggest, the mischaracterization) of *Gavenda*, a case dealing with the effect of a mathematical error in the calculation of the decimal interest credited to a royalty owner, as support for the court's holding in *Heritage Resources* stretches the rationale in *Gavenda* almost to the breaking point. The inclusion in the *Heritage Resources* division orders of language authorizing the deduction of post-production costs in calculating royalty appears no more "erroneous" than was the inclusion in the *Middleton* division orders of language authorizing the payment of royalty on an amount realized, rather than a market value, basis. Perhaps the disclaimer in the *Heritage Resources* division orders of any intent to alter or amend the terms of the applicable leases provides the basis for distinguishing *Middleton*, although the supreme court does not address this point.

The foregoing result seems even odder in light of the Texas Supreme Court's holding in *Judice v. Mewbourne Oil Co.*,[243] issued on the same day as *Heritage Resources*. In *Judice*, the applicable leases provided for the payment of royalty based on a fraction of the "market value at the well of all gas produced and saved" from the leased premises,[244] but the division orders executed by the plaintiff/royalty owners and the lessee provided for royalty settlement based either on "the gross proceeds realized at the well" or "the net proceeds realized at the well" by the lessee.[245] After noting the parties' agreement that the division orders governed royalty settlements prior to their revocation upon the filing of suit, the court stated that "we look only to the division orders to determine [the lessee's] royalty obligation prior to the time suit was filed," citing *Middleton*.[246]

C. Division Order Legislation.

In 1991, the Texas legislature amended Subchapter J of Chapter 91 of the Texas Natural Resources Code, relating to "Payment for Proceeds of Sale," to add extensive provisions relating to division orders. These provisions were expressly made effective only as to "division orders and transfer orders executed after" August 26, 1991, the effective date of the amendments.[247]

Under the 1991 amendments to Subchapter J, as a condition for the payment of proceeds from the sale of oil and gas production to a party entitled to receive them, the party obligated to make the payment is entitled to receive a signed division order from the payee containing certain statutorily prescribed elements.[248] The term "division order" is defined as "an agreement signed by the payee directing the distribution of proceeds from the sale of" production and "directs and authorizes the payor to make payment for the products taken in accordance with the division order."[249] Division orders are deemed to be binding for the time and to the extent that they have been acted on and made the basis of settlements and payments. Division orders are terminable by either party on thirty (30) days written notice, however, and, from the time that such notice is given, they cease to be binding.[250] Division orders do not amend any lease or operating agreement between an interest owner and the lessee or operator or any other contracts for the purchase of oil or gas,[251] nor do they change or relieve the lessee's specific expressed or implied obligations under an oil and gas lease, and any provision of a division order that contradicts a provision of an oil and gas lease is deemed to be invalid to the extent of the contradiction.[252] Division orders may be used, however, to "clarify royalty settlement terms in the oil and gas lease."[253]

From the standpoint of our market value royalty analysis, the most significant provision added to Subchapter J by the 1991 amendments is the statutory definition of the term "market value." According to Section 91.402(i):

> With respect to oil and/or gas sold in the field where produced or at a gathering point in the immediate vicinity, the terms "market value," "market price," "prevailing price in the field," or other such language, when used as a basis of valuation in the oil and gas lease, shall be defined as the amount realized at the mouth of the well by the seller of such production in an arm's-length transaction.[254]

The phrase "arm's-length transaction" is not defined.

D. Analysis.

The 1991 amendments to Subchapter J do little to facilitate or clarify the use and effectiveness of division orders in Texas. On the one hand, several provisions of the 1991 amendments emphasize the absolute preeminence of the provisions of the lease over those of the division order and, indeed, invalidate any provision of a division order that contradicts the provisions of the applicable lease, a position that retreats from the principles in *Middleton* and *Cabot* but that is consistent with the holding in *Heritage Resources*. On the other hand, the 1991 amendments incorporate the case law principle of the binding nature of division orders as the basis of royalty settlements and payments until revoked and appear to embrace *Middleton* and *Cabot* by purporting to convert statutorily the market value standard in conventional oil and gas leases to an amount realized standard.

The Texas courts have not yet addressed any of these inconsistencies.[255] Some commentators have suggested that the inconsistency presented by the statutory definition of "market value" should not, in fact, be read to be applicable to oil and gas leases, notwithstanding the expressed language of Section 91.402(i) to that effect, but instead should be limited in its applicability to post-August 26, 1991 division orders, given the overall context of the statute.[256] The Arkansas Supreme Court followed this approach in interpreting a similar statute, holding that the statute did not have the effect of a blanket lease amendment that converted either a market value or a fixed price royalty payment standard into an amount realized payment standard.[257]

Assuming that to be the case, Sections 91.402(h) and 91.402(i) arguably permit a post-August 26, 1991 division order to "clarify" the meaning of "market value" in leases that do not otherwise define the term without actually amending the underlying lease, with the result that the case law definition of "market value" established in *Vela, Middleton, Heritage Resources,* and *Yzaguirre* is ignored and the "amount realized at the mouth of the well" standard articulated in the statute is substituted therefor.[258] Whether such a result benefits the lessee or the royalty owner depends, of course, on whether the gas market is one of rising or declining prices. Regardless, however, at least on the issue of how royalty settlements are calculated (which, I suggest, is the most important issue addressed in a division order), it seems that the 1991 amendments to Subchapter J signal a statutory return to the principles stated in *Middleton* and *Cabot* regarding the effectiveness of division orders to modify the otherwise-applicable royalty payment standard in the applicable oil and gas lease.

VII. Conclusion

As it turns out, *Vela* and *Middleton* neither resulted in economic ruin for the oil and gas producers, as Dad had feared, nor did they provide a guaranteed roadmap for litigation success for royalty owners against producers.

Although each side won some and lost some in the market value royalty cases decided over the years, the decontrol of wellhead gas prices and the dramatic overhaul of the manner in which natural gas is marketed in the U.S. have eliminated, for the most part, the market conditions that made the "market value v. amount realized" distinction such a flashpoint for oil and gas litigation for over forty years.

As noted before, however, gas royalty calculation remains complex, and there is often significant money involved. Those circumstances alone are reason enough to anticipate more litigation in this area. *Heritage Resources'* holdings regarding post-production costs have already spawned several lawsuits based on lessor attempts to draft enforceable language preventing post-production costs from being subtracted in the calculation of royalty "at the well".[259] Perhaps the Texas Supreme Court's forthcoming decision in *Hyder*[260] will provide additional guidance in this regard.

Certainly, the witches' brew of division order cases — from *Middleton* and *Cabot*, to *Gavenda*, to *Heritage Resources* — coupled with the ambiguities in the 1991 Texas division order legislation seem very likely — indeed, are overdue — to spawn a series of lawsuits. The questions whether index prices are an appropriate measure of market value, and whether basis differentials constitute hidden post-production costs, are other questions that, in my view, are ripe for judicial consideration. Whatever the nature of the future disputes, however, *Vela, Middleton*, and now *Heritage Resources* will, for better or worse, provide the analytical framework for the legal issues that will be raised.

---

1 Partner, Jackson Walker L.L.P., Houston, Texas. Portions of this chapter appear in two prior articles by the author: Michael P. Pearson, *Royalty Calculation Issues in the Post Order 636 Gas Market*, 15th Ann. Adv. Oil, Gas & Min. L. Course, St. Bar of Tex., Paper M (1997) (hereinafter Pearson I); Michael P. Pearson, *Gas Royalty Calculation 2005 – An Update*, 30 Oil, Gas & Energy Res. L. Section Report, St. Bar of Tex., No. 3, at 4 (2006) (hereinafter Pearson II). *See also* Michael P. Pearson and Richard D. Watt, *To Share or Not to Share: Royalty Obligations Arising Out of Take-or-Pay or Similar Gas Contract Litigation*, 42D Inst. On Oil & Gas L. & Tax'n 14-1 (1991) (hereinafter Pearson and Watt).

2 429 S.W.2d 866 (Tex. 1968).

3 613 S.W.2d 240 (Tex. 1981).

4 *Exxon Corp. v. Middleton*, 571 S.W.2d 349, 351 (Tex. Civ. App. – Houston [14th Dist.] 1978), *rev'd*, 613 S.W.2d 240 (Tex. 1981). *See* Allen D. Cummings, *Today's Marketing, Yesterday's Leases, Check Stub Statutes: The Perfect Storm?*, 30th Ann. Oil, Gas & Min. L. Inst., Univ. of Texas School of Law, St. Bar OGERL Section, Paper 8, at 5-6 (2004) (hereinafter Cummings).

5 *See Exxon Corp. v. Middleton*, 571 S.W.2d at 351; Cummings, *supra* note 4, at 6.

6 *See* Cummings, *supra* note 4, at 6.

7 *A Brief History of Natural Gas Regulation*, Federal Energy Regulatory Commission (May 19, 2010), http://www.ferc.gov/students/energyweregulate/gas.htm.

8 15 U.S.C. §§ 717, et seq. (2014).

9 *Id.* at § 717a(6). The principal components of the FPC's NGA regulation consisted of limiting the construction of new pipelines to those required by the "public convenience and necessity," restricting the ability of natural gas companies to abandon their assets or service, *id.* at § 717f, and requiring that interstate pipeline transportation rates must be "just and reasonable," *id.* at § 717c. *See* Jay G. Martin, *Federal Regulation of Natural Gas – A Primer*, 2nd Gas & Power Inst., Univ. of Texas School of Law, St. Bar OGERL Section, Paper 13, at 2, 3 (2003) (hereinafter Martin).

10 15 U.S.C. § 717b.

11 347 U.S. 672 (1954).

12 *See* 15 U.S.C. § 717f. Once a producer dedicated a lease or leased acreage to a certificate of public convenience and necessity, gas produced from the dedicated acreage was required to be sold in the interstate market until the FPC granted an abandonment under Section 7 of the NGA, *id.* at § 717f(b), even if, prior to such abandonment, the underlying sales contract had expired, *Sunray Mid-Continent Oil Co. v. FPC*, 364 U.S. 137 (1960), or the underlying oil and gas lease had expired, *California v. Southland Royalty Co.*, 436 U.S. 519 (1978).

13 *Phillips Petroleum Co. v. Wisconsin*, 347 U.S. 672, 684 (1954). *See* 15 U.S.C. §717c. Initially, the FPC attempted to establish well-by-well rates for these gas sales. As the backlog of individual well rate proceedings increased, however, the FPC first attempted to establish wellhead rates on an area-wide basis, *see, e.g., Permian Basin Area Rate Cases*, 390 U.S. 747 (1968), and *Area Rate Proceedings*, 50 F.P.C. 390, 392 (1973), and later on a nation-wide basis, *see Opinion* 770, 56 F.P.C. 509 (1976).

14 *See* Bruce M. Kramer, "*Royalty Obligations Under the Gun-The Effect of Take-or-Pay Clauses on the Duty to Make Royalty Payments*," 39 Inst. On Oil & Gas L. & Tax'n 5-1, 5-4, 5-5 (1988) (hereinafter Kramer); Edward B. Poitevent II and Edel F. Blanks, *Take-or-Pay: The Aftermath*, Univ. Of Houston L. Center Adv. Oil & Gas Short Course, at B-1 (1991) (hereinafter Poitevent and Blanks).

15 *See* Carolyn Hazel, *The Gas Marketing Revolution: Sharing Values Between Lessors And Lessees*, 13th Adv. Oil, Gas & Min L. Course, St. Bar of Tex., Paper H, at H-1 (1995) (hereinafter Hazel).

16 For good discussions of the evolution of the disparity between interstate and intrastate gas markets during this period, *see* Order No. 451, *Ceiling Prices: Old Gas Pricing Structure*, [Regs. Preambles 1986-90] F.E.R.C. Stats. & Regs. (CCH) 30,700; Martin, *supra* note 9, at 3-5.

17 *Exxon Corp v. Middleton*, 571 S.W.2d 349, 353, (Tex. Civ. App. – Houston [14th Dist.] 1978), *rev'd*, 613 S.W.2d 240 (Tex. 1981). A recent commentator described this historic oil and gas industry "custom and usage" as follows:

> The words "market value at the well" were designed to enable the lessee, for royalty purposes, to construct an artificial (but fair) wellhead value by deducting transportation costs from the price he received at the purchaser's pipeline. Thus, if it costs the lessee 2¢ per mcf to transport the gas to the purchaser's pipeline, where he sells it for 10¢ per mcf, the presumed wellhead value for royalty purposes would be 8¢ per mcf.

Dick Watt, *Analysis of Royalty Clauses and Issues – Past, Present, and in the Future*, 41st Ann. Oil, Gas & Min. L. Inst., Univ. of Texas School of Law, St. Bar OGERL Section, Paper 6, at 5 (2015) (hereinafter Watt), *quoting* Thomas W. Lynch, *The Deductibility of "Post-production" Costs in Calculating Gas Royalties*, Review Of Texas Oil And Gas Law X, Energy L. Section, Dallas Bar Ass'n (1995).

18 *Texas Oil & Gas Corp. v. Vela*, 429 S.W.2d 866, 871 (Tex. 1968).

19 *Id.* at 868.

20 *Id.* at 870.

21 *Id.*

22 *Id.* at 871.

23 *Id.*

24 *Id.* at 872.

25 *Id.* at 873.

26 *Id.*

27 329 F.2d 485 (5th Cir. 1964).

28 *Id.* at 488.

29 *Id.* at 489.
30 *Id.* at 490.
31 Vela, 429 S.W.2d 866, 879-80 (Hamilton, J. dissenting).
32 "El Dorado" refers to the legendary city of gold and precious stones sought by numerous explorers of South America in the 16th – 19th centuries, including the Spaniards Gonzalo Pizarro (half-brother of Francisco Pizarro) and Francisco de Orellana, and the Englishman Sir Walter Raleigh. The legend of El Dorado is also the subject of numerous literary, art, film, and television treatments and references, including Milton's *Paradise Lost* (Book XI, pp. 408-11), the 1966 John Wayne-Howard Hawks film, *El Dorado*, and, perhaps most famously, the ballad poem, *Eldorado*, by Edgar Allen Poe, first published in 1849. *See* Kenneth Silverman, Edgar A. Poe: Mournful And Never-Ending Remembrance (Harper Perennial 1991); *El Dorado*, Wikipedia, http://www.wikipedia.org/ wiki/El_Dorado.
33 *E.g.*, Joseph W. Morris, *The Gas Royalty Clause — What Is Market Value?*, 25th Ann. Inst. On Oil & Gas L.& Tax'n 63, at 75 (1974) (hereinafter Morris) (stating that Vela "stands alone in its construction of this [market price] language and it should not be followed by the courts in other jurisdictions."). *See also* Frank G. Harmon, *Vela Today: Market Value Royalty Problems*, 27 Oil & Gas Tax Q. 185 (1978); William S. Hayes, *Vela: Legacy of Conflict Over Determination of Market Value for Royalties*, 11 St. Mary's L.J. 502 (1979); Raymond B. Kelly, III, What Price, Gas?, 7 St. Mary's L.J. 333 (1975).
34 *See* Department of Energy Organization Act, Pub. L. No. 95-91, 42 U.S.C. §§7131, 7134 (2014).
35 15 U.S.C. §§3301, *et seq*. (2014). *See* Pearson II, *supra* note 1, at 4.
36 NGPA § 102 (new onshore wells), 15 U.S.C. §3312; NGPA §103 (new onshore production wells), 15 U.S.C.. § 3313; NGPA § 107 (high-cost natural gas), 15 U.S.C. § 3317; and NGPA § 108 (stripper well natural gas), 15 U.S.C. § 3318, *all repealed*, Pub. L. No. 101-60, § 2(b), 103 Stat. 158 (1989).
37 NGPA §§ 104 (existing interstate contracts) and 106 (rollover contracts), 15 U.S.C. §§ 3314, 3316, *repealed*, Pub. L. No. 101-60, § 2(b), 103 Stat. 158 (1989).
38 NGPA § 105 (existing intrastate contracts), 15 U.S.C. § 3315, *repealed*, Pub. L. No. 101-60, § 2(b), 103 Stat. 158 (1989).
39 *See* Pearson and Watt, *supra* note 1, at 14-6, 14-10; Pearson II, *supra* note 1, at 7.
40 Texas *Oil & Gas Corp. v. Vela*, 429 S.W.2d 866, 873 (Tex. 1968). *See, e.g., Domatti v. Exxon Corp.*, 494 F. Supp. 306, 312 (W.D. La. 1980) (court noted that *Vela* did not address the problem of how the market value of gas sold in the interstate market was to be determined); *Hemus & Co. v. Hawkins*, 452 F. Supp. 861, 862 (S.D. Tex. 1978) (court concluded that *Vela* "does not really address…what sales are really comparable?").
41 For more detailed discussions of this issue, see Robert. O. Lewers, *Primary Jurisdiction and the Royalty Owner: A Misapplied Doctrine*, 23 SW. L.J. 454 (1969); Frederick K. Slicker, *An Evolving Concept of Federal Power Commission Natural Gas Rate Regulation: Will Royalty Owners Be Next?* 16 U. Kan. L. Rev. 378 (1968).
42 367 F.2d 104, 121 (5th Cir. 1966).
43 367 F.2d 84, 103 (5th Cir. 1966).
44 *Id.* In *Weymouth*, however, Judge Brown, writing for the Fifth Circuit, criticized as inadequate the district court's definition of "market price" as "that price which a willing buyer would pay and a willing seller would take, after fair negotiation, with neither party acting under compulsion", stating:

> So this "free," "willing" buyer is not so "free." Nor is his counterpart, the seller. Nor is the commodity. Nor is the business. Nor is the sale. The test in capsulated form is, then, what would a willing seller and a willing buyer in a business which subjects them and the commodity to restriction and regulation, including a commitment for a long period of time, agree to take and pay with a reasonable expectation that the FPC would approve the price (and price changes) and other terms and then issue the necessary certificate of public convenience and necessity.

Weymouth, 367 F.2d at 90.
45 463 F.2d 256, 258 (D.C. Cir. 1971), *cert. denied*, 406 U.S. 976 (1972). In so holding, the D.C. Circuit specifically overruled FPC Opinion 562, 42 F.P.C. 164, in which the FPC, on petition from the royalty owners in *Huber*, had declared that the royalty provisions of oil and gas leases constituted sales of natural gas for resale in interstate commerce subject to the provisions of the NGA.
46 *Kingery v. Continental Oil Co.*, 626 F.2d 1261, 1264 (5th Cir. 1980), *cert. denied*, 454 U.S. 1148 (1982) (the Fifth Circuit held that "where the gas has been irrevocably dedicated to the interstate market, it follows inexorably that the only comparable sales to be used in determining the market value of such gas are sales on the interstate market"); *Domatti v. Exxon Corp.*, 494 F. Supp. 306, 314 (W.D. La. 1980); *Hemus & Co. v. Hawkins*, 42 F. Supp. 861, 862 (S.D. Tex. 1978). *See also Burns v. Exxon Corp.*, 158 F.3d 336, 342 (5th Cir. 1998). *But see Sowell v. Natural Gas Pipeline Co. of America*, 789 F.2d 1151, 1154-55 (5th Cir. 1986) (court concluded that, under the "market value" royalty provisions in controversy, the lessor was entitled to royalty based on the average market price of all gas sold, whether in the interstate or intrastate markets, in a six county area).
47 *Bowers v. Phillips Petroleum Co.*, 692 F.2d 1015, 1021 (5th Cir. 1982); *Flowers v. Diamond Shamrock Corp.*, 693 F.2d 1146, 1153 (5th Cir. 1982).
48 622 S.W.2d 80 (Tex. 1980).
49 Morris, *supra* note 33, at 75.
50 *Holmes v. Kewanee Oil Co.*, 233 Kan. 544, 664 P.2d 1335 (Kan. 1983) ; *Matzen v. Cities Service Oil Co.*, 233 Kan. 337, 667 P.2d 337 (Kan. 1983); *Lightcap v. Mobil Oil Corp.*, 221 Kan. 448, 562 P.2d 1 (Kan. 1977).
51 *Montana Power Co. v. Kravik*, 179 Mont. 87, 586 P.2d. 298 (Mont. 1978), *on subsequent appeal*, 189 Mont. 369, 616 P.2d 321 (Mont. 1980).
52 *Teavee Oil & Gas Inc. v. Hardesty*, 171 W.Va. 123, 297 S.E.2d 898 (W. Va. 1982) (court held that, for purposes of the West Virginia business and occupation tax based on fair market value of gas, current market prices at the time of production should be utilized).
53 *Amerada Hess Corp. v. Conrad*, 410 N.W. 124, 130 (N.D. 1987) (North Dakota gross production tax is measured by "the current market value of the gas at the time it is produced").
54 *Piney Woods Country Life School v. Shell Oil Co.*, 726 F.2d 225 (5th Cir. 1984), *cert. denied*, 471 U.S. 1005 (1985).
55 1981 Okla. 65, 630 P.2d 1269, 1272-74 (Okla. 1981).
56 *See Texas Oil & Gas Corp. v. Vela*, 429 S.W.2d 866, 879-80 (Tex. 1968) (Hamilton, J., dissenting).
57 *Henry v. Ballard & Cordell Corp.*, 418 So. 2d 1334 (La. 1982). *But see Shell Oil Co. v. Williams*, 428 So. 2d 798, 801-02 (La. 1983) (in a case in which the parties stipulated that, under the leases in controversy, the terms "market price" and "market rate" refer to current market value, the court held that the current market value of gas dedicated to the interstate market was to be determined by reference to comparable sales in the interstate market, and not higher, unregulated intrastate sales).
58 *Hillard v. Stephens*, 276 Ark. 545, 637 S.W.2d 581 (1982). *Accord, Taylor v. Arkansas Louisiana Gas Co.*, 604 F. Supp. 779 (W.D. Ark. 1985), *aff'd*, 793 F.2d 189 (8th Cir. 1986).
59 571 S.W.2d 349 (Tex. Civ. App – Houston [14th Dist.] 1978), *rev'd*, 613 S.W.2d 240 (Tex. 1981).
60 *Middleton*, 613 S.W.2d at 241-42.
61 *Middleton*, 571 S.W.2d at 355-56.
62 *Middleton*, 613 S.W.2d at 242.
63 *Id.* at 242.
64 *Id.* at 244.
65 *Id.* (citing *Monsanto Co. v. Tyrell*, 537 S.W.2d 135, 137 (Tex. Civ. App. – Houston [14th Dist.] 1976, *writ ref'd n.r.e.*)).
66 *Id.* at 244-45 (citing *Texas Oil & Gas Corp. v. Vela*, 429 S.W.2d 866, 871 (Tex. 1968)). This result is also consistent with the terms of the Texas Uniform Commercial Code. *See* Tex. Bus. & Com. Code Ann. § 2.107(a) (Tex. U.C.C.) (West 2014) (a contract for the sale of minerals or the like, including oil and gas, is a contract for the sale of goods subject to Chapter 2 of the Texas U.C.C. if the minerals are to be severed by the seller; until severance, however, a purported present sale of such minerals that is *not* effective as a transfer of an interest in land is effective only as a contract to sell).
67 *Middleton*, 613 S.W.2d at 243.
68 *Id.* at 242.
69 *Id.* at 243.
70 *Id.* at 245 (citing *Texas Oil & Gas Corp. v. Vela*, 429 S.W.2d 866, 871 (Tex. 1968)).
71 *Id.* at 246.
72 *Id.* (citing *Texas Oil & Gas Corp. v. Vela*, 429 S.W.2d 866, 872 (Tex. 1968)).
73 559 S.W.2d 410 (Tex. Civ. App. – El Paso 1977, *writ ref'd n.r.e.*)
74 *Id.* at 413.
75 *Id.* at 412. *See* text accompanying note 62, *supra*.
76 *Butler*, 559 S.W.2d at 416.
77 *Id.* at 414.
78 *Exxon Corp. v. Middleton*, 613 S.W.2d 240, 243 (Tex. 1981).

79 *Id.* at 244. The court also noted that its holding was consistent with the federal district court holdings in *Skaggs v. Heard*, 172 F. Supp. 813 (S.D. Tex. 1959) (sale of gas at the outlet of a compressor located on the leased premises, but not less than 320 feet from any well drilled thereon, constituted a sale "at the wells"), and *Kingery v. Continental Oil Company*, 434 F. Supp. 349 (W.D. Tex. 1977), *rev'd on other grounds*, 626 F.2d 1261 (5th Cir. 1980), *cert. denied*, 454 U.S. 1148 (1982) (sale of gas at pipeline interconnect 3½ miles from the exterior boundary of the leased premises was a sale "off the premises").

80 *Middleton*, 613 S.W.2d at 251-52.

81 *Id.* at 246-47.

82 *See* text accompanying notes 46 and 47, *supra*.

83 *Middleton*, 613 S.W.2d at 246. See Richard D. Watt, Donato Ramos, and John Beckworth, *Royalty Litigation — Key Issues*, 19 TEX. OIL & GAS L.J. Nos. 1, 2, and 3, at 10 (2005) (hereinafter Watt, Ramos, and Beckworth).

84 *Middleton*, 613 S.W.2d at 245-46.

85 *Id.* at 246. Among other issues regarding the plaintiffs' expert's testimony, the court of civil appeals objected to the plaintiffs' expert's failures to (a) designate the Anahuac Field as the relevant market area, (b) calculate a mathematical average of all prices paid in the Anahuac Field, and (c) corroborate such mathematical average price with comparable sales in the field. *Id.*

86 *Id.* at 249. In particular, the Texas Supreme Court specifically rejected the court of civil appeals' objection to the failure by the plaintiffs' expert to calculate a mathematical average of the price paid in the Anahuac Field. Citing *Vela*, the court reaffirmed that "a mathematical average of all prices paid in the field is 'not a final answer to the difficult problem of determining market value at any particular time.'" *Id.* at 248.

87 *Id.*

88 *First Nat'l Bank v. Exxon Corp.*, 622 S.W.2d 80 (Tex. 1981).

89 *Id.*

90 *Id.* at 82.

91 *See* Pearson II, *supra* note 1, at 7; Pearson and Watt, *supra* note 1, at 14-6, 14-8.

92 *See Diamond Shamrock Exp. Co. v. Hodel*, 853 F.2d 1159, 1164 (5th Cir. 1988).

93 *See, e.g., Atlantic Richfield Co. v. ANR Pipeline Co.*, 768 S.W.2d 777 (Tex. App. – Houston [14th Dist.] 1989, no writ).

94 *E.g., Universal Res. Corp. v. Panhandle Eastern Pipe Line Co.*, 813 F.2d 77 (5th Cir. 1987); *The Lenape Res. Corp. v. Tennessee Gas Pipeline Co.*, 925 S.W.2d 565 (Tex. 1996); *Valero Transmission Co. v. Mitchell Energy Corp.*, 743 S.W.2d 658 (Tex. App. – Houston [1st Dist.] 1987, no writ). *See* J. Michael Medina, et al., *Take or Litigate: Enforcing the Plain Meaning of the Take-or-Pay Clause in Natural Gas Contracts*, 40 ARK. L. REV. 185 (1986); David L. Roland, *Comment: Take-or-Pay Provisions for the Natural Gas Industry*, 18 ST. MARY'S L.J. 251 (1986).

95 Order No. 436, *Regulation of Natural Gas Pipelines After Partial Wellhead Decontrol,* [Regs. Preambles 1982-85] F.E.R.C. STATS. & REGS. (CCH) ¶30,665, *order on reh'g*, Order No. 436-A, [Regs. Preambles 1982-85] F.E.R.C. STATS. & REGS. (CCH)] ¶30,675 (1985), *order on reh'g*, Order No. 436-B, [Regs. Preambles 1986-90] F.E.R.C. STATS. & REGS. (CCH) ¶30,688, *order on reh'g*, Order No. 436-C, 34 F.E.R.C. ¶61,404, *order on reh'g*, Order No. 436-D, 34 F.E.R.C. ¶61,405, *order on reh'g*, Order No. 436-E, 34 F.E.R.C. ¶61,403 (1986), *vacated and remanded sub nom. Associated Gas Distributors v. FERC*, 824 F.2d 981 (D.C. Cir. 1987), *cert. denied sub nom., Southern California Gas Co. v. FERC*, 485 U.S. 1006 (1988).

96 Order No. 636, *Pipeline Service Obligations and Revisions to Regulations Governing Self-Implementing Transportation Under Part 284 of the Commission's Regulations, and Regulation of Natural Gas Pipelines After Partial Wellhead Decontrol*, [Current] F.E.R.C. STATS. & REGS. (CCH) ¶30,939, *order on reh'g*, Order No. 636-A, [Current] F.E.R.C.STATS. & REGS. (CCH) ¶30,950, *order on reh'g*, Order No. 636-B, 61 F.E.R.C. ¶61,272 (1992), *reh'g denied*, 62 F.E.R.C. ¶61,007 (1993), *aff'd in part and remanded in part, United Distribution Cos. v. FERC*, 88 F.3d 1105 (D.C. Cir. 1996), *cert. denied sub nom., New York Public Service Comm'n v. FERC*, __ U.S. __, 117 S. Ct. 1723 (1997), and *Burlington Resources Oil & Gas Co. v. FERC*, __ U.S. __, 117 S. Ct. 1724 (1997).

97 Order No. 436, [Regs. Preambles 1982-85] F.E.R.C. STATS. & REGS. (CCH) ¶30, 665, at 31,497-31,569. For an excellent discussion of Order No. 436, *see* Thomas G. Johnson, *Order No. 436 Revisited – The Interim Rule and Then What?"*, 39th INST. ON OIL & GAS L. & TAX'N 6 1 (1988).

98 Order No. 636, F.E.R.C. STATS. & REGS.. (CCH) [Current] ¶30,939, at 30,402-13, 30,421-25, and 30,437-43.

99 Pub. L. No. 101-60, 103 Stat. 157 (1989) (codified in scattered sections of 15 U.S.C.A.).

100 For a comprehensive summary of these actions by the FERC, *see* Pearson II, *supra* note 1, at 8-12.

101 *See* Kathleen R. McLaurin, *New Financing Techniques in Gas Marketing*, 6th ANN. OIL & GAS L. INST., S. Texas College of Law, Paper G, at G-2 (1993).

102 *See* Hazel, *supra* note 15, at H-2, H-3.

103 "Firm" sales service is a higher class of service for gas that is continuous without curtailment except upon the occurrence of force majeure or other occasional, extraordinary circumstances. 8 Patrick H. Martin & Bruce M. Kramer, WILLIAMS & MEYERS OIL & GAS LAW, *Manual of Terms*, at 381 (2014) (hereinafter, Williams & Meyers).

104 *See* Pearson II, *supra* note 1, at 12, 13; Hazel, *supra* note 15, at H-2, H-3; James C.T. Hardwick & J. Kevin Hayes, *Gas Royalty Issues Arising from Direct Gas Marketing*, 43D INST. ON OIL & GAS L. & TAX'N 11-1, 11-8, 11-9 (1992) (hereinafter, Hardwick and Hayes). In the latter example, the gas price often reflects a premium over current index prices to compensate the seller for the additional risk assumed by the seller with respect to a longer term, firm sales obligation.

105 53 S.W.3d 368 (Tex. 2001). In an unpublished opinion decided two years earlier, the Dallas Court of Appeals had reached the same decision based on similar facts in *De los Santos v. Coastal Oil & Gas Corp.*, 1999 WL 619639 (Tex. App. – Dallas) (not designated for publication).

106 *Yzaguirre*, 53 S.W.3d at 371. Indeed, Tennessee had previously sought, unsuccessfully, a declaratory judgment that the gas contract did not obligate it to purchase all of the gas produced from the leases at the escalated price provided for therein. *See Lenape Res. Corp. v. Tennessee Gas Pipeline Co.,* 925 S.W.2d 565 (Tex. 1996).

107 *Yzaguirre*, 53 S.W.3d 368 at 373-74 (citing *Texas Oil & Gas Corp. v. Vela*, 429 S.W.2d 866, 870-71 (Tex. 1968), and *Amoco Prod. Co. v. First Baptist Church*, 611 S.W.2d 610 (Tex. 1980)). *Accord, Piney Woods Country Life School v. Shell Oil Co.*, 726 F.2d 225, 234 (5th Cir. 1984), *cert. denied*, 471 U.S. 1005 (1985) ("If the price of gas declines, a market value royalty clause would benefit a lessee who has contracted to sell at a favorable price.")

108 111 S.W.3d 69, 71 (Tex. 2003).

109 Tex. R. Civ. P. 42(b).

110 111 S.W.3d at 76.

111 *Id.*

112 *See, e.g.*, Watt, Ramos, and Beckworth, *supra* note 83, at 11, 12, 15-18; Baldemar Garcia, Jr., *Royalty Update*, 20th ANN. ADV. OIL, GAS & ENERGY RES. L. COURSE, St. Bar of Tex., Ch. 20, at 7 (2002).

113 *See* Allen D. Cummings, Susan Richardson, and Lisa Vaughan, *Litigating Gas Royalty Cases*, 19 OIL, GAS & MIN. L. SECTION REPORT, St. Bar of Tex., No. 3, at 25, 26 (1995) (hereinafter, Cummings, Richardson and Vaughan); Pearson and Watt, *supra* note 1, at 14-26, 14-27; David E. Pierce, *Royalty Valuation Principles in a Changing Gas Market*, 11th ANN. ADV. OIL, GAS & MIN. L. COURSE, St. Bar of Tex., Paper E, at E 12, E 13 (1993) (hereinafter D. Pierce); John S. Lowe, *Current Lease and Royalty Problems in the Gas Industry*, 23 TULSA L. J. 547 (1988)

114 Messrs. Watt, Ramos, and Beckworth argue that this analysis is flawed when applied to the facts in *Yzaguirre* because (a) the lessee bore no commodity price risk under the Tennessee Contract since the contract provided only for escalations, and no reductions, of the gas price paid thereunder and (b) the Tennessee Contract expressly indemnified the lessee against *Vela*-type royalty risk. *See* Watt, Ramos, and Beckworth, *supra* note 83, at 12.

115 Historically, Texas law has recognized three broad categories of covenants implied in all oil and gas leases which are intended, generally, to protect the interests of the lessor in connection with the development and protection of the lease and to discourage the lessee from considering only its own interests in the operation of the lease: (a) the covenant reasonably to develop the premises; (b) the covenant to protect the leasehold; and (c) the covenant to manage and administer the lease. *Amoco Prod. Co. v. Alexander*, 622 S.W.2d 563, 567 (Tex. 1981); *Cabot Corp v. Brown*, 754 S.W.2d 104, 106 (Tex. 1987). Included within the covenant to manage and administer the lease is the covenant reasonably to market the oil and gas produced from the leased premises. *Cabot Corp. v. Brown*, 754 S.W.2d 104, 106 (Tex. 1987); *Parker v. TXO Prod. Corp.*, 716 S.W.2d 644, 646 (Tex. App. – Corpus Christi 1986, no writ). The diligence required of the lessee in the performance of the implied covenants is that which would be exercised by a reasonably prudent operator under the same or similar circumstances. *Amoco Prod. Co. v. Alexander,* 622 S.W.2d 563, 567-68 (Tex. 1981).

116 754 S.W.2d 104 (Tex. 1987).

117 *Id.* at 106. The implied covenant to market is clearly applicable to royalty on gas production calculated based on the amount realized by the lessee from the sale of such production, although the implied covenant does not imply a duty to sell gas at market value. *E.g., Amoco Prod. Co. v. First Baptist Church*, 579 S.W.2d 280, 287 (Tex. Civ. App. – El Paso 1979), *writ ref'd n.r.e. per curiam*, 611 S.W.2d 610 (Tex. 1980).

118 754 S.W.2d at 106. In *Cabot*, the lessee under a lease providing for the payment of royalty based on the market value of gas production at the well actually paid royalty on such gas production, which was dedicated to and sold in interstate commerce under the NGA, pursuant to division orders executed by the royalty owner which obligated the lessee to pay royalty based on the applicable FPC ceiling rate. *Id.* at 105. The supreme court held that, until the division orders, which established a royalty payment standard different from that provided for in the lease, were revoked, the plaintiffs were precluded from asserting a claim for damages under the implied covenant to market based on the lessee's failure to seek an abandonment of the gas under the NGA so that it could be sold in the higher-priced intrastate market. *Id.* at 107 (citing *Middleton*). The division orders were deemed revoked when the lessee was served with process in this litigation, and the court remanded the case to the trial court to permit the royalty owner to establish its damages, if any, for the period after the division orders were revoked. *Id.* at 108. Because the quoted language relating to the implied covenant to market was not central to the court's decision, it is generally regarded as dictum.

119 *Yzaguirre v. KCS Res., Inc.*, 53 S.W.3d 368, 372-73 (Tex. 2001).

120 *Id.* at 373-74.

121 *Id.* This result had been called for by numerous commentators for some time. *See, e.g.*, Cummings, Richardson, & Vaughan, *supra* note 113, at 25, 26; McCartney, *Implied Covenants – Ongoing and Emerging Issues*, ADV. OIL & GAS SHORT COURSE, Univ. of Houston L. Center, Paper K, at K 21 (1997); Elizabeth N. "Becky" Miller, *Implied Covenants – An Update*, 17th ANN. ADV. OIL, GAS & MIN. L. COURSE, St. Bar of Tex., Paper K, at K 10, K 11 (1999) (hereinafter Miller).

122 *See* Watt, Ramos and Beckworth, *supra* note 83, at 21, 22.

123 *Yzaguirre v. KCS Res., Inc.*, 53 S.W.3d 368, 375 (Tex. 2001).

124 The holding in *Yzaguirre* does not, however, necessarily affect the lessee's obligation to market production with due diligence. In addition, in a footnote, the court in *Yzaguirre* suggested that a royalty owner under a market value royalty standard might have a claim under the implied covenant to market if the lessee intentionally sold gas off the leased premises in order to reduce the amount payable to the royalty owner. *Id.* at 375 n.3. *See* Watt, Ramos and Beckworth, *supra* note 83, at 22.

125 Tex. R. Civ. P. 42(a), 42(b).

126 For example, in *Union Pacific Resources Group, Inc. v. Hankins*, 111 S.W.3d 69 (Tex. 2003), the Texas Supreme Court reversed a court of appeals judgment certifying the plaintiff class and held that, "[b]ecause a covenant to obtain the best price reasonably available is implied under Texas law only to proceeds leases, not to market-value leases," the royalty owners had not established "questions of law or fact common to the class" sufficient to support certification. *Id.* at 70. After reviewing the list of common issues developed for the proposed class by the trial court, several of which asked whether the defendants had "breached the implied covenant to reasonably market," the court stated:

> Since *Yzaguirre* held that market value leases have no such implied covenant, these questions cannot satisfy the commonality requirement in a class that includes both proceeds leases and market value leases.

Id. at 75.

Similarly, in *Bowden v. Phillips Petroleum Co.*, 247 S.W.3d 690 (Tex. 2008), the Texas Supreme Court addressed efforts by royalty owners to obtain class certification under Tex. R. Civ. P. 42(b) for three classes of claimants alleging that Phillips, the common lessee, underpaid royalties as a result of Phillips' sales of gas production from the relevant leases to its gas marketing affiliate. "Subclass 3" consisted of royalty owners in the Texas Panhandle whose leases contained both amount-realized and market value provisions, where Phillips sold the gas under "percentage of proceeds" contracts with its marketing affiliate. *Id.* at 708. After addressing several royalty owner claims based on alleged implied covenant breaches by Phillips, the supreme court affirmed the refusal by the Houston Court of Appeals (14th District) to certify Subclass 3, concluding that because Subclass 3 contained both amount-realized and market value royalty provisions, and because the implied covenant to market applies to amount-realized leases but not market value leases (citing *Yzaguirre* and *Hankins*), Subclass 3 did not satisfy the "commonality" requirement of Tex. R. Civ. P. 42(b). *Id.* at 708-709.

Accord, Union Pacific Resources Group, Inc. v. Neinast, 67 S.W.3d 275 (Tex. App. – Houston [1st Dist.] 2001, *pet. denied*); and *Enron Oil & Gas Co. v. Joffrion*, 116 S.W.3d 215 (Tex. App. – Tyler 2003, *no pet.*); and in the Fifth Circuit's decision in *Stirman v. Exxon Corp.*, 280 F.3d 554, 563 (5th Cir. 2002). *But see* notes 186 and 187 and accompanying text, *infra*.

127 There are, of course, numerous distinguished commentators who do not completely share this view. *See* Watt, *supra* note 17, at 8 ("In reading these cases, one is reminded of the fable of the group of blind men, who each describe an elephant by feeling a different part of its body, with the elephant looking entirely different depending on which body part is being described. Because of this, it is becoming increasingly difficult to rationally or fairly apply these earlier holdings to current disputes. . . ."); Watt, Ramos, and Beckworth, *supra* note 83, at 12-22.

128 939 S.W.2d 118 (Tex. 1996).

129 *Exxon Corp. v. Middleton*, 613 S.W.2d 240, 245-49 (Tex. 1981); *Texas Oil & Gas Corp. v. Vela*, 429 S.W.2d 866, 872-74 (Tex. 1968). *Accord, Piney Woods County Life School v. Shell Oil Co.*, 725 F.2d 225, 234 (5th Cir. 1984), *cert. denied*, 471 U.S. 1005 (1985).

130 *Middleton*, 613 S.W.2d at 249.

131 *Vela*, 429 S.W.2d at 871.

132 In *Vela*, the defendant's expert reviewed all gas sales from the Lopeno Field during the four years prior to the commencement of the *Vela* litigation, determined the arithmetic average of these sales prices, deducted a charge for compression, and determined the market value to be $0.13047 per Mcf. *Id.* at 872-73. Although the court noted that "the mathematical average of all prices paid in the field is not the final answer" in determining market value, *id.* at 874, the court upheld the expert's finding. *Id.*

133 *Id.* at 873.

134 *Yzaguirre v. KCS Res., Inc.*, 53 S.W.3d 368, 374-75 (Tex. 2001).

135 *Id.* (citing *Texas Oil & Gas Corp. v. Vela*, 429 S.W.2d 866, 871 (Tex. 1968), and *Exxon Corp. v. Middleton,* 613 S.W.2d 240, 244-46 (Tex. 1981)).

136 *See* Garcia, *supra* note 112, at 10, 11; Watt, Ramos and Beckworth, *supra* note 83, at 15-18. In some cases, the courts have honored the applicable sales price as the proper measure of current market value. *See, e.g., Piney Woods Country Life School v. Shell Oil Co.*, 905 F.2d 840, 850 (5th Cir. 1990) (on appeal of the district court's judgment following the Fifth Circuit's remand of the case pursuant to its 1984 decision, the court held that the evidence sustained the district court's finding that the applicable contract price represented the fair market value of the gas in controversy); *Maddox v. Texas Co.*, 150 F. Supp. 175, 180 (E.D. Tex. 1957).

137 *Heritage Res., Inc. v. NationsBank*, 939 S.W.2d 118 (Tex. 1996).

138 The "work-back" or "net-back" method of calculating market value has been endorsed by the courts in other states. *See Piney Woods County Life School v. Shell Oil Co.*, 726 F.2d 225, 239 (5th Cir. 1984), *cert. denied*, 471 U.S. 1005 (1985); *Ashland Oil, Inc. v. Phillips Petroleum Co.*, 554 F.2d 381, 387 (10th Cir. 1977), *on remand*, 463 F.Supp. 619 (N.D. Okla. 1978), *aff'd in part and rev'd in part*, 607 F.2d 335, 336 (10th Cir. 1979), *cert. denied*, 446 U.S. 936 (1980) (judgment of trial court set aside based upon trial court's failure to employ the work-back method of calculating the value of helium for royalty purposes); *Montana Power Co. v. Kravik*, 586 P.2d 298, 303 (Mont. 1978) (court approved use of work-back method of calculating market value in the absence of comparable sale information, but stated that "[t]his is the least desirable method of determining market price"). *See* Williams & Meyers, *supra* note 103, §645.2 at 604, 605 & n.10.

139 *Heritage Res.*, 939 S.W.2d at 120-21.

140 *Id.* at 120.

141 *Heritage Res.*, 895 S.W.2d 833, 836-37 (Tex. App. – El Paso 1995), *rev'd*, 939 S.W.2d 118 (Tex. 1996).

142 *Heritage Res.*, 895 S.W.2d at 836.

143 *Id.* at 837.

144 *Heritage Res.*, 939 S.W.2d at 123.

145 *Id.* at 122. In her concurring opinion, Justice Owen described the so-called net-back approach as one which "determines the prevailing market price at a given point and backs out the necessary reasonable costs between that point and the wellhead." *Id.* at 130. *Heritage Resources* was cited by the Fifth Circuit as support for this proposition in *Ramming v. Natural Gas Pipeline Co.,* 390 F.3d 366, 373 (5th Cir. 2004).

146 *Heritage Res.*, 939 S.W.2d at 122-23.

147 *Id.* at 122.

148 *Id.*

149 *Id.* at 124 (Owen, J., concurring).

150 Generally, under Texas law, when gas is sold at the well, no post-production costs and expenses, other than the royalty owner's proportionate share of severance and other applicable taxes, may be charged against the royalty interest because the price paid for the gas at the wellhead is presumed to be based on its value before transportation, processing, and other post-production activities. *E.g., Piney Woods County Life School v. Shell Oil Co.*, 726 F.2d 225, 240 (5th Cir. 1984), *cert. denied*, 471 U.S. 1005 (1985). When gas is sold other than at the wellhead, however, regardless of whether a market value or an amount realized royalty payment standard is in effect, Texas courts have permitted the deduction of reasonable post-production costs in calculating royalty, absent a contrary provision in the lease. *See* 1 Ernest E. Smith & Jacqueline Lange Weaver, TEXAS LAW OF OIL & GAS § 4.6.C at 195 (2014) (hereinafter, Smith & Weaver).

151 939 S.W.2d at 127. According to the Fifth Circuit, "'At the well' means that gas has not been increased in value by processing or transportation. It has this meaning in conjunction with 'value' or 'amount realized' as well as with 'sold.' . . . On royalties 'at the well', therefore, the lessors may be charged with . . . all expenses subsequent to production relating to the processing, transportation, and marketing of gas and sulfur." *Piney Woods*, 726 F.2d at 240.

152 *Heritage Res.*, 939 S.W.2d at 129-30. In Oklahoma, Kansas, and Colorado, the courts have held that the obligation to render production marketable imposed on the lessee by these states' formulation of the implied covenant to market precludes the deduction of post-production costs of compression, dehydration, gathering, and, in some cases, transportation in calculating royalty. *E.g., Bailey v. Shell Western E&P, Inc.*, 609 F.3d 710, 723-724 (5th Cir. 2010) (applying Colorado law), *cert. denied*, __ U.S. __, 131 S. Ct. 428 (2010); *Rogers v. Westerman Farm Co.*, 29 P.3d 887, 903-06 (Colo. 2001); *Garman v. Conoco Inc.*, 886 P.2d 652 (Colo. 1994); *Wood v. TXO Prod. Corp.*, 854 P.2d 880 (Okla. 1992); *Gilmore v. Superior Oil Co.*, 192 Kan. 388, 388 P.2d 602 (Kan. 1964); *Schupbach v. Continental Oil Co.*, 193 Kan. 401, 394 P.2d 1 (Kan. 1964). Oklahoma law, at least, obligates the lessor to bear its proportionate share of transportation costs when the point of sale is off the leased premises. *Wood v. TXO Prod. Corp.*, 854 P.2d 880 (Okla. 1992); *Johnson v. Jernigan*, 475 P.2d 396 (Okla. 1970). For comprehensive treatments of the law relating to post-production costs in most of the producing states, see Robert L. Theriot and Joshua P. Downer, *Royalty and Deductions – Old Issues in New Plays*, 39 Oil, Gas & Energy Res. L. Section Report, St. Bar of Tex., No. 1, at 131 (2014); Guy Stanford Lipe and Rebecca Lynn Phillips, *Current Developments and Trends in Royalty Litigation*, 64th Ann. Inst. On Oil & Gas Law § 5.03 (2013); Mark G. Rodriguez and Rebecca L. Phillips, *Royalty and Post-Production Costs: Differences Across the Producing States*, 36 Oil, Gas & Energy Res. L. Section Report, St. Bar of Tex., No. 4, at 13 (2012); Mark G. Rodriguez and Walter R. Mayer, *Royalty and Post-Production Costs: Keeping Track of It All*, 25th Adv. Oil, Gas & Energy Res. L. Course, St. Bar of Tex., Ch. 7 (2007); Edward B. Poitevent, II, "*Post-Production Deductions From Royalty*," 29 Oil, Gas & Energy Res. L. Section Report, St. Bar of Tex., No. 1, at 38 (2004).

153 *Heritage Res.*, 939 S.W.2d at 130-31. Contrast with *Rogers v. Westerman Farm Co.*, 29 P.3d 887, 897 (Colo. 2001), in which the Colorado Supreme Court stated that the phrase "at the well" is silent as to the allocation of post-production costs.

154 *Heritage Res.*, 939 S.W.2d at 131-32.

155 40 Tex. Sup. Ct. J. 445 (Tex. 1997).

156 *Id.* at 447.

157 *Id.* After *Heritage Resources* was released, one of the Justices recused himself from further proceedings in the case. As a result, when Justices Cornyn and Spector, who originally joined in the majority opinion, joined Justices Gonzalez and Abbott in dissent, the Justices split 4-4 in ruling on the motion for rehearing. *See* Watt, *supra* note 17, at 10.

158 760 F.3d 470 (5th Cir. 2014).

159 *Id.* at 476.

160 *E.g., Warren v. Chesapeake Exploration, L.L.C.*, 759 F.3d 413 (5th Cir. 2014); *Yturria v. Kerr-McGee Oil & Gas Offshore, LLC*, 291 Fed. Appx. 626 (5th Cir. 2008) (not designated for publication); *Ramming v. Natural Gas Pipeline Co.*, 390 F.3d 366 (5th Cir. 2004); *French v. Occidental Permian Ltd.*, 440 S.W.3d 1 (Tex. 2014); *Union Pacific Resources Group v. Hankins*, 111 S.W.3d 69 (Tex. 2003); and *Tana Oil and Gas Corp. v. Cernosek*, 188 S.W.3d 354 (Tex. App. – Austin 2005, *pet. denied*).

161 *See Heritage Res.*, 939 S.W.2d at 123; Watt, Ramos and Beckworth, *supra* note 83, at 15.

162 *Heritage Res.*, 939 S.W.2d at 122, citing *Texas Oil & Gas Corp. v. Hagen*, 683 S.W.2d 24, 29 (Tex. App. – Texarkana 1984), *aff'd in part and rev'd in part*, 1984 WL 47847 (Tex. 1987), *jdgmt and op. of Tex. Supp. withdrawn, judgment of Tex. App. set aside, and cause dism'd as moot*, 760 S.W.2d 960 (Tex. 1988).

163 *Heritage Res.*, 939 S.W.2d at 123.

164 *E.g., Yzaguirre v. KCS Res. Inc.*, 53 S.W.3d 368, 374-75 (Tex. 2001); *Occidental Permian Ltd. v. Helen Jones Foundation*, 333 S.W.3d 392, 403-04 (Tex. App. – Amarillo 2011, *pet. denied*).

165 390 F.3d 366 (5th Cir. 2004).

166 *Id.* at 372.

167 *Id.* at 374.

168 760 F.3d 470 (5th Cir. 2014).

169 *Id.* at 471, *aff'g* 2013 WL 874711 at 7 (N.D. Tex. 2013) (*mem. op.*).

170 440 S.W.3d 1 (Tex. 2014).

171 *Id.* at 3-4.

172 *See* Watt, Ramos and Beckworth, *supra* note 83, at 15-16.

173 *Heritage Res.*, 939 S.W.2d at 122, *citing Texas Oil & Gas Corp. v. Hagen,* 683 S.W.2d 24, 29 (Tex. App. – Texarkana 1984), *aff'd in part and rev'd in part*, 1987 WL 47847 (Tex. 1987), *jdgmt and op. of Tex. Sup. withdrawn, jdgmt of Tex. App. set aside, and cause dism'd as moot*, 760 S.W.2d 960 (Tex. 1988). Justice Owen's concurring opinion describes "the so-called net-back approach" to determining market value at the well as establishing "the prevailing market price at a given point and back[ing] out the necessary, reasonable costs between that point and the wellhead." *Heritage Res.*, 939 S.W.2d at 130 (Owen, J., concurring).

174 *See* Watt, *supra* note 17, at 26-27; Watt, Ramos and Beckworth, *supra* note 83, at 15.

175 *E.g., Ashland Oil, Inc. v. Phillips Petroleum Co.*, 554 F.2d 381, 387 (10th Cir. 1977), *on remand*, 463 F.Supp. 619 (N.D. Okla. 1978), *aff'd in part, rev'd in part*, 607 F.2d 355 (10th Cir. 1979), *cert. denied,* 446 U.S. 936 (1980) ("Under this method, a point was selected where there can be determined an established price and the costs of processing or transportation were deducted to move back to the place where the value must be established.").

176 *See* Watt, *supra* note 17, at 27.

177 Lewis Carroll, Through The Looking Glass, And What Alice Found There (McMillan 1871).

178 *Piney Woods Country Life School v. Shell Oil Co.*, 726 F.2d 225, 240 (5th Cir. 1984), *cert. denied*, 471 U.S. 1005 (1985) ("The next best method is to examine sales of sweet gas and sulfur, to determine the market value of the products resulting from processing . . . Processing costs may then be deducted as an indirect means of determining what a buyer would have paid for the sour gas at the wellhead.").

179 *E.g., Potts v. Chesapeake Exploration, L.L.C.*, 760 F.3d 470 (5th Cir. 2014); *Ramming v. Natural Gas Pipeline Co.,* 390 F.3d 366 (5th Cir. 2004); *French v. Occidental Permian Ltd.*, 440 S.W.3d 1 (Tex. 2014).

180 *Potts*, 760 F.3d at 471.

181 *Id.* at 471-72.

182 *Id.* at 472.

183 *Id.* at 475.

184 As stated by the Texas Supreme Court, "If the parties intended royalties to be calculated on the amount realized standard, they could and should have used *only* a 'proceeds-type' clause. . . . . The parties did not use 'market value' and 'amount realized' interchangeably and we reject Exxon's assertion that the parties intended 'market value' to have essentially the same meaning as 'amount realized.'" *Exxon Corp. v. Middleton*, 613 S.W.2d 240, 245 (Tex. 1981). *Accord, Yzaguirre v. KCS Res., Inc.*, 53 S.W.3d 368, 373 (Tex. 2001); *Amoco Prod. Co. v. First Baptist Church*, 611 S.W.2d 610 (Tex. 1980); *Texas Oil & Gas Corp. v. Vela*, 429 S.W.2d 866, 872 (Tex. 1968).

185 *See, e.g., Piney Woods*, 726 F.2d at 240.

186 *See* Watt, *supra*, note 17, at 30-31. In support of this argument, the commentator cites language from the Texas Supreme Court's opinion in *Phillips Petroleum Co. v. Yarbrough*, 405 S.W.3d 70, 78 (Tex. 2013), to the effect that , "A duty to market is implied in leases that base royalty calculations on the price received by the lessee for the gas."

187 *See* notes 173 through 184 and accompanying text, supra.

188 *Heritage Res.,* 895 S.W.2d 833, 836-37 (Tex. App. – El Paso 1995), *rev'd*, 939 S.W.2d 118 (Tex. 1996).

189 *See Heritage Res.*, 939 S.W.2d at 132 (Gonzalez, J., dissenting). Interestingly, in *Judice v. Mewbourne Oil Co.*, 939 S.W.2d 133 (Tex. 1996), decided on the same day as *Heritage Resources*, the Texas Supreme Court found such a patent ambiguity in the phrase "gross proceeds realized at the well" as used in a division order. Stating that the term "gross proceeds" means that royalty is to be calculated by reference to the gross price received by the lessee, while the phrase "at the well" contemplates the deduction of post-production costs in the calculation of royalty, *id.* at 136, the court concluded that, based on the extrinsic evidence presented at trial, the parties had intended royalty to be calculated based upon the price received by the lessee without deduction for compression charges. *Id.* at 136-37.

190 *E.g., Potts v. Chesapeake Exploration, L.L.C.,* 760 F.3d 470 (5th Cir. 2014); *Ramming v. Natural Gas Pipeline Co.*, 390 F.3d 366 (5th Cir. 2004); *French v. Occidental Permian Ltd.*, 440 S.W.3d 1 (Tex. 2014).

191 *Warren v. Chesapeake Exploration, L.L.C.*, 759 F.3d 413 (5th Cir. 2014); *Yturria v. Kerr-McGee Oil Gas Onshore, LLC*, 291 Fed. Appx. 626 (5th Cir. 2008) (not designated for publication); *Chesapeake Exploration, L.L.C. v. Hyder*, 427 S.W.3d 472 (Tex. App. – San Antonio 1996, *pet. denied*); *Occidental Permian Ltd. v. Helen Jones Foundation*, 333 S.W.3d 392 (Tex. App. – Amarillo 2011, *pet. denied*); *Tana Oil and Gas Corp. v. Cernosek*, 188 S.W.3d 354 (Tex. App – Austin 2005, *pet. denied*).

192 *E.g., French v. Occidental Permian Ltd.*, 440 S.W.3d 1 (Tex. 2014); *Cartwright v. Cologne Production Co.*, 182 S.W.3d 438 (Tex. App. – Corpus Christi 2006 *pet. denied*); *Neimeyer v. Tana Oil and Gas Corp.*, 39 S.W.3d 380 (Tex. App. – Austin 2001, *pet. denied*).

193 *Heritage Res.*, 939 S.W.2d at 131 (Owen, J., concurring).
194 *Potts v. Chesapeake Exploration, L.L.C.*, 760 F.3d 470 (5th Cir. 2014).
195 *Id.* at 471-72.
196 *Id.* at 473-74.
197 *Id.* at 475.
198 759 F.3d 413 (5th Cir. 2014).
199 *Id.* at 416.
200 *Id.* at 418-19.
201 427 S.W.3d 472 (Tex. App. – San Antonio 2014, *pet. granted*).
202 *Id.* at 476.
203 *Id.* at 477.
204 *Id.* at 475. *See* note 180 and accompanying text, supra.
205 *Hyder*, 427 S.W.3d at 476.
205 *Id.* at 477.
207 *Id.*
208 *Id.* at 477-78. A similar result based on differently worded royalty provisions was reached in *Yturria v. Kerr-McGee Oil Gas Onshore, LLC*, 291 Fed. Appx. 626 (5th Cir. 2008) (not designated for publication).
209 *See* Watt, *supra* note 17, at 12.
210 *E.g., J.M. Huber Corp. v. Denman*, 367 F.2d 104, 110 (5th Cir. 1966); *Pan American Petroleum Corp. v. Long*, 340 F.2d 211, 223 (5th Cir. 1964); *Phillips Petroleum Co. v. Williams*, 158 F.2d 723, 727 (5th Cir. 1947); *Chicago Corp. v. Wall*, 156 Tex. 217, 293 S.W.2d 844, 847 (Tex. 1956);
211 156 Tex. 217, 293 S.W.2d 844 (1956).
212 *Id.* at 846-47.
213 559 S.W.2d 410 (Tex. Civ. App. – El Paso 1977, *writ ref'd n.r.e.*).
214 *Id.* at 412.
215 *Id.* at 413.
216 *Id.* at 416-17.
217 300 F.Supp. 119 (D.C. Okla. 1969), *aff'd*, 421 F.2d 236 (10th Cir. 1970).
218 367 F.2d 104 (5th Cir. 1966).
229 158 F.2d 723 (5th Cir. 1946).
220 *Wall*, 559 S.W.2d at 416-17.
221 *Exxon Corp. v. Middleton*, 613 S.W.2d 240, 249 (Tex. 1981).
222 *Id.* at 242, 249. *See* text accompanying note 62, *supra*.
223 *Middleton*, 613 S.W.2d at 249.
224 *Middleton*, 571 S.W.2d 349, 364 (Tex. Civ. App. – Houston [14th Dist.] 1978), *rev'd in part, rev'd and remanded in part*, 613 S.W.2d 240 (Tex. 1981).
225 *Middleton*, 613 S.W.2d at 250.
226 *Middleton*, 571 S.W.2d at 364.
227 *Id.* at 365.
228 *Middleton*, 613 S.W.2d at 250-51.
229 *Id.* at 250.
230 158 F.2d 723, 727 (5th Cir. 1946).
231 *Middleton*, 613 S.W.2d at 250.
232 754 S.W.2d 104, 107 (Tex. 1987).
233 705 S.W.2d 690, 692-93 (Tex. 1986).
234 *Id.* at 692.
235 *Id.*
236 *Heritage Res., Inc. v. NationsBank*, 895 S.W.2d 833 (Tex. App. – El Paso 1995), *rev'd*, 939 S.W.2d 118 (Tex. 1996).
237 *Heritage Res.*, 895 S.W.2d at 835, 838.
238 *Id.* at 839.
239 *Id.*
240 *Heritage Res.*, 939 S.W.2d at 123.
241 *Id.* at 123-24.
242 *Id.* A similar result was reached in a pre-*Middleton* case, *Stanolind Oil & Gas Co. v. Terrell*, 183 S.W. 2d 743 (Tex. Civ. App.-Galveston 1944, *writ ref'd*) (division orders prepared by lessee held not to be binding, and lessee to have been unjustly enriched, when the division orders provided for the deduction of gross production taxes from the lessor's bonus, notwithstanding an expressed lease provision to the contrary).
243 *Heritage Res.*, 939 S.W.2d 133 (Tex. 1996).
244 *Id.* at 135.
245 *Id.* at 136.
246 *Id.* at 135.
247 Acts 1991, 72nd Leg. Ch. 650, §4 (eff. Aug. 26, 1991).
248 Tex. Nat. Res. Code Ann. §91.402(c)(1) (Vernon 2014).
249 *Id.* at §91.401(3).
250 *Id.* at §91.402(g).
251 *Id.* at §91.402(c)(2).
252 *Id.* at §91.402(h).
253 *Id.* at §91.402(i).
254 *Id.* at §91.402(i).
255 In *Yzaguirre v. KCS Res., Inc.*, 53 S.W.3d 368 (Tex. 2001), the plaintiffs apparently cited Section 91.402(i) of the Texas Natural Resources Code in support of their argument that royalty should be paid on the basis of the proceeds from the Tennessee Contract. In a footnote, the Texas Supreme Court stated, "The Royalty Owners point out that the statute is consistent with their argument, but they do not argue that it controls our analysis of their 1973 lease." *Yzaguirre*, 53 S.W.3d at 373 n.3.
256 *E.g.*, 1 Smith & Weaver, *supra* note 148, §4.6.E at 195-2; Peter E. Hosey, *Follow the Money!—Oil and Gas Leases and Division Orders*, 23D Ann. Adv. Oil, Gas & Energy Res. L. Course, St. Bar of Tex., Ch. 8, at 12 (2005).
257 *Hillard v. Stephens*, 637 S.W.2d 581 (Ark. 1982).
258 *See* Hosey, *supra* note 256, at 12, 14.
269 *See* notes 188 through 209 and accompanying text, *supra*.
260 *Chesapeake Exploration, L.L.C. v. Hyder*, 427 S.W.3d 472 (Tex. App. – San Antonio 2014, *pet. granted*).

CHAPTER 15

Getty Oil Company, Petitioner, v. John H. Jones, Respondent.

COMMENTARY

by Ernest V. "Ernie" Bruchez

470 S.W.2d 618

1971

Getty Oil Company, Petitioner,
v.
John H. Jones, Respondent.

470 S.W.2d 618

1971

Clyde E. Willbern and Cloy D. Monzingo, Houston, Turpin, Smith, Dyer, Hardie & Harman, Irby L. Dyer, Midland, for petitioner.

Cayton, Gresham & Fulbright, Karl Cayton and William E. Fulbright, Lamesa, for respondent.

STEAKLEY, Justice.

John H. Jones, respondent, the surface owner of a tract of land in Gaines County, Texas, sued for an injunction to restrain Getty Oil Company, petitioner, an oil and gas lessee, from using vertical space for pumping units that prevent the use by him of an automatic irrigation sprinkler system, and for damages. Upon trial, the jury ***620** found that it was not reasonably necessary for Getty to install pumps that prevented the operation of the irrigation system; and that by doing so Getty decreased the market value of the land $117,475, and decreased the value of the use of the land from the time of erection of the pumps until the trial by $19,000. The trial court granted Getty's Motion for Judgment Non Obstante Veredicto on the ground there was no evidence that Getty used more lateral surface than reasonably necessary. Upon appeal, the court of civil appeals reversed the judgment of the trial court, holding that vertical as well as lateral space was restricted to that which is reasonably necessary. The court remanded the case, however, on the further holding that the trial court had erroneously instructed the jury. One Justice dissented. 458 S.W.2d 93. Both parties have filed applications for writ of error. We affirm the judgment of the court of civil appeals.

In 1955 Jones purchased the 635 acre tract of land in question, which was subject to prior mineral leases in which he acquired no interest. Getty holds an oil, gas and mineral lease covering 120 acres in the west half of the tract; Amerada Petroleum Corporation holds a similar lease covering the remainder of the western half of the tract. The lease for the eastern half of the tract is held by Adobe Oil Company.

Jones has drilled seven irrigation wells since 1955, five of which are used to irrigate this tract of land. Prior to 1963, he used hand-moved, and later power roll, irrigation equipment to irrigate the tract. In 1963 he installed a self-propelled sprinkler irrigation system known as the 'Valley System.' This system consists of 1,300 feet of pipe supported at a height of seven feet above the ground by a series of steel towers which rotate in a clockwise direction around a pivot point. The system can negotiate most obstacles which are less than seven feet in height. The pivot points are connected by underground pipes to the irrigation wells. Labor is required only to move the system from one pivot point to another. There are six pivot points which provide for irrigation of the entire tract except for a few corner areas. At the time Jones installed the system Getty had one producing oil well in the northwest corner of the tract. This well had a beam-type pumping unit considerably over seven feet in height; however, the unit was outside the circumference of the closest pivot point and did not interfere with operation of the sprinkler system.

In December of 1967 Getty drilled two additional wells on its 120 acres which produced but would not flow. Getty installed two beam-type pumping units, one of which is seventeen feet high at the top of its upstroke, and the other thirty-four feet high. Because of this height, the pumps preclude the use of four pivot points of Jones' irrigation system with a consequent depreciation in the value of the land because of the reduction in its production potential. Getty also has battery tanks placed on the land that are outside the circumference of the irrigation system and do not interfere with it.

Prior to the time Getty developed its two new wells, Adobe had drilled four wells on the eastern half of the Jones tract and had installed beam-type pumping units on each of the wells. Two of these wells were outside the circumference of the closest pivot points of the sprinkler system; the others would have interfered with the system and were placed in concrete cellars to provide clearance. In addition, the cellars were placed so that the support towers of the sprinkler system would pass around them. In its portion to [SIC] the tract Amerada also has two wells within the circumference of the irrigation system but both utilize hydraulic pumping units which are less than seven feet in height at the well head and hence do not interfere with the irrigation system. The power unit for these hydraulic pumps is also located so as not to interfere with the system.

The oil and gas lease grants Getty the land 'for the purpose of investigating, exploring, prospecting, drilling and mining for and producing oil, gas and all other minerals, laying pipe lines, building roads, tanks, power stations, telephone lines, houses for its employees, and other structures thereon to produce, save, take care of, treat, transport, and own said products.' The lease obligates the lessee to bury all pipe lines below ordinary plow depth when required by the lessor. The lease contains no specific provision concerning the vertical usage of the land.

Jones does not charge Getty with negligence nor deny Getty's right to determine the location of its wells and to install some type of pumping equipment when necessary for production. His position is that under the facts and circumstances it was not reasonably necessary for Getty to install pumping units in the manner which denies him the use of his irrigation equipment.

Getty's principal contention is that it has a right to exclusive use of the superadjacent airspace above the limited surface area occupied by the pumps and that only the lateral surface of the land should be subject to the established rule of reasonably necessary surface usage. We disagree. It has long been recognized that ownership of real property includes not only the surface but also that which lies beneath and above the surface. The use of land extends to the use of the adjacent air. See United States v. Causby, 328 U.S. 256, 66 S.Ct. 1062, 90 L.Ed. 1206 (1946); Broughton v. Humble Oil & Refining Co., 105 S.W.2d 480 (Tex.Civ.App.—El Paso 1937, writ ref'd); Schronk v. Gilliam, 380 S.W.2d 743 (Tex.Civ.App.—Waco 1964, no writ). Although the earlier cases were generally limited to a consideration of the lateral surface, we held in Brown v. Lundell, 162 Tex. 84, 344 S.W.2d 863 (1961), that the rule of liability of the mineral lessee for negligently and unnecessarily damaging the surface estate includes the subsurface. This decision implicitly recognized that there are vertical as well as lateral boundaries to the use of the surface estate by the oil and gas lessee. We now hold explicitly that the reasonably necessary limitation extends to the superadjacent airspace as well as to the lateral surface and subsurface of the land.

Getty further says that if it has acted in a reasonable manner in accomplishing the purposes of the oil and gas lease, its right to so use the surface and the air above is absolute, and that the consequences to the owner of the surface estate are of no legal effect. The expert witnesses agreed that the beam-type pumping units used by Getty were more economical than the hydraulic pumping units; and there was no evidence of any intrinsic value to Getty from the extra expense of constructing below-surface cellars to house the beam-type units. So, Getty argues that their placement of the beam-type pumping units on the surface was authorized by the lease as a matter of law. The question to be resolved, then, is whether evidence may be entertained to show the effect of Getty's manner of surface use upon the use of the surface by Jones, together with the nature of alternatives available to Getty, in resolving the issue of reasonable necessity.

It is well settled that the oil and gas estate is the dominant estate in the sense that use of as much of the premises as is reasonably necessary to produce and remove the minerals is held to be impliedly authorized by the lease; but that the rights implied in favor of the mineral estate are to be exercised with due regard for the rights of the owner of the servient estate. Humble Oil & Refining Co. v. Williams, 420 S.W.2d 133 (Tex.Sup. 1967); General Crude Oil Co. v. Aiken, 162 Tex. 104, 344 S.W.2d 668 (1961); Brown v. Lundell, 162 Tex. 84, 344 S.W.2d 863 (1961); see Keeton & Jones, Tort Liability and the Oil and Gas Industry, 35 Texas L.Rev. 1 (1956); Comment, Land Uses Permitted an Oil and Gas Lessee, 37 Texas L.Rev. 889 (1959); Lambert, Surface Rights of the Oil and Gas Lessee, 11 Okl.L.Rev. 373 (1958); Davis, Selected Problems Regarding Lessee's Rights and Obligations to the Surface Owner, 8 Rocky Mt.Min.L.Inst. 315 (1963). In another context we recently gave recognition to the surface soil as a natural resource in Acker v. Guinn, 464 S.W.2d 348 (Tex.Sup.1971): '(the mineral estate) owner is entitled to make reasonable use of the surface for the production of his minerals. It is not ordinarily contemplated, however that the utility of the surface for agricultural * * * purposes will be destroyed or substantially impaired.' The due regard concept defines more fully what is to be considered in the determination of whether a surface use by the lessee is reasonably necessary. There may be only one manner of use of the surface whereby the minerals can be produced. The lessee has the right to pursue this use, regardless of surface damage. Kenny v. Texas Gulf Sulphur Co., 351 S.W.2d 612 (Tex.Civ.App.—Waco 1961, writ ref'd). And there may be necessitous temporary use governed by the same principle. But under the circumstances indicated here; i.e., where there is an existing use by the surface owner which would otherwise be precluded or impaired, and where under the established practices in the industry there are alternatives available to the lessee whereby the minerals can be recovered, the rules of reasonable usage of the surface may require the adoption of an alternative by the lessee.

The only evidence regarding reasonable means of irrigating this land is found in the testimony of witnesses presented by Jones. It was their testimony that a critical shortage of labor available to farms in the area necessitates the use of automatic sprinkling equipment in irrigating the land. Indeed, Jones testified that the decreasing availability of labor was the controlling factor in his installation of the self-propelled sprinkler system in 1963. Getty sought by cross examination of the witnesses to establish that manual irrigation would suffice, or that a reversible automatic sprinkler would be an adequate alternative for Jones; all, however, rejected manual irrigation as a realistic alternative because of the labor shortage. Neither did the witnesses consider the reversible system a suitable substitute since it would require supervision night and day to avoid collision with the pumps; and that, even if supervisory labor is available, loss of a day's watering would result from moving the system to its proper position by the reversal procedures.

Although disputed by Getty, there was evidence to show that it had reasonable alternatives for obtaining its oil. A petroleum engineer presented by Jones testified that the construction of cellars adequate for the two pumping units required by Getty would have cost less than $12,000 when the pumps were initially installed, and that natural air circulation would alleviate the danger of hydrogen sulfide gas collecting in the cellars. He further testified that installation of large hydraulic pumps would have initially cost less than $5,000 more than the present pumps and would have annual operations costing from $350 to $1,000 more per year. Another witness for Jones was a contract pumper for Adobe who was currently operating two beam-type pumps in cellars, together with twenty-five beam-type pumps on the surface. He testified that less maintenance was necessary on the units in the cellars than on the ones on the surface and that there was less leakage of hydrogen sulfide gas; he also testified that the prevailing winds ventilated the cellars.

The record thus indicates that the irrigation system currently in use affords Jones the most advantageous, and perhaps the only reasonable means of developing the surface for agricultural purposes. It is also indicated that there is available to Getty the two types of pumping installations—the beam-type pumps in cellars or the hydraulic pumps on the surface—which are reasonable alternatives to its present use of the surface; and that Getty's use of an alternative method of producing its wells would serve the public policy of developing our mineral resources while, at the same time, permitting the utilization of the surface for productive agricultural uses. Under such circumstances the right of the surface owner to an accommodation between the two estates may be shown, dependent, of course, upon the state of the evidence and the findings of the trier of the facts. Here, the trial court submitted the following special issue and accompanying instruction:

'Do you find from a preponderance of the evidence that Getty Oil Company's erection of the pumping units in question at its Numbers One and Two Wells at such excess in height so that Plaintiff's sprinkler system will not pass over the same constituted a use of the surface of the land in question in a manner which is not reasonably necessary?

'In answering the foregoing Special Issue, you are instructed that a determination of whether the erection of such pumping units by Getty Oil Company constitutes a use of the surface of the land in question in a manner which is not reasonably necessary involves weighing the degree of harm or inconvenience, if any, such pumping units cause to John H. Jones against the utility, if any, of such pumping units to Getty Oil Company and the suitability of other measures, if any, which would substantially serve the purpose of such pumping units to Getty Oil Company at less or no inconvenience or harm, if any, to John H. Jones.'

We agree with the court of civil appeals that inclusion of the phrase 'at such excess in height' in the issue was erroneous as a comment upon the weight of the evidence. Additionally, and as also recognized by the court of civil appeals, the accompanying instruction erroneously calls for a weighing of harm or inconvenience to Jones against the considerations pertaining to Getty. This is not the proper test, particularly in the suggestion that inconvenience to Jones may be a controlling element. There must be a determination that under all the circumstances the use of the surface by Getty in the manner under attack is not reasonably necessary. The burden of this proof is upon Jones, the surface owner. Cf. Humble Oil & Refining Co. v. Williams, 420 S.W.2d 133 (Tex.Sup.1967). Jones sought to discharge this burden by showing that the use which Getty is making of the surface is not reasonably necessary because of non-interfering and reasonable ways and means of producing the minerals that are available to Getty, the use of which will obviate the abandonment by Jones of his existing use of the surface, and that the alternatives available to Jones would be impractical and unreasonable under all the conditions. These are the elements to be considered by the trier of facts and the jury should be so instructed in resolving the issue of the reasonable necessity of the surface use by Getty, the mineral lessee.

We further hold, as urged by Getty, that in [SIC] event it is ruled that Getty is making an unreasonable surface use, Getty will have the right to install non-interfering pumping units; and in such event Getty will not be liable in damages beyond the decrease in the value of the use of the land from the time the interfering pumps were installed to the time of their removal.

The judgment of the court of civil appeals is affirmed.

McGEE, Justice (dissenting).

I respectfully dissent.

The mineral lease under which Getty claims is dated January 15, 1948. Jones purchased the 635 acres in question in 1955, long after the execution of the lease. At the time of Jones' purchase of the surface, there was a well equipped with a rod and beam pumping unit, a tank battery and heater treater on the land. After his purchase, Jones, a cotton farmer, drilled seven water wells for the irrigation of his crops. Initially, between 1956 and 1963, Jones irrigated the land with hand-moved equipment, then later in the same period with power-moved equipment. Still later, in 1965, he installed a self-propelled irrigation system consisting of 1300 feet of pipe mounted seven feet above the ground which rotate automatically from pivot points. The only labor thus involved is the moving of the unit from one pivot point to another.

In January, 1968, Getty completed two more producing wells on the land, both requiring pumping units. One of the units extends seventeen feet above the ground and the other extends thirty-four feet above the ground (at the top of the upstroke of the beam). These pumping units prevent the operation of Jones' Valley Irrigation System.

Jones does not charge Getty with negligence or contest Getty's right to determine the location of its oil wells or its right to install some type of pumping equipment. At the time the first well was drilled and a pumping unit installed, there was no question that Getty's action in so doing was authorized under the terms of the lease. Jones bought this surface with full knowledge of the lease and the presence of the original pumping unit and the possibility of the drilling of additional wells which might also require pumping units. Now, by changing the nature of his surface operations, Jones seeks to alter the terms of the prior mineral lease and to impose additional burdens on the oil and gas lessee which are not imposed by the original oil and gas lease.

It is fundamental that by the oil and gas lease, Getty obtained the dominant estate. Getty has the right to the use of as much of the premises as is reasonably necessary to comply with the terms of the lease and to effectuate its purposes. Humble Oil & Refining Co. v. Williams, 420 S.W.2d 133 (Tex.Sup.1967); Brown v. Lundell, 162 Tex. 84, 344 S.W.2d 863 (1961); Warren Petroleum Corp. v. Monzingo, 157 Tex. 479, 304 S.W.2d 362, 65 A.L.R.2d 1352 (1957); Warren Petroleum Corp. v. Martin, 153 Tex. 465, 271 S.W.2d 410 (1954). There is no contention by Jones in this case that Getty is 'using more land than necessary' to effectuate the purposes of the lease.

There is no express provision in the lease requiring that pumping units or other structures be placed in cellars beneath the top of the ground. Indeed, the lease specifically and expressly provides to the contrary. The oil, gas and mineral lease here involved is as follows:

> '* * * grants, leases and lets, exclusively unto lessee the following described land in Gaines County, Texas: (describing W/2 Sec. 4, less 5 acres) and any and all lands or rights and interests in land owned or claimed by lessor adjacent or continuous to the land above described.'

The foregoing grant of land is modified only by a purpose clause as follows:

> '* * * for the purpose of investigating, exploring, prospecting, drilling and mining for and

> producing oil, gas, and all other minerals, laying pipe lines, building roads, tanks, power stations, telephone lines, houses for its employees and other structures thereon to produce, save, take care of, treat, transport and own said products. * * *'

The lease deals expressly with the question of the horizontal and vertical locations of Getty's equipment and installations, as follows:

> '* * * when required by Lessor, Lessee will bury all pipelines below ordinary plow depth, and no well shall be drilled within two hundred (200) feet of any residence or barn now on said land without Lessor's consent.'

This case is simple. Getty claims the right to place pumping units on the top of its well sites to a height necessary to effectuate the purposes of its lease. Jones claims a right to come over the top of the well site with his irrigation equipment at a point about seven feet above the ground. The two claimed rights cannot exist simultaneously. By the terms of the lease, Getty has the right to utilize the air space to a height above its well sites as is reasonably necessary to effectuate the purposes of the oil and gas lease.

The only specific provision of the lease requiring the lessee to bury equipment provides that the lessee must bury all pipe lines below ordinary plow depth when required by the lessor. To hold that roads, tanks, pumping units, power stations, telephone lines, houses for employees and other structures are, or might be, required to be buried by this clause or by the purpose clause is to give the lease an unreasonably strained construction. Here the parties dealt expressly with the subject of what, if any, of Getty's equipment must be buried below the surface. These express provisions require application of the principles of law stated in Freeport Sulphur Co. v. American Sulphur Royalty Co., 117 Tex. 439, 6 S.W.2d 1039:

> 'Implied covenants can only be justified upon the ground of legal necessity. Such a necessity may arise out of the terms of the contract or out of the substance thereof. One absolutely necessary to the operation of the contract and the effectuation of its purpose is necessarily implied whether inferable from any particular words or not. It is not enough to say it is necessary to make the contract fair, or that it ought to have contained a stipulation which is not found in it, or that, without such covenant, it would be improvident or unwise or would operate unjustly; for men have the right to make such contracts. Accordingly courts hesitate to read into contracts anything by way of implication, and never do it except upon grounds of obvious necessity.'

Further, it is elementary that an express stipulation upon a matter excludes the possibility of an implication upon the same subject.

This Court should not rewrite the oil and gas lease which was of record when Jones purchased the property. The majority is, in the face of express language, reading into the lease an implied covenant requiring Getty to alter its operations at its expense to accommodate Jones in order that the latter may operate his farm more efficiently whenever and wherever the uses of the surface might change. To read the lease now, 22 years after the document was executed, in this manner is contrary to, rather than in accord with, the intention of the original parties to the agreement. Warren Petroleum Corp. v. Monzingo, Supra. In Monzingo, the Court refused to imply an obligation upon the lessee to restore the surface of the leased premises to its original condition after expiration of a lease: 'Admittedly the lease contained no such provision and one is not to be read into the contract by implication.' 157 Tex. at 481, 304 S.W.2d at 363.

The majority opinion holds that testimony that pumping units could be installed in a cellar 24 feet below the top of the surface raises a fact issue as to how much air space above the top of the surface may be occupied by the oil and gas lessee's equipment which is being used to produce oil from the well. Such a holding would permit a jury to find that pumping units (and other oil and gas development and production equipment) must be located Below the surface of the earth, despite the express provisions of the oil and gas lease and the holdings of our courts, thus depriving the oil and gas lessee of its Right to occupy and use the surface for its oil and gas operations. See Warren Petroleum Corp. v. Martin, Supra; Warren Petroleum Corp. v. Monzingo, Supra; Humble Oil and Refining Co. v. Williams, Supra; Texas Co. v. Daugherty, 107 Tex. 226, 176 S.W. 717 (1915); Gregg v. Caldwell-Guadalupe Pick-Up Stations, 286 S.W. 1083 (Tex.Comm.App.1926, holding approved); Stradley v. Magnolia Petroleum Co., 155 S.W.2d 649 (Tex.Civ.App.—1941, writ ref'd); Trinity Production Co. v. Bennett, 258 S.W.2d 160 (Tex.Civ.App.—1953, writ ref'd n.r.e.); Sinclair Prairie

Oil Co. v. Perry, 191 S.W.2d 484 (Tex.Civ.App.—1945, no writ); Baker v. Davis, 211 S.W.2d 246 (Tex.Civ.App.—1948, no writ); Grimes v. Goodman Drilling Co., 216 S.W. 202 (Tex.Civ.App.—1919, writ dism'd); Placid Oil Co. v. Lee, 243 S.W.2d 860 (Tex.Civ.App.—1951, no writ); Pitzer & West v. Williamson, 159 S.W.2d 181 (Tex.Civ.App.—1942, writ dism'd); Miller v. Crown Central Petroleum Corp., 309 S.W.2d 876 (Tex.Civ.App.—1958, no writ); Parker v. Texas Co., 326 S.W.2d 579 (Tex.Civ.App.—1959, writ ref'd n.r.e.); Cozart v. Crenshaw, 299 S.W. 499 (Tex.Civ.App.—1927, no writ); and Gulf Oil Corp. v. Walton, 317 S.W.2d 260 (Tex.Civ.App.—1958, no writ).

It is difficult to believe that this Court would hold that such testimony should render useless the express grant in the oil and gas [SIC] and disregard prior court decisions. The oil and gas lease becomes a mere letter in the sand, to be washed away by the tidal wave which will be caused by the majority holding. If the majority is correct, then the lease does not mean what it says; the oil and gas lessee has the right to use the surface of the land and place the development and production equipment 'thereon.'

If the irrigation wells on Jones' land go dry and the best surface use becomes grazing cattle on the land, would this Court require the lessee to raise entrenched pumping units to avoid the danger of cattle falling into the hole or to fence around the units? I think not. Jones v. Nafco Oil and Gas, Inc., 380 S.W.2d 570 (Tex.Sup.1964); Warren Petroleum Corp. v. Martin, Supra.

It should also be noted that the Court's opinion allows Jones to have his cake and eat it too. He purchased the land in question from the original lessor subject to an oil and gas lease, and no doubt paid less for the land than if he had bought the full fee title. Now the majority allows him to recover damages because the lessee is using the land in such a way as to interfere with his farming operations. Further, the majority allows him to require the lessee to bury his equipment, thereby giving him a more valuable estate than the one he originally contracted to buy. The majority opinion, in effect, makes the dominant estate the servient estate and the servient estate the dominant estate.

Even if one agrees with the rationale of the majority, there is no reason or authority for requiring the lessee to bear the cost of burying the equipment when the only benefit insures [SIC] to the lessor or surface owner.

The majority says:

'It is well settled that the oil and gas estate is the dominant estate in the sense that use of as much of the premises as is reasonably necessary to produce and remove the minerals is held to be impliedly authorized by the lease; But that the rights implied in favor of the mineral estate are to be exercised with due regard for the rights of the owner of the servient estate.' (Emphasis added.)

We said in Brown v. Lundell, 162 Tex. 84, 344 S.W.2d 863, at 866:

'We further held that since the lessee was the owner of the dominant estate he had the right to use so much of the premises as was reasonably necessary to the exclusion of the lessor in order to carry out the purposes of the mineral grant, But even so that right must be reasonably exercised with due regard to the rights of the owner of the surface.' (Emphasis added.)

We then held, at 867:

'The ultimate issue was whether Brown was Negligent in the way and Manner in which he disposed of the salt water.' (Emphasis added.)

In Humble Oil and Refining Co. v. Williams, 420 S.W.2d 133, at 134 (Tex.Sup.1967), we said:

> 'A person who seeks to recover from the lessee for damages to the surface has the burden of alleging and proving either specific acts of negligence or that more of the land was used by the lessee than was reasonably necessary. Warren Petroleum Corp. v. Monzingo * * *; Robinson Drilling Co. v. Moses, Tex.Civ.App.1953, 256 S.W.2d 650, no writ; Finder v. Stanford, Tex.Civ.App.1961, 351 S.W.2d 289, no writ.'

The majority recognizes that Jones does not charge Getty with negligence nor deny Getty's right to determine the location of its wells and to install some type of pumping equipment when necessary for production. Jones does not contend that Getty is using more surface than necessary.

There is no evidence in this record that the use of the beam-type unit was not reasonably necessary to produce these wells. No one complains about the height of the units from the base to the top. Thus, the vertical space occupied immediately above the well is admittedly not excessive. Jones is contending that Getty, though free from negligence, is liable for damages, and should be forced to bury its equipment at Getty's expense, to permit Jones to employ a method of irrigation that can pass over the well site. This Court is rewriting the oil and gas lease covering the land subsequently purchased by Jones, simply because of inconvenience to Jones.

Prior decisions have contained statements that the oil and gas lessee and the lessor or surface owner must exercise its right with due regard for the rights of the other. None of the decisions allows recovery of damages unless the contract requires payment of damages, Meyer v. Cox, 252 S.W.2d 207 (Tex.Civ.App.—1952, writ ref'd), absent a showing that the owner of the dominant estate has exercised its rights in a negligent manner or has used more land than is reasonably necessary to effectuate the purposes of the lease. Even if the majority is of the opinion that the injunction requiring the lessee to employ a different manner of pumping its wells is justified, There is no basis in law for allowing the surface owner to recover damages. Injunctions have been granted or denied under the 'due regard' theory, but No case has been cited, nor have I been able to find one, which would allow recovery of damages on this theory.

I agree with the dissenting opinion filed in the Court of Civil Appeals, 458 S.W.2d at 97, and would affirm the judgment of the trial court that Getty's use of the land is reasonable as a matter of law.

POPE, J., joins in this dissent.

ON MOTION FOR REHEARING

STEAKLEY, Justice.

There are stated misconstructions of the Court's opinion in Getty's Motion for Rehearing and in some of the supporting briefs by friends of the Court. Some we will notice. We do not hold that a mineral lessee's surface use may be found unreasonable without regard to the surface uses otherwise available to the surface owner. The reasonableness of a surface use by the lessee is to be determined by a consideration of the circumstances of both and, as stated, the surface owner is under the burden of establishing the unreasonableness of the lessee's surface use in this light. The reasonableness of the method and manner of using the dominant mineral estate may be measured by what are usual, customary and reasonable practices in the industry under like circumstances of time, place and servient estate uses. What might be a reasonable use of the surface by the mineral lessee on a bald prairie used only for grazing by the servient surface owner could be unreasonable within an existing residential area of the City of Houston, or on the campus of the University of Texas, or in the middle of an irrigated farm. What we have said is that in determining the issue of whether a particular manner of use of the dominant mineral estate is reasonable or unreasonable, we cannot ignore the condition of the surface itself and the uses then being made by the servient surface owner. When we take judicial notice of the relatively few reported cases of conflict which have arisen between the two estates on the more than 378,000 oil and gas wells that have been drilled, operated and produced in this State, many of them within cities, parks, lakes, and bays and on farms, prison lands and industrial sites, it is indicated that the usual and customary practice of the oil and gas operators of this State is to take due consideration of the uses being made by the servient surface owner. There is evidence of this in the alternative methods employed by Amerada and Adobe under their leases of other portions of the Jones tract. As indicated in the Court's opinion, if the manner of use selected by the dominant mineral lessee is the only reasonable, usual and customary method that is available for developing and producing the minerals on this particular land then the owner of the servient estate must yield. However, if there are other usual, customary and reasonable methods practiced in the industry on similar lands put to similar uses which would not interfere with the existing uses being made by the servient surface owner, it could be unreasonable for the lessee to employ an interfering method or manner of use. These considerations involve questions to be resolved by the trier of the facts.

A single or a multiple issue submission may by [SIC] in order depending on the facts and circumstances in a given situation. The evidence and circumstances here are such that a proper initial inquiry would be whether Jones had reasonable means of developing his land for agricultural purposes other than by use of the sprinkler system in question. If this is found to be the case, Jones must yield to the surface use adopted by Getty since it is not contended that the beam-type pumps installed by Getty are otherwise unreasonable. If such is not found to be the case, Jones is under the burden of a second showing that Getty's present manner and method of use on this land is unreasonable because there are alternative methods used in the industry on this type of property which are available to Getty whereby it can produce its wells without interfering with the existing uses of the servient estate being made by Jones. If this is found to be the case, Getty is bound to convert to a noninterfering use. We have not held, as some have stated, that the issue is a question of inconvenience to the surface owner. To the contrary, the instruction accompanying the special issue submitted to the jury in this case was ruled erroneous because it indicated exactly this.

We also make clear, in response to Jones' Motion for Rehearing, that the ruling of the court of civil appeals with respect to the admissibility of evidence concerning the acts of Adobe in placing its pumps in cellars, with which we agreed, is the law of the case upon retrial.

The Motions for Rehearing are overruled.

Concurring opinion by GREENHILL, J.

WALKER, J., concurs in the Order.

McGEE, J., dissenting.

GREENHILL, Justice (concurring).

The decision in this case can rest on a narrower basis, and I would prefer a narrower holding.

As I understand the record, before Getty installed its beam type pump within the irrigated area of Jones, there were already two different types of pumping units in operation in the immediate area. Adobe Oil Company had placed its pumping units in concrete cellars; and an Adobe pumper testified that they required less maintenance, and leaked less sulphide gas than the surface pumps. Amerada had installed its two wells with non-interfering hydraulic pumps.

So when Getty got ready to put its pumps in the irrigated area, it had three choices, two of which would not have interfered with the existing irrigation system. It chose to use the surface beam type pump and thus chose to exercise what it regarded as its rights whether it injured Jones or not. In my opinion, the above facts and circumstances constitute some evidence to support the jury's finding that Getty's use of the surface was in a manner which was not reasonably necessary.

While the opinion of the court points out the facts that the irrigation system was already in existence when Getty installed its pump, and that others in the area were using different ways to produce the oil, the court's holding is not expressly limited to conditions in existence when Getty's pumps were installed on the irrigated area. Perhaps it would be dictum for the court to say more. But so that there might be no misunderstanding at least as far as I am concerned, I would limit this holding to the conditions at the time the pumps were installed. I would not hold that Getty, or anyone else, would have to move its pumps if they were in place before Jones purchased and installed his irrigation system. For example, if Jones decided to use a mobile irrigation system in the northwest corner where Getty had had its surface pump already operating, my opinion as to how the case should be decided would be different. I would think that the surface owner could not compel the oil and gas lessee to change its operations because the surface owner decided to change his operations. At least that would be a different ball game. In that event, it would seem proper to me for the surface owner to pay for the necessary changes in the oil and gas lessee's operations, or at least to contribute to such expense, depending in part on what benefit there might be to such lessee.

So I regard the holding in this case as being a narrow one, and as applying to a situation where, viewing the record in the light most favorable to the jury's verdict, the oil and gas lessee deliberately chose to install its surface pumps so as to destroy or seriously impair an existing surface irrigation system, where the evidence shows that it had at least two alternative choices which apparently seemed reasonable enough to other oil operators on the same property.

The Accommodation Doctrine:

Commentary on Getty Oil Company v. John H. Jones

by Ernest V. "Ernie" Bruchez

1. Historical Context.

In 1971, Texas had a population of 11 million people. Gaines County, Texas, where this case originates, had 7,500 people. Gaines County abuts New Mexico, on the South Plains of Texas, with surface features that drain to draws, playas, and underground water. Cedar Lake, one of the largest alkali lakes on the Texas plains, is located in Gaines County.

In 1955, Mr. John H. Jones purchased 635 acres of land in Gaines County and farmed. The land was subject to prior mineral leases in which he acquired no interest. Three lessees were operating on Mr. Jones' property. The eastern half of the property was under lease to Adobe Oil Company. Most of the western half of the property was under lease to Amerada Petroleum Corporation with the remaining 120 acres under lease to Getty Oil Company.

Jones had drilled seven irrigation wells since 1955, five of which were used for irrigation of the property. Prior to 1963, Jones used hand-moved and later power roll irrigation equipment to irrigate the property. In 1963, Jones installed a self-propelled sprinkler irrigation system known as the "Valley System." This system comprises 1,300 feet of pipe supported at a height of seven feet above the ground by steel wheels that rotate in a clockwise direction around a pivot point. This gave Jones the ability to irrigate 120 acres at a time. The system can negotiate most obstacles less than seven feet in height. The pivot points are connected by underground pipes to the irrigation wells. Labor is required only to move the system from one pivot point to another. Jones installed six pivot points. This enabled him to irrigate his entire farm except for a few corner areas.

When Jones installed the system Getty had one producing oil well in the northwest corner of the property. This well had a beam-type pumping unit considerably over seven feet in height; however, the unit was outside the circumference of the closest pivot point and did not interfere with the operation of the sprinkler system.

In 1967, Getty drilled two additional wells on its 120-acre lease that produced but would not flow. Getty installed two beam-type pumping units, one of which was seventeen feet high at the top of its upstroke, and the other thirty-four feet high. Because of this height and the location of the pumps, Jones could not use four pivot points of his irrigation system.

Before Getty developed its two new wells, Adobe had drilled four wells on the eastern half of the Jones tract and had installed beam-type pumping units on each of the wells. Two of these wells were outside the circumference of the closest pivot points of the irrigation system; the others would have interfered with the system and were placed in concrete cellars to provide clearance and located so as to not interfere with the rotation of the system. Amerada also had two wells within the circumference of the irrigation system but both utilized hydraulic pumping units that were less than seven feet in height and were likewise located so as to not interfere with the rotation of the irrigation system.

The oil and gas lease granted Getty the land *"for the purpose of investigating, exploring, prospecting, drilling and mining for and producing oil, gas and all other minerals, laying pipe lines, building roads, tanks, power stations, telephone lines, houses for its employees, and other structures thereon to produce, save, take care of, treat, transport, and own said products."* The lease obligated the lessee to bury all pipe lines below ordinary plow depth when required by the lessor. The lease contains no provision concerning the vertical usage of the land.

2. Landmark Status.

Jones did not charge Getty with negligence nor deny Getty's right to determine the location of its wells and to install some type of pumping equipment when necessary. Jones' position was that under the facts and circumstances, it was reasonably necessary for Getty to install pumping units in a manner that permitted him the use of his irrigation equipment.

Getty's principal contention was that it had the right to exclusively use the super-adjacent airspace above the limited surface area occupied by the pumps, and that only the lateral surface of the land should be subject to the established rule of reasonably necessary surface usage. Getty claimed it had the absolute right to use the surface and the air above notwithstanding the consequences to the owner of the surface estate.

Ownership of real property includes not only the surface but also that which lies beneath and above the surface. Using land extends to the use of the adjacent air.[1] Although these earlier cases were limited to a consideration of the lateral surface, the rule of liability of the mineral lessee for negligently and unnecessarily damaging the surface estate includes the subsurface.[2] This decision implicitly recognized there are vertical and lateral boundaries to the use of the surface. The "reasonably necessary" limitation extends to the super-adjacent airspace and to the lateral surface and subsurface of the land.

This is the point on the pencil. What is reasonably necessary surface usage? What does it include? To whom does the limitation apply? At what point in time does it apply? Does it change over time? May evidence be introduced to show the effect of Getty's manner of surface use upon the use of the surface by Jones together with the nature of alternatives available to Getty in resolving the issue of reasonable necessity?

The right of the mineral estate as the dominant estate to use as much of the leased premises as is reasonably necessary to produce and remove the minerals has been held to be impliedly authorized by the lease. But the rights implied in favor of the mineral estate are to be exercised with *due regard* for the rights of the owner of the servient estate.[3] In another context, the surface soil was recognized as a natural resource.[4]

The *due regard* defines more fully what is to be considered in determining whether a surface use by the lessee is reasonably necessary. If only one manner of use was available then the lessee prevails.[5] The record showed that the irrigation system installed by Jones was most advantageous to him and perhaps was the only reasonable means of developing the surface for agricultural purposes. However, the record also showed that Getty had at least two reasonable alternatives to its use of the surface, and that Getty's use of an alternative method of producing its wells would *serve the public policy of developing our mineral resources while, at the same time, permitting the utilization of the surface for productive agricultural uses* [emphasis added].

In applying the test, there must be a determination that under all the circumstances, the use of the surface by Getty in the manner under attack is not reasonably necessary. The burden of this proof is upon Jones, the surface owner.[6]

There is a powerful argument that determining the result to be had as between the surface owner and the lessee is to be based upon a snapshot on the property when the conflict arises. Said another way, the surface owner should not be able to locate or relocate his surface uses that negatively affect a preexisting use by the lessee. Future plans should not be a determinative factor, but in balancing the competing interests, preexisting permits and disclosed objectives should be considered.[7]

This limitation on the Accommodation Doctrine has been further expanded in subsequent cases by the holding that a duty of accommodation exists only if the mineral owner has a reasonable alternative on the premises involved.[8] The mineral owner may use fresh water from the land for secondary recovery operations despite evidence of resulting depletion of the aquifer, since the court held that procuring water from outside the premises was not an alternative the mineral owner could be required to adopt.[9]

3. Effect.

The dominant mineral estate has the right to reasonable use of the surface estate to produce minerals, but this right is to be exercised with due regard for the rights of the surface estate's owner.[10] This concept of "due regard," known as the Accommodation Doctrine, was first articulated in *Getty Oil* and balances the rights of the surface owner and the mineral owner in the use of the surface.[11] Upon remand of *Haupt I*, the court reiterated the elements of the accommodation doctrine established by the Supreme Court:

> [W]here there is an existing use by the surface owner which would otherwise be precluded or impaired, and where under the established practices in the industry there are alternatives available to the [mineral owner] whereby the minerals can be recovered, the rules of reasonable usage of the surface may require the adoption of an alternative by the [mineral owner].[12]

Deactivation of the Accommodation Doctrine may occur when too detailed a lease including explicit negotiations regarding surface usage by the mineral developer is negotiated, or reservations in a deed explicitly restrict operations.[13]

And while the Accommodation Doctrine preserves the mineral owner's absolute right to use the surface if there is only one way to produce the minerals, the core of the Accommodation Doctrine is:

> *Getty recognizes that if there is but one means of surface use by which to produce the minerals, then the mineral owner has the right to pursue that use, regardless of surface damage.* [emphasis added] [citation omitted]. If the mineral owner has reasonable alternative uses of the surface, one of which permits the surface owner to continue to use the surface in the manner intended (especially when there is only one reasonable manner in which the surface may be used) and one of which would preclude that use by the surface owner, the mineral owner *must* use the alternative that allows continued use of the surface by the surface owner.[14]

What, then, is the surface owner's burden of proof?

> [T]he surface owner must show that the particular manner of surface use being challenged is not reasonably necessary to the mineral owner under all circumstances.[15] This may be done by proving that the mineral owner has other reasonable means of production, besides the method under attack that will not interfere with the surface owner's existing use.[16] The surface owner must also show that any alternative uses of the surface, other than the existing use, are impracticable and unreasonable under all the circumstances.[17]All of these elements of the surface owner's burden are fact-sensitive and must be established either conclusively or by appropriate findings in determining the reasonable necessity of the mineral owner's surface use.[18]

The Water District [the surface owner] had to introduce evidence and obtain findings to establish that the plaintiffs [the mineral owners] had alternative means of access and that their use of the surface was not reasonably necessary because an alternative means of access was reasonable.[19]

Haupt stands for the proposition that economic reasonableness is one factor to consider in determining whether an alternative is reasonable. In addition, if there is only one way to produce the minerals, such as vertical drilling, the mineral owner may pursue that use regardless of damage to the surface estate.[20]

4. The Future of the Accommodation Doctrine.

Even though the surface owner's ability to rely upon the "Accommodation Doctrine" has some serious limitations, intuitively it seems that the more developed the surface becomes, the more the Accommodation Doctrine may protect the surface owner.

The Accommodation Doctrine also received a boost from drilling and zoning ordinances that have passed or are being passed by cities in Texas and elsewhere. But the Texas Senate approved House Bill 40, also known as the "Denton Fracking Bill", and it was signed by Governor Greg Abbott on May18, 2015. The bill is immediately effective and amends Section 2., Subchapter C, Chapter 81, Natural Resources Code, by adding Section 81.0523.

H.B. 40, which was passed in response to Denton's voter-approved ban on hydraulic fracturing, does more than attempt to prevent a city from halting fracking, however. It confirms the state's exclusive jurisdiction over oil and gas operations and preempts the regulation of such operations by municipalities.

In effect, the bill limits the power of cities to regulate oil and gas development. It states that "the legislature recognizes that in order to continue (the) prosperity and the efficient management of a key industry in this state, it is in the state's interest to explicitly confirm the authority for regulation of oil and gas activities within the state."

Supporters of the bill say the legislation balances local control and property rights by providing cities with the authority to reasonably regulate surface-level oil and gas activities, while also affirming that regulation of operations and production remains under the exclusive jurisdiction of the state.

Opponents worry that a lack of municipal oversight will affect a city's ability to protect the health, public safety, and property of residents living in areas with heavy drilling activities. They argue these protections are best handled at the local level.

In 1983, the Texas legislature enacted a statute that provides for a procedure for adopting a plat binding upon all affected mineral owners in certain counties and under certain circumstances.[21] A Model Surface Use and Mineral Development Accommodation Act drafted by the National Conference of Commissioners on Uniform State Laws has been circulating among oil and gas practitioners since 1990.

As noted previously, from the origin of the dominant-servient dichotomy, with no damages being owed by the mineral owner for "reasonably necessary" use of the surface, to the current trend toward specific legislation of the split estate relationship, it is clear that the dominance of the mineral estate has eroded to varying degrees in the various jurisdictions. There is little consistency. A Mississippi appeals court affirmed a state law that follows the "reasonably necessary" test only.[22] No surface damages are probable merely from the fact that the mineral owner occupies and causes damage to the surface absent negligence or unreasonable use.

Contrast the Mississippi case with the Texas case[23] where the court uses the apparent Texas standard of mixing the "reasonably necessary" standard and the "due regard/reasonable accommodation" doctrine to determine the rights of the dominant estate. Unfortunately, the court is not clear whether the "reasonably necessary" test (beneficial to the mineral estate) or the Accommodation Doctrine (beneficial to the surface estate) should take precedence.

Most mineral severances have been accomplished with no detailed attention to the relative rights of the surface and mineral owners. The parties have, intentionally or not, allowed the common law or elected officials to supply their respective rights. Essentially, the common law has been good to the mineral owners with the "dominant estate" analysis. When they weigh in, the elected officials and the agencies that operate under them, work to pare back the rights of mineral owners for the benefit of surface owners. All of this developed, and developing, law forms the backdrop for each new negotiation and is a constant point of reference for all negotiations. But the most satisfactory result regarding any given tract of land will likely come from an informed and comprehensive negotiation by the respective owners.

---

1 *United States v. Causby*, 328 U.S. 256 (1946); *Humble Oil & Refining Co.*, (Tex. Civ. App.—El Paso 1937, writ ref'd); *Schronk v. Gilliam*, (Tex. Civ. App.—Waco 1964, no writ).

2 *Brown v. Lundell*, 162 Tex. 84 (1961).

3 *Humble Oil & Ref. Co. v. Williams*, 420 S.W.2d 133 (Tex. 1967); *Gen. Crude Oil Co. v. Aiken*, 162 Tex. 104, (1961).

4 *Acker v. Guinn*, 464 S.W.2d 348, 352 (Tex. 1971) ("A grant or reservation of minerals by the fee owner effects a horizontal severance and the creation of two separate and distinct estates: an estate in the surface and estate in the minerals.").

5 *Kenny v. Texas Gulf Sulphur Co.*, (Tex.Civ.App.—Waco 1961, writ ref'd).

6 *Humble Oil & Ref. Co.*, 420 S.W.2d 133.

7 *Texas Genco, LP v. Valence Operating Co.*, 187 S.W.3d 118 (Tex. App.—Waco 2006, pet. denied).

8 *Sun Oil Co. v. Whitaker*, 483 S.W.2d 808 (Tex. 1972).

9 *Id.*

10 *Getty Oil Co. v. Jones*, 470 S.W.2d 618, 621 (Tex. 1971).

11 *Tarrant County Water Control & Improvement Dist. No. 1 v. Haupt, Inc.*, 854 S.W.2d 909, 911 (Tex. 1993) (Haupt I).

12 *Haupt, Inc. v. Tarrant County Water Control & Improvement Dist. No. 1*, 870 S.W.2d 350, 353 (Tex. App.—Waco 1994, no writ) (Haupt II) (quoting *Getty Oil*, 470 S.W.2d at 622).
13 *Landreth v. Melendez*, 948 S.W.2d 76 (Tex. App.—Amarillo 1997, no writ).
14 *Id.* (quoting Haupt I, 854 S.W.2d at 911-12) (emphasis in original); *see also id.* at 912-13 ("if reasonable alternative drilling methods exist that protect [the surface owner's existing use], then an accommodation by the mineral owners would be required") (emphasis added).
15 *Haupt*, 854 S.W.2d at 911; *Getty Oil*, 470 S.W.2d at 623.
16 *Id.*
17 *Getty Oil*, 470 S.W.2d at 623.
18 *Haupt*, 854 S.W.2d at 911; Getty Oil, 470 S.W.2d at 623.
19 *Haupt II*, 870 S.W.2d at 353; *Texas Genco*, 187 S.W.3d at 121-23 (footnote omitted) (italics in original).
20 *Haupt II*, 870 S.W.2d at 353.
21 Mineral Use of Subdivided Land Act, Tex. Nat. Res. Code Ann. § 92.001 et seq. (West).
22 *EOG Res., Inc. v. Turner*, 908 So.2d 848 (Miss. Ct. App 2005).
23 *Trenolone v. Cook Exploration Co.*, 166 S.W. 3d 498 (Tex. App.—Texarkana 2005).

CHAPTER 16

Amoco Production Company, Petitioners, v. John Alexander et al., Respondents.

COMMENTARY

by Elizabeth N. "Becky" Miller

622 S.W.2d 563

1981

Amoco Production Company, Petitioners,
v.
John Alexander et al., Respondents.

622 S.W.2d 563

1981

McGinnis, Lochridge & Kilgore, Robert C. McGinnis and John W. Stayton, Jr., Austin, Dean J. Capp and James D. Klutz, Houston, for petitioners.

Scott & Douglass, Frank Douglass and Tom Reavley, Jr., Austin, Leland B. Kee, Angleton, for respondents.

CAMPBELL, Justice.

This is an action by royalty owners for damages because of field-wide drainage. The trial court, after a jury verdict, rendered judgment for the Alexanders, lessors, for actual and exemplary damages against Amoco, lessee. The Court of Civil Appeals reformed the trial court's judgment and affirmed the judgment as reformed. 594 S.W.2d 467. We modify the judgment of the Court of Civil Appeals and affirm the judgment as modified.

The Hastings, West Field, in Brazoria County, is a water-drive field. Water and oil are in the same reservoir. Because water is heavier than oil, the water moves to the bottom of the reservoir driving the oil upward. As oil is removed, water moves up to fill the space.

As the oil is produced, the oil-water contact (a measure of the reservoir water level) gradually rises until the wells begin to produce water along with oil. As the wells are produced, the fluid from the wells contains increasingly higher percentages of water. When the wells produce almost all water, the wells are abandoned. The wells are then said to be "watered out" or "flooded out."

The Hastings, West Field, reservoir is not horizontal. It is highest (closer to the surface) in the southeast part. It is lowest in the northwest. Hence, the reservoir dips downward gradually from the southeast to the northwest. Leases on the higher part of the reservoir are called "updip leases" and on the lower, "downdip leases." The Alexanders' leases with Amoco are downdip. Amoco, with 80% of the field production, also has updip leases. Exxon, Amoco's chief competitor in the field, owns leases generally updip from the Alexanders and downdip from the remainder of the Amoco leases.

In water-drive fields, such as the Hastings, West Field, natural underground conditions and production of oil updip work to the disadvantage of downdip leases. As the oil is produced, the oil-water contact rises. The greater the production from updip leases, the sooner the wells on downdip leases will be "watered out" because of the water-drive pushing the oil to the highest part of the reservoir. The downdip leases, therefore, are the first to water out. Moreover, production anywhere in the field will cause the oil-water contact to rise and move from the downdip leases to the updip leases. This is field-wide drainage.

The Alexanders' theory of this lawsuit is that Amoco slowed its production on the Alexander-Amoco downdip leases and increased production on Amoco updip leases causing the Alexander-Amoco downdip leases to "water out" much sooner. Oil not produced from the Alexander leases will eventually be recovered by Amoco as the water pushes the oil to the Amoco updip leases. Their theory of liability is that Amoco owed the Alexanders an obligation to obtain additional oil production from the Alexander leases by drilling additional wells and reworking existing wells to increase production. If Amoco had fulfilled that obligation, additional oil would have been produced from which the Alexanders would have been paid 1/6th royalty. The Amoco updip leases pay 1/8th royalty.

The Alexanders contend they pleaded two legal theories of recovery: (1) in contract, breach of Amoco by its implied obligation to take such steps as a reasonably prudent operator would have taken to protect the Alexander leases from drainage; and (2) in tort; [SIC] for "intentional acts and omissions" undertaken by Amoco "for the purpose of increasing Amoco's production from its updip leases" and the deliberate waste of the Alexanders' royalty oil. The jury found:

(1) Amoco failed to operate the Alexander leases as a reasonably prudent operator.

(2) Amoco operated its leases under an intentional policy of maximizing its profits by producing less oil from the Alexander leases than would have been produced by a reasonably prudent operator, while increasing the drainage of oil from the Alexander leases by Amoco production on other leases.

The jury awarded actual and exemplary damages.

We must determine whether:

(1) Amoco had a duty to protect from field-wide drainage, or a duty not to drain the Alexander downdip leases by its operations updip.

(2) Amoco had a legal duty under the Alexander leases to apply to the Railroad Commission for permits to drill additional wells at irregular locations, to obtain the permits, and drill the wells [SIC]

(3) The trial court erred in admitting testimony that the Railroad Commission would have granted exception permits to allow Amoco to drill additional wells on the Alexander leases.

(4) The Alexanders are entitled to recover exemplary damages.

FIELD-WIDE DRAINAGE

Whether Amoco had a duty to protect the Alexander downdip leases from field-wide drainage, or a duty not to drain the leases by its updip operations has not been considered by the Texas courts. The Court of Civil Appeals held Amoco had a duty to protect the Alexanders from field-wide drainage.

An oil and gas lessee has an implied obligation to protect from local drainage. Local drainage is oil migration from under one lease to the well bore of a producing well on an adjacent lease. Local drainage depends upon production from wells in a specific area in a field. It will begin, increase, or decrease according to production. Local drainage may be in several directions in one field and can be prevented by drilling offset wells. Field-wide drainage in a water-drive field, however, is relatively independent of the location of particular wells. It depends on the water-drive and production from all wells in the field. Protecting from field-wide drainage, therefore, is more difficult than protecting from local drainage.

Amoco urges the Court of Civil Appeals correctly held the drainage in this case was field-wide but the court erred in holding the law imposes an obligation upon Amoco to prevent field-wide drainage, or an obligation not to drain the Alexander leases by its updip operations. Amoco recognizes the obligation to protect from local drainage, but states the Court of Civil Appeals was in error in extending that obligation to require a lessee to protect his lessor from field-wide drainage. Amoco argues this imposes a new implied obligation never previously held to exist.

Has the Court of Civil Appeals imposed a new obligation never previously held to exist? The terms "obligation," "duty," and "covenant" have been used interchangeably in oil and gas cases to describe the performance required of a lessee under an oil and gas lease. Traditionally, matters relating to the development of the lease and the protection of the lessor's interest are not expressly included in the written lease. Since the early history of oil and gas litigation, the courts have held that covenants are implied when an oil and gas lease fails to express the lessee's obligation to develop and to protect the lease. In recent years, implied covenants have been expanded to matters of management of the lease. The words "duty" or "obligation" are best used to express the requirements of a lessee in performance of the implied covenants.

Commentators differ on the classification of implied covenants in oil and gas leases. See R. Hemingway, The Law of Oil and Gas s 8.1 (1971); 5 E. Kuntz, a Treatise on the Law of Oil and Gas s 55.1 (1978); 5 H. Williams &

C. Meyers, Oil and Gas Law s 804 (1980); Walker, The Nature of the Property Interests Created by An Oil and Gas Lease in Texas, 11 Texas L.Rev. 399 (1933). These covenants are usually grouped into categories according to the factual basis of the dispute between the lessor and lessee. 5 H. Williams & C. Meyers, Oil and Gas Law s 804 (1980). However, these categories are specific applications of three broad implied covenants to particular controversies. These broad implied covenants are: (1) to develop the premises, (2) to protect the leasehold, and (3) to manage and administer the lease.

The standard of care in testing the performance of implied covenants by lessees is that of a reasonably prudent operator under the same or similar facts and circumstances. Shell Oil Co. v. Stansbury, 410 S.W.2d 187, 188 (Tex.1966); Texas Pac. Coal & Oil Co. v. Barker, 117 Tex. 418, 431-32, 6 S.W.2d 1031, 1035-36 (1928). The reasonably prudent operator concept is an essential part of every implied covenant. Every claim of improper operation by a lessor against a lessee should be tested against the general duty of the lessee to conduct operations as a reasonably prudent operator in order to carry out the purposes of the oil and gas lease.

Amoco contends the Court of Civil Appeals' holding expands the offset drilling obligation beyond the point of fairness and workability by including within it the obligation to offset field-wide or regional drainage. Field-wide drainage affects all leases in the field; and if the duty exists, each lessee may be required to drill offset wells. The drilling of offset wells increases field-wide drainage and sets off a chain reaction [SIC] the drilling of each additional well would trigger a field-wide obligation to drill more offsets and each drilling would further accelerate the field-wide drainage. Amoco argues, therefore [SIC] the end result of carrying out the obligation would be self-defeating.

Amoco also says that updip leases enjoy a natural advantage over downdip leases. If the natural drainage is to be offset, the only valid way is through field-wide regulation by the Railroad Commission regulating rates of production to protect correlative rights in the field.

The implied covenant to protect against drainage is part of the broad implied covenant to protect the leasehold. The covenant to protect the leasehold extends to what a reasonably prudent operator would do under similar facts and circumstances. "As is true of the other implied duties, it is not easy to separate the duty from the standard of performance. The lessee is required generally to do what a prudent operator would do. Protection of the leased premises against drainage is but a specific application of that general duty." 5 E. Kuntz, a Treatise on the Law of Oil and Gas s 61.3 (1978). The covenant to protect from drainage is not limited to local drainage. It extends to field-wide drainage. Oil lost by field-wide drainage is just as lost as local drainage oil. The methods of safeguarding from the loss may be different and protecting from local drainage may be easier. However, it is no defense for a lessee to say there is no duty to act as a reasonably prudent operator to protect from field-wide drainage.

A lessor is entitled to recover damages from a lessee for field-wide drainage upon proof (1) of substantial drainage of the lessor's land, and (2) that a reasonably prudent operator would have acted to prevent substantial drainage from the lessor's land. In Shell Oil Co. v. Stansbury, supra, this Court held a reasonably prudent operator would have drilled a well on the lessor's land to protect from drainage. However, because of the complexity of the oil and gas industry and changes in technology, the courts cannot list each obligation of a reasonably prudent operator which may arise. The lessee must perform any act which a reasonably prudent operator would perform to protect from substantial drainage.

The duties of a reasonably prudent operator to protect from field-wide drainage may include (1) drilling replacement wells, (2) re-working existing wells, (3) drilling additional wells, (4) seeking field-wide regulatory action, (5) seeking Rule 37 exceptions from the Railroad Commission, (6) seeking voluntary unitization, and (7) seeking other available administrative relief. There is no duty unless such an amount of oil can be recovered to equal the cost of administrative expenses, drilling or re-working and equipping a protection well, producing and marketing the oil, and yield to the lessee a reasonable expectation of profit. Clifton v. Koontz, 160 Tex. 82, 96-97, 325 S.W.2d 684, 695-96 (1959).

The Court of Civil Appeals has not imposed a new obligation upon Amoco. The jury, in finding that Amoco failed to operate the Alexander leases as a reasonably prudent operator, has determined that Amoco failed in its duties under the implied covenants to protect the leasehold.

Amoco argues the Court of Civil Appeals did not consider that Amoco has obligations to all of its lessors in the field. Anything it does to maintain or increase production from updip leases may accelerate the water drive and expose Amoco to liability to downdip lessors. If Amoco fails to maintain or increase updip production, it is exposed to liability from the updip lessors. Amoco argues the Court has placed it between contrary obligations from which there is no escape. The fulfilling of one obligation necessarily causes the breach of the other.

The conflicts of interest of Amoco, as a common lessee, cause us concern. The Alexander leases provided for 1/6th royalty while Amoco's updip leases provided for 1/8th royalty. There is no economic incentive for Amoco to increase production on the Alexander lease because it will eventually recover the Alexander's oil updip. Money invested in the Hastings, West Field, will have a longer productive life if invested updip. The greater the updip production the sooner Amoco's competitor Exxon will water out. Money spent updip will yield greater returns than money spent downdip because of higher daily production. With downdip operators out of production Amoco can produce its upper sands without competition and can begin production from its lower sands where it does not have significant production competition.

These conflicts would not occur if Amoco was not a common lessee (lessee common to downdip and updip lessors). If the Alexanders were the only Amoco lessor, their interests would more nearly coincide. Amoco's interest would be to capture the most oil possible from the Alexander leases before they watered out.

Amoco's responsibilities to other lessors in the same field do not control in this suit. This lawsuit is between the Alexanders and Amoco on the lease agreement between them and the implied covenants attaching to that lease agreement. The reasonably prudent operator standard is not to be reduced to the Alexanders because Amoco has other lessors in the same field. Amoco's status as a common lessee does not affect its liability to the Alexanders.

DUTY TO APPLY FOR ADMINISTRATIVE RELIEF

The Railroad Commission rules in the Hastings, West Field, prohibit the drilling of a well nearer than 660 feet to any other well and nearer than 330 feet to any property line or lease line. The rules allow the Railroad Commission to grant drilling permits as an exception to the spacing regulation. These exceptions are commonly referred to as Rule 37 permits. This rule provides:

> (T)he Commission in order to prevent waste or to prevent the confiscation of property will grant exceptions to permit drilling within shorter distance than above prescribed whenever the Commission shall determine that such exceptions are necessary to prevent waste or to prevent confiscation of property.

The Alexanders contend Amoco should have drilled replacement wells in the extreme updip corner of each lease. The wells would be within 50 feet of the lease line and 200 feet apart. The wells could not be drilled unless the Railroad Commission granted Rule 37 permits. Amoco did not apply for the permits.

The Court of Civil Appeals held that when Amoco determined the leases were watering out, prudent operation demanded drilling replacement wells unless it would be economically unfeasible. If Rule 37 permits were required, Amoco should have applied for them in furtherance of its duty to prudently operate the leases. Because Amoco failed to apply, the Court of Civil Appeals held, the Alexanders were entitled to show the exceptions most likely would have been granted and they suffered damages because of Amoco's failure.

Amoco states the holding of the Court of Civil Appeals amounts to the imposition of an implied covenant obligating a lessee to seek exceptions to regulations limiting the drilling and production of wells. Amoco argues there is no Texas authority for imposing an obligation to seek administrative relief and there is no duty to seek administrative relief.

[12] We disagree with Amoco's argument that there is no duty to seek administrative relief. Amoco owed the Alexanders the duty to do whatever a reasonably prudent operator would do if the Alexanders were its only lessor in the field.

The duty to seek favorable administrative action may be classified under the implied covenants to protect the lease, or to manage and administer the lease. Regardless of the category, the standard of care in testing Amoco's performance is that of a reasonably prudent operator under similar facts and circumstances. Shell Oil Co. v. Stansbury, 410 S.W.2d 187, 188 (Tex.1966); 5 H. Williams & C. Meyers, Oil and Gas Law s 804 (1980).

We do not agree with the Court of Civil Appeals if its holding means that in every case of field-wide drainage the lessee must seek Rule 37 exceptions. There may be facts where the prudent operator would not seek administrative relief. The probability that the Railroad Commission will grant or deny the permit is a consideration to be made by the prudent operator. The jury, from evidence justifying granting or denying the permit, can determine if a reasonably prudent operator would have applied for the permit.

The jury found Amoco failed to operate the Alexander leases as a reasonably prudent operator. Does this finding, based in whole or in part on Amoco's failure to apply for Rule 37 permits, establish liability for failure to drill the replacement wells? If it does not, what remedies do the Alexanders have? They have no rights in the management or operation of the oil leases. Amoco, as operator, could quickly determine when the wells began watering out. Amoco, because of its conflicting interests, had no economic incentive to protect the Alexander leases. The downdip lessors, after their leases have watered out, have no opportunity to capture the oil updip.

It is the failure to act as a reasonably prudent operator that triggers the loss. If the Railroad Commission denies the Rule 37 permits, after a reasonably prudent application, the operator has no liability for not drilling the wells. We hold that an operator, who fails to act as a reasonably prudent operator by not seeking Rule 37 permits, is liable for loss caused by the failure to drill the wells.

TESTIMONY THAT THE RAILROAD COMMISSION WOULD GRANT RULE 37 PERMITS

The Alexanders' two expert witnesses testified, in response to hypothetical questions, that the Railroad Commission would have granted approval to drill the replacement wells. Amoco contends the admission of this evidence is reversible error.

The jury question was whether Amoco operated the leases as a reasonably prudent operator. In answering this question the jury had to determine whether a reasonably prudent operator would have requested Rule 37 permits. The jury was not asked whether the Railroad Commission would have granted them.

There was other evidence on which the jury could base its decision. Amoco knew that: this was a water-drive field and the Alexander leases were downdip; these leases would water out first; the leases began watering out; a 25% increase in field production, allowed by the Railroad Commission, would speed up the watering out of the leases; there was a process by which permits could be granted; drainage was occurring as early as 1972; Amoco's action updip was accelerating the drainage; Amoco could recover the Alexander oil on its updip leases; Amoco had no economic incentive to drill replacement wells on the Alexander leases; the Alexander leases would be the first to require additional replacement wells.

There was evidence that the Railroad Commission granted twenty-two Rule 37 permits to Exxon and Amoco updip in the same fault block section of this field beginning in 1975. The jury could also consider that Amoco, in opposing a 1973 Rule 37 application on the adjacent Pearland lease, represented that the Pearland lease had 2.9 million barrels of oil originally in place. This meant that in 1973 the lease had already produced all of its recoverable oil originally in place. However, in the course of this litigation, Amoco revealed that the calculation of its own reservoir engineers showed that 3.884 million barrels of oil were originally in place under the Pearland lease.

This Court has upheld the admissibility of evidence showing the reasonable probability that zoning restrictions will be lifted. See City of Austin v. Cannizzo, 153 Tex. 324, 333-35, 267 S.W.2d 808, 814-15 (1954). However, we need not decide whether it was error to admit the answers to the hypothetical questions in this case because the answers are cumulative to other evidence presented to the jury. This Court is not of the opinion that such error, if any, amounted to such a denial of Amoco's rights as is reasonably calculated to cause and probably did cause the rendition of an improper judgment. Tex.R.Civ.P. 434, 503.

EXEMPLARY DAMAGES

Amoco argues that exemplary damages are not recoverable because the Alexanders failed to plead and prove a tort allowing recovery of exemplary damages. We agree.

The Alexanders alleged "a breach by Amoco of both its express and implied covenants ... under the lease contracts ... to protect said leases from drainage and to operate said leases as a reasonable and prudent operator" and their "royalty interest under Leases A and B has been wasted and damaged ...."

First, Amoco argues that exemplary damages are not recoverable because a breach of the implied covenant to protect against drainage is an action sounding in contract and not in tort. The rights and duties of the lessor and lessee are determined by the lease and are contractual. The lease constitutes the contract. In the absence of express provisions to the contrary, the lease imposes upon the lessee several implied covenants, including the duty to protect against drainage. Texas Pac. Coal & Oil Co. v. Barker, 117 Tex. 418, 431, 6 S.W.2d 1031, 1035 (1928); see Note, 12 St. Mary's L.J. 600, 601-602 (1980).

[16] In Texas Pac. Coal & Oil Co. v. Stuard, 7 S.W.2d 878, 882 (Tex.Civ.App. Eastland 1928, writ ref'd), the Court of Civil Appeals held that "the implication to develop after drilling the exploratory well is a part of the written contract and is governed by the four-year statute of limitation." In Indian Territory Illuminating Oil Co. v. Rosamond, 190 Okl. 46, 120 P.2d 349, 354 (1941), the Oklahoma Supreme Court held that "the implied covenant to protect against drainage is a part of the written lease as fully as if it had been expressly contained therein..." and applied the statute of limitations relating to actions on written contracts. We hold that the implied covenant to protect against drainage is a part of the lease and is contractual in nature.

Exemplary damages are not allowed for breach of contract. A. L. Carter Lumber Co. v. Saide, 140 Tex. 523, 526, 168 S.W.2d 629, 631 (1943); McDonough v. Zamora, 338 S.W.2d 507, 513 (Tex.Civ.App. San Antonio 1960, writ ref'd n. r. e.). Even if the breach is malicious, intentional or capricious, exemplary damages may not be recovered unless a distinct tort is alleged and proved. City Prods. Corp. v. Berman, 610 S.W.2d 446, 450 (Tex.1980); A. L. Carter Lumber Co. v. Saide, supra. K. W. S. Mfg. Co. v. McMahon, 565 S.W.2d 368, 372 (Tex.Civ.App. Waco 1978, writ ref'd n. r. e.). We hold that a breach of the implied covenant to protect against drainage is an action sounding in contract and will not support recovery of exemplary damages absent proof of an independent tort.

Second, Amoco argues that exemplary damages are not recoverable under a cause of action for "waste." The Alexanders as lessors under the oil and gas leases are not entitled to maintain an action for waste. Waste is defined as "permanent harm to real property, committed by tenants for life or for years, not justified as a reasonable exercise of ownership and enjoyment by the possessory tenant and resulting in a reduction in value of the interest of the reversioner or remainderman." Moore v. Vines, 474 S.W.2d 437, 439 (Tex.1971); 1 American Law of Property s 2.16e (1952).

The common law theory of waste must not be confused with an action for negligent waste or destruction of minerals which may be maintained by a mineral or royalty owner. See Elliff v. Texon Drilling Co., 146 Tex. 575, 583, 210 S.W.2d 558, 563 (1948). The Alexanders owned a 1/6th royalty interest in the leases. A royalty or royalty interest, whether created by grant or reservation or by lease, is an interest in real property and is a fee simple interest in land. Sheffield v. Hogg, 124 Tex. 290, 298, 77 S.W.2d 1021, 1024 (1934).

This is not a waste case. There has been no "waste" as defined in section 85.046(a) of the Texas Natural Resource Code. There has been no negligent waste or destruction as occurred in Elliff, supra. Nor has there been an ultimate loss by a reversionary or remainder interest. The problem is the operation, by a common lessee, of some leases to the detriment of others.

TRIAL OF COMMON LESSEE CASES

The courts that have considered the common lessee problem have considered facts different from this case. In those cases the common lessee was causing the drainage by production on adjacent or adjoining land. The drainage was caused by production independent of water-drive and was local drainage. However, those decisions are analogous because of the common lessee. Professors Williams and Meyers have put these cases in three categories. See 5 H. Williams & C. Meyers, Oil and Gas Law s 824 (1980); Meyers & Williams, Implied Covenants in Oil and Gas Leases: Drainage Caused by the Lessee, 40 Texas L. Rev. 923 (1962). First, there are cases which state the lessee was causing the drainage but place no significance on that fact. See, e. g., Billeaud Planters v. Union Oil Co. of Cal.,

245 F.2d 14, 18-19 (5th Cir. 1957); Gerson v. Anderson-Prichard Prod. Corp., 149 F.2d 444, 445-46 (10th Cir. 1945); Chapman v. Sohio Petroleum Co., 297 S.W.2d 885, 886-87 (Tex.Civ.App. El Paso 1956, writ ref'd n. r. e.). Second, other cases state that the lessee caused the drainage but hold this fact does not alter the ordinary rules of liability for failure to protect from drainage. Hutchins v. Humble Oil & Ref. Co., 161 S.W.2d 571, 573 (Tex.Civ.App. Galveston 1942, writ ref'd w. o. m.); accord, Tide Water Associated Oil Co. v. Stott, 159 F.2d 174, 177 (5th Cir. 1946). Third, there are cases holding the liability of the lessee is increased when the lessee is causing the drainage. See, e. g., Cook v. El Paso Natural Gas Co., 560 F.2d 978, 982-84 (10th Cir. 1977) (reasonable prudent operator rule inapplicable in common lessee case, proof of drainage all that is required); Bush Oil Co. v. Beverly-Lincoln Land Co., 69 Cal.App.2d 246, 158 P.2d 754, 758 (1945) (immaterial whether protection well would be profitable if drainage caused by lessee's affirmative act); Phillips Petroleum Co. v. Millette, 221 Miss. 1, 72 So.2d 176, 183 (Miss.1954) (lessee strictly liable for substantial drainage caused by own affirmative acts).

This Court in Shell Oil Co. v. Stansbury, 410 S.W.2d 187, 188 (Tex.1966), expressly overruled the Hutchins case, supra, and held that an express offset provision does not limit the lessee's obligation to protect from drainage when the lessee is the one causing the drainage. In drainage cases, Texas courts place upon the lessor the burden to prove that substantial drainage has occurred and that an offset well would produce oil or gas in paying quantities. Clifton v. Koontz, supra.

The judgment of the Court of Civil Appeals is modified to prohibit the recovery of exemplary damages and affirmed as modified.

Commentary on Amoco Production Co. v. Alexander

by Elizabeth N. "Becky" Miller

Historical Context:

Amoco Production Co. v. Alexander[1] has long been considered a landmark "implied covenant case." However, long before this case was decided, Texas courts had recognized the existence of implied covenants in every oil and gas lease.[2] The standard by which an operator is judged in his performance of the implied covenants was well recognized to be that of a reasonably prudent operator under the same or similar circumstances.[3] The duty to protect the leasehold from drainage was recognized as a specific application of the general duty of the lessee to act as a reasonably prudent operator,[4] and in *Shell Oil Co. v. Stansbury*[5] the Texas Supreme Court had specifically recognized the implied duty to prevent substantial drainage if a reasonably prudent operator would have done so under the same or similar circumstances.

What appeared to be missing was a clear framework to determine the breadth of duties that could be implied. Commentators differed on their attempts to classify the covenants and, by trying to classify them, were often interpreted as restricting them to specifically stated obligations.[6] In *Amoco v. Alexander* the court stepped into the fray and recognized three broad implied covenants (to develop, to protect, and to manage and administer the estate), but then made it clear each is defined by the standard of care required: to do whatever a reasonably prudent operator would do under the same or similar circumstances. In addition, the court tackled the question of whether, because the duties are implied, they can give rise to tort as well as contract damages.

Facts of the Case:

Amoco v. Alexander was considered a case of first impression by the court because it dealt with whether a lessee has the duty to protect the leasehold from "field-wide drainage" and not just "local drainage." The Alexanders' lease was in the downdip area of an active water-drive reservoir. In a water-drive reservoir, as oil is produced the oil/water contact rises, pushing oil updip and watering out downdip leases. Accordingly, the most efficient location for wells is on the highest part of the reservoir as they will theoretically be able to produce most if not all of the recoverable reserves.

The Alexanders sued Amoco, claiming it had failed to drill or rework wells on their downdip lease in favor of drilling wells at the top of the structure on leases taken from others. The Alexanders' lease called for a 1/6th royalty whereas the updip leases had a 1/8th royalty, making it even more advantageous for Amoco to try to move the oil off the Alexander lease to be recovered elsewhere. The Alexanders sought damages for breach of the implied duty to protect their lease from drainage and sued in tort for intentionally increasing Amoco's production from its updip leases, thereby deliberately wasting or depleting the Alexanders' downdip oil. Amoco challenged whether it had any duty at all to protect from such drainage, that its obligations to its other lessors in the field would make it impossible to protect all its leases from field-wide drainage, and that its obligations to the Alexanders did not include seeking Rule 37 (spacing) exceptions to drill wells in the extreme updip portion of the lease at closer than a regular distance from the lease line. The jury found in the Alexanders' favor and awarded actual and exemplary damages.

On appeal, Amoco argued that field-wide drainage is a different animal from local drainage. If there were a duty to protect against field-wide drainage, an operator could be required to drill offset wells on each tract he owns in the field, irrespective of whether such wells are necessary to recover the reserves. In addition, each new well drilled would hasten the water-drive, accelerating drainage and be self-defeating. Because updip leases have a "natural advantage" over downdip leases, the only valid way to protect the downdip well is through Railroad Commission regulation of production rates to protect correlative rights in the field.

The supreme court defined the issues before it as (1) whether there is an implied duty to protect from field-wide drainage; (2) whether the implied duty includes the obligation to seek Railroad Commission permits to drill wells at irregular locations; and (3) whether breach of an implied covenant gives rise to a claim for exemplary damages.

Holding:

The court held that the implied covenant to protect from drainage is not limited to local drainage. It extends to field-wide drainage as well. Drainage is drainage—oil lost by field-wide drainage is just as lost to the injured lessor as oil lost to local drainage. The mechanics of the loss and the methods to protect from the loss may differ, but not the duty. The standard for recovery under either is the same: lessor is required to prove (1) substantial drainage has occurred, and (2) a reasonably prudent operator would have acted to prevent substantial drainage. More importantly, the court makes clear that because of the complexity of the oil and gas business and the changes in technology that have occurred or may occur, it is impossible for the courts to list each specific obligation of the reasonably prudent operator to protect from drainage that may arise in any circumstance. Instead, the duty to protect cannot be separated from the standard to act as a reasonably prudent operator—to do that which a reasonably prudent operator would do under the same or similar circumstances. The duty to protect from field-wide drainage might include obligations to drill replacement wells, re-work existing wells, drill additional wells, seek field-wide regulatory action, seek Rule 37 exceptions, seek voluntary unitization, or seek other available administrative relief, depending on the facts.

While here the court found there was a duty to seek Rule 37 exceptions, it was not creating a "new duty" as Amoco had argued. Instead, it was a duty defined by the standard of care—evidence had established a reasonably prudent operator under the same or similar circumstances would have sought to obtain Rule 37 exceptions to drill more wells on the Alexander lease. The court further affirmed the duty is owed individually under each lease: Amoco's responsibilities to other lessors in the same field do not control its obligations to these lessors.

Finally, the court held that the Alexanders were not entitled to exemplary damages for breach of an implied covenant. "Breach of the implied covenant to protect against drainage is an action sounding in contract and will not support recovery of exemplary damages absent proof of an independent tort."[7] It does not matter whether the breach is malicious, intentional, or capricious, exemplary damages are not allowed for breach of contract.[8] Furthermore, there was no cause of action for negligent waste or destruction of the minerals giving rise to a claim for waste.[9] There was only drainage of oil from one tract to others, which sounds in contract and not in tort.

<u>Historical Significance</u>:

Amoco v. Alexander has probably become the most commonly cited implied covenant case in Texas jurisprudence. It is the foundation for any discussion of what implied covenants are, how they are defined, and what standard of care is required. By making clear the breadth of the duty owed is defined by the standard of care—that of a reasonably prudent operator under the same or similar circumstances—disputes are no longer argued on the basis of whether a particular duty has ever been recognized before, but whether the facts support the behavior sought. Further, *Amoco v. Alexander* has put to rest the question of whether the reasonably prudent operator standard includes a common-law or tort-like duty giving rise to exemplary damages, or otherwise raises the duty owed by the lessee from contract to something more. The same approach has continued to be taken by subsequent courts, as in *Circle Dot Ranch, Inc. v. Sidwell Oil & Gas, Inc.*,[10] where the court held the implied duty to pool in "good faith" is a contract duty defined by what a reasonably prudent operator would do under the same or similar circumstances.

---

1 622 S.W.2d 563 (Tex. 1981).

2 *Grubb v. McAfee*, 109 Tex. 527, 212 S.W. 464, 465 (1919) (approving lower court holding that the law implies the obligation to exercise reasonable diligence to continue drilling after oil encountered in the first well); *W. T. Waggoner Estate v. Sigler Oil Co.*, 118 Tex. 509, 518, 19 S.W.2d 27, 29 (1929) (when lease fails to define lessee's duty as regards development after discovery of paying production, the law implies the obligation to continue to develop and produce oil or gas with reasonable diligence).

3 *Texas Pac. Coal & Oil Co. v. Barker*, 117 Tex. 418, 431-32, 6 S.W.2d 1031, 1035-36 (1928).

4 5 Eugene Kuntz, A Treatise on the Law of Oil and Gas §61.3 (1991).

5 410 S.W.2d 187 (Tex. 1966).

6 *See* Richard W. Hemingway, The Law of Oil and Gas §8.1 (1971); 5 Eugene Kuntz, A Treatise on the Law of Oil and Gas §55.1 (1991); 5 Howard R. Williams & Charles J. Meyers, Oil and Gas Law §804 (1980), and A. W. Walker, Jr., *The Nature of the Property Interests Created by An Oil and Gas Lease in Texas*, 11 Texas L. Rev. 399 (1933).

7 622 S.W.2d at 571.

8 *A. L. Carter Lumber Co. v. Saide*, 140 Tex. 523, 526, 168 S.W.2d 629, 631 (1943).

9 *See Elliff v. Texon Drilling Co.*, 146 Tex. 575, 582-83, 210 S.W.2d 558, 562-63 (1948).

10 891 S.W.2d 342 (Tex. App.—Amarillo 1995, writ denied).

17

CHAPTER 17

Westland Oil Development Corporation et al., Petitioners, v. Gulf Oil Corporation et al., Respondents.

COMMENTARY

by Arnold J. "Arne" Johnson

637 S.W.2d 903

1982

Westland Oil Development Corporation et al., Petitioners,
v.
Gulf Oil Corporation et al., Respondents.

637 S.W.2d 903

1982

Bullock, Scott & Nesig, Maurice N. Bullock, Midland, Reynolds, Allen, Cook, Pannill & Hooper, William Pannill, Houston, Jack N. Price, Austin, for petitioners.

Stubbeman, McRae, Sealy, Laughlin & Browder, Tom Sealy, W. B. Browder, Jr. and Marc Skeen, Midland, Morgan L. Copeland and Susan R. Sewell, Houston, for respondents.

Opinion

McGEE, Justice.

This case involves the adjudication of the parties' interests in certain oil and gas leases located on six sections of land in Pecos County, Texas. We must determine the effect that a letter agreement, dated November 15, 1966 (hereinafter referred to as "the November 15, 1966, letter agreement"), had upon the respective interests in those leases. The trial court granted summary judgment in favor of Westland Oil Development Corporation and L. C. Kung (hereinafter referred to as "Westland"), petitioners herein and plaintiffs in the trial court, holding that Gulf Oil Corporation and the Superior Oil Company (hereinafter referred to as "Gulf and Superior"), respondents herein and defendants in the trial court, were on notice as a matter of law of the November 15, 1966, letter agreement, and that said agreement was enforceable as to all six sections. The court of appeals reversed the judgment of the trial court and remanded the cause for a determination of the notice issue. 620 S.W.2d 765. We reverse the judgment of the court of appeals and render judgment that Gulf and Superior were on notice of the November 15, 1966, letter agreement as a matter of law, and that the statute of frauds does not prohibit enforcement of said agreement as to three of the six sections under dispute.

Prior to August 4, 1966, Mobil Oil Corporation (hereinafter referred to as "Mobil") owned oil and gas leases covering twenty-nine sections in the Rojo Caballos Field in Pecos County, Texas. The six sections comprising the subject matter of this suit were a part of those twenty-nine sections, and are identified as sections 23, 24, 25 and 26, Block 49, and sections 19 and 30, Block 48. From this point forward, we will refer to the sections by number only and eliminate any corresponding reference to the block number.

On August 4, 1966, Mobil and Westland entered into a farmout agreement (hereinafter referred to as the Mobil/Westland farmout agreement). The leases which were the subject matter of the farmout agreement covered, among others, sections 19, 23 and 24. The agreement provided that at such time as Westland complied with its drilling obligations and completed a producing well, it would be entitled to receive an assignment of one-half of Mobil's interest in those sections. The Mobil farmout obligated Westland to commence a wildcat well by September 1, 1966. Westland sought more time, and Mobil granted an extension of time to December 1, 1966, in a letter dated August 29, 1966.

A Midland partnership, Chambers & Kennedy (hereinafter referred to as "C & K"), became interested in taking over Westland's obligations under the Mobil/Westland farmout agreement. The agreement made to accomplish this was the November 15, 1966, letter agreement. This agreement contains a provision which is the center of the controversy in this case. Under the terms of this agreement, C & K assumed all of the obligations imposed by the Mobil/Westland farmout agreement, agreed to pay Westland $50,000.00 in cash, and assigned to Westland a 1/16 of 8/8 overriding royalty interest on any acreage earned from Mobil, 1/32 of the working interest obtained from Mobil under the farmout agreement, and a production payment of $150,000.00 payable out of the production from the test well.

The November 15, 1966, letter agreement also contained what shall be referred to as an area of mutual interest agreement. This is the controversial provision referred to above. In an area of mutual interest agreement, the parties attempt to describe a geographic area within which they agree to share certain additional leases acquired by any of them in the future. This necessarily contemplates that oil and gas leasehold interests will be conveyed. Therefore, the agreement is in the nature of a contract to convey interests in oil and gas leases.

The area of mutual interest agreement was contained in paragraph 5 of the November 15, 1966, letter agreement and reads as follows:

> 5. If any of the parties hereto, their representatives or *assigns*, acquire any additional leasehold interests affecting any of the lands covered by said farmout agreement, or any additional interest from Mobil Oil Corporation under lands in the area of the farmout acreage, such shall be subject to the terms and provisions of this agreement; provided, however that in no event shall the owners of the working interest under any portion of such acreage be entitled to less than 75% working interest leases.

(emphasis added). It is this covenant or obligation which Westland seeks to enforce against Gulf and Superior.

C & K included several other investors in the farmout well, including Union Texas Petroleum, a division of Allied Chemical Corporation (hereinafter "Union Texas"). The farmout well was spudded on December 1, 1966, and completed on January 23, 1968. The well was marginal but earned the acreage. By assignment dated March 7, 1968, Mobil conveyed to C & K, Union Texas as operator, and the other investors in the well, one-half of its leasehold interests in the farmout block, which included the leases covering sections 19, 23 and 24. This assignment provided that as to all the lands and depths assigned, with one exception, the assignment would be subject to all the provisions of a certain operating agreement dated March 1, 1968. The precise language of that assignment was as follows:

> This Assignment is made without warranty to title, either express or implied. In addition, as to all the lands and depths herein assigned (except as to said Section 18), *this Assignment shall be subject to all the provisions of that certain Operating Agreement dated March 1, 1968*, by and between Assignor and Assignee.
>
> The provisions hereof shall be binding upon, and shall inure to the benefit of, the parties hereto and their respective heirs devisees, legal representatives, successors and assigns.

(emphasis added). The March 7, 1968, assignment is the only instrument mentioned thus far which was recorded. It was filed for record May 16, 1968, in the lease records of Pecos County, Texas.

The March 1, 1968, operating agreement was executed by Mobil, C & K, Union Texas, and the other owners of the interests in the six sections of land described in the Mobil/Westland farmout agreement. This operating agreement is critical to an understanding of the case because of the provisions contained within paragraph 31, the last clause of the agreement. Captioned above paragraph 31 was the heading, "OTHER CONDITIONS, IF ANY, ARE:."

Subparagraphs B and C referred to the Mobil/Westland farmout agreement and the November 15, 1966, letter agreement as follows:

> B. This Agreement shall supersede and replace that certain Operating Agreement attached as Exhibit "A" to the said Farmout Letter Agreement dated August 4, 1966 between Mobil Oil Corporation and Westland Oil Development Corporation. *In the event of any conflict between this Contract and the Farmout Letter Agreement dated August 4, 1966, between Mobil Oil Corporation and Westland Oil Development Corporation as amended by letter dated August 29, 1966, and November 11, 1966, and a Letter Agreement between Chambers and Kennedy and Westland Oil Development Corporation and L. C. Kung dated November 15, 1966, then such prior agreements shall prevail over this Agreement.*

(emphasis added).

The court of appeals quoted the last sentence of paragraph 31.B. but did not quote the next paragraph:

> C. Exhibit "A" lists all of the parties, and their respective percentage or fractional interests under this Agreement. *Such interests are specifically subject to all terms, conditions and*

reservations set forth in that Farmout Agreement Letter dated August 4, 1966 between Mobil Oil Corporation and Westland Development Corporation, as amended, and that certain Assignment dated March 7, 1968 from Mobil Oil Corporation to C. Fred Chambers and W. D. Kennedy and Union Texas Petroleum.

(emphasis added).

Gulf and Superior obtained their interests in the leases covering sections 19, 23 and 24 through dealings with one Bernard Hanson. By letter dated April 18, 1972, Mobil entered into a farmout agreement with Hanson wherein Mobil agreed that if Hanson commenced a test well on Section 25, Block 49, to a depth sufficient to test the Ellenberger formation and completed it as a producer, Mobil would assign all of its leasehold rights below a depth of 15,000 feet in section 25, and an undivided 60% of its leasehold rights in sections 19 and 30, Block 48, and Sections 23, 24 and 26, Block 49. Sections 19, 23 and 24 were the three southernmost sections involved in the Mobil/Westland farmout agreement. Sections 25, 26 and 30 abut those three sections to the south. The farmout agreement with Hanson stated that the lands and leases covering sections 19, 23 and 24 were covered by the March 1, 1968, operating agreement between Mobil, C & K and Union Texas, and that any interest earned by Hanson from Mobil would be subject to that agreement. Hanson then assigned this farmout agreement to Gulf and Superior.

Hanson also approached C & K, Union Texas and their other partners, and obtained from them farmouts similar to the one received from Mobil. These farmouts covered part of their interests in leases covering sections 19, 23 and 24 which were earned pursuant to the Mobil/Westland farmout agreement and the November 15, 1966, letter agreement. Most of these farmout agreements refer to the March 1, 1968, operating agreement. Hanson also assigned these farmout agreements to Gulf and Superior.

In 1972, Gulf and Superior drilled the test well as required by the Hanson farmout agreements. This well was completed in March 1973, as a large gas producer. Gulf and Superior thereby earned the acreage under these farmout agreements, and the earned leasehold estates were assigned directly to Gulf and Superior. The assignment from Mobil was dated May 22, 1973, and was expressly made subject to the March 1, 1968, operating agreement.

Upon learning of the last assignments from Mobil, Westland filed suit and sought a declaratory judgment that the November 15, 1966, letter agreement was valid and applied to the interests acquired by Gulf and Superior from Mobil, and would cover any acreage so acquired in the Rojo Caballos Field. Westland moved for summary judgment, their motion being based on the November 15, 1966, letter agreement, various instruments, letters between the parties which included those instruments previously referred to and several depositions. Westland contended that all of these supported their claim that Gulf and Superior were on notice of the November 15, 1966, letter agreement, and that, by references made therein to other existing instruments, their interests acquired under the letter agreement covered the interest acquired by Gulf and Superior from Mobil. The trial court granted Westland's motion for summary judgment and declared the November 15, 1966, letter agreement enforceable as to the interests and acreage acquired by Gulf and Superior from Mobil. The decree vested title in Westland in the manner set forth in the November 15, 1966, letter agreement.

Under rule 166–A of the rules of civil procedure, a plaintiff/movant must prove as a matter of law all of the issues expressly presented in order to be entitled to a summary judgment Tex.R.Civ.P. 166–A (1978). The defendant/nonmovant "must expressly present to the trial court any reasons seeking to *avoid* movant's entitlement, such as those set out in rules 93 and 94, and he must present summary judgment proof when necessary to establish a fact issue." *City of Houston v. Clear Creek Basin Authority*, 589 S.W.2d 671 (Tex.1979). Thus, it was incumbent upon Gulf and Superior to plead and present summary judgment proof establishing a fact issue on the affirmative defense of statute of frauds. Gulf and Superior also opposed the motion for summary judgment on the basis that they were innocent purchasers for value and without notice of the equitable claim of Westland. However, Gulf and Superior were not required to prove their status of innocent purchasers. The plaintiff claiming an equitable title assumes the burden of proving that the subsequent purchaser of the legal title was not a bona fide purchaser. *Walters v. Pete*, 546 S.W.2d 871 (Tex.Civ.App.—Texarkana 1977, writ ref'd n.r.e.). Therefore, in the context of this case, Westland was required to prove as a matter of law that Gulf and Superior were on notice of its equitable claim to the leases in question.

There are two questions before us in this case. The first concerns the issue of whether Gulf and Superior were on notice of Westland's prior equitable title. The second issue deals with whether the description of the leases covered by the area of mutual interest agreement contained in paragraph 5 of the November 15, 1966, letter agreement is legally insufficient, thereby rendering the agreement unenforceable under the statute of frauds. We will first address the issue of notice.

The court of appeals held that a question of fact existed as to whether Gulf and Superior, as reasonable purchasers, would have been placed on the duty to conduct complete inquiry of the operating agreement by the reference to it in their assignment from Mobil. The court believed that the normal function of an operating agreement was to define and control the development operations of a certain tract of land, and not to affect title to property. Thus, a question of fact existed as to what a reasonable purchaser would have done under the circumstances.

This, however, is not the rule with regard to references made in documents appearing in one's chain of title. It is well settled that "a purchaser is bound by *every* recital, reference and reservation contained in or fairly disclosed by any instrument which forms an essential link in the chain of title under which he claims." (emphasis added). *Wessels v. Rio Bravo Oil Co.*, 250 S.W.2d 668 (Tex.Civ.App.—Eastland 1952, writ ref'd). *See also Williams v. Harris County Houston Ship Channel Navigation District*, 128 Tex. 411, 99 S.W.2d 276 (1936); *Texas Co. v. Dunlap*, 41 S.W.2d 42 (Tex.Comm'n App.1931, jdgmt adopted); *Guevara v. Guevara*, 280 S.W. 736 (Tex.Comm'n App.1926, jdgmt adopted); *Tuggle v. Cooke*, 277 S.W.2d 729 (Tex.Civ.App.—Fort Worth 1955 writ ref'd n.r.e.); *Abercrombie v. Bright*, 271 S.W.2d 734 (Tex.Civ.App.—Eastland 1954, writ ref'd n.r.e.); Lange, Land Titles and Title Examination § 816 at 259 (1961). As stated in *Loomis v. Cobb*, 159 S.W. 305 (Tex.Civ.App.—El Paso 1913, writ ref'd),

> The rationale of the rule is that *any* description, recital of fact, or reference to other documents puts the purchaser upon inquiry, and he is bound to follow up this inquiry, step by step, from one discovery to another and from one instrument to another, until the whole series of title deeds is exhausted and a complete knowledge of *all the matters referred* to and affecting the estate is obtained.

(emphasis added) 159 S.W. at 307; *see also W. T. Carter & Bro. v. Davis*, 88 S.W.2d 596 (Tex.Civ.App.—Beaumont 1935, writ dism'd).

Since it was the duty of Gulf and Superior to make investigation of the operating agreement, they are also charged with notice of the contents of the operating agreement. *Wessels v. Rio Bravo Oil Co., supra*. Subparagraph 31.B. makes a clear reference to the November 15, 1966, letter agreement and therefore Gulf and Superior were charged with the duty of inspecting that document. We also believe that subparagraph 31.C., when read in conjunction with 31.B., is capable of a construction which would supply a reference to the November 15, 1966, letter agreement. However, it is unnecessary for us to decide this question in light of the unambiguous reference made in subparagraph 31.B.

It is not unusual for an operating agreement, as was the case here, to not be placed of record. An entirely different result might obtain on the issue of notice if, upon diligent inquiry and search, Gulf and Superior were simply unable to obtain a copy of the operating agreement. *See Loomis v. Cobb, supra*. However, Gulf and Superior have never contended such was the case, and there is evidence to the effect that Gulf and Superior had a copy of the operating agreement in their files. Therefore, we hold that the reference to the March 1, 1968, operating agreement contained in the May 22, 1973, assignment from Mobil to Gulf and Superior, as a matter of law, charged Gulf and Superior with the duty of inspecting said agreement. As a result, Gulf and Superior were charged with notice of the November 15, 1966, letter agreement and the equitable claim of Westland, and cannot enjoy the status of innocent purchasers.

We next address the issue of whether paragraph 5 of the November 15, 1966, letter agreement supplies a legally sufficient description of the property covered thereby. It is an agreement to assign an interest in an oil and gas leasehold estate, and therefore is subject to the requirements of the statute of frauds as set out in section 26.01 of the Texas Business and Commerce Code. Tex.Bus. and Com.Code Ann. § 26.01 (Supp.1980–1981); *Consolidated Gas & Equipment Co. v. Thompson*, 405 S.W.2d 333 (Tex.1966). The paragraph actually contains two different descriptions which are separated by the word "or." To illustrate this, we will insert each description separately into the body of paragraph 5. Employing this method, the first description would read as follows:

> If any of the parties hereto, their representatives or assigns, acquire *any additional leasehold interests affecting any of the lands covered by said farmout agreement*, ..., such shall be subject to the terms and provisions of this agreement,

(emphasis added). Westland contends this constitutes a sufficient description of sections 19, 23 and 24, thereby rendering the area of mutual interest agreement enforceable as to those sections.

The second description would provide:

> If any of the parties hereto, their representatives or assigns, acquire ... any additional interest from Mobil Oil Corporation *under lands in the area of the farmout acreage*, such shall be subject to the terms and provisions of this agreement; ...

(emphasis added). Westland contends this second description applies to sections 25, 26 and 30, and is legally sufficient to permit enforcement of the area of mutual interest agreement as to those three sections.

We believe the first description is legally sufficient to satisfy the statute of frauds. The operative words are "leasehold interests affecting any of the lands covered by said farmout." In the introductory paragraph to the November 15, 1966, letter agreement, the parties expressly agreed that the Mobil/Westland farmout would be referred to as "said farmout." Copies of that instrument were attached to the November 15, 1966, letter agreement. The caption to the Mobil/Westland farmout agreement reads as follows:

> PROPOSED FARMOUT OF MOBIL'S LEASEHOLD INTEREST IN THE DRILLSITE SECTION AND AN UNDIVIDED ONE–HALF OF OUR LEASEHOLD INTEREST IN SECTIONS 7, 18 and 19, BLOCK 48, TWP. 8, T. & P., AND SECTIONS 13, 23 and 24, BLOCK 49, TWP. 8, T. & P. LESS THE DRILLSITE SECTION FOR THE DRILLING OF A PROJECTED ELLENBURGER TEST TO BE LOCATED IN THE SE ¼ SECTION 13, BLOCK 49, TWP. 8, T. & P. RY. CO. SURVEY, PECOS COUNTY, TEXAS (MOC T–29063, T–29165, T–30931–C, T–31229–C, D, AND T–31230–D, E, G–O).

In *Wilson v. Fisher*, 144 Tex. 53, 188 S.W.2d 150 (1945) this court stated:

> In so far as the description of the property is concerned the writing must furnish within itself, or by *reference to some other existing writing*, the means or data by which the particular land to be conveyed may be identified with reasonable certainty.

(citation omitted) (emphasis added). *See also Kmiec v. Reagan*, 556 S.W.2d 567 (Tex.1977); *Morrow v. Shotwell*, 477 S.W.2d 538 (Tex.1972); *Owen v. Hendricks*, 433 S.W.2d 164 (Tex.1968); *Pickett v. Bishop*, 148 Tex. 207, 223 S.W.2d 222 (1949). This has been referred to as the "nucleus of description" theory. *Gates v. Asher*, 154 Tex. 538, 280 S.W.2d 247 (1945).

We believe that the words "said farmout" sufficiently provide that nucleus of description. The introductory paragraph defines "said farmout" and one is expressly directed to an instrument which contains an adequate legal description. Therefore, the area of mutual interest agreement provides a description of sections 19, 23 and 24 which is legally sufficient.

We reach a different conclusion with respect to the second description. The phrase "lands in the area of the farmout acreage" does not meet the test set out above. Westland contends that one should substitute "Rojo Caballos Area" for the word "area" contained in the phrase recited above. Westland then argues that parol evidence could be introduced to supply a legal description for "Rojo Caballos Area."

Westland's argument asks us to indulge in an impermissible inference. The description necessary to meet the requirements of the statute of frauds cannot be arrived at from tenuous inferences and presumptions of doubtful validity. *Rowson v. Rowson*, 154 Tex. 216, 275 S.W.2d 468 (1955); *Wilson v. Fisher, supra*. When resort to extrinsic evidence is proper, it should be used only for the purpose of identifying the land with reasonable certainty from the data in the memorandum, and not for the purpose of supplying its location or description. *Id*. There is nothing contained within the November 15, 1966, letter agreement which necessarily leads to the conclusion that "area" means "Rojo Caballos Area." We believe that "lands in the area of the farmout acreage" simply means lands in close proximity to the farmout acreage. Such a description, under the established authority, is not legally sufficient. We hold the second description contained within paragraph 5 of the November 15, 1966, letter agreement is within the statute of frauds and unenforceable. Accordingly, the area of mutual interest agreement cannot be enforced with respect to sections 25, 26 and 30.

Gulf and Superior contend that if one part of the paragraph 5 description does not satisfy the statute of frauds, then this court's decision in *Phillips v. Burns*, 151 Tex. 614, 252 S.W.2d 927 (1952) prohibits enforcement of the contract as to the balance of the description. In *Phillips*, the court was faced with an entirely different situation. The description in that case read,

> "One certain farm located about 6 miles south of Linden, Texas, in Cass County, a part of the A. D. Duncan Survey, and known as the old Whipple Place, together with several tracts of land adjoining it; amounting in all to about 500 acres, now owned by the lessor herein."

252 S.W.2d at 928. Thus, the contract of the parties was for 500 acres. This tract was comprised of the old Whipple Place *and* the tracts adjoining it. The court concluded that the "old Whipple Place" was a sufficient description, but the phrase, "together with several tracts of land adjoining it," was not. To hold part of the description valid and to disregard the rest, the court determined, would be writing a new contract for the parties. Implicit in the holding was that the parties never intended that the two descriptions could be enforced in the alternative. *Both* descriptions were necessary in order to obtain the 500 acres desired, and their agreement contemplated performance of the contract as to the entire acreage.

The import of paragraph 5 is not the same. The two descriptions are separated by the word "or" and it is highly probable that additional interests would be acquired in one of the areas, but not the other. In such case the assignee would be obligated to convey to Westland its proportionate interests only in the area in which the assignee acquired the additional interests. The result is that the contract would be performed as to one area, but not to the other. As such, the covenant to convey is divisible and capable of being enforceable in part and invalid in part. *See Kmiec v. Reagan*, 556 S.W.2d at 569.

The assignment from Mobil to Gulf and Superior covered sections 19, 23, 24, 25, 26 and 30. Only sections 19, 23 and 24 were "lands covered by" the Mobil/Westland farmout agreement. Therefore, the area of mutual interest agreement contained in paragraph 5 is enforceable only as to the additional leasehold interests acquired by Gulf and Superior covering those three sections.

Gulf and Superior also contend that the area of mutual interest agreement is a personal covenant between Westland and C & K, and therefore not binding upon them as assignees of C & K. They argue that privity of estate does not exist, and the covenant does not "touch and concern" the land. We disagree. The agreement contained within paragraph 5 of the November 15, 1966, letter agreement is a contract to convey interests in oil and gas leases. Such an agreement, at least with respect to sections 19, 23 and 24, involved covenants running with the land.

In order for the covenant to run with the land there must be privity of estate between the parties to the agreement. This means there must be a mutual or successive relationship to the same rights of property. Blasser v. Cass, 158 Tex. 560, 314 S.W.2d 807 (1958). Privity of estate exists in this case by virtue of the assignment of sections 19, 23 and 24 to Gulf and Superior.

We further believe that the agreement touches and concerns the land. The tests involved in making this determination are far from absolute. The courts have consistently relied upon rather general statements in their analyses of the touch and concern requirement. As stated in Reno, *Covenants, Rents and Public Rights*, 2 Amer.L. of Prop. § 9.4 (1952):

> One of the two often cited statements of the requirement is that a covenant will run 'if it affected the nature, quality or value of the thing demised, independently of collateral circumstances, or if it affected the mode of enjoying it' ...

It has also been said,

If the promisor's legal relations in respect to the land in question are lessened—his legal interest as owner rendered less valuable by the promise—the burden of the covenant touches or concerns that land; if the promisee's legal relations in respect to that land are increased—his legal interest as owner rendered more value by the promise—the benefit of the covenant touches or concerns the land.

Bigelow, *The Content of Covenants in Leases*, 12 Mich.L.Rev. 639 (1914); Williams, *Restrictions on the Use of Land: Covenants Running with the Land at Law*, 27 Tex.L.Rev. 419 (1949).

We believe that the promise to convey the prescribed interests in the leases covering sections 19, 23 and 24 clearly affected the nature and value of the estate conveyed to C & K. It burdened the promisor's estate and could be considered to have rendered it less valuable. Accordingly, we are of the opinion that the covenant affecting Gulf and Superior's interest in sections 19, 23 and 24 was one which runs with the land.

The judgment of the court of appeals is reversed. We render judgment that Gulf and Superior were on notice of the equitable claim of Westland, and that the November 15, 1966, letter agreement is enforceable as to Section 19, Block 48, and Sections 23 and 24, Block 49, and unenforceable as to Sections 25 and 26, Block 49, and Section 30, Block 48.

Dissenting opinion by WALLACE, J., in which SPEARS, J., joins.

WALLACE, Justice, dissenting.

I respectfully dissent. While I agree with the Court's holding that the description contained in Paragraph 5 of the November 15 Letter Agreement is sufficient to satisfy the Statute of Frauds as to sections 19, 23, and 24, I do not agree with the holding that Gulf and Superior were on notice, as a matter of law, of the equitable claim of Westland.

Notice, in law, is of two kinds, actual and constructive. Courts in the past have confused the distinct meaning of the two types of notice by using these terms "constructive" and "actual" notice interchangeably. Many courts have not even distinguished between the two terms, but have merely stated a party was on notice. However, there are distinctions between types of notice which should be recognized and followed.

Constructive notice is implied by law, from duly recorded instruments or from the possession of land. *Sickles v. White*, 66 Tex. 178, 17 S.W. 543 (1886). The letter agreement before us was not recorded, therefore, we are not dealing with constructive notice.

Actual notice can be of two kinds, express and implied. *Hexter v. Pratt*, 10 S.W.2d 692 (Tex.Comm.App.1928). As this Court and other courts have previously stated, actual notice is a question of fact. *O'Ferral v. Coolidge*, 149 Tex. 61, 228 S.W.2d 146 (1950); *Flack v. First National Bank of Dalhart*, 148 Tex. 495, 226 S.W.2d 628 (1950); *Nelson v. Bridge*, 39 Tex.Civ.App. 283, 87 S.W. 885 (1905, writ ref'd); *Buckalew v. Butcher-Arthur Inc.*, 214 S.W.2d 184 (Tex.Civ.App.—Beaumont 1948, writ ref'd n.r.e.); *Portman v. Earnhart*, 343 S.W.2d 294 (Tex.Civ.App.—Dallas 1960, writ ref'd n.r.e.); *Exxon v. Raetzer*, 553 S.W.2d 842 (Tex.Civ.App.—Corpus Christi 1976, writ ref'd n.r.e.); 58 Am.Jur.2d, Notice, § 5 (1971).

Express actual notice is express knowledge of a fact. *Woodward v. Ortiz*, 150 Tex. 75, 237 S.W.2d 286 (1951). Both parties admit that Gulf and Superior had no actual knowledge of the area of mutual interest clause; therefore, we are left with implied actual notice, if there is any notice at all.

Implied actual notice is an inference of fact. *Exxon v. Raetzer*, supra. This Court in *Flack*, supra, 226 S.W.2d at 632, stated the rule to be "one who has knowledge of such facts as would cause a prudent man to make further inquiry, is chargeable with notice of the facts, which by use of ordinary intelligence, he would have ascertained."

It is helpful to begin with the assignment through which Gulf and Superior gained title and work backward to see exactly what Gulf and Superior knew or should have known. To begin with, Gulf and Superior received an assignment dated May 22, 1973, from Mobil Oil of 60% of its interest in sections 19, 23, 24, 26 & 31, and 100% of its interest in section 25. This assignment was expressly made subject to the March 1, 1968 operating agreement. Gulf and Superior received this assignment by drilling a well on section 25 and earning the acreage pursuant to farmout agreements from Mobil, Chambers/Kennedy (C&K), and others. The operating agreement contains two possible references to the November 15 Letter Agreement. Paragraph 31B states:

> ... (i)n the event of any conflict between this contract and the Farmout Letter Agreement dated August 4, 1966, between Mobil Oil Corporation and Westland Oil Development, as

> amended by Letter dated August 29, 1966 and November 11, 1966 and a Letter Agreement between Chambers & Kennedy and Westland Oil Development Corporation and L. C. Kung dated November 15, 1966, then such prior agreements shall prevail over this Agreement.

Paragraph 31C states the following:

> Exhibit A lists all of the parties, and their ... interests .... Such interests are specifically subject to all terms, conditions, and reservations set forth in that Farmout Agreement Letter dated August 4, 1966 between Mobil Oil Corporation and Westland Development Corporation as amended and that certain assignment dated March 7, 1968 from Mobil to C. Fred Chambers and W. D. Kennedy and Union Texas Petroleum.

It is the letter agreement dated November 15, 1966 between Westland/Kung and Chambers/Kennedy which contains the area of mutual interest clause which Westland contends Gulf and Superior are on notice of and therefore bound by.

This Court in *Flack*, supra, 226 S.W.2d at 631, stated that the duty of inquiry extends only to matters which are fairly suggested by the facts really known. In *Texas Co. v. Dunlap*, 41 S.W.2d 42 (Tex.Comm'n App.1931, judgment adopted); *Guevara v. Guevara*, 280 S.W. 736 (Tex.Comm'n App.1926, judgment adopted); *Tuggle v. Cooke*, 277 S.W.2d 729 (Tex.Civ.App.—Fort Worth 1955, writ ref'd n.r.e.); and *W. T. Carter & Bro. v. Davis*, 88 S.W.2d 596 (Tex.Civ.App.—Beaumont 1935, writ dism'd); cited by the majority, the references were to vendor's liens and prior deeds. A deed and a vendor's lien definitely suggest matters involving title. An operating agreement and a "conflict between an operating agreement and a letter agreement" do not necessarily suggest a title matter. As pointed out by the Court of Appeals, the function of an operating agreement is to explain in detail the operation between the various interests in the development of a tract for economical production of the minerals, not to establish interests of any kind. Therefore, a reference to any conflict with an operating agreement might well have alerted a reasonably diligent purchaser to check the letter agreement if he was concerned with the operations, not for title reasons. Nor does paragraph 31B in any way suggest that the letter agreement between C&K and Westland involves title. The reference in 31C does not even refer to the November 15, Letter Agreement between Westland and C&K, unless one assumes the words "as amended," refers to it. However, "as amended," just as logically refers only to the actual amendments to the farmout between Mobil and Westland of August 29, 1966, and November 11, 1966. The letter agreement between Westland and C&K is not an amendment to the agreement between Mobil and Westland, but a new agreement between different parties.

Additionally, where circumstances claimed to be sufficient to charge a person with notice may just as reasonably be referred to some other matter, such circumstances have been held not sufficient to charge him with notice. *Houston Oil Co. of Texas v. Griggs*, 181 S.W. 833, 838 (Tex.Civ.App.—Beaumont 1916) affirmed in 213 S.W. 261 (Tex.Comm.App.1919, judgment adopted); *Exxon Corp. v. Raetzer*, supra. We do not have to decide that question, since this case is before us on summary judgment. Ordinarily, summary judgment will not be awarded where the issue is inherently one for a jury, such as the exercise of judgment. 4 McDonald, Texas Civil Practice, "Judgments" Sec. 17.2612 at 177 (rev. 1971). Actual notice is normally a question of fact, it will only become a question of law when there is no room for ordinary minds to differ as to the proper conclusion to be drawn from the evidence. *O'Ferral v. Coolidge*, supra.

I am not willing to hold that as a matter of law, Gulf and Superior were on notice of an equitable right expressed in an unrecorded farmout agreement between Westland/Kung and Chambers/Kennedy, ambiguously referred to in an operating agreement between Chambers/Kennedy and Union Texas Petroleum, which was expressly referred to in the assignment from Mobil to Gulf and Superior. That is a question of fact, raised by the summary judgment proof and properly reserved for the trier of fact.

The majority opinion fails to mention the rules regarding actual notice. It instead states that the rule concerning references made in documents appearing in one's chain of title, is that a purchaser is bound by every recital, reference, and reservation contained in or fairly disclosed by any instrument which forms an essential link in the chain of title under which he claims. Therefore, the majority concludes that Gulf and Superior were on notice as a matter of law of the contents of the operating agreement, and on notice as a matter of law of the contents of the November 15 letter agreement. Even if the rule recited by the majority were the only applicable rule, I would still not conclude that Gulf and Superior were on notice, as a matter of law, of the contents of the November 15 letter agreement.

I would agree that under the rule and the cases cited by the majority, Gulf and Superior would be on notice of the contents of the March 1, 1968 operating agreement. The May 22, 1973 assignment from Mobil to Gulf and Superior is within Gulf and Superior's chain of title, and it expressly refers to the operating agreement. Therefore, it falls directly within the rule cited by the majority. However, the March 1, 1968 operating agreement does not contain the clause under which Westland asserts its equitable rights. Nor is there any clause in the operating agreement which sets out Westlands rights. Nor is the operating agreement within Gulf and Superior's chain of title. Therefore, the rule cited by the majority does not apply to a reference to another instrument contained in the operating agreement.

It is this extra step from the March 1, 1968 operating agreement to the November 15 letter agreement which I do not believe the case authority supports. While much of the language contained in the cases cited by the majority is broad enough to cover the step from the operating agreement to the letter agreement, I do not think the facts of those cases would allow such an extension of the rule.

In every case cited by the majority, the instrument which contains the equitable right is referred to in an instrument in the purchaser's chain of title. Furthermore, the instrument referred to somehow directly suggests outstanding rights, such as deeds and vendors, [SIC] liens, namely: *Wessels v. Rio Bravo Oil Co.*, 250 S.W.2d 668 (Tex.Civ.App.—Eastland 1952, writ ref'd)—deed within purchaser's chain of title referred to an unrecorded prior contract and further stated, "excepting and reserving herefrom all the exceptions and reservations contained in the said instrument so made by the said Railway Company"; *Williams v. Harris County Houston Navigation District*, 128 Tex. 411, 99 S.W.2d 276 (1936)—purchaser's deed referred directly to another deed which was within its chain of title, that deed contained covenants regarding the execution of releases which the court held the purchaser was bound by; *Texas Co. v. Dunlap*, supra, deed within the purchaser's chain of title reserved a vendor's lien, and purchaser was charged with notice that a lien existed against said land; *Guevara v. Guevara*, supra,—purchaser's deed recited the existence of a purchase money note and retention of a vendor's lien; the court imputed knowledge of the contents of that note to the purchaser; *Tuggle v. Cooke*, supra,—reference in deed in purchaser's chain of title to an interest in 50 acres being conveyed or had been conveyed by another deed, purchaser was bound by that conveyance; *Abercrombie v. Bright*, 271 S.W.2d 734 (Tex.Civ.App.—Eastland 1954, writ ref'd n.r.e.)—reference in deeds in purchaser's chain of title stated that they were subject to a former conveyance of 11 acres; *Loomis v. Cobb*, 159 S.W. 305 (Tex.Civ.App.—El Paso 1913, writ ref'd)—original deed from the town of San Elizario to the original grantee, which was in the purchaser's chain of title, recited that it was executed by virtue of authority and in accordance with an ordinance of the town council. The deed also stated that the ordinance was for surveying, adjusting, and providing for the division and granting of the unappropriated lands. Purchaser was held to be bound by the provisions of the ordinance; *W. T. Carter & Bro. v. Davis*, supra,—recorded deed referred to another recorded deed, both deeds were links in Carter & Bro.'s chain of title, therefore the reservation of the mineral estate in the first deed was notice to Carter & Bro. that it was only acquiring the surface estate.

I would not extend the rule cited in these cases, [SIC] to the facts of this case. I would hold that a question of fact remains for the trier of fact to decide and, therefore, would remand the cause to the trial court on the issue of notice.

SPEARS, J., joins in this dissent.

Commentary on Westland Oil Development Corporation v. Gulf Oil Corporation

by Arnold J. "Arne" Johnson

On June 9, 1982, the Supreme Court of Texas sent a wake-up call to landmen prone to imprecise drafting and title examiners struggling to define the scope of their reviews amidst a steady flow of drilling activity.[1] Some might contend that *Westland Oil Development Corporation v. Gulf Oil Corporation* is not a "landmark" case because it lacks the oil and gas law roots of more traditional royalty and lease disputes. That view overlooks the real significance of the case, which is to bring other established law to the oil patch and remind us that the principles of constructive and actual notice, duty of inquiry, and the statute of frauds often flourish among shades of gray.

Background

In 1966 Lyndon Johnson was President,[2] a first-class postage stamp cost five cents,[3] *The Sound of Music* would win the Oscar for best picture,[4] and the late Don Haskins would make history by coaching the Texas Western Miners to a shocking upset of legendary Adolph Rupp's top-ranked Kentucky Wildcats to capture college basketball's national crown.[5] As summer drew to a close, Mobil Oil Corporation (Mobil) and Westland Oil Development Corporation (Westland) were putting the final touches on an August 4 farmout agreement that entitled Westland to "produce to earn" one-half of Mobil's oil and gas lease rights in six sections of land in Pecos County.[6] Westland obtained several extensions of its drilling commencement obligation before passing its rights and obligations under the agreement to a Midland partnership, Chambers and Kennedy (C & K), under a November 15 letter agreement that included a seemingly benign "area of mutual interest" provision that Westland would later seek to enforce:

> If any of the parties hereto, their representatives or *assigns*, acquire any additional leasehold interests affecting any of the lands covered by said farmout agreement, or any additional interest from Mobil Oil Corporation under lands in the area of the farmout acreage, such shall be subject to the terms and provisions of this agreement; provided, however that in no event shall the owners of the working interest under any portion of such acreage be entitled to less than 75% working interest leases.[7] (Emphasis added.)

Chambers and Kennedy (C & K) with other investors including Union Texas Petroleum (Union Texas) as operator, spud the farmout well on December 1 and completed it over a year later on January 23, 1968, earning a March 7, 1968 assignment from Mobil that was made subject to a March 1, 1968 operating agreement signed by Mobil, C & K, Union Texas, and the other owners of the interests in the farmout lands and binding on their successors.[8] That operating agreement referred to the August 4, 1966 farmout agreement and November 15, 1966 letter agreement and provided that in the event of a conflict, the August 4 and November 15 agreements would prevail.[9] It also provided that the interests of the parties were subject to all terms, conditions, and reservations set forth in the August 4 farmout agreement and March 7, 1968 assignment, although the March 7, 1968 assignment was the only instrument recorded.[10]

Gulf Oil Corporation and Superior Oil Company (collectively, "Gulf and Superior") obtained their interests in three of the six sections through an April 18, 1972 farmout agreement from Mobil that stated that the lands and leases covering the three sections were covered by the March 1, 1968 operating agreement and that any interest earned would be subject to that agreement.[11] Gulf and Superior received similar farmouts from C & K, Union Texas, and the other owners and completed a producing gas well in March 1973.[12] The March 22, 1973 assignment they earned from Mobil was expressly made subject to the March 1, 1968 operating agreement.[13]

Westland sued claiming that the area of mutual interest provision contained in the November 15, 1966 letter agreement applied to the interests acquired by Gulf and Superior from Mobil and any other acreage so acquired in the field since, and that Gulf and Superior were on notice of the obligations imposed by that agreement.[14] The trial court granted Westland's motion for summary judgment, finding that Gulf and Superior were on notice as a matter of law of the November 15, 1966 letter agreement and that the agreement was enforceable as to the interests acquired by Gulf and Superior and vested title in Westland.[15] The court of appeals reversed and remanded, holding that it was a question of fact as to whether Gulf and Superior, as reasonable purchasers, had a duty to conduct complete inquiry of the operating agreement by virtue of the reference to it in their assignment from Mobil.[16]

The Issues

The Supreme Court considered two issues.[17] The first was whether Gulf and Superior were on notice of Westland's prior equitable title.[18] The second, posed in the negative, was whether the description of the leases covered by the area of mutual interest provision of the November 15, 1966 letter agreement was insufficient under the statute of frauds and thus unenforceable.[19]

The Advocates

Westland and its assignees were represented by Maurice Bullock of the Midland firm of Bullock, Scott and Nesig; William Pannill of the Houston firm of Reynolds, Allen, Cook, Pannill and Hooper; and Austin attorney Jack N. Price.[20] Gulf and Superior were represented by Tom Sealy, W. B. Browder, Jr. and Marc Skeen of the Midland firm of Stubbeman, McRae, Sealy, Laughlin and Browder; and Morgan L. Copeland and Susan R. Sewell (Richardson) of Houston.[21]

The Holdings

As to the first issue of whether Gulf and Superior were on notice of Westland's prior equitable title, the Supreme Court noted that it was well settled that "a purchaser is bound by *every* recital, reference and reservation contained in, or fairly disclosed by, any instrument which forms an essential link in the chain of title under which he claims."[22] The court held that since it was the duty of Gulf and Superior to make investigation of the operating agreement, they were also charged with notice of its contents that referred to the November 15, 1966 letter agreement.[23] As a result, Gulf and Superior were charged with notice of that agreement and the equitable claim of Westland and thus could not enjoy the status of innocent purchasers.[24]

As to the second issue of whether the description of the leases covered by the area of mutual interest provision contained in the November 15, 1966 letter agreement was legally insufficient, thereby rendering the provision unenforceable under the statute of frauds, the court relied upon the use of the word "or" to separate the two types of lands subject to the provision.[25] The court found that the description was sufficient as to the reference to "lands covered by said farmout agreement," as the November 15, 1966 letter agreement containing the area of mutual interest provision expressly stated that the term "said farmout" meant the prior farmout from Mobil to Westland.[26] Also, a copy of the farmout agreement was attached and specifically described the leases and lands covered.[27] The court found that the reference to "lands in the area of the farmout acreage" was insufficient to satisfy the statute of frauds since the word "area" meant lands in close proximity to the farmout acreage rather than a specific area.[28] Finally, the court held that the insufficient latter description did not prohibit the enforcement of the agreement as to lands sufficiently described in the former description.[29]

The Dissent

Justice Wallace, joined by Justice Spears, agreed with the majority holding on the second issue but disagreed on the first that Gulf and Superior were on notice, as a matter of law, of Westland's equitable claim.[30] They highlighted the distinction between constructive notice implied by law— inapplicable here since the letter agreement was not recorded— and actual notice that may be express or implied and is a question of fact.[31] Here "both parties admit[ted] that Gulf and Superior had no [express] actual knowledge of the area of mutual interest" provision and implied actual knowledge must be inferred from fact.[32] Because the function of an operating agreement is to address operations matters, not title issues, a reference to any conflict within an operating agreement "might well have alerted a reasonably diligent purchaser to check the letter agreement if he was concerned with the operations," not with the title.[33]

The Legacy

The legacy of *Westland* is that it offers something for everyone. Traditional title examiners would now ruminate over its notice and duty of inquiry holding, especially as "subject to" references were becoming increasingly common in oil and gas contracts and assignments. Perhaps more importantly, landmen and in-house counsel commonly involved in agreement negotiation and preparation would be reminded that they are not immune to the effects of contemporary case law and must think as they draft, as imprecision and references to other documents can have dire consequences.

Epilogue

Upon reflection, *Westland* boasts a classic script with multiple parties of various shapes and sizes, overlapping agreements, producing wells, a rich litigation history that eventually lands at the Supreme Court of Texas for resolution, and a thoughtful dissenting opinion. It recalls a time when courtrooms showcased advocacy skills over high-tech mixed-media presentations. Susan Richardson fondly recalls Bill Pannill displaying some document enlargements in the courtroom, only to have Justice Greenhill caution: "Do you see, Mr. Pannill, who is sitting up here on this bench? We are a bunch of old men and if you think we can read those documents, you are mistaken." In revisiting the opinion, one can only applaud the resourcefulness of the lawyers on both sides and the deliberative approach taken by the courts in dissecting the issues presented. *Westland* has been cited nearly one two hundred times in the quarter of a century since it was rendered,[34] earning a well-deserved spot on the list of Texas landmark cases.

---

1 *See Westland Oil Dev. Corp. v. Gulf Oil Corp.*, 637 S.W.2d 903 (Tex. 1982).
2 *Lyndon B. Johnson*, The White House, http://www.whitehouse.gov/about/presidents/lyndonbjohnson.
3 *Rates for Domestic Letters Since 1863*, United States Postal Service, http://about.usps.com/who-we-are/postal-history/domestic-letter-rates-since-1863.pdf.
4 Peter Bart, *'Sound of Music' Wins Oscar as the Best Film of 1965; Julie Christie, Lee Marvin and Robert Wise Acclaimed*, N.Y. Times, Apr. 19, 1966, at A34.
5 Gordon S White, *MINERS WIN, 72-65; Hill, 5-10, Scores 20 Points to Help Down Team Rated No. 1 TEXAS WESTERN UPSETS KENTUCKY*, N.Y. Times, Mar. 20, 1966.
6 *Westland Oil Dev. Corp. v. Gulf Oil Corp.*, 637 S.W.2d 903, 905 (Tex. 1982).
7 *Id.* (emphasis added).
8 *Id.* at 905-06.
9 *Id.* at 906.
10 *Id.*
11 *Id.*
12 *Id.* at 907.
13 *Id.*
14 *Id.*
15 *Id.* at 904, 907.
16 *Id.* at 904, 907-08.
17 *Id.*
18 *Id.*
19 *Id.*
20 *Id.* at 904.
21 *Id.*
22 *Id.* at 908.
23 *Id.*
24 *Id.*
25 *Id.* at 908-09.
26 *Id.* at 909.
27 *Id.*
28 *Id.* at 909-10.
29 *Id.*
30 *Id.* at 911.
31 *Id.*
32 *Id.* at 912.
33 *Id.*
34 *Citing References for Westland Oil Dev. Corp. v. Gulf Oil Corp.*, WESTLAW, http://www.westlaw.com (search "Find citation" for "637 S.W.2d 903"; then follow "Go" hyperlink; then follow "Citing References" hyperlink).

18

CHAPTER 18

Clinton Manges, Petitioner,
v.
J. C. Guerra, et al., Respondents.

COMMENTARY

by M.C. Cottingham "Cottie" Miles

673 S.W.2d 180

1984

Clinton Manges, Petitioner,
v.
J. C. Guerra, et al., Respondents.

673 S.W.2d 180

1984

Pat Maloney, Adams & Hunter, Royal D. Adams, San Antonio, Luther Jones, Jr., Corpus Christi, Watson & Henderson, Murray Watson, Jr., Waco, for petitioner.

Smith, McIlheran, Lauderdale & Jones, Garland F. Smith, Weslaco, Dibrell, Dotson, Dibrell & Dibrell, T. Kellis Dibrell, San Antonio, Flores, Sanchez, Vicaurri, Munoz & Guerra, David H. Guerra, McAllen, McGinnis, Lochridge & Kilgore, Lloyd Lochridge and Thomas O. Barton, Austin, H.P. Guerra, III, Rio Grande City, for respondents.

POPE, Chief Justice.

We grant the motion for rehearing and withdraw the court's former opinion as well as the concurring and dissenting opinion.

This appeal concerns the proper exercise of the executive right of a mineral estate. The suit is one of several suits filed in the controversy among the various parties. The present suit was filed by J.C. Guerra and others against Clinton Manges, Gas Producing Enterprises and the Bank of the Southwest National Association. Clinton Manges and several members of the Guerra family were mineral co-tenants, with Manges holding the executive right to all the minerals. The Guerras sued Manges for failure to exercise diligence in leasing the minerals to third persons and for leasing a portion of the minerals to himself at allegedly unfair terms. The trial court rendered judgment removing Manges as holder of the executive rights; cancelling a lease Manges executed to himself; voiding, as to the Guerras' interests, certain transactions between Manges and third parties; and awarding the Guerras $382,608.79 in actual damages and $500,000 in exemplary damages. The court of civil appeals affirmed the judgment of the trial court. 621 S.W.2d 652.

This cause was tried by a jury and judgment was rendered on jury findings in favor of the Guerras. Those issues and findings are stated in the opinion of the court of appeals, and that court has found that each issue is supported by sufficient evidence. The issues are not attacked in this court. We affirm the judgment cancelling the lease that Manges made to himself. We affirm the award of damages for Manges' failure to lease the Guerra mineral acreage not covered by the Manges-to-Manges lease which the jury found he could have leased, and upon the basis of those actual damages we sustain the award of punitive damages. We reverse the judgment that removed Manges as the executive.

On March 31, 1969, Clinton Manges entered into a contract to purchase 72,000 acres of land in Jim Hogg and Starr counties from the M. Guerra & Son Partnership. Under the contract, Manges was to purchase all of the surface and an undivided one-half of the partnership's 55,000 to 60,000 mineral acres. The sale was to include the executive rights to the one-half mineral interest reserved by the Guerras. Litigation among members of the Guerra family resulted in the land being placed with a receiver. On August 20, 1971, the receiver executed a deed conveying the land to Manges in accordance with the contract of sale. The deed provided that Manges was not to lease the Guerras' mineral interest for less than a one-eighth royalty; also, it expressly provided that the Guerras were to participate "in all bonuses, rentals, royalties, overriding royalties and payments out of production." An agreed judgment rendered on June 11, 1974, adjudged that Manges was the owner of 53.4 percent of the minerals and the Guerras owned 46.6 percent.

In addition to the M. Guerra & Son Partnership land, between 1968 and 1970, Manges purchased the Virginia C. Guerra Estate, which consisted of 21,000 surface acres and about 16,000 mineral acres. Manges acquired the land by purchasing the undivided interests of the various Virginia C. Guerra descendants. As with the M. Guerra & Son Partnership land, Manges received all of the surface and an undivided one-half of the minerals. The sale included the executive rights to the one-half mineral interest reserved by the Guerras, subject to the limitation that Manges could not lease the minerals for less than a one-eighth royalty. The M. Guerra & Son Partnership owned an undivided one-seventh of the Virginia C. Guerra Estate land, and Manges received this interest by virtue of the June 11, 1974 agreed judgment.

The Guerras assert a number of ways that Manges used the executive powers to benefit himself with no similar benefit to the non-executives. On May 10, 1974, Manges, his wife, and Duval County Ranch Company executed a deed of trust securing a note in the principal amount of $7,028,346 held by the Bank of the Southwest National Association. This deed of trust covered, among other mineral interests, "all of the oil, gas and other mineral interests ... including ... executive rights and powers" owned or claimed by Manges and affecting lands in Starr and Jim Hogg counties.

On September 11, 1974, Manges, his wife and Duval County Ranch Company executed two instruments to Gas Producing Enterprises. One of the instruments was an option to purchase oil and gas and the other was a "Repayment Agreement, Collateral Assignment and Security Agreement." These instruments covered the mineral interest Manges purchased from the Guerras plus other properties owned by Manges in a total of thirteen Texas counties. The option contract purported to give Gas Producing Enterprises the right to purchase oil and gas produced from all of the mineral estates to which Manges held executive rights. The Gas Producing Enterprises contracts were executed in connection with a loan from Gas Producing Enterprises to Manges of $2,800,000 (later increased to $5,000,000). Manges was to use this money in drilling and developing the mineral interests. Neither contract required Manges to drill and develop the Guerra lands in particular.

J.C. Guerra sued Manges, Gas Producing Enterprises, the Bank of the Southwest, and Cove Investments, Inc., in Jim Hogg County, contending that these instruments effectively withdrew the Guerra minerals from the lease market. The other Guerras were made involuntary plaintiffs. R.R. Guerra filed a similar suit as a cross-action on the same day in Starr County. Cove Investments, Inc., intervened in the Starr County suit, claiming title to all, or alternatively, one-half of the minerals and executive rights owned by Manges. The controversy between Manges and Cove Investments was severed for a separate trial. *See Cove Investments, Inc. v. Manges*, 602 S.W.2d 512 (Tex.1980). Cove Investments, Inc., and R.R. Guerra filed notices of *lis pendens* on October 2, 1974, and September 19, 1975, respectively.

After the Guerras filed this suit, Manges discovered that Exxon had drilled wells on an adjoining tract which were draining the Guerra/Manges minerals. Manges, claiming that he was unable to lease to anyone else because of the *lis pendens* notices, leased 25,911.62 acres to himself on April 20, 1977. This lease was for a term of ten years, and provided for a one-eighth royalty and a $2 per acre annual delay rental. The lease recited a $5 bonus for the entire acreage. Purporting to act under the Manges-to-Manges lease, Manges drilled five offset wells, three of which were producing, and at the time of trial had produced over $2,000,000. Manges claimed at trial his proportionate 53.4 percent of the one-eighth royalty and 100 percent of the remaining seven-eighths of the production revenue. This money has been held in a suspense account.

On July 16, 1977, Manges, as lessee under the Manges-to-Manges lease, entered into a farm-out agreement with Joe Schero covering the same land as the Manges-to-Manges lease. Manges was to receive, in addition to his fractional share of the one-eighth royalty, a fifty percent working interest free of drilling costs. On the same day the farm-out agreement was executed, Manges gave Schero a "top lease," which was conditional on the Manges-to-Manges lease being declared void. Under the farm-out, Schero drilled an additional sixteen to eighteen other wells, all of which were nonproducing.

Trial was to a jury. The jury was instructed that:

> the possessor of an "Executive Right" as herein defined owes to the co-mineral owners the same degree of diligence and discretion in exercising the rights and powers granted under such Executive Rights as would be expected of the average land owner who because of self-interest is normally willing to take affirmative steps to seek or to cooperate with prospective lessees ... that in the exercise of the executive rights, the holder thereof is

> required to use utmost good faith and fair dealing as to the interest of the non-executive mineral interest owners. You are further instructed that the holder of the executive rights has a duty to prevent drainage of oil or gas from any lands covered by the executive rights. In any lease executed by the holder of the executive rights, the holder thereof is required to obtain all benefits that could be reasonably obtained from a disinterested third party.

Neither party objected to the instruction. The jury found that Manges had breached the duty he owed the Guerras as holder of the executive rights to their minerals covered by the June 11, 1974 agreed judgment and the six-sevenths of the Virginia C. Guerra minerals that he did not acquire by that judgment. Based on the jury findings, the trial court rendered judgment (1) removing Manges as holder of the executive rights to the Guerras' mineral interests; (2) cancelling the Manges-to-Manges lease as of the date of its execution (April 20, 1977); (3) adjudging Manges to be a drilling and producing co-tenant with the Guerras in three producing wells and two dry holes drilled by him; (4) requiring an accounting by Manges of income from production from the producing wells, less necessary and reasonable costs of drilling and production; (5) awarding the Guerras actual damages against Manges of $382,608.79 plus $500,000 exemplary damages; (6) adjudging the Bank of the Southwest National Association deed of trust to be of no force or effect insofar as it purported to cover the Guerras' mineral interests and executive rights; and (7) cancelling the two Gas Producing Enterprises contracts insofar as they purported to cover the Guerras' mineral interests and executive rights. Manges appealed and the court of civil appeals affirmed the judgment of the trial court.

The duty of utmost good faith owed by an executive has been settled since *Schlittler v. Smith*, 128 Tex. 628, 101 S.W.2d 543, 545 (1937). That standard has been repeated in *First National Bank of Snyder v. Evans*, 169 S.W.2d 754, 757 (Tex.Civ.App.—Eastland 1943, writ ref'd); *Kimsey v. Fore*, 593 S.W.2d 107, 111 (Tex.Civ.App.—Beaumont 1980, writ ref'd n.r.e.); *Portwood v. Buckalew*, 521 S.W.2d 904, 911 (Tex.Civ.App.—Tyler 1975, writ ref'd n.r.e.); and *Morriss v. First National Bank of Mission*, 249 S.W.2d 269, 276 (Tex.Civ.App.—San Antonio 1952, writ ref'd n.r.e.). The fiduciary duty arises from the relationship of the parties and not from the contract. *See English v. Fischer*, 660 S.W.2d 521, 524–25 (Tex.1983) (Spears, J., concurring). While a contract or deed may create the relationship, the duty of the executive arises from the relationship and not from express or implied terms of the contract or deed. That duty requires the holder of the executive right, Manges in this case, to acquire for the non-executive every benefit that he exacts for himself. R. Hemingway, *The Law of Oil & Gas*, § 2.2(D) (2d ed. 1983).

In our opinion Manges' conduct amounted to a breach of his fiduciary duty as found by the jury in making the lease to himself, in agreeing upon a $5 nominal bonus for 25,911.62 acres of land, and in dealing with the entire mineral interest so that he received benefits that the non-executives did not receive. His taking one hundred percent of seven-eighths of the three producing wells, his taking one-half of the working interest, free and clear of costs, by his farm-out to Schero, was also the receipt of special benefits that the non-executives did not receive. Upon the basis of his receipt of special benefits, we must cancel the lease as we did in *State v. Standard*, 414 S.W.2d 148 (Tex.1967). In *Standard* we held that the surface owner, as the exclusive agent for the state in the execution of an oil and gas lease under the Relinquishment Act, could not reserve the right to acquire for himself at a later time a one-sixteenth share of the working interest, when the state was not accorded an equal right. *Id.* at 153. The Manges-to-Manges lease was correctly cancelled.

It does not follow, however, that Manges must be removed as the executive. The Guerras elected not to cancel the executive rights even though the jury found that they had been fraudulently induced to sell their lands. Their motion for judgment stated:

> The Plaintiffs have elected, and now elect not to rescind the initial transfer to the defendant, Clinton Manges, of the executive rights to their interest in the mineral estate in the Guerra lands, as the same may be authorized by the jury's answers to Special Issues Nos. 2, 3, 4 and 4a, and elect instead to take the damages as found by the jury.

Having elected to waive their right to rescind the transfer of executive rights so they would recover damages, they will not be permitted to urge that the executive right should be cancelled. The Guerras elected to take the damages related to Manges' failure to lease Guerra lands that were not included in the Manges-to-Manges lease. The jury found that Manges could have leased those lands to a third party but did not, and that the damages for his failure to lease amounted to $800,000 in lost bonus and $120,000 in lost delay rentals. The findings are supported by evidence as found by the court of appeals. We have no power to set aside the court of appeals' findings of factual sufficiency, and there is some evidence that supports the findings. The Guerras, as owners of 46.6 percent of the minerals, are legally entitled to receive their proportionate 46.6 percent of those damages as held by the judgments below.

The Guerras brought suit for recovery of damages, actual and exemplary, for Manges' breach of his fiduciary duty. Recovery against a breaching fiduciary is not limited to an accounting of profits received by the fiduciary, but can also include exemplary damages. *Texas Bank & Trust Co. v. Moore*, 595 S.W.2d 502, 510 (Tex.1980); *International Bankers Life Insurance Co. v. Holloway*, 368 S.W.2d 567, 584 (Tex.1963). This is in contrast to a suit for breach of contract, which will not support a judgment for exemplary damages even if the agreement is maliciously breached. *Amoco Production Co. v. Alexander*, 622 S.W.2d 563, 571 (Tex.1981). The Guerras' suit was based upon a breach of an executive's fiduciary duty, and not the breach of an implied covenant to a contract, as in *Amoco*.

Based upon the actual damages and the jury findings, the Guerras are entitled to recover exemplary damages. The jury found that Manges had willfully disregarded the rights of the Guerras in several specific ways, including his failure to negotiate for mineral leases with third persons, that Manges' actions were in willful and unconscionable disregard of the interests of the Guerras, that the conduct was malicious or wanton, and that the Guerras should receive as punitive damages the sum of $500,000. Manges did not breach a contract; rather, as the jury found, he willfully, wantonly, maliciously and unconscionably breached his fiduciary duty. We affirm the judgment on the verdict for punitive damages.

After this court rendered its judgment in this cause, the Guerras filed motions that three of the justices be recused. Each of the justices is qualified under Article V, Section 11, of the Texas Constitution to serve. Prior to any further proceedings in the case and in compliance with the provisions of Rule 18b of the Texas Rules of Civil Procedure, each challenged justice certified the matter to the entire court. The court then decided the motions by a vote of the justices of the court sitting en banc, except that the challenged justice did not sit when his challenge was considered. The court has concluded that each motion to recuse should be and is denied. Another justice who did not participate in the original decision has participated on rehearing. *See Sun Oil Co. v. Whitaker*, 483 S.W.2d 808 (Tex.1972).

We reverse that part of the judgment of the courts below that removed Clinton Manges as the holder of the executive rights on behalf of the Guerras. We affirm the remaining parts of the judgments below.

RAY, J., notes his dissent.

The Duty of Utmost Good Faith and Fair Dealing: Commentary on Manges v. Guerra

by M.C. Cottingham "Cottie" Miles[*]

The mineral estate has five (5) interests: "(1) the right to develop (the right of ingress and egress), (2) the right to lease (the executive right), (3) the right to receive bonus payments, (4) the right to receive delay rentals, and (5) the right to receive royalty payments."[1] These interests constitute the "bundle of sticks" of mineral estate ownership. One of those rights, the executive right—the right to execute leases after severance from the underlying mineral interests—can often lead to issues regarding the duties owed by the executive to non-participating royalty and mineral interest owners as the executive right permits such owners "the right to take or authorize all actions that affect the exploration and development of the mineral estate."[2] Because of the broad powers that an executive holds over the mineral estate with the right to lease, Texas courts have determined the executive owes a duty to a non-executive, as exemplified in the seminal case defining the duty of the executive to the non-executive in *Manges v. Guerra*.[3]

In *Manges*, Clinton Manges ("Manges") purchased 72,000 acres of land in Jim Hogg and Starr Counties from the M. Guerra & Son Partnership (the "Partnership").[4] As a result of this purchase, Manges acquired the entire surface and an undivided one-half (1/2) of the Partnership's mineral interest in 55,000–60,000 acres.[5] Manges also obtained the executive right to the undivided one-half (1/2) mineral interest reserved by the Partnership.[6] The deed from the Partnership provided that Manges could not lease the mineral interest of the Partnership for less than a one-eighth (1/8) royalty and further provided that the Partnership would "participate 'in all bonuses, rentals, royalties, overriding royalties, and payments out of production.'"[7] Manges also purchased the interests of the Virginia C. Guerra Estate (the "Estate"), which consisted of 21,000 surface acres and about 16,000 mineral acres.[8] By such purchase, Manges received all of the surface estate and an undivided one-half (1/2) interest in the minerals of said property.[9] As to the non-participating interest reserved by the Estate, Manges could also not lease the minerals for less than a one-eighth (1/8) royalty.[10] The Estate and the Partnership are collectively referred to herein as the "Guerras."

Subsequently, Manges, his wife, and Duval County Ranch Company executed a deed of trust securing a note held by the Bank of the Southwest, National Association (the "Bank") covering all of the oil, gas, and other mineral interests, including the executive right claimed by Manges, in Starr and Jim Hogg Counties.[11] Manges also executed two instruments in favor of Gas Producing Enterprises covering the lands he had acquired from the Guerras.[12] One of the instruments was an option to purchase oil and gas from all of the lands in which Manges held the executive right, including the interest acquired from the Guerras.[13] The other instrument provided for the payment of a loan from Gas Producing Enterprises to Manges, along with an assignment of collateral and the creation of a security interest with regard to such indebtedness.[14] The Guerras sued Manges, Gas Producing Enterprises, the Bank and Cove Investments, Inc., contending that the "instruments effectively withdrew the Guerras' minerals from the lease market."[15] The Guerras also asserted that Manges had breached the duty he owed to the Guerras as an executive, and the Guerras filed notices of *lis pendens*.[16]

After the suit was filed, Manges discovered that producing wells drilled on an adjoining tract were draining the tract in which Manges and the Guerras owned mineral interests.[17] Claiming that he was unable to lease to anyone else because of the *lis pendens* notices, Manges leased 25,911.62 acres to himself for a term of ten (10) years, a one-eighth (1/8) royalty, a $2.00 per acre annual delay rental, and a $5.00 bonus for all 25,911.62 acres.[18] Manges subsequently drilled five (5) offset wells, three (3) of which produced hydrocarbons.[19] Thereafter, Manges, acting as a lessee under the Manges to Manges lease, entered into a farmout agreement with Joe Schero covering the same land as the Manges to Manges lease, whereby Manges would receive, in addition to his fractional share of the one-eighth (1/8) royalty, a fifty percent (50%) working interest free of drilling costs.[20]

Based upon jury findings, the trial court rendered judgment (i) removing Manges as holder of the executive rights to the mineral interests owned by the Guerras, (ii) canceling the Manges to Manges lease as of the date of its execution, (iii) adjudging Manges to be a drilling and producing co-tenant with the Guerras in three (3) producing wells and two (2) dry holes drilled by him, (iv) requiring Manges to account for net income from the producing wells, (v) awarding the Guerras actual and exemplary damages, (vi) adjudging the Bank deed of trust to be of no force or effect insofar as it purported to cover the mineral interest of the Guerras, and (vii) canceling the two (2) Gas Producing Enterprises contracts as to the mineral interest of the Guerras and their executive right.[21] The Court of Civil Appeals affirmed, and the Texas Supreme Court granted the application of Manges for Writ of Error.[22]

The Court considered several issues in the *Manges* case including (i) the standard of conduct required of the holder of the executive right, (ii) whether an executive must lease the minerals to another rather than develop them himself when a non-executive mineral interest is involved, (iii) whether the executive should exercise diligence in securing a lease, and (iv) whether cancellation of the executive right is an appropriate remedy for the breach of the duties owed by the executive to the non-executive interest owner.[23] The Court ruled that the holder of the executive right owes a duty to the non-executive "to acquire for the non-executive every benefit that he exacts for himself" by combining the duty of utmost good faith with a fiduciary duty, resulting in the imposition of exemplary damages upon the executive for his failure to meet such a standard.[24]

The Court clarified that "[w]hile a contract or deed may create the relationship" between the executive and non-executive, when the executive right is severed, "the duty of the executive arises from the relationship [of the parties] and not from express or implied terms of the contract or deed."[25] Therefore, while Manges became the executive by the deeds from the Guerras to Manges, because the deeds created the relationship of an executive and a non-executive, Manges owed a duty to acquire for the Guerras every benefit that Manges obtained for himself.[26] Since Manges did not do that, he breached his fiduciary duty to the Guerras, resulting in both compensatory and punitive damages being awarded against him.[27]

To determine how the Texas Supreme Court came to its conclusion in the *Manges* case, one must review the case law leading to the *Manges* decision. In *Manges*, the Court cited *Schlittler v. Smith*,[28] which is the earliest Texas case to discuss the standard of care owed by an executive to a non-executive. In *Schlittler*, the Texas Supreme Court stated in dicta that Schlittler (the executive) owed a duty of utmost good faith to Smith (the non-executive).[29] The question since *Schlittler* that remains is what does that duty of utmost good faith entail and when does it arise.

The next case considering the duty of the executive to the non-executive after *Schlittler* was *Portwood v. Buckalew*.[30] In *Portwood*, the Portwood heirs entered into a partition agreement dividing the surface of a ranch but leaving the mineral estate undivided.[31] Each of the heirs received the executive right over the surface tract provided to each of them by the partition agreement.[32] The partition agreement further provided that each of the heirs would share in all bonuses, royalties, and delay rentals in proportion to their ownership.[33] A lawsuit resulted after the defendants executed oil and gas leases providing for (i) the payment of surface damages in amounts ranging from $2.00 to $26.00 per acre, and (ii) additional overriding royalties which were assigned to such lessors who had the executive right in exchange for the release of the anticipated surface damages.[34] The Tyler Court of Appeals, citing *Schlittler*, held that an executive owes an implied covenant of utmost fair dealing "so as to protect the interest of" the non-participating owner in that the executive "must exact for the non-executive every benefit that he exacts for himself."[35] Therefore, if the executive obtains overriding royalties or cash bonuses for himself, he must do the same for the non-executive.[36] The Tyler Court of Appeals concluded that the lessors had violated the duty of utmost fair dealing owed to the owners of the non-executive mineral fee interest because they had characterized as surface damages amounts that otherwise would have been included in the bonus or royalty payments to all of the mineral co-owners.[37]

In *Kimsey v. Fore*, the plaintiffs purchased a term royalty entitling them to one-half (1/2) of royalty for five (5) years and as long thereafter as oil and gas were produced.[38] A well was drilled during the term of the non-participating royalty interests; however, it was abandoned because of mechanical problems.[39] Negotiations then ensued to enter into a second lease, but the landowners initially refused to execute a new lease until after the term royalty expired.[40] Eventually, the defendants entered into a second lease, which provided that if production was obtained before the term royalty expired, the lessee would bear the full burden of the non-participating interest owner.[41] The lease had a three (3) year primary term, and after the term royalty had expired, another well was drilled.[42] The Court of Civil Appeals ruled that the defendants had violated the duty of utmost fair dealing to the owners of the term royalty.[43] The defendants argued "that such nebulous and uncertain covenants as [a] 'duty to use utmost fair dealing' should not be implied."[44] Regardless, the Beaumont Court of Appeals ruled "that it [was] necessary to imply such covenant[s] in order to give effect to and effectuate the purpose of the contract as a whole.'"[45]

In *Federal Land Bank of Houston v. United States*, the plaintiff owned a one-sixteenth (1/16) term royalty in land which the United States later acquired for use as an air base.[46] About two (2) years before the term royalty would terminate, producing oil wells were completed on adjacent tracts.[47] The United States Government decided to lease the land; however, it wanted to adjoin additional government lands in the lease.[48] Because it took some time to adjoin these additional lands, the first producing well on the land was not completed until shortly after the plaintiff's term royalty had ended.[49] The District Court ruled that the United States Government had violated the duty that it owed to the non-executive term royalty interest because this delay only benefited the government.[50] Judge Whitaker in his dissent argued that the standard imposed upon the executive (the United States of America) was tantamount to a fiduciary standard in that the executive's liability was based upon its failure to ignore its own interest in order to protect the interest of the term royalty owner whose term royalty was about to expire.[51] The majority, while not conceding that it imposed a fiduciary duty, admitted that it was applying a stricter rule than usual, "requir[ing] the mineral fee owner to act with more celerity," because while "utmost fair dealing and diligence" normally requires the executive only to act with the diligence required of an ordinary land owner, the plaintiff's term royalty interest was about to expire.[52]

By the time of the *Manges* ruling, the body of case law had created a rule that constituted an intermediate standard between good faith and fiduciary—a duty of utmost good faith from the executive to the non-executive. The *Manges* case described the duty of utmost good faith as a fiduciary duty. However, most scholars concur that the actual language used in *Manges* outlined the scope of a duty falling short of a true fiduciary duty as a true fiduciary would be under an obligation to subordinate its own interest for that of its beneficiary. In *Manges*, the Court stated that the duty required the executive "to acquire for the non-executive every benefit that [the executive] exact[ed] for himself".[53] Although *Manges* may not have created a true fiduciary standard, a breach of the duty of utmost good faith and fair dealing could result in punitive or exemplary damages just as with the breach of a normal fiduciary standard.

After *Manges*, various Texas courts followed, distinguished, and explained the *Manges* case. The first post *Manges* decision was *Comanche Land & Cattle Co. v. Adams*.[54] In *Comanche Land & Cattle Co.*, the defendant entered into a joint venture oil and gas mining agreement for the development of a tract, which expressly negated the concept of royalties, providing some evidence that the agreement was entered into for the express purpose of defeating the rights of the [non-executive] royalty [interest] owner.[55] The executive argued that since no lease had been executed, there were no royalties payable to pay to the plaintiffs.[56] The Eastland Court of Appeals stated that while a joint venture agreement may not be a deed, the duty of utmost good faith "arises from the relationship of the parties and not from the express or implied terms of the deed."[57] Since there was evidence that the defendant could have entered into an oil and gas lease containing a one-eighth (1/8) royalty provision, the Eastland Court of Appeals ruled that the defendant violated the duty of utmost good faith to the plaintiff.[58]

The San Antonio Court of Appeals distinguished *Manges* in *Pickens v. Hope*.[59] In *Pickens*, the plaintiff owned a fixed one-sixty fourth (1/64) non-participating royalty.[60] In *Manges*, the non-executives owned one-half (1/2) of the mineral estate and were entitled to one-half (1/2) of all the benefits accruing to the mineral estate, including all royalties, delay rentals, and bonuses, thus creating "a duty on the part of Manges to manage the mineral property belonging to the Guerras."[61] Such managerial duties did not arise in the *Pickens* case because the plaintiff owned a fixed one-sixty fourth (1/64) royalty, and the plaintiff's interest was not dependent on the defendant's management of the mineral estate.[62] As no management duty was conferred upon the defendant in *Pickens*, no fiduciary relationship could have arisen.[63] Furthermore, the court did not require the executive to enter into a lease solely to save the term royalty, as an executive is permitted to consider all business terms of the situation to maximize its benefits.[64] Therefore, the San Antonio Court of Appeals ruled that there was no evidence of the defendant acting unlike "an ordinary prudent land owner" in failing to lease its lands, and the Court subsequently reversed the jury's findings that the defendant "breached the duty of 'good faith and utmost fair dealing, by failing to lease or develop the oil, gas, and other minerals under the [defendant's lands].'"[65]

In *Mims v. Beall*, the plaintiff, a one-fourth (1/4) non-participating royalty interest owner, sued the executive when the executive leased to the executive's son for a one-eighth (1/8) royalty with no bonus.[66] The non-executive plaintiff argued that a one-eighth (1/8) royalty was unreasonably low and violated the standard of utmost good faith.[67] The Texarkana Court of Appeals affirmed the jury finding in that the action of the executive in leasing to his son who subsequently assigned the lease to a third party and obtained an overriding royalty interest that the non-executive did not share, constituted a breach of the duty of utmost good faith.[68] The Texarkana Court of Appeals also confirmed that a malicious breach of the duty could support an award of exemplary damages, and further found that a lessee who participates in the executive's breach of the duty of utmost good faith against the non-executive (such as the defendant's son) could also be held liable to the non-participating interest owner.[69]

In *Dearing v. Spiller*, the plaintiff's predecessor in interest had conveyed a 600 acre tract to the defendant but reserved a one-half (1/2) non-executive mineral interest.[70] The deed also provided that any oil and gas lease obtained by the executive could not have less than a one-eighth (1/8) royalty.[71] The property had been leased to Shell in 1944, and multiple wells were drilled.[72] However, production had declined and one well was holding all 600 acres when the defendant purchased and plugged the well, thereby terminating the lease.[73] Subsequently, the executive was offered a one-fourth (1/4) royalty and a $100.00 per acre bonus from a third party.[74] However, the defendant executive rejected that offer and leased it to his related company for a one-eighth (1/8) royalty and no bonus.[75] The plaintiff non-executive sued, claiming that such action constituted self dealing and a breach of the duty of utmost good faith.[76]

The Fort Worth Court of Appeals held that when the executive enters into a transaction in which the executive and the non-executive are both interested, the executive "must exact for the non-executive every benefit that he exacts for himself."[77] The court further ruled that an executive is forbidden from any self dealing, whether it is through spouses, children (as was the case in *Mims*), agents, and all others whose interests are closely identified with that of the fiduciary.[78] Additionally, the court clarified that while an executive is not barred, as a matter of law, from developing the premises himself, if the market value of the lease is so much greater than the terms the executive grants to himself, a clear breach of the duty of utmost good faith has occurred.[79] Exemplary damages were awarded in the *Dearing* case as well.[80]

Recently, in 2003, the Texas Supreme Court reaffirmed the *Manges* ruling; however, it provided that the imposition of a fiduciary duty only begins after the execution of a mineral lease.[81] In *Bass*, the non-executive royalty owner sued the mineral estate owner alleging a breach of the implied duty to develop.[82] The defendant had contracted with Exxon to conduct a seismic survey on the land; however, the defendant never entered into a lease.[83] The plaintiffs argued that the defendant had breached the implied duty to the non-executive royalty interest owners by refusing to lease and develop the land.[84] To prove the alleged breach, the plaintiffs required the defendant to provide them access to the seismic data, as the plaintiffs claimed that the seismic data would reveal whether the development would be profitable.[85] The Court first analyzed whether the defendant owed the plaintiffs a duty to develop the land under a fiduciary duty.[86] The Court distinguished a fiduciary duty from a covenant to develop by stating that "a fiduciary duty arises out of agency law based upon a special relationship between the two parties" whereas "a duty to develop a mineral estate arises not from a fiduciary relationship, but from the implied covenant doctrine of contracts law in which courts read a duty to develop into an oil and gas lease when necessary to effectuate the parties' intent."[87] The Court emphasized that these two duties are distinct and were developed under different legal theories.[88]

The Court further stated as under *Manges*, an executive owes a non-executive a fiduciary duty; therefore, the defendant owed the plaintiff a duty to acquire every benefit for the plaintiff that the defendant would acquire for himself.[89] However, the Court stated that an executive owes a duty of the utmost good faith to protect the amount of the plaintiff's royalty only after a mineral lease is executed.[90] Because the defendant had not entered into a mineral lease in *Bass*, the Court ruled that the defendant owed no duty to protect the plaintiff's royalty reservation.[91] The Court further opined that *Manges* implied that execution of an oil and gas lease must occur before a fiduciary duty is imposed.[92] As the defendant had not executed a mineral lease, no duty could have been breached.[93] The result of this case, therefore, is that an executive may refuse to lease the minerals knowing that no fiduciary duty is applied unless a mineral lease is first entered into by the executive.

The Corpus Christi Court of Appeals in *Hlavinka v. Hancock*, affirmed the Texas Supreme Court in *Bass*, as the plaintiff in that case had argued that the defendant breached its fiduciary duty by failing to lease the land.[94] The defendant claimed that he had not leased the land yet, as he thought that he could obtain a larger bonus than what was currently being offered.[95] The *Hlavinka* court stated that "the executive did not breach a fiduciary duty to the non-executives without having exercised his executive power."[96] Furthermore, in *Hlavinka*, the plaintiffs argued that the executive breached its fiduciary duty by failing to notify or inform the non-executive of any of the lease negotiations.[97] The Corpus Christi Court of Appeals stated in response that as the defendants owned the exclusive right to enter into a lease, the non-executives were not entitled to participate in oil and gas leasing.[98] Therefore, there could not have been any breach of a duty to disclose.[99]

In *Veteran's Land Bd. v. Lesley*, the defendant was a real estate developer who owned only twenty-five percent (25%) of the minerals but all of the executive right.[100] The defendant also owned all of the surface estate.[101] Through a series of recorded restrictions, the defendant sold to individual lot owners' deeds that included a covenant against drilling for minerals.[102] Thus, while the defendant had a duty to his non-executive plaintiffs, he wanted to maximize profits from lot sales by ensuring that no drilling would ever occur on the lots that he was selling. The trial court found that the defendant had breached his duty to the non-executive plaintiff; however, the Eastland Court of Appeals, relying on the decision of the Texas Supreme Court in *Bass*, overruled the trial court by stating that because the defendant had not leased the land, the fiduciary duty had not arisen.[103] In essence, the defendant owner was allowed to use his executive right to prevent oil and gas development of the land he was trying to sell for residential real estate development.[104]

The Texas Supreme Court affirmed in part and reversed in part and struck down the restrictive covenants that had been placed on the property.[105] To explain its decision, vis-a-vis its opinion in *Bass*, the *Lesley* Court stated that while an executive may not be liable for failing to lease the minerals when never offered to do so, a refusal to lease the minerals must be considered more carefully.[106] If the refusal to lease "is arbitrary or motivated by self-interest to the non-executive's detriment, the executive may have breached his duty" to the non-executive.[107] In *Lesley*, the Court found that the executive's refusal to lease the minerals was motivated by self-interest as the main reason was to develop the land for single family residences with no future mineral development ever to occur thereon, and constituted an affirmative action by the executive to prevent future mineral leasing and production on such lands.[108]

The most recent decision regarding the duty that an executive owes to its non-executives is *KCM Fin. v. Bradshaw*.[109] In *Bradshaw*, Steadfast Financial, L.L.C. ("Steadfast") owned the minerals subject to the non-participating royalty interest of Betty Lou Bradshaw ("Bradshaw").[110] The deed creating the non-participating royalty interest provided that the executive could not execute an oil and gas lease permitting less than a one-eighth (1/8) royalty.[111]

Steadfast executed an oil and gas lease to Range Resources Corporation for a one-eighth royalty and a bonus of $7,505.00 per acre.[112] Bradshaw filed suit against Steadfast alleging that it breached its fiduciary duty by entering into a one-eighth royalty lease when Steadfast owed a duty to obtain a one-fourth royalty because, Bradshaw argued, "the 'going royalty rate in Hood County, Texas was one-fourth'" at the time.[113] With a one eighth-royalty lease, Bradshaw would receive a one-sixteenth royalty, and with a one-fourth royalty lease, Bradshaw would have received a one-eighth royalty.[114]

The Fort Worth Court of Appeals noted that the level of duty the executive owes depends on the level of control that the executive has over the rights of the non-participating royalty interest owner under the instrument creating the non-participating royalty interest.[115] That is, whether a fraction of royalty or a fractional royalty is reserved, and if it is a fraction of royalty, then the executive will be held to a higher standard of duty.[116] The court found that Bradshaw's non-participating royalty interest was a fraction of royalty; therefore, the level of control that Steadfast had over Bradshaw's royalty was greater than if it were a fixed fractional royalty.[117] The court ruled that, because Bradshaw had presented some proof that (i) a one-eighth royalty lease was below market value for Hood County, (ii) a higher royalty lease had originally been considered by Steadfast, and (iii) the bonus obtained by Steadfast was higher than market value in Hood County, a fact question existed regarding whether Steadfast had breached its fiduciary duty by engaging in self-dealing and conspiring with others to the detriment of Bradshaw.[118]

While elaborating on the scope of the executive duty, the Texas Supreme Court in *Bradshaw* concluded that the facts at hand exemplified "the essence of self-dealing."[119] The Court began by examining the executive duty generally and emphasizing how the existence of self-dealing is inquiry-determinative.[120] Self dealing is most commonly "observed in situations where the executive employs a legal contrivance to benefit himself," as "was most readily apparent in *Manges*."[121] The Court recognized the need for the executive to have a duty to its non-executives in light of an executive's ability to significantly reduce the value of the non-executive interest.[122] Although the executive is allowed considerable latitude and is not required to subordinate its interests to the non-executive, the executive's discretion is not unbridled.[123] The Court stated that "the controlling inquiry is whether the executive engaged in acts of self-dealing that unfairly diminished the value of the non-executive interest."[124]

The Court noted that the lease royalty is one of the components that affect the value of a lease.[125] While the amount of the royalty is material to the determination of whether or not the executive has breached his duty, it is not the sole determinative factor.[126] Rather, "the subject transaction must be viewed as a whole."[127] In viewing the transaction as a whole, the Court emphasized the unusually low royalty amount for both the executive and non-executives, and the unusually high bonus amount for solely the executive, which showed the intent of the executive to diminish the value of the non-executives' interest.[128] The Court summarized the facts at hand as the executive's misappropriation of a shared benefit for the executive's own benefit and concluded that "such conduct is the essence of self-dealing."[129]

CONCLUSION

An executive has the sole right to lease the minerals and to authorize any and all exploration and development of the mineral estate while the non-executive has no rights in this regard and must rely solely on the executive to lease the minerals and negotiate the royalty, bonus, and delay rentals. Texas courts have determined that with such power comes responsibility, resulting in the case law produced duty of utmost good faith and fair dealing owed by the executive to the non-executive first stated in *Schlittler*, expanded in *Portwood, Kimsey*, and *Federal Land Bank*, and culminating in *Manges*. This commentary and the case law cited herein have discussed what is entailed by this duty and when the duty arises.

By *Manges* and its progeny, the duty of the executive to the non-executive entails the executive (i) obtaining for the non-executive every benefit he obtains for himself, and (ii) never engaging in self dealing regarding leasing the minerals, thereby creating an intermediate duty between ordinary good faith and a fiduciary obligation, with a fiduciary obligation having been breached when the executive violates the above two (2) requirements. The Texarkana Court of Appeals in *Mims* and the Fort Worth Court of Appeals in *Dearing* further expounded on the duty of utmost good faith and fair dealing by providing that any self dealing with the executive's spouse, child, agent, or other person related to the executive is also prohibited.

The duty of the executive to the non-executive normally arises when the executive has leased the minerals, and not before, as provided in *Bass* and followed in *Hlavinka*. However, an executive's refusal to lease the minerals may constitute a breach of that duty as provided in the *Lesley* case. Additionally, when the executive enters into an agreement instead of oil and gas lease to defeat the interest of the non-executive, as in *Comanche Land and Cattle Co.*, such action may constitute a breach of the executive's duty. Lastly, a fiduciary duty may not exist when the non-executive interest is a fixed non-participating term royalty that cannot be altered, as in *Pickens*.

Some issues regarding the duty owed by the executive to the non-executive remain unresolved, including without limitation, what sort of actions equate to self-dealing that unfairly diminishes the value of the non-executive interest, as in *Bradshaw*. Other issues may develop as well; however, the *Manges* case has withstood the test of time and remains one of the landmark cases in Texas, as it constitutes the seminal case regarding the duty of the executive to the non-executive.

---

* Partner, Martin & Drought, P.C., San Antonio, Texas.
1 *See Altman v. Blake*, 712 S.W. 2d 117, 118 (Tex. 1986).
2 Ernest E. Smith & Jacqueline Lang Weaver, *Texas Law of Oil and Gas* § 2.6, 2-74 (2nd Edition 2006).
3 *Manges v. Guerra*, 673 S.W.2d 180 (Tex. 1984).
4 *Manges,* 673 S.W.2d at 181.
5 *Id.*
6 *Id.*
7 *Id.*
8 *Id.* at 182.
9 *Id.*
10 *Id.*
11 *Id.*
12 *Id.*
13 *Id.*
14 *Id.*
15 *Id.*
16 *Id.*
17 *Id.*
18 *Id.*
19 *Id.*
20 *Id.* at 182–83.
21 *Id.* at 183.
22 *Id.* at 181.
23 *Id.* at 183–84.
24 *Id.*
25 *Id.* at 183.
26 *Id.* at 183–84.
27 *Id.* at 184–85.
28 *Schlittler v. Smith*, 128 Tex. 628, 101 S.W.2d 543 (1937).
29 *Schlittler*, 128 Tex. at 631, 101 S.W.2d at 545.
30 *Portwood v. Buckalew*, 521 S.W.2d 904 (Tex. Civ. App.—Tyler 1975, writ ref'd n.r.e.).
31 *Portwood*, 521 S.W.2d at 909.
32 *Id.*
33 *Id.*
34 *Id.* at 914–15.
35 *Id.* at 911.
36 *Id.*
37 *Id.* at 914.
38 *Kimsey v. Fore*, 593 S.W.2d 107, 108 (Tex. Civ. App.— Beaumont 1979, writ ref'd n.r.e.)
39 *Kimsey*, 593 S.W.2d at 108.
40 *Id.*
41 *Id.*
42 *Id.* at 108–09.
43 *Id.* at 112.
44 *Id.*
45 *Id.*
46 *Federal Land Bank of Houston v. United States*, 168 F.Supp. 788, 789 (Ct. Cl. 1958).
47 *Federal Land Bank of Houston*, 168 F.Supp. at 789–90.
48 *Id.* at 790.
49 *Id.*
50 *Id.* at 791.
51 *Id.* at 792.
52 *Id.* at 791.
53 *Manges*, 673 S.W.2d at 183.
54 *Comanche Land & Cattle Co. v. Adams*, 688 S.W.2d 914 (Tex. App.— Eastland 1985, no writ).
55 *Comanche Land & Cattle Co.*, 688 S.W.2d at 915–16.
56 *Id.* at 915.
57 *Id.* at 915–16.
58 *Id.*
59 *Pickens v. Hope,* 764 S.W.2d 256 (Tex. App.— San Antonio 1988, writ denied).
60 *Pickens*, 764 S.W.2d at 266.
61 *Id.*
62 *Id.*
63 *Id.* at 268.
64 *Id.* at 270.
65 *Id.* at 271.
66 *Mims v. Beall*, 810 S.W.2d 876, 878 (Tex. App.—Texarkana 1991, no writ).
67 *Id.*
68 *Id.*
69 *Id.* at 880–81.

70 *Dearing v. Spiller*, 824 S.W.2d 728, 730 (Tex. App.—Fort Worth 1992, writ denied).
71 *Dearing*, 824 S.W.2d at 730.
72 *Id.*
73 *Id.* at 730–31.
74 *Id.* at 731.
75 *Id.*
76 *Id.*
77 *Id.* at 733.
78 *Id.*
79 *Id.* at 734.
80 *Id.*
81 *See In re Bass*, 113 S.W.3d 735, 743 (Tex. 2003).
82 *Bass*, 113 S.W.3d at 737.
83 *Id.* at 738.
84 *Id.*
85 *Id.*
86 *Id.* at 743.
87 *Id.*
88 *Id.*
89 *Id.* at 745.
90 *Id.* at 744.
91 *Id.* at 744.
92 *Id.* at 745.
93 *Id.*
94 *Hlavinka v. Hancock*, 116 S.W.3d 412, 420 (Tex. App.—Corpus Christi 2003, pet. denied).
95 *Hlavinka*, 116 S.W.3d at 419.
96 *Id.* at 420.
97 *Id.*
98 *Id.* at 421.
99 *Id.*
100 *Veteran's Land Bd. v Lesley*, 281 S.W.3d 602, 608–09 (Tex. App.—Eastland 2009, aff'd in part, rev'd in part, 352 S.W.3d 479 (Tex. 2011).
101 *Id.* at 609.
102 *Id.* at 609–10.
103 *Id.* at 619.
104 *Id.* at 620.
105 *Lesley v. Veterans Land Bd.*, 352 S.W.3d 479, 491 (Tex. 2011).
106 *Id.*
107 *Id.*
108 *Id.*
109 *KCM Fin. v. Bradshaw*, 457 S.W.3d 70 (Tex. 2015).
110 *Bradshaw v. Steadfast Fin., L.L.C.*, 395 S.W.3d 348, 350 (Tex. App.—Fort Worth 2013, pet. granted).
111 *Id.* at 352.
112 *Id.* at 353.
113 *Id.* at 351.
114 *Id.*
115 *Id.* at 370.
116 *Id.*
117 *Id.*
118 *Id.*
119 *KCM Fin. v. Bradshaw*, 457 S.W.3d 70, 83 (Tex. 2015).
120 *Id.* at 81.
121 *Id.*
122 *Id.* at 82.
123 *Id.* at 81.
124 *Id.* at 82.
125 *Id.*
126 *Id.* at 84.
127 *Id.*
128 *Id.*
129 *Id.* at 83.

19

CHAPTER 19

Margaret Lyne Moser et al., Petitioners, v. United States Steel Corporation et al., Respondents.

COMMENTARY

by Laura H. Burney

676 S.W.2d 99

1984

Margaret Lyne Moser et al., Petitioners,
v.
United States Steel Corporation et al., Respondents.

676 S.W.2d 99

1984

John H. Miller, Jr., Sinton, Luther E. Jones, Jr., Corpus Christi, Wm. G. Burnett, Sinton, for petitioners.

Bracewell and Patterson, Charles G. King, III and John L. Harvey, Houston, Robert D. Nogueria, Beeville, for respondents.

ON MOTION FOR REHEARING

CAMPBELL, Justice.

Our opinion of June 8, 1983, is withdrawn. The Motion for Rehearing is denied.

This is a suit to quiet title to an interest in uranium ore. We must determine whether uranium is included in a reservation or conveyance of "oil, gas and other minerals." The trial court awarded title to the defendant mineral owners, and the court of appeals affirmed the trial court judgment. 601 S.W.2d 731. We affirm the judgments of the courts below, and hold that uranium is a part of the mineral estate.

The Mosers, plaintiffs, and the Gefferts, defendants, own neighboring tracts of land in Live Oak County. Prior to 1949, the boundary between the Mosers' land and that of the Gefferts was a winding road. In 1949, the road was straightened and, as a result, no longer represented the true boundary between the two ranches. The new road separated a 6.77 acre tract of the Geffert ranch on the Moser side of the road and a 6.42 acre tract of the Moser ranch on the Geffert side of the road. To avoid crossing the highway to reach their tracts, the Mosers' predecessor in title and the Gefferts executed similar deeds conveying the surface estates of the isolated tracts to the other party. The 1949 deeds contain identical language reserving:

> [A]ll of the oil, gas, and other minerals of every kind and character, in, on, under and that may be produced from said tract of land, together with all necessary and convenient easements for the purpose of exploring for, mining, drilling, producing and transporting oil, gas or any of said minerals.

Substantial quantities of uranium were discovered on the 6.77 acre tract. The Mosers, as surface owners of the 6.77 acre tract, sued the Gefferts to establish ownership of the uranium. The Gefferts, as owners of the mineral estate under the 6.77 acre tract, counterclaimed to establish that uranium is one of the "other minerals" reserved from the conveyance of the surface.

At trial, the parties offered conflicting evidence on the depth of the uranium deposits and the effect its removal would have on the surface. Special issues were submitted based on the test set out by this Court in *Reed v. Wylie*, 554 S.W.2d 169 (Tex.1977) (*Reed* I): if substantial quantities of the mineral lie so near the surface that extraction, as of the date of the severance of the surface and mineral estates, would necessarily have destroyed the surface, the surface owner has title to the mineral. The jury found there would have been no substantial surface destruction at the time the deed was executed. The trial court accordingly held the uranium was a part of the mineral estate retained by the Gefferts in the 1949 deed.

After the Mosers' appeal to the court of civil appeals, but prior to final disposition by that court, we rendered our decision in *Reed v. Wylie*, 597 S.W.2d 743 (Tex.1980) (*Reed* II). The court of civil appeals held that *Reed* II should govern the appeal. In *Reed* II, we modified the rule of *Reed* I by holding that a substance "near the surface" is a part of the surface estate if it is shown that any reasonable method of production, at the time of conveyance or thereafter, would consume, deplete, or destroy the surface. 597 S.W.2d at 747. A deposit within 200 feet of the surface was held to be "near the surface" as a matter of law. In addition, we held if a surface owner establishes ownership of a substance at or near the surface, the surface owner owns the substance beneath the tract at whatever depth it may be found. *Id.* at 748. The *Moser* court of civil appeals found, as a matter of law, that at the time of trial the only reasonable method of mining uranium from the tract was by in-situ leaching or solution mining, a process which it found did not result in substantial destruction of the surface. 601 S.W.2d at 734. Accordingly, the court of civil appeals affirmed.

We have previously attempted to create a rule to effect the intent of the parties to convey valuable minerals to the mineral estate owner, while protecting the surface estate owner from destruction of the surface estate by the mineral owner's extraction of minerals. *See Reed v. Wylie*, 597 S.W.2d 743 (Tex.1980); *Reed v. Wylie*, 554 S.W.2d 169 (Tex.1977); *Acker v. Guinn*, 464 S.W.2d 348 (Tex.1971). In so doing, we decided that determinations of title should be based on whether a reasonable use of the surface by the mineral owner would substantially harm the surface. Application of this rule has required the determination of several fact issues to establish whether the owner of the surface or the mineral estate owns a substance not specifically referred to in a grant, reservation or exception. *See Reed v. Wylie*, 597 S.W.2d 743, 750 (Spears, J., concurring). As a result, it could not be determined from the grant or reservation alone who owned title to an unnamed substance. Determining the ownership of minerals in this manner has resulted in title uncertainty. We now abandon, in the case of uranium, the *Acker* and *Reed* approach to determining ownership of "other minerals" and hold that title to uranium is held by the owner of the mineral estate as a matter of law.

In Texas, the mineral estate may be severed from the surface estate by a grant of the minerals in a deed or lease, or by reservation in a conveyance. *See Humphreys-Mexia Co. v. Gammon*, 113 Tex. 247, 254 S.W. 296 (1923). This severance is often accomplished by a grant or reservation of "oil, gas and other minerals." Consequently, Texas courts have had many occasions to construe the scope of the term "other minerals." We have determined that some unnamed substances have been impliedly conveyed or reserved in mineral conveyances by cataloging each, on a substance-by-substance basis, as part of the surface or mineral estate as a matter of law. *See, e.g., Sun Oil Co. v. Whitaker*, 483 S.W.2d 808 (Tex.1972) (fresh water not included in mineral estate reservation of "oil, gas, and other minerals"); *Heinatz v. Allen*, 147 Tex. 512, 217 S.W.2d 994 (1949) (devise of "mineral rights" held not to include limestone and building stone); *Atwood v. Rodman*, 355 S.W.2d 206 (Tex. Civ. App.—El Paso 1962, writ ref'd n.r.e.) ("oil, gas, and other minerals" did not include limestone, caliche, and surface shale); *Union Sulphur Co. v. Texas Gulf Sulphur Co.*, 42 S.W.2d 182 (Tex. Civ. App.—Austin 1931, writ ref'd) (solid sulphur deposits conveyed by ordinary oil and gas lease); *Praeletorian Diamond Oil Ass'n v. Garvey*, 15 S.W.2d 698 (Tex. Civ. App.—Beaumont 1929, writ ref'd) (gravel and sand not intended to be included in lease for "oil and other minerals"); *Reed v. Wylie*, 597 S.W.2d 743 (Tex.1980) (near surface lignite, iron and coal is part of the surface estate as a matter of law).

In making these determinations of ownership, our courts have considered a number of construction aids. We have refused to employ the *ejusdem generis* rule of construction to limit the term "oil, gas and other minerals" to hydrocarbons. *Southland Royalty Co. v. Pan American Petroleum Corp.*, 378 S.W.2d 50 (Tex.1964). Likewise, we have acknowledged that the scientific or technical definition of a disputed substance is not determinative of whether it is a mineral, because the term "other minerals" would then "embrace not only metallic minerals, oil, gas, stone, sand, gravel, and many other substances but even the soil itself." *Heinatz v. Allen*, 147 Tex. 512, 217 S.W.2d 994, 997 (1949). Such a construction would eliminate any distinction between the surface and the mineral estates. We have, however, approved of considering whether the substance is thought to be a mineral within the ordinary and natural meaning of the term. *See Heinatz v. Allen*, 217 S.W.2d at 997; *Psencik v. Wessels*, 205 S.W.2d 658, 660–61 (Tex.Civ.App.—Austin 1947, writ ref'd). The knowledge of the parties of the value, or even the existence of the substance at the time the conveyance was executed [SIC] has been found to be irrelevant to its inclusion or exclusion from a grant of minerals. *See Cain v. Neumann*, 316 S.W.2d 915, 922 (Tex.Civ.App.—San Antonio 1958, no writ). *Accord Barden v. Northern Pacific Ry.*, 154 U.S. 288, 314, 14 S.Ct. 1030, 1033, 38 L.Ed. 992 (1893) ("[T]he knowledge or want of knowledge at the time [of the grant] by the grantee in such cases, of the property reserved in no respect affects the transfer to him of the title to it."). In *Acker v. Guinn*, 464 S.W.2d 348 (Tex.1971), we quoted with approval Professor Eugene Kuntz' theory that the proper focus when construing an implied grant of minerals is the general, rather than the specific, intent of the parties. We adopted the view that the general intent of parties executing a mineral deed or lease is presumed to be an intent to sever the mineral and surface estates, convey all valuable substances to the mineral owner regardless of whether their presence or value was known at the time of conveyance, and to preserve the uses incident to each estate. *Id.* at 352; Kuntz, *The Law Relating to Oil and Gas in Wyoming*, 3 Wyo. L.J. 107, 112 (1949).

Professor Kuntz suggested the apparently irreconcilable conflict between the rights of the surface owner to preserve the integrity of his surface fee and the right of a mineral owner who takes a mineral under an implied grant to extract his mineral could be compromised as follows:

> The rights of the surface owner to subjacent support and his right to the use of the top-soil in its place would have to be respected, and at the same time, the owner of the mineral fee should have a right of extraction. Since the right of extraction could only be exercised by destruction of the surface owner's enjoyment, it could only be accomplished with compensation for the damages to the surface estate.... Specific mention of the substance, however, together with the usual provisions for extraction, would demonstrate a specific intention to make the surface right subject to the rights of access for purposes of extraction and would not make the mineral owner accountable for necessary damage flowing therefrom.

Kuntz, *The Law Relating to Oil and Gas in Wyoming*, 3 Wyo. L.J. 107, 115 (1949).

We now hold a severance of minerals in an oil, gas and other minerals clause includes all substances within the ordinary and natural meaning of that word, whether their presence or value is known at the time of severance. *Heinatz v. Allen*, 147 Tex. 512, 217 S.W.2d 994 (1949); *Cain v. Neumann*, 316 S.W.2d 915 (Tex.Civ.App.—San Antonio 1958, no writ). We also hold uranium is a mineral within the ordinary and natural meaning of the word and was retained in the Gefferts' conveyance of the 6.77 acre tract to the Mosers. We continue to adhere, however, to our previous decisions which held certain substances to belong to the surface estate as a matter of law. *See, e.g., Heinatz v. Allen*, 147 Tex. 512, 217 S.W.2d 994 (1949) (building stone and limestone); *Atwood v. Rodman*, 355 S.W.2d 206 (Tex.Civ.App.—El Paso 1962, writ ref'd n.r.e.) (limestone, caliche, and surface shale); *Fleming Foundation v. Texaco*, 337 S.W.2d 846 (Tex.Civ.App.—Amarillo 1960, writ ref'd n.r.e.) (water); *Psencik v. Wessels*, 205 S.W.2d 658 (Tex.Civ.App.—Austin 1947, writ ref'd) (sand and gravel); *Reed v. Wylie*, 597 S.W.2d 743 (Tex.1980) (near surface lignite, iron and coal).

Having established that the mineral owner has title to uranium, we now must determine the issue of reasonable use of the surface estate by the uranium owner. The mineral owner, as owner of the dominant estate, has the right to make any use of the surface which is necessarily and reasonably incident to the removal of the minerals. *See Sun Oil Co. v. Whitaker*, 483 S.W.2d 808 (Tex.1972); *Getty Oil Co. v. Jones*, 470 S.W.2d 618, 627 (Tex.1971); *Humble Oil & Refining Co. v. Williams*, 420 S.W.2d 133 (Tex.1967). This is an imperative rule of mineral law; a mineral owner's estate would be worthless without the right to reach the minerals. A corollary of the mineral owner's right to use the surface to extract his minerals is the rule that the mineral owner is held liable to the surface owner only for negligently inflicted damage to the surface estate. *General Crude Oil v. Aiken Co.*, 162 Tex. 104, 344 S.W.2d 668 (1961); *Stradley v. Magnolia Petroleum Co.*, 155 S.W.2d 649 (Tex.Civ.App.—Amarillo 1941, writ ref'd); 1 H. Williams & C. Meyers, Oil and Gas Law §§ 217, 218.8 (1981).

Restricting the mineral owner's liability to negligently inflicted damage to, or excessive use of, the surface estate is justified where a mineral is specifically conveyed. It is reasonable to assume a grantor who expressly conveys a mineral which may or must be removed by destroying a portion of the surface estate anticipates his surface estate will be diminished when the mineral is removed. It is also probable the grantor has calculated the value of the diminution of his surface in the compensation received for the conveyance. This reasoning is not compelling when a grantor conveys a mineral which may destroy the surface in a conveyance of "other minerals."

We hold the limitation of the dominant mineral owner's liability to negligently inflicted damages does not control in a case such as this, in a general conveyance of "other minerals." When dealing with the rights of a mineral owner who has taken title by a grant or reservation of an unnamed substance such as this, liability of the mineral owner must include compensation to the surface owner for surface destruction.

This holding does not affect the right of the mineral owner to enter the surface estate and use so much of the surface as is reasonably necessary to remove the minerals. *Ball v. Dillard*, 602 S.W.2d 521, 523 (Tex.1980); *Harris v. Currie*, 142 Tex. 93, 176 S.W.2d 302, 305 (Tex.1943). As in the case of the mineral owner who takes under a specific grant, the mineral owner under a grant of "other minerals" is restricted in his use of the surface estate by the dictates of the "due regard" or "accommodation doctrine." This rule is applied when the surface owner and mineral owner are attempting to use the surface estate for two conflicting and incompatible uses. We held, in *Getty Oil Co. v. Jones*, 470 S.W.2d 618 (Tex.1971), that even though the mineral owner held the dominant estate, he must exercise his rights of surface use with due regard for the rights of the surface owner.

Because of the extent of public reliance on our holdings in *Acker v. Guinn*, 464 S.W.2d 348 (Tex.1971), and *Reed v. Wylie*, 597 S.W.2d 743 (Tex.1980), and because of an inability to foresee a coming change in the law, the rules announced in this case are to be applied only prospectively from the date of our original opinion, June 8, 1983. *See Sanchez v. Schindler*, 651 S.W.2d 249, 254 (Tex.1983).

We affirm the judgments of the courts below. We hold as a matter of law the Gefferts are the owners of the uranium in the 6.77 acre tract.

RAY, Justice, dissenting.

I respectfully dissent. I agree with the majority that uranium is a mineral within the ordinary and natural meaning of the word. Also, I agree with the majority that a mineral owner who takes title by an instrument containing an unspecific grant of "oil, gas and other minerals" must compensate the surface owner for the surface destruction caused by the mining of the minerals. I disagree with the majority in that its decision to apply the compensation rule prospectively prevents the Mosers from receiving compensation for the destruction of their surface estate. The rationale underlying the majority's determination to apply this decision prospectively is based on the public's reliance on our former holdings and the public's inability to foresee this change in the law. Neither of these reasons, however, applies to the case at bar. Thus, I would hold that the new compensation rule applies in this case, so that the Mosers are entitled to compensation from the mineral owners for the destruction of their surface estate.

THE MEANING OF "OTHER MINERALS"
Commentary on Moser
by Laura H. Burney

In *Moser v. United States Steel Corp.*,[1] the Texas Supreme Court addressed the meaning of the phrase "oil, gas and other minerals." That seemingly simple phrase found in countless deeds conveying or reserving property created disputes between surface and mineral owners about title to unnamed substances, such as uranium, coal, iron ore, and lignite. Surface owners argued that in order to protect their rights, such substances, which may be produced through surface-destructive methods, should belong to them. In a 1971 case, *Acker v. Guinn*[2], the Texas Supreme Court adopted that argument and formulated the "surface destruction" test as its interpretative tool for the "other minerals" phrase. A few years later in *Reed v. Wylie*[3], which reached the high court twice, the Texas Supreme Court ultimately defined that test as holding that "a substance 'near the surface' is part of the surface estate if it is shown that any reasonable method of production, at the time of conveyance or thereafter, would consume, deplete or destroy the surface."[4] Furthermore, under the test a deposit within 200 feet of the surface is "near the surface" as a matter of law, vesting the surface owner with title to "near surface" substances at whatever depths they may be found.[5]

Commentators consistently criticized the "surface destruction" test for its focus on fact issues rather than the deed records, an approach that complicates and jeopardizes the stability of land titles.[6] In *Moser*, the Texas Supreme Court agreed and replaced the "surface destruction" test with the "ordinary and natural meaning" test: "[A] severance of minerals in an oil, gas and other minerals clause includes all substances within the ordinary and natural meaning of that word, whether their presence or value is known at the time of severance."[7] To protect the rights of surface owners, the Court also modified the dominance of the mineral estate by requiring those owners to pay for any surface destruction—not just negligently inflicted damage—when they acquire title to an unnamed substance through the "other minerals" phrase.[8]

Although the *Moser* decision launched a direct hit against the "surface destruction" test (SDT) the blow was not fatal. Instead, the Court allowed the test to survive by restricting its ruling to conveyances executed after June 8, 1983, the date of the first *Moser* decision.[9] With that prospective limitation, the Court kept the test alive for all deeds executed prior to that date, including the 1949 deed at issue in the case. In other words, the *Moser* rules did not apply to the *Moser* parties.

Those parties were the Mosers, surface owners of the 6.77 acre tract where substantial quantities of uranium had been discovered, and the Gefferts, who owned the "oil, gas and other minerals." The parties' predecessors in title, who owned neighboring ranches, had included this phrase in deeds they executed to one another because a road that had been straightened no longer marked the correct boundary between the two properties. At trial, the parties dutifully complied with the SDT, providing evidence about the depth of the uranium and the effect mining it would have on the surface estate. As required by the test, fact questions were submitted to a jury. After the jury determined the uranium mining would not cause substantial destruction of the surface, the trial court awarded title to the Gefferts, as mineral estate owners. The court of appeals affirmed after applying precepts from the second *Reed* decision and finding as a matter of law that at that time of trial the only reasonable method of mining uranium was solution mining, a process that did not cause substantial surface destruction.[10]

Determined to benefit from the SDT and gain title to the uranium, the surface owners appealed to the Texas Supreme Court, which ultimately issued two opinions. In both, the Court recognized the problems caused by relying on fact questions to determine land title issues and purported to abandon the SDT. To address the rights of surface owners, the Court also adopted surface damage rules, suggested by the respected oil and gas scholar, Dean Eugene Kuntz, for substances conveyed with an "other minerals" clause. Those rules hold that "the limitation of the dominant mineral owner's liability to negligently inflicted damages does not control" when a mineral owner claims a substance through a general "other minerals" conveyance. Instead, the Court held that mineral owners of an unnamed substance acquired through these broad conveyances are liable for any destruction of the surface. As the Court explained

> Restricting the mineral owner's liability to negligently inflicted damage to, or excessive use of, the surface estate is justified where a mineral is specifically conveyed. It is reasonable to assume a grantor who expressly conveys a mineral which may or must be removed by destroying a portion of the surface estate anticipates his surface estate will be diminished when the mineral is removed. It is also probable the grantor has calculated the value of diminution of his surface in the compensation received for the conveyance. This reasoning is not compelling when a grantor conveys a mineral which may destroy the surface in a conveyance of "other minerals."[11]

These damages rules, however, were not available to the losing parties in *Moser*, the surface owners, because of the prospective ruling placed in the second opinion issued a year after the Court withdrew its first one. According to the *Moser* majority, "[b]ecause of the extent of public reliance on our holdings in [*Acker*] and [*Reed*], and because of an inability to foresee a coming change in the law, the rules announced in this case are to be applied only prospectively from the date of our original opinion, June 8, 1983."[12] One justice disagreed. In his dissenting opinion, Justice Ray stated there were no justifications for the prospective ruling; therefore, he believed the Mosers, as the surface owners, should have been entitled to compensation from the mineral owners for the destruction of their surface estate in the mining of the uranium.[13]

In addition to the prospective limitation, the second *Moser* opinion included another change from the first opinion. This one appears in the Court's list of cases establishing that certain substances belong to the surface estate as a matter of law. Specifically, it added the opinion of *Reed v. Wylie*.[14] Recall that *Reed* held that "near surface" lignite, iron, and coal belong to the surface estate as a matter of law, and that a deposit within 200 feet of the surface is "near surface" as a matter of law. In light of the *Reed* addition to the surface-substances list, factual determinations, rather than the "ordinary and natural meaning" test, continue to control title determinations for certain substances, even for deeds executed after June 8, 1983.

Post-Moser Cases: In post-*Moser* cases, the prospective limitation has remained controversial. For example, in a 1985 decision, *Friedman v. Texaco*,[15] the Texas Supreme Court applied the SDT to a 1959 deed, a date that precedes the *Acker* (1970) and *Reed* (1977 and 1980) decisions. This fact did not deter the Court from applying the test to earlier deeds. Instead, in *Friedman*, Justice Spears justified this application by claiming that while the law may have been unsettled in the 1950s, the surface destruction concept was not new.[16] Yet according to at least one writer, *Friedman* "stands as an unwarranted retroactive extension of the surface destruction test, which further detracts from the remedial goals of *Moser II*."[17]

A year after *Friedman* the Texas Supreme Court faced a case that, like *Moser* and *Reed*, reached the Court twice. Unlike those cases, however, in *Schwarz v. State*[18] the dispute arose not from a conveyance between private parties but from a reservation in patents from the State of Texas issued pursuant to early Land Sales Acts. The patents recited that "all of the minerals in the above described land are reserved to the State."[19] The State claimed that, as mineral owner, it had retained title to coal and lignite. In the first *Schwarz* opinion the State lost after the Court applied the surface-destruction test, and held that these substances belonged to the surface owner. In the process, the Court reviewed the history behind the Land Acts and rejected the State's position that the SDT should not apply to this pre-June 8, 1983 conveyance because the legislature intended to reserve all minerals "with the corresponding right to destroy the surface."[20] However, a year later, in *Schwarz II*, this rejected contention became the Court's holding. This time the Court concluded that legislative history revealed empirical evidence that the State intended a broad reservation of minerals.[21]

A concurring Justice saw the *Schwarz II* holding as an opportunity to criticize *Moser's* prospective limitation, and its addition of *Reed* to the list of cases establishing surface substances. According to Justice C. L. Ray, who was the dissenter in *Moser*, the Court had created this absurd-sounding scenario for analyzing "other minerals" clauses in Texas:

> [T]he surface belongs to the surface estate owner and the minerals belong to the mineral estate owner, except in pre-June 8, 1983 severances where nobody knows who owns what (not even a title examiner) until ownership has been litigated, in which case if some portion of a mineral is found within 200 feet of the surface, it belongs to the surface owner unless, of course, the land was purchased pursuant to the Land Sales Act of 1895, in which case even though the estates were severed before June 8, 1983, the minerals belong to the mineral estate, or the State.[22]

As Justice Ray explained, the Court could have avoided this contorted state of the law had it ruled retroactively in *Moser*.[23]

In a 1995 decision, *Plainsman Trading Co. v. Crews*,[24] a dissenting justice echoed Justice Ray's frustration with the perpetuation of the "'surface destruction test' and all its contortions."[25] In *Crews* the Court addressed a question for which appeals courts had provided different answers: whether the SDT applies to construing non-participating royalty interests (NPRIs) granted or reserved through an "other minerals" clause in pre-June 8, 1983 deeds. In that case, the Crewses were the grantees of the surface estate in a 1949 deed in which the grantor, who owned both the surface and mineral estates, had reserved the NPRI. After the Crewses executed a uranium lease, the owners of the NPRI claimed their interest attached to the uranium production. Because the SDT applied to the 1949 deed and the uranium was less than 200 feet below the surface, the lower courts held that the uranium belonged to the surface estate owner as a matter of law. The NPRI owners viewed that determination as irrelevant to their rights. Instead, they argued that the policy behind the SDT—prohibiting mineral estate owners from destroying surface estates—is not raised with NPRI owners, whose non-possessory interests present no threat to surface owners' enjoyment of their estates.

The Texas Supreme Court disagreed. Even though the grantor who had reserved the NPRI in the "oil, gas and other minerals" owned both the surface and mineral estates at the time, the majority in *Crews* concluded that, "[i]f a non-participating royalty is carved from the *mineral fee*, it cannot attach to a substance, mineral or not, which is *not a part* of the *mineral fee estate*."[26] This holding prompted the dissenting Justice to chastise the Court for having perpetuated the very problems it sought to solve in *Moser*:

> The surface destruction test should be applied only where its underlying policy is furthered. . . . We should minimize the number of situations in which land interest owners must resort to factual determinations of the depth of minerals, etc., to determine ownership because "Determining the ownership of minerals in this manner has resulted in title uncertainty." *Moser*, 676 S.W. 2d at 101. We need fewer, not more applications of the surface destruction test. Today the majority takes a giant step backward from using common sense to give words their plain (and probable intended) meaning, and decreases title certainty in the process.[27]

This dissenting opinion in *Crews*, like Justice C.L. Ray's concurrence in *Schwarz II*, identifies the effects of the *Moser* court's failure to at once end and clarify the "surface destruction" test. Instead, Justice C.L. Ray's convoluted summary of that test in *Schwarz II* remains accurate.

Conclusion: In an article written in 1987, I noted the similarities between Justice Ray's sarcastic summary and the famous "Who's on First" dialogue between the comedians Abbot & Costello. Writing in 2008, it appears another non-legal source applies to an analysis of *Moser*, the song from the classic movie *Casablanca*: "As Time Goes By." Although the prospective limitation may have been unwarranted and unfortunately allowed the "surface destruction" test to survive, drafters have heeded *Moser's* lessons for over 25 years and generally avoid the broad "other minerals" phrase in favor of specific lists of substances or other language clarifying the parties' intent.[28] Therefore, as time goes by, controversies should fade over *Moser* and the meaning of "other minerals" clauses.[29]

---

1 *Moser v. U.S. Steel Corp.*, 676 S.W. 2d 99 (Tex. 1984).
2 *Acker v. Guinn*, 464 S.W. 2d 348 (Tex. 1971).
3 *Reed v. Wylie*, 597 S.W. 2d 743 (Tex. 1980) (Reed II); 554 S.W. 2d 169 (Tex. 1977) (Reed I).
4 *Moser*, 676 S.W.2d at 100.
5 *Id.* at 101.
6 For one list of the many articles that have analyzed and criticized the "surface destruction" test and *Moser, see* E. Smith & Jacqueline Lang Weaver, The Texas Law of Oil and Gas, §§ 3-29 (2d ed. 2002).
7 *Moser*, 676 S.W.2d at 102.
8 *Id.* at 103.
9 *Id.*
10 *Id.* at 100: "After the Mosers' appeal to the court of civil appeals, but prior to final disposition by that court, we rendered our decision in [*Reed II*]. . . . In *Reed II*, we modified the rule of *Reed I* by holding that a substance 'near the surface' is a part of the surface estate if it is shown that any reasonable method of production, at the time of conveyance or thereafter, would consume, deplete, or destroy the surface." *Id.* (*citing Reed II*, 597 S.W.2d at 747).
11 *Id.* at 103.
12 *Id.*
13 *Id.* at 104 (Ray, J., dissenting).
14 The Court listed the following as substances that belong to the surface as a matter of law: water, limestone and building stone, caliche, surface shale, gravel and sand, near surface lignite, iron and coal. *Moser*, 676 S.W.2d at 102 (majority opinion).
15 *Friedman v. Texaco, Inc.*, 691 S.W. 2d 586 (Tex. 1985).
16 *Id.* at 588.
17 Laura H. Burney, "*Oil, Gas, and Other Minerals*" *Clauses in Texas: Who's on First?*, 41 Sw. L.J. 695, 702 (1987).
18 *Schwarz v. State*, 28 Tex. Sup. Ct. J. 488 (June 12, 1985) (*Schwarz I*), *opinion withdrawn on reh'g*, 703 S.W. 2d 187 (Tex. 1986) (*Schwarz II*).
19 *Schwarz II*, 703 S.W. 2d at 188.
20 *Schwarz I*, 28 Tex. Sup. Ct. J. at 491. Expert testimony had established that coal was located at a depth averaging 50 feet, which qualifies as surface as a matter of law under *Reed.*
21 *Schwarz II*, 703 S.W. 2d at 189. This time the Court viewed the legislative history as revealing that the State intended to withhold from the conveyance all of the coal or lignite, "whether or not recovery of such would destroy or deplete the surface estate." The Court also relied on the canon of construction that instruments from the State should be interpreted in its favor.
22 *Id.* at 193 (Ray, J., concurring).
23 *Id.* For another case demonstrating the adverse effects of *Moser's* prospective limitation, *see Atl. Richfield Co. v. Lindholm*, 714 S.W. 2d 390 (Tex. App.—Corpus Christi 1986, writ ref'd n.r.e.), *analyzed in* Burney, *supra* note 17 (prospective ruling in *Moser* prevented court from noting protection provided to surface owners through Surface Reclamation Statutes, which were passed after the SDT was formulated).
24 *Plainsman Trading Co. v. Crews*, 898 S.W. 2d 786 (Tex. 1995).
25 *Id.* at 792 (Gammage, J., dissenting).
26 *Id.* at 790 (majority opinion) (emphasis in original).
27 *Id.* at 792-93 (Gammage, J., dissenting).

28 In a 1988 case, an appellate court declined to apply the SDT to a deed that reserved "all minerals . . . including gold, silver, coal, oil, gas . . . with the right to take the same therefrom upon paying the grantee . . . the reasonable market value of all the land reasonably necessary for the taking of such minerals . . ." In light of this specific language, the court held the parties intended to reserve uranium, even though it might be mined through surface-destructive methods. *Wojtasczyk v. Burns*, 744 S.W. 2d 354, 355 (Tex. App.—Corpus Christi 1988, no writ).

29 Controversies between private parties have faded over the years. However, Texas courts may again address the meaning of "minerals" as that term appears in State grants, including those covered by the Relinquishment Act. *See Koch v. Tex. Gen. Land Office*, 2007 WL 2286482 (appeal to Austin appellate court from order granting State's plea to jurisdiction in declaratory judgment suit in which Appellant sought declaration that limestone and other materials were not included in the mineral estate reserved to the State under the Relinquishment Act).

In addition to patents and other conveyances, courts have applied *Moser* to ad valorem taxation disputes. *See Gifford-Hill & Co., Inc. v. Wise Cnty. Appraisal Dist.*, 827 S.W. 2d 811 (Tex. 1991) (holding that new appraisal category was improper attempt to treat limestone as a mineral rather than part of surface estate).

CHAPTER 20

Eb F. Luckel, et al.
v.
Furl White, et al.

COMMENTARY

by Laura H. Burney

819 S.W.2d 459

1991

Eb F. Luckel, et al.
v.
Furl White, et al.

819 S.W.2d 459

1991

J.M. Slator, III, Houston, Robert C. Bledsoe, and Tevis Herd, Midland, for appellants.

Claude C. Roberts, William A. Teague, Robert I. Peeples, Houston, Rex G. Fortenberry, Beaumont, Chap B. Cain, III, Liberty, Susan M. Edmonson, Seabrook, Bradford Pickett, Liberty, Thomas A. Zabel, Stanley J. Krist, Houston, and E.R. Norwood, Liberty, for appellees.

GAMMAGE, Justice.

This suit concerns the construction of a royalty deed in which the "granting," "habendum" and "warranty" clauses recite that a 1/32nd royalty interest is conveyed, but the "subject to" and "future lease" clauses state that the grantee shall be entitled to receive one-fourth of any and all royalties. The grantee's successors (Luckel, et al.) sought declaratory judgment that the deed conveyed an interest in one-fourth of the royalties reserved under all subsequent leases and an accounting for oil and gas production on the land. Both sides moved for summary judgment. The trial court construed the deed as conveying a fixed 1/32nd royalty interest, giving controlling effect to the "granting" clause and holding the "future lease" clause ineffective to convey one-fourth of future royalties on future leases. The trial court's holding follows *Alford v. Krum*, 671 S.W.2d 870 (Tex.1984). The trial court granted a partial summary judgment to the grantor's successors (White, et al.) and severed the cause to make the summary judgment final. The court of appeals affirmed. 792 S.W.2d 485. We reverse the court of appeals, overrule *Alford v. Krum*, and hold that the so-called "future lease" clause was effective to convey a one-fourth interest in all royalties as to future leases.

In 1935 Mary Etta Mayes executed the royalty deed in question to L.C. Luckel, Jr. The land was then subject to an oil and gas lease, the "Coe lease." Mayes had, contemporaneously with execution of the Coe lease, transferred one-half of her royalty interest to her children, and consequently owned only one-half the royalty payable under lease. The Coe lease provided for the usual one-eighth royalty. What Mayes conveyed to Luckel was one-half of the royalty she owned, which amounted to a 1/32nd royalty. The last clause of the deed explained that the Coe lease had reserved a one-eighth royalty and she was conveying one-half of the 1/16th royalty she owned, which conveyed royalty was one-fourth of the total royalty provided for in the Coe lease. The deed is set out in detail in the court of appeals opinion, 792 S.W.2d at 487–88, but we repeat the pertinent parts as follows (emphasis supplied):

> ["Granting" clause]
>
> I, Mary Etta Mayes, ... [convey to] L.C. Luckel, Jr. *an undivided one thirty-second (1/32nd) royalty interest in* and to the following described property, ...
>
> ["Habendum" and "Warranty" clauses]
>
> TO HAVE AND TO HOLD *the above described 1/32nd royalty interest* ... unto the said L.C. Luckel, Jr. his heirs and assigns forever ... *to warrant and forever defend ... the said 1/32nd royalty interest ...*
>
> ["Subject-to" clause]
>
> It is understood that said premises are now under lease originally executed to one Coe and that the grantee herein shall receive no part of the rentals as provided for under said lease, but *shall receive one-fourth of any and all royalties paid under the terms of said lease.*

> ["Future lease" clause]
>
> It is expressly understood and agreed that the grantor herein reserved [sic] the right upon expiration of the present term of the lease on said premises to make other and additional leases ... and the grantee shall be bound by the terms of any such leases ... [and] *shall be entitled to one-fourth of any and all royalties reserved under said leases.*
>
> [Final clause]
>
> It is understood and agreed that Mary Etta Mayes is the owner of one-half of the royalties to be paid under the terms of the present existing lease, the other one-half having been transferred by her to her children and by the execution of this instrument, Mary Etta Mayes conveyed one-half of the one-sixteenth (1/16th) royalty *now reserved by her.*

The Coe lease eventually expired. The land covered by the Mayes–Luckel deed is now the subject of five other mineral leases. Four of these leases provide for royalties of one-sixth (1/6th). The Luckel successors (Luckel) contend the future lease clause entitles them to one-fourth of all of the royalties under the current leases. As to those four leases the 1/24th royalty interest they claim would exceed the 1/32nd interest originally conveyed in the granting clause and warranted in the deed under the Coe lease. The *White* respondents argue the deed entitles Luckel only to a fixed 1/32nd royalty. In effect they contend that when the mineral estate reverted upon expiration of the Coe lease, they owned the rights to any increase in negotiated royalty in future leases because the "future lease" clause was ineffective to increase the Luckel share as to new leases with larger royalties. Thus *White, et al.* argue they are entitled to all of the increase in the royalty amount.

There is no contention that the deed is ambiguous. The construction of an unambiguous deed is a question of law for the court. *Altman v. Blake*, 712 S.W.2d 117, 118 (Tex.1986). The primary duty of a court when construing such a deed is to ascertain the intent of the parties from all of the language in the deed by a fundamental rule of construction known as the "four corners" rule. *Garrett v. Dils Co.*, 157 Tex. 92, 94–95, 299 S.W.2d 904, 906 (1957); 1 E. KUNTZ, THE LAW OF OIL AND GAS, § 16.1 (1987); 6A R. POWELL, THE LAW OF REAL PROPERTY, ¶ 899[3], at 81A–108 (P. Rohan ed. 1991). "That intention, when ascertained, prevails over arbitrary rules." *Harris v. Windsor*, 156 Tex. 324, 328, 294 S.W.2d 798, 800 (1956). The court, when seeking to ascertain the intention of the parties, attempts to harmonize all parts of the deed. *Altman v. Blake*, 712 S.W.2d at 118. "[T]he parties to an instrument intend every clause to have some effect and in some measure to evidence their agreement." *Id.* Even if different parts of the deed appear contradictory or inconsistent, the court must strive to harmonize all of the parts, construing the instrument to give effect to all of its provisions. *Benge v. Scharbauer,* 152 Tex. 447, 451, 259 S.W.2d 166, 167 (1953). The court should "not strike down any part of the deed, unless there is an irreconcilable conflict wherein one part of the instrument destroys in effect another part thereof." *Id.* The question is what effect the one-fourth language of the "future lease" clause should have, given these rules of construction.

Luckel argues that to give effect to all provisions of the deed, in particular the future lease clause, the deed must be interpreted to grant one-fourth of the royalties payable under the Coe lease (which was equal to 1/32nd of production) and, when that lease expired, one-fourth of the royalties paid under all subsequent leases. The court of appeals concluded that the granting, habendum, and warranty clauses of the deed conveyed a permanent 1/32nd royalty interest and that the future lease clause was ineffective to convey one-fourth of future reserved royalty, despite its express terms. The court of appeals offered two rationales—a "harmonizing" of the deed under the four corners rule and application of *Alford v. Krum*. We address the issues in that order.

The court of appeals reasoned that all parts of the deed could be harmonized, including the future leases clause, by assuming that the parties to the deed contemplated that all future leases would provide for one-eighth royalty. One-eighth was the "usual" royalty so standard in the 1920s and 1930s that all Texas courts took judicial notice of it. *Garrett v. Dils Co.*, 157 Tex. at 96, 299 S.W.2d at 907. The court interpreted the future lease clause as merely extending the fixed 1/32nd royalty interest conveyed in the granting, habendum and warranty clauses to future leases, creating a permanent 1/32nd royalty. Thus, by this "harmonizing," the court of appeals concluded that the clear and unambiguous language "one-fourth of any and all royalties reserved under said leases" really meant a fixed 1/32nd.

The court's reasoning is not a proper "harmonizing" under the four corners rule, and conflicts with a number of this court's decisions. We do not quarrel with the assumption that the parties probably contemplated nothing other than the usual one-eighth royalty. But that assumption does *not* lead to the conclusion that the parties intended only a fixed 1/32nd interest. It is just as logical to conclude that the parties intended to convey one-fourth of all reserved royalty, and that the reference to 1/32nd in the first three clauses is "harmonized" because one-fourth of the usual one-eighth royalty is 1/32nd. One would therefore conclude the express 1/32nd granting clause only meant to convey a one-fourth of all future royalties, which "harmonizes" the clauses to the same extent as the court of appeals' analysis. Both this reasoning and the opposite reasoning employed by the court of appeals ignore the express language used, and produce different assumptions about what the parties' actual intent was.

The assumption that the parties contemplated only the usual one-eighth royalty is equally consistent with an actual intent to convey a fixed 1/32nd interest or a one-fourth of the reserved royalty interest. Even if the court could discern the actual intent, it is not the actual intent of the parties that governs, but the actual intent of the parties *as expressed in the instrument as a whole*, "without reference to matters of mere form, relative position of descriptions, technicalities, or arbitrary rules." *Sun Oil Co. v. Burns*, 125 Tex. 549, 552, 84 S.W.2d 442, 444 (1935); *see also Woods v. Sims*, 154 Tex. 59, 65–66, 273 S.W.2d 617, 620 (1954). In particular, the labels we have given the clauses of "granting," "warranty," "habendum" and "future lease" are not controlling, and we should give effect to the substance of unambiguous provisions. The language "one-fourth of any and all royalties reserved under" future leases is clear and unambiguous; in fact, except for the use of one-fourth rather than one-half, it tracks the language of one of this court's opinions describing what an undivided one-half of all reserved royalty interest is. *See Schlitter v. Smith*, 128 Tex. 628, 630, 101 S.W.2d 543, 545 (1937). The future lease clause in the Mayes–Luckel deed recites that the grantee "shall be entitled to one-fourth of any and all royalties reserved under said leases." This language is as effective to grant an interest as the formal "do hereby grant, bargain, sell and convey" language of what we have designated as the "granting" clause. *Sun Oil Co. v. Burns*, 125 Tex. at 553–54, 84 S.W.2d at 444. "We must construe this language as it is written and we have no right to alter it by interpolation or substitution." *Dahlberg v. Holden*, 150 Tex. 179, 183, 238 S.W.2d 699, 701 (1951). In particular, we may not interpolate or substitute, as the court of appeals' "harmonizing" has done, to change the clear and unambiguous grant of an interest of one-fourth of reserved royalty to mean a fixed royalty interest of 1/32nd of production. The court of appeals erred in "harmonizing" the "future lease" clause to alter its clear and unambiguous meaning.

We now address the second reason given by the court of appeals—application of this court's decision in *Alford v. Krum*, 671 S.W.2d 870 (Tex.1984). The court of appeals correctly applied *Alford*. In that case, an undivided mineral interest was involved. The granting clause stated "one-half of the one-eighth interest in and to all of the oil, gas and other minerals in and under and that may be produced from" the described tract; the "subject to" clause stated the deed was subject to the existing lease "but covers and includes 1/16th of all the royalties due under said lease," but the "future lease" clause provided that "in the event that [the existing] lease for any reason becomes canceled or forfeited, then and in that event, the lease interests and all future rentals on said land, for oil, gas and mineral privileges shall be owned jointly by [the respective parties] each owning a one-half interest in all oil, gas and other minerals in and upon said land, together with one-half interest in all future rents." This court held that the granting clause conflicted with the future lease clause, and that the conflict was resolved in favor of the granting clause because the granting clause was the "controlling language" and "key expression of intent" but the fractional interest of the future lease clause was "nothing more than a restatement or confirmation of the interest deeded in the previous portions of the instrument," "redundant" and "unnecessary." 671 S.W.2d at 872–73.

The only significant difference between our present case and *Alford* is that *Alford* dealt with the conveyance of a fractional mineral interest and the present case deals with a fractional royalty interest. That difference is not material. A royalty interest is an interest in land that is a part of the total mineral estate. *State National Bank v. Morgan*, 135 Tex. 509, 514, 143 S.W.2d 757, 760 (1940). The royalty interest is a property interest that is one of the rights and attributes comprising the mineral estate; the other rights and attributes include the right to receive delay rentals, the right to share in benefits secured from the lessee such as production payments and the like, the right to develop and produce minerals, and the executive right. *Day & Co. v. Texland Petroleum, Inc.*, 786 S.W.2d 667, 669 & n. 1 (Tex.1990); *Altman v. Blake*, 712 S.W.2d at 118. A royalty interest derives from the grantor's mineral interest and is a nonpossessory interest in minerals that may be separately alienated. *Sheffield v. Hogg*, 124 Tex. 290, 77 S.W.2d 1021 (1934). The same instrument may convey an undivided portion of the mineral estate and a separate royalty interest, and the royalty interest conveyed may be larger or smaller than the interest conveyed in the minerals in place. *Woods v. Sims*, 154 Tex. at 65, 273 S.W.2d at 621; *Richardson v. Hart*, 143 Tex. 392, 185 S.W.2d 563 (1945). An undivided royalty interest may be conveyed as a fixed fraction of total production or as a fraction of the total royalty interest, and if conveyed as a fraction of the total royalty interest its amount (as a percentage of production) depends upon the royalty reserved in future leases. *Schlitter v. Smith*, 128 Tex. at 630, 101 S.W.2d at 544–45. Thus a royalty deed is, in general, subject to the same legal rules for construction as a mineral deed.

In Texas, a typical oil and gas lease actually conveys the mineral estate (less those portions expressly reserved, such as royalty) as a determinable fee. *Stephens County v. Mid–Kansas Oil & Gas Co.*, 113 Tex. 160, 173–74, 254 S.W. 290, 295 (1923). The "possibility of reverter" is the real property term of art for what the grantor owns as a future interest in a determinable fee grant; it is the grantor's right to fee ownership in the real property reverting to him if the condition terminating the determinable fee occurs. 2A R. POWELL, THE LAW OF REAL PROPERTY, ¶ 270[9] at 20–17 (P. Rohan ed. 1991). The royalty rights that may revert, as part of the total mineral estate that may revert, are therefore part of this possibility of reverter. Since the royalty rights may be separately alienated, they may be conveyed as part of this possibility of reverter the same as the mineral estate may be. Thus the analysis in *Alford v. Krum* applies equally to mineral deeds or royalty deeds.

Our concern is, therefore, not with the court of appeals' application of *Alford v. Krum*, but with the *Alford* opinion itself. Upon further consideration, we have concluded that the majority in *Alford* incorrectly failed to harmonize the provisions under the four corners rule and then erred in applying the "repugnant to the grant" rule in disregard of the future lease clause. Consequently, correct application of the harmonizing rule to the Mayes–Luckel deed conflicts with *Alford*. The so-called "future lease" provision in the Mayes–Luckel deed presently conveyed the possibility of reverter to one-fourth fractional interest of the royalty interest as part of the mineral estate. 3A W. SUMMERS, THE LAW OF OIL AND GAS, § 601 (2d ed. 1958). The provisions of the deed are harmonized by construing the grant to be of a 1/32nd interest (or one-fourth of the reserved royalty under the existing lease) until the existing lease expired. The interest conveyed was an undivided one-fourth of the total reserved royalty interest, which applied to all future leases. This reconciliation of the deed provisions is consistent with our analysis of the deed and method of harmonizing provisions in *Garrett v. Dils Co.*, 157 Tex. 92, 299 S.W.2d 904 (1957). *See also Richardson v. Hart*, 143 Tex. 392, 185 S.W.2d 563 (1945). Since the deed makes a present conveyance of the possibility of reverter, there is no violation of the rule against perpetuities. *See generally Delta Drilling Co. v. Simmons*, 161 Tex. 122, 127–28, 338 S.W.2d 143, 145 (1960); *Garrett v. Dils Co.*, 157 Tex. at 96–97, 299 S.W.2d at 906–907. In particular, the deed did not condition the effectiveness of the grant on the expiration of the Coe lease. *Cf. Peveto v. Starkey*, 645 S.W.2d 770 (Tex.1982). The proper way to harmonize the provisions of the Mayes–Luckel deed, consistent with our prior decisions under the four corners rule, is to hold that upon the termination of the Coe lease, Luckel owns an undivided one-fourth of the reserved royalty in all future leases. We therefore overrule *Alford v. Krum*.

We do note one distinction between the undivided royalty interest granted here and the one granted in *Schlittler v. Smith*, 128 Tex. 628, 101 S.W.2d 543 (1937). In that case, the trial court rendered judgment that the royalty deed grantee was entitled to receive one-half of not less than the usual one-eighth royalty. We observed that "although very likely neither of the parties thought it would be less," there was nothing in the deed requiring the grantee to receive at least the share the "usual" royalty would produce. *Schlittler v. Smith*, 128 Tex. at 631, 101 S.W.2d at 544–45. We therefore modified that portion of the trial court judgment. In the present case, the "granting" clause's outright grant of a 1/32nd fixed royalty means the parties did express their intent that the undivided one-fourth royalty never should fall below one-fourth of the usual one-eighth, or the 1/32nd expressly granted.

We conclude the unambiguous Mayes–Luckel deed is properly harmonized to mean that the interest conveyed was one-fourth of the royalties reserved under the existing and all future leases, provided Luckel is to receive not less than 1/32nd of production, which is one-fourth of the usual one-eighth. We reverse the judgment of the court of appeals and render judgment that the petitioners are entitled to payments from royalties under all existing and future leases on the subject land in accordance with that construction. We remand the cause to the trial court for the accounting sought by Luckel and further proceedings consistent with this opinion.

MAUZY, J., concurs and files an opinion.
PHILLIPS, C.J., joined by GONZALEZ, COOK and HIGHTOWER, JJ., dissents and files an opinion.

MAUZY, Justice, concurring.

I join the court in overruling our regrettable decision in *Alford v. Krum*, 671 S.W.2d 870 (Tex.1984). I would go one step further, however, and adopt Chief Justice Pope's dissenting opinion in that case. As Chief Justice Pope observed, our interpretation of deeds should not be dictated by arbitrary rules like the "repugnant to the grant" rule which moved the *Alford* majority. Rather, our method for understanding the meaning of a deed should be "to ascertain the intention of the parties, when it can be ascertained from a consideration of all parts of the instrument." 671 S.W.2d at 876. In the present case, the evident intention of the parties was to convey one-fourth of the royalties reserved under the existing and all future leases. For that reason, I concur.

PHILLIPS, Chief Justice, dissenting.

I respectfully dissent. I agree with both the trial court and the court of appeals that the provisions of the deed may be best harmonized by interpreting the deed to convey a fixed 1/32nd royalty interest.

The court's preoccupation with giving literal effect to the language of the future-lease clause is akin to a Ptolemaic insistence on placing the earth at the center of the universe. In focusing solely on the words of this one clause, the court has tortured the plain terms of at least three other clauses, which must be fully considered to ascertain the actual intent of the parties. *See, e.g., Altman v. Blake*, 712 S.W.2d 117, 118 (Tex.1986); *Benge v. Scharbauer*, 152 Tex. 447, 451, 259 S.W.2d 166, 167 (Tex.1953). A fair examination of the four corners of the deed, in my opinion, compels a different result.

On its face, the future-lease clause appears to grant a one-fourth interest in all royalties under future leases, regardless of the size of the royalty. But the granting, warranty, and habendum clauses of the deed all unambiguously convey and warrant a 1/32nd royalty interest forever. As the court acknowledges, when the Mayes–Luckel deed was executed in 1935, most private oil and gas leases provided for a ⅛th royalty. *See State Nat'l Bank v. Morgan*, 135 Tex. 509, 516, 143 S.W.2d 757, 761 (1940). If we take judicial notice of this fact, as we have before, we may assume that the parties were aware of this standard royalty when they drafted the deed. *See Sun Oil Co. (Delaware) v. Madeley*, 626 S.W.2d 726, 731 (Tex.1981); *Garrett v. Dils Co.*, 157 Tex. 92, 96, 299 S.W.2d 904, 907 (1957). I believe the parties failed to contemplate that a one-fourth share of future royalties might not always equal 1/32nd of production, and carelessly referred to the interest under future leases as one-fourth of all royalties rather than one fourth of a ⅛th royalty.

This interpretation allows us to harmonize the apparently contradictory language of the future-lease clause with the granting clause's permanent grant of a 1/32nd royalty interest. Construing the deed as a whole, I would conclude that the parties intended the future-lease clause merely to extend the effect of the grant of a permanent 1/32nd royalty interest to future leases.

The court argues that it is just as reasonable to suppose that the parties really intended to grant a one-fourth interest in all future royalties and that their mistake came in using language appropriate to a permanent 1/32nd royalty interest because they thought that the two interests would always be the same. Under this interpretation, the deed conveyed to Luckel (1) a present interest in one fourth of the royalties payable under the Coe lease, or a 1/32nd royalty, and (2) a separate present interest in a fraction of Mayes's possibility of reverter upon termination of the Coe lease. To avoid a breach of warranty, the court holds that Luckel's fractional interest in the possibility of reverter is now equal to one fourth of all royalties reserved under all leases, or a 1/32nd royalty, whichever is greater.

Indeed, this interpretation is one possible way of reconciling all the provisions. However, I do not believe that it truly harmonizes the provisions or that it comports with what common sense tells us was probably the intent of the parties. Although possible, it is unlikely that the grantor intended the future-lease clause to grant a separate interest in addition to that granted by the other clauses of the deed. "The oft-repeated expression that a grantor has the power to convey by one instrument different interests in the possibility of reverter and under the subsisting lease should not obscure the fact that very few grantors really intend to convey interests of different magnitude." 2 H. Williams & C. Meyers, *Oil and Gas Law* § 340.2, at 242–43 (1990). Rather than interpreting the future-lease clause as an additional grant, I would give effect to the clear and unambiguous language of the granting, habendum, and warranty clauses, all of which express the intent to grant a permanent 1/32nd interest.

Finally, despite holding that no irreconcilable conflicts exist between the provisions of the deed, the court deems it necessary to overrule *Alford v. Krum*, 671 S.W.2d 870 (Tex.1984). In that case, when confronted by what we believed to be an irreconcilable conflict between the granting clause and the future-lease clause of a deed, we gave effect to the language of the granting clause, following the "repugnant to the grant" rule. In the present case, no party has urged, nor does the court find, a conflict between the granting clause and any other clause of the deed. I therefore would reserve the question of the continued viability of *Alford* for a case that presents an actual conflict between the provisions of a deed.

GONZALEZ, COOK and HIGHTOWER, JJ., join in this dissent.

THE INTERPRETATION OF MINERAL AND ROYALTY DEEDS WITH DIFFERENT FRACTIONS:

Commentary on Luckel v. White

by Laura H. Burney[1]

In the 1991 decision *Luckel v. White*, the Texas Supreme Court addressed an issue that had vexed the judiciary and title examiners for decades: how should courts interpret mineral and royalty deeds with different fractions in different clauses?[2] And should it matter that those varying fractions inevitably are multiples of the traditional 1/8th lease royalty?[3] For example, in *Luckel* the court faced a royalty deed with the fraction 1/32 inserted in the granting clause, but with the fraction 1/4 appearing in a "subject to" clause and in a "future lease" clause.[4] Only seven years before *Luckel*, in *Alford v. Krum*, the court had adopted a bright-line rule for this conflicting-fraction problem, the canon of construction "the granting clause prevails."[5] Despite its simplicity that rule drew criticism for ignoring the preeminent principle of document interpretation—accord meaning to all language within the four corners of a deed. *Alford* was soundly criticized by the bench and bar, even earning the dubious distinction in a State Bar poll of "worst oil and gas case ever written."

Luckel v. White provided an opportunity for the court to reconsider the *Alford* rule. As in *Alford*, the document before the court in *Luckel* was a familiar form known as a two-grant or multi-clause deed form.[6] This form evolved in the 1920s in response to a problematic case, *Caruthers v. Leonard*.[7] Caruthers had determined that when a grantee received an interest in a mineral estate that was already under lease, only a reversionary interest passed, not a proportionate share of the lease benefits, such as delay rentals and royalties.[8] Twenty years later *Caruthers* was overruled and courts clarified that lease benefits are appurtenant to the mineral estate and pass to grantees as a matter of law.[9] For example, in a typical transaction today a grantor wishing to convey an undivided one-half interest in his minerals would use a deed form with one space for that fraction; that deed conveys to the grantee an undivided 1/2 mineral interest and 1/2 of the lease benefits under an existing lease and any future leases on the property.

Caruthers created an unfortunate deed-form legacy. Its now-rejected analysis suggested to drafters that the benefits provided for in an existing lease would pass to a grantee only if expressly assigned. To ensure that result, a multi-clause deed form came into vogue. The multiple clauses included the traditional granting clause with a blank for the parties to insert the fractional interest intended to be conveyed; a "subject to" clause for noting the property was currently subject to a lease but that the conveyance "covers and includes" a proportionate share of the benefits from that lease; and also a "future lease" clause, where drafters addressed the eventual termination of the existing lease and clarified that the grantee would receive lease benefits under any future leases. Although these forms contain three spaces in each clause for insertion of the fractional interest conveyed, the form was not intended to create multiple conveyances. Instead, drafters adopted this form in response to *Caruthers* to clarify that a single grant of a fractional mineral interest included a proportionate interest in benefits under existing and future leases.

The *Caruthers* form, which is still found in form books, poses few interpretative problems if the same fraction appears in each of the three clauses.[10] Unfortunately, court houses across Texas contain countless multi-clause deed forms with differing fractions. The explanation for that practice lies in another early conceptual problem. That problem, known as the "estate misconception," was the misunderstanding about the estates created in an oil and gas lease.[11] Because for decades the typical landowner's royalty in a lease was 1/8th, landowners often assumed that after executing a lease they owned only 1/8th of the minerals.[12] But as the Texas Supreme Court has since recognized, in actuality a lease conveys to the lessee a fee simple determinable in 8/8th of the minerals with the landowner/lessor retaining a non-possessory estate known as a possibility of reverter in 8/8ths of the minerals. In light of that fact, a grantor wishing to convey an undivided one-half of his minerals after having executed a lease with a 1/8th royalty would place the fraction 1/2 in each and every clause of the deed. A grantor functioning under the "estate misconception," however, would assume she owns only 1/8th of the minerals, multiply that fraction by the fractional interest she intends to convey, 1/2, and insert that fraction, 1/16, in the granting clause. Indeed, virtually every case appearing in reported Texas cases reflects this pattern: a larger fraction appears in the "subject to" and "future lease" clauses (1/2, 1/4, 1/8, or 1/12) while the fraction in the granting clause equals that fraction times 1/8th, (1/16, 1/32, 1/64, or 1/96).

The *Luckel* deed followed this pattern. In that case, the granting clause conveyed "an undivided one thirty-second (1/32nd) royalty interest."[13] The habendum/warranty clause followed and referred to the same fractional interest.[14] The "subject to" clause named an existing lease and provided that the grantee "shall receive one-fourth of any and all royalties paid under the terms of said lease."[15] The "future lease" clause stated that it is "expressly understood and agreed" that the grantee "shall be entitled to one-fourth of any and all royalties" under future leases.[16]

The controversy arose after the existing lease terminated and other leases were executed providing for not the usual 1/8th landowner's royalty, but a 1/6th royalty.[17] The grantee's successors claimed they were entitled to 1/4 of the royalty (1/24th of production).[18] The grantor's successors argued that the deed conveyed only a fixed 1/32nd royalty.[19]

The appellate court in *Luckel* dutifully followed the *Alford* decision and held the deed conveyed the fixed fraction, 1/32nd, found in the granting clause.[20] The Texas Supreme Court, however, disagreed and accomplished one task with finality: it overruled *Alford* and rejected the "granting clause prevails" approach.[21] According to the Supreme Court's majority opinion in *Luckel*, "the majority in *Alford* [had] incorrectly failed to harmonize the provisions under the four corners rule."[22] Instead, the *Luckel* majority viewed the deed as entitling the grantee's successors to 1/4 of the 1/6th royalty.[23]

Although *Luckel* clearly jettisoned the *Alford* interpretative approach, concurring and dissenting opinions disagreed about the approach the court had adopted for the problem.[24] The concurring judge agreed that the *Alford* approach should be rejected while simultaneously urging the adoption of the dissenting opinion from that case.[25] That dissenting opinion, however, advocated adoption of the "two grant" or "separate estates" view of multi-clause deeds, a view followed in pre-*Alford* cases.[26] Specifically, the *Alford* dissenter, Justice Pope, interpreted the deed in that case as having granted separate estates, a 1/16th interest under the granting clause and a 1/2 interest through the future lease clause.[27] Unlike the *Luckel* concurring opinion, the *Luckel* dissent expressed disdain for the "two grant" view and chastised the majority opinion for having applied that approach to the *Luckel* deed.[28]

In light of the mixed messages sent by the multiple *Luckel* opinions, commentators reached different conclusions about the approach the court had adopted to replace the *Alford* rule.[29] Some argued that *Luckel* had rejected the two-grant approach and viewed the future lease clause not as making a separate grant or as creating a conflict, but as evidence of the parties' intent.[30] Other writers, however, believed that Luckel likely represented the "regrettable rebirth of the two-grant doctrine" in Texas mineral deed construction.[31]

Three years after *Luckel*, another case confirmed the controversy about its legacy.[32] In *Concord Oil Company v. Pennzoil Exploration & Production Company*, the appellate court applied the two-grant doctrine to a 1937 deed with the fraction 1/96 in the granting clause and 1/12 in a subsequent clause.[33] At the time of that conveyance, the grantor owned only a 1/12th interest in the property, which was subject to an oil and gas lease providing for a 1/8th royalty.[34] Concord was the successor in interest to the grantee in the 1937 deed and Pennzoil was the successor in interest to the grantor through a quitclaim deed executed in 1961.[35] Concord claimed that because the grantor had conveyed all he owned, the 1/12th mineral interest, with the 1937 deed, the grantor had nothing to convey later to Pennzoil's predecessor in title.[36] Pennzoil pointed to the fraction 1/96 in the granting clause as describing the interest Concord owned since the existing lease had terminated years earlier.[37] The trial and appellate courts agreed with Pennzoil.[38] According to the appellate court's reading, the second clause of the 1937 deed included a "subject to" clause but not a "future lease" clause.[39] Because the existing lease had terminated, the appellate court concluded that the grantee owned only the 1/96th interest set forth in the granting clause.[40] Absent a future lease clause, the court held the grantee had not received the 1/12th interest in future leases.[41]

Concord appealed to the Texas Supreme Court where it ultimately prevailed.[42] However, the parties' complicated appellate path mirrored the confusion about *Luckel*'s legacy. At first, the Supreme Court declined to hear the case.[43] But after receiving over twenty amicus briefs urging the court to clarify the law it granted Concord's request and set the case for oral arguments on September 7, 1995.[44] Over a year later, on October 18, 1996, the court issued an opinion reversing the court of appeals decision, but four justices dissented.[45] That opinion was subsequently withdrawn when the court granted Pennzoil's motion for rehearing and heard oral arguments again on January 8, 1998.[46] In June 1998, the case was put to rest when all justices filed their final opinions and the court overruled all motions for rehearing.[47]

As in *Luckel*, the Texas high court produced multiple opinions in *Concord*. A plurality and concurring opinion ruled that the 1937 deed conveyed a 1/12th mineral interest, while the dissent agreed with the appellate court's application of the two-grant doctrine.[48] The plurality opinion, written by Justice Priscilla Owen and signed by three other justices, conducted a lengthy review of prior Texas cases, including *Luckel*.[49] According to the plurality, these cases endorsed a "harmonizing" or "four corners" approach, not the two-grant doctrine.[50] This opinion did recognize the truism that a grantor may convey two different interests in the mineral estate, but noted that in reality most grantors do not intend to do so.[51] The plurality also emphasized that the mere presence of different fractions in a multi-clause deed form does not work to convey two separate interests, one in the mineral estate and another in royalty from an existing lease.[52]

Focusing on the language in the 1937 deed, Justice Owen noted the deed twice referred to the "estate" conveyed, evidencing the grantor's intent to convey a single estate rather than two separate ones.[53] This opinion also noted that the deed effectively conveyed all attributes of a 1/12th mineral interest by conveying 1/12th of all royalties under the existing lease and under any other "mineral lease or leases."[54] Contrary to the decision of the court of appeals, Justice Owen viewed the Concord deed as containing a future lease clause but stressed that whether a deed contained that clause is not determinative.[55]

The *Concord* plurality opinion also addressed the role of the 1/8th lease royalty and the "estate misconception" in the interpretative process.[56] In explaining the effect of the "estate misconception" on drafting, the court noted that early court decisions had perpetuated this view and sanctioned the use of conflicting fractions to convey a single interest.[57] The plurality, however, did not base its decision in Concord on the "estate misconception" but considered an understanding of that theory as "instructive" but not "dispositive."[58] In fact, the opinion declined to adopt any "bright line" rules.[59] Instead, it endorsed a four corners approach and limited its opinion to the precise language in the 1937 deed.

Has *Concord* clarified *Luckel*'s legacy? A court of appeals decision rendered in 2002 caused this writer to wonder. *Neel v. Killam Oil Company* involved a deed that departed from the typical pattern because the larger fraction, 1/2, appeared in the granting and "subject to" clauses of a 1945 deed while the smaller fraction, 1/16th, was placed in a "future lease" clause.[60] The grantee argued that this deed conveyed a one-half royalty "forever," as provided in the granting clause, entitling him to 1/2 of the 1/4th royalty provided in new leases (1/8th of production).[61] In rejecting this argument and holding that the deed conveyed a fixed 1/16th interest, the court fixated on the future lease clause, an approach the Concord plurality had rejected.[62] Although the opinion cited *Concord* and *Luckel*, it failed to review the history of the multi-clause deed form or acknowledge the effect of the "estate misconception" on drafting.

The losing party in *Neel* appealed but the Texas Supreme Court declined to hear the case. However, in a 2011 opinion, *Hausser v. Cuellar*, the same court of appeals "disapproved[d] of [its] analysis in *Neel*."[63] And five years before Hausser, that appellate court had departed from its approach in *Neel* and carefully applied principles from the *Concord* plurality opinion. *Garza v. Prolithic Energy Company* centered on a 1938 contract and a deed with the fraction 1/2 in the granting and "subject to" clauses, but the fraction 1/16 in the "future lease" clause.[64] The trial court ruled that the deed conveyed a single undivided 1/2 interest and the appellate court agreed. In the process, the court acknowledged *Luckel*'s support for the two-grant approach: "*Luckel* appears to support [the] contention that the deeds in question could convey an undivided portion of the mineral estate and a separate royalty that would become smaller under future leases than the interest in the minerals in place."[65] Ultimately, the *Garza* court rejected that view.[66] Instead, the court reviewed the development of the multi-clause deed form and the effect of the "estate misconception" on drafting and held that the deed could be "harmonized" by holding that it conveyed an undivided 1/2 interest in the minerals.[67] As the court explained, "[o]ur holding is consistent with the *Concord* decision because neither the Contract nor the Mineral Deed contains any language that makes it evident that two differing estates were to be conveyed."[68]

The Texas Supreme Court declined to review both the *Garza* and *Hausser* opinions. However, those cases and other recent opinions involving conflicting fractions appear to represent *Concord*'s and *Luckel*'s legacy.[69] Specifically, these post-*Neel* opinions incorporate *Concord*'s rejection of the blanket application of the "two grant" doctrine to multi-clause deeds with different fractions, unless the deed has clear language evidencing the intent to make separate grants. Because such language is absent from those forms, they should not be viewed as making multiple grants. Instead, the conflicting fractions should be harmonized in light of the "estate misconception" and the language in the deed at issue. Until the Texas Supreme Court clearly confirms that view, however, drafters, title examiners, and courts may continue to debate the legacy of *Luckel v. White*.

---

1 Portions of this paper appear in other articles by the author: *Oil, Gas, and Mineral Titles: Resolving Perennial Problems in the Shale Era*, 62 U. Kan. L. Rev. 97 (2013); *Interpreting Mineral and Royalty Deeds: The Legacy of the One-Eighth Royalty and Other Stories*, 33 St. Mary's L.J. 1 (2001); and *The Regrettable Rebirth of the Two-Grant Doctrine in Texas Deed Construction*, 34 S. Tex. L. Rev. 74 (1993).

2 *Luckel v. White*, 819 S.W.2d 459 (Tex. 1991).

3 *Luckel*, 819 S.W.2d at 459.

4 *Id.* at 460.

5 *Alford v. Krum*, 671 S.W.2d 870, 872 (Tex. 1984), this case was *overruled by Luckel v. White*, 819 S.W.2d 459 (Tex. 1991).

6 For example, in *Luckel*, the deed includes five clauses: "Granting" clause, "Habendum" and "Warranty" clause, "Subject-to" clause, "Future lease" clause, and "Final" clause. Each clause includes different types of interests, and the percentage numbers are different. *Luckel*, at 461.

7 *Caruthers v. Leonard*, 254 S.W. 779 (Tex. Comm'n App. 1923, judgm't adopted), *overruled by Harris v. Currie*, 142 Tex. 93, 176 S.W.2d 302 (1943).

8 *Id.* at 782.

9 *See Harris v. Currie*, 142 Tex. 93, 176 S.W.3d 302 (1943).

10 But *see Hoffman v. Magnolia Petroleum Co.*, 273 S.W. 828 (Tex. Comm'n App. 1925, judgm't adopted). Writers identify *Hoffman* as the case that propagated the two-grant doctrine, but that case did not involve conflicting fractions. Instead, the problem arose when the grantor conveyed a ½ interest in a certain 90 acres of 320 acres already subject to a lease. The "subject to" clause provided that the deed included one-half of all royalties due under the existing lease. The court agreed with the grantee's claim that this language entitled him to ½ of the royalty payable from the entire lease, not just from wells drilled on the 90 acres conveyed.

11 *See Concord Oil Co. v. Pennzoil Exploration and Production Co.*, 966 S.W.2d 451, 460 (1998).

12 *See* Laura H. Burney, *Interpreting Mineral and Royalty Deeds: the Legacy of the One-eighth Royalty and Other Stories*, 33 St. Mary's L.J. 1 (2001) [hereinafter the *Legacy of the One-eighth Royalty*].

13 *Luckel*, at 461.

14 *Id.*

15 *Id.*

16 *Id.*

17 *Id.* ("The Coe lease eventually expired. The land covered by the Mayes Luckel deed is now the subject of five other mineral leases. Four of these leases provide for royalties of one-sixth").

18 *Id.* at 462.

19 *Id.*

20 *Id.*

21 *Id.* at 464.

22 *Id.*

23 *Id.*

24 *Id.* at 465.

25 *Id.* ("Rather, our method for understanding the meaning of a deed should be 'to ascertain the intention of the parties, when it can be ascertained from a consideration of all parts of the instrument'").

26 *See Legacy of the One-eighth Royalty, supra* note 12, at 90-93 (reviewing cases following two-grant doctrine from 1925 to 1955).

27 *Alford*, 671 S.W.2d at 876.

28 *Luckel*, at 466 (Phillips, C.J., dissenting).

29 *See the Legacy of the One-Eighth Royalty, supra* note 12, at 11.

30 *Id.*

31 *See* the *Legacy of the One-Eighth Royalty, supra* note 12, at 11 (reviewing articles dissecting implications of Luckel).

32 *Id.*

33 *Concord Oil Co. v. Pennzoil Exploration and Production Co.*, 878 S.W.2d 191 (Tex. App.—San Antonio 1994, writ granted), *rev'd*, 966 S.W.2d 451 (Tex. 1998).

34 *Concord*, 878 S.W.2d at 192.

35 *Id.*

36 *Id.* at 193.

37 *Id.* at 192.

38 *Id.*

39 *Id.* at 195.

40 *Id.* at 197.

41 *Id.*

42 *See Concord Oil Co. v. Pennzoil Exploration and Production Co.*, 966 S.W.2d 451 (Tex. 1998).

43 *See* the *Legacy of the One-Eighth Royalty, supra* note 12, at 13. ("The court (Texas Supreme Court) initially denied the writ in November 1994").

44 *Id.*

45 *Concord*, 966 S.W.2d at 457.

46 *Id.* at 452.

47 *See* the *Legacy of the One-Eighth Royalty, supra* note 12, at 13(describing procedural path in *Concord* and noting the author served as appellate counsel for Concord Oil in the Texas Supreme Court).

48 *Concord*, at 466. (In Justice Enoch's concurring opinion, he explained that he would have found two grants if the *Concord* deed had not, in his view, resulted in an over-conveyance under that approach). For a critique of the concurring and dissenting opinions, *see* the *Legacy of the One-Eighth Royalty, supra* note 12, at 17-21.

49 *See Concord.*

50 *Id.* at 457.

51 *See id.* (commenting that a mineral interest owner is allowed to convey any mineral estate attribute, or any fraction thereof, including "a fraction of the mineral interest, a fraction of royalties, the right to receive delay rentals, and the executive rights").

52 *See id.* at 458 (finding no language that indicated "the 1/12 interest in rents and royalties was meant to be in addition to or separate from the estate granted in the opening clause").

53 *Id.* at 457-458.

54 *Id.* at 459.

55 *Id.* at 460.

56 *See* the *Legacy of the One-Eighth Royalty, supra* note 12, at 15.

57 *Concord*, at 460.

58 *Id.*

59 *See id.* at 460-461 (rejecting Concord's recommendation that the court issue a "bright-line" test for interpreting conveyances that contain conflicting fractions). The court reasoned such firm rules would be arbitrary and would not allow the court to construe the conveyance as a whole. *Id.*

60 *Neel v. Killam Oil Company*, 88 S.W.3d 334, 338 (Tex. App.—San Antonio 2002, pet. denied).

61 *Neel*, 88 S.W.3d at 340.

62 *Id.* at 340-341.

63 345 S.W. 3d 462, 470 (Tex. App.—San Antonio 2011, pet. denied).

64 *Garza v. Prolithic Energy Company*, 195 S.W.3d 137, 139-140 (Tex. App.—San Antonio 2006, pet. denied). The case also involved another deed with the fraction "15/32nd of 1/8th" in the future lease clause.

65 *Garza*, 195 S.W.3d at 143.

66 *Id.* at 145 (the court held that the trial court properly construed the deeds).

67 *Id.*

68 *Id.* at 146.

69 For a thorough discussion of the post-*Neel* cases and the status of the two-grant doctrine in Texas and other states *see* Laura H. Burney, *Oil, Gas and Mineral Titles: Resolving Perennial Problems in the Shale Era*, at 113. This article also discusses another issue testing the *Luckel/Concord* legacy: whether fractions expressed as a double fraction, in which one fraction is invariably the once-customary 1/8th royalty, should be multiplied to create a fixed interest or analyzed and interpreted as creating a floating non-participating royalty interest. *Id.* at 114 – 121.